College Football "Bowl Games of the 21st Century" Part I {2000-2010}

Available at www.stevesfootballbible.com

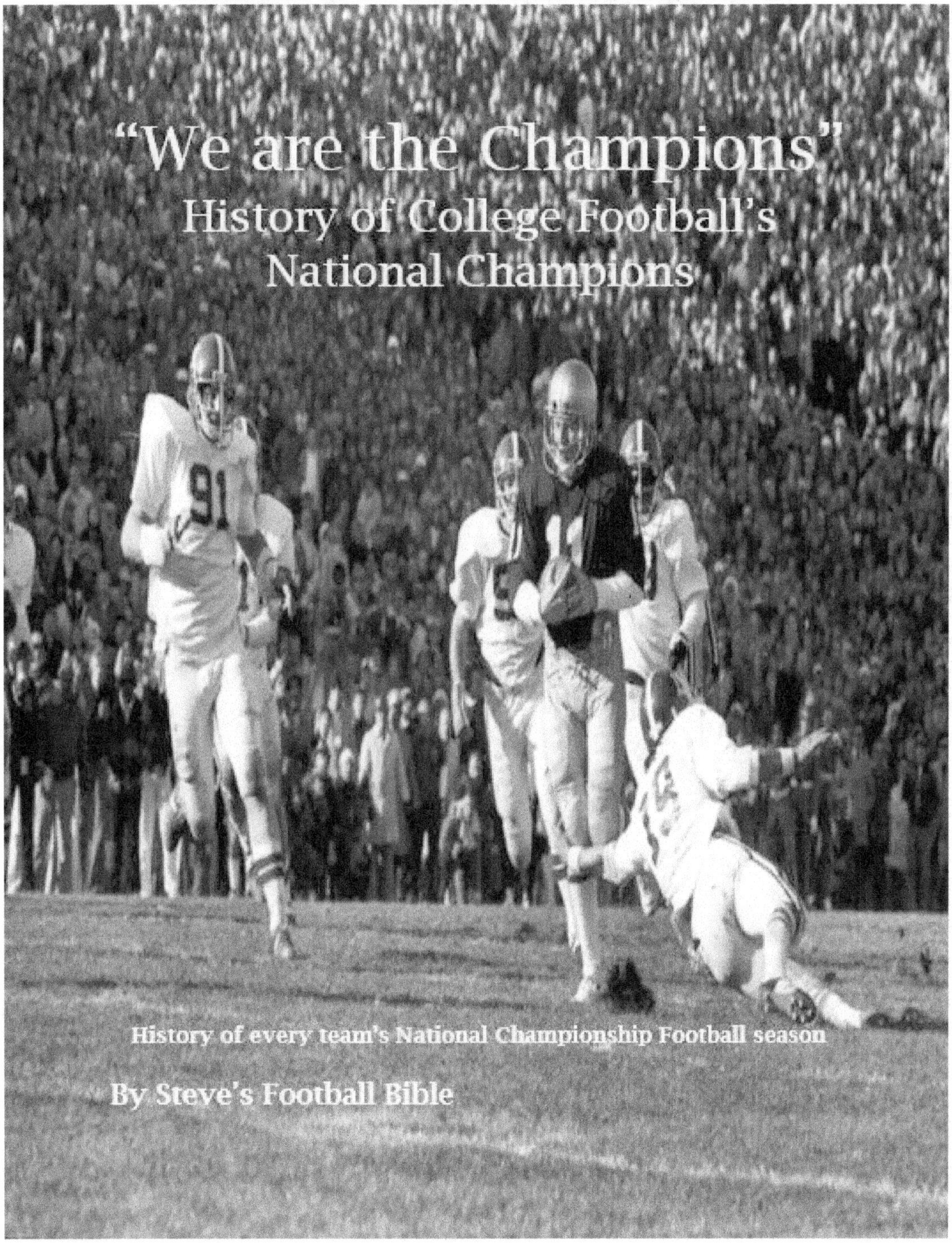

"We are the Champions"
History of College Football's National Champions

History of every team's National Championship Football season

By Steve's Football Bible

Text Copyright © 2022 by Steve's Football Bible, LLC
{2nd Edition} All Rights Reserved
Information in this book is for educational and entertainment purposes.

Information in this book was derived from numerous news services and college media guides available on the internet, including, but not limited to, Wikipedia, Arizona Daily Star, Associated Press, Bentley Historical Society, USA Today, Bleacher Report, SB Nation, "Sugar Bowl Classic: A history by Marty Mulé", Cotton Bowl Classic web site, Sun Bowl Classic web site, Orange Bowl Classic web site, Tournament of Roses web site, Washington Times , Los Angeles Times, New York Times, Philadelphia Inquirer, Washington Post, Boston Globe, NBC Sports, CBS Sportsline, Deseret News, ESPN, Black Shoes Diaries, ABC Sports Online, BCS Football.com, Sportsline USA, Chicago Tribune, Milwaukee Sentinel-Journal, UPI, Fort Worth Star-Telegram, Orlando Sentinel, Las Vegas Sun, Daily Press, San Jose Mercury News, Raycom Media, CollegeFootballPoll.com, SportsDayDFW.com, WVUIlustrated.com, GatorZone.com, Garnet and Gold, ECUPirates.com, HuskerMax.com, Lions Den, GoldenEagles.net, GoDucks.com, CU at the game, NUSports.com, Reuters News Service.

The following Colleges and Universities media guides and/or websites: Alabama, Appalachian State, Arizona, Arkansas State, Army, Auburn, Baylor, Boise State, Bowling Green, BYU, California, Central Michigan, Cincinnati, Colorado, Colorado State, Duke, East Carolina, Florida, Florida State, Fresno State, Georgia, Georgia State, Georgia Tech, Hawaii, Houston, Illinois, Indiana, Indiana, Iowa, Iowa State, Kansas State, LSU, Louisville, Marshall, Maryland, Memphis, Miami, Michigan State, Middle Tennessee, Minnesota, Mississippi, Mississippi State, Missouri, Navy, Nebraska, North Carolina A&T, North Carolina, NC State, Northern Illinois, Northwestern, Notre Dame, Ohio, Ohio State, Oklahoma, Oklahoma State, Oregon, Oregon State, Penn State, Pittsburgh, Purdue, San Diego State, Southern Miss, SMU, South Carolina, South Florida, Stanford, Syracuse, Tennessee, TCU, Texas A&M, Toledo, Troy, Tulsa, UCLA, UNLV, Utah, Utah State, Villanova, Virginia, Virginia Tech, Wake Forest, Washington.

ISBN: 9-781393067-67-2

Introduction

My love of College Football began in 1966. As a 7 year old kid I remember watching the Notre Dame-Michigan State "Game of the Century". Next, I remember the 1967 USC-UCLA game and O.J. Simpson weaving through the UCLA defense for the winning touchdown with 6 minutes left in the game. I remember the 1968 Rose Bowl, Indiana vs USC. Who was this Indiana team that went to the Rose Bowl over my beloved Minnesota Golden Gopher's? I attended my first college football game in 1971. Michigan vs Minnesota at Memorial Stadium on the Campus of the University of Minnesota. My Aunt Roberta took me. I was hooked after that. The Golden Gophers were defeated that day 35-7 by the Wolverines. George Honza of the Golden Gophers scored the only touchdown that day on a pass from Craig Curry. Ironically, I met Mr. Honza in January of 2017 while officiating a basketball game.

Growing up in a rural farming town (Alden) in southern Minnesota, as a youth I spent a lot of my Saturday's in the fall watching ABC Sports College game of the week. I don't think I missed many Michigan-Ohio State games followed by the USC-UCLA game in the afternoon every third Saturday in November. The 1971 Nebraska-Oklahoma game stands out as one of the more memorable games I watched as a kid. Every New Year's Day I spent watching all the Bowl games. Cotton and Sugar Bowl at noon, followed by the Rose Bowl in the afternoon, finishing up with the Orange Bowl in the evening. The only day of New Year's Day Bowl games I missed was in January 1978, when I was in the Army, while traveling back to Ft. McClellan, Alabama to start my A.I.T., after being on Christmas leave.

This book is for all the College Football fans, casual or diehard, historians or those who just plain love the College game. I hope everyone enjoys.

Steve Fulton

Contents

Introduction ii

Chapter 1 – 2000-2005 1

    2000 Outback Bowl 1

    2000 Gator Bowl 2

    2000 Florida Citrus Bowl 1

    2000 Cotton Bowl Classic 1

    2000 Rose Bowl 1

    2000 Orange Bowl 1

    2000 Fiesta Bowl 1

    2000 Sugar Bowl (BCS Championship Game) 2

    2000 GMAC Mobile Alabama Bowl 3

    2000 Las Vegas Bowl 4

    2000 Oahu Bowl 4

    2000 Aloha Classic 5

    2000 Galleryfurniture.com Bowl 6

    2000 Motor City Bowl 7

    2000 Humanitarian Bowl 7

    2000 Music City Bowl 8

    2000 Insight Bowl 9

    2000 Micron PC Bowl 10

    2000 Sun Bowl 11

    2000 Liberty Bowl 11

    2000 Chick-Fil-A Peach Bowl 12

    2000 Holiday Bowl 13

    2000 Alamo Bowl 14

    2000 Independence Bowl 14

    2000 Silicon Valley Football Classic 15

    2001 Outback Bowl 16

    2001 Gator Bowl 17

    2001 Florida Citrus Bowl 18

    2001 Cotton Bowl Classic 19

    2001 Rose Bowl 20

    2001 Fiesta Bowl 20

    2001 Sugar Bowl 21

    2001 Orange Bowl (BCS Championship Game) 22

    2001 New Orleans Bowl 23

    2001 GMAC Bowl 24

    2001 Tangerine Bowl 25

    2001 Las Vegas Bowl 25

    2001 Independence Bowl 26

    2001 Seattle Bowl 27

2001 Music City Bowl...28

2001 Galleryfurniture.com Bowl 28

2001 Holiday Bowl..29

2001 Motor City Bowl...30

2001 Insight Bowl..30

2001 Alamo Bowl..31

2001 Liberty Bowl...32

2001 Humanitarian Bowl..33

2001 Sun Bowl..34

2001 Silicon Valley Football Classic..35

2001 Chick-Fil-A Peach Bowl..35

2002 Outback Bowl...36

2002 Florida Citrus Bowl...37

2002 Cotton Bowl Classic...38

2002 Gator Bowl...39

2002 Fiesta Bowl...39

2002 Sugar Bowl...40

2002 Orange Bowl..41

2002 Rose Bowl (BCS Championship Game) 42

2002 New Orleans Bowl..43

2002 GMAC Bowl...44

2002 Tangerine Bowl...45

2002 Las Vegas Bowl...45

2002 Hawai'i Bowl...46

2002 Motor City Bowl...47

2002 Insight Bowl..48

2002 Independence Bowl...49

2002 Houston Bowl...50

2002 Holiday Bowl..50

2002 Continental Tire Bowl 51

2002 Alamo Bowl..52

2002 Music City Bowl...53

2002 Seattle Bowl..54

2002 Humanitarian Bowl..54

2002 Liberty Bowl...55

2002 Sun Bowl..56

2002 San Francisco Bowl...57

2002 Chick-Fil-A Peach Bowl..57

2002 Silicon Valley Football Classic..58

2003 Gator Bowl...59

2003 Outback Bowl...60

2003 Capital One Bowl..60

2003 Cotton Bowl Classic...61

2003 Rose Bowl	62
2003 Sugar Bowl	63
2003 Orange Bowl	64
2003 Fiesta Bowl (BCS National Championship Game)	66
2003 New Orleans Bowl	67
2003 GMAC Bowl	68
2003 Tangerine Bowl	68
2003 Fort Worth Bowl	69
2003 Las Vegas Bowl	70
2003 Hawai'i Bowl	70
2003 Motor City Bowl	71
2003 Insight Bowl	72
2003 Continental Tire Bowl	73
2003 Alamo Bowl	74
2003 Houston Bowl	75
2003 Holiday Bowl	75
2003 Silicon Valley Football Classic	76
2003 Independence Bowl	77
2003 Music City Bowl	78
2003 Liberty Bowl	79
2003 San Francisco Bowl	79
2003 Sun Bowl	80
2004 Gator Bowl	81
2004 Outback Bowl	81
2004 Capital One Bowl	82
2004 Rose Bowl	83
2004 Orange Bowl	84
2004 Cotton Bowl Classic	85
2004 Chick-Fil-A Peach Bowl (January)	88
2004 Fiesta Bowl	88
2004 Humanitarian Bowl	90
2004 Sugar Bowl - (Bowl Championship Series Championship Game)	91
2004 New Orleans Bowl	92
2004 Champs Sports Bowl	92
2004 GMAC Bowl	93
2004 Las Vegas Bowl	94
2004 Fort Worth Bowl	94
2004 Hawai'i Bowl	95
2004 MPC Computers Bowl	96
2004 Motor City Bowl	98
2004 Independence Bowl	98
2004 Insight Bowl	99
2004 Houston Bowl	99

2004 Alamo Bowl 100
2004 Continental Tire Bowl 101
2004 Silicon Valley Football Classic 102
2004 Emerald Bowl 103
2004 Holiday Bowl 104
2004 Liberty Bowl 105
2004 Music City Bowl 106
2004 Sun Bowl 107
2004 Chick-Fil-A Peach Bowl (December) 107
2005 Gator Bowl 108
2005 Outback Bowl 109
2005 Capital One Bowl 109
2005 Cotton Bowl Classic 110
2005 Rose Bowl 111
2005 Fiesta Bowl 112
2005 Sugar Bowl 113
2005 Orange Bowl - (BCS National Championship Game) 114
2005 New Orleans Bowl 115
2005 GMAC Bowl 117
2005 Las Vegas Bowl 118
2005 San Diego County Credit Union Poinsettia Bowl 118
2005 Fort Worth Bowl 120
2005 Hawai'i Bowl 120
2005 Motor City Bowl 121
2005 Champs Sports Bowl 122
2005 Insight Bowl 123
2005 MPC Computers Bowl 124
2005 Alamo Bowl 125
2005 Emerald Bowl 126
2005 Holiday Bowl 127
2005 Independence Bowl 128
2005 Music City Bowl 129
2005 Sun Bowl 130
2005 Chick-Fil-A Peach Bowl 131
2005 Meineke Car Care Bowl 132
2005 Houston Bowl 132
2005 Liberty Bowl 133

Chapter 2 – 2006-2010 135
2006 Gator Bowl 135
2006 Outback Bowl 136
2006 Capital One Bowl 137
2006 Cotton Bowl Classic 137
2006 Fiesta Bowl 138

2006 Sugar Bowl 139
2006 Orange Bowl 141
2006 Rose Bowl (BCS National Championship Game) 142
2006 Poinsettia Bowl 143
2006 Las Vegas Bowl 144
2006 New Orleans Bowl 145
2006 Armed Forces Bowl 146
2006 New Mexico Bowl 147
2006 PapaJohns.com Bowl 148
2006 Hawai'i Bowl 148
2006 Motor City Bowl 150
2006 Emerald Bowl 150
2006 Independence Bowl 151
2006 Texas Bowl 152
2006 Holiday Bowl 153
2006 Music City Bowl 153
2006 Liberty Bowl 154
2006 Champs Sports Bowl 155
2006 Sun Bowl 156
2006 Insight Bowl 157
2006 Meineke Car Care Bowl 158
2006 Alamo Bowl 159
2006 Chick-Fil-A Peach Bowl 160
2006 MPC Computers Bowl 160
2007 Outback Bowl 161
2007 Gator Bowl 162
2007 Capital One Bowl 163
2007 Cotton Bowl Classic 164
2007 Rose Bowl 164
2007 Fiesta Bowl 166
2007 Orange Bowl 167
2007 Sugar Bowl 168
2007 International Bowl 169
2007 GMAC Bowl 170
2007 BCS Championship Game 171
2007 Poinsettia Bowl 173
2007 New Orleans Bowl 174
2007 PapaJohns.com Bowl 174
2007 Las Vegas Bowl 175
2007 New Mexico Bowl 176
2007 Hawai'i Bowl 177
2007 Motor City Bowl 179
2007 Holiday Bowl 180

2007 Texas Bowl 181
2007 Champs Sports Bowl 182
2007 Emerald Bowl 182
2007 Meineke Car Care Bowl 183
2007 Liberty Bowl 184
2007 Alamo Bowl 185
2007 Independence Bowl 186
2007 Humanitarian Bowl 187
2007 Armed Forces Bowl 189
2007 Music City Bowl 190
2007 Sun Bowl 191
2007 Chick-Fil-A Peach Bowl 192
2007 Insight Bowl 193
2008 Gator Bowl 194
2008 Outback Bowl 195
2008 Capital One Bowl 196
2008 Cotton Bowl Classic 198
2008 Rose Bowl 199
2008 Sugar Bowl 200
2008 Fiesta Bowl 201
2008 Orange Bowl 202
2008 International Bowl 203
2008 GMAC Bowl 204
2008 BCS Championship Game 205
2008 EagleBank Bowl 207
2008 St. Petersburg Bowl 208
2008 Las Vegas Bowl 209
2008 New Mexico Bowl 210
2008 New Orleans Bowl 210
2008 Poinsettia Bowl 211
2008 Hawai'i Bowl 212
2008 Motor City Bowl 213
2008 Champs Sports Bowl 214
2008 Meineke Car Care Bowl 215
2008 Emerald Bowl 216
2008 Independence Bowl 217
2008 PapaJohns.com Bowl 218
2008 Alamo Bowl 219
2008 Humanitarian Bowl 220
2008 Texas Bowl 221
2008 Holiday Bowl 221
2008 Music City Bowl 222
2008 Armed Forces Bowl 223

2008 Sun Bowl ... 224
2008 Insight Bowl ... 225
2008 Chick-Fil-A Peach Bowl ... 226
2009 Gator Bowl ... 227
2009 Outback Bowl ... 228
2009 Capital One Bowl ... 228
2009 Rose Bowl ... 229
2009 Orange Bowl ... 231
2009 Liberty Bowl ... 232
2009 Cotton Bowl Classic ... 232
2009 Sugar Bowl ... 233
2009 International Bowl ... 234
2009 Fiesta Bowl ... 235
2009 GMAC Bowl ... 236
2009 BCS Championship Game ... 237
2009 St. Petersburg Bowl ... 239
2009 New Mexico Bowl ... 239
2009 New Orleans Bowl ... 240
2009 Las Vegas Bowl ... 241
2009 Poinsettia Bowl ... 242
2009 Hawai'i Bowl ... 243
2009 Meineke Car Care Bowl ... 244
2009 Emerald Bowl ... 245
2009 Little Caesars Pizza Bowl ... 246
2009 Music City Bowl ... 247
2009 Independence Bowl ... 248
2009 Champs Sports Bowl ... 249
2009 EagleBank Bowl ... 250
2009 Humanitarian Bowl ... 251
2009 Holiday Bowl ... 252
2009 Armed Forces Bowl ... 253
2009 Texas Bowl ... 253
2009 Sun Bowl ... 254
2009 Insight Bowl ... 255
2009 Chick-Fil-A Peach Bowl ... 256
2010 Outback Bowl ... 257
2010 Gator Bowl ... 258
2010 Capital One Bowl ... 260
2010 Rose Bowl ... 261
2010 Sugar Bowl ... 262
2010 PapaJohns.com Bowl ... 263
2010 Liberty Bowl (January) ... 264
2010 Alamo Bowl (January) ... 265

2010 Cotton Bowl Classic 267
2010 International Bowl 268
2010 Fiesta Bowl 268
2010 Orange Bowl 269
2010 GMAC Bowl 270
2010 BCS Championship Game 271
2010 New Mexico Bowl 272
2010 Humanitarian Bowl 273
2010 New Orleans Bowl 274
2010 Beef 'O' Brady's Bowl 275
2010 Maaco Bowl 276
2010 Poinsettia Bowl 277
2010 Hawai'i Bowl 278
2010 Little Caesars Pizza Bowl 279
2010 Independence Bowl 280
2010 Champs Sports Bowl 280
2010 Insight Bowl 281
2010 Military Bowl 282
2010 Texas Bowl 283
2010 Alamo Bowl (December) 284
2010 Armed Forces Bowl 285
2010 Music City Bowl 286
2010 Pinstripe Bowl 287
2010 Holiday Bowl 289
2010 Meineke Car Care Bowl 290
2010 Liberty Bowl (December) 291
2010 Sun Bowl 291
2010 Chick-Fil-A Peach Bowl 292

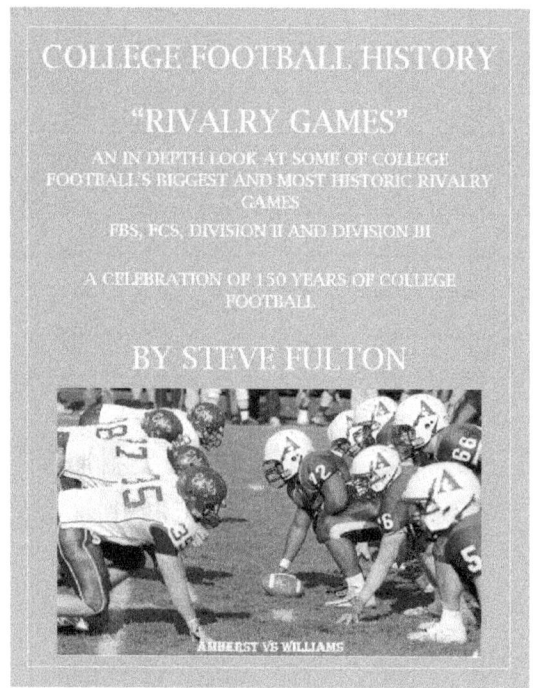

Chapter 1 – 2000-2005
2000 Outback Bowl
The 2000 edition to the Outback Bowl featured the Georgia Bulldogs and the Purdue Boilermakers.

2000 Outback Bowl	Line	1	2	3	4	OT	Final
#20 Purdue	(-5.5)	19	6	0	0	0	25
#24 Georgia	(60.0)	0	10	8	7	3	28

Scoring Summary
Purdue - Daniels 3 yard pass from Brees (Dorsch kick)
Purdue - Daniels 11 yard pass from Brees (kick failed)
Purdue - Sutherland 21 yard pass from Brees (two-point conversion failed)
Purdue - James 32 yard pass from Brees (two-point conversion failed)
Georgia - Edwards 74 yard run (Hines kick)
Georgia - Hines 32 yard Field goal
Georgia - Carter 8 yard run (Pass run for two-point conversion)
Georgia - McMichael 8 yard pass from Carter (Hines kick)
Georgia - Hines 21 yard Field goal

Associated Press Outback Bowl Game Summary - Hap Hines kicked a 21-yard field goal on the first overtime possession as 24th-ranked Georgia completed a huge comeback, rallying for a 28-25 victory over No. 20 Purdue in the Outback Bowl. The morning start time appeared to affect Georgia, which fell behind 25-0 early in the second quarter following Drew Brees' fourth touchdown pass. But the Bulldogs scored 10 points before halftime and a touchdown in each of the last two quarters to send the game to overtime. Purdue could not move the ball on its first OT possession and came up empty when Travis Dorsch sent a 43-yard field-goal attempt wide right. The Bulldogs wasted little time putting away the game. Patrick Pass gained 19 yards on two carries to move the ball into position for Hines' winning kick. It was the second bowl game ever decided in overtime. Toledo defeated Nevada, 40-37, in the 1995 Las Vegas Bowl. Overtime was nothing new for the Bulldogs, who suffered a controversial 51-48 OT loss to archrival Georgia Tech in their regular-season finale. Quincy Carter ran for one touchdown and passed for another for the Georgia (8-4), which improved to 18-4-3 in bowl games. The Bulldogs also won the Outback Bowl for the second time in three seasons after a 33-6 victory over Wisconsin in 1998. Brees, who will be among the favorites for next season's Heisman Trophy, completed 36-of-60 passes for 378 yards with an interception. His passing yards set an Outback Bowl record, surpassing the 336 posted last season by Kentucky's Tim Couch. The Boilermakers (7-5), who had won their previous two bowl appearances, fell to 6-2 all-time in the postseason. Ahead 25-18 in the fourth quarter, the Boilermakers squandered a chance to extend the lead when Dorsch missed a 38-yard field goal with just over 11 minutes remaining. The kick was ruled wide right, although television replays showed the ball made it just inside the upright. It was a rough day for Dorsch, who missed all three of his field-goal attempts and an extra point in the first quarter. Carter, also a 2000 Heisman hopeful, made an early case by engineering a 13-play, 94-yard drive that tied it at 25-25 with 79 seconds remaining. The 6-3 signal-caller kept alive that drive with a 21-yard completion to Terrence Edwards on 4th-and-12 to the Boilermakers' 7. But Carter saved his best for last when he scrambled away from a pair of defenders and threw an eight-yard TD to Randy McMichael that deflected off safety Adrian Beasley's hand. Carter, who completed 20-of-33 passes for 243 yards while adding 41 yards on 16 rushes. With a high-powered offensive attack, the Boilermakers tried to run Georgia off the field by scoring on their first three possessions. Purdue received the kickoff and drove 80 yards in 12 plays with Brees capping the drive with a three-yard touchdown toss to Chris Daniels 4:34 into the contest. Less than four minutes later, Brees and Daniels hooked up again, this time for an 11-yard score. Dorsch missed the extra point, leaving Purdue with a 13-0 lead. Daniels had a huge game with 12 catches for 103 yards. Brees finished his brilliant first quarter by taking the Boilermakers 80 yards in seven plays. This time, he found speedster Vinny Sutherland with a 21-yard TD but the two-point conversion failed. Brees was 11-of-15 for 157 yards in the period. Purdue's offense received some help early in the second quarter when Michael Greer fumbled and defensive end Warren Moore recovered on the Bulldogs' 32. On the next play, Brees hit Chris James for a 32-yard touchdown, giving Purdue a 25-0 advantage with 10:38 to play before halftime. A big play helped start Georgia's comeback. Edwards, a freshman receiver, took an end-around and raced 74 yards into the end zone to get the Bulldogs on the board. Edwards also had eight receptions for 97 yards. Hines kicked a 32-yard field goal with nine seconds left in the half, cutting Georgia's deficit to 25-10. Brees finished the half 21-of-32 for 249 yards with an interception. He found it tougher thereafter, completing 15-of-28 passes for 129 yards. Carter pulled the Bulldogs within seven with 4:36 left in the third quarter when he scored on an eight-yard draw play.

College Football "Bowl Games of the 21st Century" — Chapter 1 – 2000-2005

2000 Gator Bowl

The 2000 Gator Bowl featured the Miami Hurricanes and the Georgia Tech Yellow Jackets.

Background - The Jackets had at one point been ranked as high as 7th in the polls before two losses had made them fall to 17th. They finished 2nd in the Atlantic Coast Conference. This was their third consecutive bowl season. The Hurricanes finished 2nd in the Big East Conference with a loss to Virginia Tech late in the season costing them a share of the title. But Miami was making their third bowl appearance under Davis, who was hired to help rebuild the program after a scandal that rocked the school in 1995.

2000 Gator Bowl	Line	1	2	3	4	Final
#23 Miami	(-5.0)	7	14	0	7	28
#17 Georgia Tech	(69.5)	0	7	6	0	13

Scoring Summary
Miami- Jackson 8 yard run (Crosland kick)
Miami- King 15 yard pass from Kelly (Crosland kick)
Georgia Tech- Hamilton 17 yard run (Manget kick)
Miami- Portis 73 yard run (Crosland kick)
Georgia Tech- Manget 25 Field goal
Georgia Tech- Manget 36 Field goal
Miami- Wayne 17 yard pass from Dorsey (Crosland kick)

Associated Press Gator Bowl Game Summary - Miami stopped Georgia Tech where it mattered the most. The 23rd-ranked Hurricanes, playing on New Year's Day for the first time in five years, held Georgia Tech to its fewest points in 17 games and ended Joe Hamilton's career on a sour note with a 28-13 victory in the Gator Bowl. Clinton Portis scored on a 73-yard run as he and James Jackson each rushed for over 100 yards, and the Hurricanes (9-4) also got a touchdown pass from each of its Quarterbacks, Kenny Kelly and Ken Dorsey. But the game belonged to Miami's defense, which extended its streak to 27 quarters without giving up a touchdown pass. No. 15 Georgia Tech (8-4), which led the NCAA in total offense and was second in scoring at 40.7 points a game, scored its fewest points since a 34-7 loss last year to Florida State. And Hamilton, who set 18 school records, failed to throw a touchdown pass for the first time in 14 games. The Yellow Jackets managed 421 yards - still its lowest output of the year - but failed miserably when they got into scoring position. They had seven drives inside the Miami 30, but Hamilton threw two interceptions and Luke Manget missed two field goals. The result was Georgia Tech's first loss in a bowl since the 1978 Peach Bowl, a span of seven games. The Gator Bowl could turn out to be a big step toward Miami returning to its days of glory, when it won four national championships in nine years. Just like then, it all starts with defense. Linebacker Nate Webster, who had 14 tackles, was the first defensive player selected MVP in the Gator Bowl since 1989. Leading 21-7 at halftime, the Hurricanes three times came up with a big play to stall Georgia Tech drives and make the Yellow Jackets settle for two field goals. Miami finally got some breathing room when Reggie Wayne made a leaping catch across his body of a 17-yard touchdown pass from Dorsey for a 28-13 lead midway through the fourth quarter. Portis, the first freshman to start at tailback for Miami since 1975, finished with 117 yards on 12 carries. Jackson had 107 yards on 21 carries. Hamilton, who led the Yellow Jackets to seven comeback victories in his career, was 20-of-40 for 245 yards and two interceptions. He also carried 22 times for 49 yards. The game was played before 43,416, the smallest Gator Bowl crowd since 1958. They all came to see a shootout that never materialized, although that sure looked to be the case when the game started. Miami met little resistance on a 66-yard opening drive that ended with Jackson going virtually untouched off left tackle for an 8-yard score. Georgia Tech roared back, moving toward scoring position in just four plays until Matt Sweeney of Miami stepped. On second-and- 6 from the 31, he rushed hard at Hamilton, swatted down his pass and picked it out of the air. The Hurricanes had a chance to really make a rout in the first half, but they got nothing out of three drives inside the 25. Dan Crosland missed two field goals, and Jeff Popovich was stopped short of a first down on a fake field goal. Kelly threaded a sideline pass into Moss for 30 yards, and hit Andre King for a 15-yard score on the first play of the second half. Tech's only touchdown came when Hamilton finally discovered Dez White, with whom he shared Gator Bowl MVP honors last year. They connected three times on a 77-yard drive, and Hamilton scored on a 17-yard scramble. Two plays later, Portis bounced off two tackles and raced down the left sideline for a 73-yard touchdown run, the longest for Miami in a bowl game. After that, Tech never came closer than eight points. So effective was Miami's defense that Dan Dyke, who punted only 30 times all year, had a season-high six punts. One of them was blocked.

2000 Florida Citrus Bowl

The 2000 Citrus Bowl matched the Michigan State Spartans against the Florida Gators. Michigan State came into the game with interim coach Bobby Williams, who took over on December 5, five days after Nick Saban departed to take over the Louisiana State program.

2000 Florida Citrus Bowl	Line	1	-	2	-	3	-	4	-	Final
#9 Michigan State	(47.5)	3	-	17	-	6	-	11	-	37
#10 Florida	(-3.0)	7	-	14	-	6	-	7	-	34

Scoring Summary
Michigan State – Edinger 46-yard field goal
Florida - Taylor 12 yard pass from Johnson (Chandler kick)
Michigan State - Burress 37 yard pass from Burke (Edinger kick)
Michigan State - Turner 24 yard fumble recovery (Edinger kick)
Florida - Taylor 8 yard pass from Doug Johnson (Chandler kick)
Michigan State - Edinger 20 yard field goal
Florida - Johnson 1 yard run (Jeff Chandler kick)
Michigan State - Burress 21 yard pass from Burke (Pass failed)
Florida - Taylor 39 yard pass from Johnson (Pass failed)
Florida - Gillespie 2-yard run (Chandler kick)
Michigan State - Burress 30 yard pass from Burke (Scott pass from Burke)
Michigan State - Edinger 39 yard field goal

Michigan State Media Guide Florida Citrus Bowl Game Summary - Paul Edinger kicked a 39-yard field goal as time expired to give No. 9 Michigan State a 37-34 victory over No. 10 Florida in the 2000 Florida Citrus Bowl. It marked Michigan State's first New Year's Day bowl victory since the 1988 Rose Bowl and it ended a four-game losing streak in postseason play. There were five lead changes in the contest. The Spartans opened the scoring as an eight-play, 36-yard drive resulted in a 46- yard field goal by Edinger. Florida countered with an eight-play, 80-yard drive to take a 7-3 lead as Travis Taylor scored on a 12- yard toss from Doug Johnson. Michigan State built a 17-7 lead in the second quarter on Bill Burke's 37-yard TD strike to Plaxico Burress and a 24-yard fumble return by T.J. Turner. The Gators put together an 11-play, 83-yard drive to pull to within 17- 14 on Johnson's 8-yard TD pass to Taylor. Edinger's second field goal, a 20-yarder, gave the Spartans a 20-14 lead but Johnson capped off an 11-play, 80-yard drive with a 1-yard sneak to put Florida ahead at the half, 21-20. Burke directed a 10-play, 84- yard drive late in the third quarter, hooking up with Burress for a 21-yard scoring pass. The Gators regained the lead on the next possession as Johnson hit Taylor for another score, this time from 39 yards out. Florida's final score came off a Spartan turnover as Alex Brown recovered a fumble at the MSU 48. Six plays later, Rob Gillespie scored on a 2-yard run as Florida extended its lead to 34-26. Michigan State rallied to tie the score at 34 early in the fourth quarter as Burke found Burress alone in the end zone for a 30-yard completion then he hit Gari Scott for the two-point conversion. Lloyd Clemons' 8-yard run on third-and-2 set up Edinger's game-winning kick from the Florida 22. Burress had a school-record 13 receptions for 185 yards and three TDs to earn Citrus Bowl MVP honors. Burke completed 21-of-35 throws for 257 yards and three scores while Clemons rushed for a game-high 105 yards on 20 carries. Johnson connected on 24-of-50 passes for 288 yards and three TDs while Taylor had 11 catches for 156 yards and three scores.

2000 Cotton Bowl Classic

The 2000 SBC Cotton Bowl Classic game took place on Jan. 1, 2000 in Dallas, Texas. The Arkansas Razorbacks defeated the Texas Longhorns 27-6. The game matched longtime rivals of the old Southwest Conference.

2000 Cotton Bowl Classic	Line	1	-	2	-	3	-	4	-	Final
#24 Arkansas	(50.0)	3	-	0	-	7	-	17	-	27
#14 Texas	(-4.5)	0	-	3	-	3	-	0	-	6

Scoring Summary
Arkansas - Dodson 25 yard field goal
Texas - Stockton 35 yard field goal
Arkansas – Cobbs 30 yard pass from Stoerner (Dodson kick)
Texas - Stockton 22 yard field goal
Arkansas - Jenkins 42 yard run (Tony Dodson kick)
Arkansas - Cobbs 37 yard run (Tony Dodson kick)
Arkansas - Dodson 27 yard field goal

Cotton Bowl Classic Game Summary - Thirty years after "The Game of the Century," long-time foes Arkansas and Texas renewed their rivalry in the 64th Southwestern Bell Cotton Bowl Classic. The last time these two rivals met was in 1991 when the Razorbacks carted home a 14-13 victory prior to their departure to the Southeastern Conference from their long-time home in the Southwest Conference. However, the most famous meeting of all took place on December 6, 1969, in the final game of college football's 100th season. Texas was ranked No. 1 and Arkansas was No. 2. President Richard Nixon flew into Fayetteville to proclaim the winning team as national champions. That dreary winter day proved to be an afternoon the Hogs could never forget and one the Longhorns would point to with pride. Texas rallied from a fourth quarter 14-0 deficit in the "Big Shootout" to pull off a stunning 15-14 victory and propelled the Horns to a memorable battle with Notre Dame in the 1970 Cotton Bowl Classic. No doubt, this wouldn't be just any match-up on just any New Year's Day. It was Texas vs. Arkansas, and the stage would be the Cotton Bowl at the "Turn of the Century." And for Arkansas, it was a chance to bury some painful memories from the past. The first half turned into a textbook defensive struggle with field goals coming from Arkansas' Tony Dodson and Texas' Kris Stockton to produce a 3-3 stalemate that stretched well into the third quarter. At last, the fireworks ignited five minutes into the second half when Texas pinned the Razorbacks just outside the goal line after Ryan Long's 44-yard punt was downed on the three. On two successive plays, Arkansas narrowly avoided being trapped for a safety. First, Quarterback Clint Stoerner escaped the fierce Texas rush by diving out of the end zone to the one for a loss of two. Next, tailback Chrys Chukwuma was swarmed by three Longhorn defenders, yet somehow fought his way out of the end zone and back to the one for no gain. Then came the game's most decisive play. On third-and 12, Stoerner launched a 47-yard bomb to split end Anthony Lucas. It was the spark the Razorbacks needed to bring their offense to life. Quickly, Stoerner moved Arkansas from midfield to the Texas 30, and while scrambling to avoid another fierce pass rush, he lobbed a wobbly pass to Cedric Cobbs. The Hogs' freshman tailback turned and sprinted down the sideline and into the end zone to give Arkansas a 10-3 lead and finish a remarkable 97-yard touchdown drive. Texas came right back. Led by sophomore Quarterback Major Applewhite who connected on six-of-seven passes during the drive, the Longhorns marched 73 yards to the Arkansas one. But that's where the threat ended. The Arkansas defense rose to stop Texas on three consecutive plays and forced the Longhorns to settle again for a field goal by Stockton. Riding the momentum from its goal line stand, Arkansas pounded Texas with a 17-point barrage in the fourth quarter. The Hogs drove 86 yards in just seven plays to increase the lead to 17-6 when backup tailback Michael Jenkins broke loose up the middle for a 42-yard scoring run. Things got progressively worse for Texas. Applewhite, the Big 12's Offensive Player of the Year, was sacked on consecutive plays and suffered a torn anterior cruciate ligament in his left knee when flushed from the pocket by the Arkansas pass rush. In came freshman Quarterback Chris Simms who was promptly sacked for a six-yard loss and Texas had to punt. The short kick gave Arkansas the football at the Texas 37 and put Cobbs in position to wrap up the game's offensive MVP award. On the first play from scrimmage, the elusive freshman running back took the handoff from Stoerner, bounced outside and raced through and over Longhorn defenders for his second touchdown of the day. After Cobbs' run pushed the lead to 24-6, Arkansas coach Houston Nutt called on Dodson to add an insurance field goal, and with just 2:46 left to play the final score was in place for the Hogs, 27-6. The smothering Arkansas defense produced eight sacks for the day and held Texas to minus-27 yards rushing, a Cotton Bowl and Texas school record. The ringleader was tackle D.J. Cooper who collected two sacks and five unassisted tackles while en route to defensive MVP honors. It was the Razorbacks' first bowl victory since 1985. Finally, after 30 years, Arkansas had put to rest the ghost of the "Big Shootout."

2000 Rose Bowl

The 2000 Rose Bowl was played on January 1, 2000. It was the 86th Rose Bowl game and was played on January 1, 2000 at the Rose Bowl Stadium in Pasadena, California. The game featured the Wisconsin Badgers defeating the Stanford Cardinal by a score of 17-9. Ron Dayne, the Wisconsin running back, was named the Rose Bowl Player of the Game for the second consecutive year.

Wisconsin Badgers - Wisconsin entered the game as the sole champions of the Big Ten Conference, their first untied conference championship season since 1962 when they played in the 1963 Rose Bowl, although they had been conference co-champions in 1993 and 1998, appearing in the 1994 and 1999 Rose Bowls. The Wisconsin offense featured a powerful running game with 1999 Heisman Trophy winner Ron Dayne at running back.

Stanford Cardinal - Stanford entered the game as the champions of the Pacific-10 Conference. It was their first conference championship season since 1971 and their first Rose Bowl since 1972.

2000 Rose Bowl	Line	1	-	2	-	3	-	4	-	Final
#22 Stanford	(59.0)	0	-	9	-	0	-	0	-	9
#4 Wisconsin	(-14.0)	0	-	3	-	7	-	7	-	17

Scoring Summary
Stanford – Biselli 28 yard field goal
Wisconsin – Pisetsky 31 yard field goal
Stanford – Carter 1 yard run (two-point conversion failed)
Wisconsin – Dayne 4 yard run (Pisetsky kick)
Wisconsin – Bollinger 1 yard run (Pisetsky kick)

Rose Bowl Game Summary - Wisconsin defeats Stanford 17-9 in the 86th Rose Bowl Game on January 1, 2000 before 93,731 people. The Badgers become the first Big Ten team ever to capture the Rose Bowl Game two years in a row, and all-time national ground game leader Ron Dayne (7,125 yards in four seasons) is Player-of-the-Game on both occasions. Dayne runs 200 yards through Stanford's defense and scores the game-turning touchdown for a Rose Bowl career rushing yardage of 446 yards and a record 30 points on five touchdowns. Stanford gains 3-0 and 9-3 leads during the first half action, but it can't run the ball on the ground (a minus five yards for the day) and flubs two kicking chances to ruin Coach Tyrone Willingham's hopes of scoring an upset. Stanford's Mike Biselli and Wisconsin's Vitaly Pisetsky trade field goals to start the scoring before Stanford's Kerry Carter climaxes a 45-yard drive with a one-yard touchdown. A bad center snap ruins the extra point try. Trailing 9-3 in the third quarter, Heisman winner Dayne bolts 64 yards, his touchdown four yards around left and the successful conversion giving Coach Barry Alvarez' Badgers a 10-9 lead which they never relinquish. A 30-yard pass from Todd Husak to DeRonnie Pitts to the Wisconsin six sets the stage for a Stanford field goal try of 23 yards but a bad center snap gives Mike Echols time to block Biselli's kick. Wisconsin increases its lead to 17-9 on two passes from Brooks Bollinger to tight end John Sigmund and a Bollinger on-yard scoring keeper plus a successful conversion. Stanford experiences futility thereafter to finish the season 8-4 compared to Wisconsin's 10-2.

Aftermath - Ron Dayne was named the Rose Bowl MVP for the second time (the first time being the 1999 Rose Bowl), becoming only the third player in the history of the Rose Bowl to repeat as MVP. To this day, he is the only player from a Big Ten Conference team to accomplish this feat: Bob Schloredt of the Washington Huskies (AAWU) was the first, Charles White of USC (Pac-10) was the second, and Vince Young of the Texas Longhorns (Big 12) has subsequently become the fourth. The two teams would go on to face off again exactly thirteen years later in the 2013 Rose Bowl, with Barry Alvarez returning to serve as interim head coach for Wisconsin, but this time, Stanford would win 20-14. 2000 Rose Queen Sophia Bush has gone on to become a successful actress, starring for nine seasons as Brooke Davis on One Tree Hill, and currently as Detective Erin Lindsay on Chicago P.D.

2000 Orange Bowl

The 2000 FedEx Orange Bowl game was played between the Alabama Crimson Tide and the Michigan Wolverines on January 1, 2000, at Pro Player Stadium in Miami Gardens, Florida. Michigan defeated Alabama 35–34 in an overtime battle. The Orange Bowl was first played in 1935, and the 2000 game represented the 66th edition of the Orange Bowl. The contest was televised on ABC. Quarterback Tom Brady led Michigan to the win, throwing for 369 yards and four touchdowns, while leading the team back from a pair of 14-point deficits in regulation (14-0 in the first half, and 28-14 in the second). Brady threw the game-winning score in overtime on a bootleg to tight end Shawn Thompson. The game was won by Michigan when Alabama placekicker, Ryan Pflugner, missed a PAT following their own touchdown. This was the first overtime BCS Bowl game.

2000 Orange Bowl	Line	1	-	2	-	3	-	4	-	OT	-	Final
#5 Alabama	(-1.0)	0	-	14	-	14	-	0	-	6	-	34
#8 Michigan	(48.5)	0	-	7	-	21	-	0	-	7	-	35

Scoring Summary
Alabama - Alexander 5 yard run (Pflunger kick)
Alabama - Alexander 6 yard run (Pflunger kick)
Michigan - Terrell 27 yard pass from Brady (Epstein kick)
Michigan - Terrell 57 yard pass from Brady (Epstein kick)
Alabama - Alexander 50 yard run (Pflunger kick)
Alabama - Milons 62 yard punt return (Pflunger kick)
Michigan - Terrell 20 yard pass from Brady (Epstein kick)
Michigan - Thomas 3 yard run (Epstein kick)
Michigan - Thompson 25 yard pass from Brady (Epstein kick)
Alabama - Carter 21 yard pass from Zow (kick failed)

Bentley Historical Library 2000 ORANGE BOWL GAME SUMMARY - Michigan erased a pair of 14-point deficits in winning a thrilling 35-34 overtime game against Alabama in the 2000 FedEx Orange Bowl at Pro Player Stadium. The Wolverines played in, and won, their first overtime contest in school history. With the score knotted at 28 at the end of regulation, Michigan scored on its initial play of overtime when Quarterback Tom Brady found tight end Shawn Thompson on a 25-yard TD pass. Kicker Hayden Epstein hit the extra point to give U-M a 35-28 lead, its first of the contest. On Alabama's first possession of overtime, Andrew Zow hit Antonio Carter with a 21-yard TD pass on the second play of the drive. However, Alabama's Ryan Pflugner pushed the extra point attempt wide right and Michigan claimed the victory. Sophomore wide receiver David Terrell was named Orange Bowl MVP after setting career bests in receiving yards (150) and receiving touchdowns (three) as well as equaling his career-high in receptions (10). Brady capped his career with a career-best four TD passes on 34-of-46 passing for a UM bowl record 369 yards. During regulation, Michigan trimmed the deficit to 14-7 with 58 seconds left in the first half when Brady hit Terrell on a 27-yard scoring strike. Michigan held Alabama on its first offensive possession of the second half and marched 59 yards to even the score at 14. The Crimson Tide responded with back-to-back touchdowns from Shaun Alexander and Freddie Milons. Michigan closed the gap when Brady and Terrell connected on a 20-yard TD pass with 5:42 left in the third quarter. After holding Alabama on its next possession, Michigan tied the game (28-28) as junior tailback Anthony Thomas scored on a three-yard run. The Wolverines dominated the fourth quarter, but a fumble heading into the end zone for the go-ahead score and a blocked 36-yard field goal attempt on the final play of regulation, sent the game into overtime.

2000 Fiesta Bowl

The 2000 Tostitos Fiesta Bowl, played on January 2, 2000, was the 29th edition of the Fiesta Bowl. The game was played at Sun Devil Stadium in Tempe, Arizona between the Tennessee Volunteers (ranked #5 in the BCS) and the Nebraska Cornhuskers (ranked #3 in the BCS). The matchup featured the two most current National Championship teams. Nebraska in 1997, and Tennessee in 1998.

2000 Fiesta Bowl	Line	1	-	2	-	3	-	4	-	Final
#5 Tennessee	(45.0)	0	-	7	-	7	-	7	-	21
#3 Nebraska	(-4.0)	14	-	3	-	7	-	7	-	31

Scoring Summary
Nebraska - Alexander 7 yard run (Brown kick)
Nebraska - Newcombe 60 yard punt return (Brown kick)
Nebraska - Brown 31 yard field goal
Tennessee - Stallworth 9 yard pass from Martin (Walls kick)
Tennessee - Henry 4 yard run (Walls kick)
Nebraska - Golliday 13 yard pass from Crouch (Brown kick)
Nebraska - Buckhalter 2 yard run (Brown kick)
Tennessee - Stallworth 44 yard pass from Wilson (Walls kick)

Associated Press Fiesta Bowl Game Summary - Too much speed, too much strength. Just too much Nebraska. With lightning-quick Eric Crouch at the controls of a relentless option attack, the third-ranked Cornhuskers beat No. 5 Tennessee 31-21 in the Fiesta Bowl on Sunday night. After the Volunteers rallied from a 17-0 deficit to cut it to 17-14 early in the second half behind the passing of Tee Martin, the Huskers (12-1) finished Tennessee off with second-half touchdown drives of 96 and 99 yards. Cedric Wilson's 44-yard pass touchdown pass to Donte' Stallworth, his second TD catch of the game, came on a Tennessee trick play that reduced the lead to 31-21 with 7:25 to play. But the Vols never got the ball again. Nebraska, which finished the game with 23 consecutive rushing plays for 156 yards, drove downfield and the Tennessee (9-3) could do nothing to stop the clock from running out. It was all-too familiar for the Volunteers, who wore down in the second half two years ago in a 42-17 loss to Nebraska in the Orange Bowl. The Huskers have won their last 11 bowl matchups against SEC teams. Nebraska's Bobby Newcombe had a 60-yard punt return for a touchdown. Crouch's quickness was the problem the Volunteers expected, but he did almost as much damage with his arm. Crouch, the game's MVP, was 9-of-15 for 148 yards and a touchdown. Martin, who finished his career with a 22-3 record as a starter, was 19-of-34 for 223 yards and a touchdown. He was intercepted twice. The Huskers rushed for 321 yards and had 469 yards overall. Dan Alexander gained 108 yards on 21 carries, Willie Miller added 87 yards on eight carries, and Crouch had 64 yards on 17 carries. Tennessee managed just 44 yards rushing. After Tennessee cut the lead to 17-14, Crouch threw a 13-yard touchdown pass to wide-open tight end Aaron Golliday to boost the lead to 24-14 with 4:44 left in the third quarter. The pass, Nebraska's first for a touchdown in 19 quarters, capped a nine-play 96-yard drive that included a 17-yard pass from Crouch to another tight end, John Bowling, on third-and-13 from the Nebraska 23. Golliday and Bowling saw extra duty because Tracey Wistrom, the Huskers' all-Big-12 tight end, was out with a knee injury. Tennessee pinned the Huskers at their 1 on their next possession, but Nebraska went 99 yards in 10 plays, all on the ground, overpowering the tiring Vols defense. Correll Buckhalter ran 27 yards to the Vols 19, then scored on a 2-yard run to make it 31-14 with 12:01 left in the game. The Cornhuskers, in their NCAA record 31st consecutive bowl game, needed just four plays to score on their first possession. Crouch went 30 yards on an option play on third-and-4 to set up Dan Alexander's 7-yard touchdown run on the next play. Nebraska made it 14-0 after the Huskers' defense stopped the Volunteers deep in their own territory. Newcombe, who started the year at Quarterback but switched to wingback after two games, took the punt and shot through a hole on the right side of the field, then won a footrace to the end zone with 3:21 left in the first quarter. Crouch's 46-yard pass to Matt Davison set up Josh Brown's 31-yard field goal that put the Huskers up 17-0 with 1:37 left in the first half. The kick hit the right upright and bounced through. The Volunteers finally got their offense in gear just before halftime. Martin completed 6-of-7 passes for 66 yards, with the only incompletion an intentional spike, as Tennessee scored on an 8-play, 65-yard drive that used up just 1 minute, 19 seconds. Martin threw a 9-yard touchdown pass to Dante' Stallworth to make it 17-7 with 18 seconds left in the half. Alexander fumbled on the first play of the second half and Tennessee's Dominique Stevenson recovered at the Nebraska 25. Four plays later, Travis Henry scored on a 4-yard run to cut the lead to 17-14. It was the only turnover of the game for the Cornhuskers, who led NCAA Division I with 25 fumbles lost. Nebraska's All-America defensive back Mike Brown, playing on the same field where he won the Arizona state high school championship, intercepted a pass and was selected the game's top defensive player. Brown said defensive coordinator Charlie McBride called his players into a huddle after the game to tell them that he was retiring. McBride has coached at Nebraska for 23 years, 18 as defensive coordinator.

2000 Sugar Bowl (BCS Championship Game)

The 2000 Sugar Bowl was the Bowl Championship Series (BCS) National Championship Game and was played on January 4, 2000, at the Louisiana Superdome in New Orleans, Louisiana. The Florida State Seminoles, representing the Atlantic Coast Conference, defeated the Virginia Tech Hokies, representing the Big East Conference, by a score of 46–29. With the win, Florida State clinched the 1999 BCS national championship, the team's second national championship in its history. An estimated total of 79,280 people attended the game in person, while approximately 18.4 million US viewers watched the game on ABC television. The resulting 17.5 television rating was the third largest ever recorded for a BCS college football game. Tickets were in high demand for the game, with tens of thousands of fans from both teams attending, many using scalped tickets to gain entry. The game kicked off at 8 p.m. EST, and Virginia Tech received the ball to begin the game. Though Tech advanced down the field, Florida State scored first and took advantage of a blocked punt for a touchdown, giving the Seminoles a 14–0 lead in the first quarter. Tech answered with a touchdown drive of its own before the end of the quarter, but Florida State scored two quick touchdowns to begin the second quarter. Virginia Tech scored a touchdown before halftime, but halfway through the game, Florida State held a 28–14 lead. In the third quarter, Virginia Tech's offense gave the Hokies a lead with a field goal and two touchdowns. Tech failed to convert two two-point conversions but held a 29–28 lead at the end of the third quarter. Florida State answered in the fourth quarter, however, taking a 36–29 lead with a touchdown and successful two-point conversion early in the quarter. From this point, the Seminoles did not relinquish the lead, extending it to 46–29 with another touchdown and a field goal. For his performance in the game, Florida State wide receiver Peter Warrick was named the game's most valuable player. Although Tech lost the game, several of its players won postseason awards—most notably Michael Vick, who earned an ESPY for his performance during the Sugar Bowl and the regular season. Several players from each team entered the National Football League after graduation, being selected either in the 2000 NFL Draft or later editions of that selection process.

2000 Sugar Bowl	Line	1	-	2	-	3	-	4	-	Final
#2 Virginia Tech	(48.5)	7	-	7	-	15	-	0	-	29
#1 Florida State	(-6.0)	14	-	14	-	0	-	18	-	46

Scoring Summary
Florida State - Warrick 64 yard pass from Weinke (Janikowski kick)
Florida State - Chaney 6 yard blocked punt return (Janikowski kick)
Virginia Tech - Davis 49 yard pass from Vick (Graham kick)
Florida State - Dugans 63 yard pass from Weinke (Janikowski kick)
Florida State - Warrick 59 yard punt return (Janikowski kick)
Virginia Tech - Vick 3 yard run (Graham kick)
Virginia Tech - Graham 23 yard field goal
Virginia Tech - Kendrick 29 yard run (2-pt pass failed)
Virginia Tech - Kendrick 6 yard run (2-pt pass failed)

Florida State - Dugans 14 yard pass from Weinke (Warrick pass from Weinke)
Florida State - Janikowski 32 yard field goal
Florida State - Warrick 43 yard pass from Weinke Janikowski kick)

Postgame effects - Florida State's victory earned it the 1999 BCS national championship and brought the Seminoles' season to an end with an undefeated 12–0 record. By beginning the season at No. 1 and ending it in the same position, Florida State became the first college football team to stay ranked No. 1 for every week of the season after being ranked No. 1 in the preseason poll. Virginia Tech's loss brought it to a final record of 11–1, but the Hokies still completed their first 11-win season in school history. The 75 total points scored in the 2000 Sugar Bowl were a Sugar Bowl record at that point in the game's history.

2000 GMAC Mobile Alabama Bowl

The 2000 GMAC Mobile Alabama Bowl was played in December 2000, and featured the Southern Miss Golden Eagles, and the TCU Horned Frogs. TCU started the scoring with a 3-yard touchdown pass from Quarterback Casey Printers to wide receiver George Layne to open a 7-0 lead. Southern Miss tied it in the 1st quarter when Leo Barnes intercepted a pass and returned it 50 yards for a touchdown. In the second quarter, Jeff Kelly threw a 9-yard touchdown pass to LeRoy Handy for a 14-7 Southern Miss lead. TCU running back LaDainian Tomlinson scored on touchdown runs of 7 and 33 yards in the third quarter, as TCU took a 21-14 lead into the fourth quarter. In the fourth quarter, Jeff Kelly threw a 56-yard touchdown pass to LeRoy Handy to tie the game at 21. He threw the game winning touchdown pass with 8 seconds left, with a 29-yard pass to Kenneth Johnson.

2000 GMAC Mobile Alabama Bowl	Line	1	-	2	-	3	-	4	-	Final
TCU	(-7.0)	7	-	0	-	14	-	0	-	21
Southern Miss	(40.5)	7	-	0	-	7	-	14	-	28

Scoring Summary
TCU – Layne 3 yard pass from Printers (Kaylakie kick)
Southern Miss – Barnes 50 yard interception return (Hanna kick)
Southern Miss – Handy 9 yard pass from Kelly (Hanna kick)
TCU – Tomlinson 7 yard run (Kaylakie kick)
TCU – Tomlinson 33 yard run (Kaylakie kick)
Southern Miss – Handy 56 yard pass from Kelly (Hanna kick)
Southern Miss – Johnson 29 yard pass from Kelly (Hanna kick)

Associated Press Mobile Alabama Bowl Game Summary - It turns out Jeff Bower didn't have to trust a kicking game that had let him down all night. Jeff Kelly's 29-yard touchdown pass to freshman Kenny Johnson with eight seconds left lifted Southern Mississippi to a 28-21 victory over No. 13 Texas Christian in the Mobile Alabama Bowl on Wednesday night. That saved Bower from canceling a redshirt year for placekicker Curtis Jones for one last attempt after four missed field goals. The Golden Eagles (8-4) had lost three of their last four games entering the first major bowl game of the season. They won the showdown with the only defense in the nation rated higher than them and held All-American LaDanian Tomlinson to his lowest rushing total of the season. Tomlinson, a Heisman Trophy finalist who led the nation in rushing the past two seasons, ran for 118 yards on 28 carries and scored two TDs in the third quarter for the Horned Frogs (10-2). With 33 seconds left, the Golden Eagles took over at the TCU 43-yard line after Mobile native Etric Pruitt got a hand on Mark Haulman's punt. Kelly wasn't surprised at the second chance, who was 11-of-23 for 159 yards and three TDs. Kelly threw two incompletions, then scrambled 14 yards for a first down on the final drive. On the next play, he lofted a perfect strike over the middle just above safety LaVar Veale's outstretched arm, victimizing the nation's top defense. TCU failed to reach midfield on the ensuing kick return. The Horned Frogs endured a December coaching change and uncertainty over who would lead them into the game. In the end, former defensive coordinator Gary Patterson replaced Dennis Franchione on the sidelines. Franchione left for Alabama Dec. 1 and was initially expected to coach the bowl game. TCU officials decided late last week to allow the Patterson era to begin a season early. Franchione watched from the press box. Quarterback Casey Printers was 10-of-22 for 115 yards with two interceptions. Kelly had a big fourth quarter. He was 7-of-15 for 40 yards after three quarters. Then, he hit LeRoy Handy on a 56-yard TD strike with 7:24 left, tying it at 21. Kelly also hit Handy, who had missed the past three years with a shoulder injury, on a 9-yarder in the third quarter. Tomlinson had a previous low of 119 yards against Tulsa. Southern Miss safety Leo Barnes returned an interception 50 yards for a TD in the first quarter. It was his fourth interception return for a score of the season. Southern Miss had two chances for a go-ahead score with just over two minutes left. For the fourth time, Brant Hanna kicked a low line drive, this one a 32-yarder that failed to clear TCU's defensive line. It was the second block of the night for the junior, who was 12-of-18 in the regular season. That prompted Bowers to tell Johnson, a junior college transfer, he would get his first shot if necessary. TCU couldn't get a first down against the nation's second-rated defense, which held the Horned Frogs to 265 yards and set up a pair of TDs with interceptions. Backup Southern Miss tailback Kelby Nance outshined Tomlinson, carrying 16 times for 104 yards. It was the first career 100-yard game for the senior, who started the season as a third teamer.

2000 Las Vegas Bowl

The 2000 edition to the Las Vegas Bowl was the 9th edition of that annual game. It featured the Arkansas Razorbacks, and the hometown UNLV Rebels. Arkansas scored first on a 7-yard touchdown pass from Quarterback Robby Hampton to wide receiver Rod Stinson for a 7-0 Razorback lead. In the second quarter, UNLV tied the score at 7, following a 19-yard touchdown pass from Jason Thomas to Nate Turner. Arkansas answered with a 25-yard touchdown pass from Hampton to Boo Williams, giving the Razorbacks a 14-7 lead. But with Thomas and Turner connecting for their second score, the game became a 14-14 tie at intermission. In the third quarter, Jason Thomas notched his third passing touchdown of the game, a 54 yarder to Troy Mason, giving UNLV a 21-14 lead, it wouldn't relinquish. In the fourth quarter, Dillon Pieffer kicked a 26-yard field goal to increase the Rebels lead to 24-14. Kevin Brown's 14 yard touchdown run made the final margin 31-14.

2000 Las Vegas Bowl	Line	1	-	2	-	3	-	4	-	Final
Arkansas	(-1.5)	7	-	7	-	0	-	0	-	14
UNLV	(44.0)	0	-	14	-	7	-	10	-	31

Scoring Summary
Arkansas -Stinson 7 pass from R Hampton (Odonohoe kick)
UNLV -Turner 19 pass from Thomas (Pieffer kick)
Arkansas -B Williams 25 pass from Hampton (Odonohoe kick)
UNLV -Turner 5 pass from Thomas (Pieffer kick)
UNLV -Mason 54 pass from Thomas (Pieffer kick)
UNLV - Pieffer 26 yard Field goal
UNLV -Brown 18 run (Pieffer kick)

UNLV Media Guide Las Vegas Bowl Game Summary - Playing before a national ESPN2 audience and a Las Vegas Bowl-record 29,113 fans, UNLV (8-5) won its fourth straight for the first time since 1984 and moved to 3-0 all-time in bowl games with a surprisingly one-sided 31-14 victory over Arkansas (6- 6), the Rebels' first over a team from the powerful Southeastern Conference. UNLV Quarterback Jason Thomas earned MVP honors by completing 12 of 17 pass attempts for 217 yards and three scores without an interception as well as rushing for 32 yards on 10 carries. Thomas' favorite target was Nate Turner, who ended his career with 126 yards on eight catches – all in the first half. Jeremi Rudolph gained 92 yards on 14 carries and Kevin Brown had 78 on 13 attempts. Arkansas, which was fresh from two consecutive victories over ranked SEC opponents to become bowl eligible, opened the scoring with the only points of the first quarter. UNLV answered with a Thomas-to-Turner 19-yard pass, which was the first TD given up by the Razorbacks in 11 quarters. Two minutes later the Hogs used Robby Hampton's second scoring throw of the game to take a 14-7 lead. UNLV, however, struck again to square things before halftime with a five-yard Turner TD. Things stayed tied until with just over two minutes left in the third, Thomas found Troy Mason with a stunning 54-yard TD strike that was the second longest in bowl history. After a Dillon Pieffer field goal put UNLV up 24-14, the Razorbacks elected to go for it on fourth and 10 from the Rebel 37 with more than 12 minutes remaining. The UNLV defense forced an incompletion, and the inspired Rebels eventually closed their shocking 24-point scoring run with an 18-yard Brown run. The Rebels outgained the bigger Hogs, who had defeated seven straight non-conference opponents and were 6-0 vs. MW teams, 476 to 298. UNLV also held its opponent to under 200 yards rushing (115) for the 12th time in 2000. The Rebels, who moved to 2-0 in Las Vegas Bowls, earned their most victories in a season since 1984 and finished the season a perfect 6-0 at Sam Boyd Stadium. Head Coach John Robinson improved to 8-1 in bowl games during his career, which made him the winningest bowl coach in NCAA D-I history with a percentage of .889.

2000 Oahu Bowl

The 2000 Jeep Oahu Bowl was the 3rd and final game named Oahu Bowl and became the Seattle Bowl for the 2001 contest. (It was later shut down after 2 years as the Seattle Bowl.) The game was played on December 24, 2000, at Aloha Stadium in Honolulu, Hawai'i. The game matched the Georgia Bulldogs against the Virginia Cavaliers and was televised on ESPN. The 24th ranked Georgia Bulldogs won the game, 37-14. The game marked the final game as head coach for Jim Donnan of Georgia and George Welsh of Virginia, both of whom retired from head coaching after the season.

College Football "Bowl Games of the 21st Century" — Chapter 1 – 2000-2005

2000 Oahu Bowl	Line	1	-	2	-	3	-	4	-	Final
#24 Georgia	(-7.5)	17	-	7	-	0	-	13	-	37
Virginia	(47.0)	0	-	7	-	7	-	0	-	14

Scoring Summary
Georgia - Bennett 35 yard field goal
Georgia - Edwards 40 yard run (Bennett kick)
Georgia - Curry fumble recovery in end zone (Bennett kick)
Virginia - Dotson 14 yard run (Greene kick)
Georgia - Haynes 3 yard run (Bennett kick)
Virginia - Thweatt 58 yard fumble recovery (Greene kick)
Georgia - Gary 21 yard pass from C. Phillips (Bennett kick)
Georgia - Burnett 4 yard fumble recovery (Bennett kick failed)

Georgia Media Guide Oahu Bowl Game Summary - The 24th-ranked Georgia Bulldogs (8-4) defeated the Virginia Cavaliers 34-17 in the 2000 Jeep O'ahu Bowl in front of an Aloha Stadium crowd of 24,187 and an ESPN national television audience on Christmas Eve. The Bulldogs were led by sophomore receiver Terrence Edwards (below), who was named the game's Most Valuable Player. Georgia jumped out to a 17-0 lead in the first quarter. The Bulldogs got on the board with a 35-yard field goal by freshman kicker Billy Bennett. On the Bulldogs' next series, one play after a successful fake punt, Edwards scampered 40 yards into the end zone on a reverse to give Georgia a 10-0 lead. On Virginia's next possession, junior running back Tyree Foreman was hit by freshman cornerback Dantra Clements, who caused a fumble that was recovered by freshman safety Kentrell Curry in the end zone for the 17-0 lead. Virginia got on the board on its next possession, going 97 yards on five plays, capped by a 14-yard touchdown run by senior receiver Demetrius Dotson to bring the score to 17-7. Georgia answered on its next possession with a four-play, 80-yard scoring drive keyed by a 57-yard run by Edwards and capped by a three-yard touchdown run by senior running back Verron Haynes, increasing the Bulldogs' lead to 24-7. The Cavaliers pulled within 24-14 in the third quarter as senior linebacker Byron Thweatt returned a Georgia fumble 58 yards, but that was as close as Virginia would get. Georgia added two more touchdowns for the final margin, a 21-yard pass from sophomore Quarterback Cory Phillips to freshman receiver Damien Gary and a four-yard fumble return by sophomore safety Cap Burnett after senior linebacker Kendrell Bell knocked the ball loose. Edwards led the Bulldogs in both receiving and rushing with eight catches for 79 yards and five rushes for 97 yards and one touchdown.

2000 Aloha Classic

The 2000 Aloha Bowl was held on December 25, 2000 in Honolulu, Hawaii. It featured the Boston College Eagles of the Big East Conference, and the Arizona State Sun Devils of the Pacific-10 Conference. Boston College won the game, 31–17. This was the final Aloha Bowl.

2000 Aloha Classic	Line	1	-	2	-	3	-	4	-	Final
Boston College	(55.0)	10	-	0	-	14	-	7	-	31
Arizona State	(-3.5)	7	-	3	-	0	-	7	-	17

Scoring Summary
Arizona State - Pace 14 yard run (Barth kick)
Boston College - Washington 10 yard run (Sutphin kick)
Boston College - Sutphin 50 yard Field goal
Arizona State - Barth 28 yard Field goal
Boston College - Dewalt 58 yard pass from Hasselbeck (Sutphin kick)
Boston College - Read 40 yard pass from Hasselbeck (Sutphin kick)
Boston College - Washington 11 yard run (Sutphin kick)
Arizona State - Dennard 31 yard pass from Cooper (Barth kick)

Associated Press Aloha Classic Game Summary - Tim Hasselbeck and several other seniors from Boston College put a rocky ride behind them. Bruce Snyder was not as lucky. Hasselbeck threw a pair of long touchdown passes in the third quarter as Boston College defeated Arizona State, 31-17, in the Aloha Bowl. It was the final game for Hasselbeck and other members of the Eagles' senior class, which began their collegiate careers amidst controversy following a 1996 gambling scandal within the program. Cedric Washington added a pair of scoring runs as Boston College (7-5) handed Snyder a loss in his coaching finale for Arizona State (6-6). Snyder was within a win of the national championship in 1996 but went 17-18 over his final three seasons for the Sun Devils and already had been told this would be his last game. Hasselbeck fired a 58-yard TD pass to Dedrick Dewalt and a 40-yarder to Ryan Read in a 2:56 span of the third quarter as Boston College built a 24-10 lead. The brother of Green Bay Packers backup Quarterback Matt Hasselbeck, Tim completed 9-of-21 passes for 209 touchdowns with an interception and was named his team's Most Valuable Player. Mike Sutphin kicked a 50-yard field goal for the Eagles, members of the Big

East Conference who won a bowl game for the first time since 1994 and improved to 1-1 under Coach Tom O'Brien in the postseason. The Eagles fell behind early as Tom Pace scored on a 14-yard run 3:10 into the game to cap a six-play, 46-yard drive and give the Sun Devils a 7-0 lead. But just 67 seconds later, Boston College tied it on a 10-yard TD run by Washington. Hasselbeck set up the score with a run of 52 yards, more than a third of his rushing total entering the day. Hasselbeck, who had 68 yards on two carries with a brace on his knee. Later in the first half, Sutphin and Mike Barth exchanged field goals for a 10-10 tie at intermission. Hasselbeck went to work in the third quarter. After completing 1-of-2 passes on the Eagles' opening possession of the half, he found Dewalt from 58 yards on the only play of the next drive. Boston College began its next series of downs on its own 46-yard line and needed only three plays to score as Hasselbeck threw a 40-yard pass to Read in the end zone for a 24-10 lead. After a shaky first half, Hasselbeck went 5-of-7 for 124 yards in the third quarter. Also, a senior, Washington carried 22 times for 113 yards. He made it 31-10 with his second TD of the game, an 11-yard run 3 1/2 minutes into the fourth quarter. Third-string Quarterback Matt Cooper capped the scoring with a 31-yard pass to Ryan Dennard in the final minute, but it was not enough for Arizona State. Sun Devils freshman starter Jeff Krohn went 6-of-10 for 74 yards with an interception in his return from mononucleosis. Pace totaled 139 yards on 25 carries for Arizona State, which had possession for over 35 1/2 minutes and 360 yards of offense but committed five of the game's seven turnovers. Sophomore safety Alfred Williams was named MVP for the Sun Devils. He had an interception, 10 tackles and forced a fumble as Arizona State closed the season with its fourth loss in five games.

2000 Galleryfurniture.com Bowl

The 2000 Galleryfurniture.com Bowl was played between the Texas Tech Red Raiders from the Big 12 Conference and the East Carolina Pirates from Conference USA (C-USA) at the Astrodome in Houston, Texas on December 27, 2000. It was the inaugural game in the bowl's history.

2000 Galleryfurniture.com Bowl	Line	1	-	2	-	3	-	4	-	Final
East Carolina	(53.0)	20	-	14	-	6	-	0	-	40
Texas Tech	(-1.0)	0	-	7	-	7	-	13	-	27

Scoring Summary
East Carolina - Garrard 6 yard run (kick failed)
East Carolina - Stokes 71 yard punt return (Miller kick)
East Carolina - Henry 1 yard run (Miller kick)
East Carolina - Collier 44 yard pass from Garrard (Miller kick)
East Carolina - Henry 1 yard run (Miller kick)
Texas Tech - Dorris 7 yard pass from Kingsbury (Birkholz kick)
Texas Tech - Jones 65 yard pass from Kingsbury (Birkholz kick)
East Carolina - Miller 36 yard Field goal
East Carolina - Miller 35 yard Field goal
Texas Tech - Roberts 17 yard pass from Kingsbury (Birkholz kick)
Texas Tech - Dorris 3 yard pass from Kingsbury (two-point conversion failed)

Associated Press Galleryfurniture.com Bowl Game Summary - When it was over, only the East Carolina Pirates and their gleeful fans went home happy. East Carolina scored 34 straight first-half points, including two 1-yard runs by Leonard Henry and a 71-yard punt return by Keith Stokes, as the Pirates stunned Texas Tech 40-27 in the first galleryfurniture.com Bowl on Wednesday night. Pirates Quarterback David Garrard voted the game's most valuable player and offensive player of the game. A crowd of 33,899 saw the first bowl game played in the Astrodome since the last Bluebonnet Bowl in 1987. But ticketing problems caused hundreds of fans to miss much of the first half standing at the will-call window waiting to get their tickets. In a game expected to be an offensive shootout, only East Carolina came through in the first half with an assortment of trick plays and fancy running by Stokes. He had 266 total yards in the game and was voted the special team's player of the game. Stokes had five kickoff returns for 105 yards, three punt returns for 82 yards, rushed for 33 yards on two carries and caught five passes for 46 yards. Stokes returned the opening kickoff 37 yards and Garrard capped the drive with a 6-yard touchdown run. The Pirates followed with an on-side kick that was recovered by Marcellus Harris. Although that surprise play didn't result in any points on the drive, Stokes took Tech's next punt 71 yards for a touchdown and Henry scored on a 1-yard run with 4:26 left in the first, completing a 20-point opening period. Garrard hit Derrick Collier with a 44-yard touchdown pass and Henry scored on another 1-yard run for a 34-0 lead in the second quarter. Garrard completed 17 of 27 passes for 229 yards and rushed 33 yards on 13 carries. Tech rallied behind Kliff Kingsbury, who threw four touchdown passes, three in the second half to cut the Pirates' big first-half bulge. The Red Raiders finally got on the board with a 7-yard touchdown pass from Kingsbury to Derek Dorris with 1:39 left in the half. The Raiders kept charging in the second half as Kingsbury hit Darrell Jones with a 65-yard touchdown pass with 13:11 to go in the third quarter to make it 34-14. After

East Carolina's Kevin Miller kicked field goals of 36 and 35 yards, Kingsbury threw a touchdown pass of 17 yards to Cole Roberts and a 3-yard pass to Dorris to make it 40-27. The last college bowl game played in the Astrodome was on Dec. 21, 1987, when Texas defeated Pittsburgh 32-27, ending a 28-year run for the bowl. Tech's bowl record dropped to 5-18-1, and the Red Raiders have lost five of their last six postseason games. East Carolina improved its bowl record to 7-2.

2000 Motor City Bowl

The 2000 Motor City Bowl was played between the Marshall Thundering Herd of the MAC defeated the Cincinnati Bearcats of the Conference USA 25–14. It was played on December 27, 2000 at the Pontiac Silverdome in Pontiac, Michigan. Cincinnati kicker Jonathan Ruffin was an All-America and had won the Lou Groza Award as the nation's best placekicker. Quarterback Deontey Kenner led the Bearcat offense, while 330 lb. defensive tackle Mario Monds led the defense. Marshall's offense was led by future NFL Quarterback Byron Leftwich, its defense was led by four-year starter Paul Toviessi. This year marked the 30th anniversary of the tragic 1970 plane crash which took the lives of 75 Marshall Football players, coaches, administrators, and boosters on November 14. Marshall Quarterback Byron Leftwich was named the game's MVP. The game was the 4th installment of the Motor City Bowl, matching the Conference USA against the Mid-American Conference for the first time in its history.

2000 Motor City Bowl	Line	1	-	2	-	3	-	4	-	Final
Cincinnati	(-2.0)	7	-	7	-	0	-	0	-	14
Marshall	(54.5)	9	-	0	-	13	-	3	-	25

Scoring Summary
Marshall – Darius 77 yard pass from Leftwich (Jenkins kick)
Cincinnati – McCleskey 2 yard run (Ruffin kick)
Marshall – Safety Jackson tackled by Owens in end zone
Cincinnati – McCleskey 2 yard run (Ruffin kick)
Marshall – Leftwich 1 yard run (Leftwich pass failed)
Marshall – Wallace 4 yard run (Jenkins kick)
Marshall – Jenkins 25 yard Field goal

Byron Leftwich threw a 77-yard touchdown pass on the fourth play of the game and rushed for a score, making up for two turnovers in the second quarter. Leftwich was 17-of-30 for 221 yards. Marshall scored touchdowns on its first two drives of the second half after Cincinnati went three-and-out on consecutive possessions. The Thundering Herd sealed the win on a 25-yard field goal from J.R. Jenkins with 43 seconds left. Marshall took a 7-0 lead when Leftwich connected with Darius Watts for the 77-yard touchdown. Leftwich threw the ball about 20 yards while Watts raced through the Bearcats defense the rest of the way for the score. The Bearcats also scored a touchdown on their first possession when DeMarco McCleskey dove for a 1-yard touchdown. Marshall's Michael Owens, who was named the game's top lineman, eluded a blocker and tackled Ray Jackson for a safety to give the Thundering Herd a 9-7 lead late in the first quarter. The Bearcats scored after the second turnover by Leftgwich to take a 14-9 lead with 1:44 left in the half. On a fourth-and-1, McCleskey took an option pitch and ran in easily for a 2-yard touchdown. Marshall also scored on its first possession of the second half on Leftwich's 1-yard sneak. Frank Wallace, who rushed for 78 yards, capped an 11-play drive with a 4-yard run to put Marshall ahead 22-14, as Leftwich was 6-of-7 for 54 yards during the 56-yard drive.

2000 Humanitarian Bowl

The 2000 edition to the Humanitarian Bowl was the 4th edition of the bowl game. It featured the Boise State Broncos, and the UTEP Miners.

2000 Humanitarian Bowl	Line	1	-	2	-	3	-	4	-	Final
Texas-El Paso	(67.5)	0	-	10	-	3	-	10	-	23
Boise State	(-9.0)	7	-	10	-	7	-	14	-	38

Scoring Summary
Boise State - Swillie 28 yard pass from Hendricks (Calaycay kick)
Boise State - Calaycay 41 yard field goal
UTEP - Knapp 9 yard pass from R. Perez (Bishop kick)
UTEP - Bishop 28 yard field goal
Boise State - Hendricks 12 yard run (Calaycay kick)
Boise State - Hendricks 77 yard run (Calaycay kick)
UTEP - Bishop 43 yard field goal
Boise State - Forsey 41 yard run (Calaycay kick)
UTEP - Bishop 47 yard field goal
UTEP - Porter 3 yard run (Bishop kick)
Boise State - Hendricks 11 yard pass from Banks (Calaycay kick)

Associated Press Humanitarian Bowl Game Summary - Bart Hendricks ran for two touchdowns, threw for another and caught a late scoring pass as Boise State beat Texas-El Paso 38-23 on Thursday in the Humanitarian Bowl. Hendricks was 17-of-29 for 247 yards and ran for another 57 yards. The two-time player of the year in the Big West was selected the game's most valuable player for the Broncos (10-2). It was a rousing sendoff for Boise State coach Dirk Koetter, working in his last game before taking over at Arizona State. Making its first bowl trip since 1988 and only the second since 1967, Western Athletic Conference co-champion UTEP (8-4) looked out of place on the frosty blue turf in Idaho. The Miners insisted all week that weather wouldn't be a factor, yet as the afternoon wore on with the temperature near the freezing mark, more and more UTEP players donned long coats and wool caps on the sideline. Hendricks gave the Broncos a 24-10 lead with a 77-yard TD run on Boise State's first play from scrimmage in the second half. It started as a keeper to the left, but Hendricks cut into open field and outraced two defenders. He also worked the clock in the closing minute of the first half before scoring on a 12-yard run with 18 seconds left. That gave the Broncos a 17-10 lead. Hendricks got the game's last touchdown on a 10-yard pass from receiver Andre Banks with 3:35 on the clock. He capped Boise State's first possession with a 28-yard TD strike to Jay Swillie. Not bad for a player who led the nation with 35 touchdowns and a 170.6 efficiency rating, better than Oklahoma's Josh Heupel, Drew Brees of Purdue or Heisman Trophy winner Chris Weinke of Florida State. Boise State broke it open with a daring fake punt on the first play of the fourth quarter. On fourth-and-4, punter Jeff Edwards stepped into a channel on the right side of the line and ran 22 yards for a first down. On the next play, Brock Forsey went for a 42-yard TD run and a 31-13 lead. They didn't touch UTEP Quarterback Rocky Perez in the first half. But after increasing the pressure in the second half, and Perez was sacked five times in the first 10 minutes of the third quarter. The Miners pulled to 31-23 with 7:45 to play when Chris Porter scored on a 3-yard run.

2000 Music City Bowl

In the 2000 Music City Bowl, West Virginia defeated Ole Miss 49–38. This game was also West Virginia Mountaineers football coach Don Nehlen's final game. Although West Virginia won the game, it was notable because of a second half comeback by freshman Eli Manning. Down 49–16 in the fourth quarter, Ole Miss Coach David Cutcliffe inserted Manning. Ole Miss scored 22 unanswered points in the fourth quarter.

2000 Music City Bowl	Line	1	-	2	-	3	-	4	-	Final
Mississippi	(-3.5)	3	-	6	-	7	-	22	-	38
West Virginia	(51.5)	7	-	28	-	14	-	0	-	49

Scoring Summary
West Virginia - Ours 40 yard pass from Lewis (Rauh kick)
Mississippi - Binkley 23 yard Field goal
West Virginia - Ivy 11 yard pass from Lewis (Rauh kick)
Mississippi - Binkley 47 yard Field goal
West Virginia - Brown 35 yard pass from Lewis (Rauh kick)
Mississippi - Binkley 26 yard Field goal
West Virginia - Brown 60 yard pass from Lewis (Rauh kick)
West Virginia - Ours 1 yard run (Rauh kick)
West Virginia - Terry 99 yard kickoff return (Rauh kick)
West Virginia - Ivy 10 yard pass from Lewis (Rauh kick)
Mississippi - Miller 7 yard run (Binkley kick)
Mississippi - Armstrong 23 yard pass from Manning (Binkley kick)
Mississippi - Rayford 18 yard pass from Manning (Binkley kick)
Mississippi - Sanford 16 yard pass from Manning (Taylor pass from Manning)

Associated Press Music City Bowl Game Summary - Finally, the biggest blemish on Don Nehlen's record has been removed. Nehlen avoided his ninth-straight bowl loss heading into retirement as West Virginia beat Mississippi 49-38 in the Music City Bowl behind a record performance from oft-injured Quarterback Brad Lewis and a wild finish. Nehlen, who finishes with a 202-128-8 record in 30 seasons as a coach, had not won a bowl game since the 1984 Bluebonnet. That also was the final game as a player for his replacement, Rich Rodriguez, who was hired last month. In fact, Nehlen had not enjoyed a lead in a bowl since 1994, a span of four games. Two years ago, the last time it went to a bowl, West Virginia fell behind 24-3 at halftime to Missouri in the Insight.com Bowl and never recovered. This time, West Virginia (7-5) turned the tables behind five TD passes and 318 yards from Lewis, who had played much of the season with a sore knee and throwing hand and had eight TDs in the regular season. There was an indication this game would be different. Nehlen said all week he planned to open his lethargic offense and have some fun. With season-long problems on special teams - including blocked punts and bad snaps — he went as far as saying he might not want to punt on fourth down. He didn't have to. The Mountaineers' first punt came in the final seconds of the third quarter with his team enjoying a 40-point lead. Once West Virginia got a big lead, Nehlen, who turns 65 on New Year's Day, didn't stop coaching. He chased down the referees on a pair of defensive penalties in the third quarter. After Mississippi (7-5) made the game interesting midway through the fourth quarter, Nehlen jumped into sideline huddles and pointed his finger at his players. They weren't going to let this one slip away. Lance Frazier's 40-yard interception return with three minutes left finished Mississippi's chances of a miracle comeback. In the end, West Virginia fans chanted, "Nehlen, Nehlen!" If there was a team that had a reason not to be focused, it was the Mountaineers, who had endured a month's worth of distractions. Besides the bowl streak and Nehlen's final game, Rodriguez made people on campus nervous by saying he would not retain the majority of Nehlen's assistants, who also were coaching their final games Thursday. Also, Rodriguez said in his first news conference that no jobs among the players were secure. So, some, including Lewis, a junior, wondered if they were starting their final games. Lewis responded. He threw two TD passes apiece to Khori Ivy and Antonio Brown. Wes Ours caught a 40-yard TD pass and scored on a 1-yard run. Shawn Terry returned the second-half kickoff 99 yards for a score. The Mountaineers needed just 18 total plays to score five first-half touchdowns. West Virginia's eight straight bowl losses had tied it with South Carolina. Although the NCAA doesn't keep records for bowl futility, the streak was believed to be the longest in Division I-A. South Carolina's streak was from 1946 to 1998 before it beat the Mountaineers in the 1995 Carquest Bowl.

2000 Insight Bowl

The 2000 Insight.com bowl was the 12th edition of the bowl game. It featured the Iowa State Cyclones and the Pittsburgh Panthers. Pitt scored first on a 72-yard touchdown pass from John Turman to Antonio Bryant, taking an early 7-0 lead. Iowa State answered with a 23-yard pass from Sage Rosenfels to Chris Anthony, tying the game at 7, at the end of the 1st quarter. In the second quarter, Joe Woodley scored on a 1-yard touchdown run for ISU making it 13-7. Ennis Haywood added a 3-yard touchdown run making it 20-7. Sage Rosenfels threw his second TD pass of the game, a 9 yarder to Chris Anthony, as Iowa State made it 27-7 at halftime. In the third quarter, Pitt Quarterback Rod Rutherford scored on a 2-yard touchdown run, making it 27-14. John Turman later threw a 44-yard touchdown pass to Antonio Bryant making it 27-20. In the fourth quarter, Iowa State's JaMaine Billups scored on a 72-yard punt return, bringing Iowa State to 34-20. Pitt's Nick Lotz kicked a 25-yard field goal, cutting the deficit to 34-23. Kevan Barlow scored on a 3-yard touchdown run, but the 2-point conversion attempt failed, leaving the score at 34-29. Iowa State's Carl Gomez kicked a 41-yard field goal to cap the scoring at 37-29. Sage Rosenfels and Reggie Hayward got the MVPs. This was Iowa State's first bowl victory in school history after four previous losses.

2000 Insight Bowl	Line	1	-	2	-	3	-	4	-	Final
Pittsburgh	(-3.0)	7	-	0	-	13	-	9	-	29
Iowa State	(53.5)	7	-	20	-	0	-	10	-	37

Scoring Summary
Pittsburgh - Bryant 72 yard pass from Turman (Lotz kick)
Iowa State - Anthony 23 yard pass from Rosenfels (Gomez kick)
Iowa State - Woodley 1 yard run (two-point conversion failed)
Iowa State - Haywood 3 yard run (Gomez kick)
Iowa State - Anthony 9 yard pass from Rosenfels (Gomez kick)
Pittsburgh - Rutherford 2 yard run (Lotz kick)
Pittsburgh - Bryant 44 yard pass from Turman (kick failed)
Iowa State - Billups 72 yard punt return (Gomez kick)
Pittsburgh - Lotz 25 yard Field goal
Pittsburgh - Barlow 3 yard run (two-point conversion failed)
Iowa State - Gomez 41 yard Field goal

Associated Press Insight Bowl Game Summary - On an historic night at Bank One Ballpark, Iowa State cashed in. The Cyclones defeated Pittsburgh, 37-29, in the Insight.com Bowl for their first bowl victory and the school's first nine-win season in 94 years. Sage Rosenfels threw a pair of touchdown passes and JaMaine Billups had a key 72-yard punt return for a score as Iowa State (9-3) emerged victorious in its first postseason contest since the 1978 Hall of Fame bowl. The Cyclone fans at the first football game at the home of baseball's Arizona Diamondbacks stormed the field and tore down one of the goalposts moments after Dan McCarney received a postgame Gatorade shower from his players. Iowa State had appeared in four bowl games prior to tonight, losing the 1978 Hall of Fame Bowl (Texas A&M), 1977 Peach Bowl (North Carolina State), 1972 Liberty Bowl (Georgia Tech) and 1971 Sun Bowl (Louisiana State). But the school became a laughingstock during the 1990s, going the entire decade without a winning season, including a nightmarish 0-10-1 campaign in 1994. The Cyclones were 4-7 in 1999. The Panthers (7-5) received two touchdown passes from John Turman but were unable to rebound from Iowa State's 27-point outburst during a 16 1/2-minute span of the first half. After falling behind 7-0, the Cyclones scored four straight touchdowns as Rosenfels threw for scores of 23 and nine yards to Chris Anthony and Joe Woodley and Ennis Haywood each added short scoring runs. The Panthers rallied and were within 27-20 with 2:05 left in the third quarter following Turman's 44-yard touchdown pass to Antonio Bryant, who finished with 155 yards and two TDs on five receptions. Turman completed 20-of-36 attempts for 347 yards and was intercepted once. But in the first minute of the final quarter, Billups field a punt at his own 28-yard line, raced toward the right sideline and was gone for Iowa State's first punt return for a score in a bowl game and its first in eight seasons. It was also the first career touchdown for the freshman running back, who is the first high school Player of the Year from the state of Nebraska to attend Iowa State. The Insight.com Bowl moved to Bank One Ballpark this year after taking place previously in Tucson.

2000 Micron PC Bowl

The 2000 MicronPC.com Bowl was the 11th edition of the college football bowl game which featured the Minnesota Golden Gophers and the North Carolina State Wolfpack.

2000 Micron PC Bowl	Line	1	-	2	-	3	-	4	-	Final
Minnesota	(-4.0)	21	-	3	-	0	-	6	-	30
NC State	(57.5)	0	-	8	-	17	-	13	-	38

Scoring Summary
Minnesota - Redmon 12 yard run (Nystrom kick)
Minnesota - Redmon 3 yard run (Nystrom kick)
Minnesota - Cole 2 yard run (Nystrom kick)
Minnesota - Nystrom 27 yard Field goal
NC State - Vanderveer 2 yard pass from Rivers (Robinson pass from Rivers)
NC State - Robinson 19 yard run (Leak pass from Rivers)
NC State - Passingham 37 yard Field goal
NC State - Robinson 3 yard run (two-point conversion failed)
Minnesota - Nystrom 23 yard Field goal
NC State - Robinson 23 yard pass from Rivers (Pass failed)
Minnesota - Nystrom 29 yard Field goal
NC State – R. Robinson 8 yard run (Passingham kick)

Associated Press MicronPC Bowl Game Summary - N.C. State, which rallied for five fourth-quarter wins during the regular season, spotted Minnesota a 24-point lead, then roared back behind Philip Rivers and Koren Robinson to beat the Golden Gophers 38-30 on Thursday night. Robinson scored on a 19-yard reverse in a 17-point third quarter, then scored the go-ahead touchdown on a 23-yard pass from Rivers with 11:01 left as the Wolfpack finished 8-4. Minnesota (6-6) led 24-8 at the half but wasted a Micron Bowl-record 246-yard rushing performance from Tellis Redmon as the Gophers fell victim to yet another Wolfpack comeback. Rivers, N.C. State's 18-year-old freshman Quarterback, was selected the most valuable player, going 24-of-39 for 310 yards. Robinson added a Micron-record 157 receiving yards. The Wolfpack clinched it with 3:16 left on an 8-yard run by Ray Robinson just five seconds after Minnesota QB Travis Cole fumbled deep in his own territory. Redmon's 42 carries and his rushing yardage broke the marks of North Carolina's Leon Johnson in 1995 when Johnson carried 29 times for 195 yards against Arkansas. Rivers threw for an Atlantic Coast Conference freshman record 3,054 yards and 25 TDs but was off his game early. He was limited to 45 yards in the first quarter as the Gophers bolted to a 24-0 lead in front of virtually empty upper deck at Pro Player Stadium. Rivers completed 50 passes of 20 or more yards this year but managed no pass longer than 14 yards in the first half against a Minnesota defense that finished in the middle of the pack in the Big Ten and was missing secondary starters Willie Middlebrooks (broken ankle) and Delvin Jones (suspension). He warmed up in the second half, along with Koren Robinson. N.C. State trailed 24-8 at halftime but got back into the game with a big third quarter. A blocked punt by Brian Williams set up a 19-yard reverse by Koren Robinson and Kent Passingham's 37-yard field goal closed the gap to 24-19. Koren Robinson's key TD catch early in the fourth improved the Wolfpack to 6-0 in the fourth-quarter comebacks in 2000 in Amato's first bowl game as a head coach. It didn't take long for the Gophers to find N.C. State's weakness, rushing for 131 yards in the opening quarter. While Minnesota was chewing up big yardage on the ground, Rivers was shaky on the Wolfpack's first few drives. Rivers threw just 10 interceptions in 441 attempts during the regular season but was picked off 50 seconds in and later in the first quarter as N.C. State fell into a big hole. Rivers' second pass bounced off the chest of Ray Robinson and into the arms of Justin Hall at the Wolfpack 23. Four plays later, Redmon raced in from 12 yards and Minnesota led 7-0 less than two minutes into the game. A 40-yard pass to a wide open Ron Johnson to the N.C. State 16 set up Redmon's second score of the quarter — a 3-yard pitch around right end. The Gophers drove 72 yards after Andre Brown's interception, which bounced off Jimmy Henry right to him. Redmon set up Cole's 2-yard QB keeper with runs of 12 and 32 yards in the drive as he gained 93 yards in the opening 15 minutes.

2000 Sun Bowl

The 2000 Wells Fargo Sun Bowl featured the UCLA Bruins, and the Wisconsin Badgers. Wisconsin opened the scoring, after Quarterback Brooks Bollinger threw a 54-yard touchdown pass to wide receiver Lee Evans for an early 7-0 lead. UCLA responded when Cory Paus threw a 64-yard touchdown pass to Freddie Mitchell to even the score at 7. UCLA's Chris Griffin added a 31-yard field goal to push UCLA's lead to 10-7. In the second quarter, running back DeShaun Foster rushed 7 yards for a touchdown, to increase the lead to 17-7. In the third quarter, Chris Griffin kicked his second field goal of the game, a 25 yarder, to move the lead to 20-7. Brooks Bollinger later found wide receiver Chris Chambers for a 3-yard touchdown pass, cutting the lead to 20-14. Michael Bennett's 6-yard touchdown run gave the Badgers a 21-20 lead, and eventually the ball game.

2000 Sun Bowl	Line	1	-	2	-	3	-	4	-	Final
UCLA	(54.5)	10	-	7	-	3	-	0	-	20
Wisconsin	(-6.0)	7	-	0	-	7	-	7	-	21

Scoring Summary
Wisconsin - Evans 54 yard pass from Bollinger (Pisetsky kick)
UCLA - Mitchell 64 yard pass from Paus (Griffith kick)
UCLA - FG Griffith 31 yard Field goal
UCLA - Foster 7 yard run (Griffith kick)
UCLA - FG Griffith 25 yard Field goal
Wisconsin - Chambers 3 yard pass from Bollinger (Pisetsky kick)
Wisconsin - Bennett 6 yard run (Pisetsky kick)

Associated Press Sun Bowl Game Summary - Michael Bennett's six-yard touchdown run with 8:55 to play lifted Wisconsin to a come-from-behind 21-20 victory over UCLA in the Sun Bowl. Having beaten the Bruins in Pasadena on January 1, 1999 for the first of back-to-back Rose Bowl titles, the Badgers (9-4) trailed 17-7 at halftime this afternoon before Bennett and Quarterback Brook Bollinger went to work. Bennett ran for 50 of his 83 yards after intermission, including the winning score. It capped a 12-play, 70-yard drive that began when UCLA kicker Chris Griffith was stopped short of a first down on a fake field goal. Bollinger completed 8-of-16 passes for 107 yards and ran for 55 yards on 16 carries, tossing touchdown passes in each half. He opened the scoring when he found Lee Evans with a 54-yard TD strike just 1:44 into play. But the Bruins struck back immediately as Cory Paus found Freddie Mitchell for a 64-yard TD pass on the ensuing drive, knotting the score at 7-7. Griffith kicked a 31-yard field goal and DeShaun Foster's seven-yard run with 3:53 left in the first half gave UCLA a 10-point cushion. Griffith's second field goal, a 25-yarder 5:49 into the third quarter, extended the Bruins' lead to 20-7, but Bollinger hit Chris Chambers with a three-yard TD toss with 4:38 left in the period to spark the Badgers' comeback. Mitchell caught nine passes for 180 yards but was unable to get open on the Bruins' final drive, which ended near midfield when All-American cornerback Jamal Fletcher picked off Scott McEwan with just over a minute left. Mitchell was flagged for unsportsmanlike conduct when he turned to taunt Wisconsin defenders on his way to the end zone on the tying score. Although he set a Sun Bowl record for receiving yards, he could not prevent Wisconsin from pulling out its sixth victory in the last seven bowl appearances. UCLA leads the series, 7-4, but the Badgers have won the last three meetings, all in bowl games. The Bruins failed to score at least 27 points for the first time in eight games as Wisconsin's defense tightened after yielding 239 yards in the first half. Foster rushed for 107 yards on 26 carries and Paus was 8-of-15 for 135 yards. McEwan came on and completed 12-of-18 passes for 135 yards but thwarted the Bruins' last gasp with an interception. UCLA outgained Wisconsin, 396 yards to 307. Trailing 20-7 midway through the third quarter, the Badgers clearly were sparked when Bennett returned Griffith's kickoff 54 yards to the Bruins' 43. The ensuing nine-play march resulted in Bollinger's TD toss to Chambers, pulling the Badgers within six points.

2000 Liberty Bowl

The 2000 AXA Liberty Bowl was played between the Colorado State Rams and the Louisville Cardinals on December 29, 2000, at Liberty Bowl Memorial Stadium in Memphis, Tennessee. Colorado State won the game 22–17; Colorado State running back Cecil Sapp, the game's MVP, ran for 160 yards and a touchdown, a career record.

2000 Liberty Bowl	Line	1	-	2	-	3	-	4	-	Final
#23 Colorado State	(53.0)	3	-	13	-	3	-	3	-	22
#22 Louisville	(-1.0)	7	-	3	-	0	-	7	-	17

Scoring Summary
Colorado State – Hurst 23 yard Field goal
Louisville – Dorsey 58 yard pass from Ragone (Smith kick)
Louisville – Smith 23 yard Field goal
Colorado State – Sapp 2 yard run (Hurst kick)
Colorado State – Rice 16 yard run (Kick failed)
Colorado State – Hurst 21 yard Field goal
Louisville – Branch 14 yard pass from Ragone (Smith kick)
Colorado State – Hurst 23 yard Field goal

Associated Press Liberty Bowl Game Summary - Cecil Sapp and the Colorado State Rams played a great game of keep away Friday. The sophomore ran for a career-high 160 yards, and C.W. Hurst kicked three field goals as the No. 23 Rams held onto the ball for more than 35 minutes in beating Louisville 22-17 in the Liberty Bowl. Louisville (9-3) came in looking for only its second 10-victory season and first since 1990 with an offense that averaged 35.3 points and the nation's fourth-stingiest defense against the run. But Sapp wore down the 22nd-ranked Cardinals, who had allowed only Florida State's Travis Minor to top 100 yards this season. Sapp said it all went according to plan for the Rams (10-2). Sapp, had a bowl-record 36 carries, topping the 35 attempts by Colorado's Bob Anderson in 1969 against Alabama. Running the ball was an excellent idea on a day where the temperature dipped into the mid-20s by halftime with the wind chill hovering at 0 due to wind gusting up to 28 mph. Sapp, a Florida native, said his job is to carry the ball and that he ignored the weather. Louisville end Dewayne White said Sapp took advantage of the Rams' big bodies on the offensive line, popping out whenever he saw light. Teammate Rashad Harris said Colorado State just controlled the game. The weather didn't bother Louisville as much as Colorado State's defense. The Cardinals had scored at least 32 points in every victory this season outgained the Rams 397 yards to 315, but they had only the ball for 25 offensive plays in the first half. The Rams also shut out Louisville in the third quarter, only the second time that's happened this season. The Cardinals also had forced more turnovers this season than any other Division I-A team except Florida. But Colorado State recovered three fumbles, one of which it converted into a 16-yard reverse by Frank Rice that made it 16-10 at halftime. Dave Ragone, Conference USA's offensive player of the year, tried to rally a team that had won four games this season despite trailing at halftime. He pulled the Cardinals within 19-17 early in the fourth quarter with a 14-yard touchdown pass to Deion Branch, who tied a bowl record with 10 receptions. But that would be all the Cardinals would get, and their final drive ended with 3:10 left as John Howell sacked Ragone on fourth-and-7. Ragone was 24-of-37 for 321 yards and two touchdowns, while Branch finished with 170 yards receiving. Colorado State earned redemption after losing this game 23-17 last year to Southern Mississippi with the slimmest margin of victory since Georgia beat Arkansas 20-17 in 1987 in the bowl now sponsored by the AXA Financial Group. The Rams trailed 10-3 when they scored 13 straight points with a 2-yard TD run by Sapp and Rice's reverse for the halftime lead. Hurst also had field goals of 24, 21 and 32 yards. Ragone put Louisville up 7-3 with a 58-yard TD pass to Damien Dorsey who scored on a catch-and-run in the first quarter. But the Cardinals missed some opportunities against a Rams defense that was stingiest near the goal line. Louisville settled for a 24-yard field goal by Nathan Smith for a 10-3 lead early in the second quarter. On the first play of their next series, Rams cornerback Terrence Gibson knocked the ball away from receiver Ronnie Ghent and Rick Crowell recovered for Colorado State.

2000 Chick-Fil-A Peach Bowl

The 2000 Peach Bowl was the 33rd Peach Bowl game and featured the Georgia Tech Yellow Jackets, and the LSU Tigers.

2000 Chick-Fil-A Peach Bowl	Line	1	-	2	-	3	-	4	-	Final
LSU	(55.0)	3	-	0	-	6	-	19	-	28
#15 Georgia Tech	(-9.5)	7	-	7	-	0	-	0	-	14

Scoring Summary
LSU - Corbello 32 yard Field goal
Georgia Tech - Burns 32 yard run (Manget kick)
Georgia Tech - Hatch 9 yard run (Manget kick)
LSU - Banks 3 yard pass from Davey (kick failed)
LSU - Reed 9 yard pass from Davey (Reed pass from Davey)
LSU - Corbello 49 yard Field goal
LSU - Banks 3 yard pass from Davey (Robinson pass from Davey)

Associated Press Chick-Fil-A Peach Bowl Game Summary - Josh Booty watched a relief pitcher get the win for Louisiana State. Rohan Davey replaced Booty in the second half and passed for three touchdowns as LSU roared back for a 28-14 victory over 17th-ranked Georgia Tech in the Peach Bowl. Booty, who abandoned a baseball career to return to college football, was ineffective as the Tigers (8-4) fell behind at halftime, 14-3. He watched from the sidelines as Davey was virtually flawless in the second half, completing 17-of-25 passes for 174 yards and three scores. Two of the TD tosses went to 265-pound fullback Tommy Banks, while 5-11 sophomore Josh Reed had nine receptions for 96 yards in the second half, including a nine-yard score and the ensuing two-point conversion. While LSU extended its bowl winning streak to four games, first-year coach Nick Saban got his first postseason victory after three losses. Georgia Tech (9-3) came undone after a dominant first half and suffered its second straight bowl loss after a five-game postseason winning streak. The Yellow Jackets had six turnovers after committing just 12 during the season. Former Georgia Tech offensive coordinator Ralph Friedgen watched from the stands at the Georgia Dome, exactly one month after he was named Maryland coach. Davey started LSU's comeback on its first possession of the second half, lofting a three-yard TD toss to Banks. But the extra point failed, leaving the Tigers behind, 14-9. LSU took the lead on the second play of the final quarter as Reed caught a nine-yard pass at the back of the end zone and managed to keep one foot in bounds. He also grabbed the two-point conversion. Linebacker Bradie James recovered freshman receiver Nate Curry's fumble two plays later and the Tigers cashed in as John Corbello kicked a career-long 49-yard field goal just 90 seconds into the period. After forcing a punt, LSU drove 91 yards in 13 plays to the clinching score. Davey again hooked up with Banks from three yards with 3:12 remaining. Georgia Tech's George Godsey was 19-of-36 for 177 yards with a pair of interceptions before leaving late in the fourth quarter with an apparent leg injury. After Corbello opened the scoring with a 32-yard field goal, the Yellow Jackets went ahead on a 32-yard run by Greg Burns and a nine-yard scoring jaunt by Jermaine Hatch.

2000 Holiday Bowl

The 2000 Holiday Bowl was played December 29, 2000 in San Diego, California. It featured the Oregon Ducks and the Texas Longhorns. Oregon won the game by a final score of 35–30.

2000 Holiday Bowl	Line	1	-	2	-	3	-	4	-	Final
#12 Texas	(-7.0)	0	-	21	-	0	-	9	-	30
#11 Oregon	(55.0)	14	-	0	-	7	-	14	-	35

Scoring Summary
Oregon - Peelle 1 yard pass from Harrington (Frankel kick)
Oregon - Harrington 18 yard pass from Howry (Frankel kick)
Texas - Mitchell 3 yard run (Stockton kick)
Texas - Simms 4 yard run (Stockton kick)
Texas - Brown 23 yard interception return (Stockton kick)
Oregon - Morris 55 yard pass from J Harrington (Frankel kick)
Oregon - Harrington 9 yard run (Frankel kick)
Texas - Ike 93 yard kickoff return (Stockton kick)
Oregon - Willis 4 yard run (Frankel kick)
Texas – Safety - Team tackled in end zone

Associated Press Holiday Bowl Game Summary - Joey Harrington and the Oregon Ducks fit right in at the Holiday Bowl. Sure, it hurt that the Ducks had blown a Rose Bowl berth six weeks earlier. But Harrington bounced back by having a hand in four touchdowns — one of them reminiscent of Steve Young — as the No. 11 Ducks beat No. 12 Texas 35-30 on Friday night in another wild Holiday Bowl. Harrington, who threw for two touchdowns, ran for one and caught a halfback pass for another. The Ducks (10-2) finished the first 10-win season in their 105-year history. After Harrington had six turnovers in a 23-13 loss at Oregon State on Nov. 18 that cost Oregon the Pacific-10 Conference's Rose Bowl berth, Coach Mike Bellotti told him he had to bounce back. Still, it wasn't settled until a desperation pass by Texas sophomore Chris Simms fell incomplete in the end zone as time ran out. Harrington had three straight completions to set up the winning score, a 4-yard end-around by Jason Willis with 5:46 left. The Longhorns moved to the Ducks' 22 with about three minutes to play, but their two heralded freshmen wide receivers, B.J. Johnson and Roy Williams, each dropped a pass in the end zone. Johnson dropped another one at the 15 that he might have scored on. Brown commended Simms for his composure at the end. The Longhorns got the ball back with 1:37 to play when De'Andre Lewis recovered a fumble on a botched handoff. But two plays later, Bauman capped a big game by the Ducks' defense with an interception at the 16. It wasn't over yet though. Oregon took a safety with 21 seconds left and the free kick went to the Texas 37. The Longhorns got to the Ducks' 39 before Simms' final pass. Simms, son of former New York Giants Quarterback Phil Simms, finished with four interceptions. Harrington personally gave the Ducks a 14-0 first quarter lead. He froze the 'Horns with play-action and threw a 1-yard touchdown pass to wide-open tight end Justin Peelle in the right corner of the end zone. After Oregon's Jed Boice recovered a fumble by Johnson at the Texas 18, Harrington got to play receiver. He pitched the ball to wide receiver Keenan Howry, who had lined up in the backfield, then slipped out to the left flat. Howry threw across the field to Harrington, who caught it at the 10 and stumbled the rest of the way into the end zone. Harrington wasn't the first

Quarterback to catch a TD pass in the Holiday Bowl, though. Young caught a 14-yard halfback pass with 23 seconds left in the 1983 game to give Brigham Young a 21-17 win over Missouri. Harrington completed 19 of 30 passes for 273 yards, with one interception. Simms was 17-of-33 for 245 yards and ran for one touchdown. Texas' leading rusher, Hodges Mitchell, left with a sprained right knee early in the third quarter after being hit by Bauman and didn't return. The Longhorns scored three times in the second quarter for a 21-14 lead. Mitchell and Simms scored on short runs and Greg Brown returned an interception 23 yards. Oregon tied it on the first drive of the second half on a 55-yard pass from Harrington to running back Maurice Morris. Morris caught a short pass and, following a block by guard Ryan Schmid, raced down the right sideline. Harrington gave the Ducks a 28-21 lead on a 9-yard draw with 9:43 to play, capping a 90-yard drive set up when Keith Lewis intercepted Simms' pass. That lead didn't last, though, as Victor Ike returned the ensuing kickoff 93 yards, the Longhorns' first for a touchdown since 1978.

2000 Alamo Bowl

The 2000 Alamo Bowl featured the Northwestern Wildcats, and the Nebraska Cornhuskers. Despite both teams being ranked, it was the biggest blowout in the game's history. Nebraska broke an NCAA bowl record by scoring 66 points, and the Huskers also set ten other Alamo Bowl records, including those for most yards of total offense (636) most rushing yards (476), most first downs (28), and most yards per play (7.7).

2000 Alamo Bowl	Line	1	-	2	-	3	-	4	-	Final
#9 Nebraska	(-14.0)	7	-	31	-	21	-	7	-	66
#18 Northwestern	(64.0)	3	-	14	-	0	-	0	-	17

Scoring Summary
Nebraska - Alexander 15 yard run (Brown kick)
Northwestern - Long 44 yard Field goal
Northwestern - Johnson 10 yard pass from Kustok (Long kick)
Nebraska - Crouch 50 yard run (Brown kick)
Nebraska - Alexander 2 yard run (Brown kick)
Nebraska - Buckhalter 2 yard run (Brown kick)
Nebraska - Brown 51 yard Field goal
Northwestern - Anderson 69 yard run (Long kick)
Nebraska - Newcombe 58 yard pass from Crouch (Brown kick)
Nebraska - Davison 11 yard pass from Crouch (Brown kick)
Nebraska - Crouch 2 yard run (Brown kick)
Nebraska - Davison 69 yard pass from Newcombe (Brown kick)
Nebraska - Diedrick 9 yard run (Brown kick)

Nebraska Media Guide Alamo Bowl Game Summary - The Nebraska offense saved its best game of the season for last, dominating Big Ten co-champion Northwestern, 66-17, in the 2000 Alamo Bowl. The 66 points were an NU and NCAA bowl record, along with the Huskers' nine offensive touchdowns. Nebraska got off to a quick start, as the Huskers scored on their first possession. Dan Alexander capped the drive with a 15-yard touchdown run, just a part of his Alamo Bowl and NU bowl-record 240 rushing yards. As a team, the Huskers had an Alamo Bowl-record 476 rushing yards. The Wildcats came right back, as Quarterback Zak Kustok marched down the field before Tim Long ended Northwestern's drive with a 44-yard field goal. Another Northwestern score made it look like the game was going to be close with NU trailing, 10-7. But Nebraska had a different plan. Quarterback Eric Crouch started NU's NCAA bowl-record tying 31-point second quarter with a 50-yard touchdown run. NU then scored 24 straight points before Northwestern's Damien Anderson ran for a 69-yard score. Bobby Newcombe's 58-yard touchdown reception gave NU a 38-17 halftime lead. The NU defense went on to shut out the Wildcats in the final two quarters. Free safety Dion Booker had a career-high eight tackles, while rush end Kyle Vanden Bosch had a career-high six Quarterback hurries, seven tackles, with three tackles for a loss, and two pass breakups. A 21-point third quarter, including Matt Davison's 69-yard touchdown reception, put NU ahead 59-17. Place-kicker Josh Brown tied the NCAA bowl record for extra-point kick attempts (9) and extra-point kicks made (9)

2000 Independence Bowl

The 2000 Sanford Independence Bowl took place on December 31, 2000 at Independence Stadium in Shreveport, Louisiana. The competing teams were the Mississippi State Bulldogs, representing the Southeastern Conference, and the Texas A&M Aggies from the Big 12 Conference. The game was later referred to as "The Snow Bowl", as a snowstorm (rare for the Shreveport area) began just before kickoff, blanketing the field in powder, and continued throughout the entire game. Mississippi State won the game in overtime, 43–41.

2000 Independence Bowl	Line	1	-	2	-	3	-	4	-	OT	-	Final
Mississippi State	(44.0)	0	-	14	-	7	-	14	-	8	-	43
Texas A&M	(-2.0)	14	-	6	-	0	-	15	-	6	-	41

Scoring Summary
Texas A&M - Whitaker 9 yard run (Kitchens kick)
Texas A&M - Toombs 4 yard run (Kitchens kick)
MSU - Walker 40 yard run (Westerfield kick)
MSU - Miller 5 yard pass from Madkin (Westerfield kick)
Texas A&M - Ferguson 42 yard pass from Farris (kick failed)
MSU - Walker 1 yard run (Westerfield kick)
Texas A&M - Johnson 35 yard pass from Farris (Whitaker run)
Texas A&M - Toombs 13 yard run (Kitchens kick)
MSU - Walker 32 yard run (Westerfield kick)
MSU - Lee 3 yard pass from Madkin (Westerfield kick)
Texas A&M - Toombs yard 25 run (kick failed)
MSU - 2 point defensive conversion by Jul Griffith
MSU - Madkin 6 yard run

Game summary - Prior to the game, the Bulldogs (8-4) had not scored in overtime in regular-season losses to Louisiana State and Arkansas. And things looked bleak for Mississippi State after Texas A&M's Ja'Mar Toombs rambled 25 yards for a touchdown on the first play of overtime. But defensive tackle Willie Blade blocked the extra point. Eugene Clinton grabbed the ball and lateraled to Julius Griffith, who went the distance to cut the deficit to 41-37. "They were blocking down on me, but I kept fighting and fighting to get through and finish the play," Blade said. On the Bulldogs' first play from scrimmage, Madkin turned a busted play into a 19-yard gain. After Dontae Walker lost a yard, Madkin went up the middle from the 7-yard line to give Mississippi State its second straight bowl win after four consecutive losses. Playing in a steady snow that obscured the yard markers and made footing treacherous, Madkin completed 9-of-19 passes for 71 yards and a pair of touchdowns. Walker carried 16 times for 143 yards and three scores. Toombs set a Texas A&M bowl record with 35 carries for 193 yards and three TDs. The yardage was the second-highest total in Aggies' bowl history, trailing only the 276 Curtis Dickey rolled up in the 1978 Hall of Fame Bowl. Trailing 21-20 after three quarters, Texas A&M grabbed the lead on a 35-yard touchdown pass from Mark Farris to Bethel Johnson. Richard Whitaker ran for the two-point conversion and Toombs scored on a 13-yard run to give the Aggies a 35-21 cushion. Just over a minute later, Walker broke off a 32-yard touchdown. With less than three minutes remaining, safety Marco Minor intercepted Farris at the Aggies' 4-yard line. Madkin threw a three-yard TD toss to Donald Lee to tie it with 90 seconds left. Whitaker and Toombs ran for first-quarter touchdowns to stake Texas A&M to a 14-0 lead. The Bulldogs tied it in the second as Walker raced 40 yards for a score (video) and Madkin found Dicenzo Miller for a five-yard TD. The Aggies took a 20-14 lead into the locker room after Farris and Robert Ferguson hooked up for a 42-yard touchdown. Texas A&M has lost four straight and seven of its last eight bowl appearances. Sherrill, the winningest coach in Mississippi State history, improved to 2-4 in bowl games with the Bulldogs and 8-6 overall. Slocum, who has won 78 percent of his games at Texas A&M, fell to 2-8 in bowls. About 30 minutes before kickoff snow blew into Shreveport with strong wind whipping from one end zone to the other. The game started with the synthetic grass field a mix of green and white. By the second quarter, the turf was blanketed by snow. Plows were used during timeouts to make the goal lines, end lines and hash marks visible. As the snow fell throughout the game, at times it came down so hard it made watching the game like looking through television static. Many of the 36,974 fans at Independence Stadium left at halftime.

2000 Silicon Valley Football Classic

The 2000 Silicon Valley Football Classic was played between the Air Force Falcons and the Fresno State Bulldogs on December 31, 2000, at Spartan Stadium in San Jose, California. Air Force won the game 37–34; while Air Force led 34–7 at halftime, Fresno State came within three points of tying the game before failing to score on a fake field goal in the last minute of the game.

2000 Silicon Valley Classic	Line	1	-	2	-	3	-	4	-	Final
Air Force	(52.5)	19	-	15	-	3	-	0	-	37
Fresno State	(-1.0)	7	-	0	-	13	-	14	-	34

Scoring Summary
Air Force - Adams 37yard Field goal
Air Force - Mckay 29 yard pass from Thiessen (Adams kick)
Air Force - Adams 46 yard Field goal
Air Force - Mckay 13 yard pass from Thiessen (Run failed)
Fresno State - Gaines 73 yard pass from Carr (Asparuhov kick)
Air Force - Thiessen 1 yard run (Adams kick)
Air Force - Thiessen 9 yard run (Jessop pass from Thiessen)
Fresno State - Greco 2 pass from Carr (Asparuhov kick)
Air Force - Adams 24 yard Field goal
Fresno State - Burch yard 8 pass from Carr (Pass failed)
Fresno State - Berrian yard 47 pass from Carr (Asparuhov kick)
Fresno State - Berrian yard 51 pass from Carr (Asparuhov kick)

Associated Press Silicon Valley Classic Game Summary - Trailing 37-34 to Air Force with 14 seconds left, Fresno State was going to go for the win, not the tie. The Bulldogs faked a field goal, but holder Jason Simpson's pass to Giachino Chiaramonte fell incomplete in the end zone and Air Force claimed the inaugural Silicon Valley Classic on Sunday. Fresno State had practiced the fake, knowing Air Force's kick-blocking abilities. When the Falcons put two jumpers — linebackers Corey Nelson and Kevin Runyon — in the middle, the play was called. Just before the fake, Fresno State's David Carr spiked the ball on third-and-7 and called a timeout. Hill said the spike was a miscommunication. It could have given the Bulldogs an edge, however, because Air Force put all its focus on the kick and left Chiaramonte and another receiver open. Simpson's pass simply went too long. Fresno State had climbed back from a 34-7 halftime deficit but couldn't quite overcome the Falcons' first-half outburst. Mike Thiessen hit Scotty McKay with two touchdown passes and ran for two more scores — all in the first half. Thiessen completed 12 of 24 passes for 204 yards. Dave Adams added field goals of 37, 46 and 24 yards for Air Force, which finished the season 9-3. Carr completed 22 of 33 passes for 291 yards and five touchdowns. But Fresno State (7-5) appeared unprepared for all the passing from the option-oriented Falcons. Thiessen threw on the first play from scrimmage and hit Brian LaBasco with a season-long 35-yard pass on the same drive. Adams kicked a 37-yard field goal to cap the series. Fresno State took over, but not for long. Carr's pass was intercepted by Joel Buelow. A play later, Thiessen found McKay with a 29-yard touchdown pass to put the Falcons up 10-0. Thiessen threw for 1,687 yards during the regular season, the most for an Air Force Quarterback since 1969. He had 13 touchdown passes, along with 10 scoring runs. Adams added a 46-yard field goal — the longest kicked by Air Force in a bowl game — with 3:06 left in the first quarter to put the Falcons ahead 13-0. Rodney Wright's fumble on Fresno State's own 14 gave the ball back to the Falcons, and Thiessen hit McKay with a 13-yard scoring pass. A 2-point conversion attempt failed. Fresno State finally got on the board with a 73-yard touchdown pass from Carr to Paris Gaines with 23 second left in the opening quarter. It was the longest reception of Gaines' career. Air Force opened the second quarter with Thiessen's 1-yard touchdown run to go up 26-7. Thiessen also ran 9 yards for a touchdown with 1:06 left in the first half. Again, the Falcons tried the conversion, and this time it worked: Thiessen's pass to Chris Jessop gave Air Force a 34-7 lead. Fresno State mounted a comeback in the second half. The Bulldogs took a chance on fourth-and-2 in the third quarter and Carr's completion to Alec Greco in the end zone made it 34-14. After Adams booted his 24-yard field goal for Air Force, Carr threw an 8-yard scoring pass to Donnell Burch to narrow the margin to 37-20. It was Burch's first career reception. Adams attempted a 30-yard field goal with 10:47 left in the game, but Fresno State's Terence Brown blocked the kick. That set up a scoring drive that ended with Carr's 47-yard pass to Bernard Berrian. Berrian caught a 51-yard pass from Carr a little more than three minutes later, and the crowd — mostly Fresno State fans — went wild. Air Force finished the season ranked ninth in the country in total offense with 451.9 yards per game. On Sunday, the Falcons had 471 yards of total offense. Air Force leads the overall series against Fresno State 4-2.

2001 Outback Bowl

The 2001 edition of the Outback Bowl featured the South Carolina Gamecocks and the Ohio State Buckeyes. Ohio State's head coach, John Cooper, was fired following the game.

2001 Outback Bowl	Line	1	-	2	-	3	-	4	-	Final
South Carolina	(42.0)	0	-	3	-	7	-	14	-	24
#18 Ohio State	(-5.5)	0	-	0	-	7	-	0	-	7

Scoring Summary
South Carolina - Corse 23 yard Field goal
South Carolina - Brewer 7 yard run (Corse kick)
Ohio State - Gurr recovered fumble in end zone (Stultz kick)
South Carolina - Brewer 28 yard pass from Petty (Corse kick)
South Carolina - Brewer 2 yard run (Corse kick)

Associated Press Outback Bowl Game Summary - Derek Watson's loss was Ryan Brewer's gain. Getting an opportunity for increased playing time with the suspension of Watson, the Ohio native almost single-handedly helped South Carolina cap its turnaround season with a 24-7 victory over No. 18 Ohio State in the Outback Bowl. A 1,000-yard rusher, Watson was suspended for the game by South Carolina coach Lou Holtz for an unspecified violation of team rules. Brewer, who was recruited by Ohio State, filled in more than capably, accounting for 219 all-purpose yards and scoring all three South Carolina touchdowns. He rushed for a seven-yard TD early in the third quarter, caught a 28-yard TD pass 43 seconds into the fourth period and ran for a two-yard score with six minutes remaining. The 5-10, 205-pound sophomore, a former Mr. Ohio, burned his home state team by rushing for 109 yards on 19 carries and catching three passes for 92 yards. He also had two punt returns for 18 yards. In their second year under Holtz, the Gamecocks (8-4) shook off a season-ending three-game losing streak to reach eight wins for the first time since 1988. South Carolina entered the campaign with a 21-game losing streak. Holtz has become immensely popular in Columbia, signing a lucrative contract extension during the season. The win was a milestone of sorts for Holtz, who has taken all six teams he has coached to a bowl game in his second season at the helm. Holtz, who captured a national championship at Notre Dame following the 1988 season, defeated Ohio State for the first time in five meetings. South Carolina earned its first bowl victory since defeating West Virginia, 24-21, in the 1995 Carquest Bowl. Ohio State coach John Cooper, who has been frequently criticized by Buckeyes' fans, will not receive as favorable a welcome. The Buckeyes (8-4) were disappointed they did not get a berth in the Rose Bowl and seemed disinterested throughout most of Monday's contest. The first half was a defensive struggle, with South Carolina managing only a 3-0 lead on Jason Corse's 23-yard field goal with 12:48 remaining in the second period. But South Carolina's stingy defense continued to dominate as the Gamecocks converted three Ohio State turnovers into a pair of touchdowns during a 21-point second half. South Carolina did most its damage on the ground, rushing for 218 yards on 51 carries. Petty completed 9-of-19 passes for 175 yards with an interception. Ohio State was held to 258 yards, including just 85 on the ground. Facing constant pressure, Steve Bellisari connected on 14-of-25 for 157 yards with an interception. The Buckeyes had a chance to tie it at halftime, but Dan Stultz missed a 47-yard field goal as time expired. South Carolina forced a turnover on Ohio State's first possession of the season as linebacker Kalimba Edwards jarred the ball loose after sacking Bellisari. Tackle Cleveland Pinkney recovered the fumble at the Buckeyes 28. Seven plays later, Brewer scored around right end, giving South Carolina a 10-0 lead with 10:53 left in the third quarter. Ohio State finally got a big play as Ken-Yon Rambo's 62-yard reception gave the Buckeyes a 1st-and-goal at the 1. Mike Gurr recovered Jonathan Wells' fumble in the end zone to pull the Buckeyes within 10-7 with 4:51 left in the period. But South Carolina put it away with a pair of scores in the final quarter. After Petty and Brewer combined for a 28-yard TD on a screen pass, the first of DeAndre Eiland's two interceptions set up Brewer's final score.

2001 Gator Bowl

The 2001 Gator Bowl was played between the Virginia Tech Hokies and the Clemson Tigers at Alltel Stadium in Jacksonville, Florida on January 1, 2001.

Virginia Tech entered the game headed by star Quarterback Michael Vick, who led the Hokies to a 10–1 regular-season record despite being injured for a part of the season. Clemson entered the game with a regular-season record of 9–2 under the command of head coach Tommy Bowden, who was in the second year of his tenure. The contest featured two high-scoring offenses that emphasized different aspects of the game. These aspects were exemplified in the game, which saw Clemson pass for more yards than Virginia Tech, while the Hokies ran for more yards than the Tigers. In recognition of his performance in leading his team to a victory, Michael Vick was named the game's most valuable player.

2001 Gator Bowl	Line	1	-	2	-	3	-	4	-	Final
#16 Clemson	(61.0)	0	-	10	-	3	-	7	-	20
#6 Virginia Tech	(-5.5)	14	-	7	-	13	-	7	-	41

Scoring Summary
Virginia Tech – Ferguson 23 yard pass from Vick (Warley Kick)
Virginia Tech – Vick 6 yard run (Warley Kick)
Clemson- Zachery 23 yard pass from Dantzler (Hunt Kick)
Clemson - Hunt 28 yard Field goal
Virginia Tech – Suggs 3 yard run (Warley Kick)
Virginia Tech – Suggs 1 yard run (kick failed)
Clemson – Hunt 26 yard Field goal
Virginia Tech – Ferguson 5 yard run (Warley Kick)
Clemson – Gardner 23 yard pass from Simmons (Hunt Kick)
Virginia Tech – Suggs 5 yard run (Warley Kick)

USA Today Gator Bowl Game Summary - The Michael Vick "Will he or won't he?" Tour steamrolled through Alltel Stadium and Clemson's defense Monday, but the final stop — back to Blacksburg, Va., or on to the NFL draft — remained a mystery. All that we know now is that the Virginia Tech Quarterback was named MVP of the Gator Bowl after throwing for 205 yards and a touchdown and rushing for 19 yards and another score in the No. 5 Hokies' 41-20 victory against No. 13 Clemson. Vick appeared to be wavering on his decision to return for his junior year in the days leading to the bowl game. He left the field Monday to the chants of "One more year! One more year!" from Tech fans. He has until Jan. 12 to declare himself eligible for the NFL draft. When given the chance, though, Vick remained as noncommittal as a lifetime bachelor. Given the way the Hokies (11-1) handled Clemson (9-3) and that the team will lose only five starters -- one on defense -- to graduation, Vick might have to weigh being a potential No. 1 pick against returning for seasoning and a shot at a national title. Clemson, which knew it needed an error-free game, opened the game with a mistake. A bad snap to punter Jamie Somaini put Virginia Tech at the Clemson 23-yard line for its first play, and right away Vick hit running back Jarrett Ferguson for a touchdown. Trailing 14-0, Clemson would try to make a game of it with 10 consecutive points in the second quarter, but Virginia Tech put the game out of reach with three more touchdowns -- two by running back Lee Suggs -- to make it 34-13 with 5:14 left in the third quarter. Shortly thereafter, Clemson junior Quarterback Woodrow Dantzler, drawing comparisons to Vick all season, was replaced by freshman Willie Simmons. The Tigers, meanwhile, struggled to get any kind of offensive continuity going, and when they did, it didn't last very long. Special teams weren't kind to Clemson, either. In addition to the bad punt snap, the Tigers were penalized for roughing the punter on Virginia Tech's first drive of the second half, and the Hokies scored two plays later to make it 27-10. The only thing left to debate at that point was Vick's future.

2001 Florida Citrus Bowl

The 2001 Florida Citrus Bowl was held on January 1, 2001 at the Florida Citrus Bowl in Orlando, Florida. The Michigan Wolverines, co-champions of the Big Ten Conference, defeated the Auburn Tigers, champions of the Southeastern Conference's Western Division, 31-28. Michigan running back Anthony Thomas was named the game's MVP.

2001 Florida Citrus Bowl	Line	1	-	2	-	3	-	4	-	Final
#20 Auburn	(49.5)	0	-	14	-	7	-	7	-	28
#15 Michigan	(-7.5)	7	-	14	-	10	-	0	-	31

Scoring Summary
Michigan - Terrell 31 yard pass from Henson (Epstein kick)
Auburn - Daniels 19 yard pass from Leard (Duval kick)
Auburn - Robinson 20 yard pass from Leard (Duval kick)
Michigan - Askew 4 yard pass from Henson (Epstein kick)
Michigan - Thomas 11 yard run (Epstein kick)
Michigan - Thomas 25 yard run (Epstein kick)
Auburn - Johnson 12 yard run (Duval kick)
Michigan - Epstein 41 yard Field goal
Auburn - Green 21 yard pass from Leard (Duval kick)

Bentley Historical Library 2001 FLORIDA CITRUS BOWL GAME SUMMARY - An efficient passing offense and a relentless ground attack led Michigan to a 31-28 victory over Auburn in the 2001 Florida Citrus Bowl. Drew Henson completed 15-of-20 passes for 294 yards and a pair of touchdowns, while tailback Anthony Thomas rushed 32 times for 182 yards and two touchdowns. On its second possession, Michigan brought a trick out of the bag, using a flea-flicker to fool the Tigers' defense and score a 31-yard touchdown pass from Henson to David Terrell. This 76-yard drive in 70 seconds set Michigan's efficient tempo for the game. Auburn struck back early in the second quarter when senior Quarterback Ben Leard hooked up with wideout Ronney Daniels on a 19-yard touchdown pass. Leard hit Clifton Robinson for a 20-yard touchdown on the Tigers' next drive. Leard threw for 394 yards on the day, mostly to keep up with the Wolverine offense. Michigan scored the next three touchdowns of the game due in large part to Thomas' punishing running. He racked up two touchdowns and became U-M's all-time leading rusher and scorer. During the Wolverines' offensive explosion, sophomore safety Julius Curry and senior safety DeWayne Patmon each made key interceptions to halt Auburn drives into Michigan territory. Other defensive stars for the Wolverines included junior linebackers Eric Brackins and Larry Foote with 13 and eight tackles, respectively, and senior lineman Eric Wilson with six tackles and a sack. Though Leard and junior running back Rudi Johnson tried to bring Auburn back, junior kicker Hayden Epstein connected on a 41-yard field goal towards the end of the third quarter, giving U-M a 31-21 lead. Auburn added another late touchdown, but Michigan recovered an onside kick with 2:22 remaining and held on for the victory.

2001 Cotton Bowl Classic

The 2001 Southwestern Bell Cotton Bowl Classic was played on January 1, 2001, at the Cotton Bowl in Dallas, Texas, USA. The bowl game featured the Tennessee Volunteers from the SEC and the Kansas State Wildcats from the Big 12 and was televised on Fox.

2001 Cotton Bowl Classic	Line	1	-	2	-	3	-	4	-	Final
#21 Tennessee	(52.5)	0	-	14	-	0	-	7	-	21
#11 Kansas State	(-3.0)	7	-	14	-	14	-	0	-	35

Scoring Summary
Kansas State – Beasley 14 yard run (Rheem kick)
Tennessee – Martin 17 yard pass from Clausen (Walls kick)
Kansas State – Morgan 56 yard pass from Beasley (Rheem kick)
Kansas State – Morgan 10 yard pass from Beasley (Rheem kick)
Tennessee – Greer 78 yard interception return (Walls kick)
Kansas State – Scobey 12 yard run (Rheem kick)
Kansas State – Scobey 6 yard run (Rheem kick)
Tennessee – Henry 81 yard run (Walls kick)

Cotton Bowl Classic Game Summary - The 65th Southwestern Bell Cotton Bowl Classic proved to be a battle of experience against youth. The wily veterans of Kansas State had one last bit of unfinished business. Tennessee was all that stood between the Wildcats and their fourth-consecutive 11-win season. Entering the Classic, Tennessee was on a tear. The Volunteers, 8-3, led by freshmen Quarterback Casey Clausen, rolled off six straight wins and had outscored their opponents 206-107 in that stretch, despite having only two senior starters on offense. Tennessee's defense was anchored by John Henderson, the fifth Outland Trophy winner to play in the Classic. Kansas State, 10-3, was fresh from a narrow loss to Oklahoma, the eventual national champion, in the Big 12 Championship. The Wildcats, with 11 senior starters on offense and defense, were hungry to finish the year on a positive note. An overnight winter storm blanketed the Cotton Bowl's playing surface in white but did nothing to dampen Kansas State's offensive attack as the Wildcats stormed to a 35-21 victory. K-State senior Quarterback Jonathan Beasley ushered in the New Year by throwing for two touchdowns and rushing for another while en route to earning Outstanding Offensive Player honors. After halftime, most of the snow had evaporated along with Tennessee's chances of winning. The No. 21 Volunteers saw a 21-14 halftime deficit expand to 35-14 just five minutes into the third quarter. K-State junior running back Josh Scobey scored twice in the third quarter on runs of 12 and six yards. However, it was Beasley's steady control of the offense that made the difference. His 308 yards in total offense were the second-most in Cotton Bowl history. Entering the Classic, Beasley had compiled only 500 rushing yards all season, but he saved his best rushing performance for last. He ran for 98 yards on 17 carries, including a 14-yard touchdown run to open the scoring at 5:46 in the first quarter. The Vols responded to Beasley's challenge when Clausen connected with wide receiver David Martin on a 17-yard touchdown pass to tie the score at 7-7 in the opening minutes of the second quarter. He became only the second true freshman to start at Quarterback in a bowl for Tennessee behind Peyton Manning. Clausen was also the third true-freshman Quarterback to ever start in a Cotton Bowl Classic. The Wildcats regained the lead a minute later when Beasley threw a 56-yard touchdown strike to Quincy Morgan. Morgan, a senior from Garland, Texas, put on a show for the hometown crowd and added another touchdown reception on the Wildcats' next possession, hooking up with Beasley one more time on a 10-yard pass play. He finished the day with 145 yards on seven receptions. In front 21-7, Kansas State was hoping to put the game out of reach on its ensuing drive, but Tennessee's Jabari Greer picked off Beasley and returned the interception 78 yards for a touchdown. Greer's defensive heroics trimmed the lead to 21-14 at halftime and brought a wild first half to a close. The combined total points in the first 30 minutes was the second highest total in Cotton Bowl history. By the start of the third quarter, Tennessee's struggle was not with the elements, but rather, finding a way to stop Kansas State's unrelenting ground attack. The Wildcats rolled up 179 yards rushing in the second half on a Tennessee defense that had allowed just 74.3 rushing yards a game during the season. Scobey finished with 147 yards on 28 carries, including his two third-quarter touchdown runs. With a 35-14 score at the end of the third quarter, the outcome of the Classic seemed inevitable. Kansas State's defense kept Tennessee at bay by holding Clausen to 7-of-25 passing for 120 yards and three interceptions. Senior defensive end Chris Johnson, the Outstanding Defensive Player of the game, accounted for both of K-State's sacks. Tennessee's bright spot offensively came from senior tailback Travis Henry who managed 180 rushing yards on 17 carries, including an 81-yard touchdown scamper with 2:44 remaining, the second longest scoring run in the game's 65-year history. Henry's 10.6 average yards per carry also was a notable achievement as the second best rushing effort at the Cotton Bowl. Yet it wasn't enough. The sea of purple-clad Kansas State fans numbering nearly 35,000 were witness to a dominant performance on both sides of the ball by a veteran Wildcat team. K-State's offense totaled 507 yards, the sixth-most in Cotton Bowl history, while the defense held a potent Tennessee offense to 298 total yards. In the end, experience won out, 35-21.

2001 Rose Bowl

The 2001 Rose Bowl was played on January 1, 2001. It was the 87th Rose Bowl game. The University of Washington Huskies football team defeated the Purdue University Boilermakers football team 34-24. Washington senior Quarterback Marques Tuiasosopo was named the Rose Bowl Player of The Game.

2001 Rose Bowl	Line	1	-	2	-	3	-	4	-	Final
#14 Purdue	(62.0)	0	-	10	-	7	-	7	-	24
#4 Washington	(Pk)	14	-	0	-	6	-	14	-	34

Scoring Summary
Washington – Cleman 1 yard run (Anderson kick)
Washington – Tuiasosopo 5 yard run (Anderson kick)
Purdue – Sutherland 5 yard pass from Brees (Dorsch kick)
Purdue – Dorsch 26 yard field goal
Washington – Anderson 47 yard field goal
Purdue – Sutherland 24 yard pass from Brees (Dorsch kick)
Washington – Anderson 42 yard field goal
Washington – Elstrom 8 yard pass from Tuiasosopo (Anderson kick)
Washington – Hurst 8 yard run (Anderson kick)
Purdue – Brown 42 yard run (Dorsch kick)

USA Today Rose Bowl Game Summary - With Drew Brees and Marques Tuiasosopo on the field, it seemed certain a Quarterback would decide the Rose Bowl. But as the third quarter was ending and the drama building Monday, there was still a question which Quarterback it would be: Brees, Purdue's record-setting thrower, or Tuiasosopo, Washington's jitterbugging two-way threat. Then Tuiasosopo jogged off the field with a banged-up right shoulder, giving the Huskies, ahead 20-17, a momentary sense of dread. But Tuiasosopo's teammates, who have seen their Quarterback take a lot of big hits this year and keep getting up, said they weren't as alarmed. He didn't, and it turned out that Tuiasosopo, despite a whopper of a mistake, got the better of Brees and led his team to a 34-24 victory. Tuiasosopo, a senior whose father, Manu, was a star defensive lineman for UCLA and in the NFL, missed the last three plays of the third quarter. He returned to face a fourth-and-1 at the Purdue 35-yard line — an ideal situation for Tuiasosopo's sneaky running ability on the option. Tuiasosopo got the first down on a 3-yard run and, moments later, he lofted a perfect throw into the end zone to 6-3 wide receiver Todd Elstrom, who towered over Purdue's 5-7 cornerback, Chris Clopton, for an 8-yard touchdown pass and a 27-17 lead. Another fourth-and-1 run with 2:42 left pretty much sealed it. He finished the game 16-for-22 for 138 yards and a touchdown, along with 15 carries for 75 yards and another touchdown. He was named MVP. Tuiasosopo gave his teammates another fright when, with a 34-24 lead, he broke into the clear for a first down but, at midfield, attempted an ill-advised lateral that Elstrom couldn't handle. Purdue recovered. But Purdue's challenge fizzled when Brees missed on three consecutive passes from the Washington 24 and Travis Dorsch missed a 42-yard field goal that would have brought the Boilermakers to within a touchdown with 4:54 left. Brees finished 23-for-39 for 275 yards and two touchdowns.

2001 Fiesta Bowl

The 2001 Tostitos Fiesta Bowl, played on January 1, 2001, was the 30th edition of the Fiesta Bowl. The game was played at Sun Devil Stadium in Tempe, Arizona, between the Oregon State Beavers (ranked number 5 in the AP Poll) and the Notre Dame Fighting Irish (ranked number 10 in the AP Poll).

2001 Fiesta Bowl	Line	1	-	2	-	3	-	4	-	Final
#10 Notre Dame	(53.0)	0	-	3	-	0	-	6	-	9
#6 Oregon State	(-4.0)	3	-	9	-	29	-	0	-	41

Scoring Summary
Oregon State - Cesca 32 yard Field goal
Oregon State - Cesca 29 yard Field goal
Oregon State - Johnson 74 yard pass from Smith (Pass failed)
Notre Dame - Setta 29 yard Field goal
Oregon State - Houshmandza 23 yard pass from Smith (Cesca kick)
Oregon State - Roberts 45 yard punt return (Prescott pass from Smith)
Oregon State - Johnson 4 yard pass from Smith (Cesca kick)
Oregon State - Simonton 4 yard run (Cesca kick)
Notre Dame - Fisher 1 yard run (Pass failed)

USA Today Fiesta Bowl Game Summary - Sixth-ranked Oregon State buried the ghost of its woeful football past and rattled the spirit of Knute Rockne himself Monday. Two years removed from their 28th consecutive losing season, an NCAA record, the Beavers capped their best season in school history with a 41-9 victory against No. 10 Notre Dame in the 30th Fiesta Bowl. The loss was the second worst in the Irish's storied 23-game bowl history. Nebraska beat Notre Dame 40-6 in the 1973 Orange Bowl. Now this, an 11-1 masterpiece capped with a blowout victory against college football's most legendary program. Quarterback Jonathan Smith led the onslaught, throwing for 305 yards and three touchdowns as the Beavers got their first major bowl victory in 59 years. Notre Dame crossed midfield only twice in the first half and surrendered 29 points in a turnover-marred third quarter to end the season 9-3 with its fifth bowl loss in a row. Oregon State linebacker Darnell Robinson forced a fumble and intercepted a pass to set up two touchdowns in the Beavers' 29-point third quarter. Chad Johnson caught touchdown passes of 74 and 4 yards, but he got away with a big mistake on the first one when officials didn't see him drop the ball two yards short of the goal line. Ken Simonton, Oregon State's big-talking 5-foot-8 tailback, gained 85 yards on 18 carries, including a 4-yard touchdown run. In the process, he broke his own single-season school rushing record. Notre Dame's 18-year-old freshman Quarterback Matt LoVecchio, under extreme pressure most of the night, threw two interceptions and fumbled the ball away - all in the third quarter. LoVecchio completed 13 of 33 passes for 138 yards. He was sacked six times. LoVecchio, who was 7-0 as a starter going into the game, had thrown just one interception and Notre Dame had just eight turnovers — tying an NCAA record — through the regular season. The Irish had five turnovers against the Beavers. The Irish lost their fifth consecutive bowl game. The Beavers had a 278-98 advantage in yardage at halftime but led just 12-3. Any doubts ended, though, with four touchdowns in a span of 7:10 in the third quarter. Notre Dame forced the Beavers to punt for the first time, but LoVecchio fumbled on a blindside hit by Robinson. Eric Manning recovered for the Beavers at the Irish 26. Two plays later, Smith lofted a perfect 23-yard scoring pass to T.J. Houshmandzadeh to make it 19-3 with 12:04 to play in the quarter. Notre Dame punted on its next possession. Houshmandzadeh returned it up the middle to midfield, then fumbled. Teammate Terrell Roberts picked the ball up at the 45 and ran to the end zone. The two-point conversion pass from Smith to Robert Prescott put Oregon State up 27-3 with 9:08 to go in the third. It got worse for LoVecchio, who threw a pass right into the hands of Robinson to give Oregon State the ball on the Irish 22. The Beavers scored in four plays, Smith throwing 4 yards to Johnson for the score, and it was 34-3 with 7:02 left in the quarter. The final touchdown came on Simonton's 4-yard run at the end of a five-play, 55-yard drive to put the Beavers up 41-3 with 4:54 to go in the third. The most interesting play was Johnson's long touchdown catch. He raced down the sidelines and casually dropped the ball as if he had crossed the goal line. But television replays clearly showed he was two yards short of the end zone. No official saw it, though, and the touchdown put Oregon State up 12-0 with 4:18 to play in the half. Consecutive sacks of LoVecchio pinned the Irish at third-and-31 on their own 2, but Oregon State free safety Calvin Carlyle was called for a personal foul for shoving down a player after the play. Notre Dame got a first down, LoVecchio threw 40 yards to Javin Hunter and the Irish ended the half with Nick Setta's 29-yard field goal. The Beavers drove to the Irish 15, 10 and 1 on their first three possessions but had to settle for field goals of 32 and 29 yards by Ryan Cesca to go up 6-0.

2001 Sugar Bowl

The 2001 Sugar Bowl a 2000–2001 BCS game was played on January 2, 2001. This 67th edition to the Sugar Bowl featured the Florida Gators, and the Miami Hurricanes, in an in-state rivalry game. Miami came into the game ranked 3rd in the BCS, 2nd in both the Coaches and AP Poll, at 10–1, whereas Florida came into the game ranked 7th in the BCS at 10–2.

2001 Sugar Bowl	Line	1	-	2	-	3	-	4	-	Final
#2 Miami	(-7.0)	10	-	3	-	14	-	10	-	37
#7 Florida	(57.0)	7	-	3	-	7	-	3	-	20

Scoring Summary
Florida - Wells 23 yard pass from Grossman (J Chandler kick)
Miami - Sievers 44 yard Field goal
Miami - Shockey 8 yard pass from Dorsey (Sievers kick)
Miami - Sievers 29 yard Field goal
Florida - Chandler 51 yard Field goal
Florida - Graham 36 yard run (J Chandler kick)
Miami - Williams 19 yard pass from Dorsey (Sievers kick)
Miami - Davenport 2 yard pass from Dorsey (Sievers kick)
Florida - Chandler 26 yard Field goal
Miami - Sievers 29 yard Field goal
Miami - Davenport 3 yard run (Sievers kick)

USA Today Sugar Bowl Game Summary - It was a good and gritty Sugar Bowl for Miami, with both adversity and the Florida Gators to overcome. Now the Hurricanes wait to see if it was good enough. No. 2 Miami's closing argument for a slice of the national championship came with three Ken Dorsey touchdown passes and a second half surge Tuesday night, sweeping past No. 7 Florida 37-20 to possibly force the voters' hand in the final AP media poll. The 11-1 Hurricanes had no easy night, losing top rusher James Jackson midway through the game, having All-American receiver Santana Moss slowed by injury, sometimes struggling with the Florida defense, occasionally baffled by Steve Spurrier's passing plans. But carry on they did, with 270 passing yards from game MVP Dorsey and three Todd Sievers field goals, and a 50-yard PAT kick for icing. Now they have rooting to do. Fate and the Bowl Championship Series make strange bedfellows. Miami must now hope old enemy and No. 3 Florida State beats No. 1 Oklahoma in the Orange Bowl. That could clear the road for the Hurricanes to finish ahead of Florida State in the Associated Press poll, for a share of their fifth national title. For Miami, the Sugar hardly could have been sweeter. It was not just any victory, but one over a despised neighbor whom the Hurricanes had not seen in 13 years, except for their brouhaha last week on Bourbon Street. And not just any trampling of Florida, but one that left the No. 1 door ajar. But who is better, the Miami team that just whipped the Gators or the Florida State team that beat Florida 30-7 in Tallahassee in November? The high stakes of Tuesday's game apparently did little to hype the gate. The crowd was announced as 64,407, or 15,000 below capacity. It was a raw, physical, often inelegant fight, full of penalty flags and swinging momentum, two Quarterbacks desperately looking for time to making their potent passing games work, two coaches who often had to turn to the ground game to try to get by. There were three lead changes, 91 passes — 52 by halftime — and 20 penalties, 11 by the Gators for 109 yards. The night changed for good in the third period, when Miami erased a 17-13 Florida lead with two quick touchdowns. The first was Dorsey's 19-yard pass to D.J. Williams, on a drive hugely aided by Florida defensive tackle Gerald Warren's roughing penalty, when he yanked down Dorsey long after the pass left. The second came on a two-yard pass to Najeh Davenport, after Daryl Jones' 44-yard punt return put Miami close. The 27-17 lead the Hurricanes took into the fourth period seemed imposing enough. Since 1985, they are 140-2 when leading after three quarters. Florida closed to within 27-20 in the final period, but Miami answered with its own field goal, and then Davenport's touchdown dive, set up by Philip Buchanon's interception of Rex Grossman, the second of the game for the Florida Quarterback and the last pass he threw, yanked then for Jesse Palmer. Two Miami penalties after the touchdown — one for unsportsmanlike conduct by the team mascot — forced Sievers to look at a 50-yard bomb for the PAT. He nailed it anyway. By then, the night had turned magic for Miami. Without Jackson and his sprained foot, the Hurricanes had turned to Clinton Portis, who rushed for 93 of his 97 yards in the second half. With Moss off the punt return unit after a hip pointer, Jones had the big return. Miami coaxed a 13-10 lead out of the first half of a game shot out of a cannon. There were 27 passes in the first period alone. Grossman's 23-yard touchdown pass to an outrageously open tight end Kirk Wells gave the Gators a 7-0 lead, Miami came back with a field goal, then an eight-yard Dorsey touchdown pass to tight end Jeremy Shockey, then another field goal for a 13-7 lead. Jeff Chandler's 51-yard field goal for Florida cut the Miami halftime lead to 13-10. It was hardly the show of power that Miami had in mind to show the voters, and the second half began even worse. Dorsey was sacked, then threw an interception. Florida followed with Earnest Graham's 36-yard touchdown run and 17-13 lead. Graham finished with a 136-yard rushing night and was called "our lone bright spot" by Spurrier.

2001 Orange Bowl (BCS Championship Game)

The 2001 FedEx Orange Bowl game was the BCS National Championship game between the University of Oklahoma Sooners and the Florida State Seminoles on January 3, 2001, at Pro Player Stadium in Miami Gardens, Florida. Oklahoma defeated FSU 13-2 in a defensive battle to claim the National Championship as head coach Bob Stoops' completed just his second season as the coach of the Sooners. The Orange Bowl was first played in 1935, and the 2001 game represented the 67th edition. The contest was televised on ABC.

2001 Orange Bowl	Line	1	-	2	-	3	-	4	-	Final
#3 Florida State	(-10.0)	0	-	0	-	0	-	2	-	2
#1 Oklahoma	(56.0)	3	-	0	-	3	-	7	-	13

Scoring Summary
Oklahoma - Duncan 27 yard Field goal
Oklahoma - Duncan 42 yard Field goal
Oklahoma - Griffin 10 yard run (Duncan kick)
Florida State - Safety, Team tackled in end zone

USA Today Orange Bowl Game Summary - In the end, the little guy, the overlooked guy, won. When Quentin Griffin, Oklahoma's 5-6 running back, hid behind the wide bodies on his offensive line and squirted into the end zone for the game-clinching touchdown in Wednesday night's national championship game against Florida State, little guys everywhere rejoiced. Little guys like Quarterback Josh Heupel, the former junior college player whose wobbly passes matched the circuitous route he took to Oklahoma. Overlooked guys like Oklahoma's defensive players, who played in the shadow of their record-breaking offense all season and thoroughly dominated the Seminoles. No one expected the Sooners to be in the national championship game this season, let alone win it, but they did just that, beating Florida State 13-2 in the Orange Bowl at Pro Player Stadium. Oklahoma secured the victory shortly after Sooners linebacker Rocky Calmus knocked the ball from Quarterback Chris Weinke's hand deep in Florida State territory with 8:30 remaining. Cornerback Roy Williams recovered the fumble and Griffin's run put the game away with his score. Now, the once-giant Sooners stand tall again. After several downtrodden years, Oklahoma (13-0) capped its perfect season with its first championship in 15 years and its seventh overall. Oklahoma's win also dimmed No. 2-ranked Miami's chances for a shared national title. The Hurricanes completed their season 11-1, including victories against Florida State during the regular season and Florida in Tuesday night's Sugar Bowl. The Orange Bowl winner automatically is ranked No. 1 in the final USA TODAY/ESPN Coaches' Poll. Voters in the Associated Press media poll chose their champion early this morning. All week, Oklahoma coach Bob Stoops, the former defensive coordinator at Florida, was asked if his experience with the Gators had prepared him to stop the Seminoles (11-2). After his team's suffocating defensive performance, the answer is yes. In 1997, Stoops' Florida defense derailed FSU's hopes for a national championship in the Sugar Bowl. The first half of Wednesday's game was dominated by defense, as both teams had more punts than points. Florida State punted six times, Oklahoma four. The Sooners led 3-0 at halftime behind a 27-yard field goal from Tim Duncan. Who would have expected that from two of the nation's top scoring teams? Keeping with tradition, Florida State's best chance to score came down to a familiar theme: wide right. Midway through the second quarter, FSU coach Bobby Bowden went for a field goal instead of going for the first down on fourth-and-1 from Oklahoma's 13-yard line. But freshman kicker Brett Cimorelli didn't reward Bowden's confidence in him. He kicked a low line drive that badly missed to the right. Field goal kicking has been the Seminoles' weakness all season; entering the game, they had missed eight PAT attempts and were 14 of 24 on field goal tries. As this attempt missed, Cimorelli punched the air with his fist, then dropped his head. Not again. In October, Florida State lost to Miami 27-24 when Matt Munyon's 49-yard field goal attempt sailed right as time expired. In the third quarter Wednesday, Oklahoma also had field goal heartache when Duncan's 37-yard attempt just missed to the right. Minutes later, though, Duncan redeemed himself by making a 42-yarder that gave the Sooners a 6-0 lead, and eventually the win.

2001 New Orleans Bowl

The 2001 New Orleans Bowl featured the North Texas Mean Green and the Colorado State Rams. It was the inaugural playing of the game. North Texas became the first team in NCAA history to make a bowl game after starting the season 0-5. They were the Sun Belt Conference Champions, despite having a losing record, and with the conference championship, had earned the automatic bid, staying consistent with rules in other NCAA sports (most notably basketball) where the conference champion earns an automatic postseason bid, regardless of record.

2001 New Orleans Bowl	Line	1	-	2	-	3	-	4	-	Final
Colorado State	(-12.0)	17	-	7	-	7	-	14	-	45
North Texas	(47.5)	0	-	14	-	0	-	6	-	20

Scoring Summary
Colorado State - Svoboda 2 yard run (Naughton kick)
Colorado State - Naughton 46 yard Field goal
Colorado State - Ochoa 8 yard pass from Van Pelt (Naughton kick)
North Texas - Dean 5 yard pass from Hall (Ball kick)
Colorado State - Van Pelt 6 yard run (Naughton kick)
North Texas - Branch 42 yard pass from Hall (Ball kick)
Colorado State - Gallimore recovered blocked punt in end zone (Naughton kick)
Colorado State - Dixon 2 yard run (Naughton kick)
Colorado State - Vomhof 20 yard run (Naughton kick)
North Texas - Blount 13 yard pass from Bridges (Pass failed)

Associated Press New Orleans Bowl Game Summary - North Texas waited 42 years to get back to a bowl. It took Colorado State less than eight minutes to make it a long night for the Mean Green. Colorado State jumped to a 17-point lead midway through the first quarter and coasted to a 45-14 victory in the inaugural New Orleans Bowl at the Superdome. Bradlee Van Pelt had modest numbers for the Rams (7-5), but he connected with Pete Rebstock for a 56-yard completion on the first play from scrimmage. Brad

Svoboda scored on a two-yard run just 79 seconds into the contest and Colorado State never looked back. After forcing a punt, Colorado State went up 10-0 on Kent Naughton's 46-yard field goal with 8:22 left. Cornerback Justin Gallimore, who returned a blocked punt for a touchdown in the third quarter, recovered a fumble on North Texas' next possession, setting up Van Pelt's eight-yard TD toss to Jose Ochoa that made it 17-0 with 7:08 to go in the first period. North Texas (5-7) ended the nation's longest bowl drought, last playing in the postseason in the 1959 Sun Bowl. The Sun Belt Conference champion become the first team to play in a bowl after a 0-5 start and the third to receive a bowl bid despite a losing record. The Mean Green also were the first team to take advantage of an NCAA waiver that allows a conference champion to play in a bowl game without the mandated six victories. North Texas tried to make a game of it, closing to 24-14 on Hall's 42-yard touchdown pass to Ja'Mel Branch with 40 seconds left in the first half. But Gallimore scored off a blocked punt to give Colorado State a 17-point cushion with 4:35 to go in the third quarter and Chad Dixon ran two yards for a TD to make it 38-14 three minutes into the final period. Colorado State took a 45-14 lead on Michael Vomhof's 20-yard run before backup Richard Bridges tossed a meaningless 13-yard TD strike to Andy Blount with 2:11 left. Kevin Galbreath rushed for 106 yards on 22 carries for the Mean Green. The win enabled Colorado State to extend a school record by winning at least seven games for the eighth straight season.

2001 GMAC Bowl

The 2001 GMAC Bowl was held on December 19 at Ladd-Peebles Stadium in Mobile, Alabama, pitted the Marshall Thundering Herd, then of the Mid-American Conference, against the East Carolina Pirates from Conference USA. This game featured what was then the biggest comeback in NCAA Division I-A (now Division I FBS) bowl history, as Marshall came back from a 38-8 halftime deficit to force overtime and eventually win 64-61 in double overtime. It was also the highest-scoring bowl game in history, breaking the previous record set when Texas Tech defeated Air Force 55-41 in the 1995 Copper Bowl. Although the record for greatest bowl comeback was broken by Texas Tech when it returned to the Copper Bowl, by then renamed the Insight Bowl, in 2006, the 2001 GMAC Bowl remains the highest-scoring bowl game ever. The game, with an official attendance of 40,139, was telecast on ESPN2. It was a rematch of one of Marshall's most historically significant games. On November 14, 1970, the two teams met at East Carolina, with the Pirates winning 17-14. That night, the plane carrying the Herd back to Huntington, West Virginia crashed just before landing, killing all 75 on board. The two teams had only met one time since the crash, a 45-0 East Carolina win in 1978.

2001 GMAC Bowl	Line	1	-	2	-	3	-	4	-	OT	-	OT	-	Final
Marshall	(66.5)	0	-	8	-	28	-	15	-	7	-	6	-	64
East Carolina	(-2.0)	21	-	17	-	3	-	10	-	7	-	3	-	61

Scoring Summary
East Carolina - Hunt 12 yard interception return (Miller kick)
East Carolina - Steward 43 yard fumble return (Miller kick)
East Carolina - Garrard 9 yard run (Miller kick)
East Carolina - Miller 25 yard Field goal
Marshall - Watts 35 yard pass from Leftwich (Buggs run)
East Carolina - Henry 7 yard run (Miller kick)
East Carolina - Garrard 6 yard run (Miler kick)
Marshall - Street 25 yard interception return (Head kick)
Marshall - Leftwich 9 yard run (Head kick)
East Carolina - Miller 22 yard Field goal
Marshall - Tarpley 25 yard interception return (Head kick)
Marshall - Wallace 15 yard run (Head kick)
East Carolina - Miller 32 yard Field goal
Marshall - Marriott 30 yard pass from Leftwich (pass failed)
East Carolina - Henry 55 yard run (Miller kick)
Marshall - Head 27 yard Field goal
Marshall - Watts 11 yard pass from Leftwich (kick failed)
Marshall - Wallace 2 yard run (Head kick)
East Carolina - Henry 25 yard run (Miller kick)
East Carolina - Miller 37 yard Field goal
Marshall - Davis 8 yard pass from Leftwich

Records - Leftwich's 576 passing yards for the game tied the bowl-game record set by Ty Detmer of BYU in the 1989 Holiday Bowl (however, Detmer's record was set in regulation). This record still stands as of 2007. East Carolina earned the dubious honor of scoring the most points ever by a losing team in a bowl game. The two teams combined for 16 touchdowns and 125 points, also bowl game records. Until 2011 this game remained the highest-scoring bowl game at the end of regulation time, with the total 102 points scored in regulation. The only other bowl game, at that time, to see 102 total points scored was the 2003

Hawai'i Bowl, in which Hawai'i defeated Houston 54-48 in three overtimes. These games edged out the 101 points scored in California's 52-49 win over Virginia Tech in the 2003 Insight Bowl. The University of Washington and Baylor University broke the record for most points in regulation in the 2011 Alamo Bowl scoring 123 combined points with Baylor winning 67-56.

2001 Tangerine Bowl

The 2001 Visit Florida Tangerine Bowl was the 12th edition to the college football bowl game, successing the MicronPC.com bowl. It featured the NC State Wolfpack and the Pittsburgh Panthers. This was the first year since 1982 that the Tangerine Bowl was played; the original version is now known as the Capital One Bowl.

2001 Tangerine Bowl	Line	1	-	2	-	3	-	4	-	Final
NC State	(48.0)	3	-	7	-	0	-	9	-	19
Pittsburgh	(Pk)	3	-	21	-	3	-	7	-	34

Scoring Summary
Pittsburgh - Lotz 27 yard Field goal
NC State - Kiker 32 yard Field goal
Pittsburgh - Bryant 15 yard pass Priestly (Lotz kick)
Pittsburgh - Bryant 2 yard pass from Priestly (Lotz kick)
NC State - Greg Golden 90 yard kick return (Kiker kick)
Pittsburgh - Rutherford 1 yard run (Lotz kick)
Pittsburgh - Lotz 33 yard Field goal
NC State – Edwards 5 yard pass from Rivers (kick failed)
NC State - Kiker 19 Field goal
Pittsburgh - Young 16 yard fumble recovery

Associated Press Tangerine Bowl Game Summary - When Walt Harris talks to future Pittsburgh teams, he'll likely refer to the 2001 players in proud terms. After a 1-5 start, the Panthers refused to give up, closing their season with a 34-19 victory over North Carolina State in the Tangerine Bowl, capping one of the program's greatest turnarounds. "Our football players have really done something in the way of fighting back from adversity," Harris said after Thursday night's victory, his team's sixth straight. Antonio Bryant, a question mark heading into the game with an injured right ankle, caught two touchdown passes to earn the game's MVP award. As he was presented with the trophy, Pitt fans chanted "One More Year," hoping to convince the star junior receiver to return to school and not head to the NFL. Despite what some believe was Bryant's last college game, he gave no indication he was ready for the pros. Bryant, who caught all seven of his passes for 101 yards in the opening half as the Panthers built a 24-10 lead. Bryant wasn't the only Pitt hero Thursday night. David Priestley, who had 13 TD passes and one interception during Pitt's winning streak, threw for 271 yards. And Pitt's defense, which allowed a combined 37 points in its previous five games, came up big after N.C. State (7-5) closed to 27-19. Lewis Moore sacked Philip Rivers and forced a fumble that was returned 16 yards by Tyre Young for a touchdown with 6:15 left. Pittsburgh's winning streak is its longest since 1983. Harris earned his first bowl win in three tries in his five seasons with Pitt. The Panthers got their first postseason victory since beating Texas A&M in the John Hancock Bowl 12 years ago. Bryant hurt his ankle in the regular-season finale against Alabama-Birmingham on Dec. 1. But the 2000 All-American and two-time Big East wide receiver was on his game early. He caught TDs of 15 and 2 yards as the Panthers went up by 14 at halftime. Meanwhile, N.C. State wasn't the same team on defense after losing first-team All-America linebacker Levar Fisher early in the second quarter to a broken left forearm. The teams traded field goals in a closely played first quarter before the Panthers took control in the second, scoring on drives of 80, 98 and 70 yards. Pittsburgh took the lead for good with 10:17 left in the second quarter when Priestley completed a 32-yard screen pass to Marcus Furman and a 22-yard swing pass to Raymond Kirkley before Bryant beat Wolfpack safety Julius Patterson on a 15-yard TD. A 49-yard completion to Bryant sparked Pitt's next long march. Priestley also found Bryant for 16 yards on a third-and-11 play and capped the drive with a 2-yard scoring pass to his star receiver for a 17-3 lead. The Wolfpack was called for roughing the punter to keep Pitt's final scoring drive of the half alive. Three plays after the penalty, Lousaka Polite ran 35 yards to the 1, and Rod Rutherford scored on a keeper.

2001 Las Vegas Bowl

The 2001 edition to the Las Vegas Bowl was the 10th edition of that annual game. It featured the USC Trojans, and the Utah Utes. The game was dominated by defense. Utah opened the scoring on a 3-yard touchdown run by Adam Tate, leading 7–0. They increased their lead to 10–0 in the second quarter, with a 26-yard field goal from Ryan Kaneshiro. That would be their final score of the game. In the third quarter, USC's Sunny Byrd scored a touchdown from 2 yards out, but the extra point missed leaving the score 10–6. Utah held on to win the game over USC.

2001 Las Vegas Bowl	Line	1	-	2	-	3	-	4	-	Final
Utah	(44.0)	7	-	3	-	0	-	0	-	10
USC	(-3.5)	0	-	0	-	6	-	0	-	6

Scoring Summary
Utah - Tate 3 yard run (Kaneshiro kick)
Utah - Kaneshio 26 Field goal
USC - Byrd 2 yard run (kick failed)

Associated Press Las Vegas Bowl Game Summary - Southern California was on a roll before being bowled over by Utah. Behind its two bruising senior running backs, the Utes edged the Trojans, 10-6, for their second win in three years at the Las Vegas Bowl. Adam Tate and Dameon Hunter combined for 197 yards and a score for Utah (8-4), which limited USC (6-6) to one yard rushing in a dominating defensive effort. The Trojans had won four straight games and entered Sam Boyd Stadium with a ton of confidence. But Tate and Hunter proved to be too much for Carson Palmer and a quiet USC offense. The 6-1, 229-pound Tate carried 23 times for 103 yards and a touchdown, opening the scoring with a three-yard run in the first quarter. Hunter, a punishing 5-11, 236-pounder, finished with 94 yards on 17 carries. Lance Rice helped when he could, completing 12-of-21 passes for 136 yards. Rice may have made the biggest play of the game, throwing a 20-yard pass to tight end Michael Richardson on 3rd-and-14 from Utah's 9-yard line with 3 1/2 minutes left. Richardson, who also has played guard and center for Utah, had three catches for 35 yards. With under 2 1/2 minutes to play, Tate salted away the win with a 17-yard run off a draw on 3rd-and-6. Behind their two-man show, the Utes finished with 358 yards of total offense to 151 for the Trojans. Utah also controlled the ball for more than 38 minutes. The Utes have had incredible success in Vegas, where they have claimed each of their last two bowl wins. They won twice at Sam Boyd Stadium this season, posting a 42-14 victory over Nevada-Las Vegas on November 3. Palmer went 15-of-26 for just 150 yards for the Trojans, who played for the first time in more than five weeks. USC had an impressive drive to start the second half, going 80 yards in 12 plays. Sunny Byrd scored from two yards, but David Davis missed the extra point, and the Trojans trailed, 10-6. Davis also missed a 47-yard field goal in the first half after making 12 straight attempts. The game turned sloppy following Byrd's TD as USC committed a pair of turnovers around a shanked punt by Utah's Brian Lewis. Both turnovers -- the only two of the game -- came in Utes' territory.

2001 Independence Bowl
ALABAMA 14 IOWA STATE 13

The 2001 MainStay Independence Bowl took place on December 27, 2001, at Independence Stadium in Shreveport, Louisiana. The competing teams were the Alabama Crimson Tide, representing the Southeastern Conference (SEC), and the Iowa State Cyclones of the Big 12 Conference (Big 12). Alabama won the game, 14–13 in what was the first all-time game between the programs.

2001 Independence Bowl	Line	1	-	2	-	3	-	4	-	Final
Alabama	(-6.5)	0	-	7	-	0	-	7	-	14
Iowa State	(51.5)	3	-	7	-	3	-	0	-	13

Scoring Summary
Iowa State - Yelk 36 yard Field goal
Iowa State - Woodley 1 yard run (Yelk kick)
Alabama - Zow 8 yard run (Thomas kick)
Iowa State - Yelk 41 yard Field goal
Alabama - Jones 27 yard pass from Zow (Thomas kick)

Associated Press Independence Bowl Game summary - Alabama will have something to build on as it heads into the offseason. Andrew Zow, playing with a bruised calf, tossed a 27-yard touchdown pass to Terry Jones with 4:44 remaining as the Crimson Tide ended coach Dennis Franchione's first season with a 14-13 victory over Iowa State in the Independence Bowl. Iowa State's defense dominated throughout, but Alabama free safety Waine Bacon blocked Tony Yelk's punt, giving the Crimson Tide possession at the Cyclones' 29-yard line. Two plays later, Zow connected with Jones for the winning score, enabling Alabama (7-5) to rally from a 10-0 deficit and finish the season with a winning record. It was a four-game improvement from last season, when the Tide went 3-8. Zow, who was sacked four times, completed 11-of-19 passes for 119 yards with an interception. The Crimson Tide were held to just 150 yards on the ground. Iowa State (7-5) had a chance to regain the lead in the final minute, but Yelk's 47-yard field goal was wide right with 46 seconds left. It was his third miss of the game. Seneca Wallace drove the Cyclones into field-goal range on their final possession. He converted a 2nd-and-25 with a 26-yard completion to Jack Whitver at midfield, then kept alive the drive by hitting Lane Danielson for 14 yards on 4th-and-7 from the Alabama

47. Wallace completed 25-of-42 passes for 284 yards. But Yelk's field goal missed the upright by inches and Zow took two snaps to run out the clock. Yelk kicked a 36-yard field goal to open the scoring 1:42 into the contest before Joe Woodley scored on a one-yard TD run to make it 10-0 36 seconds into the second quarter. But Alabama got on the board on Zow's eight-yard TD run with 9:19 left in the second and Yelk failed to extend the lead, missing a 25-yard field goal with 26 seconds left in the half. He converted a 41-yarder to make it 13-7 with 2:11 left in the third period but kept Alabama within one score by missing a 40-yarder 4:22 into the final period. The Cyclones were trying to win consecutive bowl games for the first time in school history. Last season, they defeated Pittsburgh in the Insight.com Bowl for their first bowl win after four losses in the postseason. Ennis Haywood rushed for 125 yards on 20 carries, marking the first time Iowa State lost in 13 games when its leading runner surpassed the century mark. Ahmad Galloway paced Alabama on the ground with 90 yards on 16 carries. The Crimson Tide were making their NCAA-record 52nd postseason appearance. They snapped a two-game bowl losing streak and improved to 30-19-3 in postseason play.

2001 Seattle Bowl

The 2001 Jeep Seattle Bowl was the first edition of the college football bowl game (previously known as the Oahu Bowl), and was to be played at Safeco Field in Seattle, Washington. The game pitted the Georgia Tech Yellow Jackets from the ACC and the Stanford Cardinal from the Pac-10. The game resulted in a 24–14 Georgia Tech upset victory over the 11th ranked Stanford team. The game was played at Safeco Field because Qwest Field had not yet been completed.

2001 Seattle Bowl	Line	1	-	2	-	3	-	4	-	Final
Georgia Tech	(61.0)	7	-	10	-	0	-	7	-	24
Stanford	(-5.0)	0	-	3	-	3	-	8	-	14

Scoring Summary
Georgia Tech - Glover 5 yard run (Manget kick)
Stanford - Biselli 35 yard Field goal
Georgia Tech - Campbell 34 pass from Godsey (Manget kick)
Georgia Tech - Manget 20 yard Field goal
Stanford - Biselli 26yard Field goal
Stanford - Johnson 4 yard pass from Lewis (Wells pass from Lewis)
Georgia Tech - Campbell 2 yard run (Manget kick)

Georgia Tech website Seattle Bowl Game Summary - Georgia Tech's players chanted "We want Mac! We want Mac!" as they accepted the inaugural Seattle Bowl trophy. Their words were a statement of support for interim coach Mac McWhorter. So was their play. George Godsey passed for a touchdown, Kelly Campbell scored twice, and the defense made an early goal-line stand as the Yellow Jackets beat No. 11 Stanford 24-14 Thursday in the Seattle Bowl. McWhorter coached Georgia Tech on Thursday because George O'Leary left the Yellow Jackets this month to become the head coach at Notre Dame. O'Leary resigned five days later, though, because of inaccuracies on his resume. McWhorter, O'Leary's assistant head coach and offensive line coach, appreciated the support his players showed by yelling his nickname after the game. Campbell's second touchdown was a 2-yard run with 1:29 left, sealing the victory for Georgia Tech (8-5) before a crowd of 30,144 at Safeco Field, home of the Seattle Mariners. That capped a 13-play, 63-yard drive. Stanford (9-3) had drawn to 17-14 with 11:39 remaining, when backup Quarterback Chris Lewis threw a 4-yard touchdown pass to Teyo Johnson, then added a 2-point conversion pass. Georgia Tech's defense set the tone on the game's first drive, stopping Stanford three times at the 1-yard line. Brian Allen was stopped on two runs from the 1, and linebacker Daryl Smith dropped Kerry Carter for a 2-yard loss on fourth down. That helped the Yellow Jackets take a 17-3 halftime lead. They went up 7-0 thanks to a 97-yard drive - their longest of the season - on 16 plays, capped by Will Glover's 5-yard run. Stanford drove from its 20 to Georgia Tech's 18 before settling for Mike Biselli's 35-yard field goal at the start of the second quarter, before Godsey teamed with Campbell for a 34-yard touchdown pass for the Yellow Jackets. Gregory's 54-yard run set up a 20-yard field goal by Luke Manget with two seconds left in the first half. Gregory's run was the longest from scrimmage for Georgia Tech this season. Gregory, who became a starter when Joe Burns was ruled academically ineligible before the Seattle Bowl, ran 19 times for 91 yards. Stanford blew a chance for a touchdown in the third quarter. The Cardinal had second down on Georgia Tech's 2 but had to settle for a 26-yard field goal by Biselli. The first football game at Safeco was played with one end zone in left field and the other near home plate - the infield dirt was part of the field. The teams lined up alongside one another, sharing a sideline. The Seattle Bowl moved from Hawaii, where it was called the Oahu Bowl. Organizers hope to play the 2002 Seattle Bowl in the Seattle Seahawks' new outdoor stadium, opening next season. Godsey was 23-for-37 for 266 yards and one touchdown, with no interceptions, while Stanford Quarterback Randy Fasani was 11-for-21 for 115 yards.

Lewis, who replaced Fasani in the fourth quarter, was 6-for-13 for 110 yards and one TD. Campbell caught 10 passes for 106 yards.

2001 Music City Bowl

The 2001 Music City Bowl was the fourth edition of the bowl game held. It was played on December 28, 2001 at LP Field in Nashville, Tennessee, and featured the Georgia Bulldogs and the Boston College Eagles.

2001 Music City Bowl	Line	1	-	2	-	3	-	4	-	Final
Boston College	(52.0)	3	-	10	-	0	-	7	-	20
#19 Georgia	(-4.0)	7	-	3	-	6	-	0	-	16

Scoring Summary
Georgia - Gibson 15 yard pass from Greene (Bennett kick)
Boston College - Sciortino 25 yard Field goal
Boston College - Dewalt 10 yard pass from St. Pierre (Sciortino kick)
Boston College - Sciortino 26 yard Field goal
Georgia - Bennett 24 yard Field goal
Georgia - Haynes 1 yard run (kick failed)
Boston College - Green 7 yard run (Sciortino kick)

Associated Press Music City Bowl Game Summary - Boston College will not have to spend the offseason listening to talk about how it cannot beat ranked teams. William Green, shut down for most of the second half, scored on a seven-yard run with 4:43 remaining as the Eagles ended a 21-game losing streak against ranked opponents with a 20-16 victory over No. 19 Georgia in the Music City Bowl. It was Boston College's first win over a top-25 team since defeating Virginia Tech in 1995. The nation's second-leading rusher, Green ran for just 26 of his 149 yards in the second half. However, he kept alive the Eagles' winning drive by converting on 4th-and-1 from the Georgia 34. Brian St. Pierre hit Dedrick Dewalt for 23 yards to move Boston College (8-4) to the 10. Green, who carried 35 times, scored two plays later, ending what might have been his final college game on a high note. He has hinted he will forgo his senior year to enter the NFL draft. Green was suspended for last season's Aloha Bowl win over Arizona State for violating team rules and sat out a heartbreaking loss to top-ranked Miami earlier this season after missing practice without permission. The Bulldogs (8-4) had a final chance, taking over at their 48 with 14 seconds left. But an incomplete pass and a sack ended Georgia's hopes. Freshman David Greene completed 22-of-38 passes for 288 yards with two interceptions for the Bulldogs. The loss snapped Georgia's four-game bowl winning streak, which matched a school record. The Eagles survived a poor game by St. Pierre, who completed just 9-of-26 passes for 109 yards. Georgia committed four turnovers but erased a 13-10 halftime deficit on Verron Haynes' one-yard touchdown run with 5:26 remaining in the third quarter. Haynes rushed for 132 yards on 27 carries. However, the Bulldogs were offside on the extra point, which turned out to be a critical mistake as Billy Bennett missed his first conversion of the season, leaving Georgia ahead by just three points. After Green's TD, the Bulldogs marched into Boston College territory, but an offensive pass interference penalty on Terrence Edwards on 2nd-and-1 from the Eagles' 37 stalled the drive. Facing a 4th-and-17 at his own 43 with less than two minutes remaining, Georgia coach Mark Richt elected to punt. The Bulldogs needed just 55 seconds to open the scoring as Greene tossed a 15-yard TD pass to Fred Gibson after Decory Bryant's 81-yard return on the opening kickoff. Georgia appeared ready to make it 14-0 on its next possession, but Haynes fumbled at the Boston College 19. The Eagles put together an 18-play drive, closing to 7-3 on Sandro Sciortino's 25-yard field goal with 1:43 left in the first quarter. Taking advantage of three Georgia turnovers, the Eagles went ahead, 13-7, in the second quarter on St. Pierre's 10-yard TD toss to Dewalt and Sciortino's 26-yard field goal. Bennett converted a 24-yard field goal with 39 seconds to left to pull the Bulldogs within 13-10 at halftime. The Bulldogs keyed on Green in the second half, holding him to three yards in the third quarter. Boston College had a 3rd-and-1 at the Georgia 35 early in the final period, but Green twice was stopped for no gain. But Musa Smith fumbled a handoff at the Boston College 33 on the Bulldogs' ensuing possession and the Eagles took advantage, moving 63 yards on nine plays for the go-ahead score.

2001 Galleryfurniture.com Bowl

The 2001 Galleryfurniture.com Bowl was the second edition of the college football bowl game (renamed the Houston Bowl the following year), and was played at the Reliant Astrodome in Houston, Texas. The game pitted the Texas A&M Aggies from the Big 12 Conference and the TCU Horned Frogs from Conference USA (C-USA). The teams were rivals in the Southwest Conference for many years.

2001 Galleryfurniture.com Bowl	Line	1	-	2	-	3	-	4	-	Final
TCU	(43.0)	0	-	7	-	0	-	2	-	9
Texas A&M	(-6.0)	0	-	14	-	7	-	7	-	28

Scoring Summary
Texas A&M – Farris 1 yard run (Scates kick)
TCU – Owens 89 yard fumble recovery (Blankenship kick)
Texas A&M – Weber 2 yard run (Scates kick)
Texas A&M – Weber 14 yard run (Scates kick)
Texas A&M – Jones 82 yard pass from Farris (Scates kick)
TCU – Team safety

Texas A&M media guide Galleryfurniture.com Bowl Game Summary - Not a bad way to begin a career. Freshman Byron Jones intercepted three passes in his first start, and Joe Weber scored two touchdowns, helping Texas A&M end a four-game bowl losing streak with a 28-9 victory over TCU in the Galleryfurniture.com Bowl on Friday. Jones, one of five freshmen in the lineup, helped the Aggies beat their former Southwest Conference rivals for the 24th straight time. A&M won a bowl game for the first time since a 22-20 victory over Michigan in the 1995 Alamo Bowl. The Aggies ended the season 8-4 after losing their final three regular-season games. The Horned Frogs (6-6) haven't beaten the Aggies since 1972 and trail the series 56-29-7. Weber, voted offensive player of the game, broke a 7-7 second-quarter tie with a 2-yard touchdown run and added a 14-yard run that put the Aggies in control with 1:14 left in the third quarter. TCU's Casey Printers was intercepted four times, including the first three of Jones' career. Aggies safety Wes Bautovich got A&M's fourth interception. On the next play, Mark Farris hit Mickey Jones for an 82-yard touchdown pass and a 28-7 lead with 14:40 left in the game. Weber broke straight up the middle on his second touchdown, knocking aside two tacklers and running into the end zone. He finished with 59 yards on nine carries. Jones was the game's MVP and was the defensive player of the game. He had three tackles and ran back his interceptions a total of 77 yards. Starting in place of the injured Sean Weston, Jones had only two broken-up passes on his defensive chart in 11 games before he returned his first interception 62 yards in the first quarter to the Frogs' 35. The Aggies couldn't score on that chance, but Jones had a 15-yard interception return to TCU's 1-yard line in the second quarter, setting up Farris' Quarterback keeper for the score. Charlie Owens scooped up a fumble by A&M running back Derek Farmer and returned it 89 yards for a TCU touchdown with four minutes left in the half, tying the game 7-7. It was the second-longest fumble return in school history. Thomas returned the ensuing kickoff 43 yards, and Carriger, a converted defensive lineman, lumbered 19 yards with his second reception of the season to set up Weber's 2-yard touchdown run with 1:06 left in the half.

2001 Holiday Bowl
The 2001 Culligan Holiday Bowl was played December 28, 2001, in San Diego, California. It featured the Washington Huskies against the Texas Longhorns. Texas won 47–43 after a dramatic comeback in the 4th quarter, scoring the winning touchdown with 38 seconds left. Earlier, Washington had carried a 36-20 lead into the 4th quarter.

2001 Holiday Bowl	Line	1	-	2	-	3	-	4	-	Final
#21 Washington	(57.5)	0	-	23	-	13	-	7	-	43
#9 Texas	(-13.0)	0	-	14	-	6	-	27	-	47

Scoring Summary
Washington – Anderson 43 yard field goal
Washington – Anderson 43 yard field goal
Washington – Johnson 38 yard interception return (Anderson kick)
Texas – Johnson 43 yard pass from Applewhite (Mangum kick)
Texas – Williams 25 yard pass from Applewhite (Mangum kick)
Washington – Collier 4 yard pass from Pickett (Anderson kick)
Washington – Anderson 40 yard field goal
Washington – Stevens 17 yard pass from Pickett (Anderson kick)
Texas - Mangum 26 yard field goal
Washington - Hurst 4 yard run (Pass failed)
Texas - Mangum 24 yard field goal
Texas - Trissel 2 yard pass from Applewhite (Pass failed)
Texas - Williams 1 yard run (Mangum kick)
Texas - Scaife 4 yard pass from Applewhite (Mangum kick)
Washington - Hurst 34 yard run (Anderson kick)
Texas - Williams 3 yard run (Mangum kick)

Culligan Holiday Bowl Game Summary - It took the Washington Huskies and Texas Longhorns a quarter to get warmed up, but once they did it was a classic, record-setting Holiday Bowl as No. 9 ranked Texas rallied from behind twice in the fourth quarter for a breath-taking 47-43 win. After a scoreless first quarter, the teams posted a record 37-point second quarter, with the Huskies taking a 23-14 lead over the turnover-plagued Longhorns. When Willie Hurst scored from 4 yards out with 3:51 left in the third quarter, Washington was well on its way to an upset win with a 36-17 lead. Behind senior Quarterback Major

Applewhite, the Longhorns launched a furious aerial assault and scored 23 points in a little over ten minutes to take a 40-36 lead with 6 minutes to play. Hurst capped a Washington drive with a 34-yard touchdown run to put the Huskies back on top, 43-40 with 1:49 to go. Then it was Applewhite's turn. He moved Texas down the field, primarily on 25 and 36 yard completions to B.J. Johnson. Ivan Williams scored on a 3-yard run with 38 seconds left to play to give the Longhorns a thrilling victory. The aerial circus shattered existing Holiday Bowl records for passing attempts by both teams (109) and completions (64).

2001 Motor City Bowl

The 2001 Motor City Bowl was played between Toledo Rockets of the MAC defeated the Cincinnati Bearcats of the Conference USA 23–16. It was played on December 29, 2001 at the Pontiac Silverdome in Pontiac, Michigan. The Bearcats were C-USA runners-up fresh off the wins from five of their last six games, which included Syracuse and #20 Southern Mississippi. Toledo was the Mid-American Conference Champ defeating Marshall University November 30, 2001 in the Glass Bowl 41-36. This game marked the first time the Bearcats and Rockets appeared in the Motor City Bowl.

2001 Motor City Bowl	Line	1	-	2	-	3	-	4	-	Final
Cincinnati	(59.0)	0	-	13	-	0	-	3	-	16
Toledo	(-4.0)	3	-	0	-	10	-	10	-	23

Scoring Summary
Toledo - France 28 yard Field goal
Cincinnati - Ruffin 29 yard Field goal
Cincinnati - Walker 28 yard pass from Guidugli (Ruffin kick)
Cincinnati - Ruffin 46 yard Field goal
Toledo - France 42 yard Field goal
Toledo - Bolden 28-yd run (France kick), 1:44
Toledo - France 30 yard Field goal
Cincinnati - Ruffin 25 yard Field goal
Toledo - Taylor 24 yard run (France kick)

Game Summary (University of Cincinnati) - Chester Taylor rushed for a bowl-record 190 yards, including a game-winning 24-yard touchdown with 3:23 left to lead Toledo to a 23-16 win over Cincinnati in the 2001 Motor Bowl. Cincinnati had a chance to tie the game in the closing moments but could not score following a first down at the 11 yard line. Tavares Bolden was 14-for-28 for 135 yards and ran for 99 yards, which helped the Rockets set a Motor City Bowl-record with 322 yards rushing. Toledo held Cincinnati to just 13 yards on the ground, also a record in the five-year history of the bowl. Taylor's 24-yard touchdown capped an 80-yard drive, which he sparked with three carries for 52 yards. The third-team all-America selection had a bowl-record 31 carries. After Todd France gave Toledo a 3-0 lead on a 28-yard field goal with 9:24 left in the first quarter, the Bearcats ran off 13 straight points to take a 13-3 halftime lead. Jonathan Ruffin sandwiched field goals from 29 and 46 yards, the latter coming as time expired in the first half, around a 28-yard Gino Guidugli touchdown pass to Tim Walker. Toledo pulled even after three quarters as France connected on a 42-yard field goal and Quarterback Tavares Bolden scored on a 28-yard run with 1:44 left in the third. Both teams put together long drives on the first two possessions of the fourth quarter but settled for field goals. The Rockets went 76 yards on 14 plays over five minutes but stalled at Cincinnati's 13. France's 30-yard field goal gave them a 16-13 lead with 9:42 left. The Bearcats then stalled at Toledo's 8 after driving 73 yards. Ruffin's 25-yard kick tied the game with 6:26 to go. The Rockets then drove 80 yards in seven plays with Taylor breaking loose up the middle for the winning score with 3:23 left. Gino Guidugli was 29-for-46 for 283 yards and a touchdown. Tye Keith caught a bowl-record nine passes for 63 yards.

2001 Insight Bowl

The 2001 Insight.com Bowl was the 13th edition of the Insight.com Bowl. It featured the Kansas State Wildcats, and the Syracuse Orangemen, and it was a rematch of the 1997 Fiesta Bowl, played in nearby Tempe.

2001 Insight Bowl	Line	1	-	2	-	3	-	4	-	Final
#18 Syracuse	(47.0)	7	-	12	-	0	-	7	-	26
Kansas State	(-5.5)	3	-	0	-	0	-	0	-	3

Scoring Summary
Syracuse - Mungro 65 yard run (Barber kick)
Kansas State - Rheem 29 yard Field goal
Syracuse - Mungro 1 yard run (kick failed)
Syracuse - Mungro 1 yard run (kick failed)
Syracuse - Morant 52 yard pass from Anderson (Barber kick)

Associated Press Insight Bowl Game Summary - Syracuse felt it was worthy of a New Year's Day bowl. Instead, the 18th-ranked Orangemen got a belated Christmas present in the desert. James Mungro rushed for 112 yards and three touchdowns as Syracuse took advantage of three first-half turnovers to rout Kansas State, 26-3, in the Insight.com Bowl at Bank One Ballpark. The Orangemen (10-3) reached 10 wins for the fifth time in school history and avenged a loss to Kansas State in the 1997 Fiesta Bowl. Mungro rumbled 65 yards for a touchdown midway through the first quarter, then added a pair of one-yard scoring runs in the second period. Syracuse's first three scoring drives took a combined 74 seconds. Mungro eclipsed the century mark for the seventh time this season and tied Jim Brown's school record for rushing touchdowns in a bowl game. Brown ran for three scores in the 1957 Cotton Bowl. The Orangemen, who registered just seven first downs, were not content to sit on the ball as R.J. Anderson tossed a 52-yard TD pass to Johnnie Morant with 3:22 left in the fourth quarter. Syracuse won 10 of its final 11 games following a 0-2 start. However, the one loss during that span was a 59-0 drubbing at top-ranked Miami on November 17, one of the reasons Syracuse was shut out of a New Year's Day bowl. Kansas State (6-6) was making its ninth straight bowl appearance but managed only Joe Rheem's 29-yard field goal with four minutes left in the opening period. Linebacker Clifton Smith led Syracuse's defensive effort with 12 tackles, including a sack. The Wildcats came into the game averaging 255 rushing yards per game but were held to 33 on 34 attempts. Ell Roberson completed just 2-of-15 passes for 70 yards for Kansas State before giving way to Marc Dunn, who was 12-of-25 for 151 yards. Following a punt, Syracuse needed just two plays to take a 7-0 lead on Mungro's 65-yard TD with 7:38 left in the first period. The game turned when Kansas State punter Mike Ronsick dropped a snap inside the Wildcats 5. Barry Baker recovered at the 4 and Mungro scored two plays later to give the Orangemen a 14-0 lead 3:21 into the second period. On Kansas State's next possession, cornerback Willie Ford intercepted Roberson at the Wildcats 43. Anderson hit Morant for a 41-yard reception, setting up Mungro's third TD just 48 seconds later. Kansas State outgained Syracuse, 254 yards to 222, but most of that came in the second half, when the Wildcats were forced to play catchup. After Mungro's first touchdown, the Wildcats made their only big play -- a 47-yard completion to Aaron Lockett to the Syracuse 36. Josh Scobey ripped off a 27-yard gain, giving Kansas State 1st-and-goal. But the Wildcats went backwards with two straight penalties and had to settle for a field goal. Kansas State had a chance to close within 19-6 at halftime, but Rheem missed a 41-yard field goal with 36 seconds left. The Wildcats also had a chance to get back in the game on its first possession of the second half, but Roberson fumbled on first down at the Syracuse 30. The teams combined for 20 punts, including 11 by Syracuse's Mike Shafer.

2001 Alamo Bowl
The 2001 Alamo Bowl featured the Iowa Hawkeyes, and the Texas Tech Red Raiders. It was a rematch of the 1996 Alamo Bowl.

2001 Alamo Bowl	Line	1	-	2	-	3	-	4	-	Final
Iowa	(61.0)	3	-	7	-	3	-	6	-	19
Texas Tech	(-1.0)	0	-	3	-	7	-	6	-	16

Scoring Summary
Iowa - Kaeding 36 yard Field goal
Iowa - Greving 1 yard run (Kaeding kick)
Texas Tech - Greathouse 50 yard Field goal
Texas Tech - Welker 20 yard pass from Kingsbury (Treece kick)
Iowa - Kaeding 31 yard Field goal
Iowa - Kaeding 46 yard Field goal
Texas Tech - Treece 23 yard Field goal
Texas Tech - Treece 37 yard Field goal
Iowa - Kaeding 47 yard Field goal

Associated Press Alamo Bowl Game Summary - Iowa spoiled Kliff Kingsbury's homecoming. Nate Kaeding kicked a 47-yard field goal -- his fourth of the game -- with 44 seconds left as the Hawkeyes earned their first bowl win in five years with a 19-16 victory over Texas Tech in the Alamo Bowl. Iowa overcame a pregame hamstring injury to leading rusher Ladell Betts to record its first bowl victory since beating Texas Tech, 27-0, in the 1996 Alamo Bowl. The Hawkeyes (7-5) also clinched their first winning season since 1997. Betts, who rushed for 1,056 yards in the regular season, tweaked his left hamstring during warmups and played in only two series. But Aaron Grevey picked up the slack, rushing for a career-high 115 yards on 25 carries. Betts carried only twice for four yards. He spent most of the first half riding a bike in an attempt to get loose but did not return to the game. A native of nearby New Braunfels, Texas, Kingsbury passed for a school-record 3,502 yards during the season and led the nation with 364 completions. He completed 29-of-49 passes for 309 yards Saturday but was intercepted twice, once late in the third quarter after engineering a tying drive on the opening possession of the second half. Kingsbury threw a pass right into the hands of 280-pound tackle Derrick Pickens, who returned it 11 yards to the Red Raiders' 11-yard line. The Texas Tech defense held, but Kaeding kicked a 31-yard field goal to give Iowa a 13-10 lead with 5:12 left in the period. The Hawkeyes forced a punt on Texas Tech's next possession and Kaeding booted a 46-yarder to make it 16-10 four seconds into the final quarter. Texas Tech's Robert Treece kicked a 23-yard field goal with 8:29 left, then converted a 37-yarder to tie it again with 2:05 to go. A scrambling Kingsbury nearly converted on 3rd-and-10, but he dove just short of the first-down marker at the 20 and Leach elected to kick the tying field goal. But Kyle McCann, who completed 19-of-26 passes for 161 yards, went to work for Iowa, hitting Kahlil Hill for 21 yards and scrambling for 16 more to the Texas Tech 26. After Jeremy Allen ran for two yards on first down, McCann was called for intentional grounding while trying to avoid a sack. The penalty pushed the Hawkeyes back to the 30, but following another incompletion, Kaeding's kick slid just inside the right upright. Kingsbury tried to get Texas Tech into field-goal range, hitting Charles Francis for 10 yards to give the Red Raiders a first down at their 49. Texas Tech's hopes ended when Bob Sanders intercepted Kingsbury's "Hail Mary" pass in the end zone on the final play of the game. The loss continued Texas Tech's postseason frustration as the Red Raiders (7-5) suffered their fourth straight bowl loss. Despite passing for more than 6,000 yards in his career, Kingsbury is 0-2 in bowl play. With 35,000 Texas Tech fans on hand, Saturday's contest felt like a home game for the Red Raiders. But Iowa kept Kingsbury off the field for most of the first quarter, opening the contest with a nearly 10-minute drive that Kaeding capped with a 36-yard field goal. Iowa took a 10-0 lead on Aaron Greving's two-yard run with 3:19 left in the second quarter and appeared in position to get more points before halftime. But Kaeding missed a 31-yard field goal with 33 seconds left. Texas Tech took advantage as Kingsbury found Nehemiah Glover over the middle for 35 yards. After an incompletion, punter Clinton Greathouse kicked a 50-yard field goal as time expired to make it 10-3 at halftime. With momentum on its side, Texas Tech looked like a different team on its initial possession of the second half. Using a no-huddle offense and spread formations, Kingsbury drove the Red Raiders 65 yards in less than 3 1/2 minutes and tied it with a 20-yard TD pass to Wes Welker.

2001 Liberty Bowl

The 2001 AXA Liberty Bowl was played between the Louisville Cardinals and the BYU Cougars on December 31, 2001, at Liberty Bowl Memorial Stadium in Memphis, Tennessee. Louisville won the game, 28–10.

2001 Liberty Bowl	Line	1	-	2	-	3	-	4	-	Final
#19 BYU	(67.5)	0	-	7	-	3	-	0	-	10
#23 Louisville	(-3.5)	7	-	7	-	7	-	7	-	28

Scoring Summary
Louisville – Miller 1 yard run (Smith kick)
BYU – Rykert 10 yard run (Payne kick)
Louisville – Mattingly 1 yard pass from Ragone (Smith kick)
BYU – Payne 29 yard field goal
Louisville – Branch 34 yard pass from Ragone (Smith kick)
Louisville – Ghent 27 yard pass from Ragone (Smith kick)

Deseret News Liberty Bowl Game Summary - BYU's 2001 football odyssey opened on a sweltering August afternoon in Provo with the Cougars scoring 10 touchdowns and 70 points against a Conference USA team, Tulane. It ended on a frigid afternoon Monday at the Liberty Bowl, where the once-mighty BYU offense could manage only one touchdown — by an offensive lineman — and a field goal against the C-USA Champions, Louisville. The weather conditions in those two games paralleled the stark contrast between the performances of the Y. offense in those contests: Scorching hot and ice cold. The No. 19 Cougars lost to the No. 23 Cardinals, 28-10, before an announced crowd of 58,968. It was another disappointing conclusion to a season for BYU. It marked its third consecutive bowl loss and its second consecutive defeat of the year, after posting 12 straight wins. Of course, the Cougars, boasting the nation's highest-scoring offense (46 points per game), were without their All-America running back, Luke Staley, and they looked almost powerless without him. BYU gained only 84 yards on the ground. The Cougars' top pass-catcher, Reno Mahe, played only one half after it became clear he could barely run on his ailing knee. He underwent surgery a couple of weeks ago. No, it wasn't a shootout, though the first play of the game indicated that it might be. Louisville's Zek Parker returned the opening kickoff 70 yards to set up the Cardinals' first touchdown. Confidence didn't come as easily to the Cougar offense. The only time BYU managed to cross the goal line was when Quarterback Brandon Doman rolled out right and threw a lateral to 6-foot-7, 301-pound offensive tackle Dustin Rykert, who rumbled into the end zone for a 10-yard touchdown. Sophomore Dewayne White, the Cardinals' star defensive end, wasn't surprised by the Cougars' trickery. With that TD,

BYU tied the score at 7-all midway through the second quarter. Later in the period, though, another trick play cost the Cougars. On fourth-and-five from its own 40-yard line, BYU tried one of its famous Ned Stearns-fake-punt-attempts. Stearns took the snap, took a couple of steps and was swarmed under for no gain. The opportunistic Cardinals then drove 40 yards and scored on a one-yard touchdown pass from Quarterback Dave Ragone to tight end Chip Mattingly with 14 seconds remaining in the first half to send them into the locker room with a 14-7 lead. The Cougars didn't seem to be too affected on their first possession of the third quarter — a 14-play, 57-yard drive that ate up seven minutes off the clock and resulted in a 29-yard field goal by Matt Payne. But Louisville answered by scoring the next time it had the ball on a 34-yard TD pass from Ragone to receiver Deion Branch. Doman struggled for much of the game and overthrew his receivers several times. The most crucial one came late in third quarter when he sailed a pass intended for Mike Rigell into the arms of Louisville safety Curry Burns. That play pretty much closed the door on the Cougars. It took the Cards just five plays to grab a 28-10 advantage on a 27-yard touchdown toss from Ragone to tight end Ronnie Ghent.

2001 Humanitarian Bowl

The 2001 edition of the Humanitarian Bowl was the fifth edition of the bowl game. It featured the Clemson Tigers versus the Louisiana Tech Bulldogs.

Background - This was the Bulldogs first bowl game since the 1990 tie in the Independence Bowl. They were looking to win a bowl game for the first time since 1977. They had won the Western Athletic Conference championship (in their first season there), which was their first conference championship since they won the Southland Conference in 1984. This was Clemson third consecutive bowl game and seventh in 10 seasons. They were looking to win a bowl game for the first time since the 1993 Peach Bowl. They had finished fourth in the Atlantic Coast Conference.

2001 Humanitarian Bowl	Line	1	-	2	-	3	-	4	-	Final
Clemson	(-6.5)	7	-	7	-	28	-	7	-	49
Louisiana Tech	(63.0)	3	-	7	-	0	-	14	-	24

Scoring Summary
Louisiana Tech - Scobee 29 yard Field goal
Clemson - Bailey 10 yard pass from Dantzler (Hunt kick)
Louisiana Tech - McCown 11 yard run (Scobee kick)
Clemson - Crosby 53 yard pass from Dantzler (Hunt kick)
Clemson - Hall 5 yard pass from Dantzler (Hunt kick)
Clemson - Rambert 62 yard pass from Dantzler (Hunt kick)
Clemson - Rambert 21 yard run (Hunt kick)
Clemson - Currie 19 yard run (Hunt kick)
Clemson - Hamilton 57 yard pass from Simmons (Hunt kick)
Louisiana Tech - Daigre 34 yard pass from McCown (Simon pass from McCown)
Louisiana Tech - Smith 2 yard run (Pass failed)

Associated Press Humanitarian Bowl Game Summary - After Clemson's up-and-down season, dazzling Woodrow Dantzler is happy with any bowl victory. Even in the snow. Even in Boise. Dantzler tied a school record with four touchdown passes and Clemson coach Tommy Bowden got his first postseason victory as the Tigers beat Louisiana Tech 49-24 in the Humanitarian Bowl on Monday. With snow falling from kickoff into the third quarter, Dantzler completed 15 of 23 passes for 218 yards. He ran 15 times for 57 yards before leaving with the Tigers ahead 42-10 after the third quarter. Both warm-weather teams struggled in the first half, but Clemson (7-5) took over in the third quarter, turning up the intensity on both sides of the ball to score 28 straight points on the Bulldogs (7-5). This fall, Dantzler became the first Division I-A player to pass for 2,000 yards and rush for 1,000 in the same season. He went out with a bang in his final performance, throwing two scoring passes in the first six minutes of the third quarter as the Tigers (7-5) extended a 14-10 halftime lead to 42-10. Dantzler found tight end Ben Hall for a 5-yard score. Later, he threw in the flat to Bernard Rambert, who was almost stopped short of a first down near midfield but broke away from a mass of tacklers and sprinted 62 yards for a TD. Rambert rushed for 101 yards and one TD and caught three passes for 77 yards. The Bulldogs, champions of the Western Athletic Conference in their first season in the league, tackled poorly in the cold weather and Quarterback Luke McCown's two third-quarter interceptions led to two Clemson TDs. Everything went right for the Tigers in the third. It was 42-10 after receiver Airese Currie hid a handoff from Dantzler, stood still while the play flowed deceptively to the right and then raced left for a 19-yard score. The 32-degree weather was better suited for the Winter Olympics than a college bowl game, with the blue turf at Boise State's Bronco Stadium looking more like a frozen hockey pond. It was the Clemson's first game in the snow since 1936. Louisiana Tech's last snow game was the 1968 Grantland Rice Bowl in Murfreesboro, Tenn., when Terry Bradshaw directed a victory over Akron. The Tigers made the best of it. Someone built a snow-statue replica of Howard's Rock, the good luck charm that Clemson players touch before each home game. They did it in Idaho, too, although the "rock" fell after too much contact. The Tigers also snapped a string of five straight bowl losses.

2001 Sun Bowl

The 2001 Wells Fargo Sun Bowl edition to the Sun Bowl featured the Washington State Cougars and the Purdue Boilermakers.

2001 Sun Bowl	Line	1	-	2	-	3	-	4	-	Final
Purdue	(50.0)	0	-	20	-	0	-	7	-	27
#13 Washington State	(-8.0)	14	-	3	-	13	-	3	-	33

Scoring Summary
Washington State - David 45 yard interception return (Dunning kick)
Washington State - Bush 46 yard pass from Gesser (Dunning kick)
Purdue - Lowe 1 yard run (Dorsch kick)
Purdue - Dorsch 28 yard Field goal
Washington State - Dunning 47 yard Field goal
Purdue - Stubblefield 3 yard pass from Orton (Dorsch kick)
Purdue - Dorsch 50 yard Field goal
Washington State - Dunning 34 yard Field goal
Washington State - Gesser 1 yard run (Dunning kick)
Washington State - Dunning 30 yard Field goal
Washington State - Dunning 37 yard Field goal
Purdue - Stubblefield 51 yard pass from Orton (Dorsch kick)

Associated Press Sun Bowl Game Summary - Washington State, the Pac-10 Conference's most surprising team in 2001, gave the league something to smile about -- but not without a few anxious moments in the final minutes. The 13th-ranked Cougars became the first Pac-10 team to win a bowl game this season, holding on for a 33-27 victory over Purdue in the Sun Bowl that gave them 10 wins for just the third time in school history. Washington State appeared in control, taking a 33-17 lead with 7:37 remaining on Drew Dunning's 37-yard field goal, his fourth of the game. But Kyle Orton, who attempted 74 passes, tossed a 50-yard touchdown to Taylor Stubblefield with 1:53 left and Purdue recovered the ensuing onside kick when the ball glanced off the helmet of Washington State safety Billy Newman into the hands of receiver John Standeford. Orton drove the Boilermakers to the Washington State 22 with completions of 21 and eight yards to Standeford. But he threw three straight incompletions, and the Cougars ran out the clock to seal the win. Orton completed 38 passes for a career-high 419 yards. Washington State (10-2), which trailed, 20-17, at halftime, also recorded 10 wins in 1929 and 1997, when Ryan Leaf led the Cougars to the Rose Bowl. This was their first bowl win since 1993. The Pac-10 had been 0-3 in the postseason, with Southern California, Stanford and Washington suffering bowl losses. The conference will get another chance for a win Tuesday, when Oregon -- hoping for a share of the national championship -- faces Colorado in the Fiesta Bowl. Washington State tied for second in the Pac-10 this year, losing to Stanford and Washington. The loss continued Purdue's late season slide as the Boilermakers (6-6) lost five of their last six games following a 5-1 start. Washington State's Jason Gesser completed only six of his first 27 passes but responded with several big completions in the second half. He finished 15-of-40 for 281 yards. Gesser's 50-yard pass to Jerome Riley set up his one-yard sneak that snapped a 20-20 tie with 3:04 left in the third quarter. Dunning converted three field goals in the second half. Leading 30-20, Washington State missed a chance to put away the contest when cornerback Antwaun Rogers intercepted Gesser in the end zone. Orton drove Purdue to the Cougars' 20, but the Boilermakers came up empty when Lamont Thompson picked off a pass in the end zone. Thompson, the Pac-10's all-time leader in interceptions, finished his career with 24, including two in this game. Dunning kicked a 37-yard field goal to extend Washington State's lead with 7:37 left. Purdue turned over the ball on downs when Orton's pass was incomplete on 4th-and-1 at the Washington State 25 with just over three minutes left. But the Boilermakers forced the Cougras to punt, and Orton went to work with his belated comeback attempt. Washington State jumped to a 14-0 lead just over eight minutes into the first quarter on cornerback Jason David's 45-yard interception return and Gesser's 46-yard TD strike to Mike Rush. But the Boilermakers erupted for 20 points in the second period. They tied it, 17-17, on Orton's three-yard toss to Taylor Stubblefield with 1:56 left in the quarter and took a 20-17 halftime lead on Travis Dorsch's 51-yard field goal with 37 seconds left. Purdue had two receivers top 100 yards. Standeford caught 12 passes for 103 yards and Stubblefield nine for 196 yards. Tim Stratton also had 12 receptions for 86 yards for the Boilermakers.

2001 Silicon Valley Football Classic
The 2001 Silicon Valley Football Classic was between the Michigan State Spartans and the Fresno State Bulldogs on December 31, 2001, at Spartan Stadium in San Jose, California. It was the second time the Silicon Valley Football Classic was played. Michigan State defeated Fresno State 44–35. Future NFL players David Carr, Jeff Smoker, Charles Rogers, TJ Duckett, and Bernard Berrian all played in this game.

2001 Silicon Valley Classic	Line	1	-	2	-	3	-	4	-	Final
Michigan State	(64.0)	17	-	20	-	0	-	7	-	44
Fresno State	(-5.0)	14	-	7	-	7	-	7	-	35

Scoring Summary
Fresno State – Spach 5 yard pass from Carr (Asparuhov kick)
Michigan State – Rogers 72 yard pass from Smoker (Rayner kick)
Fresno State – Wright 36 yard pass from Carr (Asparuhov kick)
Michigan State – Dave Rayner 41 yard Field goal
Michigan State – Duckett 5 yard run (Rayner kick)
Fresno State – Wright 79 yard pass from Carr (Asparuhov kick)
Michigan State – Duckett 39 yard run (Rayner kick)
Michigan State – Rogers 69 yard pass from Smoker (Kick failed)
Fresno State – Gaines 2 yard run (Asparuhov kick)
Fresno State – Gaines 15 yard pass from Carr (Asparuhov kick)
Michigan State – McCoy 5 yard pass from Smoker (Rayner kick)

Associated Press Silicon Valley Football Classic Bowl Game Summary - Charles Rogers set a Michigan State record with 270 yards receiving — and he wasn't even the most prolific pass-catcher on the field at the Silicon Valley Football Classic. It was that kind of a day in San Jose, as Rogers caught two of Jeff Smoker's three touchdown passes during the Spartans' phenomenal first half in a 44-35 victory over Fresno State on Monday. In a matchup of two potent offenses that combined for 1,146 total yards, Smoker and Rogers outdueled Fresno State's high-profile combo of David Carr and Rodney Wright, who finished with 13 catches for a school-record 299 yards and two TDs. After an inconsistent season in which they finished eighth in the Big Ten and barely qualified for a bowl, the Spartans (7-5) gained 405 yards and scored 37 points before halftime. Carr threw for 531 yards to Smoker's 376, but the Spartans' big early lead proved too large to overcome. After Fresno State (11-3) pulled within two points in the final minutes, the Spartans made one last scoring drive to clinch their second bowl victory under Coach Bobby Williams. T.J. Duckett rushed for 184 yards and two scores as Michigan State overwhelmed the Bulldogs, whose high-octane offense was expected to dominate the game. Instead, Fresno State ended its breakout season with its first loss in four games against teams from BCS conferences. Carr, who won the Johnny Unitas award as the nation's top senior Quarterback, ended his prolific career with another amazing game, but he couldn't play defense. Fresno State fell to 0-4 in bowl games during Pat Hill's otherwise successful tenure. After the teams exchanged handshakes, Michigan State defensive end Nick Myers, the game's defensive MVP, planted the school flag at midfield. Trailing 37-28 with 6:52 left, Fresno State's Bryce McGill blocked Craig Jarrett's punt and returned it to the Spartans 16. Two plays later, Paris Gaines caught a screen pass and ran through several blocks for a TD. But Michigan State came alive once again for a 77-yard drive. After a 43-yard reception by Rogers, Smoker hit Ivory McCoy for a 5-yard TD with 1:59 left. After just two seasons, this unassuming lower-tier bowl game is building a reputation for exciting, bizarre football. Last season, the Bulldogs overcame a 27-point deficit, but lost the inaugural game to Air Force when a superbly executed fake field goal failed in the closing seconds. Though Spartan Stadium was dominated by thousands of red-clad fans who made the two-hour drive from Fresno, Michigan State had a large rooting section of transplanted Michiganders and thousands of fans who made the trip for the bowl and the Michigan State basketball team's game against Stanford last Saturday. Fresno State opened the frenzied first half by driving 63 yards in four plays for the first TD just 59 seconds in. Less than eight minutes later, Michigan State replied with a 72-yard TD pass from Smoker to Rogers. In the first quarter alone, the Spartans had the longest rush in the school's bowl history, the second-longest pass in their bowl history, their longest field goal of the season and their first defensive touchdown of the year. With a 69-yard TD pass to Rogers 3:05 before halftime, Michigan State went ahead 37-21. The teams combined for 752 total yards in the first half.

2001 Chick-Fil-A Peach Bowl
The 2001 edition to the Peach Bowl featured the North Carolina Tar Heels and the Auburn Tigers. North Carolina scored on a 10-yard Willie Parker touchdown run, as UNC led 7-0 after 1 quarter of play. In the second quarter, Jeff Reed kicked a 22-yard field goal, extending North Carolina's lead to 10-0. In the third quarter, Quarterback Ronald Curry scored on a 62-yard touchdown run giving North Carolina a 16-0 lead.

In the fourth quarter, Damon Duval kicked a 34-yard field goal, and Daniel Cobb threw a 12-yard touchdown pass to Lorenzo Diamond, as North Carolina made the final score 16-10.

2001 Chick-Fil-A Peach Bowl	Line	1	-	2	-	3	-	4	-	Final
North Carolina	(-2.5)	7	-	3	-	6	-	0	-	16
Auburn	(45.0)	0	-	0	-	0	-	10	-	10

Scoring Summary
North Carolina - Parker 10 yard run (Reed kick)
North Carolina - Reed 22 yard Field goal
North Carolina - Curry 62 yard run (kick failed)
Auburn - Duval 34 yard Field goal
Auburn - Diamond 12 yard pass from Cobb (Duval kick)

Associated Press Chick-Fil-A Peach Bowl Game Summary - Ronald Curry put a spectacular end to his career and coach John Bunting's first season at North Carolina. Curry scrambled 62 yards for a touchdown in the third quarter and the Tar Heels used a smothering defensive effort to record a 16-10 victory over Auburn in the Peach Bowl. While never living up to his vast potential, Curry went out a winner as North Carolina (8-5) overcame a 0-3 start and extended its bowl winning streak to five games. The Tar Heels had not played a postseason game since the 1998 Las Vegas Bowl. The Tar Heels had a 10-0 lead when Curry turned a busted play into the clinching touchdown with the longest run of his career. Once a win away from playing in the Southeastern Conference championship game, Auburn (7-5) did not reach the end zone until late in the fourth quarter, when Daniel Cobb threw a 12-yard touchdown toss to Lorenzo Diamond. But fullback Richard Moore recovered the ensuing onsides kickoff and North Carolina ran out the clock. The Tar Heels limited Auburn to 176 total yards, including just 31 on the ground. Cornerback Michael Waddell forced Tim Carter to fumble early in the first quarter and defensive end Joey Evans returned it 18 yards to the Auburn 9. Two plays later, Willie Parker scored from the 10 to put the Tar Heels ahead for good, 7-0. North Carolina covered 84 yards essentially in two plays late in the second quarter. Parker broke off a 43-yard run, and freshman Darian Durant connected with Sam Aiken for a 41-yard pass, but the Tar Heels had to settle for Jeff Reed's 22-yard field goal and a 10-0 halftime lead. Curry's keeper extended it to a 16-point advantage, but Auburn finally got on the board on a 34-yard field goal by Damon Duval 1:44 into the fourth quarter. Parker rushed for 131 yards on 19 carries and Curry added 67 on 10 attempts. But he completed 5-of-6 passes for just 65 yards while Durant was 7-of-14 for 76 yards and an interception. Cobb split time with freshman Jason Campbell split and was 6-of-10 for 71 yards. Campbell completed 12-of-18 passes for 74 yards before bruising his rotator cuff.

2002 Outback Bowl

The 2002 edition to the Outback Bowl featured the South Carolina Gamecocks, and the Ohio State Buckeyes. South Carolina had blown out Ohio State in the previous year's game, 24-7.

2002 Outback Bowl	Line	1	-	2	-	3	-	4	-	Final
#23 Ohio State	(42.0)	0	-	0	-	7	-	21	-	28
#14 South Carolina	(-1.0)	0	-	14	-	14	-	3	-	31

Scoring Summary
South Carolina - Pinnock 1 yard run (Weaver kick)
South Carolina - Scott 7 yard pass from Petty (Weaver kick)
South Carolina - Gause 50 yard pass from Petty (kick failed)
South Carolina - Pinnock 10 yard pass (Watson pass from Petty)
Ohio State - Bellisari 2 yard run (Nugent kick)
Ohio State - Sanders 16 yard pass from Bellisari (Nugent kick)
Ohio State - Wells 1 yard run (Nugent kick)
Ohio State - Sanders 9 yard pass from Bellisari (Nugent kick)
South Carolina - Weaver 42 yard Field goal

Associated Press Outback Bowl Game Summary - Sheldon Brown and Daniel Weaver spoiled what could have been the greatest comeback in New Year's Day bowl history. Brown's 34-yard interception return set up Weaver's 42-yard field goal on the final play of the game as No. 14 South Carolina edged 23rd-ranked Ohio State, 31-28, in the Outback Bowl. South Carolina, which also beat the Buckeyes, 24-7, in last year's Outback Bowl, appeared to be cruising after opening a 28-0 lead late in the third quarter. But Steve Bellisari, seeing his first action since his arrest on a drunk driving charge in mid-November, rallied the Buckeyes for four touchdowns over the final 15 minutes. He completed 20-of-33 passes for 285 yards and two touchdowns. Bellisari was suspended from the team after getting arrested prior to Ohio State's game against Illinois on November 17 and did not play in the Buckeyes' last two regular season games. Bellisari entered Tuesday's game in the first half but was ineffective until scoring on the final play of the third quarter to get the Buckeyes on the board. He engineered three drives in the final period and pulled the Buckeyes even with a nine-yard TD pass to Darnell Sanders with 1:54 left. Ohio State got back the ball on Derek Ross' interception but were penalized for excessive celebration and started the drive at the 15. The Buckeyes appeared content to play for overtime but after one running play, Bellisari lofted an ill-advised pass into traffic that was returned by Brown to the Ohio State 29 with 23 seconds left. Following two incompletions, Phil Watson picked up five yards on third down. Ohio State called two timeouts to ice Weaver, whose kick barely cleared the crossbar. The biggest comeback in New Year's Bowl history occurred two years ago in the Outback Bowl, when Georgia rallied from a 25-point deficit to defeat Purdue, 28-25, in overtime. Marshall erased a 30-point halftime to defeat East Carolina, 64-61, in double overtime in this year's GMAC Bowl. Phil Petty tossed two touchdown passes and Andrew Pinnock scored twice for the Gamecocks (9-3), who reached nine wins for the first time since going 10-2 in 1994 under Joe Morrison. Petty, who injured his shoulder in the first half, completed 19-of-37 passes for 227 yards in his final game for South Carolina. Lou Holtz, who went 0-11 in his first season at South Carolina in 1999, became the first Gamecocks' coach to win consecutive bowl games. Prior to Holtz's arrival, South Carolina had won only one of its previous nine bowl appearances, a 24-21 victory over West Virginia in the 1995 Carquest Bowl. Ohio State (7-5), which parlayed a 26-20 victory over rival Michigan into a berth in this game, came out flat in its first bowl appearance under Tressel. For the Buckeyes, their performance in the first three quarters was all too familiar to last year's loss to the Gamecocks, when they seemed disinterested. Coach John Cooper lost for the eighth time in 11 bowl games and was fired the next day. After a scoreless first period, South Carolina took control in the second with a pair of scores. Pinnock only rushed for 48 yards on 12 carries but scored on a one-yard TD run 2:23 into the period before Petty and Brian Scott connected on a seven-yard TD pass that made it 14-0 with 7:54 left in the half. South Carolina scored on its first possession of the second half, taking a 20-0 lead on Petty's 50-yard TD pass to Andrea Gause just 2:04 into the third quarter. The Gamecocks extended their lead to 28-0 on Pinnock's 10-yard TD run and Petty's conversion pass to Watson with 5:38 left in the third quarter. After Ohio State closed to 28-14 on Bellisari's 16-yard TD pass to Sanders with 10:12 left in the contest, the Buckeyes' appeared to be dashed when Bellisari fumbled a snap at the South Carolina 23 with six minutes left. But Ohio State got back the ball one player later when Watson fumbled the handoff. Bellisari found Michael Jenkins for 22 yards before Jonathan Wells bowled in from the 1 two plays later to make it 28-21 with 5:02 left. South Carolina went three-and-out on its next possession and Bellisari again drove the Buckeyes down the field, completing all five passes for 63 yards during the tying drive.

2002 Florida Citrus Bowl

The 2002 Florida Citrus Bowl was held on January 1, 2002 at the Florida Citrus Bowl in Orlando, Florida. The Tennessee Volunteers, champions of the Southeastern Conference's Eastern Division, defeated the Michigan Wolverines, second-place finishers in the Big Ten Conference, 45-17. Tennessee Quarterback Casey Clausen was named the game's MVP. This was the last Citrus Bowl before the game was renamed the Capital One Bowl.

2002 Florida Citrus Bowl	Line	1	-	2	-	3	-	4	-	Final
#15 Michigan	(47.0)	0	-	10	-	0	-	7	-	17
#8 Tennessee	(-3.5)	10	-	14	-	7	-	14	-	45

Scoring Summary
Tennessee - Walls 32 yard Field goal
Tennessee - Washington 3 yard pass from Clausen (Walls kick)
Tennessee - Clausen 1 yard run (Walls kick)
Michigan - Askew 14 yard pass from Navarre (Epstein kick)
Tennessee - Clausen 1 yard run (Walls kick)
Michigan - Epstein 28 yard Field goal
Tennessee - Witten 64 yard pass from Clausen (Walls kick)
Tennessee - Washington 37 yard pass from Clausen (Walls kick)
Tennessee - Stephens 3 yard run (Walls kick)
Michigan - Bell 24 yard pass from Navarre (Epstein kick)

Bentley Historical Library 2002 Florida Citrus Bowl Game Summary - No. 8-ranked Tennessee won the first-ever meeting between the two schools and in the process ended Michigan's streak of four straight Jan. I bowl victories with a 45-17 win on New Year's Day. Tennessee scored the first 17 points of the game, then added another 21 unanswered points to start the second half. B.J. Askew was named the Michigan Offensive MVP and senior linebacker Larry Foote garnered the Defensive MVP by the media. Tennessee Quarterback Casey Clausen was named the game's Most Valuable Player. Askew gained 71 rushing yards on nine carries and added a 14-yard touchdown on a screen pass. Marquise Walker caught five passes for 100 yards and junior/sophomore quarter-back John Navarre completed 2 1-of- 39 passes for 240 yards and two TDs. Foote recorded a team-high nine tackles and two pass breakups with outside linebacker Victor Hobson adding eight stops. Tennessee jumped out to a 17-0 lead on a 32-yard field goal by Alex Walls, a three-yard slant to Kelley Washington and Clausen's one-yard scramble to begin the second quarter. Michigan trimmed the deficit to 17-7 as Navarre completed a 14-yard screen pass to Askew for a touchdown. The punt rush team set up U-M's best field position of the game by forcing a six-yard punt by the Volunteers. Tennessee answered on the ensuing possession as Clausen scored his second straight touchdown on a one-yard keeper. Utilizing their two-minute offense, the Wolverines moved inside the 10-yard line but settled for a 28-yard field goal by Hayden Epstein with 37 seconds left in the half. The Volunteers struck quickly in the third quarter as Clausen completed a 64-yard TD pass to Witten that gave UT a 31-10 lead. Tennessee scored a pair of touch-downs in the fourth quarter as Washington caught a 37-yard TD reception and Travis Stephens scored on a three-yard run. The Wolverines found the end zone with 9:32 remaining as Navarre completed a 24-yard TD pass to wide receiver Calvin Bell.

2002 Cotton Bowl Classic

The 2002 Cotton Bowl Classic matched the Arkansas Razorbacks and the Oklahoma Sooners.

Background - This was the Sooners first Cotton Bowl Classic appearance ever. The Sooners finished 2nd in the Big 12 South after two crucial losses to Nebraska and Oklahoma State This was the first appearance for the Razorbacks since 2000. Despite finishing 5th in the SEC West, they were invited to this game.

2002 Cotton Bowl Classic	Line	1	-	2	-	3	-	4	-	Final
#10 Oklahoma	(-13.0)	7	-	0	-	3	-	0	-	10
Arkansas	(46.0)	0	-	0	-	0	-	3	-	3

Scoring Summary
Oklahoma – Hybl 1 yard run (Duncan kick)
Oklahoma – Duncan 32 yard Field goal
Arkansas – O'Donohoe 32 yard Field goal

Cotton Bowl Classic Game Summary - The walk down the end zone tunnel was no different. The Sooner nation made the accustomed trek down Interstate-35. Even the title sponsor was unchanged. Another border war was to erupt, but this battle was of a different sort compared to the traditional SBC Red River Shootout. The opposing chant of "Hook'em Horns" gave way to "Woooo Pig Sooooooooie!" as 72,955 red–clad Oklahoma and Arkansas fans converged on Dallas for the 66th SBC Cotton Bowl Classic. The clash between the crimson of Oklahoma and the cardinal of Arkansas renewed a rivalry that dates as far back as 1899. The Razorbacks finished the regular season as one of the hottest teams in college football, having won six of their final seven games to finish 7-4 and 4-4 in the Southeastern Conference. Oklahoma, ranked 10th nationally, brought a defensive unit into the New Year's Day Classic that had sparked a successful run at a national title the year before and led the team to a 10-2 record and a 6-2 mark in the Big 12. The Sooners were accustomed to playing under pressure, and pressure is exactly what OU applied to Arkansas for the greater part of four quarters. With a defensive roster loaded with weapons, it was only fitting that Butkus Award winner Rocky Calmus would thwart Arkansas' comeback attempt by pouncing on a loose ball coughed up by Razorback Quarterback Matt Jones with 1:42 remaining. Despite Oklahoma's defensive effort that limited Arkansas to 50 yards on 55 plays of total offense, the Razorbacks went into their final drive with a chance to tie the game. A similarly impressive defensive effort by Arkansas held the Sooner offense in check and limited OU to 231 total yards. Arkansas opened the fourth quarter with a 12-play, 52-yard drive that culminated in a 32-yard field goal by Brennan O'Donohoe with 9:46 remaining. The Razorbacks best shot to tie the score came with less than three minutes to play. Arkansas drove to near midfield before linebacker Teddy Lehman sacked Jones and knocked the ball loose. Calmus recovered the fumble and ended any hope of a Hog comeback. The Sooners created numerous openings in the Arkansas offensive line and rang up nine Quarterback sacks, tying the SBC Cotton Bowl record set by Miami against Texas in 1991. The 50 yards of total offense by Arkansas was the third fewest in Classic history. The game's only touchdown came in the first quarter when Oklahoma put together a 13-play, 63-yard drive, including a fourth-and-one conversion at the Arkansas 16. Quarterback Nate Hybl scored on a sneak from the 1-yard line for the only points Oklahoma would need. Oklahoma added a field goal early in the second half when Tim Duncan connected on a 32-yard field goal with 8:45 remaining in the third quarter. Hybl eventually found a way to maneuver through the Arkansas defense to complete 24 passes, surpassing the previous SBC Cotton Bowl record of 21 held by Navy's Roger Staubach (1964) and BYU's Steve Sarkisian (1997). Hybl finished with 175 yards on 24-32 passing. The offensive MVP award went to OU running back Quentin Griffin. The junior rushed for 56 yards and caught nine passes for 32 yards, extending to 30 his school record for consecutive games with a reception. His nine catches, at the time, ranked second in Cotton Bowl history behind Arkansas' Bobby Crockett who had 10 against LSU in 1966. Oklahoma safety Roy Williams took the defensive MVP honor. The Bronko Nagurski and Jim Thorpe award winner was in on six tackles, including three tackles-for-loss for minus-17 yards. In the end, the Sooner defense with its star power outlasted the Razorbacks, 10-3, and left Arkansas seeing red.

2002 Gator Bowl
The 2002 Gator Bowl was between the Virginia Tech Hokies and the Florida State Seminoles at Alltel Stadium in Jacksonville, Florida on January 1, 2002.

2002 Gator Bowl	Line	1	-	2	-	3	-	4	-	Final
#24 Florida State	(52.0)	0	-	10	-	3	-	17	-	30
#15 Virginia Tech	(-2.0)	0	-	3	-	0	-	14	-	17

Scoring Summary
Virginia Tech - Warley 36 yard Field goal
Florida State - Rix 1 yard run (Beitia kick)
Florida State - Beitia 50 yard Field goal
Virginia Tech - Jones 5 yard run (Warley kick)
Florida State - Beitia 47 yard Field goal
Virginia Tech - Davis 55 yard pass from Noel (Warley kick)
Florida State - Walker 77 yard pass from Rix (Beitia kick)
Florida State - Beitia 35 yard Field goal
Florida State - Walker 23 yard pass from Rix (Beitia kick)

Gator Bowl Game Summary - The 2002 Gator Bowl kicked off on January 1, 2002 at Alltel Stadium in Jacksonville, Florida, exactly one year since the Hokies had last played in the game. The game's early going seemed promising for the defense-minded Hokies. In the first quarter, Tech held Florida State scoreless despite only managing a single field goal on offense. In the second quarter, however, Florida State began to find gaps in the Hokie defense and scored 10 points. At halftime, Florida State held a 10–3 lead. In the third quarter, Tech struck back. The Hokies scored 14 points in the quarter, while Florida State managed just a field goal. The Hokies' All-American tailback Lee Suggs had suffered a season-ending injury in the first game of the season, but freshman Kevin Jones had carried the offense for the season and continued to perform well in the post-season Gator Bowl game. With a 5-yard run from Jones and a 55-yard pass from Grant Noel to André Davis, Tech took a 17–13 lead going into the fourth quarter. But the lead quickly evaporated on a 77-yard catch and run from Chris Rix to Javon Walker.

2002 Fiesta Bowl
The 2002 Tostitos Fiesta Bowl, played on January 1, 2002, was the 31st edition of the Fiesta Bowl. The game was played at Sun Devil Stadium in Tempe, Arizona between the Colorado Buffaloes (ranked #3 in the BCS) and the Oregon Ducks (ranked #4 in the BCS). Oregon was ranked #2 in both the AP Poll and Coaches Poll, leading to some controversy that Oregon should have played for the 2002 BCS National Championship. In the game, Oregon Quarterback Joey Harrington threw for 350 yards and 4 touchdowns and led the Ducks to a 38–16 victory. Harrington was named offensive player of the game. Oregon cornerback Steve Smith had three interceptions, a Fiesta Bowl record, and was named defensive player of the game. This was the first edition of the Fiesta Bowl to match two schools from the Western United States. Previous editions had either only one representative from the West, or none.

2002 Fiesta Bowl	Line	1	-	2	-	3	-	4	-	Final
#2 Oregon	(60.0)	7	-	14	-	7	-	10	-	38
#4 Colorado	(-3.0)	7	-	0	-	0	-	9	-	16

Scoring Summary
Colorado – Drumm 1 yard run (Brougham Kick)
Oregon – Howry 28 yard pass from Harrington (Siegel kick)
Oregon – Parker 79 yard pass from Harrington (Siegel kick)
Oregon – Smith 6 yard pass from Harrington (Siegel kick)
Oregon – Morris 49 yard run (Siegel kick)
Oregon - Siegel 47 yard Field goal
Oregon – Peelle 4 yard pass from Harrington (Siegel kick)
Colorado – Flores 39 yard Field goal
Colorado – Graham 4 yard pass from Ochs (kick failed)

Oregon Media Guide Fiesta Bowl Game Summary - Joey Harrington threw for four touchdowns and Steve Smith intercepted a bowl-record three passes as No. 2 Oregon pounded No. 3 Colorado in the 31st Fiesta Bowl. Heisman Trophy finalist Harrington became the first Pac-10 Quarterback to lead his team to three bowl wins and ended his career third at Oregon in passing yards (6,911) and touchdowns (59). After a first-quarter Buffalo touchdown, the Ducks scored 38 consecutive points. The game's offensive MVP led the charge with a 28-yard scoring strike to Keenan Howry and a season-long 79-yard TD pass to Samie Parker on subsequent drives. The latter marked Oregon's longest scoring play in bowl history and tied for the longest pass in Fiesta Bowl history. On the ground, Maurice Morris brought the crowd to its feet in the second half with a dazzling 49-yard touchdown scamper though a half-dozen would-be tacklers, as he rolled off the back of another. His 89 rushing yards at game's end also made him the first back in Oregon history to run for 1,000 yards in consecutive seasons (1,049). Freshman kicker Jared Siegel also booted a career-long 47-yard field goal early in the fourth quarter. Colorado tried its luck in the air in the second half and salvaged a couple of late scores to avoid the biggest defeat in Fiesta Bowl history. The Duck defense held the Buffalo rushers to a combined 49 yards — far below their previous 228.5 avg. that ranked eighth nationally. Wesly Mallard and Dave Moretti led the Duck defenders with 13 and 11 tackles, respectively, while Smith earned the game's top defensive award.

2002 Sugar Bowl

The 2002 Sugar Bowl was played on January 1, 2002. This 68th edition to the Sugar Bowl featured the Illinois Fighting Illini, and the LSU Tigers. Illinois came into the game 10–1, and ranked 8th in the BCS, whereas LSU came into the game 9–3, and ranked 13th in the BCS. Domanick Davis started the scoring with a 4-yard touchdown run to open a 7–0 LSU lead. In the second quarter, he posted touchdown runs of 25 and 16 yards, as LSU opened a 21–0 lead. Quarterback Rohan Davey found wide receiver Josh Reed in the end zone for a 28–0 lead. Quarterback Kittner threw a touchdown pass to Hodges to close the deficit to 28–7. Rohan Davey added another touchdown pass before the half to open a 34–7 half-time lead. Illinois tried to rally but were too far behind, and LSU ended up winning 47–34.

2002 Sugar Bowl	Line	1	-	2	-	3	-	4	-	Final
#7 Illinois	(56.0)	0	-	7	-	14	-	13	-	34
#12 LSU	(-2.0)	7	-	27	-	7	-	6	-	47

Scoring Summary
LSU - Davis 4 yard run (Corbello kick)
LSU - Davis 24 yard run (Kick blocked)
LSU - Davis 16 yard run (Corbello kick)
LSU - Reed 5 yard pass from Davey (Corbello kick)
Illinois - Hodges 2 yard pass from Kittner (Christofilakos kick)
LSU - Royal 7 yard pass from Davey (Corbello kick)
Illinois - Lloyd 17 yard pass from Kittner (Christofilakos kick)
LSU - Reed 32 yard pass from Davey (Corbello kick)
Illinois - Lloyd 10 yard pass from Kittner (Christofilakos kick)
Illinois - Young 17 yard pass from Kittner (Christofilakos kick)
LSU - Davis 4 yard run (Pass failed)
Illinois - Young 40 yard pass from Lloyd (Pass failed)

Sugar Bowl Recap excerpted from the book "Sugar Bowl Classic: A History" by Marty Mulé
This Sugar Bowl was one for the books - the record books. In a game being played more for poll position and the old-time bowl goal of pure fun than anything else, LSU was rollicking in the first 30 minutes, by halftime sending press box statisticians flipping furiously through the records. By then the one faint doubt of the outcome was whether Kurt Kittner would once again manage to bring his team a come-from-behind victory, which he had done five times during the regular-season. In that opening half the Illini simply could not slow down the Tigers. After a couple of self-inflicted miscues (both by tight ends - a flag on Robert Royal that killed one drive and a drop by Joe Domingeaux that could have gone the distance), LSU scored touchdowns on five of its next six possessions. That span included the biggest scoring spurt in Sugar Bowl history, with 27 Tiger points in the second quarter. It came down to this: Tiger receivers were running helter-skelter across the Superdome rug almost unimpeded, through an Illini secondary that featured three All-Big Ten athletes. After Domanick Davis, on his way to an unprecedented four Sugar Bowl touchdowns, scrambled in from the 2 in the opening period; he added two more in the second quarter - reaching the end zone on a quick-hitter from 25 yards out and then scoring from the 16. Both times Illinois was trying to shoot the gaps with its cornerbacks and both times Davis ran into the vacant spaces untouched. In the air, even when Davey was missing his mark, Illinois was unable to cover the Tiger wideouts, which showed in the first-half stat sheets: 33 Davey passes and 19 completions, covering 246 yards. As it turned out, Davey's two touchdowns came when LSU was at point-blank range, and both came on third down with Illinois playing zone defense. First, from the 5-yard line after Josh Reed found his way to the back of the end zone where Davey speared him. Then, from the 7, Royal did the same thing for the final points of the half. The LSU defense was no less spectacular. Illinois simply couldn't hold out the Tiger rush, coming at Kittner with hands high to disrupt his low passing trajectory. It was a successful strategy, making a basket case of Kittner, who was trying to throw over a picket fence of outstretched limbs and digits. He had more first-half

passes batted down at the line of scrimmage than completed ones. At one point he was 1-for-13 for a grand total of one yard. One play told the story of Illinois' frustration: Illini go-to receiver Brandon Lloyd's only catch of the first half resulted in an LSU touchdown, when corner Randall Gay stripped him after a four-yard gain, picked up the fumble and returned it 19 yards to the Illini 5. Moments later the score was jacked to 27-0 when Davey hit the embarrassingly open Reed. Kittner finished the first half 5-of-17 passing for 80 yards and a touchdown. But 75 of those yards came on a three-play scoring drive, leaving Illinois' best quarterback in history 2-for-14 for five yards the rest of the half. At intermission the Tigers had a commanding edge in total offense, 344-134, and led 34-7. The Sugar Bowl was over, but Illinois showed its mettle by making it respectable in the second half. Kittner completed 7-of-10 passes for 142 yards and three touchdowns in the third quarter, and he ended the night 14-of-35 for 262 yards for four touchdowns and one interception. When the smoke cleared, no fewer than a dozen records were set in the highest-scoring Sugar Bowl in history, including 595 yards of total offense, 444 passing yards by Davey, and 239 receiving yards by Reed on yet another record 14 receptions.

2002 Orange Bowl

The 2002 FedEx Orange Bowl game was between the Florida Gators and the ACC champion Maryland Terrapins on January 2, 2002. Florida defeated Maryland 56–23. The Orange Bowl was first played in 1935, and the 2002 game was the 68th edition of the Orange Bowl. The contest was televised on ABC. This was Steve Spurrier's last game as coach of the Florida Gators as he resigned two days after the game.

2002 Orange Bowl	Line	1	-	2	-	3	-	4	-	Final
#5 Florida	(-15.0)	14	-	14	-	21	-	7	-	56
#6 Maryland	(58.0)	7	-	3	-	0	-	13	-	23

Scoring Summary
Florida - Graham 1 yard run (Chandler kick)
Florida - Jacobs 46 yard pass from Berlin (Chandler kick)
Maryland - Williams 64 yard pass from S Hill (Novak kick)
Maryland - Novak 20 yard Field goal
Florida - Jacobs 15 yard pass from Grossman (Chandler kick)
Florida - Gaffney 4 yard pass from Grossman (Chandler kick)
Florida - Graham 6 yard run (Chandler kick)
Florida - Gillespie 11 yard run (Chandler kick)
Florida - Gaffney 33 yard pass from Grossman (Chandler kick)
Maryland - Riley 1 yard run (Novak kick)
Florida - Perez 10 yard pass from Grossman (Chandler kick)
Maryland - Riley 10 yard run (two-point conversion failed)

Associated Press Orange Bowl Game Summary - Florida coach Steve Spurrier followed through on his promise to bench Rex Grossman for a curfew violation. He kept the Heisman Trophy runner-up on the bench for the first six series. It hardly mattered. Grossman and fifth-ranked Florida barely missed a beat, rolling to a 56-23 victory over No. 6 Maryland in the Orange Bowl. The sophomore shook off the benching to throw touchdown passes on his first two series as the Gators (10-2) broke open a close game in the final three minutes of the first half. Maryland was defenseless against Grossman, who led Florida to touchdowns on six straight possessions before the Gators finally punted for the first time in the second half with just over four minutes left. Overall, Grossman completed 20-of-28 passes for 248 yards and an Orange Bowl record-tying four touchdowns in just under 2 ½ quarters. The 79 combined points set an Orange Bowl mark. Florida amassed 659 total yards and 456 yards through the air, also Orange Bowl records. Ranked first in the preseason, Florida will finish in the top five for the first time since 1998. However, losses to Auburn and Tennessee kept the Gators out of the Southeastern Conference championship game -- and a chance at the national title. Berlin directed two scoring drives in his first start of the season. But he threw two interceptions and Florida only led, 14-10, when Grossman replaced him with six minutes remaining in the first half. Grossman tossed a 15-yard TD pass to Taylor Jacobs with 2:18 left. Florida forced a punt, and Grossman struck again, finding Jabar Gaffney in the back of the end zone for a four-yard TD with three seconds remaining that gave the Gators a 28-10 lead. With Maryland keying on receivers Reche Caldwell and Gaffney, the contest turned into a coming-out party for Jacobs, who caught 10 passes for 170 yards and was named the game's Most Valuable Player. Maryland was one of the best stories in college football this season, winning the Atlantic Coast Conference title in its first season under alumnus Ralph Friedgen. The Terrapins reached 10 wins for the first time since 1976 but faced no team as explosive as the Gators and received a dose of reality. Berlin and Grossman combined for more than 300 yards passing in the first half alone. Friedgen, whose team led the ACC in defense, believed the game turned when Grossman entered. Although thrilled to be playing in a major bowl, Maryland found little joy in the "Sunshine State" this season as the Terrapins suffered their only two losses in Florida by a combined 108-54. They suffered a 52-

31 loss at Florida State on October 27. Florida even got production out of its running game as Earnest Graham ran for 152 yards and two touchdowns on 16 carries. After Berlin's 46-yard TD pass to Jacobs gave Florida a 14-0 lead with 12 seconds left in the first quarter, Maryland quickly answered as Shaun Hill tossed a 64-yard TD pass to Jafar Williams on the final play of the period. The Terrapins forced three turnovers in the first half but only turned them into three points. After Williams' TD, Maryland cornerback Dennard Wilson returned an interception 37 yards to the Florida 3, but the Terrapins had to settle for Nick Novak's 20-yard field goal with 12:02 left in the first period. Florida's Earnest Graham fumbled at the Maryland 24 on the next drive. The Terrapins drove to Florida's 28, but Novak missed a 46-yard field goal with 6:03 left. Spurrier decided he had seen enough of Berlin and went to Grossman, who picked apart the Maryland secondary. Florida tacked on three scores in the third quarter. After Graham and Robert Gillespie scored on TD runs of six and 11 yards, respectively, the Gators showed no mercy. Grossman and Gaffney combined for a 33-yard TD pass that made it 49-10 with 2:52 left. Grossman also tossed a 10-yard TD strike to Carlos Perez early in the fourth quarter. Maryland was making its first bowl appearance since tying Louisiana Tech, 34-34, in the 1990 Independence Bowl.

2002 Rose Bowl (BCS Championship Game)

The 2002 Rose Bowl, played on January 3, 2002. It was the 88th Rose Bowl game and was the BCS National Championship Game of the 2001 college football season. The game featured the Miami Hurricanes and the Nebraska Cornhuskers, marking the first time since the 1919 Rose Bowl, and only the third time in the game's history, that neither the Big Ten nor the Pac-10 Conferences had a representative in this game. The Hurricanes won the game, 37–14, for their fifth national title. Miami Quarterback Ken Dorsey and wide receiver Andre Johnson were named the Rose Bowl Players of the Game.

Teams - Because the Rose Bowl was hosting the BCS Championship game, as part of the agreement begun in the 1998 season, the Tournament of Roses committee would get the number one and number two ranked teams in the Bowl Championship Series system. However, this was the third Rose Bowl number one versus two pairing, with the first two in the 1963 and 1969 games. Nebraska became the first team from outside the Southern United States to play in a BCS title game, as the previous three title games were all-Southern affairs.

2002 Rose Bowl	Line	1	-	2	-	3	-	4	-	Final
#4 Nebraska	(55.0)	0	-	0	-	7	-	7	-	14
#1 Miami	(-8.5)	7	-	27	-	0	-	3	-	37

Scoring Summary
Miami – Johnson 50 yard pass from Dorsey (Sievers kick)
Miami– Portis 39 yard run (Sievers kick)
Miami – Lewis 47 yard interception return (Sievers kick)
Miami – Shockey 21 yard pass from Dorsey (Kick failed)
Miami – Johnson 8 yard pass from Dorsey (Sievers kick)
Nebraska – Davies 16 yard run. (Brown kick)
Nebraska – Groce 71 yard punt return (Brown kick)
Miami – Sievers 37 yard field goal.

Associated Press Rose Bowl Game Summary - Forget that the BCS was a mess. Miami made it a moot point. The top-ranked Hurricanes completed their return to the top of the college football world, using three touchdown passes by Ken Dorsey to build a big early lead and defeat No. 4 Nebraska, 37-14, in the 88th Rose Bowl. Andre Johnson caught seven passes for 199 yards and two scores for the Hurricanes (12-0), who laid claim to their fifth national title and first since 1991. The victory continued the magical ride of Larry Coker, a 53-year-old career assistant who was promoted to coach last January after the sudden departure of Butch Davis to the NFL's Cleveland Browns. Miami players lobbied hard for Coker to get the job and he proved worthy of the support, taking a program that was placed on NCAA probation five years ago and becoming the first rookie coach to win a national title since Michigan's Bennie Oosterbaan in 1948. Dorsey and Johnson shared Most Valuable Player honors and were helped by Clinton Portis, who carried 20 times for 104 yards and a score. Miami forced an NCAA-high 45 turnovers this season and three in the first half alone Thursday night, including a pivotal interception by James Lewis, to roar to a 34-0 halftime lead and hand Nebraska a second straight humbling defeat. Only a series of upsets allowed the Cornhuskers to gain a controversial invitation to the Bowl Championship Series title game, and Nebraska did little early in the game to prove it deserved to be here. Routed by Colorado, 62-36, in its regular-season finale, Nebraska (11-2) has dropped consecutive games for the first time since 1990, when it lost its season finale to Oklahoma and the Citrus Bowl to Georgia Tech. Oregon will complain that it could have given Miami a better game, particularly after it dominated Colorado in Tuesday's Fiesta Bowl. That might be the case, but if the Ducks were anywhere near as good as Miami, they would not have lost a regular-season game. Miami was the only major college football team to finish without a blemish. In fact, the Hurricanes have won 22 straight games since losing to Washington in September 2000. Dorsey, a native of Orinda, California, completed 22-of-35 passes for 362 yards, including 258 in the first half. He improved to 26-1 as a starter and joined Bernie Kosar, Steve Walsh, Craig Erickson and Gino Torretta in the fraternity of Quarterbacks who have won national titles with the Hurricanes. Dorsey finished third in the Heisman Trophy voting and enjoyed a far more enjoyable evening than Nebraska counterpart Eric Crouch, who won the sport's highest individual honor but concluded his college career with two straight losses. Crouch committed a pair of costly turnovers in the first half but managed to rush for 114 yards on 22 carries. His best run was a 36-yarder in the fourth quarter, and he completed 5-of-15 passes for 62 yards. Substantially more than half the crowd of 93,781 was dressed in Cornhusker red. Yet Husker nation was quieted in a hurry as the quick-strike Hurricanes jumped to the big halftime lead. Miami outscored opponents, 273-33, in the first half this season. The last thing Nebraska could afford was turnovers, but Crouch was stripped of the ball by linebacker D.J. Williams midway through the opening quarter and tackle William Joseph recovered near midfield. Dorsey went right to work, tossing a 49-yard touchdown pass to a wide-open Johnson with 6:51 left in the period. Johnson danced past cornerback Keyou Craver, who fell near the line of scrimmage and tried vainly to grab at Johnson. Josh Davis fumbled the ensuing kickoff, but an unsportsmanlike conduct penalty pushed the Hurricanes back and they were forced to punt. The respite proved temporary as Dorsey quickly moved Miami downfield. Johnson again beat Craver, this time for a 34-yard gain along the sideline, before Portis bounced off several tackles and raced outside for a 39-yard touchdown 27 seconds into the second quarter. The troubles continued for Crouch minutes later when a short pass to Tracey Wistrom sailed high and off the fingers of the tight end and into the chest of safety James Lewis, who raced 47 yards for a 21-0 lead with 12:52 left in the second quarter. Dorsey needed just two plays on Miami's next possession, connecting with Johnson on a 45-yard pass before finding tight end Jeremy Shockey for a 27-0 bulge with 10:40 to go before halftime. Shockey caught five passes for 88 yards. The dissection of Nebraska's once-vaunted defense continued with Dorsey completing passes of 24 yards to Johnson and 17 to Shockey before Johnson caught an eight-yard TD toss for a 34-0 lead. Miami finished with 472 total yards. Nebraska showed life in the second half, beginning with a 16-yard touchdown run by fullback Judd Davies late in the third quarter. DeJuan Groce cut the deficit to 20 points by scoring on a 71-yard punt return 36 seconds into the final period. Miami blunted some of the Cornhuskers' momentum with an 11-play drive that took 4:24 off the clock and ended with a 37-yard field goal by Todd Sievers. Any chance of a miracle comeback by Nebraska ended when running back Thunder Collins was stopped on 4th-and-6 from the Miami 16 with 4 1/2 minutes left. Dahrran Diedrick, the leading rusher in the Big 12 Conference, was held to 47 yards on 15 carries. Miami has won five straight bowl games since a 24-17 loss to Nebraska in the Orange Bowl following the 1994 season, a victory that gave Tom Osborne his first national title.

2002 New Orleans Bowl

The 2002 Wyndham New Orleans Bowl featured the North Texas Mean Green and the Cincinnati Bearcats. It was North Texas' second consecutive New Orleans Bowl appearance.

2002 New Orleans Bowl	Line	1	-	2	-	3	-	4	-	Final
Cincinnati	(-8.0)	7	-	0	-	6	-	6	-	19
North Texas	(44.5)	3	-	14	-	7	-	0	-	24

Scoring Summary
Cincinnati - Keith 6 yard Pass from Guidugli (Ruffin kick)
North Texas – Bazaldua 30 yard Field goal
North Texas – Cobbs 27 yard Run (Bazaldua kick)
North Texas – Pearl 20 yard interception return (Bazaldua kick)
North Texas – Galbreath 35 yard Run (Bazaldua kick)
Cincinnati – Ruffin 29 yard Field goal
Cincinnati – Ruffin 33 yard Field goal
Cincinnati - Callicott 43 yard Fumble return (Pass failed)

Associated Press New Orleans Bowl Game Summary - Kevin Galbreath made sure North Texas would not waste a career-high five interceptions by Gino Guidugli. Galbreath rushed for 130 yards and a touchdown and helped the Mean Green hold off mistake-prone Cincinnati in the New Orleans Bowl, 24-19. North Texas (8-5), which closed a season with seven straight victories for the first time since 1941, converted four first-half interceptions by Guidugli into 17 points to take a 10-point advantage into the break. But after Galbreath scored on a 35-yard run 2:02 into the second half to give the Mean Green a 24-7 advantage, the Bearcats (7-7) chipped away. Cincinnati climbed within 24-19 on two third-quarter field goals by Jonathan Ruffin and a 43-yard fumble return by Franklin Callicott with 5:15 to play. LaDaris Vann dropped Guidugli's ensuing two-point conversion pass, however, and Galbreath picked up two key first downs down the stretch to help the Mean Green run out the clock. It was the first bowl victory by North Texas since the defunct Optimist Bowl in 1946. The Mean Green improved to 2-3 all-time in bowl contests, while Cincinnati fell to 3-4. Guidugli completed 19-of-34 passes for 224 yards and one touchdown, a six-yard pass to Tye Keith that opened the scoring with 8:36 left in the first quarter. North Texas took the lead for good, 10-7, on a 27-yard run by Patrick Cobbs 4:07 into the second quarter after Guidugli threw his third interception, this time to Chris Hunt. Jeremy Pearl capped the first-half scoring with a 20-yard interception return for a touchdown with 2:46 left in the quarter. Andrew Smith connected on just 9-of-22 passes for 126 yards and one interception for the Mean Green, who improved to 9-7-1 all-time against their former Missouri Valley Conference rival. North Texas outgained Cincinnati on the ground, 192-85.

2002 GMAC Bowl

The 2002 GMAC Bowl was the 5th edition of the GMAC Bowl. It was played in December 2002, and featured the Louisville Cardinals, and the Marshall Thundering Herd. Marshall started the scoring with a 9-yard touchdown pass from Byron Leftwich to wide receiver Denero Marriott for a 7-0 lead. In the second quarter, Marshall's Curtis Head kicked a 23-yard field goal to give Marshall a 10-0 lead. Byron Leftwich later tossed an 8-yard touchdown pass to wide receiver Demetrius Doss for a 17-0 lead. Louisville got on the board with a 2-yard TJ Patterson touchdown run, making the score 17-7. In the third quarter, Byron Leftwich again connected with Demetrius Doss for a 12-yard touchdown pass and a 24-7 lead. He later found Denero Marriott for a 26-yard touchdown pass in the fourth quarter. Franklin Wallace added a 15-yard touchdown run to give Marshall a 38-7 lead. With 13 seconds left in the game, Quarterback Dave Ragone found Tiger Jones in the end zone for a Louisville touchdown. The two-point conversion to Jones made the final score 38-15.

2002 GMAC Bowl	Line	1	-	2	-	3	-	4	-	Final
Marshall	(-2.5)	7	-	10	-	7	-	14	-	38
Louisville	(62.0)	0	-	7	-	0	-	8	-	15

Scoring Summary
Marshall – Marriott 9 yard pass from Leftwich (Head kick)
Marshall – Head 23 yard Field goal
Marshall – Doss 8 yard pass from Leftwich (Head kick)
Louisville – Patterson 2 yard sun (Smith kick)
Marshall – Doss 12 yard pass from Leftwich (Head kick)
Marshall – Marriott 26 yard pass from Leftwich (Head kick)
Marshall – Wallace 15 yard run (Head kick)
Louisville – Jones 11 yard pass from Ragone (Jones pass from Ragone)

Associated Press GMAC Bowl Game Summary - Byron Leftwich and Marshall didn't need a miracle comeback this time in the GMAC Bowl. Leftwich became the first player in Division I-A history to throw four touchdown passes in two bowl games, leading Marshall to a 38-15 victory over Louisville on Wednesday night. Marshall (11-2) won a bowl for the fifth consecutive year, the longest such streak in the nation. Top-ranked Miami has won four straight. Leftwich led Marshall to three of the bowl wins. This year's was special because it came in his last game -- and practically on one leg. Already slowed by a sore shin injured in early November, he took several hits in the first quarter and hobbled back to the huddle. In last year's GMAC Bowl, the Thundering Herd came from 30 points down to beat East Carolina 64-61 in double-overtime behind Leftwich's 576 yards passing in the highest-scoring bowl game ever. No such comebacks were needed this time for the Mid-American Conference champions as they took a 17-0 lead early in the second quarter. By then, word had filtered down to the Louisville players that coach John L. Smith was a candidate for the vacant coaching job at Michigan State. Smith said he'll meet with Michigan State on Thursday but declined further comment. ESPN has learned that Smith will accept the Spartans job, possibly by the end of the week. Louisville (7-6) finished with its worst record in Smith's five years. The Cardinals were 11-2 last year. Louisville got inside the Marshall 30 just twice and went 0-for-13 on third downs. The Cardinals gained just 88 yards in the first half. The game was billed as a matchup of two of the nation's top Quarterbacks. Leftwich, picked as the game's Most Valuable Player, did his part, going 22-of-44 for 249 yards. He threw TD passes of 8 and 13 yards to backup receiver Demetrius Doss -- who had one scoring catch all season -- and 9 and 26 yards to Denero Marriott. Marriott had 10 catches for 137 yards. Ragone went 20-of-45 for 193 yards. He'll get another chance when he returns to Mobile on Jan. 18 for the Senior Bowl. Midway through the fourth quarter, Jamus Martin stripped Ragone and Jonathan Goddard recovered the fumble. A personal foul penalty gave Marshall the ball at the Louisville 16, and Butchie Wallace scored on first down for a 38-7 lead. It was a disappointing finish to an up-and-down season for Louisville. The Cardinals started ranked 17th but lost the opener at home to Kentucky. There also was a win over then-No. 4 Florida State and a loss at 4-7 Houston to finish the regular season.

2002 Tangerine Bowl

The 2002 Tangerine Bowl was the 13th edition of the Tangerine bowl game. It was played on December 23, 2002, and featured the Clemson Tigers and the Texas Tech Red Raiders.

2002 Tangerine Bowl	Line	1	-	2	-	3	-	4	-	Final
Texas Tech	(-5.0)	17	-	17	-	7	-	14	-	55
Clemson	(66.0)	0	-	2	-	7	-	6	-	15

Scoring Summary
Texas Tech – Treece 29 yard Field goal
Texas Tech – Glover 46 yard pass from Kingsbury (Treece kick)
Texas Tech – Peters 19 yard pass from Kingsbury (Treece kick)
Texas Tech – Henderson 10 yard run (Treece kick)
Clemson – Team Safety
Texas Tech – Welker 59 yard punt return (Treece kick)
Texas Tech – Treece 40 yard Field goal
Clemson – Hall 10 yard pass from Whitehurst (Hunt kick)
Texas Tech – Francis 2 yard pass from Symons (Bishop kick)
Clemson – Jasmin 2 yard run (pass failed)
Texas Tech – Welker 9 yard pass from Kingsbury (Bishop kick)
Texas Tech – Henderson 26 yard pass from Symons (Bishop kick)

Associated Press Tangerine Bowl Game Summary - Kliff Kingsbury went out in style. The senior Quarterback passed for 375 yards and three touchdowns in his final appearance for Texas Tech as the Red Raiders routed Clemson, 55-15, in the Tangerine Bowl. Kingsbury suffered a sprained right ankle early in the third quarter when defensive end Dekhaleed Vaughn rolled on his leg. The Quarterback limped noticeably and had to be helped off the field but got his ankle taped and returned after missing just one series. Kingsbury ended his career ranked fourth on the NCAA's all-time passing list with 12,429 yards, trailing only Ty Detmer, Tim Rattay and Chris Redman. Kingsbury's Texas Tech career officially ended when he tossed a 19-yard pass to Carlos Francis with 6:13 remaining. The completion enabled him to join Detmer and David Klingler as the only Quarterbacks in NCAA history to pass for than 5,000 yards in a season. The native of New Braunfels, Texas completed 32-of-43 passes to end the year 479-of-712 for 5,017 yards and 45 touchdowns. His final TD pass, the 95th of his career, was a nine-yard strike to Wes Walker with 9:18 remaining in the fourth quarter. Kingsbury also earned his first bowl victory, having lost to East Carolina in the 2000 Galleryfurniture.com Bowl and to Iowa in last year's Alamo Bowl. Texas Tech (9-5) recorded its first postseason win since beating Air Force in the Copper Bowl in 1995, which also was the last time the Red Raiders won nine games. They are 6-18-1 all-time in bowl play. Texas Tech wasted no time taking control, opening a 24-0 lead early in the second quarter and stretching its advantage to 34-2 at halftime. The Tigers (7-6) got their only points of the half when a punt was blocked through the end zone. Kingsbury left with 10:12 to go in the third quarter. Backup B.J. Symons led Texas Tech to a score, tossing a two-yard TD strike to Francis that made it 41-9 with 6:12 left in the period. Kingsbury left for good with about six minutes remaining and Symons threw a second TD, a 26-yard shovel pass to Taurean Henderson that completed the scoring with 5:32 left. The 55 points matched an all-time bowl high for Texas Tech, equaling their total in the Copper Bowl seven years ago. Clemson surrendered its most points in a bowl game. The Tigers were forced to play from behind virtually from the outset as Robert Treece opened the scoring with a 29-yard field goal 4:49 into the contest. Kingsbury followed with TD passes of 46 yards to Nehemiah Glover and 19 yards to Mickey Peters to make it 17-0. The Red Raiders extended their lead on Henderson's 11-yard TD run 2:51 into the second quarter. Texas Tech made it 31-2 on Walker's 59-yard punt return with 3:52 left in period. The Red Raiders tacked on three more points on Treece's 40-yard field as time expired in the first half. The Red Raiders held a 555-360 edge in total offense. Charlie Whitehurst completed 20-of48 passes for 263 yards with a TD for Clemson but threw four interceptions.

2002 Las Vegas Bowl

The 2002 SEGA Sports Las Vegas Bowl was the 11th edition of the annual game. It featured the UCLA Bruins, and the New Mexico Lobos. The Bruins defeated the Lobos 27-13. Notably the game was the first Division I-A college football game to have a female player on the field, Katie Hnida. Also, UCLA coach Ed Kezirian was victorious in his one and only appearance as a head coach, giving him a perfect coaching record.

2002 Las Vegas Bowl	Line	1	-	2	-	3	-	4	-	Final
New Mexico	(51.5)	6	-	0	-	0	-	7	-	13
UCLA	(-10.5)	3	-	3	-	7	-	14	-	27

Scoring Summary
UCLA — Fikse 49 yard field goal.
New Mexico — Black 55 yard interception return (Kick blocked)
UCLA — Fikse 39 yard field goal.
UCLA — Bragg 74 yard punt return (Fikse kick)
UCLA — Page 29 yard interception return (Griffith kick)
UCLA — Ebell 1 yard run (Fikse kick)
New Mexico — Manning 11 yard pass from Kelly (Byrd kick)

Associated Press Las Vegas Bowl Game Summary - Kicker Katie Hnida made Division I-A college football history for New Mexico, which unfortunately had no one to boost its offense. Craig Bragg returned a punt 74 yards for a touchdown in the third quarter and freshman Jarrad Page took an interception 29 yards for a score as UCLA snapped its two-game bowl losing skid with a 27-13 victory over New Mexico in the Las Vegas Bowl. Bragg recorded the longest punt return in Las Vegas Bowl history, surpassing the 45-yard effort by Nevada's Bryan Reeves in 1992. UCLA's last punt return for a TD came against Washington in 1998. Hnida became the first woman to appear in a Division I-A college football game, but had her extra point blocked with 8:20 to play in the first quarter, when New Mexico owned a 6-3 lead. The 21-year-old Hnida took the field with 8:20 remaining in the first quarter after cornerback Desmar Black intercepted Drew Olson's pass and returned it 55 yards to give New Mexico a 6-3 lead. A 5-9, 150-pounder, Hnida was activated four weeks ago by New Mexico. The Littleton, Colorado native also became the first woman to dress for a bowl team. Under the guidance of interim coach Ed Kezirian, the Bruins (8-5) then scored 24 unanswered points and won a post-season game for the first time since beating Texas A&M in the 1998 Cotton Bowl. The Bruins ended the regular season with one-sided losses to Southern California and Washington State and fired Coach Bob Toledo. Kezirian, currently the director of academic services and an assistant coach from 1982-92, was named interim coach. Former UCLA receiver and Denver Broncos assistant Karl Dorrell already has been hired as Toledo's replacement but was not on the sidelines at Sam Boyd Stadium. Nate Fikse sparked the Bruins' outburst with his second field goal to knot the contest with 4:53 remaining in the half. Freshman Tyler Ebell then capped it, recording his 10th rushing TD of the season to open a 27-6 cushion with 8:41 left in the contest. New Mexico's Casey Kelly struggled, completing 18-of-32 passes for 237 yards with a TD, an interception and a fumble. He was sacked four times - twice by Bruins defensive end David Tautofi - and the Lobos' offense eventually contributed with just 5 1/2 minutes to play when Kelly connected with receiver Joe Manning on an 11-yard TD pass. The Lobos (7-7) fell to 2-4-1 all-time in bowl games after winning six of their final seven regular-season contests to earn just a third post-season berth in 41 years. Moore accounted for 17 of New Mexico's season-low 45 yards rushing. Neither team impressed offensively. The freshmen Quarterback duo of Olson and Matt Moore combined to complete just 12-of-22 passes for 94 yards and an interception for UCLA, which registered just 73 rushing yards. Momentum swung to the Bruins early in the third when Bragg broke a tackle on a punt return and cruised down the left sideline to help UCLA grab a 13-6 advantage.

2002 Hawai'i Bowl

The 2002 ConAgra Foods Hawai'i Bowl was the inaugural Hawai'i Bowl game and matched the hometown Hawaii Warriors with the Tulane Green Wave. Hawaii came into the game 10–2 and Tulane came into the game 6–5.

2002 Hawaii Bowl	Line	1	-	2	-	3	-	4	-	Final
Hawaii	(-12.5)	7	-	7	-	0	-	14	-	28
Tulane	(64.0)	0	-	6	-	20	-	10	-	36

Scoring Summary
Hawaii – Mitchell 1 yard run (Ayat Kick)
Hawaii – Galeai 2 yard run (Ayat Kick)
Tulane – Marler 22 yard Field goal
Tulane – Marler 37 yard Field goal
Tulane – Elpheage 60 yard punt return (Pass failed)
Tulane – Losman 1 yard run (Losman Run)
Tulane – Moore 25 yard run (Pass failed)
Hawaii – Colbert 57 yard pass from Withy-Allen (Ayat Kick)
Tulane – Losman 3 yard run (Losman Pass to Davis)
Hawaii – Colbert 31 yard pass from Withy-Allen (Ayat Kick)
Tulane – Team Safety

Associated Press Hawaii Bowl Game summary - Star Quarterback Timmy Chang suffered an injury and Hawaii never quite recovered. Lynaris Elphepage returned a punt 60 yards for a touchdown and Quarterback J.P. Losman ran for two scores as Tulane rallied from 14 points down and held on for a 36-28 triumph over Hawaii in the inaugural Hawaii Bowl. Hawaii owned a 14-3 lead when Chang, who directs the nation's top passing attack, left the game with less than five minutes left until halftime. The sophomore sustained a jammed thumb and, though X-rays were negative, it was too swollen for Chang to return. Elphepage and Losman recorded TDs in the third and Mewelde Moore ran in for another score to give the Green Wave (8-5) a 26-14 lead. Backup Quarterback Shawn Withy-Allen connected with Justin Colbert for two touchdowns and the Warriors (10-4) pulled within 34-28 with 5:12 to go in the contest. But Tulane got a safety when Withy-Allen fumbled the ball out of the end zone and the Green Wave ran out the clock. Tulane improved to 2-0 in bowl games under Coach Chris Scelfo, who received a two-year contract extension prior to the game, and raised its all-time bowl mark to 4-6. The Green Wave were successful in their first bowl appearance since beating Brigham Young, 41-27, in the 1998 Liberty Bowl to complete the first 12-0 season in school history. During the regular season, Chang completed 335-of-603 passes for 4,350 yards and 25 touchdowns in Hawaii's "Run-and-Shoot" offense. But the sophomore was limited to completing 14-of-21 passes for 124 yards and engineering a pair of touchdown drives before being sidelined. Withy-Allen completed 18-of-31 passes for 239 yards with a pair of TDs and an interception. But Chang and his replacement were sacked a combined eight times. Colbert was Hawaii's offensive star, making nine catches for 158 yards, and fellow receiver Jeremiah Cockheran also tallied nine receptions for 87 yards. Tulane was trailing at halftime, 14-6, but Elphepage's punt return just 4:16 into the third quarter sliced the Green Waves' deficit to two points and provided momentum. An All-Conference USA selection, Elphepage recorded four punt returns for 143 yards and a pair of kickoff returns for 57 yards. Elphepage set up Tulane's go-ahead score, returning a punt 56 yards to the Hawaii 17. Losman had a one-yard TD run and made the two-point conversion on a Quarterback draw to give the Green Wave a 20-14 advantage with 6:17 to go in the third. Moore had 30 carries for 116 yards, including a 25-yard TD run with 21 seconds to go in the third that increased Tulane's lead to 12 points. The junior running back also led the Green Wave with six catches for 80 yards.

2002 Motor City Bowl

The 2002 Motor City Bowl was played on December 26, 2002, at Ford Field in Detroit, Michigan. Boston College scored touchdowns on its first six possessions and routed Toledo 51-25. It was the sixth time the Motor City Bowl had been played.

2002 Motor City Bowl	Line	1	-	2	-	3	-	4	-	Final
Boston College	(-4.0)	14	-	28	-	6	-	3	-	51
Toledo	(59.5)	3	-	15	-	7	-	0	-	25

Scoring Summary
Boston College – Knight 2 yard run (Sciortino kick)
Boston College – Adams 17 yard pass from St. Pierre (Sciortino kick)
Toledo – Robbins 35 yard Field goal
Boston College – Hazard 40 yard pass from St. Pierre (Sciortino kick)
Toledo – Dawson 2 yard run (Robbins kick)
Boston College – Dodd 15 yard run (Sciortino kick)
Boston College – Adams 40 yard pass from St. Pierre (Sciortino kick)
Boston College – Brokaw 1 yard run (Sciortino kick)
Toledo – Ford 9 yard pass from Jones (Robbins kick)
Boston College – Sciortino 35 yard Field goal
Boston College – Sciortino 23 yard Field goal
Toledo – Johnson 30 yard pass from Jones (Robbins kick)
Boston College – Sciortino 45 yard Field goal

Associated Press Motor City Bowl Game Summary - Boston College played like a team on a mission. Brian St. Pierre led the Eagles to touchdowns on their first six possessions and Boston College beat Toledo 51-25 in the Motor City Bowl on Thursday night. St. Pierre, the game's most valuable player, completed 25 of 35 passes for a career-high 342 yards and three touchdowns as Boston College capped one of the most successful four-year runs in school history. The Eagles' senior class, which includes St. Pierre, won its 32nd game, tying the 1981-84 group for the most wins in a four-year span in the past 60 years. Boston College became the ninth team in school history to win at least nine games and the first since 1993. Boston College appeared in a bowl game for a fourth consecutive season. The Eagles, who are 32-17 over that span, finished the season with four straight wins. Toledo (9-5) wasn't able to take advantage of a partisan crowd at Detroit's new Ford Field, which is located about an hour north of the Rockets' campus. The bowl's previous five games were played at the Silverdome in suburban Pontiac. Boston College faced the challenge of the Rockets' unpredictable spread offense, but it was the Eagles who dominated with a more traditional approach. The Eagles set a Motor City Bowl record for most points. The previous record was set in Marshall's 48-29 win over Louisville in 1998. It was the most points the Eagles scored since a 55-3 win over Connecticut on Oct. 7, 2000. Toledo scored the lone touchdown of the second half when Brian Jones connected with Manny Johnson on a 30-yard score with 25 seconds remaining in the third quarter to make it 48-25. Jones, who set several single-season Toledo passing records this year, completed 27 of 41 passes for 331 yards, two touchdowns and two interceptions. Carl Ford caught 10 passes for 112 yards, including a 9-yard touchdown pass with 24 seconds to go in the second quarter. Down 28-10 with less than six minutes to go in the first half, Toledo gambled, going for it on a fourth-and-1 from its own 40, but Jones' pass fell incomplete. Boston College took possession, and on the next play, Grant Adams caught St. Pierre's pass across the middle, eluded a defender and raced into the end zone for a 35-10 lead. A 1-yard TD run by Brandon Brokaw with 1:31 to go in the half made it 42-10. Boston College set a school bowl record for points in a half, surpassing the 31 points the Eagles scored in the first half of the 1985 Cotton Bowl, a 45-28 win over Houston. They also set a Motor City Bowl record for points in a half. Toledo left tackle Nick Kaczur was ejected near the end of the first half for twice punching Boston College defensive end Phil Mettling during a scrum after a 2-point conversion by the Rockets made it 42-18. As a result, the teams were not allowed to go into the tunnel together at halftime. Officials halted the Rockets near the end zone as Boston College's players made their way into the locker room. A second Toledo player, defensive back Brock Dodrill, was ejected early in the third quarter when he hit St. Pierre out of bounds. Toledo, coming off a 49-45 loss to Marshall in the MAC championship game, failed to defend its Motor City Bowl title from a season ago. MAC teams had won the previous four Motor City Bowl games. Toledo cut the Eagles' advantage to 21-10 when Trinity Dawson scored on a 2-yard run with 10:47 remaining in the first half. Boston College made it 21-3 a minute into the second period when St. Pierre delivered a third-and-8 pass to Joel Hazard, who made a defender miss along the sideline, cut up field and dove into the end zone for a 40-yard score. Boston College ran almost exclusively on its first scoring drive, which covered 76 yards over 11 plays, culminating in Derrick Knight's 2-yard run. On their second possession, the Eagles passed on seven of nine plays and took a 14-0 lead on St. Pierre's 17-yard pass to Adams.

2002 Insight Bowl

The 2002 Insight Bowl was the 14th edition to the Insight Bowl, formerly known as the Copper Bowl and the Insight.com Bowl. It featured the Panthers of the University of Pittsburgh and the Beavers of Oregon State University.

2002 Insight Bowl	Line	1	-	2	-	3	-	4	-	Final
Pittsburgh	(45.0)	7	-	3	-	14	-	14	-	38
Oregon State	(-2.5)	7	-	3	-	3	-	0	-	13

Scoring Summary
Pittsburgh – Fitzgerald 40 yard pass from Rutherford (Abdul Kick)
Oregon State – Newson 65 yard pass from Anderson (Yliniemi Kick)
Oregon State – Yliniemi 50 yard Field goal
Pittsburgh – Abdul 45 yard Field goal
Pittsburgh – Rutherford 1 yard Run (Abdul Kick)
Pittsburgh – Robinson 66 yard Punt return (Abdul Kick)
Oregon State – Yliniemi 31 yard Field goal
Pittsburgh – Miree 7 yard Run (Abdul Kick)
Pittsburgh – Palko 8 yard Run (Abdul Kick)

Game Summary - Pittsburgh scored first after a 40-yard touchdown pass from Quarterback Rod Rutherford to wide receiver Larry Fitzgerald, taking a 7–0 lead. Oregon State responded with a 65-yard touchdown pass from Derek Anderson to James Newsome, tying it at seven. In the second quarter, Oregon State took a 10–7 lead after Karl Yliniemi kicked a 50-yard field goal. David Abdul kicked a 45-yarder for Pitt, and the game was tied at ten at the half. Rod Rutherford scored for Pitt on a 1-yard touchdown run in the third quarter to take a 17–10 lead. Late in the quarter, Panthers kick-returner Shawn Robinson scored on a 66-yard punt return, pushing the Panther lead to 24–10. Karl Yliniemi responded for Oregon State with a 31-yard field goal, making it 24–13 at the end of three quarters. The Panthers extended their lead in the fourth quarter when Brandon Miree scored on an 8-yard touchdown run and Tyler Palko scrambled in for an 8-yard touchdown run to close out the scoring in the game, which ended in a final score of 38–13 in favor of Pitt.

2002 Independence Bowl

The 2002 Independence Bowl was between the Nebraska Cornhuskers and the Ole Miss Rebels on December 27, 2002, at Independence Stadium in Shreveport, Louisiana. Ole Miss won the game 27–23; Ole Miss Quarterback Eli Manning, who passed for 313 yards and a touchdown, was the offensive player of the game. After the loss, Nebraska finished the season 7–7, ending a forty-year streak of winning seasons for the Cornhuskers.

2002 Independence Bowl	Line	1	-	2	-	3	-	4	-	Final
Nebraska	(-6.5)	3	-	14	-	3	-	3	-	23
Mississippi	(51.5)	0	-	14	-	10	-	3	-	27

Scoring Summary
Nebraska - Brown 29 yard Field goal
Nebraska - Herian 41 yard pass from Lord (Brown kick)
Ole Miss - Johnson 11 yard pass from Manning (Nichols kick)
Nebraska - Groce 60 yard punt return (Brown kick)
Ole Miss - Sanford 1 yard run (Nichols kick)
Ole Miss - Nichols 37 yard Field goal
Nebraska - Brown 23 yard Field goal
Ole Miss - Sanford 1 yard run (Nichols kick)
Nebraska - Brown 29 yard Field goal
Ole Miss - Nichols 43 yard Field goal

Associated Press Independence Bowl Game Summary - Nebraska has become a mediocre football team -- and now the Cornhuskers have the record to prove it. Eli Manning threw for 313 yards and a touchdown as Mississippi ended Nebraska's 40-year streak of winning seasons with a 27-23 victory Friday in the Mainstay Independence Bowl. Nebraska managed just one offensive touchdown on Jammal Lord's pass to Matt Herian in the second quarter. Josh Brown kicked three field goals and DeJuan Groce had a punt return for a score. The Cornhuskers (7-7) had finished above .500 every year since 1961, when they went 3-6-1. Their seven losses this year are their most since going 3-7 in 1958. Manning was 25-for-44 for Ole Miss (7-6) and became the school's career passing leader in what could be his final college game. The highly touted junior said he will take some time after the season to decide if he will enter the NFL draft. Manning, the offensive player of the game, said he has no timetable for deciding. Nebraska was No. 8 in the country after a 3-0 start this season. But the Cornhuskers' startling demise prompted Solich to make sweeping changes to his coaching staff after the regular season. Solich fired his defensive coordinator and two other defensive assistants and said he will hire an offensive coordinator next season. Solich has acted as his own offensive coordinator since taking over for Tom Osborne in 1998. Nebraska defensive end Chris Kelsay had two sacks and was defensive player of the game. Nebraska had its option working in the first half with 207 of its 262 yards on the ground. But Ole Miss adjusted in the second half and held Nebraska to 97 yards and no touchdowns. Dahrann Diedrick had 92 yards rushing and Lord had 176 total yards. The win enabled the Rebels to avoid their first losing season since 1996. It was their third Independence Bowl victory in the past five years. Ole Miss took its first lead of the game four plays after a curious play call by Nebraska. On a fourth-and-12 from their own 35, the Cornhuskers faked a punt, letting upback Judd Davies throw a pass that fell incomplete. The play was an audible called at the line by Davies. Toward Sanford went over the top for his second 1-yard touchdown run of the game moments later to give Ole Miss a 24-20 lead with 3:24 left in the third. Brown's third field goal of the game, a 29-yarder made it 24-23 with just under eight minutes left. But Jonathan Nichols made a 43-yarder with 4:30 left and Nebraska never threatened after that. After a quiet first quarter, the Cornhuskers and Rebels took turns scoring touchdowns in a 28-point second quarter. Lord's first completion of the game went for a 41-yard touchdown to Herian that made it 10-0. Von Hutchins' interception and 27-yard return to the Nebraska 27 setup the Rebels' first score -- an 11-yard pass from Manning to Kerry Johnson. Groce got the Cornhuskers' lead back to 10 on a record-tying punt return. Groce brought Cody Ridgeway's kick back 60 yards for his fourth punt return touchdown of the season, tying an NCAA record. Groce caught the ball near the left sideline, ran clear across field, before turning it up. Once he did, he was hardly touched by an Ole Miss defender. The score made it 17-7 with 2:43 left in the half. Manning needed a little more than a minute to answer, driving the Rebels 88 yards on nine plays, the last a TD run by Sanford. Mississippi coach David Cutcliffe has been the subject of much speculation in recent days. A report last week said he was planning to leave the Rebels to fill the coaching vacancy at Kentucky. Cutcliffe released a statement last Saturday saying he was not a candidate for the Kentucky job, but that has not stopped the speculation. Before the game Ole Miss athletic director Pete Boone said he has not spoken with Cutcliffe about Kentucky since Saturday, and he would be surprised if the coach left.

2002 Houston Bowl

The 2002 Houston Bowl was the third edition of the college football bowl game (known in its first two years as the "Galleryfurniture.com Bowl"), and was played at Reliant Stadium in Houston, Texas. The game pitted the Oklahoma State Cowboys from the Big 12 Conference and the Southern Miss Golden Eagles from Conference USA (C-USA). The game resulted in a 33–23 Oklahoma State victory.

2002 Houston Bowl	Line	1	-	2	-	3	-	4	-	Final
Southern Miss	(48.5)	3	-	10	-	10	-	0	-	23
Oklahoma State	(-7.5)	10	-	10	-	0	-	13	-	33

Scoring Summary
Oklahoma State – Denard 3 yard pass from Fields (Phillips kick)
Oklahoma State - Phillips 46 yard field goal
Southern Miss - Jones 38 yard field goal
Southern Miss - Almond 13 yard run (Jones kick)
Oklahoma State - Phillips 52 yard field goal
Southern Miss - Jones 24 yard field goal
Oklahoma State - Woods 51 yard pass from Fields (Phillips kick)
Southern Miss - Walley 2 yard run (Jones kick)
Southern Miss - Jones 30 yard field goal
Oklahoma State - Phillips 28 yard field goal
Oklahoma State - Bell 22 yard run (Phillips kick)
Oklahoma State - Phillips 24 yard field goal

GoldenEagles.net Houston Bowl Game Summary - Rashaun Woods caught nine passes for 165 yards, and Luke Phillips kicked four field goals to help lead Oklahoma State to a 33-23 win over Southern Mississippi in the Houston Bowl at Reliant Stadium. Josh Fields threw for 297 yards and two touchdowns on 20-of-39 attempts for the Cowboys (8-5), who posted 13 straight points in the fourth quarter to record their fourth straight win and overcome a 23-20 deficit. Phillips converted a 29-yard field goal on the first play of the fourth quarter. The play gave Oklahoma State a 23-23 tie, the fourth of the game. Tatum Bell's 22-yard touchdown run put the Cowboys ahead 30-23 with 8:07 remaining in the fourth. Phillips added a 23-yarder with 5:16 remaining to extend the lead to 33-23. Bell ended with 159 yards on 12 carries for Oklahoma State and finished the season with 1,105 yards. Dustin Almond completed 10-of-25 passes for 171 yards for the Golden Eagles (7-6), who lost three of their final four games. Chris Johnson caught five of his throws for 67 yards, and Curt Jones kicked three field goals. Mike Denard's three-yard touchdown catch and a 46-yard field goal by Phillips gave the Cowboys a 10-0 lead midway through the first quarter. The Eagles forged a 10-10 tie 4:28 into the second quarter on a 13-yard touchdown run by Almond. Jones kicked a 38-yard field goal with 2:51 left in the first quarter. Phillips tied his personal best with a 52-yard kick to put Oklahoma State ahead 13-10 with 8:05 left in the second quarter. Jones responded for Southern Miss with a 24-yard field goal 5:28 later to force a 13-13 tie. But the Cowboys took a 20-13 lead 1:38 before the half on a 51-yard touchdown reception by Woods. The Eagles forced the game's third tie, at 20-20, on James Walley's three-yard touchdown run 4:10 into the third quarter. They took a 23-20 lead, their first of the game, on a 30-yard field goal by Jones with 4:13 left in the third quarter.

2002 Holiday Bowl

The 2002 Holiday Bowl was played December 27, 2002 in San Diego, California. It featured the Arizona State Sun Devils against the Kansas State Wildcats. Kansas State won the game by a 34-27 final score.

2002 Holiday Bowl	Line	1	-	2	-	3	-	4	-	Final
#6 Kansas State	(-17.5)	0	-	14	-	0	-	20	-	34
Arizona State	(62.5)	0	-	20	-	0	-	7	-	27

Scoring Summary
Arizona State – Taplin 6 yard pass from Walter (Barth kick)
Arizona State – Barth 26 yard Field goal
Kansas State – Sproles 41 yard run (Rheem kick)
Arizona State – Hill 9 yard run (Barth kick)
Arizona State – Barth 39 yard Field goal
Kansas State – Roberson 32 yard run (Rheem kick)
Kansas State – Roberson 3 yard run (Rheem kick)
Arizona State – Williams 10 yard pass from Walter (Barth kick)
Kansas State – Roberson 1 yard run (Rheem kick)
Kansas State – Evans 10 yard pass from Roberson (Rheem kick)

Associated Press Holiday Bowl Game Summary - The oddsmakers should know better than to set an 18-point line for the Pacific Life Holiday Bowl. K-State QB Ell Roberson passed for 1,580 yards and ran for another 1,032 last season. Yes, favored Kansas State won, but certainly not the way they were expected to.

Ell Roberson rallied the sixth-ranked Wildcats with three fourth-quarter touchdowns, including a 10-yard pass to Derrick Evans with 1:15 to play for a 34-27 victory over scrappy Arizona State on Friday night. Roberson also scored on sneaks of 2 yards and 1 yard in the fourth quarter to add to the Holiday Bowl's history of wild finishes. He had four TDs overall, having also scored on a 32-yard run just before halftime. Kansas State (11-2), the highest-ranked team not in a Bowl Championship Series game, trailed 20-14 entering the fourth quarter and seemed on the verge of what would have been a shocking upset. By then, though, Roberson was well on his way to leading a 16-play, 65-yard drive that took 7 minutes, 13 seconds. His 2-yard plunge pulled the Wildcats into a 20-20 tie with 12:36 left in the fourth quarter, but they blew the extra point because of a low snap. ASU needed just 1:46 to go ahead 27-20 on Andrew Walter's 10-yard misdirection screen pass to Mike Williams, when the Quarterback rolled right and threw left. Walter was 6-of-8 for 78 yards on the drive. But Roberson came back and led an 80-yard drive that he finished with 1-yard sneak for a 27-27 tie with 6:41 left. All-American cornerback Terence Newman, used as a wide receiver, set up the winning score with a 34-yard punt return. Once a 10-yard holding penalty against K-State was marched off, the Wildcats started the winning drive on their 41. Roberson, the game's offensive MVP, hit Evans on a slant pattern for K-State's first lead of the game. From 4:29 left in the third quarter until the winning TD pass, Roberson was 8-for-12 passing for 127 yards, and carried nine times for 44 yards. Arizona State had one last shot at the upset, but Walter's desperation pass on fourth-and-15 from his 49 was knocked down inside the 5. Ever since the bowl matchups were set, the Sun Devils were constantly reminded that the point spread was the biggest of all 28 bowls. Kansas State won its sixth straight game. It was the fifth time in six seasons the Wildcats finished with 11 wins. Arizona State (8-6) lost for the fourth time in five games. Roberson completed 11 of 28 passes for 215 yards and one TD and rushed 18 times for 63 yards and three scores. Walter was 28-of-57 for 293 yards and two touchdowns, with one interception. The Wildcats had only 17 yards rushing on 26 carries. Kansas State's Darren Sproles rushed 21 times for 118 yards and a score. Arizona State All-American defensive end Terrell Suggs harassed Roberson for most of the first half and had two sacks, pushing his NCAA record to 24. Suggs is a junior and is undecided whether he'll turn pro. Fans chanted "One more year! One more year!" when he collected the trophy for defensive MVP. After a scoreless first quarter, Arizona State took off, but K-State kept it close with big plays. Walter threw a 6-yard TD pass to Justin Taplin and Mike Barth kicked a 26-yard field goal for a 10-0 lead. The Wildcats came right back on Sproles' 41-yard scoring run, highlighted by his spin move to evade two tacklers at the line of scrimmage. The play was set up by Newman's 36-yard catch. Two possessions later, on third-and-1 from the K-State 9, Arizona State hurried to the line of scrimmage to surprise the Wildcats, coming out with two tight ends and a full-house backfield. Tailback Hakim Hill took the handoff and ran untouched around right end for the score and a 17-7 lead. Sproles' fumble set up Mike Barth's 39-yard field goal for a 20-7 lead, but again K-State responded quickly. On second-and-10 from the 32, Roberson was flushed from the pocket by Suggs, but ended up scoring, evading four defenders along the way, to pull the Wildcats to 20-14. Roberson set up the score with a 41-yard pass to Taco Wallace.

2002 Continental Tire Bowl

The 2002 Continental Tire Bowl was between the Virginia Cavaliers (UVA) and the West Virginia Mountaineers at Ericsson Stadium in Charlotte, North Carolina, on December 22, 2002. It was the first edition of the Continental Tire Bowl. West Virginia represented the Big East Conference (Big East) in the game; Virginia represented the Atlantic Coast Conference (ACC).

2002 Continental Tire Bowl	Line	1	-	2	-	3	-	4	-	Final
#15 West Virginia	(-5.5)	10	-	0	-	6	-	6	-	22
Virginia	(52.0)	7	-	21	-	10	-	10	-	48

Scoring Summary
West Virginia – James 27 yard Field goal
Virginia – Lundy 14 yard pass from Hagans (Hughes kick)
West Virginia – Cobourne 6 yard run (James kick)
Virginia – Schaub 1 yard run (Hughes kick)
Virginia – Hagans 69 yard punt return (Hughes kick)
Virginia – Lundy 4 yard run (Hughes kick)
Virginia – Lundy 48 yard pass from Schaub (Hughes kick)
Virginia – Hughes 27 yard Field goal
West Virginia – Marshall 1 yard run (Pass failed)
Virginia – Hughes 30 yard Field goal
West Virginia – Cobourne 1 yard run (Pass failed)
Virginia – Lundy 31 yard run (Hughes kick)

Associated Press Continental Tire Bowl Game Summary - Wali Lundy spent most of his life chasing Avon Cobourne. In their first head-to-head meeting, he finally passed him. Lundy scored four touchdowns and gained 239 all-purpose yards as Virginia snapped a four-game bowl losing streak Saturday with a 48-22 victory over No. 15 West Virginia in the inaugural Continental Tire Bowl. Cobourne, who was four years ahead of Lundy at Holy Cross High School in southern New Jersey, ran for 117 yards and two touchdowns for West Virginia. Lundy, who came in averaging 53.8 yards rushing and 27.6 receiving, ran for 127 and caught five passes for 76 yards. He scored touchdowns on runs of 4 and 31 yards. He caught a 14-yard TD pass from Marques Hagans and a 48-yard TD pass from Matt Schaub. He said Cobourne had little to say to him after the game. Cobourne, who said he barely knows Lundy, still praised his performance. Schaub, the ACC player of the year, threw for 182 yards and a score and Hagans returned a punt 69 yards for his second touchdown as the Cavaliers (9-5) won their first postseason game since the 1995 Peach Bowl. Virginia did an excellent job slowing down Cobourne, the Big East's all-time leading rusher, who came into the game averaging 141 yards a game. He ran for 54 in the first quarter and scored on a 6-yard run but didn't gain a single yard in the second quarter. He finished with 117 yards -- the 28th 100-yard game of his career. Cobourne added a 1-yard touchdown in the fourth quarter, but a 2-point conversion attempt by the Mountaineers (9-4) failed, and the TD only cut the score to 41-22 with 7:17 to play. Cobourne ended his career with 5,039 yards, ninth-best in NCAA Division I-A history. But it was the bowl win he most wanted, especially a convincing victory, to prove that the Mountaineers deserved to be in a bigger bowl. They were passed over for the Gator Bowl despite finishing second in the Big East when officials took Notre Dame instead. West Virginia coach Rich Rodriguez turned the Mountaineers around from a 3-8 record last season. The Cavaliers also felt slighted at being in the Tire Bowl. They finished second in their conference and felt they deserved a berth in a New Year's Day game. The initial disappointment wore off when fans from both schools snapped up the 73,535 tickets -- painting Ericsson Stadium in a sea of blue-and-gold West Virginia fans and orange-and-blue Cavs supporters. But Virginia, which quietly went about its business all week, felt a second slight by the Mountaineers' confidence, and rumors that West Virginia players had guaranteed a victory. The Mountaineers were uncharacteristically sloppy. They came into the game with the second-best turnover margin in the nation at plus-21, but Quarterback Rasheed Marshall was intercepted by Almondo Curry in the third quarter, and Phil Braxton's pass after a pitch from Marshall was intercepted by Darryl Blackstock.

Continental Tire Bowl Game Notes - For his performance in the 2002 Continental Tire Bowl—4 touchdowns and 203 total yards receiving and rushing—Virginia running back Wali Lundy was named the most valuable player of the game. He led the Cavaliers in both rushing—22 carries, 127 yards—and receiving—five catches, 76 yards—while scoring four touchdowns.

2002 Alamo Bowl

The 2002 Alamo Bowl featured the Wisconsin Badgers and the Colorado Buffaloes.

2002 Alamo Bowl	Line	1	-	2	-	3	-	4	-	OT	-	Final
Colorado	(-7.0)	14	-	0	-	14	-	0	-	0	-	28
Wisconsin	(53.0)	7	-	14	-	0	-	7	-	3	-	31

Scoring Summary
Colorado – Strickland 91 yard Interception Return (Brougham Kick)
Wisconsin – Davis 4 yard run (Allen Kick)
Colorado – Hackett 10 yard pass from Hodge (Brougham Kick)
Wisconsin - Williams 10 yard pass from Bollinger (Allen Kick)
Wisconsin – Charles 7 yard pass from Bollinger (Allen Kick)
Colorado – Brown 4 yard run (Brougham Kick)
Colorado – Hackett 11 yard pass from Colvin (Brougham Kick)
Wisconsin – Bollinger 1 yard run (Allen Kick)
Wisconsin - Allen 37 yard Field Goal

Associated Press Alamo Bowl Game Summary - For much of the Alamo Bowl, Wisconsin looked like a team that had lost six of its final eight regular-season games. Then Brooks Bollinger and Mike Allen played like world-beaters. Bollinger came up with a series of clutch plays at the end of regulation, including the tying touchdown in the final minute, and Allen kicked a 37-yard field goal in overtime as the Badgers overcame four turnovers to defeat No. 14 Colorado, 31-28. The Badgers (8-6) won the coin toss in overtime and elected to play defense first. They pushed the Buffaloes (9-5) backward, forcing a 45-yard field goal attempt by Pat Brougham that was pushed well right. Wisconsin ran the ball up the middle three straight plays, setting up Allen's kick, which sailed through the middle of the uprights to give the Badgers a fourth straight bowl victory and seventh in eight tries under coach Barry Alvarez. Wisconsin tied it, 28-28, on a one-yard keeper by Bollinger with 51 seconds left in regulation. Bollinger, a senior, completed two fourth-down passes on the drive, including a 30-yarder to Darrin Charles to the Colorado 1. One play earlier, freshman Jonathan Orr got behind the defense but let a sure TD pass slip through his hands at the

Buffaloes' 5. Colorado trailed at halftime, 21-14, after Wisconsin converted three interceptions by Robert Hodge into touchdowns. But early in the third quarter, Jim Leonhard fumbled a punt at the Badgers' 26, setting up a five-yard TD run by Chris Brown that tied it. On Wisconsin's ensuing possession, running back Anthony Davis lost the ball after a hit by safety Medford Moorer, who recovered the fumble at the Badgers' 17. Backup Quarterback Zac Colvin threw an 11-yard TD pass to D.J. Hackett to give Colorado a 28-21 lead with 5:58 left in the quarter. Brown left with a concussion early in the fourth quarter after rushing an Alamo Bowl-record 28 times for 97 yards. The Buffaloes also were down two starting offensive lineman by the end of the game. Davis carried 25 times for 99 yards and a touchdown and Bollinger had 82 yards and a score on 20 rushes. Bollinger also completed 12-of-24 passes for 163 yards with two TDs and an interception. Hodge was harried into 6-of-13 passing for 62 yards with a touchdown and three interceptions. Colvin was 3-of-5 for 15 yards and a score. Colorado lost its second straight bowl game after winning its previous six. The Buffaloes fell to 4-1-1 all-time against the Badgers. Barnett is 1-4 all-time in bowls, losing two of three with Colorado. The Buffaloes took a 7-0 lead on an Alamo Bowl-record 91-yard interception return by cornerback Donald Strickland 3:53 into the contest. Wisconsin tied it with 4:54 left in the quarter on a four-yard run by Davis after Scott Starks intercepted Hodge deep in Colorado territory. The Buffaloes went back in front on a 10-yard fade pass from Hodge to Hackett on the final play of the first quarter. But Wisconsin took advantage of two more interceptions by Hodge in the second quarter, scoring on an 11-yard pass from Bollinger to Brandon Williams and a seven-yard toss to Darrin Charles to take a seven-point lead into halftime.

2002 Music City Bowl

The 2002 Gaylord Hotels Music City Bowl was the fifth edition of the bowl game. It was played at LP Stadium in Nashville, Tennessee on December 30, 2002, and featured the Arkansas Razorbacks and the Minnesota Golden Gophers.

2002 Music City Bowl	Line	1	-	2	-	3	-	4	-	Final
Arkansas	(-8.0)	7	-	0	-	0	-	7	-	14
Minnesota	(47.0)	6	-	6	-	7	-	10	-	29

Scoring Summary
Arkansas – Wilson 2 yard pass from Jones (Carlton Kick)
Minnesota – Nystrom 24 yard Field Goal
Minnesota – Nystrom 45 yard Field Goal
Minnesota – Nystrom 21 yard Field Goal
Minnesota – Nystrom 22 yard Field Goal
Minnesota – Utecht 19 yard pass from Abdul-Khaliq (Nystrom Kick)
Minnesota – Nystrom 29 yard Field Goal
Minnesota – Tapeh 33 yard run (Nystrom Kick)
Arkansas – Smith 10 yard pass from Sorahan (Carlton Kick)

Associated Press Music City Bowl Game Summary - Kicker Dan Nystrom became the Big Ten Conference's all-time leading scorer as Minnesota shook off a four-game losing streak with a 29-14 victory over Arkansas in the Music City Bowl. In his final game for the Golden Gophers, Nystrom tied a school record with five field goals, helping Minnesota (8-5) register its first bowl win in 17 years. He ended his career with 367 points, breaking the Big Ten mark of 355 set by Purdue's Travis Dorsch from 1998-2001. Nystrom also set a Big Ten record with 71 career field goals, three more than Dorsch. The Golden Gophers, who closed the regular season with losses to Ohio State, Michigan, Iowa and Wisconsin, reached eight wins for just the eighth time in school history and the first since 1999. Minnesota improved to just 3-5 in the postseason, earning its first bowl win since defeating Clemson in the 1985 Independence Bowl. The victory snapped a three-game bowl losing streak. Arkansas (9-5) ended its season with a two-game slide. The Razorbacks won six in a row to capture the Southeastern Conference West Division title but were routed by Georgia, 30-3, in the SEC championship game. Arkansas continued to struggle offensively as it was shut down after driving 74 yards on its first possession and taking a 7-0 lead on Matt Jones' two-yard pass to George Wilson. The postseason woes continued for the Razorbacks, who have dropped three straight bowls and 10 of their last 11. They fell to 10-20-3 all-time in bowl play. Nystrom kicked field goals of 24 and 45 yards in the first quarter and converted from 21 and 22 yards in the second to give the Golden Gophers a 12-7 halftime lead. Minnesota broke it open in the second half as Asad Abdul-Khaliq tossed a 19-yard TD pass to tight end Ben Utecht with 2:44 left in the third quarter and Thomas Tapeh ripped off a 33-yard touchdown run with 7:49 left. Tapeh broke several tackles on his way to the end zone, extending the lead to 29-7. Between the touchdowns, Nystrom kicked his fifth field goal, a 29-yarder three minutes into the fourth period. Minnesota held a 434-288 edge in total offense. Abdul-Khaliq completed 16-of-31 passes for 216 yards. Arkansas got a late TD on backup Ryan Sorahan's 10-yard strike to Richard

Smith. Sorahan took over for Jones early in the fourth quarter with the Razorbacks trailing, 22-7. But Fred Talley fumbled, and defensive end Mark Losli recovered for Minnesota at midfield. Another mistake allowed the Golden Gophers to retain possession as Arkansas was penalized for having 12 men on the field during a punt on 4th-and-4. The Golden Gophers cashed in the TD run by Tapeh, who rushed for 99 yards on 19 carries. Arkansas, which led the SEC in rushing, was held to 80 yards on the ground. Jones and Sorahan combined to complete just 18-of-40 passes for 208 yards. Michael Lehan led Minnesota's defensive effort with two of the team's three interceptions. In their first 12 games, the Golden Gophers had just four interceptions.

2002 Seattle Bowl

The 2002 Seattle Bowl was the second and final edition of the college football bowl game (known for the previous 3 years as the Oahu Bowl, before moving to Seattle), and was played at Qwest Field in Seattle, Washington. The game pitted the University of Oregon Ducks from the Pac-10 and the Wake Forest University Demon Deacons from the ACC. The game resulted in a 38–17 Wake Forest victory.

2002 Seattle Bowl	Line	1	-	2	-	3	-	4	-	Final
Wake Forest	(58.5)	7	-	14	-	10	-	7	-	38
Oregon	(-7.5)	3	-	7	-	7	-	0	-	17

Scoring Summary
Oregon - Siegel 45 Field goal
Wake Forest - Mughelli 1 yard run (Wisnosky kick)
Wake Forest - Anderson 57 yard pass from MacPherson (Wisnosky kick)
Wake Forest - MacPherson 1 yard run (Wisnosky kick)
Oregon - Parker 7 yard pass from Kellen Clemens (Siegel kick)
Wake Forest - Wisnosky 43 yard Field goal
Oregon - Floberg 1 yard run (Siegel kick)
Wake Forest - Anderson 63 yard pass from MacPherson (Wisnosky kick)
Wake Forest - Barclay 12 yard run (Wisnosky kick)

GoDucks.com Seattle Bowl Game Summary - Attempts to rebound from a disappointing last half of its regular season proved futile as big plays and a ball-control offense contributed to Oregon's first post-season setback in four tries. After jumping onto the scoreboard first via a Jared Siegel field goal, the Ducks were unable to secure their second first down of the game until staring at a 14-3 deficit in Seahawks Stadium. Despite completing only nine passes, Wake Forest's offense took advantage of maintaining possession of the football for 34:34 while scoring on two of four plays longer than 30 yards to account for a second bowl win over Oregon in 11 years. Redshirt freshman Quarterback Kellen Clemens came off the bench to replace Jason Fife to open the second quarter — responding with his first touchdown pass as a collegian in his most extensive play to date — and helped the Ducks bounce back from an 18-point deficit. A 43-yard Keenan Howry punt return, followed by the school's career receiving leader's 36-yard run, led to Matt Floberg's lone scoring run of the year to close the gap to 24-17 late in the third quarter. Yet the Oregon offense was unable to take advantage of the momentum as it was limited to only two more first downs the remainder of the afternoon. Linebackers David Moretti and Kevin Mitchell led the defense with 17 and 15 tackles, respectively, while George Wrighster's five catches propelled him to the top of the school's list for most single season catches by a tight end ever (41).

2002 Humanitarian Bowl

The 2002 edition to the Humanitarian Bowl was the 6th edition of the bowl game. It featured the Boise State Broncos and the Iowa State Cyclones. Iowa State got on the board first after a 30-yard field goal from Adam Benike, taking a 3-0 lead. In the second quarter, Boise State's Brock Forsey scored from 4 yards out for Boise State to jump ahead 7-3. Iowa State Quarterback Seneca Wallace threw a 6-yard touchdown pass to wide receiver Jamaul Montgomery, and Iowa State took a 10-7 lead to halftime. In the third quarter, Brock Forsey gave Boise State the lead again, as he rumbled in from 2 yards out to place the Broncos in front 14-10. Quarterback Ryan Dinwiddie later scored on a 1-yard Quarterback sneak to make it 21-10. In the fourth quarter, Brock Forsey added his third touchdown of the game, a 9 yarder, as Boise State built a 27-10 lead, and pulled away from Iowa State. Lane Danielson scored on a four-yard run making it 27-16, but Ryan Dinwiddie threw a 3-yard touchdown pass to Lou Fanucchi to cap the scoring and give Boise State a 34-16 win.

2002 Humanitarian Bowl	Line	1	-	2	-	3	-	4	-	Final
Iowa State	(67.0)	3	-	7	-	0	-	6	-	16
#18 Boise State	(-12.0)	0	-	7	-	14	-	13	-	34

Scoring Summary
Iowa State - Benike 30 yard Field goal
Boise State - Forsey 4 yard run (Calaycay kick)
Iowa State - Montgomery 6 yard pass from Wallace (Benike kick)
Boise State - Forsey 2 yd run (Calaycay kick)
Boise State - Dinwiddie 1 yard run (Calaycay kick)
Boise State - Forsey 9 yard run (Pass failed)
Iowa State - Danielsen 4 yard run (Pass failed)
Boise State - Fanucchi 3 yard pass from Dinwiddie (Calaycay kick)

Associated Press Humanitarian Bowl Game Summary - A cold, wet and dreary morning turned into a delightful afternoon for Boise State. The weather didn't improve, but it hardly mattered to the Broncos (No. 15 ESPN/USA Today, No. 18 AP) as they beat Iowa State 34-16 Tuesday in the Humanitarian Bowl. Brock Forsey ran for three touchdowns to lead the Broncos. Forsey, who scored on runs of 4, 2 and 9 yards, finished the season with 32 touchdowns, the second-highest season total in Division I-A. Barry Sanders has the record with 39 for Oklahoma State in 1988. With temperatures in the low 40s and a steady rain falling, the conditions were hardly typical for a bowl game. It didn't discourage 30,446 fans, nearly all of whom showed up to cheer on the Broncos (12-1). Boise State won its third Humanitarian Bowl in four seasons. The Broncos also won it in 2000 and 1999. The Western Athletic Conference champions went 7-0 at home this season. Bobby Hammer was voted MVP of the game after he had 10 tackles, including three for a loss. The Cyclones (7-7), who opened the season at 6-1 and reached the top 10 for the first time in school history, had a 1-6 finish. Wallace hyperextended his knee in the first quarter and missed a couple of series. The Cyclones' offense never recovered. Boise State scored at least 34 points in each of its victories this season. The Broncos needed only half that as they shut down Iowa State. Wallace, the Cyclone Quarterback who was an early Heisman Trophy contender, had been averaging 268.6 yards of total offense. He had 190 Tuesday, most of it coming after Boise State already had taken command. Iowa State's loss dropped Big 12 Conference teams to 3-3 in bowl games with No. 8 Oklahoma and No. 9 Texas still to play. Three Iowa State starters were ruled ineligible for the game because of low grades. They might not have been much help as the Cyclones battled a boisterous crowd in Bronco Stadium all day. The crowd was at its loudest to start the second half with the Broncos trailing 10-7. Boise State forced Iowa State into going three-and-out on the Cyclones' first four possessions of the second half, and the Broncos capitalized with two touchdowns to take a lead they would not relinquish. Ryan Dinwiddie completed passes of 11, 17 and 16 yards to Billy Wingfield before Forsey scored from 2 yards to make it 14-10, ending a quick drive that started at the Boise State 46. After a punt set up the Broncos at their own 49, Lou Fanucchi took a reverse 25 yards to help set up Dinwiddie's 1-yard TD run that put the Broncos up 21-10 with 4 minutes left in the third. Forsey, who had 24 carries for 78 yards, added a 9-yard TD run in the fourth quarter and Dinwiddie threw a 3-yard TD pass to Fanucchi with 27 seconds left in the game. Dinwiddie was 17-for-32 for 160 yards and ran for a touchdown. Wallace missed two series after getting hit on the left knee in the first quarter as the Cyclones drove to the Boise State 13. Backup Cris Love and the Cyclone offense went backward on the first two plays, and Iowa State settled for a 30-yard field goal by Adam Benike. By the time Wallace returned, the Broncos had taken a 7-3 lead on a 4-yard run by Forsey. Iowa State regained the lead on a 6-yard touchdown pass from Wallace to Jamaul Montgomery with 2:29 left in the half.

2002 Liberty Bowl

The 2002 AXA Liberty Bowl was played between the TCU Horned Frogs and the Colorado State Rams on December 31, 2002, at Liberty Bowl Memorial Stadium in Memphis, Tennessee.

2002 Liberty Bowl	Line	1	-	2	-	3	-	4	-	Final
TCU	(52.5)	0	-	7	-	0	-	10	-	17
#23 Colorado State	(-5.0)	0	-	0	-	3	-	0	-	3

Scoring Summary
TCU – Dunbar 2 yard pass from Stilley (Browne kick)
Colorado State – Babcock 46 yard Field goal
TCU – Browne 25 yard Field goal
TCU – Madison 3 yard run (Browne kick)

Associated Press Liberty Bowl Game Summary - Texas Christian figured out how to stop Colorado State standout Cecil Sapp after just two runs in the AXA Liberty Bowl. Sapp reeled off big gains of 59 and 25 yards on the Rams' first two possessions, and the Horned Frogs -- who rank first in the nation against the run -- knew something had to change. Sapp had 22 yards the rest of the game, and TCU tailback Ricky Madison stole the show with 111 yards rushing and a touchdown as the Horned Frogs beat Colorado State 17-3 on Tuesday. It was the Horned Frogs' 500th victory in school history. Madison ran for 107 of his yards in the rainy second half as TCU's offense came alive after a sloppy opening by both teams. In the first half, the teams combined for three lost fumbles, two interceptions, a missed field goal and an unsuccessful faked field goal. Their sloppy play made for the lowest scoring first half of a Liberty Bowl since Penn State led Tulane 6-0 in 1979. TCU (10-2) finally put together a seven-play, 62-yard scoring drive led by Lonta Hobbs in the closing minutes of the second quarter. The freshman ran for 39 yards in the drive, capped when Sean Stilley threw a 15-yard touchdown pass to LaTarence Dunbar with 1:21 remaining to put TCU up 7-0 at the break. Colorado State (10-4) countered quickly in the third quarter with a 46-yard field goal by Jeff Babcock at 11:22. The score -- which tied Babcock's career long -- came on a four-play drive for negative-6 yards. The Rams had another opportunity for points on their next possession, when short back-to-back runs by Sapp brought them to the TCU 22. But two penalties and a play for negative yardage pushed them back to the 38, and they had to punt. The Rams were held to 89 yards rushing -- compared with 197 for TCU -- for their lowest total of the season. TCU also outgained Colorado State 338-149. TCU added cushion in the fourth when Nick Browne scored on a 25-yard field goal with 6:57 remaining. Madison then scored just over three minutes after the field goal for the final margin. Sapp's first run -- the longest allowed by TCU from scrimmage this season -- brought Colorado State to the TCU 11, but the Rams couldn't capitalize. Though they set up for a field goal, they instead attempted a fake with holder Joey Cuppari passing to an open Brandon Alconcel in the end zone. But Alconcel dropped the pass. Sapp finished with 106 yards -- although 84 of them came on those first two runs. Despite that, the total gives him his ninth 100-yard game of the season, tying a school record set by Steve Bartalo in 1986.

2002 Sun Bowl

The 2002 Wells Fargo Sun Bowl featured the Washington Huskies, and the Purdue Boilermakers. This game was a rematch of the 2001 Rose Bowl.

2002 Sun Bowl	Line	1	-	2	-	3	-	4	-	Final
Washington	(-3.0)	17	-	0	-	0	-	7	-	24
Purdue	(57.5)	0	-	14	-	17	-	3	-	34

Scoring Summary
Washington – Reddick 7 yard pass from Pickett (Anderson Kick)
Washington – Cooper 31 yard fumble return (Anderson Kick)
Washington – Anderson 38 yard Field goal
Purdue – Standeford 7 yard pass from Orton (Lacevic Kick)
Purdue – Williams recovered fumble in end zone (Lacevic Kick)
Purdue – Lacevic 22 yard Field Goal
Purdue – Harris 10 yard run (Lacevic Kick)
Purdue – Gardner 19 yard fumble return (Lacevic Kick)
Purdue – Lacevic 29 yard Field Goal
Washington - Reddick 12 yard pass from Pickett (Anderson Kick)

Associated Press Sun Bowl Game Summary - First Wisconsin, then Minnesota, now Purdue. The Boilermakers became the third underdog from the Big Ten Conference to win a bowl game this month, rallying from an early 17-point deficit to defeat Washington, 34-24, in the Sun Bowl. Linebacker Gilbert Gardner's 19-yard fumble return for a touchdown late in the third quarter highlighted the comeback as Purdue roared back from a 17-0 first-quarter deficit with 34 straight points. The Big Ten improved to 3-0 in bowl play and has four more teams in action over the next three days, including No. 2 Ohio State, which faces top-ranked Miami in the national championship game on Friday in the Fiesta Bowl. At the other end of the spectrum is the Pac-10 Conference, which dropped to 1-4 in bowl play. The Pac-10 has two teams - Southern California and Washington State - involved in BCS bowls. Making its second straight Sun Bowl appearance, Purdue (7-6) avenged a loss to Washington in the 2000 Rose Bowl and defeated the Huskies for just the second time in 10 all-time meetings (2-7-1). The win kept alive Tiller's streak of never having a losing season in six years at Purdue. Washington (7-6) appeared ready to turn the game into a blowout as Cody Pickett tossed a seven-yard TD pass to Patrick Reddick, Marquis Cooper returned a fumble 31 yards for a score and John Anderson kicked a 39-yard field in the first 11 minutes. In the first quarter, Washington had 94 yards to Purdue's minus-8. But the Boilermakers' defense settled down, as the Huskies' next seven possessions resulted in five punts, an interception and a fumble. Purdue got on the board on Kyle Orton's seven-yard TD toss to John Standeford with 5:09 left in the second quarter, then closed to 17-14 when wide receiver Ray Williams recovered Brandon Jones' fumble in the end zone with 35 seconds left in the half. Orton threw for 283 yards and completed 25-of-37 passes—exactly half his attempts in last year's 33-27 Sun Bowl loss to Washington State. He threw for 702 yards in the two bowl games. Standeford caught 10 passes for 105 yards, while Taylor Stubblefield grabbed seven for 92. While Pickett was 25-of-54 for 272 yards, the Huskies rushed for just 44 yards on 24 carries. The defeat saddled Washington with just its second six-loss season in 25 years. The Huskies won their final three regular-season games to avoid their first losing year since 1976. Following a 22-yard field goal by Berin Lacevic early in the second half, the Boilermakers took the lead for good on Jones' 10-yard run with 3:33 left in the third quarter. Just 85 seconds later, Gardner stripped Pickett, scooped up the fumble and went the distance to make it 31-17. The Boilermakers kept the ball out of Pickett's hands with a seven-minute possession in the fourth quarter that Lacevic capped with a 29-yard field goal with 5:52 to go. Purdue rolled up 408 yards over the final three quarters and finished with a 400-316 advantage. A large chunk of Washington's total came on its final two possessions. The Huskies got within 10 on Pickett's 12-yard TD strike to Patrick Reddick with 3:31 left before Anderson missed a 23-yard field goal with 15 seconds to play.

2002 San Francisco Bowl

2002 San Francisco Bowl was the inaugural edition of the college football bowl game between the Virginia Tech Hokies and the Air Force Falcons at Pacific Bell Park in San Francisco, California on December 31, 2002. The 2002 San Francisco Bowl kicked off in clear, 69 °F weather, but the field was soggy after several days of rain.

2002 San Francisco Bowl	Line	1	-	2	-	3	-	4	-	Final
Air Force	(54.5)	10	-	0	-	0	-	3	-	13
#21 Virginia Tech	(-11.5)	7	-	3	-	7	-	3	-	20

Scoring Summary
Air Force – Ward 15 yard run (Ashcroft kick)
Air Force – Ashcroft 45 yard Field goal
Virginia Tech – Suggs 16 yard run (Warley kick)
Virginia Tech – Warley 23 yard Field goal
Virginia Tech – Suggs 2 yard run (Warley kick)
Air Force – Ashcroft 21 yard Field goal
Virginia Tech – Warley 37 yard Field goal

San Francisco Bowl Game Summary - In the first seven minutes of the game, Air Force scored 10 consecutive unanswered points. The Tech defense eventually clamped down on the Falcons' offense, however, and only allowed three points for the remainder of the game. The Virginia Tech offense slowly climbed back from the initial 10-point deficit, scoring a touchdown in the first quarter and a field goal in the second. By halftime, the Hokies had equalized the score at 10–10. In the second half, defense continued to dominate as Tech gradually built a lead. The Hokies scored the only points of a third quarter as running back Lee Suggs ran into the end zone from one yard out, allowing Tech to take a 17–10 lead into the fourth quarter. The Falcons didn't give up easily, however. Air Force kicker Joey Ashcroft cut into the Tech lead with a 21-yard field goal. Tech matched the score later in the quarter to restore the one-touchdown lead. As time ran down, Air Force had one final chance to tie the game and send it into overtime. Beginning at its own 18-yard line with 4:11 left to play, the Falcons drove deep into Tech territory. With seven seconds remaining, Air Force Quarterback Chance Harridge tried to scramble into the end zone but was stopped before the goal line by Tech cornerback Ronyell Whitaker. The defensive stop preserved the 20–13 Hokie victory, and Tech Quarterback Bryan Randall was named the game's most valuable player.

2002 Chick-Fil-A Peach Bowl

The 2002 edition of the Peach Bowl featured the Maryland Terrapins and the Tennessee Volunteers. The game was played December 31st, 2002 at the Georgia Dome in Atlanta, Georgia.

2002 Chick-Fil-A Peach Bowl	Line	1	-	2	-	3	-	4	-	Final
Tennessee	(Pk)	0	-	3	-	0	-	0	-	3
Maryland	(47.0)	7	-	10	-	3	-	10	-	30

Scoring Summary
Maryland – McBrien 1 yard run (Novak kick)
Maryland – Cox 54 yard interception return (Novak kick)
Tennessee – Walls 38 yard Field Goal
Maryland – Novak 48 yard Field Goal
Maryland – Novak 44 yard Field Goal
Maryland – McBrien 6 yard run (Novak kick)
Maryland – Novak 25 yard Field goal

Associated Press Chick-Fil-A Peach Bowl Game Summary - Maryland never gave Tennessee or its partisan crowd at the Georgia Dome a chance to get in the game. Quarterback Scott McBrien rushed for a pair of touchdowns as the 18th-ranked Terrapins routed the Volunteers, 30-3, in the Peach Bowl to complete a remarkable turnaround. Maryland (11-3) won 10 of its final 11 games after a 1-2 start and recorded its first bowl victory since beating Syracuse, 35-18, in the 1985 Cherry Bowl. The only loss for the Terrapins during that stretch was a 48-13 setback to Virginia that snapped an eight-game winning streak.

Last season, Coach Ralph Friedgen led Maryland to its first Atlantic Coast Conference title in 17 years, but the Terrapins were drubbed by Florida State, 56-23, in the Orange Bowl. A year later, Maryland reached 11 wins for only the second time in the 110-year history of the program. The Terrapins' only other 11-win campaign came in 1976, when they went 11-0 in the regular season before losing to Houston in the Cotton Bowl and ending the season ranked eighth in the country. The defeat ended a disappointing campaign for Tennessee (8-5), which suffered its first five-loss season during Phillip Fulmer's 12-year tenure as coach. Maryland appeared better prepared for the contest, holding the Volunteers to a season-low 45 rushing yards. Tennessee's previous low was 59 yards against Alabama. The Terrapins repeatedly pressured Casey Clausen, who was sacked six times. He completed 23-of-37 passes for 242 yards. Linebacker E.J. Henderson, the Butkus and Bednarik Award winner, spearheaded Maryland's defensive effort with 12 tackles—including four for losses - and two sacks. The Volunteers were held without a touchdown in a bowl game for the first time since the 1957 Gator Bowl, when they lost to Texas A&M, 3-0. Tennessee reached the Maryland 16 with nine minutes left but turned the ball over on downs. McBrien scored the only touchdown the Terrapins needed on a one-yard keeper with six minutes left in the first quarter and went in from six yards just over two minutes into the final period to make it 27-3. McBrien was 11-of-19 for 120 yards and rushed seven times for 36 yards. Steve Suter's Peach Bowl-record 79-yard punt return set up Nick Novak's third field goal of the game, a 25-yarder with four minutes to go. Novak also converted from 44 and 48 yards. Cornerback Curome Cox returned an interception 55 yards to give Maryland a 14-0 lead 3:28 into the second quarter.

2002 Silicon Valley Football Classic

The 2002 Silicon Valley Football Classic was between the Georgia Tech Yellow Jackets and the Fresno State Bulldogs on December 31, 2002, at Spartan Stadium in San Jose, California.

2002 Silicon Valley Classic	Line	1	-	2	-	3	-	4	-	Final
Georgia Tech	(-6.5)	7	-	0	-	14	-	0	-	21
Fresno State	(49.0)	3	-	10	-	7	-	10	-	30

Scoring Summary
Fresno State - Asparuhov 22 yard field goal
Georgia Tech - Watkins 35 yard pass from Suggs (Manget kick)
Fresno State - Asparuhov 42 yard field goal
Fresno State - Meza 48 yard interception return (Asparuhov kick)
Georgia Tech - Bilbo 1 yard run (Manget kick)
Fresno State - Davis 3 yard run (Asparuhov kick)
Georgia Tech - Smith 42 yard pass from Bilbo (Manget kick)
Fresno State - Asparuhov 33 yard field goal
Fresno State - Davis 28 yard run (Asparuhov kick)

Associated Press Silicon Valley Football Classic Game Summary - Rodney Davis' phone rang in the locker room just before Fresno State took the field for the Silicon Valley Classic. It was his brother and teammate, calling to wish the Bulldogs good luck. Starting receiver Marque Davis was at home, one of seven players who couldn't participate because of academic problems. So, Rodney Davis ran for them. He carried 37 times for 153 yards and two touchdowns as Fresno State won its first bowl game in 10 years, defeating Georgia Tech 30-21 on Tuesday. The Bulldogs (9-5) had not won a postseason game since beating Southern California in the 1992 Freedom Bowl, a string of four straight losses. And they were even more proud they did it with a depleted roster. Fresno State suited only 45 players and was missing five starters. A new Western Athletic Conference rule requires athletes to pass at least six credits to play in a bowl game, and seven didn't meet the requirement. Asen Asparuhov kicked a 33-yard field goal with 3:43 left, one of his three in the game, and Davis clinched the victory with a 28-yard TD run just more than a minute later for the Bulldogs. And the Fresno State defense did an impressive job after halftime of weathering a strong second-half comeback attempt by Georgia Tech freshman backup Quarterback Damarius Bilbo. Bilbo passed for a touchdown and ran for another after replacing the ineffective A.J. Suggs, but Bilbo also threw four interceptions as the Yellow Jackets (7-6) committed seven turnovers. Georgia Tech was the only team in the ACC to throw more interceptions (14) than touchdowns (13) this season. The game turned into a muddy mess after hard rain fell Monday night. It took only a few plays for Georgia Tech's gleaming white uniforms to turn a dull brown, and there were plenty of slips and missed plays. In a lackluster first half, the teams struggled to take advantage of their scoring opportunities, with Fresno State leading 13-7 at halftime. Dee Meza's 48-yard interception return for a touchdown with 14 seconds left in the second quarter highlighted the half. Fresno State was playing in the Silicon Valley Classic for the third straight year, and Bulldogs fans took up most of the seats at Spartan Stadium. Georgia Tech was trying to protect the nation's top bowl record in its sixth straight postseason appearance, and the Yellow Jackets thought their chances were good with Fresno State missing so many key players. Georgia Tech is now 20-11 after coming into the game tied with Penn State for a .667 bowl winning percentage. Yellow Jackets placekicker Luke Manget made three extra points to give him 160 straight PATs, one shy of the NCAA record for consecutive extra points of 161, set by John Becksvoort of Tennessee from 1991-94.

2003 Gator Bowl

The 2003 Gator Bowl was between the NC State Wolfpack and the Notre Dame Fighting Irish at Alltel Stadium in Jacksonville, Florida on January 1, 2003. The game ended in a 28–6 victory for NC State.

Background - The Wolfpack had finished 4th in the Atlantic Coast Conference and were playing in a bowl game for the third consecutive year. This was their first appearance in the Gator Bowl since 1992. Notre Dame was in their first season under Tyrone Willingham and in their first bowl game since 2001. This was Notre Dame's first Gator Bowl appearance since 1999.

2003 Gator Bowl	Line	1	-	2	-	3	-	4	-	Final
#17 NC State	(-1.0)	0	-	21	-	0	-	7	-	28
#11 Notre Dame	(41.0)	3	-	0	-	3	-	0	-	6

Scoring Summary
Notre Dame – Setta 23 yard field Goal
NC State – McClendon 2 yard run (Kiker kick)
NC State – McClendon 3 yard run (Kiker kick)
NC State – Cotchery 9 yard pass from Rivers (Kiker kick)
Notre Dame – Setta 41 yard Field Goal
NC State – Berton 7 yard pass from Rivers (Kiker kick)

Associated Press Gator Bowl Game Summary - New coach, same result. No. 17 North Carolina State knocked out Carlyle Holiday early, then added to Notre Dame's bowl woes by routing the 12th-ranked Fighting Irish, 28-6, in the Gator Bowl. Phillip Rivers picked apart Notre Dame's secondary in the first half, completing 13-of-15 passes for 134 yards in the opening 30 minutes and directing three long scoring drives in the second quarter. North Carolina State (11-3) closed the most successful season in school history on a high note. After setting a school record by winning their first nine games, the Wolfpack endured a three-game losing streak. But they ended the year with wins over Florida State and Notre Dame. Safety Rod Johnson led North Carolina State's dominant defensive effort with three interceptions. The three picks set a record for a Notre Dame opponent. Tyrone Willingham brought some excitement back to Notre Dame in his first year in South Bend, but the season ended in disappointing fashion for the Fighting Irish (10-3), who suffered their sixth straight bowl loss. Notre Dame lost its last two games by a combined score of 72-19. The Fighting Irish ended the regular season with a 44-13 setback at Southern California. North Carolina State pounded Notre Dame physically as tight end Gary Godsey and Holiday suffered injuries in the first quarter and did not return. Godsey suffered a leg injury on Notre Dame's first series and hobbled to the locker room on crutches. Holiday's 12-pass completion to Arnaz Battle gave the Fighting Irish a first-and-goal on the North Carolina State 2 on their next possession, but the Wolfpack's defense stiffened. After Ryan Grant was held to a one-yard gain on first down, Holiday was knocked out of the game after being stopped for no gain on second down. He was slammed to the turf by linebacker Antonio Burnette, suffering a separated shoulder. Notre Dame settled for Nicholas Setta's 23-yard field goal and a 3-0 lead with 5:12 left in the first quarter, but the goal line stand clearly changed the complexion of the game. North Carolina State scored touchdowns on its next three possessions, starting with a 96-yard drive, and opened a 21-3 lead at halftime. Backup Pat Dillingham finished the game at Quarterback for Notre Dame and was ineffective. The Fighting Irish came into the game ranked 107th out of 117 teams in Division I-A in total offense and played like it. Dillingham completed 19-of-37 passes for 166 yards, a large chuck of its on Notre Dame's final drive. To add to the frustration, the Fighting Irish reached the North Carolina State 1 before turning the ball over on downs in the final minute. The six points matched a bowl low for Notre Dame, which suffered a 40-6 loss to Nebraska in the 1973 Orange Bowl. The Fighting Irish were held to just 86 yards on the ground. The defense came out inspired in the third quarter, giving the Fighting Irish a chance to climb back into the game. Notre Dame twice drive into North Carolina State territory but could only come away with Setta's 41-yard field goal with 1:44 left in the third. The Wolfpack put away the contest on Rivers' seven-yard TD pass to Sean Berton with 10:41 left in the fourth quarter. Rivers finished 23-of-37 passes for 228 yards and a pair of touchdowns. Jerricho Cotchery repeatedly burned the Irish, catching 10 passes for 127 yards. Freshman T.A. McLendon capped off North Carolina State's first two scoring drives with TD runs of two and three yards. Rivers tossed a nine-yard TD pass to Cotchery to make it 21-3 with 1:16 left in the first half.

2003 Outback Bowl

The 2003 Outback Bowl was held on January 1, 2003 at Raymond James Stadium in Tampa, Florida. The Michigan Wolverines, third-place finishers in the Big Ten Conference, defeated the Florida Gators, who finished second the Eastern Division of the Southeastern Conference, 38-30. Michigan running back Chris Perry was named the game's MVP.

2003 Outback Bowl	Line	1	-	2	-	3	-	4	-	Final
#22 Florida	(47.5)	0	-	16	-	7	-	7	-	30
#12 Michigan	(Pk)	7	-	14	-	14	-	3	-	38

Scoring Summary
Michigan – Perry 4 yard run (Finley kick)
Florida - Graham 2 yard run (Leach kick)
Florida - Graham 1 yard run (Run failed)
Michigan - Perry 1 yard run (Finley kick)
Florida - Leach 29 yard field goal
Michigan - Bellamy 8 yard pass from Navarro (Hines kick)
Florida - Ratliff 33 yard pass from Grossman (Leach kick)
Michigan - Perry 7 yard run (Finley kick)
Michigan - Perry 12 yard run (Finley kick)
Florida - Walker 3 yard pass from Grossman (Leach kick)
Michigan - Finley 33 yard field goal

Bentley Historical Library 2003 OUTBACK BOWL GAME SUMMARY - Michigan claimed a 38-30 victory in a back-and-forth affair against No 22 Florida in the 2003 Outback Bowl at Raymond James Stadium. Tailback Chris Perry earned Outback Bowl MVP honors after setting a bowl game record and a modem era Michigan bowl record with four touchdowns. Perry matched his career high with 28 carries for 85 yards and four TDs and added a career-best six receptions for 108 yards. Quarterback John Navarre completed 21-of-36 passes for a career-high 319 yards and one TD. Defensively, Victor Hobson sealed the win for the Wolverines with his interception on Florida's final drive. Hobson tallied a career-best 12 tackles and two tackles for loss. Michigan took advantage of a Florida turnover as Perry scored on a four-yard touchdown run late in the first quarter. U-M gained possession at the Florida three-yard line after recovering an errant shotgun snap. Florida, however, answered to take a 13-7 lead early in the second quarter on a pair of TD runs by tailback Ernest Graham. U-M took control of the game on a 12-play scoring drive as Perry leaped over the goal line on a fourth-down play from the one-yard line. The Gators regained the lead, 16-14, with 1:37 left in the first half as placekicker Matt Leach connected on a 29-yard field goal, but Michigan responded to take a 21-16 halftime advantage as Navarre completed an eight-yard touchdown pass to Bellamy with 27 seconds left. Florida scored on its opening possession of the second half to gain a 23-21 lead. The Wolverines answered the Gators' TD and took the lead for good, 28-23, on a seven-yard TD run by Perry. U-M extended its lead to 35-23 as Perry scored his fourth TD of the game, a 12-yard run through the middle of the defense. Florida trimmed the deficit to 35-30 with 8:21 remaining as Grossman fired a three-yard TD pass to tight end Aaron Walker. On the Gator's next possession, a Hobson sack forced Florida to punt the ball away. U-M got the ball back at its 34-yard line and proceeded to put the game away as kicker Adam Finley connected on a 33-yard field goal for a 38-30 lead with 2:20 left. The Gators attempted to mount one final drive to tie the game. After reaching the Wolverine 37-yard line, Florida tried a little trickery on a wide receiver reverse pass, but it was intercepted by Hobson and returned 42 yards to seal Michigan's victory.

2003 Capital One Bowl

The 2003 Capital One Bowl was between the Penn State Nittany Lions and the Auburn Tigers on January 1, 2003, at the Citrus Bowl in Orlando, Florida. Auburn won the game 13–9; Auburn running back Ronnie Brown was the game's MVP, rushing for 184 yards and two touchdowns.

2003 Capital One Bowl	Line	1	-	2	-	3	-	4	-	Final
#10 Penn State	(-7.0)	3	-	3	-	0	-	3	-	9
#19 Auburn	(49.5)	0	-	0	-	7	-	6	-	13

Scoring Summary
Penn State – Gould 21 yard Field goal
Penn State – Gould 27 yard Field goal
Auburn – Brown 1 yard run (Duval kick)
Penn State – Gould 32 yard Field goal
Auburn – Brown 17 yard run (Kick failed)

Associated Press Capital One Bowl Game Summary - Ronnie Brown scored on a 17-yard touchdown run with 2:19 left and outplayed Heisman Trophy finalist Larry Johnson as No. 19 Auburn beat 10th-ranked

Penn State 13-9 Wednesday in the Capital One Bowl. Brown rushed 37 times for 184 yards and two touchdowns, and the Tigers (9-4) shut down Penn State's offensive stars for their first bowl win since 1998. Johnson, who rushed for 2,015 regular-season yards, was limited to 72 yards on 20 carries as Penn State (9-4). The Nittany Lions fell to 1-4 when he failed to reach 100 yards. Penn State Quarterback Zach Mills was temporarily benched in the second half and couldn't convert two late drives into points. He threw two straight incompletions before getting intercepted by Roderick Hood. That gave the Tigers the ball at Penn State's 27 with 1:49 left, but four straight runs by Brown only worked the clock down to 42 seconds. With no timeouts left, Mills moved it to Auburn's 43 with a 14-yard scramble and two short passes to Matt Kranchick. His shuffle pass under pressure fell short of a first down on fourth down. Penn State's four losses came by a total of 20 points, as coach Joe Paterno failed to pad his NCAA record 20 bowl wins after a two-year postseason absence. The Tigers beat their third Top 10 opponent of the season. Brown, voted the game's MVP, passed the 1,000-yard mark despite not making his first start until the eighth game and missing the regular-season finale against Alabama with a sprained ankle. Down 9-7, the Tigers started their winning drive at Penn State's 40 with 5:05 left after Robbie Gould's 36-yard punt. Brown carried on five of the six plays, but Jason Campbell's pass on the two-point attempt fell short. Mills' first five passes of the second half fell incomplete and he finished 8-of-24 for 67 yards and was replaced on two series by Michael Robinson. All-Big Ten receiver Bryant Johnson was held without a catch. The Nittany Lions' only points came on Gould's field goals of 21, 27 and 31 yards. He missed a 33-yarder in the first half. The Tigers borrowed a chapter from Paterno's playbook to take a 7-6 lead with 3:52 left in the third quarter. They ran it 13 straight times and milked nearly seven minutes off the clock, with Brown twisting into the end zone on fourth down from the goal line. He carried on the first six plays and the last four, gaining 59 yards on the drive. The Nittany Lions had gone nearly 10 quarters without giving up a point in the postseason. Penn State lost 10 yards on the next drive, setting up Auburn in good field position. The Tigers drove to the 26 before Jimmy Kennedy stuffed Campbell's Quarterback sneak inches short on fourth down. Then, the Nittany Lions replaced struggling Mills with the do-it-all Michael Robinson. Robinson hit Tony Johnson for a 34-yarder and scrambled for 20 yards down to the 19. The drive stalled but Gould's 31-yard field goal - his third of the game - gave Penn State a 9-7 lead with 10:10 left. The Nittany Lions were stymied after that. Neither team managed much offensively, with Auburn gaining 278 yards and Penn State 268. The much-hyped running backs were trumped by turnovers, costly penalties and not-so special teams in the first half. Johnson, who had 1,037 yards in his last four games, lost 6 yards on his first five carries. The Tigers, however, had two turnovers and 74 yards in penalties and got Damon Duval's 24-yard field goal try blocked by Derek Wake to trail 6-0 at half-time. Campbell lost a fumble on the Tigers' third play at their own 15. Penn State had to settle for Gould's 21-yarder, and the offense was similarly ineffective from that point.

2003 Cotton Bowl Classic

The 2003 SBC Cotton Bowl Classic was between the Texas Longhorns and the LSU Tigers on January 1, 2003, at the Cotton Bowl in Dallas, Texas.

2003 Cotton Bowl Classic	Line	1	-	2	-	3	-	4	-	Final
LSU	(47.0)	10	-	7	-	0	-	3	-	20
#9 Texas	(-10.5)	7	-	14	-	7	-	7	-	35

Scoring Summary
LSU – Corbello 26 yard FG
Texas – Jackson 46 yard fumble return (Mangum kick)
LSU – Toefield 20 yard pass from Randall (Corbello kick)
LSU – Davis 10 yard run (Corbello kick)
Texas – R. Williams 51 yard pass from Simms (Mangum kick)
Texas – Benson 1 yard run (Mangum kick)
Texas – R. Williams 39 yard run (Mangum kick)
Texas – I. Williams 8 yard pass from Simms (Mangum kick)
LSU – Corbello 39 yard FG

Cotton Bowl Classic Game Summary - Forty years to the day after Texas and LSU's last meeting, the Longhorns and Tigers picked up where they left off – at the SBC Cotton Bowl Classic. Their last encounter came in the 1963 Cotton Bowl as LSU knocked off an undefeated Longhorn squad, 13-0. This time around, Texas came away from New Year's Day as victors after an opportunistic Longhorn defense forced three turnovers en route to a memorable 35-20 win in the 68th Classic. The No. 9 Longhorns (11-2) grabbed their 11th Field Scovell Trophy as champions of the Cotton Bowl and posted consecutive 11-win seasons for the first time in school history. In the opening period, LSU (8-5) seemed on the verge of running away to another Classic upset, holding Texas to only three offensive plays and no first downs. It was the Texas defense that opened the scoring for the Longhorns. Senior linebacker Cory Redding blew by his blocker and knocked the ball loose from LSU Quarterback Marcus Randall. Linebacker Lee Jackson snatched the ball off the ground and raced 46 yards for a touchdown to make it 7-3. It was the first touchdown off a fumble return in Cotton Bowl history. The quick score forced the Longhorn defense to stay on the field, and LSU took advantage. Randall marched the Tiger offense down the field and connected with running back LaBrandon Toefield on a 20-yard pass to give LSU a 10-7 lead after the first quarter. Randall looked like an instant SBC Cotton Bowl Hall of Famer as he led the Tigers to scores on three of their first four possessions. LSU extended its lead to 17-7 early in the second. On a designed QB draw play, Randall picked up 76 yards before UT's Nathan Vasher finally pulled him down. Domanick Davis finished the drive with a 10-yard run up the middle. LSU had 287 yards on those first four possessions and was averaging 8.2 yards per play. The Longhorn defense was forced to adjust, and Texas finally turned on the light switch in the second quarter. The combination of Texas Quarterback Chris Simms and split end Roy Williams got the offense moving and LSU couldn't find a way to stop the duo. Williams cut into LSU's 17-7 lead three minutes into the second quarter when Simms connected with the junior on a quick post route for a 51-yard touchdown. Texas caught LSU in single coverage on Williams again later in the second period. Williams turned a short post pass into a long gain, going 75 yards before stepping out of bounds at the 5. Cedric Benson finished off the drive with a 1-yard dive into the end zone to give the Longhorns a 21-17 lead heading into the locker rooms at the half. Williams put the game solidly in Texas' favor in the third quarter when he cut back twice inside LSU defenders on a reverse and scored a 39-yard touchdown. The touchdown play was set up by another fumble recovery by linebacker Lee Jackson. In all, Williams produced 181 yards on five touches en route to being voted Outstanding Offensive Player. Outstanding Defensive Player honors went to senior defensive end Cory Redding, who in the second half forced LSU's offense out of rhythm. Texas went to increased zone blitzes, and the changes allowed Redding to harass Randall and Toefield. Redding finished with eight tackles, including four tackles for a loss of 23 yards. After gaining 310 yards in the first half, LSU's offense was limited to 131 the rest of the game. The Longhorns pulled away at the beginning of the fourth quarter when Simms connected with Ivan Williams on an 8-yard pass to extend the lead to 35-17. LSU added a John Corbello 39-yard field goal with 7:41 remaining in the game. After his final game as a Longhorn, Redding let his emotions come rushing out after walking off the Cotton Bowl field a winner and accepting the Outstanding Defensive Player trophy.

2003 Rose Bowl

The 2003 Rose Bowl was played on January 1, 2003. It was the 89th Rose Bowl game. It was a match-up between the Oklahoma Sooners and the Washington State Cougars. Nate Hybl who played Quarterback for the Sooners, was named the Rose Bowl Player of The Game.

Teams - Prior to the BCS, this pairing never would have occurred. Oklahoma came into the game Big 12 Champions, while Washington State came in co-champions of the Pac-10. The Rose Bowl normally features the champions of the Big Ten and the Pac-10. However, because the Buckeyes had finished #2 in the BCS, they were set to play in the 2003 Fiesta Bowl for the national championship against Miami (Fla.) earlier in the season, Ohio State had defeated Washington State 25-7. The Orange Bowl had the next pick after the Fiesta Bowl pairing, and #3 (#5 BCS) Iowa was chosen. The Rose Bowl had the next BCS selection. The next, best available team to choose was #8 (#7 BCS) Oklahoma, who won the Big 12 Championship Game, to play Pac-10 winner Washington State. When it came time for the Orange Bowl and Sugar Bowl to make a second pick, both wanted USC. However, a BCS rule stated that if two bowls want the same team, the bowl with the higher payoff has the option. The Orange Bowl immediately extended an at-large bid to the number 5 ranked Trojans and paired them with at-large number 3 Iowa in a Big Ten/Pac-10 "Rose Bowl" matchup in the 2003 Orange Bowl. Rose Bowl committee executive director Mitch Dorger was not pleased with the results. This left the Sugar Bowl with #14 BCS Florida State, the winner of the Atlantic Coast Conference. Notre Dame at 10-2 and #9 in the BCS standings was invited to the 2003 Gator Bowl. Kansas State at #8 also was left out.

2003 Rose Bowl	Line	1	-	2	-	3	-	4	-	Final
#8 Oklahoma	(-6.5)	3	-	14	-	3	-	14	-	34
#7 Washington State	(55.0)	0	-	0	-	0	-	14	-	14

Scoring Summary
Oklahoma - DiCarlo 45 yard field goal
Oklahoma - Savage 12 yard pass from Hybl (DiCarlo kick)
Oklahoma - Perkins 51 yard punt return (DiCarlo kick)
Oklahoma - DiCarlo 30 yard field goal
Oklahoma - Fagan 9 yard pass from Hybl (DiCarlo kick)
Washington State - Riley 37 yard pass from Gesser (Dunning kick)
Oklahoma - Griffin 19 yard run (DiCarlo kick)
Washington State - Moore 89 yard kickoff return (Dunning kick)

Associated Press Rose Bowl Game Summary - This Rose Bowl presented by PlayStation 2 was one to remember for the Sooners. And it was one Mike Price would sooner forget. Price chose to coach seventh-ranked Washington State in the bowl game after accepting the Alabama coaching job two weeks ago. But No. 8 Oklahoma gave him rude send-off, winning 34-14 Wednesday. Washington State (10-3) was held to a season-low 243 yards -- just 4 on the ground -- and didn't score until the final six minutes, by which time Oklahoma had a 27-0 lead. Jason Gesser, the Cougars' star Quarterback, was 17-of-34 for 239 yards and two interceptions and was sacked six times. Oklahoma (12-2) was burned by deep passes in its two losses, but Gesser became another topflight Quarterback handcuffed by the Sooners. They had previously throttled Seneca Wallace of Iowa State, Kliff Kingsbury of Texas Tech and Chris Simms of Texas. While the defense was controlling Washington State, Nate Hybl was solid at Quarterback and Quentin Griffin had his 10th straight 100-yard game. Hybl, like Griffin playing his final game, was 19-of-29 for 240 yards, two touchdowns and no interceptions. He was voted the game's MVP. Griffin, who had 1,740 yards during the regular season, had 144 yards on 30 carries and scored the Sooners' final touchdown on a 19-yard run. The Sooners outgained Washington State by a 2-to-1 margin in the first half but had just a 3-0 lead before scoring twice in the final 1:51. The first touchdown came on a 12-yard pass from Hybl to Antwone Savage. Hybl also had completions of 30 and 19 yards in the 65-yard drive. The Cougars were forced to punt on their next possession and Antonio Perkins returned the kick 51 yards for a touchdown that made it 17-0. Perkins was due -- he had two other big returns wiped out by penalties in the first quarter. After being shut out in the first half for the first time this season, the Cougars put together a nice drive to open the third quarter. They moved from their 8 to the Oklahoma 41 before Gesser was intercepted on a tipped ball. Oklahoma turned that into a field goal and a 20-0 lead. Washington State moved to the Oklahoma 34 early in the fourth quarter but turned it over on downs, failing to convert a fourth-and-1 play. The Sooners then drove 66 yards in 11 plays, with Hybl hitting Curtis Fagan on a 9-yard scoring pass to make it 27-0 with 8:02 to play. The Cougars came in averaging just under 35 points but didn't score until Gesser's 37-yard pass Jerome Riley with 6:08 remaining, avoiding their first shutout since 1984. After Oklahoma's final touchdown, Sammy Moore scored on an 89-yard kickoff return for the Cougars. The Sooners were playing in their 36th bowl game but their first Rose Bowl. They got invited after the Orange Bowl picked Iowa and Southern California for its game. That left the Rose Bowl without a Pac-10-Big 10 matchup for the first time since 1947, not counting last year when this game was the site of the BCS national championship game between Miami and Nebraska. Price will get to see the Sooners again shortly. His second game as the Crimson Tide's coach will be against Oklahoma. The crowd of 86,848 on a sunny, 70-degree day was the smallest at this game since 1944, when 68,000 watched USC beat Washington 29-0.

Aftermath - This game drew one of the fewest attendance numbers in the modern history of the Rose Bowl. It was the first time that the stadium held less than the nominal capacity for the Rose Bowl game since before the 1947 Rose Bowl and the agreement between the PAC-10 and Big Ten conferences. The 1944 Rose Bowl had the third smallest crowd played in the Rose Bowl stadium at 68,000. The 1931 Rose Bowl had the second smallest crowd at 60,000. The smallest crowd at the Rose Bowl stadium was the 1934 Rose Bowl at 35,000. University of Michigan coach Bo Schembechler remarked, "Didn't watch it," when asked what he thought of this game and about the Nebraska-Miami Rose Bowl the previous year During the early 2010s cycle of conference realignment, the Pac-10 eyed six Big 12 members as possible additions to the conference, including Oklahoma. However, the only Big 12 School that did join the Pac-10 (now the Pacific-12) was Colorado.

2003 Sugar Bowl

The 2003 Sugar Bowl was held on January 1, 2003. This 69th edition to the Sugar Bowl featured the Florida State Seminoles, and the Georgia Bulldogs. Florida State came into the game 9–4 and ranked 14th in the BCS, whereas Georgia came into the game 12–1 and ranked 3rd in the BCS. Seminoles defensive tackle Darnell Dockett was suspended from the game after pleading guilty to a misdemeanor theft charge.

2003 Sugar Bowl	Line	1	-	2	-	3	-	4	-	Final
#16 Florida State	(49.0)	0	-	7	-	6	-	0	-	13
#4 Georgia	(-8.0)	3	-	14	-	6	-	3	-	26

Scoring Summary
Georgia - Bennett 23 yard field goal
Florida State - Boldin 5 yard pass from Walker (Beitia kick
Georgia - Thornton 71 yard interception return (Bennett kick)
Georgia - Edwards 37 yard pass from Shockley (Bennett kick)
Georgia - Bennett 42 yard field goal
Georgia - Bennett 25 yard field goal
Florida State - Thorpe 40 yard pass from Boldin (Boldin rush failed)
Georgia - Bennett 35 yard field goal

Associated Press Sugar Bowl Game Summary - Georgia finished its memorable season in style, though the Bulldogs made it sound like the Nokia Sugar Bowl was only the beginning. Certainly, they don't plan to go another 20 years between championships. MVP Musa Smith rushed for 145 yards, Bruce Thornton returned an interception for a touchdown and backup Quarterback D.J. Shockley tossed a scoring pass in his only throw of the night. Billy Bennett kicked four field goals as the Bulldogs went conservative, throwing a season-low 15 passes. All they had to do was let Fabian Walker, making his first start at Quarterback for the Seminoles, beat himself. Walker obliged, throwing two interceptions and also losing a fumble. The Seminoles had only one turnover in their last four regular-season games. The Bulldogs (13-1) became the first team in school history to win 13 games, capping a breakthrough season in which Richt steered the program back to national prominence in just his second season. Richt even got the satisfaction of beating his mentor. He served 14 years on Bobby Bowden's staff at Florida State before moving to Georgia in 2001. Plenty of Georgia fans were on hand to savor their team's return to the national stage. Red and black dominated the Superdome as the Bulldogs made their first Sugar Bowl appearance since the 1982 season -- also the year of their last Southeastern Conference championship. Florida State (9-5), playing in the Sugar Bowl for the sixth time in 15 years, was viewed as the most unworthy team in the Bowl Championship Series. Their performance did little to change that perception, handing Bowden his first five-loss season since 1981. In all fairness, the Seminoles might have given a better showing at full strength. But they lost their top two Quarterbacks and had to go with third choice Walker, who had thrown only eight passes in his career. Why was Walker playing? Adrian McPherson was kicked off the team in late November for allegedly stealing a check, while Chris Rix was suspended from the bowl after he overslept and missed a final exam. Walker, a Georgia native, threw both interceptions when trying to force passes to well-covered receivers while being pressured. Thornton took his interception 71 yards for a touchdown, putting the Bulldogs ahead for good with 6½ minutes left in the first half. Walker was 7-of-12 for 68 yards. On Florida State's first offensive play of the second half, Walker was stripped of the ball by Will Thompson and Ken Veal recovered for the Bulldogs, setting up Bennett's third field goal of the night and a comfortable 23-7 lead. The Seminoles gave star receiver Anquan Boldin a shot at Quarterback, hoping he could spark the offense. It might have worked, too, if Talman Gardner had not dropped a perfectly thrown deep pass near the goal line. Boldin hopped up and down in dismay after the ball slipped through Gardner's hands. On the next play, Boldin bruised his left hand when dragged down behind the line, knocking him out for the rest of the first half. After getting his hand checked out, Boldin came back to throw a 40-yard touchdown pass to Craphonso Thorpe on the final play of the third quarter. It wasn't enough. Boldin also caught a touchdown pass, hauling down a 5-yarder from Walker early in the second quarter to give the Seminoles a short-lived 7-3 lead. Georgia's offense didn't do much, managing just one touchdown on its own -- and even that score was set up by Damian Gary's 26-yard punt return. Shockley, who played four series in relief of starter David Greene, took advantage of Gary's long return right away, lofting a 37-yard touchdown pass to Terrence Edwards on his only throw of the night. On his way down the field to celebrate, Shockley jawed with a couple of Florida State players, undoubtedly a holdover from a fumble on his first possession. That was Georgia's only turnover. The Bulldogs went conservative, relying on one of the nation's top-ranked defenses to shut down the Seminoles. Smith had 18 of his 23 carries in the second half, rushing for 108 yards over the final two quarters. Richt saw no reason to open the offense. The Bulldogs allowed just 262 yards. Bennett connected on field goals of 23, 42, 25 and 35 yards to give him 130 points for the season, breaking Garrison Heart's school record of 126 in 1992. Florida State, which earned an automatic BCS bid by winning the Atlantic Coast Conference, was the only team playing in a major bowl with more than two losses. For the second year in a row, the Seminoles failed to win 10 games -- a standard that used to be automatic in Tallahassee. In fact, Florida State has lost nine games the last two years -- equaling its total number of defeats from 1992-99.

2003 Orange Bowl

The 2003 FedEx Orange Bowl game was between the Iowa Hawkeyes and the USC Trojans on January 2, 2003, at Pro Player Stadium in Miami Gardens, Florida. The Orange Bowl was first played in 1935, and the 2003 game represented the 69th edition of the Orange Bowl. The contest was televised on ABC.

Teams - Prior to the BCS, the New Year's Day pairings never would have occurred. The Rose Bowl normally features the champions of the Big Ten (in 2002, the Ohio State Buckeyes) and the Pac-10. However, because the Buckeyes had finished No. 2 in the BCS, they were set to play in the 2003 Fiesta Bowl for the national championship against Miami (Fla.) The Orange Bowl had the next pick after the Fiesta Bowl pairing, and No. 3 (#5 BCS) Iowa was chosen. The Rose Bowl had the next BCS selection. The next, best available team to choose was No. 8 (#7 BCS) Oklahoma, who won the Big 12 Championship Game, to play Pac-10 winner Washington State in the 2003 Rose Bowl. When it came time for the Orange Bowl and

Sugar Bowl to make a second pick, both wanted USC. However, a BCS rule stated that if two bowls want the same team, the bowl with the higher payoff has the option. The Orange Bowl immediately extended an at-large bid to the number 5 ranked Trojans and paired them with at-large number 3 Iowa in a Big Ten/Pac-10 "Rose Bowl" matchup in the 2003 Orange Bowl.

2003 Orange Bowl	Line	1	-	2	-	3	-	4	-	Final
#5 USC	(-6.0)	7	-	3	-	14	-	14	-	38
#3 Iowa	(57.0)	10	-	0	-	0	-	7	-	17

Scoring Summary
Iowa – Jones 100 yard kickoff return (Kaeding kick)
USC – Fargas 4 yard run (Killeen kick)
Iowa – Kaeding 35 yard field goal
USC – Killeen 35 yard field goal
USC – Williams 18 yard pass from Palmer (Killeen kick)
USC – Fargas 50 yard run (Killeen kick)
USC – McCullough 5 yard run (Killeen kick)
USC – Byrd 6 yard run (Killeen kick)
Iowa – Brown 18 yard pass from Banks (Kaeding kick)

Associated Press Orange Bowl Game Summary - Carson Palmer has yet another trophy for his shelf: Orange Bowl MVP. The Heisman Trophy winner dominated his duel with Heisman runner-up Brad Banks, throwing for 303 yards and a touchdown to help No. 5 Southern California beat No. 3 Iowa 38-17 Thursday night in the FedEx Orange Bowl. Palmer led scoring drives of 79, 80, 99, 85 and 61 yards, helping the Trojans to a 16-minute advantage in time of possession. They mounted long touchdown marches on their first three possessions of the second half to blow open a game that was 10-10 at halftime. Banks was limited to 204 yards passing and failed to lead the Hawkeyes' normally high-powered offense to the end zone until the final minute. Their biggest play came when C.J. Jones returned the opening kickoff 100 yards for a touchdown, an Orange Bowl record. Southern California (11-2) beat a Top 25 team for The Trojans outscored UCLA, Notre Dame and Iowa 134-51 over their final three games, a showing that might be impressive enough to vault them to second in the final rankings behind the Fiesta Bowl winner between No. 1 Miami and No. 2 Ohio State. That would be USC's highest finish since 1979. Palmer completed 21 of 31 passes, feasting on a defense that ranked last in the Big Ten against the pass. His 65-yard bomb to Kareem Kelly set up Southern Cal's first score, but mostly Palmer made short throws to keep drives alive. Banks, a Florida native who had dozens of relatives watching from the stands, went 15-for-36 and threw his first interception since Oct. 19. Iowa's muscle was a concern for Southern California coming into the game, but instead the fleet Trojans wore down the Hawkeyes. USC gained 363 yards in the second half to finish with 550. The matchup was dubbed the Rose Bowl of the East because Pasadena is the more traditional ultimate postseason reward for both teams, but USC thrived in the unfamiliar setting. Justin Fargas rushed for 122 yards, including touchdowns of 4 and 50 yards. Williams caught six passes for 99 yards, including his 14th touchdown reception of the season to tie an NCAA freshman record. After Jones scored on the opening kickoff, more than 40,000 Iowa fans in attendance had little to cheer about. While Iowa fans sat mostly silent, such former Trojans stars as Keyshawn Johnson, Tony Boselli and Rodney Peete rooted from their team's sideline. There were no sightings of O.J. Simpson, who lives in Miami and showed up at a USC practice last week. The Hawkeyes were hurt by 13 penalties, two turnovers and several missed opportunities. In the first half, they had first-and-goal at the 2 and at the 1, but they came away with only three points from the two possessions. A sack by Matt Grootegoed stymied the first threat, and Iowa settled for a 35-yard field goal by Nate Kaeding. The Hawkeyes earned a first down at the 1 with 10 seconds left in the half, but after Banks overthrew Brown in the end zone, they sent in the field goal team. Consecutive false-start penalties pushed the ball to the 11, and Bernard Riley then blocked Kaeding's 29-yard attempt, ending the half with the score tied. Iowa never recovered from that deflating sequence. USC took the lead for good by driving 80 yards on the first possession of the second half and scoring on Williams' acrobatic catch. A punt then pinned the Trojans at their 1, and on third down a scrambling Palmer was stopped short of a first down. But Bob Sanders was flagged for a late hit, sustaining a drive that ended with Fargas' long touchdown sprint. Another Iowa punt was followed by another USC score, Sultan McCullough's 4-yard run. Playing for the first time since Nov. 16, the Hawkeyes still managed a quick start. Jones took the opening kickoff at the goal line, broke into the clear thanks to a block by Jermelle Lewis and scored untouched. The Trojans quickly came back. Palmer's first pass was negated by a penalty. His second was the long strike to Kelly, setting up Fargas' 4-yard touchdown run. USC spent much of the second quarter in Iowa territory but couldn't score until the final 72 seconds, when Ryan Killeen kicked a 35-yard field goal after Lewis lost a fumble at midfield.

2003 Fiesta Bowl (BCS National Championship Game)

The 2003 Tostitos Fiesta Bowl took place on January 3, 2003 in Tempe, Arizona at Sun Devil Stadium. The Ohio State Buckeyes defeated the Miami Hurricanes by a score of 31–24 in double overtime. It also served as the BCS National Championship Game for the 2002 NCAA Division I-A football season. The game was the second overtime result in either the Bowl Championship Series, or its predecessors, the Bowl Alliance or the Bowl Coalition, the first being the January 1, 2000 Orange Bowl between Alabama and Michigan.

Game summary - The Buildup - Throughout the season the defending national champion Miami Hurricanes continued a historic winning streak. The regular season ended with a perfect record extending the streak to 34 games. Their roster included future NFL players on both offense and defense including Willis McGahee, Ken Dorsey, Andre Johnson, Kellen Winslow Jr., Jonathan Vilma, D.J. Williams, William Joseph, Jerome McDougle, Antrel Rolle, Kelly Jennings, and Sean Taylor. Their offensive line had also produced 3 straight 1,000 yard seasons by 3 different running backs and were leading the nation in fewest sacks allowed. They were an overwhelming favorite to win their 2nd consecutive national title. Ohio State had started the season ranked #13 after losing to South Carolina in the Outback Bowl the previous year. It was head Coach Jim Tressel's second year with the team, and he had the experienced Buckeyes looking to win the Big Ten title. After gaining national respect by beating a top 10 Washington State team, Ohio State would go on to ride their strong defense and surprising offense to a 13-0 regular season. Freshman star Maurice Clarett highlighted their elite rushing attack, while Quarterback Craig Krenzel managed the games well by throwing to talented wideouts Michael Jenkins and Chris Gamble. They had won 6 games by 7 points or fewer, and the last 3 games by a slim margin of 16 points. The Buckeyes took advantage and finished their season with a close win against Michigan, who were ranked 9th nationally. They held on to a 14-9 lead with an interception in the end zone by safety Will Allen in the final seconds. Even though they were undefeated, the Buckeyes were heading into the Fiesta Bowl as 2 touchdown underdogs. But they had a lot of motivation from strong leaders like 3x All-American safety Mike Doss.

2003 Fiesta Bowl	Line	1	-	2	-	3	-	4	-	OT	-	2OT	-	Final
#2 Ohio State	(49.0)	0	-	14	-	3	-	0	-	7	-	7	-	31
#1 Miami	(-12.0)	7	-	0	-	7	-	3	-	7	-	0	-	24

Scoring Summary
Miami – Parrish 25 yard pass from Dorsey (Sievers kick)
Ohio State – Krenzel 1 yard run (Nugent kick)
Ohio State – Clarett 7 yard run (Nugent kick)
Ohio State – Nugent 44 yard field goal
Miami – McGahee 9 yard run (Sievers kick)
Miami – Sievers 40 yard field goal
Miami – Winslow. 7 yard pass from Dorsey (Sievers kick)
Ohio State – Krenzel 1 yard run (Nugent kick)
Ohio State – Clarett 5 yard run (Nugent kick)

Miami Media Guide Fiesta Bowl Game Summary - Miami's 34-game winning streak came to an end in as Ohio State defeated the Hurricanes 31-24 in double overtime to win the Fiesta Bowl and the BCS National Championship. Maurice Clarett scored his second touchdown on a five-yard run in the second overtime. Craig Krenzel had a pair of touchdown runs for the Buckeyes (14-0), who ended Miami's winning streak -- the sixth-longest in college football history -- in a game of high drama that was prolonged by a controversial pass interference call. It was the first-ever overtime in a BCS title game, despite Miami turning the ball over five times and losing Willis McGahee to a knee injury in the fourth quarter. On the final play of regulation, Todd Sievers kicked a 40-yard field goal to tie it at 17-17. Kellen Winslow Jr. caught a seven-yard TD pass from Ken Dorsey in the first overtime. A controversial pass interference penalty allowed Ohio State to tie the game. On 4th-and-goal from the 5, Glenn Sharpe batted away a pass intended for Chris Gamble. Miami began its celebration, but Sharpe was flagged. Krenzel then scored on a one-yard run.

The Aftermath - The amount of future NFL talent that played in the game is considered highly exceptional. Of the 43 players who started in the game (OSU's Chris Gamble started on both offense and defense), 37 of them were eventually NFL draft picks (including 18 first-rounders). Of the 100 players who played in the game, 52 went on be drafted and 58 went on to play in the NFL. The pass at the end of the first overtime was ruled incomplete by the side judge. A few seconds later, another official threw a flag, initially signaling holding before changing the call to a pass interference against Miami. When asked why it took him so long to make the call, official Terry Porter said he wanted to make sure that the call was correct, explaining "I replayed it in my mind. I wanted to make double sure that it was the right call." "The Call" has since been defended by most sportswriters as a good one, however a few sportswriters have denounced the call, including Sports Illustrated's Rick Reilly, and CBS Sports Dennis Dodd, who wrote: I saw a piece somewhere before the BCS title game on Porter and his refusal to back down from doing anything wrong. I've written about his call extensively over the year. It wasn't until I saw that piece again recently that I realize how much Porter choked. What the piece failed to mention was that the Big 12 tried to spin it a different way. The flag wasn't for pass interference, they said, but HOLDING. It appears that Miami's Glenn Sharpe did hold Chris Gamble off the line, but that would make the call even more ridiculous. That means that Porter threw the flag a good 10 seconds after the snap. It should also be noted that Dodd later changed his opinion and wrote the following: Terry Porter was right. Six and a half months after the most controversial call of the Bowl Championship Series era, the Big 12 field judge has been vindicated. The call was subsequently validated by the National Association of Sports Officials and was also selected by Referee Magazine as one of the "Best 18 Calls of All Time." "The Call" was also discussed on the ESPN Classic show, The Top 5 Reasons You Can't Blame..., in an episode titled, "The Top 5 Reasons You Can't Blame the Referees for Miami losing the 2003 Fiesta Bowl.

2003 New Orleans Bowl

The 2003 Wyndham New Orleans Bowl featured the North Texas Mean Green and the Memphis Tigers. It was North Texas's third consecutive New Orleans Bowl appearance. Kicker Nick Bazaldua got North Texas on the board first with a 47-yard field goal to give the team an early 3-0 lead. Memphis Quarterback Danny Wimprine scored on a 7-yard touchdown run to give Memphis a 7-3 lead. In the second quarter, Wimprine found Chris Kelley for a 10-yard touchdown pass, and a 14-3 lead. Stephen Gostkowski connected on a 21-yard field goal before halftime, to increase the lead to 17-3. In the third quarter, running back Patrick Cobbs scored on a 35-yard touchdown run to bring the score to 17-10. In the fourth quarter, running back LaKendus Cole scored on a 5-yard touchdown run to increase the lead to 24-10. Patrick Cobbs scored his second touchdown on a 2-yard run to bring the score to 24-17. Stephen Gostkowski finished the scoring with a 42-yard field goal, to make the final 27-17.

2003 New Orleans Bowl	Line	1	-	2	-	3	-	4	-	Final
Memphis	(-4.0)	7	-	10	-	0	-	10	-	27
North Texas	(48.0)	3	-	0	-	7	-	7	-	17

Scoring Summary
North Texas – Bazaldua 47 yard Field goal
Memphis – Wimprine 7 yard run (Gostkowski kick)
Memphis – Kelley 10 yard pass from Wimprine (Gostkowski kick)
Memphis – Gostkowski 21 yard Field Goal
North Texas – Cobbs 35 yard run (Bazaldua kick)
Memphis – Cole 5 yard run (Gostkowski kick)
North Texas – Cobbs 2 yard run (Bazaldua kick)
Memphis – Gostkowski 42 yard Field Goal

Associated Press New Orleans Bowl Game Summary - Memphis made its first bowl appearance in 32 years a successful one. Danny Wimprine passed and rushed for touchdowns in a near flawless first half as the Tigers posted a 27-17 victory over North Texas in the New Orleans Bowl. Wimprine completed 10-of-11 passes for 162 yards in the opening half. He rushed for a seven-yard touchdown and tossed a 10-yard TD strike to Chris Kelly, helping Memphis (9-4) build a 17-3 lead. The Tigers, who tied for third in Conference USA, posted their first bowl victory since defeating San Jose State, 28-9, in the 1971 Pasadena Bowl. Wimprine, a New Orleans native finished 17-of-23 for 254 yards. Memphis burned North Texas with big plays in the first half as a 63-yard completion to Darren Garcia and a 50-yard strike to Mario Pratcher set up the scores. Kevin Moore elected to return the ensuing kickoff from seven yards deep in the end zone, and the move backfired as he fumbled at the 10-yard line. Cato Mott recovered for Memphis, and Stephen Gostkowski kicked a 21-yard field goal to make it 17-3. Patrick Cobbs, the nation's leading rusher, came alive in the second half, scoring two touchdowns for North Texas (9-4) and finishing with 107 yards - 50 below his average. But the turning point came early in the fourth quarter. With North Texas trailing, 17-10, Cobbs' 46-yard run was called back because of a holding penalty. It would have given the Mean Green a first down at the Memphis 13-yard line. Penalties also hurt North Texas as the Mean Green were called for a 15-yard face mask after stopping Memphis on third down on the ensuing possession. The penalty gave the Tigers a first down at the North Texas 21, and they took advantage, grabbing a 24-10 lead on Lakendus Cole's five-yard TD run with 9:08 remaining. North Texas' Adam Hall overthrew his receivers all night, completing just 9-of-21 passes for 152 yards.

2003 GMAC Bowl

The 2003 GMAC Bowl was played on December 18th, 2003 at the Mercedes Benz Superdome between the Louisville Cardinals, and the Miami-Ohio RedHawks.

2003 GMAC Bowl	Line	1	-	2	-	3	-	4	-	Final
Miami-Ohio	(-14.0)	21	-	14	-	0	-	14	-	49
Louisville	(70.5)	0	-	21	-	7	-	0	-	28

Scoring Summary
Miami-Ohio - Larkin 28 yard pass from Roethlisberger (Parseghian Kick)
Miami-Ohio - Murray 2 yard run (Parseghian Kick)
Miami-Ohio - Nance 12 yard pass from Roethlisberger (Parseghian Kick)
Louisville – Gates 1 yard run (Smith Kick)
Miami-Ohio - Brandt 16 yard pass from Roethlisberger (Parseghian Kick)
Miami-Ohio - Larkin 26 yard pass from Roethlisberger (Parseghian Kick)
Louisville – Russell 31 yard pass from Bush (Smith Kick)
Louisville – Russell 2 yard pass from LeFors (Smith Kick)
Louisville – Russell 24 yard pass from LeFors (Smith Kick)
Miami-Ohio - Smith 3 yard run (Parseghian Kick)
Miami-Ohio - Pusateri 35 yard interception return (Parseghian Kick)

Associated Press GMAC Bowl Game Summary - Ben Roethlisberger ended his college career in style. Roethlisberger threw for 376 yards and four touchdowns as 15th-ranked Miami Ohio tied a school record with its 13th straight win, a 49-28 victory over Louisville in the GMAC Bowl. At 6-5 and 240 pounds, the strong-armed Roethlisberger has been projected as a high first-round pick in the NFL draft. But he did not reveal his intentions until after the GMAC Bowl, when he announced he will skip his senior season and head to the pros. "I love this guy, it's the right thing to do for him," Miami coach Terry Hoeppner said. Roethlisberger did nothing to hurt his NFL stock by throwing all of his touchdown passes in the first half, when the RedHawks (13-1) jumped to a 35-7 lead. J.R. Russell caught three TD passes to help Louisville cut the deficit to 35-28 after three quarters, but the RedHawks regained a 14-point cushion early in the fourth on a three-yard run by Mike Smith. Any chance of a comeback ended when safety Matt Pusateri picked off Stefan LeFors and returned the interception 35 yards for a score with 7:57 left. LeFors threw for 224 yards and was intercepted three times. The RedHawks (13-1) own the nation's longest current winning streak and matched the school record set from 1972-74. The only loss for Miami Ohio was its season opener against Iowa. "When they got within seven, the character of this football team was revealed once again, Hoeppner said. The wide-open affair featured 1,089 total yards, including 597 by the RedHawks. Martin Nance of Miami caught nine passes for 168 yards, including a 12-yard TD from Roethlisberger late in the first quarter that made it 21-0. Roethlisberger, who completed 21-of-33 passes, also threw TD passes of 28 and 26 yards to Michael Larkin and 16 yards to Matt Brandt. Miami was playing its first bowl game since the 1986 California Bowl. It was the RedHawks' first bowl win since a 20-7 triumph over South Carolina in the 1975 Tangerine Bowl

2003 Tangerine Bowl

The 2003 Tangerine Bowl was the 14th edition of the college football bowl game and was played on December 22, 2003, featuring the NC State Wolfpack, and the Kansas Jayhawks.

2003 Tangerine Bowl	Line	1	-	2	-	3	-	4	-	Final
NC State	(-11.5)	21	-	7	-	14	-	14	-	56
Kansas	(65.0)	7	-	3	-	10	-	6	-	26

Scoring Summary
NC State – Washington 45 yard pass from Rivers (Kiker Kick)
Kansas – Gordon 23 yard pass from Whittemore (Brooks Kick)
NC State – Washington 14 yard pass from Rivers (Kiker Kick)
NC State – McLendon 1 yard run (Kiker Kick)
Kansas – Brooks 28 yard Field Goal
NC State – McLendon 3 yard pass from Rivers (Kiker Kick)
Kansas – Green 11 yard pass from Whittemore (Brooks Kick)
NC State – Clark 40 yard pass from Rivers (Kiker Kick)
NC State – Davis 10 yard run (Kiker Kick)
Kansas – Bech 39 yard field goal
Kansas – Whittemore 9 yard run (Pass failed)
NC State – Cotchery 21 yard pass from Rivers (Kiker Kick)
NC State – McLendon 26 yard run (Kiker Kick)

Associated Press Tangerine Bowl Game summary - The Tangerine Bowl again saw a prolific passer close his college career with a game to remember. Philip Rivers passed for a career-high 475 yards and five touchdowns as North Carolina State closed an inconsistent season with a 56-26 rout of Kansas. The 2002 Tangerine Bowl saw Texas Tech's Kliff Kingsbury throw for 375 yards and three touchdowns in a 55-13 win over Clemson. This one had a similar outcome as Rivers raised the bar and the Wolfpack toyed with an overmatched opponent. The Atlantic Coast Conference Player of the Year, Rivers threw for more than 4,000 yards in the regular season and had his No. 17 retired prior to a November game against Maryland. He showed he deserved the honor, throwing a 45-yard TD pass to Richard Washington just 62 seconds into the contest to set the tone. Rivers connected on a 14-yard touchdown toss to Washington in the second quarter and found running back T.A. McLendon for a three-yard score that made it 28-10 at halftime. Rivers completed TD passes of 40 yards to Brian Clark in the third quarter and 21 yards to Jerricho Cotchery - who had 13 catches for 171 yards - in the fourth. Rivers completed 37-of-45 passes and received a warm ovation when he was removed with 7 1/2 minutes left. McLendon also had a pair of rushing touchdowns for North Carolina State (8-5), which lost its final two regular-season games. Kansas (6-7) completed its second season under Coach Mark Mangino with its first bowl appearance since the 1995 Aloha Bowl. It was a long night for the Jayhawks - not just because the game took more than 3 1/2 hours to complete. Kansas allowed 653 yards and its highest point total since last season's 64-0 setback to Kansas State. Bill Whittemore threw a pair of touchdown passes and ran for another for Kansas.

2003 Fort Worth Bowl

The 2003 edition to the Fort Worth Bowl, the inaugural edition of the game, featured the Boise State Broncos and the TCU Horned Frogs. The title sponsor for the game was PlainsCapital Bank.

2003 Fort Worth Bowl	Line	1	-	2	-	3	-	4	-	Final
#19 TCU	(59.0)	14	-	10	-	7	-	0	-	31
#18 Boise State	(-10.0)	7	-	17	-	3	-	7	-	34

Scoring Summary
TCU – Rodgers 3 yard run (Browne Kick)
Boise State – Acree 27 yard pass from Dinwiddie (Jones kick)
TCU – Rodgers 22 yard pass from Hassell (Browne kick)
TCU – Hassell 21 yard run (Browne kick)
Boise State – Carpenter 54 yard pass from Dinwiddie (Jones kick)
Boise State – Mikell 75 yard run (Jones kick)
TCU – Browne 32 yard Field goal
Boise State – Jones 23 yard Field Goal
Boise State – Jones 37 yard field goal
TCU – Hobbs 7 yard run (Browne kick)
Boise State – Schouman 18 yard pass from Dinwiddie (Jones kick)

Associated Press Fort Worth Bowl Game Summary - Ryan Dinwiddie went out a winner. The NCAA's all-time leader in passing efficiency, Dinwiddie threw for 325 yards and three touchdowns as 16th-ranked Boise State rallied from a 14-point deficit to defeat No. 19 Texas Christian, 34-31, in the inaugural Fort Worth Bowl. Dinwiddie, who passed for 9,809 yards in his career with 82 TDs and just 20 interceptions. Boise State (13-1) rallied from a 21-7 first-half deficit to win a bowl game on the road for the first time in school history. The winning score was set up when rover Chris Carr recovered Lonta Hobbs' fumble at the Horned Frogs' 29 early in the fourth quarter. Dinwiddie gave the Broncos a 34-31 lead with an 18-yard touchdown pass to Derek Schouman 2:17 into the final period. "I will definitely be voting our team in the top 10," Boise State coach Don Hawkins said. Playing at home after challenging for a BCS bid most of the season, the Horned Frogs (11-2) had a chance to tie, converting two fourth downs on their final drive, including a 28-yard completion to Reggie Harrell. But with regular kicker Nick Browne hampered by a strained quadriceps muscle, Mike Wynn's 51-yard field goal attempt with seven seconds left was well short. Wynn handles TCU's kickoff chores. The loss snapped TCU's school-record 13-game home winning streak. The teams combined for more than 600 yards in the first half while battling to a 24-24 tie. But Boise State blanked TCU after the Horned Frogs grabbed a 31-27 lead on Hobbs' seven-yard scamper 5 1/2 minutes into the third quarter. Boise State burned TCU with its quick-strike offense, needing less than four minutes combined on its four touchdown drives. In the first half, Dinwiddie threw TD passes of 27 yards to T.J. Acree and 54 yards to Jeff Carpenter. But it was Boise State's defense that turned around the game in the second half, getting more pressure on Brandon Hassell. He completed 13-of-26 passes for 160 yards with a TD and interception and rushed for 117 yards and a score on 23 carries. Hassell was not as sharp in the second half. After taking the 31-27 lead, the Horned Frogs picked up just one first down on their next five possessions, turning over the ball twice.

2003 Las Vegas Bowl

The 2003 Las Vegas Bowl was the 12th edition of that annual game. It featured the Oregon State Beavers, and the New Mexico Lobos. Oregon State's 55 points scored remains a Las Vegas Bowl record. Their 41-point victory margin is also a record.

2003 Las Vegas Bowl	Line	1	-	2	-	3	-	4	-	Final
Oregon State	(-2.5)	17	-	14	-	10	-	14	-	55
New Mexico	(52.0)	7	-	0	-	0	-	7	-	14

Scoring Summary
Oregon State – Jackson 34 yard pass from Anderson (Yliniemi Kick)
Oregon State – Yliniemi 21 yard Field goal
New Mexico – Baskett 27 yard pass from Kelly (Zunker Kick)
Oregon State – Hass 42 yard pass from Anderson (Yliniemi Kick)
Oregon State – Jackson 3 yard run (Yliniemi Kick)
Oregon State – Jackson 11 yard run (Yliniemi Kick)
Oregon State – Jackson 6 yard run (Yliniemi Kick)
Oregon State – Yliniemi 31 yard Field goal
Oregon State – Jackson 1 yard run (Yliniemi Kick)
New Mexico – Counter 17 yard pass from McKamey (Zunker Kick)
Oregon State – Hawkins 19 yard pass from Rothenfluh (Yliniemi Kick)

Associated Press Las Vegas Bowl Game Summary - Steven Jackson had a happy homecoming, matching a bowl record with five touchdowns in leading Oregon State to a 55-14 rout of New Mexico in the Las Vegas Bowl. A Las Vegas native, Jackson rushed for 149 yards and four touchdowns and caught five passes for 51 yards and another score in his final collegiate game. Afterward, he announced he will skip his senior season and enter the NFL draft. Only two others have scored five TDs in a bowl game, including Oklahoma State's Barry Sanders against Wyoming in the 1988 Holiday Bowl. The other was San Jose State's Sheldon Canley vs. Central Michigan in the 1990 California Bowl. Jackson is considered one of the best running backs in the country and a certain first-round pick in next year's draft. Derek Anderson complemented his star running back, passing for 322 yards and two TDs as the Beavers (8-5) finished a somewhat disappointing season on a high note. They had lost four of their previous six games. Anderson became just the second Pac-10 Conference Quarterback to throw for at least 4,000 yards in a season, joining Cody Pickett, who did it last year for Washington. Oregon State's defense was on top of its game as well, holding New Mexico (8-5) to 127 yards of total offense - six rushing—and seven first downs. Lobos' running back DonTrell Moore set a school record with 1,438 rushing yards during the regular season, but he picked up only five on 11 carries. Mike Hass and Josh Hawkins added TD catches for the Beavers, who rebounded from last year's 38-13 loss to Pittsburgh in the Insight Bowl. Hurt by early penalties, the Lobos dropped their third straight bowl game and second in as many years. New Mexico got itself in an early hole as Jackson finished off an 84-yard drive - the first of the game - with a 34-yard TD catch off a screen on 3rd-and-19. The Lobos had held on 4th-and-1 before taking an unsportsmanlike conduct penalty. Using their best player as a decoy, the Beavers increased their lead to 17-7 when Jackson took a handoff and flipped the ball back to Anderson, who threw a 42-yard TD to Hass off a flea-flicker. Jackson added touchdown runs of three and 11 yards on consecutive possessions as Oregon State built a 31-7 lead with 7:01 left in the first half. He also found the end zone from six and one yards in the second half. After scoring for the final time, Jackson walked off the field pulling back each finger on his left hand before holding it up to the crowd of 25,437 at Sam Boyd Stadium, signifying his school-record five TDs. Recognized by his trademark dreadlocks, Jackson spent most of the final quarter celebrating with family members, fans and teammates, some of whom had him sign their jerseys. The Beavers didn't exactly need Jackson, playing against an offense that didn't pick up its second first down until the fourth quarter. New Mexico averaged only 2.2 yards on 57 plays. Penalties didn't help, either. New Mexico got to Oregon State's 14-yard line on a 19-yard completion in the first quarter, but a clipping call pushed them back 15 yards. A field goal made it 10-7. The Beavers' defense made its share of big plays as well. Chaz Scott and Richard Seigler combined for a sack that ended a drive and set up Jackson's second TD of the night. On the Lobos' next possession, Scott recovered a fumble by Moore. While the Beavers doused Coach Riley with Gatorade in the closing moments, they did the same to defensive coordinator Mark Banker, who helped orchestrate the most decisive win in the 12-year history of the Las Vegas Bowl.

2003 Hawai'i Bowl

The 2003 Sheraton Hawai'i Bowl matched the hometown Hawaii Warriors with the Houston Cougars. The game is also memorable for a fight between both teams that occurred after the game was over. Players from each team got into shouting matches and punches were thrown.

2003 Hawaii Bowl	Line	1	-	2	-	3	-	4	-	OT	-	Final
Houston	(75.5)	10	-	10	-	0	-	14	-	14	-	48
Hawaii	(-10.5)	3	-	10	-	14	-	7	-	20	-	54

Scoring Summary
Houston – McCullar 34 yard pass from Kolb (Bell Kick)
Houston – Bell 21 yard Field Goal
Hawaii – Miranda 19 yard field goal
Hawaii – Herbert 48 yard pass from Chang (Miranda Kick)
Houston – Battle 2 yard run (Bell Kick)
Houston – Bell 35 yard Field Goal
Hawaii – Miranda 29 yard Field Goal
Hawaii – Brewster 1 yard run (Miranda Kick)
Hawaii – Rivers 7 yard pass from Chang (Miranda Kick)
Houston – Battle 2 yard run (Bell Kick)
Hawaii – Rivers 4 yard pass from Chang (Miranda Kick)
Houston – Marshall 81 yard pass from Kolb (Bell Kick)
Hawaii – Komine 11 yard pass from Chang (Miranda Kick)
Houston – Evans 6 yard run (Bell Kick)
Houston – Battle 4 yard run (Bell Kick)
Hawaii – Rivers 18 yard pass from Chang (Miranda Kick)
Hawaii – Brewster 8 yard run (Two point conversion failed)

Associated Press Hawaii Bowl Game summary - The Hawaii Bowl had a little bit of everything, minus the Christmas cheer. In a wild shootout that featured snipers in the stadium, three overtimes and a helmet-throwing postgame brawl, Timmy Chang passed for 475 yards and five touchdowns, leading Hawaii to a 54-48 victory over Houston in the Hawaii Bowl. The teams combined for 1,158 yards of offense, 81 improbable ones coming on a pass from Houston freshman Kevin Kolb to Vincent Marshall for a touchdown that tied the game at 34-34 with 22 seconds left in regulation. After both clubs scored easily on each of their first two overtime possessions, Michael Brewster scored on an eight-yard run, giving Hawaii a 54-48 lead. The ensuing two-point conversion failed. That gave the Cougars (7-6) a chance to win, but they failed to get into the end zone, sending the Warriors into hysterics when they were stopped on a 4th-and-5 from the 20-yard line. The amount of security guards were doubled when a suspicious package arrived at Aloha Stadium, but they came in handy after the game when the teams met at midfield and a handful of players exchanged punches and threw helmets. The incident soured an otherwise wild game that saw one of the most prolific passers in NCAA history at his best. Chang came off the bench early in the second quarter and led all seven of Hawaii's touchdown drives. Benched two games ago, Chang entered when senior starter Jason Whieldon injured his non-throwing shoulder. A junior from Oahu, Chang completed 26-of-42 passes for 475 yards with just one interception. The performance allowed Chang to jump four spots on the NCAA's all-time passing list, going from seventh to third. With 12,814 yards, he trails Phillip Rivers for second place by 195 and record-holder Ty Detmer by 2,217. Chang's TD passes were from 48, seven, four, 11 and 18 yards. Three of them went to Jason Rivers, his former high school teammate who grabbed seven passes for 143 yards. Jeremy Cockheran had five catches for 162 yards. Even without standout receiver Chad Owens, Hawaii totaled 641 yards of offense. With one of the most balanced offenses in the country, the Cougars weren't bad either. Bruising freshman Jackie Battle ran for 124 yards and three scores and Kolb passed for 332 yards and two TDs.

2003 Motor City Bowl

The 2003 Motor City Bowl was between the Northwestern Wildcats and the Bowling Green Falcons on December 26, 2003, at Ford Field in Detroit, Michigan. The game between the Mid-American Conference (MAC) team Bowling Green and Big Ten Conference Northwestern was played at neutral-site Ford Field. As then organized the Motor City Bowl matched a MAC team and a team from either the Big Ten, the Big East Conference, or an at-large team. Bowling Green accepted a bid for the Motor City Bowl after losing to Miami-Ohio in the MAC Championship Game. It was Bowling Green's first appearance in a bowl game since the 1992 Las Vegas Bowl. Northwestern was the first Big Ten team to play in the Motor City Bowl and had not appeared in a bowl game since the 2000 Alamo Bowl. Bowling Green and Northwestern last played each other on November 17, 2001, a meeting that Bowling Green won 42–43. Unusually for the Motor City Bowl there were two MVPs: Bowling Green Quarterback Josh Harris and Northwestern running back Jason Wright. Harris passed for 386 yards, including three touchdown passes, and rushed for Bowling Green's fourth touchdown. Harris' completion record of 38/50 and total offense of 454 yards set Motor City Bowl records. Wright had 21 carries for 237 yards, including a 77-yard touchdown run which was the second-longest in Motor City Bowl history.

2003 Motor City Bowl	Line	1	-	2	-	3	-	4	-	Final
Northwestern	(55.5)	7	-	3	-	7	-	7	-	24
Bowling Green	(-7.0)	0	-	7	-	7	-	14	-	28

Scoring Summary
Northwestern – Herron 40 yard run (Huffman kick)
Northwestern – Huffman 31 yard Field Goal
Bowling Green – Harris 4 yard run (Suisham kick)
Northwestern – Wright 77 yard run (Huffman kick)
Bowling Green – Magner 7 yard pass from Harris (Suisham kick)
Bowling Green – Sanders 11 yard pass from Harris (Suisham kick)
Northwestern – Herron 2 yard run (Huffman kick)
Bowling Green – Magner 3 yard pass from Harris (Suisham kick)

Associated Press Motor Bowl Game Summary - Northwestern took away Bowling Green's running game. So, Josh Harris beat the Wildcats through the air. Harris passed for 386 yards and three touchdowns to lead Bowling Green to a 28-24 victory over Northwestern in the Motor City Bowl on Friday night. Bowling Green (11-3) took the lead for good on Harris' 3-yard touchdown pass to Cole Magner with 4:06 left. Harris, who also ran for a TD, set a Motor City Bowl record for completions with 38 in 50 attempts. Magner also set a game record for catches, finishing with 12 for 97 yards and two touchdowns. Jason Wright ran for 237 yards on 21 carries and finished with 336 all-purpose yards for Northwestern (6-7). He had a 77-yard TD run — the second-longest run in Motor City Bowl history — to give the Wildcats a 17-7 lead early in the third quarter and an 88-yard kickoff return early in the fourth to set up Noah Herron's 2-yard touchdown run that made it 24-21. Wright said he took offense to being called slow by one of the announcers during ESPN's Hawaii Bowl broadcast Thursday night. Bowling Green used two 80-yard scoring drives to take a 21-17 lead early in the fourth. Harris threw a 7-yard TD pass to Magner and put the Falcons on top with an 11-yarder to Steve Sanders. Northwestern opened the scoring on Herron's 40-yard fourth-down run in the first quarter and made it 10-0 on Brian Huffman's 31-yard field goal. Bowling Green answered with a 67-yard drive, capped by Harris' 4-yard run. With Bowling Green's victory, the Mid-American Conference finished the bowl season with a 2-0 record. Miami of Ohio beat Louisville last week in the GMAC Bowl.

2003 Insight Bowl

The 2003 Insight Bowl was between the Virginia Tech Hokies and the California Golden Bears at Bank One Ballpark in Phoenix, Arizona, on December 26, 2003. Cal and Virginia Tech combined for 101 points; only the 2001 GMAC Bowl saw more points scored by two teams in a bowl game without overtime.

2003 Insight Bowl	Line	1	-	2	-	3	-	4	-	Final
California	(56.5)	7	-	14	-	21	-	10	-	52
Virginia Tech	(-3.0)	21	-	7	-	0	-	21	-	49

Scoring Summary
California – Rodgers 1 yard run (Fredrickson kick)
Virginia Tech – Randall 2 yard run (Warley kick)
Virginia Tech – Willis 3 yard pass from Randall (Warley kick)
Virginia Tech – Vick 36 yard pass from Randall (Warley kick)
California – Lyman 33 yard pass from Rodgers (Fredrickson kick)
Virginia Tech – Jones 11 yard run (Warley kick)
California – Arrington 13 yard pass from Rodgers (Fredrickson kick)
California – Manderino 3 yard run (Fredrickson kick)
California – Echemandu 9 yard run (Fredrickson kick)
Virginia Tech – Willis 22 yard pass from Randall (Pace kick)
California – Strang 13 yard run (Fredrickson kick)
Virginia Tech – Shreve 28 yard pass from Randall (Pace kick)
Virginia Tech – Hall 52 yard punt return (Warley kick)
California – Fredrickson 35 yard Field goal

Virginia Tech Media Guide Insight Bowl Game Summary - It wasn't New Year's Eve, but the Virginia Tech Hokies and the California Golden Bears certainly blasted off more than their fair share of fireworks. Unfortunately for the Hokies, Cal got to fire off the final round. Cal kicker Tyler Fredrickson, who came into the game having made just 14 of 29 field-goal attempts all season, drilled a 35-yarder at the final horn to lift Cal past the Hokies 52-49 in a thrilling Insight Bowl game played in front of a record crowd of 42,364 fans at Bank One Ballpark in Phoenix. The loss marked Tech's fifth in its final seven games this season. The Hokies finished the season 8-5 overall and fell to 6-11 in bowl games, including a 5-6 mark under head coach Frank Beamer. Cal, playing in a bowl for the first time since 1996, finished its season 8-6 overall. The loss marked a bitter end to Tech's season, particularly from a defensive standpoint. Looking to rebound from several poor performances down the stretch, the Hokies instead gave up 530 yards of total offense. The Bears held the ball for more than 37 minutes and converted 13-of-17 on third down. And Cal Quarterback Aaron Rodgers shredded the Hokies for 394 yards and two touchdowns, completing 27-of-35. Trailing by seven at halftime, Cal scored touchdowns on its first four possessions of the second half, taking a 49-35 lead on a 13-yard run by Vincent Strang with 6:26 left in the game. Strang's touchdown capped a 65-yard drive that ate 7:09 off the clock. But the Hokies rallied, scoring 14 unanswered themselves. After Strang's touchdown, Tech went 80 yards in less than two minutes and Quarterback Bryan Randall found Chris Shreve for a 28-yard touchdown that cut the Cal lead to seven, 49-42, with 4:28 left. Tech forced the Bears to punt on Cal's next possession - Cal's only punt of the second half. Tech punt returner DeAngelo Hall got the ball and tied the game at 42 when he took that punt 52 yards for a touchdown with 3:11 remaining. That marked Hall's third punt return for a touchdown this season and the fifth of his career. He became Tech's all-time leader for career punt returns for touchdowns, breaking the mark of four held by André Davis and Frank Loria. But on the ensuing kickoff after Hall's touchdown, Tech's Brandon Pace kicked the ball out of bounds, giving the Bears the ball at the 35. Cal marched 47 yards on seven plays, reaching the Tech 18 before calling a timeout with two seconds in the game. The Hokies also called a timeout, trying to ice Fredrickson. But the senior from Santa Clara, Calif., booted it through the uprights to give Cal the win. The loss overshadowed a brilliant game by Tech's offense, and most notably, Randall. On the money for the entire game, the senior from Williamsburg, Va., completed 24-of-34 for 398 yards and four touchdowns. He also scored a touchdown rushing, thus accounting for five of Tech's seven scores. Seniors Keith Willis, Ernest Wilford and Shreve also enjoyed huge games in their final contests as Hokies. Willis, a tight end from Norfolk, Va., became the first Tech player ever to catch two touchdown passes in a bowl game - his first two touchdowns of the season - and Wilford broke Antonio Freeman's career mark for receptions. The senior from Richmond caught eight passes for 110 yards, giving him 126 catches for his career. Freeman had held the record of 121 for the past nine years. Shreve, from Mouth of Wilson, Va., caught three passes for 93 yards and the touchdown. The catches mark his first since the Rutgers game, when he hauled in four, including two for touchdowns. Junior Kevin Jones, also playing his final game as a Hokie before heading to the NFL, rushed for 153 yards on 16 carries and scored a touchdown. Tech finished with 551 yards of total offense.

Insight Bowl Game Notes - For his performance in the 2003 Insight Bowl, California Quarterback Aaron Rodgers was named the offensive player of the game. Rodgers completed 27 of his 35 passes for 394 yards and two touchdowns in the winning effort. Rodgers' performance tied Cal's bowl records for most completions, most touchdowns, and most rushing touchdowns, and was the third-highest offensive output by a single player in California history.

2003 Continental Tire Bowl

The 2003 Continental Tire Bowl featured the Pittsburgh Panthers, and the Virginia Cavaliers. The game was the second edition to this bowl game. The game was played on Saturday, December 27, 2003. The win by Virginia made them 2–0 all time in the game.

2003 Continental Tire Bowl	Line	1	-	2	-	3	-	4	-	Final
Pittsburgh	(55.0)	0	-	13	-	3	-	0	-	16
Virginia	(-2.5)	7	-	10	-	3	-	3	-	23

Scoring Summary
Virginia – Miller 52 yard pass from Schaub (Hughes kick)
Pittsburgh – Brockenbrough 13 yard pass from Rutherford (Abdul kick)
Virginia – Lundi 1 yard run (Hughes kick)
Pittsburgh – Miree 18 yard pass from Rutherford (Kick failed)
Virginia – Hughes 44 yard Field Goal
Virginia – Hughes 30 yard Field Goal
Pittsburgh – Gibboney 29 yard Field Goal
Virginia – Hughes 39 yard Field Goal

Associated Press Continental Tire Bowl Game Summary - Matt Schaub capped his career as the Virginia Cavalier's most prolific Quarterback by taking a knee on his second consecutive Continental Tire Bowl victory. Larry Fitzgerald could only watch from the Pittsburgh Panthers sidelines, hands on his hips in yet another disappointing loss in what might have been the final game for one of the greatest players in Panthers history. Virginia made it 2-for-2 in the 2-year-old Tire Bowl by using solid defense to snap Fitzgerald's record touchdown streak at 18 games in a 23-16 victory on Saturday. The Cavaliers (8-5) did it by limiting the looks in Fitzgerald's direction with a steady pass-rush that led to five sacks and only six throws to Fitzgerald. The Heisman Trophy runner-up, who could petition the NFL for early entry into the draft, was held to five catches for 77 yards and failed to score a touchdown for Pittsburgh (8-5) for the first time since Oct 12, 2002, against Notre Dame. His 18 consecutive games with a touchdown is an NCAA record. Then he said he still wasn't sure what his future holds, just that he plans to be enrolled in classes at Pitt next month. So what could have been Fitzgerald's swan song instead became Schaub's big day. He threw for a 244 yards and a touchdown -- the 56th of his career, a Virginia record -- to earn the MVP award in the second-year bowl. The Cavs beat West Virginia here last season and marked the sweep by running as a team to the far end zone and celebrating with the Virginia-dominated crowd. Schaub, whose touchdown was a 52-yard strike to Heath Miller, wasted little time on sentimentality. But his coach felt otherwise, taking time to credit Schaub for leading the Cavs to consecutive bowl victories for just the second time in school history. But the game was also won with defense. Virginia used a goal-line stand on Pitt's first drive of the game. The Panthers were stopped on four straight plays from the 1 and Fitzgerald was not on the field for any of them. The Cavaliers also sacked Rod Rutherford on fourth-and-10 near the end of the first half and forced him into a costly fumble that basically sealed the game. Connor Hughes kicked a 39-yard field -- his third of the game -- to give Virginia a 23-16 lead with 2:28 to play. But with Fitzgerald on the field, it seemed almost a given the Panthers would be able to move down field. They got 45 yards from TuTu Ferguson on the ensuing kickoff, but Rutherford was sacked by Brennan Schmidt on the first play and Kai Parham recovered on the Pitt 37. The Cavaliers then put the game away with a 17-yard run by Wali Lundy that moved them to the 17 and allowed them to run out the clock. Lundy, who scored four touchdowns in this bowl last year, finished with 90 yards and a 1-yard touchdown run. Charlotte native Alvin Pearman, who missed the game last year with an injury, marked his homecoming with 104 yards rushing and six catches for 32 yards. Brandon Miree ran for 110 yards for Pitt and added four catches for 43 yards, including a 17-yard touchdown. The scoring pass from Rutherford was his 37th of the season, tying the school record Dan Marino set in 1981. Rutherford finished with 246 yards passing, two touchdowns, an interception and a fumble. His mistakes weren't the only ones for Pitt, though. The Panthers also missed a conversion and a field goal, critical errors for a team extremely disappointed at even being in the second-tier bowl.

2003 Alamo Bowl

The 2003 Alamo Bowl was between the Michigan State Spartans and the Nebraska Cornhuskers played December 29, 2003 at the Alamodome in San Antonio, Texas. In a defensive game, Nebraska scored first, leading 3–0 on a 29-yard field goal kicked by David Dyches. Michigan State's Dave Rayner tied the score at 3 at the end of the 1st quarter, kicking a 46-yard field goal. In the second quarter, running back Cory Ross scored on touchdown runs of 2 and 6 yards, to give Nebraska a 17–3 lead. There was no further scoring, and the game ended with Nebraska defeating Michigan State, 17–3.

2003 Alamo Bowl	Line	1	-	2	-	3	-	4	-	Final
Michigan State	(49.5)	3	-	0	-	0	-	3	-	3
#22 Nebraska	(-3.0)	3	-	14	-	0	-	0	-	17

Scoring Summary
Nebraska – Dyches 29 yard Field Goal
Michigan State – Rayner 46 yard Field Goal
Nebraska – Ross 2 yard run (Dyches kick)
Nebraska – Ross 6 yard run (Dyches kick)

Associated Press Alamo Bowl Game Summary - Bo Pelini got Nebraska to play like the "Blackshirts" of old. The 21st-ranked Cornhuskers shut down Michigan State's high-powered offense and used two short second-quarter touchdown runs by Cory Ross to defeat the Spartans, 17-3, in the Alamo Bowl. Ross rushed for a career-high 138 yards on 37 carries for Nebraska (10-3), which was playing in its NCAA-record 35th consecutive bowl game. Named interim coach when Frank Solich was fired at the end of the regular season, Pelini is not considered a serious candidate for the job. But as the Cornhuskers' defensive coordinator, he devised a game plan that stifled Michigan State Quarterback Jeff Smoker. After the teams traded field goals in the first quarter, Ross scored on runs of two and six yards, giving Nebraska a 17-3 halftime lead. Jamaal Lord rushed for 79 yards on 10 attempts for the Cornhuskers, including a career-long 66-yard scamper that set up Ross' second score. The fiery Pelini gave Michigan State (8-5) an opening when he was flagged for an unsportsmanlike conduct penalty with the Spartans facing 4th-and inches in the fourth quarter. Pelini was upset the officials did not give the ball to Nebraska after Smoker fumbled a snap. The penalty gave Michigan State a first down at the Nebraska 34 with more than seven minutes left. But two plays later, cornerback Pat Ricketts sealed the win with the Cornhuskers' school-record 31st interception, which also is tops in Division I-A. Nebraska recorded three interceptions and five sacks while holding Michigan State to 18 rushing yards and 174 total, more than 200 below its average. Smoker completed 21-of-39 passes for 156 yards. His final pass for the Spartans was intercepted by cornerback Fabian Washington with 1:08

remaining. Safety Josh Bullocks' interception gave Nebraska a first down at the Spartans 36 early in the second quarter and led to Ross' first TD.

2003 Houston Bowl

The 2003 Houston Bowl was between the Navy Midshipmen and the Texas Tech Red Raiders on December 30, 2003, at Reliant Stadium in Houston, Texas. It was the fourth time the Houston Bowl was played. Texas Tech defeated Navy 38–14. The Houston Bowl was Navy's first bowl game since the 1996 Aloha Bowl, in which Navy defeated California 42–38 Texas Tech, representing the Big 12 conference, was playing in its fourth straight bowl game, stretching back to the inaugural Houston Bowl (then the Galleryfurniture.com Bowl).

2003 Houston Bowl	Line	1	-	2	-	3	-	4	-	Final
Navy	(74.0)	0	-	0	-	7	-	7	-	14
Texas Tech	(-12.0)	0	-	14	-	10	-	14	-	38

Scoring Summary
Texas Tech – Peters 4 yard pass from Symons (Toogood kick)
Texas Tech – Glover 17 yard pass from Symons (Toogood kick)
Navy – Candeto 2 yard run (Rolfs kick)
Texas Tech – Henderson 4 yard run (Toogood kick)
Texas Tech – Toogood 24 yard Field Goal
Navy – Candeto 2 yard run (Rolfs kick)
Texas Tech – Hicks 13 yard pass from Symons (Toogood kick)
Texas Tech – Peters 5 yard pass from Symons (Toogood kick)

Associated Press Houston Bowl Game Summary - B.J. Symons completed the most prolific passing season in Division I-A history by throwing for 497 yards and four touchdowns to lead the Red Raiders to a 38-14 victory over Navy in the Houston Bowl on Tuesday, then admitted afterward he's been playing with a torn ligament in his left knee for more than two months. Neither he nor the school ever had revealed how badly Symons hurt himself Oct. 11 while jumping to celebrate a TD pass to teammate Wes Welker. After finishing his career by extending his single season passing record to 5,833 yards, he told reporters that he will undergo reconstructive surgery on his anterior cruciate ligament Jan. 6. His gritty performance, the seventh on the bad leg, lifted Tech (8-5) to the first back-to-back bowl victories in school history. The game ended a remarkable turnaround season for Navy (8-5), which won just three games over the previous three years. Quarterback Craig Candeto, at the controls of Coach Paul Johnson's top-ranked rushing offense, ran for 90 yards and both touchdowns in his last game. Candeto's 2-yard TD run early in the third quarter pulled Navy within 14-7 against the larger, faster and more highly recruited Red Raiders. Navy did it all with virtually no threat of the pass as Candeto completed just two for 33 yards. The Red Raiders' No. 1 passing offense responded, with Symons leading them back quickly to set up a four-yard TD run by Taurean Henderson. Keith Toogood tacked on a 21-yard field goal for a 24-7 lead. Tech's 110th-ranked defense never quite stopped Navy, which rolled up 289 yards rushing, but slowed the Midshipmen enough despite a fourth-quarter scoring plunge by Candeto. Symons poured it on at the end with TD passes to Jarrett Hicks and Mickey Peters. Tech, which beat Clemson in last year's Tangerine Bowl, improved its postseason record to 7-19-1. Symons ended his senior year with 52 TD passes, second only to the 54 thrown by Houston's David Klingler in 1994. His favorite target, Welker, tied an NCAA record by catching a pass in his 47th consecutive game. Johnson, unaware of how banged up Symons was, came away duly impressed. Candeto headed into his five-year service commitment with 33 career touchdowns rushing, pulling ahead of Navy's all-time rushing leader Napoleon McCallum to No. 2 on the academy's TD list. Johnson gambled early in the second quarter when Navy fell short on a fake punt near midfield. Moments later, Symons lobbed a perfect timing pass to Peters on the right side of the end zone for the game's first score. Late in the quarter Navy appeared to stop Tech when Shalimar Brazier clobbered Symons for an 18-yard loss, but he bounced back to hit Nehemiah Glover three straight times for gains of six and 12 yards, and a 17-yard score and a 14-0 lead.

2003 Holiday Bowl

The 2003 Holiday Bowl was played December 30, 2003 in San Diego, California. It featured the Washington State Cougars against the Texas Longhorns. Washington State pulled off a major upset by winning 28-20.

2003 Holiday Bowl	Line	1	-	2	-	3	-	4	-	Final
#15 Washington State	(59.0)	0	-	7	-	19	-	2	-	28
#5 Texas	(-9.5)	0	-	10	-	0	-	10	-	20

Scoring Summary
Texas – Benson 1 yard run (Pino kick)
Washington State – Moore 12 yard pass from Kegel (Dunning kick)
Texas – Pino 39 yard Field goal
Washington State – Moore 54 yard pass from Kegel (Dunning kick)
Washington State – Smith 12 yard run (Dunning kick)
Washington State – David 18 yard fumble return (Dunning kick)
Texas – Pino 19 yard Field goal
Washington State – Safety
Texas – Williams 30 yard pass from Mock (Pino kick)

Holiday Bowl Game Summary - Washington State's Cougars, ranked No. 15 in the nation entering the game, used an aggressive defense and an MVP performance by punter Kyle Basler to defeat the No. 5 rated Texas Longhorns, 28-20 in another nail biting finish. Texas controlled the ball for over 39 minutes in the game to establish a Holiday Bowl record, but Washington State's defense had seven Quarterback sacks and forced three turnovers. Texas led 10-7 at the half before the Cougars went on a 19-0 run in the third quarter to take a 26-10 lead. A 54-yard Matt Kegel to Sammy Moore touchdown, a 12-yard Jonathan Smith run and an 18-yard Jason David fumble recovery for a touchdown put the Cougars in the driver's seat. In true Holiday Bowl tradition, Texas rallied in the fourth quarter on a David Pino field goal and a 30-yard Chance Mock to Roy Williams touchdown pass, but Washington State's defense turned back Texas on two late possessions to hold on for the win.

2003 Silicon Valley Football Classic

The 2003 Silicon Valley Football Classic was between the UCLA Bruins and the Fresno State Bulldogs on December 30, 2003, at Spartan Stadium in San Jose, California. It was the fourth time the Silicon Valley Football Classic was played. Fresno State defeated UCLA 17-9. It was the sixth time the two teams had met on the field and the first victory for Fresno State. For the 2003 bowl season the Silicon Valley Classic had contractual tie-ins with the Western Athletic Conference (WAC) and the Pacific-10 Conference (Pac-10). The SVC organizers had a choice between UCLA and the Washington Huskies, both of whom finished the season 6-6 and bowl eligible, to represent the Pac-10. The SVC invited UCLA, citing UCLA's victory against Washington earlier in the season. Since the beginning of the bowl in 2000, the Fresno State Bulldogs represented the WAC. Fresno State and the Tulsa Golden Hurricane finished the season tied for second in the WAC and available for the SVC. Fresno State returned to the SVC for the fourth straight year, while Tulsa went to the Humanitarian Bowl.

2003 Silicon Valley Classic	Line	1	-	2	-	3	-	4	-	Final
UCLA	(-3.0)	0	-	7	-	2	-	0	-	9
Fresno State	(43.0)	14	-	3	-	0	-	0	-	17

Scoring Summary
Fresno State – Sumlin 1 yard run (Visintainer kick)
Fresno State – Sumlin 44 yard pass from Pinegar (Visintainer kick)
Fresno State – Visintainer 44 yard Field Goal
UCLA – Bragg 27 yard pass from Olson (Medlock kick)
UCLA – Team Safety

Associated Press Silicon Valley Football Classic Game Summary - Pat Hill used to watch Rodney Davis grind out yards in the snow and mud in high school - so Fresno State's coach knew the star senior would be well suited for the conditions Tuesday night. Davis rushed for 77 yards to win his second straight Silicon Valley Classic offensive MVP award in Fresno State's 17-9 victory over UCLA on a messy field at Spartan Stadium. Nearly one year ago, Davis rushed for 153 yards and two TDs -- the last being the game-clincher -- in Fresno State's victory over Georgia Tech. It sure seemed to be bad for the Bruins. Though even a dry field might have caused them problems the way their offense has been performing. UCLA (6-7) lost its last five games to turn what once was a promising season into a disappointment under first-year coach Karl Dorrell. The inefficient offense was again the culprit, going 2-for-14 on third-down conversions. Bryson Sumlin made his first career touchdown catch and ran for a score for Fresno State (9-5), which made its school-record fifth straight bowl appearance and fourth in a row in this game. Sumlin, a sophomore backup who began his Fresno State career as a cornerback, capitalized on two big chances to score and helped the Bulldogs beat the Bruins for the first time in six meetings. And once again, the Bulldogs seized the opportunity to spoil things for a bigger, more prominent program in a game dominated by defense. Paul Pinegar passed for 133 yards, but Fresno State didn't exactly need a prolific offense to beat the inept Bruins, who managed just 164 total yards - 97 in one series shortly before halftime. Manuel Sanchez intercepted Bruins Quarterback Drew Olson with 2:42 left and several Bulldogs celebrated their win by sliding face-first through the mud. Fresno State seemed to be in control until a drive midway through the third quarter in which a series of mistakes left the Bulldogs facing fourth-and-37. Asi Faoa blocked the ensuing punt in the end zone for a UCLA safety. Later in the quarter, Pinegar fumbled when he attempted to throw, and left Fresno State stranded at its own 1. But the Bruins bailed out the Bulldogs by roughing punter Mike Lingua, and UCLA never mounted another significant drive. The Bruins swore they were happy with their less than glamorous bowl destination, but they sure didn't play that way. UCLA seemed disinterested and disorganized, struggling to stop Fresno State's offense and failing to move the ball through the air or on the ground while falling behind 17-0 early in the second quarter. After Fresno State stopped UCLA on fourth-and-1 late in the first quarter, Pinegar completed a 44-yard TD pass to Sumlin, who also had a 1-yard scoring run earlier in the period. When Fresno State downed a punt inside the 3 shortly before halftime, the Bruins briefly woke up. UCLA went 97 yards in just seven plays, with Craig Bragg making a spectacular 27-yard diving catch in the corner of the end zone 20 seconds before halftime for the Bruins' first score. UCLA starting safety Jarrad Page was ejected 5 seconds later after apparently throwing the final shove in a scuffle involving many players. Dorrell hollered at referee David Witvoet as they ran, they off the field at halftime. Dorrell admitted Monday that he had turned down opportunities to play Fresno State during the regular season, essentially because the Bruins have nothing to gain by facing the upset-minded Bulldogs. Fresno State lost the first two Silicon Valley Classics, including a thrilling last-second defeat on a failed fake field goal in the inaugural game. The Bulldogs beat Georgia Tech in the game last season, overcoming several injuries for the school's first bowl victory since 1992. The win makes the Western Athletic Conference 3-0 this bowl season. Boise State beat TCU 34-31 in the Fort Worth Bowl and Hawaii defeated Houston 54-48 in triple overtime in the Hawaii Bowl. The last WAC team to play will be Tulsa, which faces Georgia Tech in the Humanitarian Bowl on Saturday.

2003 Independence Bowl

The 2003 Independence Bowl was between the Arkansas Razorbacks and the Missouri Tigers on December 31, 2003, at Independence Stadium in Shreveport, Louisiana. Arkansas made their sixth straight bowl appearance but had lost the last three. Missouri, on the other hand, was making their first bowl appearance since 1998. This was Missouri's first bowl game under Head Coach Gary Pinkel.

2003 Independence Bowl	Line	1	-	2	-	3	-	4	-	Final
Missouri	(54.0)	7	-	0	-	7	-	0	-	14
Arkansas	(-2.5)	3	-	18	-	3	-	3	-	27

Scoring Summary
Arkansas – Balseiro 33 yard Field Goal
Missouri – Abron 1 yard run (Matheny kick)
Arkansas – Balseiro 28 yard Field Goal
Arkansas – Jones 1 yard run (Wilson pass from Jones)
Arkansas – Cobbs 41 yard run (Balseiro kick)
Arkansas – Balseiro 25 yard Field Goal
Missouri – Smith 5 yard run (Matheny kick)
Arkansas – Balseiro 24 yard Field Goal

Associated Press Independence Bowl Game Summary - Arkansas' bowl drought is over, thanks to a big game from Cedric Cobbs and an opportunistic defense. Cobbs ran for 141 yards, including a 41-yard touchdown, to help the Razorbacks end a three-game bowl losing streak with a 27-14 victory over Missouri in the Independence Bowl on Wednesday night. Arkansas' defense made two key fourth-and-1 stops, one of them at the goal line, as the Razorbacks won for only the second time in their last 12 bowl games. In six seasons under coach Houston Nutt, Arkansas is 2-4 in bowl games. Chris Balseiro kicked four short field goals, an Independence Bowl record, as Arkansas (9-4) rebounded from a 31-point loss to LSU in the regular-season finale. Arkansas' 300 yards rushing also was an Independence record. Backup DeCori Birmingham added 85 yards on 10 carries and Quarterback Matt Jones had 74 yards on seven carries. The Razorbacks likely benefited from a largely pro-Arkansas crowd. That state's border is only 30 miles away, and there were about twice as many Arkansas supporters as there were for Missouri. Special teams were a problem area for Missouri (8-5), which lost 41 yards to its own 3 after a high snap went over punter Brock Harvey's head _ essentially handing the Razorbacks a touchdown. Arkansas' Tom Crowder intercepted a fake field pass by holder and backup Quarterback Sonny Riccio on the last play of the first half, and Crowder also blocked a punt in the fourth quarter. Brad Smith of Missouri had 155 yards passing and 96 yards rushing to set the school career total yardage record in just his second season. He scored on a 5-yard run late in the third quarter to cut the gap to 10 points. But he fell 23 yards short of becoming the first player in NCAA history to pass for 2,000 yards and run for 1,000 in two seasons. Zack Abron added 137 yards on 19 carries for Missouri, making its first bowl appearance in five years and only the school's third in 20 seasons. The Tigers had a 407-385 edge in total yardage but didn't have a lot to show for their 407 total yards. Cobbs set a school record with his seventh 100-yard rushing game this season, the 11th of an injury-plagued career. He's totaled 460 yards in his last three games and was named the game's offensive MVP. The only time he was touched on his second-quarter scoring run was when he collided with Jones on the handoff. He ran for 99 yards in the first half to help Arkansas take a 21-7 lead. Missouri was hurt when it came up empty on consecutive 10-play drives, one at the end of the first half and another at the start of the third quarter. Freshmen Keith Jackson Jr. and Jeremy Harrell stuffed Abron on fourth-and-1 at the Razorbacks 12 with 1:59 left. Then Lerinezo Robinson intercepted a rollout pass from Smith on fourth-and-goal from the 1 as Arkansas preserved its 21-7 lead. During the regular season, Missouri was 13-for-15 on fourth-and-1. The Tigers also were thwarted on fourth-and-goal from the 8 with about five minutes to go. Missouri led 7-6 when Zach Strom's snap sailed high above the head of Harvey and rolled to the Tigers 3. Jones slipped two would-be tacklers on a 1-yard run three plays later, and his conversion pass to George Wilson put the Razorbacks ahead to stay at 14-7. Arkansas scored on consecutive plays, making it 21-7, as Cobbs scored following a three-and-out for Missouri. Balseiro was 4-for-4 on field goals, connecting from 33, 28, 25 and 24 yards. Balseiro didn't get the kicking job until the fourth game of the year and finished 11-for-15 on field goal attempts.

2003 Music City Bowl

The 2003 Gaylord Hotels Music City Bowl (presented by Bridgestone) was played on December 31, 2003 in Nashville, Tennessee, and featured the Auburn Tigers and the Wisconsin Badgers. It was the sixth edition of the game. Both teams were awarded $912,912 for their participation in the game.

2003 Music City Bowl	Line	1	-	2	-	3	-	4	-	Final
Wisconsin	(46.0)	0	-	6	-	0	-	8	-	14
Auburn	(-3.0)	0	-	7	-	7	-	14	-	28

Scoring Summary
Wisconsin – Allen 20 yard Field Goal
Auburn – Brown 1 yard run (Vaughn Kick)
Wisconsin – Allen 35 yard Field goal
Auburn – Williams 1 yard run (Vaughn Kick)
Wisconsin – Evans 12 yard pass from Sorgi (Daniels pass from Sorgi)
Auburn – Brown 2 yard run (Vaughn kick)
Auburn – Williams 1 yard run (Vaughn kick)

Associated Press Music City Bowl Game Summary - Auburn cornerback Carlos Rogers got the last laugh. Burned by wide receiver Lee Evans two series earlier, Rogers made the key defensive play that led to Ronnie Brown's go-ahead two-yard touchdown run with 3:30 remaining as Auburn posted a 28-14 victory over Wisconsin in the Music City Bowl. The win enabled the Tigers (8-5) to cap a turbulent season that began with national championship aspirations on a high note. "The best way to get a positive light on our university after what we've been through was to get this win," said Tigers coach Tommy Tuberville, who signed a one-year contract extension after school officials secretly met with Louisville's Bobby Petrino about a possible coaching change. With 8:52 left in the fourth quarter, Evans jumped over Rogers' back in the end zone for spectacular 12-yard TD pass. Jim Sorgi then hit Owen Daniels for the conversion pass that tied the contest, 14-14. The TD appeared to spark the Badgers, who forced a three-and-out, but on Wisconsin's ensuing possession, Rogers deflected a deep pass intended for Evans into the hands of safety Will Herring for an easy interception. The Tigers (8-5) needed just 76 seconds to drive 87 yards for the winning score as Jason Campbell set up Brown's short TD run with completions of 51 yards to Jeris McIntyre and 28 yards to Silas Daniels. Linebacker Karlos Dansby delivered the knockout punch on the next series, sacking Sorgi, who fumbled at the one-yard line. Carnell Williams, who ran for 68 yards on 18 attempts, scored his second TD on the next play to give Auburn a 28-14 cushion with 1:37 remaining. Brown also scored twice for the Tigers, whose defense overpowered Wisconsin, holding the Badgers to 58 yards rushing and 203 overall. End Reggie Torbor led that effort with seven tackles and 3 1/2 sacks. Campbell completed 10-of-22 passes for 138 yards and rushed for 67 yards on nine carries. The Badgers (7-6) dropped to 7-2 in bowl play under Barry Alvarez, who was denied his 100th victory at Wisconsin. Williams' one-yard drive over the top capped a 16-play, 80-yard march that gave the Tigers a 14-6 lead with 1:32 left in the third period.

College Football "Bowl Games of the 21st Century"   Chapter 1 – 2000-2005

2003 Liberty Bowl

The 2003 AXA Liberty Bowl, played on December 31, 2003, was the 45th edition of the Liberty Bowl. The game was played between the Utah Utes, and the Southern Mississippi Golden Eagles, in front of 55,989 fans.

2003 Liberty Bowl	Line	1	-	2	-	3	-	4	-	Final
#25 Utah	(-2.5)	0	-	7	-	0	-	10	-	17
Southern Mississippi	(44.5)	0	-	0	-	0	-	0	-	0

Scoring Summary
Utah – Warfield 5 yard run (Borreson kick)
Utah – Borreson 19 yard Field Goal
Utah – Scalley 74 yard fumble recovery (Borreson kick)

Associated Press Liberty Bowl Game Summary - With a convoy of teammates leading the way, Morgan Scalley hopped into the end zone to seal a milestone victory for Utah and make a case for these being the best Utes ever. Scalley returned a fumble for a touchdown late in the game and set up the only other TD by causing a turnover, leading No. 25 Utah to a 17-0 victory over Southern Mississippi in the Liberty Bowl on Wednesday. The Mountain West Conference champions finished the season with back-to-back shutouts and tied a school record set in 1994 with 10 victories. In a lackluster game dominated by hard-hitting defense and sloppy offense, Scalley provided a little excitement. The junior safety scooped up a fumble after a completed pass and raced 74 yards for a score behind a wall of blockers with 1:36 left to play. Scalley said he just got lucky after Dave Revill and Eric Weddle jarred the ball from Terrell Browden's grasp. Southern Miss (9-4) managed to get deep into Utah territory just once in the second half when Anthony Harris broke free for a 41-yard run to the 18 with about eight minutes left and Utah up 7-0. But the Utes (10-2) stiffened, and on fourth-and-2 from the 10 Revill and Ray Holdcraft combined to sack Micky D'Angelo. Southern Miss Coach Jeff Bower said the Utes didn't fool and surprise the Golden Eagles' offense, they just "whipped us." The fourth-down stop seemed to inspire Utah's offense momentarily. Alex Smith hit Paris Warren deep down the middle for 49 yards on the next play. That led to Bryan Borreson's 19-yard field goal to make it 10-0 with 3:24 left. Brandon Warfield had 91 yards rushing on 27 carries for Utah and scored the only offensive touchdown in the second quarter. Warfield bulled into the end zone from 5 yards out, two plays after Scalley forced a fumble by Southern Miss Quarterback Dustin Almond deep in Golden Eagles' territory. The shutout was the first in the Liberty Bowl since 1994, when Illinois beat East Carolina 30-0. Utah didn't allow a point in its final 10 quarters. Southern Miss, the Conference USA champs, had its six-game winning streak snapped, despite a stellar game by linebacker Rod Davis and the Golden Eagles' swarming defense. The teams combined for just 441 yards, 228 by Utah. The Utes ended the regular season with a 3-0 victory over BYU, but that was in a snowstorm. Weather had nothing to do with the offensive ineptitude on Wednesday. Almond, who made great strides after a poor start to the season, was 11-for-33 for 122 yards. He was relieved by D'Angelo to start the fourth quarter. D'Angelo was 2-for-6 for 22 yards and sustained a concussion on the fourth-down sack. Smith wasn't much better for the Utes. He went 8-for-19 for 124 yards. The Pac-10 officials were busy throughout, calling 24 penalties - 12 on each team - for 177 yards.

2003 San Francisco Bowl

The 2003 San Francisco Bowl was the second edition of the San Francisco bowl between the Colorado State Rams and the Boston College Eagles at Pacific Bell Park in San Francisco, California on December 31, 2003.

2003 San Francisco Bowl	Line	1	-	2	-	3	-	4	-	Final
Boston College	(Pk)	21	-	0	-	0	-	14	-	35
Colorado State	(54.0)	0	-	7	-	7	-	7	-	21

Scoring Summary
Boston College – Knight 5 yard run (Sciortino kick)
Boston College – Lester 50 yard pass from Peterson (Sciortino kick)
Boston College – Knight 3 yard run (Sciortino kick)
Colorado State – Green 7 yard run (Babcock kick)
Colorado State – Anderson 40 yard pass from Van Pelt (Babcock kick)
Boston College – Lester 19 yard pass from Peterson (Sciortino Kick)
Boston College – Knight 28 yard run (Sciortino kick)
Colorado State – Van Pelt 1 yard run (Babcock kick)

Associated Press San Francisco Bowl Game Summary - Derrick Knight ran for 122 yards and three touchdowns and Larry Lester caught two scoring passes in Boston College's fourth straight bowl victory, 35-21 over Colorado State in the San Francisco Bowl on Wednesday night Paul Peterson passed for 224 yards and T.J. Stancil had three interceptions for the Eagles (8-5), who finished their season on a three-game winning streak by shutting down the Rams and senior Quarterback Bradlee Van Pelt in decisive fashion. Knight secured the victory on a winding 27-yard TD scamper with 9:29 to play. The Eagles' school rushing leader finished his standout career without a loss in a bowl game, and he'll have plenty of time to celebrate: He plans to stay in San Francisco for the East-West Shrine Game next weekend. Boston College, the Big East representative in the second edition of this bowl, also won the Aloha, Music City and Motor City bowls during Knight's career under coach Tom O'Brien, who has led the Eagles to five straight winning seasons. Van Pelt passed for 163 yards and ran for 65 and a score despite sitting out the first quarter for the Mountain West representative Rams (7-6), who fell behind 21-0 in the first quarter and never recovered. Van Pelt, the Rams' hard-running Quarterback, played his final college game with a 2.50-inch titanium rod in his broken throwing hand, but his aggressive style was mostly ineffective against BC's sturdy defense. He threw three interceptions, and backup Jesse Holland threw two more. David Anderson had a career-high 10 catches for 134 yards, setting Colorado State's single-season records for receptions and yards. He also made a 40-yard TD catch midway through the third quarter, briefly pulling the Rams within 21-14. Stancil, a junior safety, had just one interception in his college career before tying the school single-game record with three. His third pick set up Lester's second TD catch with 12:31 left. The game matched the top offenses from the schools' respective conferences, but Colorado State had difficulty making big plays. Boston College made enough big plays in the first and fourth quarters to secure an easy victory. The Eagles scored touchdowns on their first three possessions, with Knight rushing for two short scores. Lester also caught a 50-yard TD pass from Peterson, impressively outrunning Colorado State's safeties to the end zone. Van Pelt's hand, broken in the regular-season finale, apparently swelled up enough to convince coach Sonny Lubick to sit out his star. The Rams were in trouble by the time Lubick put Van Pelt in the game, even though Holland completed six of his seven passes. Van Pelt immediately engineered a 68-yard scoring drive, with Green rushing for a 7-yard score. Dexter Wynn, the Rams' feared kick return specialist, made his first reception of the season during a later drive, but it ended with Stancil's second interception in the end zone. Boston College had several thousand vocal supporters in the stands at Pacific Bell Park on a surprisingly warm night on San Francisco's waterfront. The Eagles gathered in front of the school band afterward, raising their helmets to wild cheers.

2003 Sun Bowl

The 2003 Wells Fargo Sun Bowl featured the Minnesota Golden Gophers, and the Oregon Ducks, a rematch of the 1999 Sun Bowl. After a scoreless first quarter, Oregon Quarterback Kellen Clemens passed to wide receiver Dante Rosario for a 19 yard touchdown pass, giving Oregon an early 7-0 lead. Minnesota used its power running game to answer back, as they pounded the ball down the field, and capped off the drive with a yard run by fullback Thomas Tapeh, knotting the game at 7-7. Samie Parker, who had a monster game with over 200 yards receiving, caught an 18 yarder from Clemens, putting Oregon up 14-7. Minnesota continued to use its running game, and Tapeh rushed for his second 1 yarder of the game again tying the game at 14. Jared Siegel's 30 yard field goal before halftime gave the Ducks a 17-14 half time lead. In the third quarter Tapeh recorded his third rushing touchdown of the game, with a 6 yarder, giving Minnesota its first lead at 21-17. Oregon responded by Samie Parker catching his second touchdown reception of the game, a 40 yarder from Clemens, his third touchdown pass of the game, and Oregon reclaimed the lead 24-21. Lawrence Maroney rushed for a 22 yard touchdown later in the quarter giving Minnesota a 28-24 lead. In the fourth quarter, Jared Siegel connected on a 32 yard field goal to pull Oregon to within 28-27. His last field goal, a 47 yarder with less than 5 minutes left in the game, gave Oregon a 30-28 lead. Minnesota's kicker, Rhys kicked a 42 yard field goal, with 23 seconds left, giving Minnesota a 31-30 win.

2003 Sun Bowl	Line	1	-	2	-	3	-	4	-	Final
#24 Minnesota	(-4.0)	0	-	14	-	14	-	3	-	31
Oregon	(60.5)	0	-	17	-	7	-	6	-	30

Scoring Summary
Oregon – Rosario 9 yard pass from Clemens (Siegel kick)
Minnesota – Tapeh 1 yard run (Lloyd kick)
Oregon – Parker 18 yard pass from Clemens (Siegel kick)
Minnesota – Tapeh 1 yard run (Lloyd kick)
Oregon – Siegel 30 yard Field Goal
Minnesota – Tapeh 6 yard run (Lloyd kick)
Oregon – Parker 40 yard pass from Clemens (Siegel kick)
Minnesota – Maroney 22 yard run (Lloyd kick)
Oregon – Siegel 32 yard Field Goal
Oregon – Siegel 47 yard Field Goal
Minnesota – Lloyd 42 yard Field Goal

Associated Press Sun Bowl Game Summary - Minnesota waited nearly a century for a season like this. Rhys Lloyd kicked a 42-yard field goal with 23 seconds remaining as the 20th-ranked Golden Gophers edged Oregon, 31-30, in a wild Sun Bowl to reach 10 wins for the first time since 1905. Minnesota (10-3) overcame a spectacular effort by Oregon wide receiver Samie Parker, who caught a career-high and Sun Bowl-record 16 passes for 200 yards and two touchdowns in his final appearance for the Ducks. Jared Siegel kicked a 47-yard field goal with 4:16 remaining to give Oregon (8-5) a 28-27 lead, but Asad Abdul-Khaliq patiently ran Minnesota's offense, keeping the ball on the ground to get the Golden Gophers into field goal range. With no timeouts remaining and Minnesota scrambling on third down, Oregon coach Mike Bellotti called timeout to ensure his team got back the ball. But the move may have helped the Gophers, who set up the field goal with one more running play. Oregon's hopes ended when safety Justin Isom intercepted Kellen Clemens on the first play after the kickoff. Clemens completed 32-of-43 passes for 363 yards with three TDs and an interception. Laurence Maroney rushed for 135 yards on 15 carries for Minnesota, which avenged a 1999 Sun Bowl loss to Oregon in which the Ducks rallied for a 24-20 victory. Fullback Thomas Tapeh ran for three TDs for the Golden Gophers. Abdul-Khaliq was 12-of-21 for 172 yards. His favorite target was Aaron Hosack, who had six receptions for 105 yards. After a scoreless first quarter, the offense picked up in the second, when the teams combined for 31 points. Siegel's 30-yard field goal as time expired gave the Ducks a 17-14 halftime lead. There were five lead changes in the second half as the offenses continued to dominate.

2004 Gator Bowl

The 2004 Gator Bowl was between the Maryland Terrapins and the West Virginia Mountaineers at Alltel Stadium in Jacksonville, Florida on 1 January 2004. The game ended in a 41–7 victory for Maryland. The Maryland Terrapins (more often, simply 'Terps') earned a bid to the Gator Bowl following a 9–3 record during the 2003 regular season. It was Ralph Friedgen's third season as Maryland head coach and third consecutive bowl game, making him just the second Maryland head coach to do so in his first three seasons—the other being Bobby Ross. At the conclusion of this game, Friedgen also became the first Atlantic Coast Conference coach to ever win at least ten games in his first three seasons. Going into the game, Maryland's 30-win three seasons was the best three-year total in school history. The West Virginia Mountaineers had finished the regular season with a record of 8–4, which already included a defeat at the hands of Maryland. Like Friedgen, it was Rich Rodriguez's third year as head coach of his program. West Virginia entered the game on a seven-game winning streak, as co-champions of the Big East conference. The game took place in front of a crowd of 78,892 fans.

2004 Gator Bowl	Line	1	-	2	-	3	-	4	-	Final
#23 Maryland	(-3.5)	10	-	14	-	10	-	7	-	41
#20 West Virginia	(51.0)	0	-	0	-	7	-	0	-	7

Scoring Summary
Maryland – Novak 27 yard Field Goal
Maryland – Williams 31 yard pass from McBrien (Novak kick)
Maryland – Suter 76 yard Punt return (Novak kick)
Maryland – Williams 22 yard pass from McBrien (Novak kick)
Maryland – McBrien 2 yard run (Novak kick)
West Virginia – Marshall 15 yard run (Cooper kick)
Maryland – Novak 24 yard Field goal
Maryland – Walker 14 yard pass from McBrien (Novak kick)

Maryland Media Guide Gator Bowl Game Summary - Former Mountaineer Scott McBrien threw for a career-high 381 yards to help Maryland to a 41-7 victory over West Virginia in the Gator Bowl, a rematch of a regular-season game that was almost as lopsided. Playing against the team he left in 2001, McBrien threw for three scores and ran for another. His teammate, Steve Suter, returned a punt for a touchdown and made a highlight-reel catch to help the Terrapins reach 10 wins for the third-straight year under Coach Ralph Friedgen.

2004 Outback Bowl

IOWA 37   FLORIDA 17
The 2004 Outback Bowl featured the Florida Gators, and the Iowa Hawkeyes.

2004 Outback Bowl	Line	1	-	2	-	3	-	4	-	Final
#13 Iowa	(47.0)	7	-	13	-	14	-	7	-	37
#17 Florida	(-3.5)	7	-	0	-	3	-	7	-	17

Scoring Summary

Florida – Knight 70 yd pass from Leak (Leach kick)

Iowa – Brown 3 yd pass from Chandler (Kaeding kick)

Iowa – Kaeding 47 yd Field goal

Iowa – Chandler 5 yd run (Kaeding kick)

Iowa – Kaeding 32 yd Field goal

Iowa – Melloy recovered blocked punt in end zone (Kaeding kick)

Florida – Leach 48 yd Field goal

Iowa – Russell 34 yd run (Kaeding kick)

Iowa – Kaeding 38 yd Field goal

Florida – Baker 25 yd pass from Leak (Leach kick)

Associated Press Outback Bowl Game Summary - Iowa took another step forward in its resurgence under coach Kirk Ferentz. Fred Russell rushed for 150 yards on 21 carries, including a back-breaking 34-yard touchdown run late in the third quarter, as the 12th-ranked Hawkeyes routed No. 17 Florida, 37-17, in the Outback Bowl. Iowa (10-3) recorded its first January bowl win since 1959 and has posted back-to-back seasons with at least 10 wins under Ferentz. The Hawkeyes also won their first game in the state of Florida after going 0-5 in their previous visits. The loss likely will put more heat on Florida coach Ron Zook, who completed his second straight 8-5 campaign after Steve Spurrier led the Gators to 12 straight double figure win seasons. Florida fans likely will be clamoring for the return of Spurrier, who is out of a job after resigning his Washington Redskins' post earlier this week. Russell's TD completed a dramatic turnaround that broke open the contest. Florida appeared to close within 27-17 on Dallas Baker's lunging 33-yard TD grab in the end zone. But the play was nullified due to offensive interference and the Gators were forced to punt. Russell's TD staked the Hawkeyes to a 34-10 cushion with 4:37 left in the third period. Getting continued stellar play from its special teams, the Hawkeyes dominated after Chris Leak's 70-yard TD strike to Kelvin Kight gave the Gators a 7-0 lead midway through the first quarter. Nate Kaeding, Iowa's all-time leading scorer, kicked three field goals and Matt Melloy recovered his own a blocked punt in the end zone to make it 27-7 just 54 seconds into the second half. It was Iowa's fifth blocked kick this season and the third for a touchdown. Nathan Chandler was steady, if not spectacular, in his final game for Iowa, completing 13-of-25 passes for 170 yards with no interceptions. After a solid freshman season, Leak struggled in his first bowl game, completing 22-of-41 passes for 268 yards.

2004 Capital One Bowl
GEORGIA 34 PURDUE 27

The 2004 Capital One Bowl was between the Purdue Boilermakers and the Georgia Bulldogs on January 1, 2004, at the Citrus Bowl in Orlando, Florida. Georgia entered the game after a disappointing loss in the SEC Championship Game, while Purdue entered as the Big Ten runner-up. 64,565 people came out to watch a rematch of the 2000 Outback Bowl, a game Georgia won in Overtime.

2004 Capital One Bowl	Line	1	-	2	-	3	-	4	-	OT	-	Final
#11 Georgia	(-3.5)	14	-	10	-	0	-	3	-	7	-	34
#12 Purdue	(42.0)	0	-	10	-	0	-	17	-	0	-	27

Scoring Summary

Georgia – Gibson 6 yard pass from Greene (Bennett kick)

Georgia – Gibson 4 yard pass from Greene (Bennett kick)

Georgia – Bennett 28 yard Field goal

Georgia – Brown 11 yard pass from Greene (Bennett kick)

Purdue – Orton 17 yard run (Jones kick)

Purdue – Jones 27 yard Field goal

Purdue – Orton 2 yard run (Jones kick)

Georgia – Bennett 40 yard Field goal

Purdue – Chambers 3 yard pass from Orton (Jones kick)

Purdue – Jones 44 yard Field goal

Georgia – Lumpkin 1 yard run (Bennett kick)

Associated Press Capital One Bowl Game Summary - Kregg Lumpkin stood along the sideline, head drooping. The freshman was disconsolate about the stunning fumble that cost Georgia a chance to wrap up the Capital One Bowl. He wanted another chance. He got it in overtime. Lumpkin redeemed himself by scoring on a 1-yard, fourth-down dive in the first overtime, giving No. 11 Georgia a 34-27 victory over No. 12 Purdue on Thursday. The Bulldogs (11-3) built a 24-0 lead in the first half. The Boilermakers tied it with a 17-point fourth quarter. Georgia finally won it when Lumpkin slipped into the end zone, then Tony Taylor made a game-ending interception. Richt wasn't in such a good mood at the end of regulation. The Boilermakers (9-4) tied it up thanks to a remarkable turn of events with just over a minute remaining. Purdue was out of timeouts when Richt called a run on second down instead of ordering Quarterback David Greene to take a knee. The coach was trying to avoid a punt with a few seconds left, but he quickly regretted his decision. Lumpkin got hemmed up deep in the backfield and tried to run the other way, but Shaun Phillips stripped the ball. After a wild scramble, Niko Koutouvides recovered for Purdue at the Georgia 34. Ben Jones kicked a 44-yard field goal with 49 seconds remaining to keep the game going, tied at 27. It was reminiscent of the "Miracle of the Meadowlands," a 1978 NFL game in which the New York Giants fumbled trying to run out the clock. Philadelphia scooped up the loose ball and ran it in for the winning touchdown. This time, Georgia had a chance to make up for its mistake in overtime. As the teams prepared for the extra period, Richt noticed Lumpkin standing along the sideline, his head down. Taking the ball first, the Bulldogs got to the 3 with the help of a pass interference penalty on Bobby Iwuchukwu, then went for it on fourth down from inside the 1. Lumpkin managed to slide through a crease for the touchdown. Purdue had a chance to keep the game going. Georgia appeared to get the clinching stop when Kyle Orton threw an incomplete pass on fourth-and-goal from the 8, but the Bulldogs were offsides. Orton's final pass was intercepted by Taylor in the end zone, setting off a wild celebration by the Georgia players after a game that lasted nearly four hours. The game was like the only other meeting between the schools, the 2000 Outback Bowl. In that one, Purdue built a 25-0 lead early in the second quarter but was stunned by one of the greatest comebacks in bowl history. Georgia rallied for a 28-25 victory in overtime. Greene passed for three touchdowns in the first half and the Bulldogs seemed on the verge of their own blowout. He finished 27-of-37 for 327 yards and was the game's MVP. But Greene's performance was overshadowed by Purdue's thrilling comeback, led by Orton. The Quarterback ran for two TDs and threw a 3-yard scoring pass to Anthony Chambers with 1:41 remaining, pulling the Boilermakers to 27-24. When the onside kick went out of bounds, the game was over, right? Not so fast. Jones, who had missed an overtime kick in a loss to Ohio State, got a chance when Lumpkin fumbled. The kicker came through with his second field goal of the game. Orton was knocked out briefly with a dislocated thumb on his non-throwing hand and finished with a plate in his shoe, having sustained a sprained toe. But he led the Purdue rally, completing 20-of-34 for 230 yards. Georgia's Billy Bennett kicked a pair of field goals, giving him 87 for his career and 31 for the season -- NCAA records.

2004 Rose Bowl
USC 28   MICHIGAN 14

The 2004 Rose Bowl was held on January 1, 2004 at the Rose Bowl in Pasadena, California. It was the 90th Rose Bowl Game. The USC Trojans, champions of the Pacific-10 Conference, defeated the Michigan Wolverines, champions of the Big Ten Conference, 28-14. USC Quarterback Matt Leinart was named the Rose Bowl Player of the Game. The events leading up to the 2004 Rose Bowl were the subject of controversy. Although USC was ranked #1 in both the AP Poll and the Coaches Poll, the Trojans were not invited to the BCS National Championship Game, the 2004 Sugar Bowl. Even though the Oklahoma Sooners lost on December 5, 2003 in the 2003 Big 12 Championship Game to the Kansas State Wildcats, by virtue of their dominance earlier in the season, they remained #1 in the final BCS rankings issued at the outset of the bowl season. Oklahoma faced the LSU Tigers, #2 in both polls and the BCS rankings, in the Sugar Bowl.

2004 Rose Bowl	Line	1	-	2	-	3	-	4	-	Final
#4 Michigan	(58.5)	0	-	0	-	7	-	7	-	14
#1 USC	(-7.0)	7	-	7	-	14	-	0	-	28

Scoring Summary

USC - Colbert 25 yard pass from Leinart (Killeen kick)

USC - White 6 yard pass from Leinart (Killeen kick)

USC - Colbert 47 yard pass from Leinart (Killeen kick)

Michigan - Massaquoi 5 yard pass from Navarre (Rivas kick)

USC - Leinart 15 yard pass from Williams (Killeen kick)

Michigan - Perry 2 yard run (Rivas kick)

Bentley Historical Library 2004 ROSE BOWL GAME SUMMARY - Top-ranked Southern California aired it out in a 28-14 win against No. 4 Michigan in the 90th Rose Bowl game, claimed its ninth Associated Press national title. USC Quarterback Mart Leinart, who was voted the game's most valuable player, completed 23 of his 34 pass attempts for 327 yards and three touchdowns. USC managed to score four receiving touchdowns on Michigan's top rated pass defense. U-M Quarterback John Navarre finished his career by completing 27 of his 46 passes for 271 yards and a touchdown. Navarre was sacked a season-high nine times. Tailback Chris Perry carried 23 times for 85 yards and one score. Braylon Edwards added 10 catches for 107 yards. The Wolverines threatened on their opening possession of the game, as they moved from their own 20 to the Trojans' 2 1. However, freshman kicker Garrett Rivas' 48-yard field goal attempt was blocked by USC Shaun Cody. The Trojans took over and needed just four plays to score. The td came on a 25-yard strike down the left hash marks to Keary Colbert. Michigan began its next-to-last drive of the first half at its own 6. The Wolverines gained a first down, but on third-and-18 from their 9, Navarre's pass bounced off Edwards' heel and into the hands of USC linebacker Lofa Tatupu. On third down from the six, Leinart tossed a soft pass to LenDale White in the left flat and he scrambled into the end zone for a 14-0 lead at the half Behind 2 1 -0 early in the third quarter, Michigan answered with a 16-play, 76-yard drive. On second down from the USC five-yard line, Navarre fired a strike to tight end Tim Massaquoi. The touchdown pass was the 72nd of Navarre's career, breaking a tie with Elvis Grbac for the U-M all-time passing td lead. The Trojans answered with an eight-play, 72-yard drive to take a 28-7 lead. The Mike Williams took a reverse pitch and fired a 15-yard strike to a wide-open Leinart. Michigan opened the fourth quarter with an 11 -play, 85-yard drive to cut the USC lead to 28-14 with 11:06 remaining. From the two-yard line, Perry took a toss from Navarre and followed his blockers around the right side for the td. Leinart then fumbled a snap, which resulted in a turnover. Michigan was unable to take advantage and turned the ball over on downs. The Trojans ran out the clock.

Aftermath - LSU defeated Oklahoma 21-14 in the Sugar Bowl. The Coaches Poll chose the winner of that game, the LSU Tigers, as the BCS National Champions. The AP Poll, however, selected the Rose Bowl champion USC Trojans, resulting in the first split national title since the 1997-98 season, the year before the creation of the Bowl Championship Series.

2004 Orange Bowl
MIAMI 16   FLORIDA STATE 14

The 2004 FedEx Orange Bowl game was between the Miami Hurricanes and the Florida State Seminoles on January 1, 2004, at Pro Player Stadium in Miami Gardens, Florida. The Orange Bowl was first played in 1935, and the 2004 game represented the 70th edition of the Orange Bowl. The contest was televised in the United States on ABC.

2004 Orange Bowl	Line	1	-	2	-	3	-	4	-	Final
#10 Miami	(46.0)	3	-	10	-	3	-	0	-	16
#9 Florida State	(-2.0)	0	-	14	-	0	-	0	-	14

Scoring Summary

Miami – Peattie 32 yard Field goal

Florida State – Booker 9 yard run (Beitia kick)

Florida State – Henshaw 7 yard pass from Rix (Beitia kick)

Miami – Moss 3 yard run (Peattie kick)

Miami – Peattie 44 yard Field goal

Miami – Peattie 51 yard Field goal

Game Summary - Miami received the ball to begin the game and scored on the first possession off a 32-yard field goal from Jon Peattie. That was the only scoring of the first quarter as both teams' Quarterbacks threw interceptions. Sean Taylor intercepted Seminole Quarterback Chris Rix while Jerome Carter intercepted Miami Quarterback Brock Berlin. Carter's interception set up the Seminoles with the ball on their own 30-yard line. Chris Rix found Chauncey Stovall for a 52-yard gain putting the Seminoles in Miami territory. On the first play of the second quarter Florida State took the lead off a direct snap to Lorenzo Booker that he ran into the end zone, giving the Seminoles the lead. Florida State got the ball back after forcing Miami to punt. Greg Jones had a 24-yard run during the Seminoles possession to set up a Chris Rix touchdown pass to Matt Henshaw. Florida State now had a 14-3 lead. On Miami's ensuing possession Jarrett Payton took a handoff on third and two for 47 yards. The Hurricanes would get another five yards off a penalty to put them on the Seminoles 25-yard line. Three plays later Tyrone Moss ran into the end zone on a 3-yard rush. Aided by a five-yard penalty the Hurricanes were able to get the Seminoles to go three and out and got the ball back with three minutes and forty four seconds at their own 24-yard line. After a penalty on the Hurricanes, Brock Berlin found wide receiver Ryan Moore open for a 41-yard gain putting the Hurricanes on the Seminoles 35-yard line. The Hurricanes were able to move to as close as the Seminoles 13-yard line, however two sacks forced the Hurricanes to settle for a field goal and go into halftime down 13-14. On the opening kickoff of the second half Antonio Cromartie was only able take the kickoff four yards and the Seminoles got the ball on their own 13-yard line. The Seminoles were unable to do anything and were forced to punt the ball which Miami would return 7 yards to their own 47-yard line. On third and seven Berlin was able to find Kellen Winslow for a 12-yard gain. On third and thirteen Miami completed a 2-yard pass to Jason Geathers coming up 11 yards short of a first down. However, Florida State was penalized five yards on the play. This was crucial because now the Hurricanes could attempt a 51-yard field goal as opposed to a 56-yard field goal. The Hurricanes did attempt the 51-yard field goal and it was good. Jon Peattie gave the Hurricanes a 16-14 lead. Both teams' offense were stagnant the rest of the game. The Seminoles did not cross the 50-yard line the remainder of the quarter. The Hurricanes had a great opportunity to capitalize when Jonathan Vilma recovered a Seminole fumble at the Hurricane 40-yard line. On the ensuing Hurricane possession Berlin found Geathers on third down for a 25-yard gain to put the Hurricanes in Seminole territory. However, Berlin threw an interception on the offense's following third down to Eric Moore. The Seminoles were unable to capitalize on the turnover and went three and out. The Hurricanes defense stepped up big in the fourth quarter. Randy Shannon's defense forced the Seminoles to go three and out on their first two drives of the fourth quarter. Following the Seminoles second punt of the quarter the Hurricanes faced a third and one situation on their own 30. Berlin was unable to rush for the first down on third down and the Hurricanes decided to go for it on fourth down. Berlin would end up fumbling the ball on fourth down giving the Seminoles the ball on the Hurricanes 30-yard line. Once again though the Seminoles offense would be on the field for only three plays as the Hurricanes stopped the Seminoles on a crucial third and three. Seminole kicker Xavier Beitia would line up to attempt a 39-yard field goal to give the Seminoles the lead. The previous season Beitia had an opportunity to beat the top ranked Hurricanes at the Orange Bowl on a 43 yard attempt, Beitia missed the kick wide left, and the Seminoles lost. Beitia would miss this kick as well as it sailed wide right and the Seminoles still trailed, 14-16. The Hurricanes got the ball back and were not able to do anything on their first three downs, and it appeared they would punt on fourth down. However, the Hurricanes faked a punt on a direct snap to D.J. Williams who rushed up the middle for 33 yards. This gave the Hurricanes good field position in Seminole territory. The Hurricanes would run the ball with Payton on two straight play to ice the clock. On third and two the Seminoles defense stopped Payton and the Hurricanes and forced them to attempt a field goal. Jon Peattie would attempt a 45-yard field goal that would be no good. The Seminoles would get one final possession to try and beat the Hurricanes however they were not able to do anything with it and the Hurricanes won by the final score of 16-14.

2004 Cotton Bowl Classic
MISSISSIPPI 31   OKLAHOMA STATE 28

The 2004 Cotton Bowl Classic was between the Ole Miss Rebels and the Oklahoma State Cowboys on January 2, 2004, at the Cotton Bowl in Dallas, Texas. Ole Miss represented the Southeastern Conference (SEC) while Oklahoma State represented the Big 12 Conference. It was Ole Miss's first January bowl victory since the 1970 Sugar Bowl and first Cotton Bowl Classic appearance since 1962.

2004 Cotton Bowl Classic	Line	1	-	2	-	3	-	4	-	Final
#21 Oklahoma State	(60.0)	7	-	7	-	0	-	14	-	28
#16 Mississippi	(-2.5)	7	-	10	-	7	-	7	-	31

Scoring Summary

Mississippi – Turner 16 yard pass from Manning (Nichols kick)

Oklahoma State – Morency 4 yard run (Phillips kick)

Oklahoma State – Bell 3 yard run (Phillips kick)

Mississippi – Espy 25 yard pass from Manning (Nichols kick)

Mississippi – Nichols 33 yard Field Goal

Mississippi – Turner 2 yard run (Nichols kick)

Mississippi – Manning 1 yard run (Nichols kick)

Oklahoma State – Morency 1 yard run (Phillips kick)

Oklahoma State – Wood 17 yard pass from Fields (Phillips kick)

Cotton Bowl Classic Game Summary - Mississippi All-America Quarterback Eli Manning came to Dallas aware of the legacy of high-profile senior signal callers at the SBC Cotton Bowl. Such greats as Theismann, Montana and Aikman finished their memorable college careers by leading their teams to victories in the Cotton Bowl. Now, add one more name to the distinguished list. Manning guided the 16th-ranked Rebels to a 31-28 win over No. 21 Oklahoma State, while throwing for two touchdowns and running for another in front of a sellout crowd of 73,928 at the 69th Classic. It was Ole Miss' first major bowl victory since Eli's father, Archie, accomplished the feat 34 years earlier in the Sugar Bowl. The Rebels finished the season 10-3, marking their first 10-win season since 1971. Manning, winner of the Maxwell and Unitas Awards, was chosen as the Classic's Outstanding Offensive Player after completing 22 (second highest in Cotton Bowl history) of 31 passes for 259 yards with one interception. Not to be outdone, OSU junior Quarterback Josh Fields put on a show of his own, completing 21 of 33 passes for a Cotton Bowl record 307 yards and one touchdown. Fifty-nine years had passed since Oklahoma State's last trip to the Cotton Bowl, and the Cowboys were returning to the sight of the first-ever bowl appearance with a trio of offensive stars, including Fields, wide receiver Rashaun Woods and running back Tatum Bell. OSU jumped out to a 14-7 lead in the second quarter after Bell took a Fields handoff in for a three-yard touchdown. The Rebels took the ensuing kickoff and drove deep inside OSU territory. On the seventh play of the drive, Manning found flanker Mike Espy for a 25-yard touchdown pass to tie the score at 14-14. Despite the offensive output, the biggest play of the contest may have come on the defensive side of the ball. OSU drove to the Ole Miss 30 with 4:03 remaining in the half. On fourth down, the Cowboys passed on the 47-yard field goal attempt. Instead, OSU went for the first down, but Ole Miss defensive end Josh Cooper put an end to the Cowboys' scoring threat by sacking Fields for an 8-yard loss. Cooper was chosen the Classic's Outstanding Defensive Player after being credited with two key tackles resulting in 11 yards in losses, including his fourth down sack on Fields. That stop helped the Rebels gain a 17-14 halftime edge when Jonathan Nichols, the Lou Groza award winner, kicked a 33-yard field goal with 15 seconds remaining in the second quarter. After Nichols' kick, the Rebels never looked back. Ole Miss, making its first SBC Cotton Bowl Classic appearance since 1962, held a 31-14 lead after Manning's one-yard touchdown sneak with 12:32 to play in the game. The Rebels burned slightly over five minutes in clock time to drive 97 yards in 13 plays for what seemed to be a comfortable lead. The Cowboys were not about to give the game to Ole Miss without a fight. OSU turned to its most potent weapon that had carried the Cowboys all the way to the SBC Cotton Bowl – the combination of Fields to Woods. OSU pulled within a touchdown with 4:38 to play after Fields floated the ball just over the reach of an Ole Miss defender and into the hands of Woods for a 17-yard score. Woods' presence was felt in the Ole Miss defensive backfield all day. The senior wide out collected 11 catches for a Cotton Bowl record 223 yards. Oklahoma State's defense had to come up with a stop to give the offense one last shot to tie up the game. Ole Miss had other thoughts. Mississippi's offense converted on three separate third-down conversions on a drive that lasted 10 plays and covered 65 yards. More importantly, OSU could not stop the clock and time ran out on the Cowboys' comeback attempt. The Rebels had won their second Cotton Bowl trophy and the school's first since 1956. The first-ever meeting between OSU and Ole Miss will forever be remembered not only as the warmest Cotton Bowl in history with a 74-degree temperature at kickoff, but also for the scorching play by two high-octane offenses.

2004 Chick-Fil-A Peach Bowl (January)
CLEMSON 27 TENNESSEE 14

The 2004 Peach Bowl featured the Clemson Tigers, and the Tennessee Volunteers.

2004 Chick-Fil-A Peach Bowl	Line	1	-	2	-	3	-	4	-	Final
Clemson	(47.5)	10	-	14	-	0	-	3	-	27
#6 Tennessee	(-5.0)	7	-	7	-	0	-	0	-	14

Scoring Summary

Clemson – Coleman 8 yard run (Hunt kick)

Clemson – Hunt 23 yard Field goal

Tennessee – Hannen 19 yard pass from Clausen (Wilhoit kick)

Clemson – Jasmin 15 yard run (Hunt kick)

Tennessee – Jones 30 yard pass from Clausen (Wilhoit kick)

Clemson – Browning 8 yard run (Hunt kick)

Clemson – Hunt 28 yard Field goal

Associated Press Chick-Fil-A Peach Bowl Game Summary - After saving coach Tommy Bowden's job, Clemson finished the season with a flourish. Charlie Whitehurst passed for 246 yards and Chad Jasmin rushed for a career-high 130 yards and a touchdown on just 15 carries as the Tigers upset seventh-ranked Tennessee, 27-14, in the Peach Bowl. Two months ago, Bowden's job appeared to be in jeopardy, but the Tigers (9-4) won their last three regular-season games, including victories over intrastate rival South Carolina and nationally ranked Florida State. Bowden received a contract extension in December, and Clemson carried the momentum into the Peach Bowl. The Tigers drove 80 yards on the game's opening possession as Whitehurst's 35-yard completion to Kevin Youngblood set up Duane Coleman's nine-yard TD run just 2:10 into the game. Bowden even resorted to some trickery as backup running back Kyle Browning rushed for an eight-yard touchdown run on a "fumblerooskie" play with 5:36 left in the first half to give the Tigers a 24-14 lead. Browning had just seven carries in his previous seven games. Whitehurst completed 22-of-40 passes. Tennessee safety Rashad Baker admitted the Volunteers were caught off guard. Tennessee never recovered as it unraveled in the second half with undisciplined play. They were whistled for 10 penalties for 119 yards and were held to just 38 yards rushing. Casey Clausen threw two TDs in the first half and finished with a career-high 373 yards but could not get much going in the second half. The second-winningest Quarterback in school history behind Peyton Manning, Clausen finished his career 34-10.

2004 Fiesta Bowl
OHIO STATE 35   KANSAS STATE 28

The 2004 Tostitos Fiesta Bowl, played on January 2, 2004, was the 33rd edition of the Fiesta Bowl. The game pitted #7 Ohio State against #8 Kansas State. It was a match-up between a perennial powerhouse in Ohio State, and a school that was only recently accustomed to winning in Kansas State. Despite Kansas State's historically losing record, head coach Bill Snyder had turned around the program in the decade prior to the bowl game, and K-State was making its second Fiesta Bowl appearance in 7 years. Kansas State was the Big 12 Conference Champion and came into the game on a seven game win streak, winning those games by an average of 39–9. In the game immediately prior to the Fiesta Bowl, Kansas State had soundly defeated #1-ranked Oklahoma 35–7 in the Big 12 Championship Game. However, the K-State team was badly distracted one night before the bowl game when its Quarterback and team leader Ell Roberson was accused of sexual assault. (No charges were ultimately filed against Roberson.) In fact, it was not known whether Roberson would play until game time. Kansas State had been favored to win by 7 points, but some casinos pulled the line over the uncertainty about Roberson. Despite being outgained 378–337 in the bowl game, and having a turnover margin of -1, Ohio State prevailed 35–28. It was Ohio State's second straight Fiesta Bowl win; they went on to win another one in 2006.

2004 Fiesta Bowl	Line	1	-	2	-	3	-	4	-	Final
#8 Kansas State	(-7.0)	0	-	7	-	7	-	14	-	28

| #7 Ohio State | (43.5) | 14 | - | 7 | - | 14 | - | 0 | - | 35 |

Scoring Summary

Ohio State – Hollins blocked punt recovered in end zone (Nugent kick)

Ohio State – Holmes 6 yard pass from Krenzel (Nugent kick)

Ohio State – Jenkins 17 yard pass from Krenzel (Nugent kick)

Kansas State – Sproles 6 yard run (Rheem kick)

Kansas State – Roberson 14 yard run (Rheem kick)

Ohio State – Jenkins 8 yard pass from Krenzel (Nugent kick)

Ohio State – Holmes 31 yard pass from Krenzel (Nugent kick)

Kansas State – Saba 3 yard run (Rheem kick)

Kansas State – Roberson 1 yard run (Rheem kick)

Associated Press Fiesta Bowl Game Summary - Craig Krenzel carried the MVP trophy off the Fiesta Bowl field for the second year in a row. His counterpart, Kansas State Quarterback Ell Roberson, left knowing he might have cost his team dearly. Krenzel, who finished his Ohio State career 24-3 as a starter, matched his career high with four touchdown passes -- two apiece to Michael Jenkins and Santonio Holmes -- and the Buckeyes (No. 6 ESPN/USA Today; No. 7 AP) held off the Wildcats (No. 10 ESPN/USA Today; No. 8 AP) 35-28 on Friday night. Krenzel should love the Fiesta Bowl. He directed the Buckeyes' dramatic 31-24 double-overtime victory over Miami for the national championship a year ago. Roberson got the start despite a sexual-assault accusation by a woman early Thursday. He was awful early in Kansas State's first Bowl Championship Series game, but nearly brought the Wildcats back from deficits of 21-0 and 35-14. After a 3-for-13 start, Roberson completed 20 of 51 passes for 294 yards and one interception. He ran for 32 yards. Roberson was not available for comment after the game. Ohio State (11-2) led 35-14 entering the fourth quarter, but Kansas State scored twice. Maurice Mack's 37-yard kickoff return to the Ohio State 46 and Roberson's 19-yard pass to James Terry helped set up Ayo Saba's 3-yard run. Roberson threw 24 yards to Davin Dennis to the Ohio State 15, and after a facemask penalty, Roberson sneaked over from the 1 to cut it to 35-28 with 2:47 left. Kansas State (11-4) got the onside kick but was called for a false start. Ohio State's Bobby Carpenter recovered the second onside kick and the Buckeyes held on. The Wildcats had one more chance, but Roberson's desperation pass from midfield was batted down at the 2. Kansas State started from its 8 with 1:12 to go, and Roberson's passing moved the Wildcats to the Ohio State 48. Krenzel's four TD passes were his most in a non-overtime game. He had four in a triple-overtime victory over North Carolina State on Sept. 12, but three came in overtime. Krenzel -- offensive MVP of last year's Fiesta Bowl national championship game -- was 11-for-24 for 189 yards with two interceptions. Jenkins had five catches for 96 yards to pass David Boston as Ohio State's career reception leader. Ohio State, with the top-ranked rushing defense in the country, held All-American Darren Sproles to a season-low 38 yards on 13 carries. Kansas State rolled into Arizona on a seven-game winning streak, the latest a 35-7 pounding of then-No. 1 and unbeaten Oklahoma in the Big 12 title game. But the Roberson case was an ugly turn of events for Snyder, whose team appeared in its 11th consecutive bowl game. A woman accused Roberson of sexual assault at the team hotel about 3:30 a.m. Thursday. Roberson acknowledged having sex, but said it was consensual. A police report was filed, and earlier Friday the university said its own investigation found no criminal wrongdoing. Snyder allowed Roberson to start but said the Quarterback could face punishment for violating team rules. Whatever that punishment is will remain a mystery. Krenzel became the second player to win consecutive MVP awards in the 33-year history of the Fiesta Bowl. Curt Warner of Penn State did it in the 1980-81 seasons. The Buckeyes gave up an average of 1.9 yards per carry this season but were burned for 179 yards on the ground in their regular-season finale at Michigan. They talked all week about regaining their reputation, then held Kansas State to 84 yards on the ground. The Buckeyes' first score came when Harlen Jacobs blocked Jared Brite's punt and John Hollins returned it 7 yards for a touchdown. Krenzel's 36-yard pass to Bam Childress set up his scrambling, 6-yard touchdown pass to Holmes that made it 14-0. After Chris Gamble's interception at the Kansas State 17, Krenzel threw over the middle to Jenkins for a TD and it was 21-0 with 37 seconds left in the first quarter. Kansas State's offense, which rolled up 519 yards against Oklahoma, finally showed some life with a 70-yard, 11-play touchdown drive, capped by Sproles' 6-yard run with 3:01 to play in the half. Roberson threw 17 yards to Thomas Hill, then ran 14 yards for a score to slice the lead to 21-14 with 8:59 left in the third quarter. But the Buckeyes took the kickoff and went 74 yards in nine plays to go up 28-14.

2004 Humanitarian Bowl

The 2004 Humanitarian Bowl was the 7th edition of the bowl game. The game was played on January 4th, 2004. The next edition was played in December 2004, almost a year from this game, and the name was changed after this contest to the "MPC Computers Bowl". This game featured the Georgia Tech Yellow Jackets, and the Tulsa Golden Hurricane. In this game Georgia Tech set several Humanitarian Bowl records. The 42 point margin of victory is a bowl game record. This was the third meeting between the schools - both previous meetings were also bowl games.

2004 Humanitarian Bowl	Line	1	-	2	-	3	-	4	-	Final
Georgia Tech	(-7.5)	7	-	3	-	21	-	21	-	52
Tulsa	(48.0)	0	-	3	-	0	-	7	-	10

Scoring Summary
Georgia Tech – Daniels 9 yard run (Burnett kick)
Tulsa – DeVault 22 yard Field goal
Georgia Tech – Burnett 29 yard Field goal
Georgia Tech – Daniels 1 yard run (Burnett kick)
Georgia Tech – Woods 2 yard run (Burnett kick)
Georgia Tech – Daniels 33 yard run (Burnett kick)
Georgia Tech – Daniels 38 yard run (Schroeder kick)
Georgia Tech – Hatch 1 yard run (Schroeder kick)
Tulsa – Mills 13 yard pass from Smith (DeVault kick)
Georgia Tech – Hatch 8 yard run (Schroeder kick)

Associated Press Humanitarian Bowl Game Summary - P.J. Daniels just about made sure Georgia Tech had a seventh straight winning season all by himself. Daniels ran for 307 yards, the second-highest total in school history, and four touchdowns to lead the Yellow Jackets to a 52-10 rout of Tulsa on a frigid Saturday afternoon in the Humanitarian Bowl. The Yellow Jackets (7-6) haven't had a losing season since going 5-6 in 1996. Tech faced suggestions that perhaps it didn't deserve to be in a bowl, even the distant outpost of the Humanitarian Bowl. Not many could say that after Saturday. Tulsa (8-5) closed the regular season on a five-game winning streak for the school's first bowl berth since 1991, but Saturday's appearance was hardly memorable. The Golden Hurricane didn't score a touchdown until the fourth quarter and finished with 144 total yards -- less than half of Daniels yardage. They were sacked seven times and held to minus-56 yards rushing. A few inches of overnight snow remained beneath the aluminum seats in Bronco Stadium and small drifts and piles had been swept from the blue artificial turf to the sidelines. The temperature at kickoff was 20 degrees and it didn't get much warmer, even after the sun broke through the clouds at halftime. But the weather did nothing to cool off Daniels, a sophomore who just earned a scholarship after last season. Tech's previous rushing high in a bowl game was 199 yards by Eddie Prokop in the 1944 Sugar Bowl, a 20-18 win over Tulsa. Daniels had 104 yards at halftime, broke Prokop's record early in the third quarter and kept going. He scored on runs of 9, 1, 33 and 38 yards. Daniels already was second on Tech's rushing list for a game with 240 yards against North Carolina on Nov. 15. Only Eddie Lee Ivery's 356 yards against Air Force in 1978 is higher in the Yellow Jackets' record book. Tech recovered six Tulsa fumbles, scored six touchdowns in the second half and broke the school bowl record for points set in a 45-21 win over Nebraska in the 1991 Florida Citrus Bowl. With the win, Atlantic Coast Conference teams went 5-1 in bowl games this season. League champion Florida State, which lost 16-14 to Miami on Thursday, was the only ACC team to lose. Even without the draw of hometown favorite Boise State, which went to the Fort Worth Bowl instead of staying in town for the second straight year, the stadium was about two-thirds full with 23,118 fans. Most of the crowd was cheering for Tulsa, which finished tied for second behind Boise State in the Western Athletic Conference, but there wasn't much to celebrate about the Golden Hurricane. Tulsa had just 20 yards of offense in the first half, thanks much to minus-29 yards rushing. The Golden Hurricane lost nearly half that on one play when Quarterback James Kilian tripped over his own feet while backing up on a pass play for a loss of 12, and they lost another 18 yards on an intentional grounding call. Tech led only 10-3 at halftime, then took over in the second half after both teams had struggled to move the ball. Daniels also set several records in the seventh Humanitarian Bowl. His yardage total more than doubled Brock Forsey's 152 yards for Boise State against Louisville in 1999, and he broke Forsey's mark of three touchdowns scored last season in a win over Iowa State. Daniels left not long after topping the 300-yard mark as Gailey substituted freely and tried to get everyone who made the long trip into the game.

2004 Sugar Bowl - (Bowl Championship Series Championship Game)

The 2004 Sugar Bowl, the BCS title game for the 2003 college football season, was played on January 4, 2004 at the Louisiana Superdome in New Orleans, Louisiana. The teams were LSU Tigers and the Oklahoma Sooners. The Tigers won the BCS National Championship, defeating the Sooners by a score of 21-14.

Set-up - BCS #2 ranked LSU came into The National Championship Title Game 12-1, with their one loss at home to #17 Florida 19-7. Top-ranked Oklahoma (but #3 in the AP poll) was 12-1, with the lone defeat coming at a neutral site in the Big 12 Championship Game against Kansas State 35-7. There was substantial media and fan controversy as to which teams deserved to play in the National Title game. USC was ranked #3 in the BCS standings but #1 by both human polls, the ESPN/USA Today Coaches Poll and the AP poll, which made up a portion of the BCS Standings. Southern Cal owned a record of 11-1, with its one loss coming in triple overtime at unranked Cal 34-31. Once the game commenced, LSU's #1 ranked defense held the country's most prolific offense, which had averaged 45.2 points and 461 yards per game, to 154 total yards (32 in the first half) and just one touchdown until midway through the fourth quarter. The Sooners' Heisman Trophy-winning QB Jason White completed only 13 of his 37 passing attempts for just 102 yards. He was also sacked seven times and intercepted twice. LSU's offense was largely supplied by freshman running back and Sugar Bowl MVP Justin Vincent, who rushed for 117 yards and a touchdown. As a result, LSU won their second National Championship Title and first since 1958. Most of the coaches voted LSU National Champions as contractually required by the BCS. There were three dissenting coaches (Ron Turner of Illinois, Mike Bellotti of Oregon and Lou Holtz of South Carolina) who voted USC #1. BCS #3 USC won the Rose Bowl against #4 ranked Michigan and was voted the National Champion in the AP Poll.

2004 Sugar Bowl	Line	1	-	2	-	3	-	4	-	Final
#2 LSU	(48.5)	7	-	7	-	7	-	0	-	21
#3 Oklahoma	(-6.5)	0	-	7	-	0	-	7	-	14

Scoring Summary
LSU – Green 24 yard run (Gaudet kick)
Oklahoma – Jones 1 yard run (DeCarlo kick)
LSU – Vincent 16 yard run (Gaudet kick)
LSU – Spears 20 yard interception return (Gaudet kick)
Oklahoma – Jones 1 yard run (DeCarlo kick)

Associated Press Sugar Bowl Game Summary - LSU's defense wasn't too impressed with the highest-scoring team in the country. The blitzes came from everywhere. Heisman Trophy winner Jason White took a brutal beating. And, when 297-pound defensive end Marcus Spears rumbled to the end zone with an interception, the purple-and-gold revelers got started on their first national title celebration in 45 years. Make no mistake: defense wins championships. Just ask Oklahoma Sooners, which came up short 21-14 in a Sugar Bowl that settled half the argument about who's No. 1. While Chad Lavalais was willing to share the national title with Southern Cal, he wasn't going to concede anything on defense. Not to the Trojans. Not to anyone. The Sooners, averaging 45.2 points, needed help from their special teams and defense just to score their two touchdowns. Without Brandon Shelby's blocked punt and Brodney Poole's interception, it wouldn't have been close. LSU was not very impressed with Oklahoma's lofty numbers. Oklahoma had a chance at the end when LSU's defense wilted just a bit. But the Tigers came through again, turning away the Sooners' chance at a tying touchdown with less than three minutes to go. Oklahoma got the ball once more, but White threw three straight incompletions, then ended up on his back in his final play of the season. Lionel Turner blitzed up the middle and crushed the Sooners Quarterback, who never had a chance to get rid of the ball. White picked himself off the turf and trudged to the sideline, having completed just 13 of 37 for 102 yards and two interceptions -- by far his worst performance in a brilliant season. Overall, the Sooners managed just 154 yards on 70 plays from scrimmage -- 2.2 yards a try. Hardly to be expected from a team that had been piling up 461.4 yards per game, beating opponents with numbers that looked more like basketball than football. Then again, LSU had been doing this all season. The Tigers were the stingiest defense in the country, allowing just over 10 points a game. Oklahoma barely made a dent in that average. There were some hairy moments for LSU. Trailing by a touchdown, Oklahoma drove from its own 42 to the LSU 12 late in the game. First down. A dozen yards from overtime. But LSU's defenders had come too far to let this one slip away. White threw a couple of incompletions, his receivers too well covered. Then came the play that epitomized LSU's gambling style -- safety Jessie Daniels blitzed up the middle and Kejuan Jones was left running all alone toward the middle of the end zone. But Daniels flattened White as he threw, the ball fluttering over Jones' outstretching, pleading hands. Oklahoma went for it on fourth down, White delivering another pass over the middle. The ball was deflected, and Sooners receiver Mark Clayton nearly came up with it, only to have it scrape the turf with 2:46 remaining. Incomplete. Yes, this night belonged to the LSU defense. Spears provided the points that ultimately decided the game. On the first play of the second half, he sacked White. Then, he fooled the Oklahoma Quarterback by dropping back in coverage on second down. White threw the ball straight to Spears, who rumbled 20 yards for a touchdown that gave LSU a 21-7 lead. It was the seventh touchdown of the year for the Tigers' defense, a school record. And now they have a national championship, too. Who cares that it will have to be shared with USC, No. 1 in The Associated Press media poll? The LSU defense proved itself worthy of being No. 1.

2004 New Orleans Bowl

The 2004 Wyndham New Orleans Bowl featured the North Texas Mean Green and the Southern Miss Golden Eagles. It was North Texas's fourth consecutive New Orleans Bowl appearance.

2004 New Orleans Bowl	Line	1	-	2	-	3	-	4	-	Final
Southern Mississippi	(-6.0)	14	-	3	-	0	-	14	-	31
North Texas	(54.0)	0	-	3	-	0	-	7	-	10

Scoring Summary
Southern Miss - Graves 37 yard pass from Almond (McCaleb Kick)
Southern Miss - Almond 1 yard run (McCaleb Kick)
North Texas - Bazaldua 24 yard Field Goal
Southern Miss - McCaleb 45 yard Field Goal
Southern Miss - Boley 62 yard interception return (McCaleb Kick)
Southern Miss - Moore 1 yard run (McCaleb Kick)
North Texas - Quinn 11 yard pass from Hall (Bazaldua Kick)

Associated Press New Orleans Bowl Game Summary - Just 10 days after getting burned by the country's No. 2 rusher, Southern Mississippi stuffed the nation's leader. The Golden Eagles limited North Texas freshman Jamario Thomas to 92 yards - just two in the second half - en route to an easy 31-10 triumph over the Mean Green in the Wyndham New Orleans Bowl, the first of 28 postseason games this season. Dustin Almond completed 16-of-30 passes for 247 yards and both ran and threw for a score for Southern Miss (7-5), which concluded its regular season with a 26-16 home loss to California on December 4 in which J.J. Arrington ran for 261 yards for the Golden Bears. In this one, Thomas - who had averaged a national-best 189.89 rushing yards this season - gained 90 yards on 18 carries in the first half, which ended with Southern Miss leading 17-3. But Thomas was stymied after the break as the Golden Eagles pulled away, and he came up 63 yards shy of surpassing Ron Dayne's NCAA freshman rushing record. Thomas, who had five consecutive games of 200 yards rushing before sitting out the regular-season finale because of a sore hamstring. Southern Miss linebacker Michael Boley, was voted the game's MVP after recording four tackles for losses, including two sacks, and returning an interception 62 yards for a touchdown. Almond opened the scoring by finding tight end Otho Graves for a 37-yard touchdown pass four minutes into the contest. Just under five minutes later, he connected on a 48-yard pass to Tavarres Williams to the 3, then ran it in from a yard out two plays later to double the advantage. Southern Miss, which finished tied for second in Conference USA, opened a 24-3 cushion just over two minutes into the fourth quarter when Boley intercepted a pass by Scott Hall and ran it back for his first touchdown since 2002. Sherron Moore capped the team's scoring with a one yard run with 1:26 to play, two plays after the Eagles recovered a fumble at the North Texas 3. Hall, who was 15-of-30 for 134 yards with two interceptions and five sacks, found Johnny Quinn for an 11-yard TD with one second remaining for the Sun Belt Conference champion Mean Green (7-5), who have appeared in all four New Orleans Bowls but have won only once.

2004 Champs Sports Bowl

The 2004 Champs Sports Bowl was the 15th edition of the bowl game and was played on December 21, 2004, featuring the Georgia Tech Yellow Jackets, and the Syracuse Orange.

2004 Champs Sports Bowl	Line	1	-	2	-	3	-	4	-	Final
Syracuse	(44.0)	6	-	0	-	0	-	8	-	14
Georgia Tech	(-5.0)	21	-	14	-	14	-	2	-	51

Scoring Summary
Georgia Tech – Reis 20 yard interception return (Bell kick)
Syracuse – Patterson 21 yard run (Kick failed)
Georgia Tech – Johnson 10 yard pass from Ball (Bell kick)
Georgia Tech – Curry 80 yard pass from Ball (Bell kick)
Georgia Tech – Daniels 2 yard run (Bell Kick)
Georgia Tech – Johnson 5 yard run (Bell kick)
Georgia Tech – Ball 11 yard run (Bell kick)
Georgia Tech – Daniels 1 yard run (Bell kick)
Syracuse – Gregory 25 yard pass from Patterson (Darlington pass from Rhodes)
Georgia Tech – Team Safety

Associated Press Champs Sports Bowl Game Summary - Georgia Tech scored 41 seconds into the game and had a season high in points by halftime in a 51-14 rout of Syracuse in the Champs Sports Bowl. Chris Reis returned an interception 20 yards for a score on the second play from scrimmage and Calvin Johnson had two TDs in the first half for Georgia Tech (7-5), which led 35-6 at halftime. Johnson caught a 10-yard TD pass from Reggie Ball in the first quarter and scored on a five-yard run just before the half to give the Yellow Jackets a 29-point lead at intermission. Georgia Tech's best offensive output during the season was a 30-10 win over Connecticut on November 13. Ball completed 9-of-15 passes for 192 yards and two TDs in the first half, including an 80-yard scoring strike to Nate Curry with 11 seconds left in the first quarter that made it 21-6. Syracuse (6-6) was unable to stop Georgia Tech when it mattered and could not get its offense on track against the nation's 14th-ranked defense. The Orange allowed 321 yards in the first half while managing only 65 yards rushing on 20 carries. Syracuse, which entered the game ranked 23rd in the country in rushing at 190.36 yards per game, finished with 51 on 31 carries. Georgia Tech rolled up 514 total yards, including 294 yards rushing and 228 yards passing. Ball finished 12-of-19 for 207 yards and was intercepted once, and he added 38 yards rushing and a TD on nine carries. It was the Yellow Jackets' best offensive output since they had 560 yards against Virginia on November 10, 2001. It was a big win to cap a successful but somewhat frustrating season for Georgia Tech. Each of the Yellow Jackets' five losses came to bowl-bound teams. They managed to earn a trip to a bowl for the eighth straight season, one of just eight teams with a streak that long. Syracuse's Perry Patterson scored on a 21-yard run with 6:24 left in the first quarter, but Collin Barber missed the extra point and Georgia Tech maintained a 7-6 lead. After Patterson's score, Georgia Tech scored 42 consecutive points before Syracuse finally found the end zone again in the fourth quarter. P.J. Daniels rushed for 119 yards and two TDs on 17 carried for Georgia Tech and Curry finished with three catches for 105 yards. Georgia Tech improved its bowl record to 22-11 with the victory. The Yellow Jackets rank sixth all-time in bowl victories, one behind Penn State, Tennessee and Oklahoma which are tied for third.

2004 GMAC Bowl

The 2004 GMAC Bowl was played in December 2004, and featured the Memphis Tigers, and the Bowling Green Falcons.

2004 GMAC Bowl	Line	1	-	2	-	3	-	4	-	Final
Bowling Green	(-3.5)	21	-	14	-	7	-	10	-	52
Memphis	(70.0)	7	-	21	-	0	-	7	-	35

Scoring Summary
Bowling Green - Pope 1 yard run (Suisham Kick)
Bowling Green - Sharon 18 yard pass from Jacobs (Suisham Kick)
Memphis - Doucette 42 yard pass from Wimprine (Gostkowski Kick)
Bowling Green - Sharon 36 yard pass from Jacobs (Suisham Kick)
Memphis - Kelley 60 yard pass from Wimprine (Gostkowski Kick)
Bowling Green - Sanders 31 yard pass from Jacobs (Suisham Kick)
Memphis - Avery 38 yard pass from Wimprine (Gostkowski Kick)
Memphis - Williams 31 yard run (Gostkowski Kick)
Bowling Green - Sanders 17 yard pass from Jacobs (Suisham Kick)
Bowling Green - Pope 13 yard pass from Jacobs (Suisham Kick)
Bowling Green - Suisham 37 yard Field Goal
Bowling Green - Pope 1 yard run (Suisham Kick)
Memphis - Doucette 14 yard pass from Wimprine (Gostkowski Kick)

Associated Press GMAC Bowl Game Summary - Bowling Green Quarterback Omar Jacobs had some pretty high standards to live up to in the GMAC bowl. Unfortunately for Memphis, he surpassed them. Jacobs threw five touchdown passes and became the third different Mid-American Conference Quarterback to win the GMAC Bowl MVP award in the last four seasons in Bowling Green's 52-35 dismantling of Memphis. Ben Roethlisberger of Miami of Ohio and Marshall's Byron Leftwich both have starred in this bowl before going on to success in the NFL. Roethlisberger, a rookie sensation with the

Pittsburgh Steelers, was the MVP last season and Leftwich, the starter for the Jacksonville Jaguars, won the MVP award in 2001 and 2002. A sophomore, Jacobs is well on his way to following in their footsteps after throwing for 365 yards and setting a MAC single-season record for TD passes with 41. The previous record of 39 was held by another successful NFL Quarterback, Chad Pennington of the New York Jets, who set the previous record while at Marshall. Bowling Green (9-3) took the lead for good, 35-28, just 37 seconds before the half when Jacobs found Steve Sanders for a 17-yard score. The Falcons then dominated the second half, scoring 17 consecutive points before Memphis (8-4) capped the scoring with a 14-yard TD pass from Danny Wimprine to John Doucette. Wimprine completed 26-of-39 passes for 324 yards and four TDs and was intercepted once. Memphis running back DeAngelo Williams, the Conference USA Offensive Player of the Year, rushed for 120 yards on 18 carries before fracturing his right fibula in the third quarter. Bowling Green entered the game having outscored opponents by 163-27 in the first quarter this season and the Falcons wasted no time jumping on the Tigers in this one. P.J. Pope scored on a one-yard TD run just under five minutes into the game to give Bowling Green a 7-0 lead. The Falcons were successful with an onside kick, setting up an 18-yard TD pass to Charles Sharon from Jacobs, who completed 26-of-44 passes. Pope, who finished with 151 yards and two TDs on 28 carries, scored both of Bowling Green's second-half TDs. He hauled in a 13-yard pass from Jacobs in the third quarter and his one-yard TD run with 8:01 to play gave the Falcons a 52-28 lead. Down 21-7 after the first quarter, Memphis (8-4) rallied to tie the game, 28-28, on a 31-yard TD run by Williams. Bowling Green is 4-3 in seven bowl appearances with four straight wins.

2004 Las Vegas Bowl

The 2004 Pioneer PureVision Las Vegas Bowl was the 13th edition of the annual game. It featured the UCLA Bruins and the Wyoming Cowboys. Wyoming won its first ever Las Vegas Bowl title.

2004 Las Vegas Bowl	Line	1	-	2	-	3	-	4	-	Final
UCLA	(-12.0)	0	-	14	-	7	-	0	-	21
Wyoming	(57.5)	10	-	0	-	0	-	14	-	24

Scoring Summary
Wyoming – Yaussi 39 yard Field Goal
Wyoming – Holden 10 yard pass from Bramlet (Yaussi kick)
UCLA – Taylor 29 yard pass from Olson (Medlock kick)
UCLA – Bragg 17 yard pass from Koral (Medlock kick)
UCLA – Bragg 25 yard pass from Koral (Medlock)
Wyoming – Raterink 22 yard pass from Bouknight (Yaussi kick)
Wyoming – Wadkowski 12 yard pass from Bramlet (Yaussi kick)

Associated Press Las Vegas Bowl Game Summary - Corey Bramlet made Wyoming's first trip to a bowl game in 11 years' worth the wait. Bramlet threw a pair of touchdown passes, including a 12-yard strike to John Wadkowski with 57 seconds remaining, to lead the Cowboys to a 24-21 victory over UCLA in the Las Vegas Bowl. The Cowboys took a 10-0 lead in the first quarter only to have UCLA reel off 21 consecutive points and take a 21-10 lead heading into the fourth quarter. Wyoming cut the deficit to 21-17 on a 22-yard reverse pass from wide receiver Jovon Bouknight to backup Quarterback J.J. Raterink just over two minutes into the fourth quarter. Trailing by four with just over four minutes to play, Wyoming (7-5) took the lead on a 10-play, 72-yard drive that Bramlet capped with his second TD pass of the game. He finished 20-of-34 for 307 yards and was intercepted once. Bramlet's first scoring strike of the game, a 10-yard pass to Tyler Holden, gave Wyoming a 10-0 lead with 4:11 to play in the opening quarter. UCLA (6-6) scored 14 points in the second quarter to take the lead but lost starting Quarterback Drew Olson to a sprained left knee. Olson, who finished 6-of-12 for 96 yards and a TD, did not return. David Koral came on after Olson went down and completed 7-of-12 passes for 89 yards and two scores both to Craig Bragg. Their first connection, from 17-yards out, gave the Bruins their first lead, 14-10, 1:50 before the half. Koral found Bragg again midway through the third for a 25-yard TD to extend the Bruins lead to 21-10. Maurice Drew rushed for 126 yards on 25 carries for UCLA, which was hampered by three turnovers. Wyoming rushed for just 76 yards on 30 carries.

2004 Fort Worth Bowl

The 2004 edition to the Fort Worth Bowl, the second edition, featured the Marshall Thundering Herd, and the Cincinnati Bearcats. It had a title sponsor of PlainsCapital Bank. The game was particularly notable because it featured an incoming school (Marshall) to and outgoing school (Cincinnati) from Conference USA.

2004 Fort Worth Bowl	Line	1	-	2	-	3	-	4	-	Final
Marshall	(53.0)	14	-	0	-	0	-	0	-	14
Cincinnati	(-1.5)	10	-	14	-	0	-	8	-	32

Scoring Summary
Cincinnati - Giddens 9 yard blocked punt return (Lovell Kick)
Cincinnati - Lovell 23 yard Field Goal
Marshall - Davis 14 yard pass from Hill (O'Connor Kick)
Marshall - Smith 32 yard interception return (O'Connor Kick)
Cincinnati - Celek 15 yard pass from Guidugli (Lovell Kick)
Cincinnati - Jackson 8 yard pass from Guidugli (Lovell Kick)
Cincinnati - Lovell 19 yard Field Goal
Cincinnati - Team safety
Cincinnati - Lovell 35 yard Field Goal

Associated Press Fort Worth Bowl Game Summary - What a difference Gino Guidugli made for Cincinnati. Guidugli threw a pair of touchdown passes and the defense totally controlled Marshall in Cincinnati's 32-14 victory in the Fort Worth Bowl. The last time Cincinnati took the field, it was handed a season-ending 70-7 drubbing at Louisville. However, the Bearcats played without Guidugli, who was sidelined with a fractured hand. Guidugli, who holds every Cincinnati career passing and total offense record, completed 24-of-36 passes for 231 yards. He threw two TD passes in the second quarter as the Bearcats took a 24-14 lead into halftime. The senior Quarterback also broke Greg Cook's 36-year-old school record for touchdown passes in a season, finishing the game with 26 in 11 games. Guidugli played equally well both under center and in shotgun formation while nursing an injured hand suffered against South Florida in the team's next-to-last regular season game. The Bearcats trailed 14-10 after the first quarter due to Guidugli's lone miscue of the game. Junior defensive back Willie Smith picked his pass by Guidugli and raced 32 yards for a touchdown to give Marshall the lead. The Bearcats (7-5) then took the lead for good when tight end Brent Celek hauled in a 15-yard scoring strike from Guidugli with 4:31 to play in the half. Earnest Jackson then capped an 11-play, 87-yard drive with an eight-yard TD catch with just 18 seconds left. Cincinnati opened the second half with a pair of 18-play drives that ate up most of the time in the third quarter and the beginning of the fourth. The Bearcats came up empty on the first series as a pass from a fake field goal was deflected and intercepted at the line of scrimmage. Marshall drove to the Cincinnati 42 in its opening possession of the second half, but a third down pass over the middle from Quarterback Stan Hill was tipped by linebacker Jamey Murphey and intercepted by Kevin Hazel. It was the only time the Thundering Herd had the ball in the quarter. Guidugli moved the Bearcats 61 yard in 18 plays on their next series, capping it with a 19-yard field goal by Kevin Lovell to make the score 27-14. On the following possession, Marshall's Ian O'Connor had his second punt blocked in the game, going out of the back of the end zone for a safety. Marshall defensive end Jonathan Goddard expressed dismay at his team's inability to put more pressure on Guidugli, especially on third down situations. Marshall (6-6) was unable to get anything going offensively, managing only 11 first downs and 134 total yards. Hill was 14-of-30 for 137 yards, one TD and one interception, but the Thundering Herd were held to minus-3 yards on the ground in 21 attempts. Marshall Coach Bob Pruett said his team had not seen much contact since the regular season finale Nov. 20, and it showed on the field. Hannibal Thomas hauled in nine receptions for 102 yards for Cincinnati, setting a Fort Worth Bowl record for receptions in a game. Cincinnati scored just one minute into the game when Tyjuan Hagler blocked a punt that Antwaun Giddens scooped up and took 10 yards for the score. With 6:23 to play in the first quarter, Lovell tacked on a 23-yard field goal to stretch the margin to 10-0. Marshall responded with two touchdowns in the final minute of the quarter. Hill connected with Josh Davis on a 14-yard scoring strike with 1:00 to play, and then Smith followed with his interception return to put the Thundering Herd on top, 14-10. The game-time temperature was 28 degrees with a wind chill factor of 17 degrees, but Hill refused to use that as an excuse for his team's poor performance. Guidugli was named player of the game for Cincinnati, while Davis took the honors for Marshall.

2004 Hawai'i Bowl

The 2004 Sheraton Hawai'i Bowl took place on December 24, 2004, at Aloha Stadium in Honolulu, Hawaii. The competing teams were the UAB Blazers, representing Conference USA (C-USA) and the Hawaii Warriors, representing the Western Athletic Conference (WAC). Hawaii won the game 59–40.

2004 Hawaii Bowl	Line	1	-	2	-	3	-	4	-	Final
Hawaii	(-3.5)	21	-	7	-	17	-	14	-	59
Alabama-Birmingham	(76.0)	13	-	13	-	7	-	7	-	40

Scoring Summary
UAB – White 51 yard pass from Hackney (Kick failed)
Hawaii – Rivers 74 yard pass from Chang (Ayat kick)
UAB – Burks 4 yard run (Hayes kick)
Hawaii – Keliipki 4 yard run (Ayat kick)
Hawaii – Welch 29 yard pass from Chang (Ayat kick)
UAB – Hayes 22 yard Field Goal
Hawaii – Owens 13 yard pass from Chang (Ayat kick)
UAB – Drinkarrd 10 yard run (Hayes kick)
UAB – Hayes 37 yard Field goal
Hawaii – Owens 15 yard pass from Chang (Ayat kick)
Hawaii – Owens 59 yard punt return (Ayat kick)
Hawaii – Ayat 43 yard Field goal
UAB – Hackney 4 yard run (Hayes kick)
Hawaii – Chang 4 yard run (Ayat kick)
UAB – Rhodes 17 yard pass from Hackney (Hayes kick)
Hawaii – Komine 42 yard kick-off return (Ayat kick)

Associated Press Hawaii Bowl Game Summary - Timmy Chang capped his record-setting career in style. Chang became the first college Quarterback to pass for 17,000 yards, throwing for four touchdowns and running for another to lead Hawaii over Alabama-Birmingham 59-40 in the Hawaii Bowl on Friday night. The fifth-year senior from Honolulu went 31-of-46 for 405 yards with no interceptions, spoiling the Blazers' first trip to a bowl game. Co-MVP Chad Owens caught eight passes for 114 yards and two TDs for Hawaii (8-5), which made its third straight appearance in the 3-year-old bowl. Owens also scored on a 59-yard punt return in the decisive third quarter, and teammate Jason Rivers added 11 receptions for 148 yards and a TD. Clinging to a two-point lead, Hawaii scored 17 straight points in the third to take a 45-26 lead, and UAB (7-5) never recovered. On Owens' spectacular return, he caught the ball at the Hawaii 41, broke a tackle near midfield and streaked down the left sideline for a touchdown. It was his fifth punt return for a score this season and his third TD of the game. The senior also made an over-the-shoulder catch on a 15-yard pass from Chang, pushing Hawaii's lead to 35-26. With that pass, Chang became the first college Quarterback to break the 17,000-yard mark for his career. He finished more than 2,000 yards ahead of Ty Detmer, who ranks second on the NCAA list. Chang's 4-yard TD run in the fourth sealed the victory. He left to a standing ovation with 5:40 remaining. Chang owns NCAA marks for yards passing (17,072), attempts (2,436), completions (1,388), interceptions (80) and total offense (16,910). With 117 TD passes, he overtook Danny Wuerffel (114) and Tim Rattay (115) and is second all-time to Detmer (121). Chang threw for 4,258 yards this season, with a career-best 38 TDs. He was 19-of-27 for 308 yards and three TDs in the first half of this one. It was the Warriors' eighth straight victory at Aloha Stadium, though they were designated the visiting team for this game. UAB was led by Quarterback Darrell Hackney, who finished 31-of-54 for 417 yards and two touchdowns. He also had a rushing TD and earned MVP honors for the Blazers. Roddy White, the second-leading receiver in the nation, had six receptions for 113 yards. A 10-yard TD run by Norris Drinkard and a 36-yard field goal by Nick Hayes cut Hawaii's lead to 28-26 at halftime, but the Blazers couldn't get any closer. A 17-yard pass from Hackney to Lance Rhodes drew UAB within 12 points with 2:06 left, but Britton Komine returned UAB's onside kick 42 yards for a touchdown to end any hopes of a rally. The game featured 1,079 yards of offense, including 699 in the first half. Both high-powered offenses got off to a quick start on a 75-degree Christmas Eve, scoring five touchdowns in the first 10 minutes. The teams traded leads until a 4-yard touchdown run by West Keliikipi and a 29-yard scoring pass from Chang to Gerald Welch put Hawaii up 21-13. Hackney threw a dart to his favorite target, White, on a slant play that went 67 yards for a touchdown on UAB's opening series. On the next play, Hawaii took a 7-6 lead on a 74-yard pass from Chang to Rivers, who waltzed along the sideline before breaking across the field.

2004 MPC Computers Bowl

The 2004 MPC Computers Bowl was between the Fresno State Bulldogs and the Virginia Cavaliers on December 27, 2004, at Bronco Stadium in Boise, Idaho. Fresno State won the game 37-34 in overtime on a 25-yard touchdown pass from Quarterback Paul Pinegar to Stephen Spach. Virginia had a complicated route to the MPC Computers bowl. Strong hopes based on a 5-0 start and a #6 ranking were dashed by a 36-3 blowout loss to Florida State and a third-place finish in the ACC. The Champs Sports Bowl typically took the fourth-place bowl eligible ACC team, but Virginia declined the bid as the game (played on December 21) would have conflicted with final exams. For a time the Independence Bowl was a possibility, as the Southeastern Conference (SEC) failed to produce enough bowl-eligible teams, but this was contingent on the MPC Computers Bowl getting a Big East school—either Boston College, Connecticut or Syracuse—to replace an ACC team. The MPC Computers bowl normally had the sixth choice of ACC teams, which would have been Georgia Tech or Clemson. Clemson declined all bowl invitations after a season-ending brawl, while Georgia Tech took Virginia's place at the Champs Sports Bowl. The Big East declined to send a team to the MPC Computers Bowl, so on December 1 Virginia accepted the bid. Fresno State accepted a bid on December 1 as well, after finishing third in the Western Athletic Conference. It was Fresno State's six straight bowl game and its first one outside of California since the 1999 Las Vegas Bowl. Virginia and Fresno State had never played each other before.

2004 MPC Computers Bowl	Line	1	-	2	-	3	-	4	-	OT	-	Final
Virginia	(-5.0)	14	-	7	-	3	-	7	-	3	-	34
Fresno State	(52.0)	7	-	3	-	7	-	14	-	6	-	37

Scoring Summary
Virginia - Pearman 13 yard run (Hughes kick)
Fresno State - Jennings 12 yard pass from Pinegar (Visintainer kick)
Virginia - McGrew 7 yard pass from Hagans (Hughes kick)
Virginia - Hagans 8 yard run (Hughes kick)
Fresno State - Visintainer 49 yard Field Goal
Fresno State - Jamison 22 yard pass from Pinegar (Visintainer kick)
Virginia - Hughes 33 yard Field Goal
Fresno State - Wood 22 yard pass from Pinegar (Visintainer kick)
Virginia - Lundy 20 yard run (Hughes kick)
Fresno State - Fairman 3 yard pass from Pinegar (Visintainer kick)
Virginia - Hughes 26 yard Field Goal
Fresno State - Spach 25 yard pass from Pinegar

Daily Press MPC Computers Bowl Game Summary - Up 14 points in the second quarter, Virginia fails to put Fresno State away and falls in overtime in the MPC Computers Bowl. Everything Virginia talked about -- a third consecutive bowl victory, a nine-win season, maybe even its highest-ever final ranking -- went poof Monday afternoon with a stunning second-half collapse nearly 2,400 miles from home. On the verge of blowing the MPC Computers Bowl wide open by halftime, the Cavaliers paid for their mistakes in a 37-34 overtime loss to Fresno State at Bronco Stadium. The Bulldogs trailed by two touchdowns in the final seconds of the first half and by seven points in the final seconds of regulation, but Quarterback Paul Pinegar's 25-yard scoring pass to Stephen Spach won it in OT. A couple hours before Spach's catch, many probably figured the game was over. Virginia scored touchdowns on its first three possessions and took a 21-7 less than three minutes into the second quarter. But the Cavs (8-4) not only let Fresno hang around, but they also let the Bulldogs get back in it. From Virginia's perspective, the end wasn't pretty. The Cavs gave up 285 total yards after halftime but still would have come away with the win had somebody wearing white made a play with 11 seconds remaining in regulation. Instead, as he rolled right and nearly ran out of room, Pinegar found a leaping Jaron Fairman in the back of the end zone for the tying (after the point-after) touchdown. Virginia coach Al Groh said the play reminded him of Dwight Clark's famous catch a couple decades ago. That being the case, Cavalier cornerback Marcus Hamilton played the role of Everson Walls -- his decent coverage wasn't decent enough. Then, after Fresno won the overtime coin toss and put Virginia on offense first, the Cavs had a first-and-goal from the 8 after Wali Lundy's 17-yard run. Yet all Virginia got was a 26-yard field goal by Connor Hughes for a 34-31 lead. Another wasted opportunity. Fresno immediately went for the win. One of two tight ends in the formation, Spach ran a post route. Backpedaling in coverage, Virginia safety Jermaine Hardy bumped into an official. Cornerback Tony Franklin was left one-on-one, and Pinegar's throw was perfect. Spach, who only had four catches during the regular season, caught it inside the 10-yard line. Franklin did his best to wrap up Spach, who outweighs him by 65 pounds, and replays indicate he should have been ruled down at the 1-yard line. But had that been the case, the Bulldogs would have been first-and-goal from the 1. Either way, Virginia would have fallen to 0-4 all-time in overtime games. The way Virginia looks at things, it shouldn't have come to that. In their first three offensive possessions, the Cavs had 196 yards, 10 first downs and 21 points. In their final three drives of the half, they had 55 yards, three first downs and no points. With a chance to put it away, Virginia did itself in. After Marques Hagans' 8-yard run made it 21-7 with 12:50 remaining in the second quarter, the Cavs were inside Fresno State territory three times before the break. Nothing came of it. Then, after taking over at its 13-yard line with 55 seconds left, the Bulldogs managed to get close enough for a 49-yard field goal by Brett Visintainer on the final play of the half. Instead of being up, say, 28-7, Virginia went into halftime ahead 21-10.

2004 Motor City Bowl

The 2004 Motor City Bowl was held on December 27, 2004 at Ford Field in Detroit, Michigan.

Team selection - The Toledo Rockets entered the game as the champions of the Mid-American Conference as they defeated Miami University on December 2, 2004 in the MAC Championship Game by a score of 35–27. This was Toledo's third trip to the bowl. They also appeared in 2001 and 2002. The Connecticut Huskies qualified for their first ever bowl appearance by finishing 7–4 and had a Big East Conference record of 3–3. Connecticut was invited to the game when the Big Ten could not provide a qualifying team.

2004 Motor City Bowl	Line	1	-	2	-	3	-	4	-	Final
Connecticut	(66.0)	17	-	13	-	3	-	6	-	39
Toledo	(-3.5)	0	-	7	-	3	-	0	-	10

Scoring Summary
Connecticut - Nuzie 35 yard Field Goal
Connecticut - Williams 32 yard pass from Orlovsky (Nuzie kick)
Connecticut - Taylor 68 yard punt return (Nuzie kick)
Toledo - Gradkowski 1 yard run (Robbins kick)
Connecticut - Sparks 7 yard pass from Orlovsky (Nuzie kick)
Connecticut - Nuzie 37 yard Field Goal
Connecticut - Nuzie 25 yard Field Goal
Toledo - Robbins 27 yard Field Goal
Connecticut - Nuzie 36 yard Field Goal
Connecticut - Lawrence 11 yard run (Kick blocked)

Motor City Bowl Game Notes - Dan Orlovsky was named the game's MVP by completing 21 of his 40 passes for 239 yards and two touchdowns. Tyler King, playing in his first game since breaking his leg in the Huskies 29–17 win over Pittsburgh on September 30, was awarded the United Auto Workers Lineman of the Game Award.

Aftermath - In the late summer of 2007, ESPN reported that the Toledo football team, and specifically running back Harvey "Scooter" McDougle and Quarterback Bruce Gradkowski, were under federal investigation for a point shaving scandal. The 2004 Motor City Bowl was one of the games in question.

2004 Independence Bowl

The 2004 Independence Bowl was between the Iowa State Cyclones and the Miami-Ohio RedHawks on December 28, 2004, at Independence Stadium in Shreveport, Louisiana. It was the twenty-ninth time the Independence Bowl had been played and the final game of the 2004 NCAA Division I FBS football season for both teams. Iowa State defeated Miami 17-13.

2004 Independence Bowl	Line	1	-	2	-	3	-	4	-	Final
Miami-Ohio	(-2.0)	0	-	7	-	6	-	0	-	13
Iowa State	(50.5)	7	-	3	-	0	-	7	-	17

Scoring Summary
Iowa State - Hicks 4 yard run (Culbertson kick)
Iowa State - Culbertson 23 yard field goal
Miami-Ohio - Clemens 28 yard pass from Betts (Parseghian kick)
Miami-Ohio - Smith 2 yard run (Soderquist kick blocked)
Iowa State - Kock 1 yard run (Culbertson kick)

Associated Press Independence Bowl Game Summary - Iowa State returned to its foundation to finally get the Big 12 a victory in the Independence Bowl. Stevie Hicks and Quarterback Bret Meyer each went for more than 100 yards in a revived running game that carried Iowa State to a 17-13 win over Miami of Ohio on Tuesday night. After building its program under Coach Dan McCarney around running the ball, Iowa State struggled in that area much of the season. But the Cyclones (7-5) piled up 295 yards on the ground -- a school record in a bowl -- to spoil Terry Hoeppner's final game as Miami's coach. Hoeppner is leaving to become the coach at Indiana. Vander Sanden helped spring Hicks for 159 yards on 27 carries, including a 4-yard touchdown run on an option pitch from Meyer, who was named the game's offensive MVP. Meyer, a freshman, carried a season-high 23 times for 122 yards and added 114 yards on 10-for-28 passing. His weaving 23-yard run set up the go-ahead touchdown early in the fourth quarter and Iowa State held on to end the Big 12's drought in the Independence Bowl. Big 12 teams had been 0-6 in this game, including Iowa State's 14-13 loss to Alabama in 2001. Just before the game, Miami athletic director Brad Bates told the team that offensive coordinator Shane Montgomery would succeed Hoeppner as coach. If the timing of that announcement was meant to inspire the RedHawks (8-5), it didn't do so right away. Miami fell behind 10-0 before rallying to a 13-10 lead in the third quarter. But the Cyclones, who were averaging just 128 yards a game rushing, kept pounding away at the Miami defensive front and finally regained the lead on Ryan's 1-yard plunge with 13:02 left. On the play before, Meyer took the snap in shotgun formation, ran to his left, cut back to his right and then danced back and forth through the secondary before being brought down just short of the end zone. Ellis Hobbs sealed the victory by stepping in front of receiver Ryan Busing to intercept Josh Betts' pass in the final minute. It was the first time in the 29-year history of the Independence Bowl that two players on the same team rushed for more than 100 yards. Betts kept Miami moving at times, but once Iowa State got its running game revved up, the RedHawks couldn't keep the Cyclones' offense off the field. Betts' 28-yard touchdown pass to Luke Clemens with 25 seconds left in the first half cut the lead to 10-7 and the RedHawks carried that momentum into the first possession of the second half, driving 80 yards in 11 plays to take the lead on Mike Smith's 2-yard run. Iowa State helped Miami on both scoring drives with penalties. A personal foul on Tim Dobbins put the RedHawks in position for their first touchdown. On their second drive, they got first downs on two pass interference penalties and a holding penalty when they had been forced to punt. Betts finished 20-of-44 for 240 yards and the one interception. Miami's Michael Larkin caught two passes to extend his NCAA record to 50 straight games with a reception. Iowa State bounced back from a 2-10 record in 2003 to share the Big 12 North title and play in a bowl game for the fourth time in five years.

2004 Insight Bowl

The 2004 Insight Bowl was the 16th edition of the bowl game. It featured the Notre Dame Fighting Irish, and the Oregon State Beavers.

2004 Insight Bowl	Line	1	-	2	-	3	-	4	-	Final
Notre Dame	(51.0)	0	-	7	-	7	-	7	-	21
Oregon State	(-4.0)	14	-	7	-	3	-	14	-	38

Scoring Summary
Oregon State – Gillett 12 yard pass from Anderson (Serna kick)
Oregon State – Newton 11 yard pass from Anderson (Serna kick)
Oregon State – Haines 11 yard pass from Anderson (Serna kick)
Notre Dame – Fasano 13 yard pass from Quinn (Fitzpatrick kick)
Oregon State – Serna 38 yard Field Goal
Notre Dame – Walker 5 yard run (Fitzpatrick kick)
Oregon State – Newton 1 yard pass from Anderson (Serna kick)
Notre Dame – McKnight 18 yard pass from Quinn (Fitzpatrick kick)
Oregon State – Wright 2 yard run (Serna kick)

Associated Press Insight Bowl Game Summary - Derek Anderson's final collegiate game was a memorable one. Anderson passed for 358 yards and four touchdowns as Oregon State easily defeated Notre Dame, 38-21, in the Insight Bowl. Anderson, who completed 28-of-45 passes, tossed two touchdowns to Joe Newton and one each to George Gillett and Dan Haines as he moved into second place on the Pac-10 Conference's all-time list in career TDs (79) and passing yards (11,249). Anderson was the game's Offensive MVP. Oregon State (7-5) opened a 14-0 first-quarter cushion behind TD tosses of 12 yards to Gillett and 11 yards to Newton. Anderson's 11-yard TD pass to Haines made it 21-0 with 7:49 left in the second quarter, and the Beavers led by at least 10 points thereafter. The first two scores were set up by a long punt return by Sammie Stroughter and a blocked punt by Derrick Doggett, respectively. Notre Dame (6-6), which has lost seven straight postseason games since beating Texas A&M in the 1994 Cotton Bowl, was playing its one and only game under Kent Baer, their defensive coordinator under Tyrone Willingham, who was fired on November 30. Notre Dame Quarterback Brady Quinn completed 17-of-29 passes for 214 yards and two TDs. After getting spurned by Utah coach Urban Meyer and several other candidates, the Irish named New England Patriots offensive coordinator Charlie Weis their new coach. But Baer - whose future is uncertain - was allowed to coach this one. Oregon State middle linebacker Trent Bray was named Defensive MVP. He finished with 10 tackles and one sack. Anderson's four touchdown passes tied an Insight Bowl record, matching Virginia Tech's Bryan Randall in 2003, West Virginia's Marc Bulger in 1998 and Brigham Young's John Walsh in 1994.

2004 Houston Bowl

The 2004 EV1.net Houston Bowl was the fifth edition of the bowl game, and was played at Reliant Stadium in Houston, Texas. The game pitted the Colorado Buffaloes from the Big 12 Conference and the UTEP Miners from the Western Athletic Conference (WAC).

2004 Houston Bowl	Line	1	-	2	-	3	-	4	-	Final
Texas-El Paso	(59.0)	14	-	7	-	0	-	7	-	28
Colorado	(-3.5)	3	-	10	-	6	-	14	-	33

Scoring Summary
Colorado - Crosby 26 yard field goal
UTEP - Jackson 7 yard run (Schneider kick)
UTEP - Chamois 1 yard run (Schneider kick)
Colorado - Charles 1 yard run (Crosby kick)
Colorado - Crosby 54 yard field goal
UTEP – Boyd 17 yard pass from Palmer (Schneider kick)
Colorado - Crosby 37 yard field goal
Colorado - Crosby 20 yard field goal
UTEP – Higgins 4 yard pass from Palmer (Schneider kick)
Colorado - Klopfenstein 78 yard pass from Klatt (Crosby kick)
Colorado - Judge 39 yard pass from Klatt (Crosby kick)

CU at The Game Houston Bowl Game Summary - Joel Klatt bounced back from a career-worst performance against Oklahoma to throw for 333 yards, leading Colorado to a 33-28 win over Texas El-Paso in the 2004 EV1.Net Houston Bowl. Mason Crosby contributed four field goals as the Buff held off the Miners late for Colorado's first bowl win in five years. After Colorado took an early 3-0 lead, UTEP took control of the contest, holding the lead for almost three full quarters. Running back Howard Jackson scored on a seven-yard run to cap an eight-play, 80-yard drive to put the Miners up, 7-3, midway through the first quarter. A Josh Chamois one-yard run made the score 14-3 after the first quarter. Colorado mounted a comeback in the second stanza. Freshman running back Hugh Charles scored from a yard out, and Mason Crosby hit a 54-yard field goal to cut the UTEP lead to 14-13, but Jordan Palmer hit Jayson Boyd from 17 yards out to give the Miners a 21-13 halftime advantage. The second half witnessed a Colorado defensive resurgence, with the Buff defense giving the Buff offense the ball near midfield on three consecutive possessions. The Colorado offense could not respond, garnering only three points from those three opportunities, making the score 21-16. A third Mason Crosby field goal, this time from 20 yards out, cut the UTEP lead to 21-19 heading into the fourth quarter. UTEP seemed in control after scoring early in the fourth quarter to go up 28-19. But, as the Buffs had done all season, their resiliency showed through. On the first play after the UTEP touchdown, Joel Klatt hit tight end Joe Klopenstein on a catch-and-run which covered 78 yards. Later, Klatt hit Evan Judge from 39 yards out to give the Buffs their first lead since early in the first quarter. The game-winning drive was kept alive by a fake punt, with punter John Torp covering 22 yards to give the Buffs a first down and much needed momentum. UTEP had two possessions after the Judge score, but never mounted a serious threat, as the Buffs held on to win, 33-28. Two plays turned the tide for the Buffs. The first was the Klopenstein touchdown covering 78 yards to pull Colorado to within two at 28-26. The 6' 6" junior tight end caught the ball near midfield, stiff-armed one defensive back, and then outraced another to the end zone. The second play was the Torp fake punt. Facing a fourth-and-three at the Buff 35, down 28-26 with ten minutes remaining, Barnett decided to gamble. The win gave the Buffs an 8-5 final record. Iowa State, with a 17-13 win over Miami (Ohio) in the Independence Bowl, finished at 7-5. The other four Big 12 North teams finished with losing records. While the Buffs had not dominated many games during the season (even falling behind North Texas 7-0 and 14-7), the eight wins still were the envy of the Big 12 North. Not bad for a team who practiced in the spring without a head coach and was the subject of bad publicity nationwide. Not bad for a team with only four senior starters on offense, and only one senior starter on defense. Not bad at all.

2004 Alamo Bowl

The 2004 Alamo Bowl featured the Ohio State Buckeyes and the Oklahoma State Cowboys.
Ohio State got on the board first, when Quarterback Justin Zwick connected with wide receiver Anthony Gonzalez for a 23-yard touchdown pass, and a 7–0 lead. Mike Nugent connected on field goals of 37 and 35 yards in the first quarter as well, as Ohio State built a 13–0 lead over Oklahoma State. In the second quarter, running back Lydell Ross rushed for a 1-yard touchdown and a 20–0 lead. He finished the game with 12 carries for 99 yards. Nugent connected on his third field goal of the game, this one from 41 yards out, as Ohio State increased its lead to 23–0, before halftime. In the third quarter, Ted Ginn, Jr. rushed five yards for a touchdown, increasing Ohio State's lead to 30–0. Nugent kicked his final field goal in the fourth quarter, a 37 yarder to give Ohio State a 33–0 lead. Shaun Willis rushed for a 4-yard touchdown at the end of the game, to make the final score 33–7.

2004 Alamo Bowl	Line	1	-	2	-	3	-	4	-	Final
Oklahoma State	(-3.5)	0	-	0	-	0	-	7	-	7
Ohio State	(48.5)	13	-	10	-	7	-	3	-	33

Scoring Summary
Ohio State – Gonzales 23 yard pass from Zwick (Nugent kick)
Ohio State – Nugent 37 yard Field goal
Ohio State – Nugent 35 yard Field goal
Ohio State – Ross 1 yard run (Nugent kick)
Ohio State – Nugent 41 yard Field goal
Ohio State – Ginn 5 yard run (Nugent kick)
Ohio State – Nugent 37 yard Field goal
Oklahoma State – Willis 4 yard run (Ricks kick)

Associated Press Alamo Bowl Game Summary - Ohio State proved it knows how to win in the face of adversity. Playing without starting Quarterback Troy Smith, 22nd-ranked Ohio State dominated Oklahoma State, 33-7, in the Alamo Bowl. Ohio State (8-4) posted a 4-1 record in Smith's five starts this season, including a 37-21 upset of archrival Michigan. Smith passed for 241 yards and two touchdowns and rushed for 145 yards and a score against the Wolverines amid the distraction of former Buckeye Maurice Clarett's claims of improper benefits being given to players by coaches and boosters. Justin Zwick, who was benched after the Buckeyes lost their first three Big Ten Conference contests, was back as the starter and played well, while Ohio State's defense was dominant. The Buckeyes opened the scoring just under three minutes into the game when Zwick hit Anthony Gonzalez for a 23-yard touchdown. Ohio State raced out to a 23-0 lead at the half and never looked back. Zwick completed 17-of-27 passes for 189 yards with no interceptions. Mike Nugent, the 2004 Lou Groza Award winner, kicked four field goals for Ohio State - including three in the first half. Oklahoma State (7-5) never was able to get anything going against Ohio State's swarming defense. Shawn Willis scored on a four-yard run midway through the fourth quarter to avoid a shutout. Vernand Morency, who entered the game eighth in the country in rushing at 145.4 yards per game, was limited to 20 on eight carries for Oklahoma State.

2004 Continental Tire Bowl

The 2004 Continental Tire Bowl featured the Boston College Eagles, and the North Carolina Tar Heels. The game was played on Thursday, December 30, 2004. The game was the third edition to this bowl game, but the last one under the name *Continental Tire Bowl*. It would later be renamed the Meineke Car Care Bowl. This edition was particularly notable because Boston College would join the Atlantic Coast Conference, which North Carolina also plays in, the following year.

2004 Continental Tire Bowl	Line	1	-	2	-	3	-	4	-	Final
Boston College	(52.0)	14	-	7	-	0	-	16	-	37
North Carolina	(-2.0)	7	-	14	-	3	-	0	-	24

Scoring Summary
Boston College - Whitworth 3 yard run (Ohliger kick)
North Carolina - McGill 12 yard pass from Durant (Barth kick)
Boston College - Adams 2 yard pass from Peterson (Ohliger kick)
North Carolina - Wright 5 yard pass from Durant (Barth kick)
North Carolina - Mitchell 51 yard pass from Durant (Barth kick)
Boston College - Kashetta 1 yard pass from Peterson (Ohliger kick)
North Carolina - Barth 27 yard Field Goal
Boston College - Callender 1 yard run (Kick failed)
Boston College - Ohliger 21 yard run (Troost kick)
Boston College - Troost 18 yard Field Goal

Associated Press Continental Tire Bowl Game Summary - Boston College Quarterback Paul Peterson cheered the play of the game while lying on a stretcher. Kicker Ryan Ohliger ran for a 21-yard touchdown on a fake field goal - one play after Peterson was carted off the field with a broken left leg - as Boston College defeated North Carolina, 37-24, in the Continental Tire Bowl. Playing with a plate and five screws in his surgically repaired right hand, Peterson turned in a gritty performance, completing 24-of-33 passes for 236 yards and two touchdowns. Peterson broke his hand against Temple on November 20 and did not play in Boston College's 43-17 loss to Syracuse the following week that cost the Eagles a berth in the Bowl Championship Series. After undergoing surgery, he returned to practice on December 19. With the Eagles (9-3) nursing a 27-24 lead early in the fourth quarter, Peterson suffered a broken leg when he was stopped for a one-yard loss on 3rd-and-1 from the Tar Heels 20. When played resumed, Boston College coach Tom O'Brien stunned the Tar Heels (6-6) with his call for a fake. Holder Matt Ryan - the Eagles backup Quarterback - handed off to Ohliger, who broke a tackle en route to the end zone and a 34-24 lead with 10:32 remaining. Peterson was diagnosed with a broken tibia. Despite the discomfort, he pumped his fists and clapped his hands as he was taken off the field. It was redemption for Ohliger, who missed a 22-yard field goal in the first half and a potentially critical extra point after the Eagles had taken a 27-24 lead on Andre Callender's one-yard TD run 46 seconds into the fourth period. Callender rushed for 174 yards on

26 carries, including a 38-yard run that set up his go-ahead score. Boston College, which becomes an official member of the Atlantic Coast Conference next season, recorded its fifth straight bowl win in as many seasons. The Eagles are the only team in the country with such a streak. North Carolina's Darian Durant threw three TD passes in the first half but was shut down in the second as the Tar Heels were held to a field goal. He completed 23-of-41 passes for 259 yards. The offenses dominated in the first half as the Quarterbacks exchanged scores. Peterson was especially sharp in the opening 30 minutes, completing 18-of-23 passes for 187 yards and both his TDs. Peterson's one-yard TD toss to David Kashetta tied the game, 21-21, with 17 seconds left in the half. Connor Barth's 27-yard field goal gave the Tar Heels a 24-21 lead with 4 1/2 minutes left in the third quarter. Backup kicker William Troost converted an 18-yard field goal for the Eagles with just over four minutes remaining in the contest.

2004 Silicon Valley Football Classic

The 2004 Silicon Valley Football Classic was between the Troy Trojans and the Northern Illinois Huskies on December 30, 2004, at Spartan Stadium in San Jose, California. It was the fifth and final time the Silicon Valley Football Classic was played. For the 2004 bowl season the Silicon Valley Classic had contractual tie-ins with the Western Athletic Conference (WAC) and the Pacific-10 Conference (Pac-10); neither conference had enough bowl-eligible teams. In previous years the SVC had an agreement to take the Pac-10's No. 6 team but was displaced by the new Emerald Bowl and had to settle for No. 7, if one existed. Organizers obtained permission from the Pac-10 to look elsewhere, and on November 16 announced an agreement with the Mid-American Conference, which had five bowl-eligible teams but as yet only two bowls. Left without a WAC team, organizers turned to the Troy Trojans of the Sun Belt Conference. Troy had never played in a bowl game before, having just moved up to Division I in 2001 and joined the Sun Belt in 2004.

2004 Silicon Valley Classic	Line	1	-	2	-	3	-	4	-	Final
Troy	(-2.0)	14	-	0	-	0	-	7	-	21
Northern Illinois	(44.0)	14	-	10	-	3	-	7	-	34

Scoring Summary
Troy - McDowell 1 yard run (Whibbs kick)
Troy - Richardson 23 yard pass from McDowell (Whibbs kick)
Northern Illinois - Wolfe 50 yard run (Nendick kick)
Northern Illinois - Haldi 1 yard run (Nendick kick)
Northern Illinois - Nendick 30 yard Field Goal
Northern Illinois - Haldi 1 yard run (Nendick kick)
Northern Illinois - Nendick 39 yard Field Goal
Northern Illinois - Harris 4 yard run (Nendick kick)
Troy - McDowell 4 yard run (Whibbs kick)

Associated Press Silicon Valley Football Classic Game Summary - Josh Haldi passed for 146 yards and rushed for two touchdowns to lead Northern Illinois through mud and rain to its first bowl victory in 21 years, 34-21 over Troy on Thursday night in the Silicon Valley Football Classic. The Huskies (9-3) overcame a steady downpour, lighting problems and a delayed kickoff by scoring 34 straight points in this unlikely postseason matchup of two schools with one previous bowl appearance between them. Garrett Wolfe, the NCAA's scoring co-leader, rushed for his 21st touchdown of the season for Northern Illinois before leaving with a hip injury. But A.J. Harris filled in with 120 yards rushing and another score as the Huskies methodically erased a quick start by the Trojans (7-5), who scored two touchdowns in the first nine minutes of Troy's first bowl game in just its fourth season in Division I-A. D.T. McDowell threw a touchdown pass and rushed for two more scores for the Trojans, but they got stuck in the mud at Spartan Stadium and were unable to move the ball effectively or stop the Huskies' rushing attack. The victory is a high point in Coach Joe Novak's impressive rebuilding job at Northern Illinois, which didn't get a bowl invitation last year despite going 10-2 and beating Maryland. But when the Pac-10 and WAC didn't produce enough bowl-eligible teams to fill their Silicon Valley slots, Northern Illinois and Troy took advantage. Haldi and the Huskies overcame more than Troy's vaunted defense, which was among the national leaders in several statistical categories. A day of intermittent rain left the Spartan Stadium field slick and soaked, and though more than 21,000 tickets were distributed, no more than 5,000 fans braved the miserable conditions for the fifth edition of a low-profile bowl game played without Fresno State for the first time. In addition, an electrical transformer outside the stadium malfunctioned shortly before kickoff, affecting the television crew and two stanchions of lights. The game began 23 minutes late under the remaining banks of lights while crews tried unsuccessfully to fix things. Yet both teams insisted on throwing long passes despite the miserable conditions and two offenses unfamiliar with such fireworks. McDowell threw 10 straight incompletions at one point, and Haldi was scarcely better _ but Northern

Illinois mixed in enough runs to keep moving consistently. Troy curiously cast aside its usual offensive caution and opened with aggressive downfield throws _ and for a little while, it worked. On the game's seventh play, McDowell hit Jason Samples with a 45-yard pass to the Northern Illinois 1 for the Trojans' longest pass of the season. McDowell scored on a keeper and then led another scoring drive, hitting Richardson with a 23-yard screen pass. But Northern Illinois responded with a 50-yard TD run by Wolfe, who set the school record for rushing touchdowns with the score. After Haldi scored on the next drive, the rain limited both teams' offenses until Haldi scored again on a 1-yard keeper 34 seconds before halftime. The slick grass and mud obviously affected both teams' defenders, who couldn't pursue and change direction with much speed. Harris scored on a 3-yard run early in the fourth quarter, and Chris Nendick kicked two field goals.

2004 Emerald Bowl

The 2004 Emerald Bowl was between the New Mexico Lobos and the Navy Midshipmen on December 30, 2004 at SBC Park in San Francisco, California, United States. The game, which Navy won with a final score of 34–19, was highlighted by a 26-play drive from the Midshipmen that took up almost 15 minutes of game time and set the record for the longest drive in a NCAA college football game. The contest was the third time the Emerald Bowl was played. The conference independent Navy Midshipmen, who finished the regular season with a 9–2 record, accepted an invitation to play in the game on November 22, 2004. Eight days later, the 7–4 New Mexico Lobos agreed to fill the open spot reserved for a Mountain West Conference team. Leading up to the game, sports writers predicted that a major highlight of the contest would be the rushing offenses of Midshipmen head coach Paul Johnson and Lobos head coach Rocky Long; both teams ranked in the top rushing offenses in the Football Bowl Subdivision (FBS). The Lobos also ranked as one of the nation's top rushing defenses. The game began in rainy conditions that had affected the San Francisco Bay Area for days before the contest. The Lobos scored a touchdown on the game's first drive to take an early lead, but the Midshipmen scored three touchdowns to bring the score to 21–7 early in the second quarter. After the Lobos narrowed that lead to 12 points by the end of the third quarter, the Midshipmen began a long drive which took up much of the fourth quarter. The drive ended with a field goal, which gave Navy a 15-point lead with a little over two minutes remaining in the game. On the next drive from the Lobos, the Midshipmen forced a turnover on downs and ran out the clock with their last possession to win the game. Midshipmen players Aaron Polanco and Vaughn Kelley were named the game's offensive and defensive Most Valuable Players, respectively. The win caused the Midshipmen to finish the season with a 10–2 record, their best record since the 1905 season. After the game, the Associated Press College Poll and the USA Today Coaches' Poll ranked the team as the 24th best in the nation. The loss caused the Lobos' record to fall to 7–5.

2004 Emerald Bowl	Line	1	-	2	-	3	-	4	-	Final
New Mexico	(-2.5)	7	-	12	-	0	-	0	-	19
Navy	(40.0)	14	-	10	-	7	-	3	-	34

Scoring Summary
New Mexico – Hall 17 yard pass from McKamey (Zunker kick)
Navy – Polanco 14 yard run (Blumenfield kick)
Navy – Polanco 1 yard run (Blumenfield kick)
Navy – Dryden 61 yard pass from Polanco (Blumenfield kick)
New Mexico – Ferguson 4 yard run (Kick failed)
Navy – Blumenfield 27 yard Field goal
New Mexico – McKamey 3 yard run (Kick failed)
Navy – Polanco 27 yard run (Blumenfield kick)
Navy – Blumenfield 22 yard Field goal

Game summary - The 2004 Emerald Bowl began with a 1:35 p.m. PST kickoff time in SBC Park. Because the field had been converted from the baseball diamond typically used by the San Francisco Giants, both teams shared the same sideline during the game. Rainy conditions caused the field's natural grass surface to become muddier as the game progressed. Although 30,563 tickets were sold, an increase of 19 percent from the 2003 game, official in-stadium attendance was listed at 28,856, an increase of 28 percent over the previous year. Despite New Mexico's closer proximity to the bowl site, Midshipmen fans comprised a large portion of the crowd; Navy directly sold 18,000 tickets prior to the game and was given credit for 22,000. The game aired live on ESPN2, with Eric Collins and Andre Ware serving as announcers. With a Nielsen rating of 2.04, the game was watched by over four million households, approximately 65 percent more viewers than the previous year.

2004 Holiday Bowl

The 2004 Holiday Bowl was held on December 30, 2004. The game was held at Qualcomm Stadium in San Diego, pitting the Pac-10's California Golden Bears and the Big 12's Texas Tech Red Raiders. Cal was edged out for a BCS bowl berth by Texas in the last week of the regular season.

Teams - In 2004 Cal posted a 10–1 record under head coach Jeff Tedford and Quarterback Aaron Rodgers, with their only regular season loss coming against the eventual national champion, USC. They finished the regular season ranked No. 4 according to polls and appeared to have an excellent chance to receive an at-large BCS bowl berth, most likely in the Rose Bowl. Under normal circumstances, the Bears, as Pac-10 runner-up, would have had first crack at a Rose Bowl berth since conference champion USC was playing for the national championship. The Bears entered their final game of the regular season ranked No. 4 in BCS standings and a 24-point favorite over Southern Miss. They won 26–16 in a closer than-expected game. With 13 seconds left in the game and Cal with the ball at the Southern Miss 22-yard, Tedford elected to run out the clock instead of attempting to increase the margin of victory to possibly impress some voters. Leading up to the game, Tedford said he had no interest to run up the score. In a controversial case, the Texas coach Mack Brown made impassioned pleas to media asking poll voters reconsider their final votes. Several Associated Press (AP) voters were besieged by fan emails and phone calls attempting to sway their votes, apparently spurred from Brown's pleas to rank Texas ahead of other "less deserving teams." Nine of the 65 AP voters switched Texas ahead of Cal, and three of them were from Texas. In the Coaches Poll, four voters moved Cal down to No. 7 and two to No. 8, when the week before none had them lower than No. 6. Meanwhile, two coaches moved Texas up to No. 3 when the team did not play that week. The Los Angeles Times wrote that accusations were raised about coaches manipulated voting, but the individual coach's votes were not released to prove or disprove the allegations. The AP Poll makes its voters' records public. No. 6 Texas gained 23 points on No. 4 Cal in the AP poll, and the fifth-ranked Longhorns closed 43 points on the fourth-ranked Bears in the coach's poll. That allowed Texas to earn a BCS berth, finishing .0129 points ahead of Cal in the BCS standings after being .0013 points behind. The Longhorns went on to beat Michigan 38–37 in the Rose Bowl. In part because of the controversy with Cal's BCS ranking, the AP poll withdrew from the BCS after the season. Texas Tech entered the game with a 7-4 overall record and a 5-3 record in the Big XII. The Red Raiders entered the game with the top-ranked passing offense in the NCAA, averaging just over 399 yards per game, and with the NCAA season leader in passing yardage, Sonny Cumbie. Earlier in the season, Tech had shown its offensive prowess with a 70-10 victory over Nebraska, the most points ever given up by Nebraska in the team's history.

2004 Holiday Bowl	Line	1	-	2	-	3	-	4	-	Final
#23 Texas Tech	(65.0)	7	-	17	-	14	-	7	-	45
#4 California	(-11.0)	14	-	0	-	3	-	14	-	31

Scoring Summary
Texas Tech – Hicks 9 yard pass from Cumbie (Trlica kick)
California – Arrington 2 yard run (Schneider kick)
California – Lynch 5 yard run (Schneider kick)
Texas Tech – Trlica 22 yard Field goal
Texas Tech – Hicks 5 yard pass from Cumbie (Trlica kick)
Texas Tech – Henderson 5 yard run (Trlica kick)
Texas Tech – Filani 60 yard pass from Cumbie (Trlica kick)
California – Schneider 29 yard Field goal
Texas Tech – Mack 11 yard run (Trlica kick)
California – Cross 11 yard pass from Rodgers (Schneider kick)
Texas Tech – Henderson 1 yard run (Trlica kick)
California – Rodgers 1 yard run (Schneider kick)

Associated Press Holiday Bowl Game Summary - The California Golden Bears have been messed over something fierce by teams from Texas this month. If getting knocked out of the Rose Bowl by the Texas Longhorns wasn't bad enough, the No. 4 Golden Bears were flat out humiliated 45-31 by the No. 23 Texas Tech Red Raiders in the Holiday Bowl on Thursday night. Cal coach Jeff Tedford was quick to address the question that's been on everyone's mind for a month. In that case, it looks as if Mack Brown isn't such a villain, after all. Cal had been in position to go to the Rose Bowl for the first time in 46 seasons but was leapfrogged in the final Bowl Championship Series standings by Brown's Longhorns, who ended up in Pasadena to face Michigan on Saturday. The day the BCS pairings were released, Cal Quarterback Aaron Rodgers said Brown "was a little classless" for begging for poll votes to help his Longhorns, and that the system was "faulty." Tedford said votes in the coach's poll should be made public. The Longhorns, by the way, beat Texas Tech 51-21 at Lubbock on Oct. 23. Texas Tech fans mocked Cal with chants of "Overrated!" in the closing minutes. The Golden Bears (10-2), who were 11½-point favorites, simply had no answer against the Red Raiders (8-4) and their efficient spread offense, which uses four wide receivers most of the time. Tech senior Sonny Cumbie threw for a career-high 520 yards and three touchdowns, including a 60-yarder to Joel Filani, and safety Vincent Meeks set up a score with a 48-yard interception return. Cumbie was 39 of 60 and broke the Holiday Bowl attempts record of 59 set by BYU's Ty Detmer in 1989. He was short of Detmer's Holiday Bowl record of 576 yards, also set in 1989. Cal's J.J. Arrington became just the third running back in Pac-10 history to rush for 2,000 yards in a season. The senior from Nashville, N.C., carried 25 times for 173 yards, ending his season with 2,018 yards. Southern Cal's Marcus Allen had 2,427 yards in 1981 and Charles White had 2,050 in 1979. Both won the Heisman Trophy. Arrington scored on a 2-yard run in the first quarter, his 15th rushing TD of the season, a school record. He had been tied with Lindsey Chapman and Russell White. The Golden Bears were undisciplined on defense -- they had two personal fouls on one Tech drive -- and Rodgers looked confused at times. California was without career receptions leader Geoff McArthur, who broke his left leg in the fourth quarter of a 26-16 win at Southern Mississippi on Dec. 4. Cal's only other loss was to No. 1 USC, 23-17 on Oct. 9. Texas Tech (8-4) had four scoring drives that took less than two minutes each. Trailing 14-7 after the first quarter, the Red Raiders scored 24 straight points and had a commanding 31-14 lead by early in the third quarter. Cumbie threw a 5-yard touchdown pass to Jarrett Hicks for a 17-14 lead with 8:57 left before halftime. The short drive was set up by Meeks' interception return. Tech piled it on with Taurean Henderson's 2-yard run late in the second quarter and Cumbie's 60-yard scoring pass to Filani on the opening drive of the second half for a 17-point lead. Filani caught the ball at the Cal 40 and raced past cornerback Daymeion Hughes into the end zone. Hicks also had a 9-yard TD catch in the first quarter. Rodgers threw an 11-yard TD pass to Garrett Cross and scored on a 1-yard sneak, both in the fourth quarter. Rodgers was 24 of 42 for 246 yards, with one interception.

2004 Liberty Bowl

The 2004 AutoZone Liberty Bowl, played on December 31, 2004, was the 46th edition of the Liberty Bowl. The game was played between Boise State, and Louisville, in front of 58,355 fans. This bowl game was notable for being the highest ranked non-BCS bowl game in the nation that year, with Boise State ranked 9th and Louisville ranked 10th. Boise State played in place of the Mountain West Conference champions, the Utah Utes, who played in the Fiesta Bowl instead.

2004 Liberty Bowl	Line	1	-	2	-	3	-	4	-	Final
#10 Boise State	(80.0)	10	-	21	-	3	-	6	-	40
#7 Louisville	(-12.0)	14	-	7	-	14	-	9	-	44

Scoring Summary
Boise State – Jones 48 yard Field goal
Louisville – Barnidge 7 yard pass from Lefors (Carmody kick)
Boise State – Avalos 92 yard interception return (Jones kick)
Louisville – Douglas 65 yard run (Carmody kick)
Louisville – Clark 30 yard pass from Brohm (Carmody kick)
Boise State – Lau fumble recovery in end zone (Jones kick)
Boise State – Acree 19 yard pass from Zabransky (Jones kick)
Boise State – Zabransky 1 yard run (Jones kick)
Boise State – Jones 42 yard Field goal
Louisville – Russell 14 yard pass from LeFors (Carmody kick)
Louisville – Lefors 1 yard run (Carmody kick)
Boise State – Helmandollar 2 yard run (Pass failed)
Louisville – Shelton 1 yard run (Pass failed)
Louisville – Carmody 19 yard Field goal

Associated Press Liberty Bowl Game Summary - In the highest scoring Liberty Bowl ever, it was a defensive play by Louisville that ended Boise State's 22-game winning streak. Louisville safety Kerry Rhodes intercepted a pass in the end zone as time expired to preserve Louisville's 44-40 victory over 10th-ranked Boise State on Friday. Now Louisville (No. 8 ESPN/USA Today; No. 7 AP) will enter the Big East Conference in grand style after handing Boise State its first loss since September 2003 in a game that was the most important in school history for both programs. Eric Shelton scored on the go-ahead touchdown on a 1-yard run with 6:48 left. Stefan LeFors threw two touchdowns and ran for a third as the Cardinals (11-1), who have never finished ranked higher than 13th, matched a school record for victories in a season. The Cardinals won their third Liberty Bowl in their final appearance as a Conference USA team. The Broncos (11-1) had one last chance to win after Art Carmody's 19-yard field goal with 1:10 left put Louisville up four. Quarterback Jared Zabransky drove the Broncos to the Louisville 30 before his final pass into the end zone as time expired was intercepted by Rhodes. He more than atoned for his missed interception opportunity in a 41-38 loss on Oct. 14 to then-No. 3 Miami. The win was a welcome end to a week in which the Cardinals were forced to deal with the news that Petrino had interviewed with LSU about its open coaching job. They certainly didn't seem distracted against the Broncos. Petrino kept referring to the Cardinals as "we," and asked if that would remain the same, he had a short answer. Everyone expected a high-scoring game in a bowl pairing the nation's top two offenses, and the teams didn't disappoint as they swapped the lead five times. The 84 combined points topped the 80 points by Colorado and Alabama in 1969 and was one of a handful of records set. Louisville won only for the second time in seven bowls despite a season-high four turnovers. The Cardinals rolled up 564 yards, topping 500 yards for the ninth time this season. LeFors was 18-of-26 for 193 yards and ran 12 times for 76 yards. The Cardinals rushed for 329 yards against a defense that had been the nation's fourth-best against the run. This was the biggest game in school history for Boise State, a program that moved up to Division I-A in 1996. The Broncos, who played their first three bowls on their home field known for its blue turf, thought they could keep up with an offense that had trailed only Louisville for most yards and points. But the Broncos, who lost 12 starters from their 2003 squad, finished with 284 yards offense, well below their 511.6-yard average. The teams still rewrote the Liberty Bowl record book. They combined for the most points in the first quarter with 24, and their 52 points were the most for the first half. Boise State kicker Tyler Jones had a record 48-yard field goal on the Broncos' first drive, and Broncos linebacker Andy Avalos had a 92-yard interception return off LeFors in the first quarter that bested the 79-yarder by Michael Jordan of Tulane in 1998. Boise State led as much as 34-21 early in the third quarter after scoring 24 straight points. The Cardinals settled down when LeFors drove them on an 81-play drive in eight plays, which he capped with a 14-yard TD toss to J.R. Russell. LeFors then gave Louisville the lead back at 35-34 when he ran in from a yard out with 2:17 left in the third. Boise State last led at 40-35 when Jon Helmandollar plunged in from 2 yards with 10:51 left.

2004 Music City Bowl

The 2004 Gaylord Hotels Music City Bowl (presented by Bridgestone) was held on December 31, 2004, in Nashville, Tennessee at The Coliseum. The game featured the Alabama Crimson Tide, of the SEC, and the Minnesota Golden Gophers, of the Big Ten. The game was ultimately won by Minnesota, 20–16. Alabama was led by head coach Mike Shula and entered a game with a 6–5 record, as the team ended their 2004 regular season by losing three of their final four games. The Crimson Tide offense was led by Quarterback Spencer Pennginton, who was a backup at the beginning of the season but was put into the starting role when Brodie Croyle was injured versus Western Carolina. Pennington led the Crimson Tide to a 3–4 record as a starter and was the starting Quarterback in the bowl game. Alabama also entered to the second-ranked overall defense in the country. Glen Mason led the Golden Gophers into the bowl game, who also had a 6–5 record. The Golden Gophers ended their 2004 regular season by losing five of their final six games after a 5–0 start. The Minnesota offense was led by two 1,000-yard rushers in Laurence Maroney and Marion Barber III, the latter of which would be named MVP of the bowl game. The two running backs combined for 2,617 yards and twenty-three touchdowns.

2004 Music City Bowl	Line	1	-	2	-	3	-	4	-	Final
Alabama	(-2.0)	7	-	7	-	0	-	2	-	16
Minnesota	(48.5)	7	-	10	-	3	-	0	-	20

Scoring Summary
Alabama - McClain 2 yard pass from Pennington (Bostick kick)
Minnesota - Lipka fumble recovery in End Zone (Lloyd kick)
Minnesota - Barber 5 yard run (Lloyd kick)
Minnesota - Lloyd 27 yard Field Goal
Alabama - McClain 1 yard run (Bostick kick)
Minnesota - Lloyd 24 yard Field Goal
Alabama - Team safety

Alabama Media Guide Music City Bowl Game Summary - Minnesota's tailback tandem of Marion Barber III and Laurence Maroney rushed for a combined 292 yards in a 20-16 win over Alabama at the 2004 Music City Bowl at The Coliseum in Nashville. Alabama managed just 21 yards rushing but Quarterback Spencer Pennington hit 22 of 36 passes for 243 yards and one touchdown to keep the Crimson Tide in contention. Barber rushed for 187 yards and a touchdown on 37 carries as Minnesota overcame three turnovers in the first quarter. The Golden Gophers (7-5) wore down Alabama (6-6) with a potent ground attack, rushing for nearly 300 yards against the nation's second-ranked run defense. Maroney also surpassed the century mark with 105 yards on 29 attempts. It marked the first time all season that Alabama had allowed a 100-yard rusher. Barber and Maroney became the first pair of running backs in NCAA history to each rush for 1,000 yards in consecutive seasons. Meanwhile, Alabama was 0-for-11 on third down conversions. Alabama used an opportunistic defense to forge an early lead. The Crimson Tide struck first when Pennington, after a fumble recovery by linebacker Freddie Roach at the Gopher 2-yard line, hit fullback Le'Ron McClain with a two-yard touchdown pass to give Alabama a 7-0 lead just 48 seconds into the game. The Tide had a chance to extend the lead a few moments later when Barber was intercepted in the end zone by cornerback Anthony Madison on an option pass from the Alabama 4. However, the Crimson Tide turned the ball over twice in a wild opening quarter, including a critical mistake by Pennington, who fumbled at his own 1. Defensive end Keith Lipka scooped up the fumble and dove into the end zone for the tying score with 4:21 left in the first period. Minnesota also converted a fumble by backup Quarterback Tyrone Prothro into the go-ahead score as Barber's five-yard touchdown run on the first play of the second quarter made it 14-7 with 14:57 left in the first half. UM's Rhys Lloyd tacked on a field goal with 8:07 to play in the first half to go up 17-7 but Alabama answered when McClain capped a 10-play, 73-yard drive with a one-yard run to make it 17-14 at the half. Lloyd drilled his second field goal of the game to put UM up 20-14 with 10:16 left to play in the third. His 24-yarder capped an 11-play, 68-yard drive to open the second half. Following an Alabama punt, Minnesota was pinned deep in its own territory and opted for a safety when Lloyd stepped out of the end zone, instead of punting, with 3:11 left in the game to pull the Crimson Tide to within 20-16. Alabama began its next possession from its own 48-yard line after the Minnesota free kick and reached the Golden Gophers' 15 where the Crimson Tide faced a third down situation. A Pennington pass missed an open Prothro in the end zone, a play that would have given Alabama the lead. Pennington's ensuing fourth down pass to DJ Hall was also incomplete with 1:23 remaining and Minnesota ran out the clock.

2004 Sun Bowl

The 2004 Vitalis Sun Bowl featured the Arizona State Sun Devils and the Purdue Boilermakers. Arizona State's place kicker, Jessie Ainsworth kicked a 22-yard field goal in the first quarter to give the Sun Devils a 3-0 lead. Arizona State's running back, Preston Jones was tackled in the end zone by Purdue's Brandon Villareal, for a safety, putting Purdue on the board 3-2. The defenses held, and that score held up in the locker room. In the third quarter, Purdue's Kyle Orton connected with wide receiver Brian Hare for a long 80-yard touchdown pass to give Purdue a 9-3 lead. Arizona State Quarterback, Sam Keller found Derek Hagan in the end zone for a 27-yard touchdown to put Arizona State back on top 10-9. He finished the game with 370 yards passing. Early in the fourth quarter, Orton found all-American Taylor Stubblefield for a 5-yard touchdown pass, reclaiming the lead for Purdue, 16-10. Arizona State moved the ball on their ensuing drive, but it stalled, and they had to settle for a field goal. Ainsworth connected on a 34-yard field goal, trimming the margin to 16-13. Keller later threw to Rudy Burgess for a 41-yard touchdown, giving ASU a 20-16 lead. Purdue reclaimed the lead with a 6-yard touchdown pass from Orton to Charles Davis giving them a 23-20 lead. Sam Keller's final touchdown to Rudy Burgess proved to be the game winner, as ASU held off Purdue by a 27-23 margin.

2004 Sun Bowl	Line	1	-	2	-	3	-	4	-	Final
#21 Arizona State	(55.5)	3	-	0	-	7	-	17	-	27
Purdue	(-7.5)	0	-	2	-	7	-	14	-	23

Scoring Summary
Arizona State – Ainsworth 22 yd Field goal
Purdue – Safety – Jones tackled in end zone by Villarreal
Purdue – Hare 80 yd pass from Orton (Jones kick)
Arizona State – Hagan 27 yd pass from Keller (Ainswoirth kick)
Purdue – Stubblefield 5 yd pass from Orton (Jones kick)
Arizona State – Ainsworth 34 yd Field goal
Arizona State – Burgess 41 yd pass from Keller (Ainsworth kick)
Purdue – Davis 6 yd pass from Orton (Jones kick)
Arizona State – Burgess 19 yd pass from Keller (Ainsworth kick)

2004 Chick-Fil-A Peach Bowl (December)

The 2004 Peach Bowl featured the Miami Hurricanes and the Florida Gators. Miami took a 7–0 lead when it blocked a Florida field goal attempt, and Devin Hester returned the ball 78 yards for a touchdown. In the second quarter, Matt Leach kicked a 34-yard field goal to make it 10–3. Roscoe Parrish scored on a 72-yard punt return giving Miami a 17–3 lead at halftime, even though it didn't score an offensive touchdown. In the third quarter, Brock Berlin threw a 20-yard touchdown pass to Ryan Moore, and the Hurricanes led 24–3. Florida's Chris Leak threw a 45-yard touchdown pass to Jemalle Cornelius as the Gators got within 24–10. A 32-yard field goal from Miami gave the Hurricanes the 27–10 win.

2004 Chick-Fil-A Peach Bowl	Line	1	-	2	-	3	-	4	-	Final
#20 Florida	(53.0)	0	-	3	-	7	-	0	-	10
#14 Miami	(-3.5)	7	-	10	-	7	-	3	-	27

Scoring Summary
Miami – Hester 78 yard return of blocked field goal (Peattie kick)
Florida – Leach 34 yard Field goal
Miami – Peattie 47 yard Field goal
Miami – Parrish 72 yard punt return (Peattie kick)
Miami – Moore 20 yard pass from Berlin (Peattie kick)
Florida – Cornelius 45 yard pass from Leak (Leach kick)
Miami – Peattie 32 yard Field goal

Associated Press Chick-Fil-A Peach Bowl Game summary - With no national championship to play for, No. 14 Miami will have to settle for state bragging rights. Devin Hester and Roscoe Parrish each scored return touchdowns and the Hurricanes' defense dominated Florida in Miami's 27-10 Peach Bowl victory. Miami (9-3) jumped out to a 17-3 lead at the half despite failing to score an offensive touchdown. Hester scored his fifth return TD of the season as he scooped up a blocked field goal and raced 79 yards for the score. Neither team managed much offense during the first two quarters. After trading second-quarter field goals, Miami struck again on special teams. Parrish picked up a few blocks on a punt return and was off to the races for a 73-yard TD, capping the first-half scoring. The Hurricanes offense got involved in the third quarter when Brock Berlin, who transferred to Miami from Florida, hit Ryan Moore with a 20-yard scoring strike to extend the lead to 24-3. Florida (7-5) never was able to establish any rhythm on offense and Chris Leak was harassed into one of his poorest performances as a Gator. Leak completed only 19-of-39 passes for 263 yards and a TD while being sacked five times and intercepted twice. The Hurricanes have won their last six meetings with the Gators and swept Florida and Florida State for the second consecutive season.

2005 Gator Bowl

The 2005 Gator Bowl was between the Florida State Seminoles and the West Virginia Mountaineers on January 1, 2005, at Alltel Stadium in Jacksonville, Florida. West Virginia represented the Big East Conference while Florida State represented the Atlantic Coast Conference (ACC).

2005 Gator Bowl	Line	1	-	2	-	3	-	4	-	Final
#17 Florida State	(-9.0)	10	-	3	-	10	-	7	-	30
#23 West Virginia	(45.5)	12	-	0	-	3	-	3	-	18

Scoring Summary
Florida State - Washington 69 yard Run (Beitia Kick)
Florida State - Beitia 32 yard Field Goal
West Virginia - Harris 36 yard Pass (Cooper Kick-failed)
West Virginia - Harris 1 yard Run (Good Kick-failed)
Florida State - Beitia 28 yard Field Goal
Florida State - Beitia 28 yard Field Goal
West Virginia - Good 44 yard Field Goal
Florida State - Thorpe 14 yard Pass (Bietia Kick)
West Virginia - Good 34 yard Field Goal
Florida State - Coleman 1 yard Run (Bietia Kick)

Associated Press Gator Bowl Game Summary - Nice recovery, Chris Rix. The Florida State Seminoles Quarterback struggled for most of his career, and nothing had changed in the Gator Bowl, his final game. Coach Bobby Bowden stuck with Rix, who eventually gave the Seminoles a spark. Rix crafted two long second-half touchdown drives, leading Florida State (No. 15 ESPN/USA Today, No. 17 AP) to a 30-18 victory over West Virginia (No. 23 ESPN/USA Today) on Saturday. At least it didn't end with a loss. The Seminoles (9-3) overcame mistake after mistake to avoid an unprecedented third straight bowl setback. Bowden, facing his former school for the first time since the 1982 Gator Bowl, moved within one bowl win of Joe Paterno's NCAA record of 19 at Penn State. Rix fumbled three times and threw two interceptions, one of which led to a touchdown. So, at halftime, Bowden thought about replacing Rix. Rix eventually settled down, completing five straight passes during a 90-yard drive late in the third quarter, capped by his 14-yard TD pass to Craphonso Thorpe. Thorpe leaped for the ball over Dee McCann in the right corner of the end zone for a 23-15 lead. It was only Rix's third TD pass of the season. Rix also led an 80-yard scoring drive in the fourth, capped by James Coleman's 1-yard run. Rix finished 16-of-31 for 157 yards. Leon Washington carried Florida State much of the day, finishing with 195 yards rushing. Quarterback Rasheed Marshall and West Virginia's platoon of running backs shredded the nation's top run defense for 238 yards. Kay-Jay Harris carried 25 times for 134 yards and scored twice. But the Mountaineers (8-4) failed to find the end zone three times after advancing inside the 20-yard line. West Virginia has lost 11 of its last 12 bowls games and is 0-5 in the Gator. West Virginia continued special team's miscues that were costly in losses to Boston College and Pittsburgh to end the regular season. In the first half, two kickers missed extra points, Brad Cooper booted a kickoff out of bounds, and the Mountaineers later faked a 27-yard field goal attempt but couldn't convert the first-down run. Backup Andy Good practiced his kicks feverishly before the start of the third quarter, and it paid off. He made field goals of 44 and 34 yards to cut the deficit to 23-18 early in the fourth period. The game featured the preseason favorites of the Big East and Atlantic Coast Conference who couldn't secure BCS berths. The Seminoles needed only six plays to score a season-high 10 points in the first quarter. Washington went 69 yards down the right sideline on the game's second play for the longest TD run in Gator Bowl history. He had 135 yards by halftime and had only 12 carries for the game, or else he might have challenged the Gator Bowl record of 216 yards by Syracuse's Floyd Little against Tennessee in 1966. West Virginia's Adam Jones fumbled the ensuing kickoff and Gerard Ross recovered at the Mountaineers 17, leading to one of three Xavier Beitia field goals. It was a start like last year's Gator Bowl, when Maryland scored 10 early points, led 24-0 at halftime and beat West Virginia 41-7. This time, West Virginia fought back. Harris scored on a 36-yard screen pass on the Mountaineers' first offensive series. McCann intercepted Rix later in the quarter and Marshall threw a 40-yard pass to Chris Henry to the 1. Harris took it in for a 12-10 lead. After the game, Henry, a junior who set a school record with 12 TD catches this season, said he intends to enter next spring's NFL draft. Florida State's Lorenzo Booker had 101 yards rushing on 20 carries. The Seminoles were penalized 17 times for 174 yards, both Gator Bowl records.

2005 Outback Bowl

The 2005 edition to the Outback Bowl featured the Georgia Bulldogs and the Wisconsin Badgers. Both teams came into the game ranked and with only 2 losses.

2005 Outback Bowl	Line	1	-	2	-	3	-	4	-	Final
#8 Georgia	(-7.5)	3	-	7	-	14	-	0	-	24
#16 Wisconsin	(40.5)	3	-	3	-	7	-	8	-	21

Scoring Summary
Georgia – Coutu 20 yard Field goal
Wisconsin – Allen 46 yard Field goal
Wisconsin – Allen 44 yard Field goal
Georgia – Gibson 19 yard pass from Greene (Coutu kick)
Georgia – Thomas 24 yard pass from Greene (Coutu kick)
Georgia – Brown 29 yard run (Coutu kick)
Wisconsin – Charles 19 yard pass from Stocco (Allen kick)
Wisconsin – Crooks 11 yard interception return (Orr pass from Stocco)

Associated Press Outback Bowl Game Summary - Freshman Thomas Brown made sure David Greene and David Pollack went out as winners for Georgia. Brown rushed for 49 of his 111 yards on Georgia's final possession as the seventh-ranked Bulldogs held off No. 16 Wisconsin, 24-21, in the Outback Bowl. Unable to generate much offense for nearly three quarters against Georgia's stingy defense, the Badgers mounted a late rally after falling behind, 24-6. Wisconsin (9-3) closed within a field goal when freshman linebacker Andy Crooks, celebrating his 19th birthday, returned an interception 11 yards for a touchdown with 4:30 remaining. But the Bulldogs (10-2) were able to run out the clock behind Brown, who carried six times on the ensuing drive. With 1:38 remaining, Brown sealed the win by gaining 11 yards on 4th-and-1 from the Wisconsin 15. Greene, the winningest Quarterback in Division I-A history, threw two touchdowns, including one to Jeremy Thomas in the third quarter that caromed off a Wisconsin defender. Greene concluded his career with a 42-10 record, surpassing Peyton Manning's previous mark of 39 wins. He also leaves Georgia as the Southeastern Conference's leader in career passing yards and total offense. Pollack, who joins Herschel Walker as Georgia's only three-time All-Americans, registered four tackles, including three sacks. Pollack appeared to deliver the knockout punch when he sacked John Stocco and recovered a fumble on the same play. The seniors finished with 42 victories, the second most in school history behind the class of 1983 (43-4-1). Crooks made things interesting by picking off Greene on the first play of the next possession, but the Bulldogs were able to run out the clock by keeping the ball on the ground. Anthony Davis led the Badgers with 79 yards rushing on 21 carries. Quarterback John Stocco threw for 170 yards but was sacked seven times as the Badgers ended the season with a three-game losing streak.

2005 Capital One Bowl

The 2005 Capital One Bowl was between the Iowa Hawkeyes and the LSU Tigers on January 1, 2005, at the Citrus Bowl in Orlando, Florida. Spread bettors favored LSU by seven points, but Iowa won, 30–25, when Quarterback Drew Tate completed a 56-yard pass to wide receiver Warren Holloway for a touchdown as time expired. Prior to the game, LSU head coach Nick Saban announced that he was leaving LSU to become the head coach for the Miami Dolphins. Iowa coach Kirk Ferentz also drew attention from NFL teams, but ultimately signed a contract extension through 2012. The Hawkeyes were co-Big Ten champions with Michigan; however, the Wolverines were granted the Big Ten's automatic BCS bid due to their 30–17 victory over Iowa on September 25, 2004. The game had 70,229 fans in attendance; Tate was named the game's Most Valuable Player. LSU became the first defending BCS national champion to lose a non-BCS bowl the following year by losing this game. Tate was the game's leading passer, throwing for all 287 of Iowa's passing yards. JaMarcus Russell was LSU's leading passer, throwing for 128 yards and two touchdowns, both to Skyler Green. Iowa's Jonathan Babineaux led the game in sacks, with three. Babineaux also led the game in tackles for loss, with 4.5. LSU intercepted Tate twice during the game; Marcus Randall was intercepted once by the Hawkeyes. Both teams fumbled the ball once, though neither time was the ball recovered by the other team.

2005 Capital One Bowl	Line	1	-	2	-	3	-	4	-	Final
#11 Iowa	(41.5)	7	-	7	-	3	-	13	-	30
#12 LSU	(-6.5)	0	-	12	-	0	-	13	-	25

Scoring Summary
Iowa – Solomon 57 yard pass from Tate (Schlicher kick)
LSU – Jackson 29 yard Field goal
LSU – Jackson 47 yard Field goal
Iowa – Considine 7 yard blocked punt return (Schlicher kick)
LSU – Broussard 74 yard run (Kick failed)
Iowa – Schlicher 19 yard Field goal
Iowa – Simmons 4 yard run (Schlicher kick)
LSU – Green 22 yard pass from Russell (Jackson kick)
LSU – Green 3 yard pass from Russell (Jackson kick)
Iowa – Holloway 56 yard pass from Tate (no PAT)

Associated Press Capital One Bowl Game Summary - Iowa spoiled Nick Saban's farewell party with one of the most dramatic plays in bowl history. Drew Tate tossed a 56-yard touchdown pass to a wide-open Warren Holloway as time expired, lifting the 13th-ranked Hawkeyes to a stunning 30-25 victory over No. 11 Louisiana State in the Capital One Bowl. Tate completed 20-of-32 passes for 287 yards and two TDs. It was the final game at LSU for the 53-year-old Saban, who signed a five-year contract with the Miami Dolphins last month. He led the Tigers to a share of the national championship last season. Third-string Quarterback JaMarcus Russell appeared to send Saban out in style, throwing two TD passes in the final 8 1/2 minutes to Skyler Green, including a three-yard strike with 46 seconds left, as LSU rallied from a 24-12 deficit. Russell completed 12-of-15 passes for 128 yards after taking over for Marcus Randall, who was knocked out of the game late in the first half with a rib injury. But four plays later, Tate took advantage of a huge lapse by LSU's secondary as Holloway inexplicably got free several yards behind the defense. Tate hit Holloway in stride at the 15 and the receiver danced into the end zone, completing one of the most memorable plays in school history and overcoming a fourth-quarter collapse. A senior wide receiver, Holloway scored his only TD at Iowa on the final play of his career. Iowa gained only 77 yards in the first half but held a 14-12 lead at the intermission. Tate tossed a 57-yard TD pass to Clinton Solomon in the first quarter and Sean Considine returned a blocked punt seven yards for a score late in the second quarter. The Hawkeyes appeared to grab control in the second half, taking a 24-12 lead on Marques Simmons' four-yard TD run just over two minutes into the fourth quarter. But Russell, who started four games in the regular season, began LSU's comeback with a 22-yard TD pass to Skyler with 8:21 remaining. Randall, who had trouble breathing in the second half, completed 10-of-15 passes for 89 yards before being forced to leave. Alley Broussard rushed for 109 yards on 13 carries for the Tigers, including a 74-yard TD with 38 seconds left in the first half.

2005 Cotton Bowl Classic

The 2005 Cotton Bowl Classic was between the Tennessee Volunteers and the Texas A&M Aggies on January 1, 2005, at the Cotton Bowl in Dallas, Texas. Tennessee represented the Southeastern Conference (SEC) while Texas A&M represented the Big 12 Conference.

2005 Cotton Bowl Classic	Line	1	-	2	-	3	-	4	-	Final
#15 Tennessee	(55.5)	14	-	14	-	10	-	0	-	38
#22 Texas A&M	(-3.5)	0	-	0	-	0	-	7	-	7

Scoring Summary
Tennessee – Fayton 57 yard pass from Clausen (Wilhoit kick)
Tennessee – Anderson 12 yard pass from Clausen (Wilhoit kick)
Tennessee – Houston 8 yard run (Wilhoit kick)
Tennessee – Brown 13 yard pass from Clausen (Wilhoit kick)
Tennessee – Riggs 9 yard run (Wilhoit kick)
Tennessee – Wilhoit 37 yard Field goal
Texas A&M – Taylor 5 yard pass from McNeal (Pegram kick)

Cotton Bowl Classic Game Summary - The Tennessee Quarterback position was a revolving door during the 2004 campaign. Two signal callers had gone down to injury during the season, and the Volunteers were down to their third QB against a resurgent Texas A&M squad in the 69th SBC Cotton Bowl. Rick Clausen easily erased any doubts the Vols had at Quarterback. The junior looked like an all-conference performer from the opening drive, and when the 2005 Classic was over, Clausen walked away with the J. Curtis Sanford Offensive MVP Trophy after leading Tennessee to a surprising 38-7 win over the Aggies. The No. 15 Vols (10-3) raced to a 28-0 lead midway through the second quarter behind Clausen's passing, then rode their bruising running game to finish off No. 22 Texas A&M (7-5). Clausen was 18 of 27 passing for 222 yards and a career-high three touchdown passes. The Tennessee defense gave Clausen and the Vols ample opportunities by forcing A&M into a season-high five turnovers. The Aggies had only turned the ball over eight times in the first 11 games. The crowd of 75,704 was the fourth largest in Cotton Bowl history and the biggest since the 1978 Notre Dame-Texas game. The largely maroon-clad crowd had turned out in droves to support their Aggies, who were making their first bowl appearance since December 2001. Tennessee wasted little time in gaining momentum by taking the opening drive 80 yards, capped off by a 57-yard pass from Clausen to C.J. Fayton for the Vols' first score. Tennessee had squelched any home-field advantage the Aggies might have enjoyed. Ultimately penalties and missed tackles also doomed A&M. An off-side penalty kept alive Tennessee's first drive. Two plays later, the Aggies missed a tackle on Fayton after his catch that he turned into the Vols' first touchdown. A&M responded by driving to the Tennessee 23 but running back Courtney Lewis couldn't hold on to the errant pitch from Quarterback Reggie McNeal, and the Vols' Turk McBride recovered the fumble. On the first snap of the Aggies' next drive, McNeal had the ball pop loose at his 28-yard line as his helmet came flying off after a jarring hit by Tennessee's Justin Harrell. The sophomore defensive tackle went on to earn the Felix McKnight Defensive MVP Trophy. Tennessee's Corey Campbell recovered the loose ball for the Vols. Four plays later, Tennessee scored on a 12-yard pass from Clausen to Cory Anderson for a 14-0 lead. Then, just when A&M appeared to be gaining some momentum early in the second quarter, Erik Mayes muffed a punt. The Vols' Corey Larkins recovered at A&M's 8-yard line, and Tennessee's offense needed one play to go up 21-0 on a Cedric Houston run. The Volunteer ground assault grinded out the clock in the second half behind the running of Houston, Gerald Riggs and David Yancey. The three backs combined for 223 yards on 44 carries. Riggs led all rushers with 102 yards on 18 carries. The junior tailback scored the Vols final touchdown on a 9-yard run in the third quarter. Tennessee added a 37-yard field goal from James Wilhoit to take a commanding 38-0 lead. A&M's highly touted offense led by McNeal was held in check until the junior Quarterback connected with Earvin Taylor of a 5-yard pass for the Aggies' only touchdown with just over five minutes left in the fourth quarter. McNeal still was able to establish a new school single-season passing record of 2,791 yards on a pass to Taylor to start the game. McNeal's mark stood as one of the few highlights for the Aggies. Rather, the Vols set new highs, and in the process, the 2005 SBC Cotton Bowl Champions gave Tennessee fans great optimism heading into the year ahead.

2005 Rose Bowl

The 2005 Rose Bowl Game was the 91st edition of the college football bowl game, held on January 1, 2005 at the Rose Bowl stadium in Pasadena, California. The Texas Longhorns, second-place finishers in the Big 12 Conference's South Division, defeated the Michigan Wolverines, co-champions of the Big Ten Conference, 38-37. Texas Quarterback Vince Young and Michigan linebacker LaMarr Woodley were named the Rose Bowl Players of the Game, the first time that the Rose Bowl separately recognized an offensive and defensive player of the game. The contest marked the first time Texas and Michigan faced each other in football, despite the long history of each school's football program, and marked the first Rose Bowl in which a Big Ten team appeared without an opponent from the Pacific-10 Conference. ABC broadcast the game nationally in 720p format, the first time the Rose Bowl was telecast in HDTV in the United States.

2005 Rose Bowl	Line	1	-	2	-	3	-	4	-	Final
#13 Michigan	(53.5)	0	-	14	-	17	-	6	-	37
#6 Texas	(-7.0)	7	-	7	-	7	-	17	-	38

Scoring Summary
Texas - Young 20 yard run (Mangum kick)
Michigan - Edwards 39 yard pass from Henne (Rivas kick)
Texas - Thomas 11 yard pass from Young (Mangum kick)
Michigan - Edwards 8 yard pass from Henne (Rivas kick)
Texas - Young 60 yard run (Mangum kick)
Michigan - Steve Breaston 50 yard pass from Henne (Rivas kick)
Michigan - Edwards 9 yard pass from Henne (Rivas kick)
Michigan - Rivas 44 yard field goal

Texas - Young 10 yard run (Mangum kick)
Michigan - Rivas 32 yard field goal
Texas - Young 23 yard run (Mangum kick)
Michigan - Rivas 42 yard field goal
Texas - Mangum 37 yard field goal

Bentley Historical Library 2005 ROSE BOWL GAME SUMMARY - senior kicker Dusty Mangum's 37-yard field goal as time expired gave No. 6 Texas a 38-37 win over the No. 13 Michigan in the 91st Rose Bowl Game. U-M was led by wide receiver Braylon Edwards with 10 receptions for 109 yards and three touchdowns. Edwards became Michigan's and the Big Ten's career receiving TD leader, closing his career with 39 scores. After an early Texas touchdown, Edwards evened the score at 7-7 in the second quarter on a 39-yard touchdown pass from Henne. Hart had runs of five, three and three yards to move the chains prior to the scoring play. Texas regained the lead at 14-7, but U-M took advantage of the game's first turnover and knotted the score at 14 apiece at halftime as Henne tossed an eight-yard TD pass to Edwards. The Wolverines gained their first lead, 28-2 1, as Henne completed a nine-yard TD pass to Edwards on a slant pass from the left side at 6:29 of the third quarter. After a Michigan field goal, Texas Quarterback Vince Young scored his third rushing TD of the game, a 10-yard run at 9:51 of the fourth quarter and trimmed the deficit to 31-28. The Wolverines boosted their lead to 34-28 with 6:09 left in regulation as Rivas hit a 32-yard field goal. Texas responded and quickly drove down the field for another touchdown, taking a 35-34 lead. Breaston began the Wolverines' next drive with a 53-yard kickoff return for a Michigan single-game bowl record, surpassing his previous season- and career-best set earlier in the game. It was his sixth kickoff return of the game for a total of 221 yards, setting Michigan and Rose Bowl records. Hart carried for 18 yards in the next three plays, ending on the 25-yard line, where Rivas completed the drive with a 42-yard field goal with 3:04 remaining on the clock. This was his third of the game, tying the Rose Bowl record. Mangum capped the Longhorns' 10-play game winning drive with his 37-yard field goal as time expired.

2005 Fiesta Bowl

The 2005 Tostitos Fiesta Bowl, played on January 1, 2005, was the 34th edition of the Fiesta Bowl. The game was played between Utah and Pittsburgh, in front of 73,519 fans. It is notable for being the first BCS game to feature a team from a non-BCS conference, and the only BCS bowl to feature a non-BCS team prior to the 2006 season, making the trip more impressive. (In 2006, the eligibility rules became less strict: the BCS increased from four games to five, and entry required a top 12 finish instead of a top 6.) Utah was led by co-head coaches Urban Meyer and Kyle Whittingham, and Quarterback Alex Smith directed his spread offense. The Utes were nothing short of unstoppable during the regular season, having won all their games by at least 14 points, and held an average lead of 40–14 after three quarters. They played key out-of-conference games against Texas A&M and North Carolina and defeated five bowl teams by an average of 23.2 points. Utah was a very successful team that broke many school records, including most wins in a single season with 12, 16 straight wins (which would reach 18 in 2005), and 544 points scored in one season. Going into the game, Utah had been ranked in the Top 10 for 8 consecutive weeks. Pittsburgh was 8–3 and the Big East Conference champion. Utah raced to a 28–0 lead and held on for a convincing 35–7 win. Alex Smith had a magnificent showing, completing 29 of 37 passes for 328 yards and 4 touchdowns, as he went on to impress NFL scouts and became the number 1 overall draft pick.

2005 Fiesta Bowl	Line	1	-	2	-	3	-	4	-	Final
#19 Pittsburgh	(67.0)	0	-	0	-	7	-	0	-	7
#5 Utah	(-15.5)	7	-	7	-	21	-	0	-	35

Scoring Summary
Utah – Ganther 4 yard run (Carroll kick)
Utah – Madsen 6 yard pass from Smith (Carroll kick)
Utah – Johnson 18 yard pass from Smith (Carroll kick)
Utah – Warren 23 yard pass from Smith (Carroll kick)
Pittsburgh – Lee 31 yard pass from Palko (Cummings kick)
Utah – Warren 18 yard pass from Smith (Carroll kick)

Associated Press Fiesta Bowl Game Summary - Utah looked like a powerhouse that deserved a better final test to its BCS-busting season. Behind the cool efficiency of Alex Smith, the Utes (No. 6 ESPN/USA Today; No. 5 AP) used their baffling spread offense and an underrated defense to dominate Pittsburgh (No. 20 ESPN/USA Today; No. 19 AP) 35-7 in the Fiesta Bowl on Saturday night. Utah was a 16-point favorite, the biggest margin of any of the bowls, and it was a safe bet. Smith completed 29 of 37 passes, four of them for touchdowns, for 328 yards and the Utes sacked Pitt's Tyler Palko nine times, a Fiesta Bowl record. Smith, a Heisman Trophy finalist who is considering going to the NFL after this, his junior, season, also rushed 15 times for 68 yards. Paris Warren caught 15 passes, breaking the Fiesta record of 11 set by Kellen Winslow of Miami in the 2003 national championship loss to Ohio State. Warren, who transferred from Oregon in 2002, had 198 yards receiving, third-most in Fiesta Bowl history. Smith's 78 percent completion rate was also a Fiesta Bowl mark. Smith and Warren shared the offensive MVP award, and Utah nose guard Steve Fifita was named the defensive MVP. Meyer punctuated two memorable years in Salt Lake City with the Utes' first unbeaten, untied season since 1930. He leaves for Florida after making Utah the first team from outside the six BCS conferences to force its way into a Bowl Championship Series game. Tens of thousands of Utah fans who made up at least three-fourths of the sellout crowd of 73,519 were not disappointed. Utah scored touchdowns on five of its first seven possessions, including all three in the third quarter. Out of a dizzying array of formations, the Mountain West Conference champs kept the Panthers off balance all night with everything from option plays to a handful of shovel passes. The Utes set up one touchdown with a reverse and scored another on the old "hook-and-ladder" play. On that play, Smith threw to Steve Savoy, who flipped the ball to Warren. Warren dashed 18 yards for the score, capping a 10-play, 94-yard drive, to put the Utes up 35-7 with 25 seconds left in the third quarter. Pitt (8-4) was overmatched in its final game under Coach Walt Harris, who is leaving for Stanford after eight seasons with the Panthers. Pittsburgh was the unwanted team among the eight BCS squads. The Panthers automatically qualified for one of the four elite games as Big East champions, even though they were only 21st in the BCS rankings. Dave Wannstedt, who resigned this season as coach of the Miami Dolphins, has been hired to replace Harris. As the BCS buster with a huge following, Utah was welcomed by the Fiesta Bowl organizers, but they had no choice but to invite Pitt as the opponent. In the first half, the Panthers accomplished their goal of controlling the ball and keeping Utah's offense off the field as much as possible. Pitt had a seven-minute advantage in time of possession, but the Utes still led 14-0, even though they had the ball only four times, the last with just 49 seconds to go in the half.

2005 Sugar Bowl

The 2005 Sugar Bowl was between the Virginia Tech Hokies and the Auburn Tigers at the Louisiana Superdome in New Orleans, Louisiana, on January 3, 2005. It was the 71st edition of the annual Sugar Bowl football contest. Virginia Tech represented the Atlantic Coast Conference (ACC) in the contest, while Auburn represented the Southeastern Conference (SEC). In a defensive struggle, Auburn earned a 16–13 victory despite a late-game rally by Virginia Tech.

2005 Sugar Bowl	Line	1	-	2	-	3	-	4	-	Final
#9 Virginia Tech	(44.5)	0	-	0	-	0	-	13	-	13
#3 Auburn	(-6.0)	6	-	3	-	7	-	0	-	16

Scoring Summary
Auburn – Vaughn 23 yard Field goal
Auburn – Vaughn 19 yard Field goal
Auburn – Vaughn 24 yard Field goal
Auburn – Aromashodu 5 yard pass from Campbell (Vaughn kick)
Virginia Tech – Morgan 29 yard pass from Randall (Pass failed)
Virginia Tech – Morgan 80 yard pass from Randall (Pace kick)

Recap excerpted from the book "Sugar Bowl Classic: A History" by Marty Mulé

The Auburn Tigers wanted to make a statement. What they made was sort of more of a stammer. Starting out like it was going to show the college football world what an injustice its omission from the national championship game had perpetuated, the Tigers could never put Virginia Tech away - and, in fact, could well have lost the game along with their argument in the end. Early though, the Tigers were making a strong case. On the night's first series, Quarterback Jason Campbell drove Auburn to the Hokies' 8. But the Tigers couldn't put the ball in the end zone. John Vaughn kicked a 21-yard field goal. An interception of Tech Quarterback Bryan Randall by Junior Rosengreen eventually put the Tigers at the 1 - where the Hokies forced a second Vaughn field goal. Auburn was in front and in charge - but not convincingly, even though Virginia Tech was unable to seriously dent the formidable Tiger defense. By the end of the quarter, Tech had two first downs and just 30 yards of offense, nine of which came on scrambles by Randall. The first real signs of offensive life for Virginia Tech came in the second period when Randall drove the Hokies to the Tiger 2 and the opportunity to seize the lead against an Auburn team that was settling for field goals instead of touchdowns. After two futile plays, on third down Randall ran a Quarterback draw and, for an instant, had a clear path to the end zone. But free safety Will Henning shot up the middle and stopped Randall a yard short. Then, on fourth down, passing up a field goal and with everyone expecting another power run, Randall rolled out and flung a pass between two defenders to sophomore fullback Jesse Allen - who had it for an instant, then dropped it. The ball may have been brushed by a defender's finger, but no one was certain. Coach Frank Beamer explained his rationale in going for seven points instead of the almost sure three at that point thusly: Instead, not only did Virginia Tech fail to take the lead but Auburn took over at the 1, and then proceeded to march 92 yards to the Hokies' 7, where John Vaughn kicked another field goal, this one of 24 yards. The 9-0 halftime lead gave Auburn breathing room, and then, on the opening drive of the third quarter, the Tigers extended the lead with their lone touchdown of the night. Campbell hit Anthony Mix with a 53-yard completion to the Tech 13, then threw five yards to Devin Aronashodu for the TD that put Auburn up 16-0. An indication of Auburn's control of the game at this point would be that at the end of three quarters, the Hokie running backs had a total net of 26 yards. Virginia Tech, though, was about to throw a major scare into the Tigers. A recovered fumble led to Tech's first points with a 29-yard scoring pass from Randall to Josh Morgan. Time was running out, but Tech made the ending a heart-stopper when Randall-to-Morgan struck again, this time on a stunning 80-yard pass - the longest against the Tigers all season - with 2:01 remaining. Suddenly Tech, dominated almost all evening long, had a chance to steal the Sugar Bowl - and the thunder from Auburn's argument that it may well have been the nation's best college football team. Cooper Wallace's recovery of Tech's on-sides kick, though, ended matters for all practical purposes. In a way, Tech deserved a better fate. The Hokies, whose running backs had only 34 yards but lived on a controlled passing offense, outgained the Tigers 375-299, and the Tech defense turned in a sterling performance, holding Auburn in check for all but five plays. Those five plays, though, were the difference. The Tigers gained 179 yards on their five plays of 20 yards or longer. Auburn had 120 on its other 54 plays. "We held them to field goals, but the big plays hurt us," Hokies cornerback Eric Green said. Williams and Brown combined for 129 yards, 60 less than their season average. Still, Auburn became just the 10th school in NCAA history to finish a seasons 13-0 or better. It didn't do the Tigers any good, however. They still were left in the cold as far as national recognition went. Coach Tommy Tuberville got something out of the memorable season, however. He cracked after the Sugar Bowl that maybe if the more recognized national media polls didn't pick Auburn No. 1, perhaps someone else would, like maybe *Golf Digest*. The tongue-in-cheek comment brought a quick response. A representative of the magazine contacted the Tiger coach and informed him that he would be receiving a lifetime subscription.

2005 Orange Bowl - (BCS National Championship Game)

The 2005 Orange Bowl was the BCS National Championship Game of the 2004 NCAA football season and was played on January 4, 2005 at Pro Player Stadium in Miami Gardens, Florida. The game matched the USC Trojans against the Oklahoma Sooners. Both teams entered with undefeated, 12–0 records. The game featured many firsts regarding the Heisman Trophy: Leinart had won the 2004 Heisman award the month prior to the game, and Oklahoma Quarterback Jason White had won the award the previous season, making it the first game to have two past-Heisman winners on the same field (and on opposite teams). The game featured four of the five Heisman finalists that year: Leinart (winner), Oklahoma running back Adrian Peterson (first runner-up), White (second runner-up) and USC running back Reggie Bush (fourth runner-up); Bush would win the award the following season (although USC returned its copy of Bush's trophy and Bush forfeited the award following the institution of NCAA sanctions in 2010).

2005 Orange Bowl	Line	1	-	2	-	3	-	4	-	Final
#2 Oklahoma	(53.5)	7	-	3	-	0	-	9	-	19
#1 USC	(-2.0)	14	-	24	-	10	-	7	-	55

Scoring Summary
Oklahoma – Wilson 5 yard pass from White (Hartley kick)
USC – Byrd 33 yard pass from Leinart (Killeen kick)
USC – White 6 yard run (Killeen kick)
USC – Jarrett 54 yard pass from Leinart (Killeen kick)
USC – Smith 5 yard pass from Leinart (Killeen kick)
Oklahoma – Hartley 29 yard Field goal
USC – Smith 33 yard pass from Leinart (Killeen kick)
USC – Killeen 44 yard Field goal
USC – Smith 4 yard pass from Leinart (Killeen kick)
USC – Killeen 42 yard Field goal
USC – White 8 yard run (Killeen kick)
Oklahoma – Safety (Leinart tackled in end zone)
Oklahoma – Wilson 9 yard pass from White (Hartley kick)

Associated Press Orange Bowl Game Summary - Matt Leinart and his Southern California teammates bounced around the end zone, then broke into a victory dance. The celebration was on -- and it was only halftime. Playing to perfection, the Heisman Trophy winner threw a record five touchdown passes and the Trojans overwhelmed Oklahoma 55-19 Tuesday night in the Orange Bowl, ending the season just as they started: No. 1. Even better, there's no one they must share it with. The much-anticipated battle of unbeatens, No. 1 vs. No. 2, turned into a coronation for USC, which had to settle for a share of the national championship last year after being left out of the Bowl Championship Series title game. That was no consolation for unbeaten Auburn, the odd team out of the BCS title game this season. The Tigers (13-0) stated their case with a 16-13 victory over Virginia Tech in the Sugar Bowl on Monday night and could have done no worse than Oklahoma against USC. But they finished second in the final Associated Press poll. USC became the first team to repeat as AP national champions since Nebraska in 1994-95 and joined Florida State in 1999 as the only teams to go wire-to-wire -- from preseason to post bowls -- as No. 1. Auburn coach Tommy Tuberville was on hand to witness the rout in a game he believed his team should have been playing in. USC was shut out of last season's BCS title game, despite topping both the AP Top 25 and ESPN/USA Today Coaches' poll at the end of the regular season. The BCS computer rankings favored Oklahoma, even though the Sooners lost the Big 12 title game 35-7. Oklahoma then washed out in the BCS championship game, losing to LSU in the Sugar Bowl 21-14 to give the Tigers the top spot in the ESPN/USA Today Coaches' poll. The Trojans wrapped up their 2003 national title three days before the BCS championship game by beating Michigan 28-14 in the Rose Bowl. They didn't have to wait for their trophy this season. With the aid of four Oklahoma turnovers, the Trojans (13-0) ambushed the Sooners (12-1) with 38 points in the final 20 minutes of the first half. The first meeting of Heisman winners couldn't have been more one-sided. Leinart set an Orange Bowl record with his five scoring tosses and Jason White spent another BCS title game running for his life. Oklahoma's 2003 Heisman winner finished 24-of-36 for 244 yards with three interceptions and two touchdowns. Leinart was 18-of-35 for 332 yards, and he had the USC band playing "Fight On" all night. The laid-back Californian who replaced Carson Palmer became the first Heisman winner to win a national title since Michigan's Charles Woodson in 1997. Leinart looked nothing like the overrated Quarterback for an average offense, as Oklahoma defensive end Larry Birdine described him. Leinart tossed four scores in the first half as the Trojans turned an early 7-0 deficit into a 38-10 halftime lead. And when the demolition had ended, the Trojans grooved in the end zone as Outkast's "Hey Ya!" blared through Pro Player Stadium. Meanwhile, the Sooners trudged off having already allowed more points in a bowl game than any team in school history. Leinart shrugged off Birdine's comment and played great in what could be his farewell to college football. The junior could be a top pick in the next NFL draft. He also got plenty of help. The Trojans reached a season high for points and turned the game into a USC highlight reel, with Leinart making pinpoint passes and his receivers making spectacular catches. Steve Smith caught an Orange Bowl-record three touchdowns, LenDale White ran for 118 yards and two scores and the USC's defense smothered Oklahoma's freshman sensation Adrian Peterson. Peterson, the Heisman runner-up to Leinart, managed just 82 yards on 25 carries. Senior Mark Bradley made a freshman mistake that set off one of those USC runs that have done in so many opponents during the Trojans' 22-game winning streak. The Sooners' most versatile player and the son of former Oklahoma Quarterback Danny Bradley tried to scoop up a punt that had bounced inside the Oklahoma 5. Collin Ashton grabbed on to Bradley, the ball squirted away, and USC recovered at the 6. Bradley trudged back to the sideline, where he received some pats on the head and back. His mood no doubt worsened on the next play, when LenDale White reached the ball over the goal line to give the Trojans a 14-7 lead late in the first quarter. USC made it 21 straight points with the help of Oklahoma's second turnover. Under pressure, Jason White heaved a deep ball into quadruple-coverage and Jason Leach came up with USC's 20th interception of the season. Then the Trojans went to work on Oklahoma freshman cornerback Marcus Walker with their own star freshman, Dwayne Jarrett. The 6-foot-5 Jarrett went over the 5-11 Walker for an 18 yard gain on third-and-8. Walker ended up in no-man's land on the next play. He looked like he wanted to blitz but stopped. Meanwhile, Jarrett ran straight down the sideline and hauled in a perfect throw from Leinart for a 54-yard score. The USC deluge continued. White was upended while throwing and was picked off by Eric Wright deep in Sooners territory. This time Leinart found Smith alone in the end zone from 5 yards out, to cap a four-touchdown barrage. In a span of 10:10, USC turned a 7-0 deficit into a 28-7 lead that left the Sooners looking dumbfounded. Oklahoma drove for a field goal on the next possession, but all it did was give USC enough time to catch its breath. Reggie Bush ripped off a 33-yard run to start the Trojans on their way and Leinart again picked on a secondary that looked like Oklahoma's soft spot much of the season. Leinart went deep to Smith, who hauled in a 33-yarder while hitting the ground to make it 35-10. Carroll greeted Leinart with a hug after the left-hander's fourth touchdown pass. Leinart gave a sly grin as he glanced up at the scoreboard. Oklahoma's season-high fourth turnover, led to Ryan Killeen's 44-yard field goal just before halftime.

2005 New Orleans Bowl

The 2005 New Orleans Bowl featured the Arkansas State Indians (now the Red Wolves) and the Southern Miss Golden Eagles. Due to the destruction caused by Hurricane Katrina, the game was played at Cajun Field in Lafayette, Louisiana instead of at the Louisiana Superdome in New Orleans. For Arkansas State, the game represented the Indians' first bowl game since the 1970 Pecan Bowl. The team had won the Sun

Belt Conference with a 6–5 record. Meanwhile, the Southern Miss Golden Eagles (representing Conference USA) also came in with a 6–5 record.

2005 New Orleans Bowl	Line	1	-	2	-	3	-	4	-	Final
Southern Miss	(-16.5)	0	-	10	-	14	-	7	-	31
Arkansas State	(49.5)	0	-	10	-	9	-	0	-	19

Scoring Summary
Southern Miss - McCaleb 31 yard Field goal
Arkansas State - Neihouse 44 yard Field goal
Southern Miss - Mason 5 yard run (McCaleb kick)
Arkansas State - Noce 4 yard run (Neihouse kick)
Southern Miss - Hull 1 yard run (McCaleb kick)
Arkansas State - Burton 2 yard pass from Noce (Neihouse kick)
Southern Miss - Nelson 29 yard pass from Almond (McCaleb kick)
Arkansas State - Team safety
Southern Miss - Nelson 6 yard pass from Almond (McCaleb kick)

Associated Press New Orleans Bowl Game Summary - Southern Mississippi's win in the New Orleans Bowl was a lot like the rest of the Golden Eagles' season -- a struggle. Shawn Nelson caught two second-half touchdowns and Cody Hull added 161 yards rushing to lead Southern Mississippi over Arkansas State 31-19 on Tuesday night in the first of the season's 28 bowl games. Southern Miss endured plenty of turmoil long before arriving in Lafayette, where the New Orleans Bowl was moved because of Hurricane Katrina. The Golden Eagles had two games postponed in September because of hurricanes Katrina and Rita, had to relocate temporarily to Memphis and played nine games in nine weeks to end the regular season. Against Arkansas State, the Golden Eagles fumbled on their first two drives, but they finally took control in the second half. Arkansas State tied the game at 17 in the third quarter on Nick Noce's 2-yard pass to Manuel Burton, but Dustin Almond answered with a 29-yard toss to Nelson to make it 24-17. The Indians scored on a safety when Southern Miss punter Luke Johnson knocked the ball out of the back of the end zone after a bad snap. The Golden Eagles made it 31-19 on Almond's 6-yard pass to Nelson with 8:22 remaining in the game. Arkansas State (6-6) was in its first bowl since moving back up from Division I-AA. The Indians were in I-AA from 1982-91; before that, their last postseason appearance was against Central Missouri State in the 1970 Pecan Bowl. Southern Mississippi (7-5) made its fourth straight postseason appearance and eighth in nine years. The Golden Eagles beat North Texas 31-10 in last year's New Orleans Bowl. Southern Miss, a double-digit favorite, appeared on its way to an easy win when Almond found Nelson for a 37-yard completion on the first play from scrimmage. But after the Golden Eagles drove to the 1-yard line, Almond fumbled a snap and the Indians recovered. Southern Mississippi's next drive ended with another fumble, this one at the Arkansas State 48. The teams exchanged field goals in the second quarter, and Cole Mason put the Golden Eagles ahead 10-3 with a 5-yard run with 2:05 to play in the half. The Indians answered with an eight-play, 80-yard drive, capped by Noce's 4-yard run with 5.8 seconds remaining. Southern Mississippi went ahead early in the third quarter. Kevis Coley recovered Noce's fumble at the Arkansas State 15 and returned it to the 10, setting up Hull's 1-yard scoring run. The Indians came back again. On first-and-goal from the 2, Noce faked a Quarterback draw and then backed up and threw to an open Burton in the back of the end zone. Antonio Warren rushed for only 20 yards for Arkansas State, finishing the season with 1,066. Warren left in the first half after reinjuring the ankle he sprained earlier in the year. He returned in the third quarter but wasn't much of a factor. His fumble at the Arkansas State 25 set up Southern Mississippi's final touchdown. Noce went 10-of-19 for 213 yards with an interception. He also ran for 55 yards. Almond went 17-of-32 for 253 yards in his final college game. He set several season school records in the game, including yards passing (2,860), completions (216), passing attempts (394) and total offense (2,763 yards). Brett Favre set the previous record for attempts with 381 in 1989. Hull, a sophomore, surpassed 100 yards for the first time. Nelson, a freshman, had six catches for 121 yards -- both career highs. He was named the game's most valuable player. Arkansas State's Darren Toney had a scintillating kickoff return nullified by a holding penalty in the second quarter. Toney ran about 25 yards up field, retreated several steps and then streaked down the sideline for what would have been a 93-yard touchdown. Arkansas State was the first Sun Belt Conference team besides North Texas to represent the league in the New Orleans Bowl. North Texas went the last four years, winning once.

2005 GMAC Bowl

The 2005 GMAC Bowl was the 8th edition of the GMAC Bowl. It was played in December 2005, and featured the UTEP Miners, and the Toledo Rockets.

2005 GMAC Bowl	Line	1	-	2	-	3	-	4	-	Final
Toledo	(-3.0)	7	-	21	-	3	-	14	-	45
Texas-El Paso	(61.5)	3	-	10	-	0	-	0	-	13

Scoring Summary
Toledo - Allen 10 yard pass from Gradkowski (Robbins kick)
UTEP - Schneider 34 yard Field goal
Toledo - Washington 33 yard pass from Gradkowski (Robbins kick)
UTEP - Higgins 18 yard pass from Palmer (Schneider kick)
UTEP - Schneider 23 yard Field goal
Toledo - Odom 31 yard pass from Gradkowski (Robbins kick)
Toledo - Thomas 37 yard interception return (Robbins kick)
Toledo - Robbins 29 yard Field goal
Toledo - Powell 22 yard pass from Gradkowski (Robbins kick)
Toledo - Hopkins 13 yard pass from Gradkowski (Robbins kick)

Associated Press GMAC Bowl Game Summary - Bruce Gradkowski and the Toledo offense ran, passed and scored almost at will. David Thomas and the defense shut down a potent UTEP offense and even scored once, too. And another GMAC Bowl resulted in a big MAC victory. Gradkowski threw five touchdown passes, Trinity Dawson ran for 132 yards and Thomas returned an interception 37 yards for a touchdown, leading the Rockets to a 45-13 victory over the Miners on Wednesday night. The Miners certainly weren't arguing that point after getting victimized by a dominant all-around performance and extending their string of postseason futility one more year. Toledo (9-3) had lost its last two bowl games, but left little doubt in this one, running the Mid-American Conference's record to 5-0 in the Mobile bowl. Mike Alston contributed two big tackles for the Rockets to end the first half, when UTEP was threatening to cut into a 28-13 deficit. It was the last time the Miners (8-4) appeared set to mount a rally. UTEP ended its season with a defeat for the 19th consecutive year and dropped to 0-4 in bowls since 1967, despite making big strides in two years under Mike Price. Price was fired from Alabama in May 2003 after an evening cavorting with strippers an hour down the road in Pensacola, Fla. He has led UTEP to back-to-back postseason games for the first time in 50 years, but the Miners finished the season with three losses in a row. Toledo's offense was just the latest from the MAC to shine in the GMAC Bowl. And the Rockets' defense was stout, too. Gradkowski completed 18-of-32 passes for 298 yards with TDs to five different receivers. He was intercepted twice, but it hardly mattered. The senior threw five TD passes in a game for the first time this season and third time in his career. The Rockets harried UTEP's prolific passer, Jordan Palmer, into an off night. He was just 14-of-33 for 163 yards with an interception and sat out several series in the second half after spraining his left ankle on the final play before halftime. UTEP was sixth nationally in passing offense, averaging 310.5 yards per game. Toledo, meanwhile, was 3-of-3 on fourth-down conversions and had three players catch passes of 30-plus yards. And Dawson pounded away, too, leaving the UTEP defenders shaking their heads. The Rockets effectively decided this game in the final three minutes before halftime. Gradkowski & Co. took over with 2:56 left and opened with four straight runs by Dawson, with a 15-yard facemask penalty tacked onto the fourth. Then, Gradkowski faked it to Dawson again and launched a 31-yard TD pass to a wide-open Steve Odom with 1:13 to play. The Miners then moved to the 15 after a sure interception bounced off Toledo cornerback Jason Flowers' hands into the grasp of receiver Joe West for a 28-yard gain. But Alston, who had also deflected the ball to Thomas for an interception, tackled Palmer on the final two plays and the clock ran out. The Toledo was able to only figuratively light up the scoreboard, though. The clock for the only functional scoreboard didn't work most of the game, forcing officials to keep time on the field. Gradkowski was chosen as the game's MVP while Dawson (offense), Alston (defensive) and Odom (special teams) also won game honors.

Point shaving - In 2007, members of the Toledo football team were charged with participating in a point shaving scandal. Members of the football team related to Detroit-area gamblers and were paid to intentionally affect the final score so that certain point spreads were covered. The 2005 GMAC Bowl was mentioned as a game that was affected. In 2011, Toledo running back Quinton Broussard pleaded guilty in connection with the point scandal. In the plea, Broussard admitted to receiving $500 for intentionally losing a fumble in the first half, when Toledo held a small lead. **Toledo was a 3 point favorite and the total on the game was 61.5**

2005 Las Vegas Bowl

The 2005 edition of the Pioneer Las Vegas Bowl was the 14th edition of that annual game. It featured the California Golden Bears, and the BYU Cougars.

2005 Las Vegas Bowl	Line	1	-	2	-	3	-	4	-	Final
BYU	(60.5)	0	-	14	-	0	-	14	-	28
California	(-7.0)	7	-	14	-	14	-	0	-	35

Scoring Summary
California – Lynch 3 yard run (Schneider kick)
BYU – Brown 19 yard pass from Bech (McLaughlin kick)
California – Lynch 23 yard run (Schneider kick)
BYU – Tahi 3 yard run (McLaughlin kick)
California – Jackson 42 yard pass from Levy (Schneider kick)
California – Lynch 35 yard run (Schneider kick)
California – Jackson 22 yard pass from Levy (Schneider kick)
BYU – Harline 7 yard pass from Beck (McLaughlin kick)
BYU – Watkins 9 yard pass from Beck (McLaughlin kick)

Associated Press Las Vegas Bowl Game Summary - Marshawn Lynch had no time for a loose shoelace. He was too busy carrying California to a victory in the Pioneer PureVision Las Vegas Bowl -- and during his second touchdown run, his untied shoe stayed on him better than any BYU tackler. Anybody who watched his performance in the Golden Bears' 35-28 over Brigham Young probably wouldn't believe him -- but everybody got a look at the wealth of offensive talent coming back to Cal in 2006. Lynch rushed for career highs of 195 yards and three touchdowns to win the MVP award, and DeSean Jackson caught two scoring passes before Cal's defense held off Brigham Young on Thursday night in an entertaining meeting of two programs with big aspirations for next season. Steve Levy passed for 228 yards in his second career start for the Golden Bears (8-4), who hung on against BYU's fourth-quarter comeback in a high-octane game featuring 915 total yards. Jackson capped his impressive freshman season with six catches for 130 yards. Cal took a 21-point lead into the final quarter after Lynch's 35-yard scoring run and Jackson's exceptional 22-yard diving TD catch in the third. But BYU Quarterback John Beck responded with scoring passes to Jonny Harline and Todd Watkins, whose 9-yard grab with 5:35 left cut Cal's lead to seven points. The Bears improbably tried a 50-yard field goal with 2:20 to play, and Tom Schneider's kick was well short. But the Cougars moved just 7 yards before Beck's arm was hit by Cal lineman Phillip Mbakogu, and Daymeion Hughes intercepted the wobbling pass to seal the Bears' second bowl victory in three postseason trips under Coach Jeff Tedford. Beck set Las Vegas Bowl records in BYU's spread offense, going 35-for-53 for 352 yards and three TDs. In their first bowl game in four years, the Cougars (6-6) mounted three scoring drives longer than 90 yards and moved the ball consistently. The Bears' stars were the difference. Jackson scored on a 42-yard romp through the BYU secondary 3 seconds before halftime, while Lynch had scoring runs of 3, 23 and 35 yards along with a handful of jaw-dropping second-effort rushes. His yards and touchdowns also were Cal bowl records. Nathan Meikle had career highs with 12 catches for 93 yards for BYU, which hasn't won a bowl game since 1996. But the season was a success for the once-proud Cougars, who got back to the postseason in Mendenhall's rookie season. Most of the bowl-record crowd of 40,053 at Sam Boyd Stadium was made up of BYU fans, but they got the biggest thrills from Lynch, who finally had a game worthy of the hype entering his sophomore campaign. Lynch was expected to dominate the Pac-10 this season after averaging 8.8 yards per carry as a freshman. Lynch was undeniably good, finishing the regular season with 1,052 yards, but he missed two games with a broken finger and was benched during another for fumbling twice. Cal scored on the game's opening drive when Lynch followed Philip, a Mormon with extensive family ties to BYU, into the end zone. The Cougars finally got going late in the first quarter with a 15-play, 92-yard drive culminating in Curtis Brown's 19-yard TD catch. After Lynch's shoelace shuffle, BYU tied it on Fahu Tahi's 3-yard scoring run 38 seconds before halftime, capping a 91-yard drive in just five plays. But the Bears got a long kickoff return and a pass-interference call before Jackson, who didn't arrive in Las Vegas until Monday night because of finals, ran a simple hook pattern and eluded three defenders for a score.

2005 San Diego County Credit Union Poinsettia Bowl

The 2005 Poinsettia Bowl was between the Colorado State Rams and the Navy Midshipmen on December 22, 2005 at Qualcomm Stadium in San Diego, California, United States. The game, which the Midshipmen won with a score of 51–30, was the inaugural edition of the Poinsettia Bowl.

2005 Poinsettia Bowl	Line	1	-	2	-	3	-	4	-	Final
Colorado State	(61.0)	10	-	0	-	14	-	6	-	30
Navy	(-3.0)	7	-	20	-	14	-	10	-	51

Scoring Summary
Colorado State - Bell 1 yard run (Smith kick)
Navy - Campbell 55 yard pass from Owens (Bullen kick)
Colorado State - Smith 34 yard Field goal
Navy - Nelson 22 yard run (Bullen kick)
Navy - Campbell 22 yard run (Bullen kick)
Navy - Campbell 2 yard run (Bullen kick)
Navy - Campbell 21 yard run (Bullen kick)
Colorado State - Osborn 10 yard pass from Holland (Smith kick)
Colorado State - Osborn 20 yard pass from Holland (Smith kick)
Navy - Campbell 34 yard pass from Owens (Bullen kick)
Navy - Nelson 21 yard run (Bullen kick)
Colorado State - Walker 22 yard pass from Holland (Smith kick)
Navy - Bullen 25 yard Field goal

Associated Press Poinsettia Bowl Game Summary - Only five players have scored five touchdowns in a bowl game, and two of them did it in San Diego. Reggie Campbell, meet Barry Sanders. "That's pretty exciting," Campbell, the small, speedy Navy slotback, said after being told he had matched Sanders' five-TD performance that came 17 years earlier on the same field. Campbell's thrilling performance, which included 290 all-purpose yards, led Navy to a 51-30 win over Colorado State in the San Diego County Credit Union Poinsettia Bowl at Qualcomm Stadium. The 5-foot-6 sophomore had touchdown catches of 55 and 34 yards and scoring runs of 22, 2 and 21 yards. Sanders scored five touchdowns and ran for 222 yards in the 1988 Holiday Bowl, leading Oklahoma State to a 62-14 win over Wyoming at what was then called Jack Murphy Stadium. Sanders won the Heisman Trophy that year. The other players with five TDs in a bowl were Michigan's Neil Snow against Stanford in the 1902 Rose Bowl, San Jose State's Sheldon Canley against Central Michigan in the 1990 California Bowl and Steven Jackson of Oregon State, who did it in the 2003 Las Vegas Bowl. Campbell was spectacular practically every time he touched the ball for Navy (8-4), which was playing in a third straight bowl game for the first time in academy history. He ran 16 times for 116 yards, caught two passes for 89 yards and returned four kickoffs for 85 yards. Navy, the nation's top-ranked rushing team with an average of 305.2 yards, ran for 467 yards and had 611 yards in total offense. The Rams (6-6) had 572 total yards as the teams combined for a bowl-record 1,183 offensive yards. Campbell's first TD was a stunner, a 55-yard reception on Navy's first play from scrimmage. Already hard to stop because of its triple-option rushing attack, Navy surprised everyone, especially Colorado State's defense, when Owens faked a handoff and threw deep to Campbell, who had gotten behind the coverage and scored easily for a 7-7 tie 4:07 into the game. Campbell was already warmed up, having returned a kickoff 28 yards after the Rams scored on the opening drive. Navy totally fooled Colorado State midway through the second quarter, when Campbell took a pitch and ran 22 yards untouched through a huge hole in the right side of CSU's defense to put the Middies ahead 20-10. Just before halftime, Campbell had the most pedestrian of his TDs, taking a toss and running in from 2 yards out a 27-10 lead. Campbell capped the first drive of the second half with a razzle-dazzle 21-yard TD run, when he took a pitch and started outside before cutting inside to put Navy up 34-10. Colorado State pulled within 10 late in the third quarter after Dustin Osborn caught touchdown passes of 10 and 20 yards from Holland on consecutive possessions. Holland was 26-of-33 for 381 yards. But Navy came right back and Campbell caught a 34-yard scoring pass from Owens for a 41-24 lead. Navy was coming off a 42-23 win over Army in which it rushed for 490 yards, including a 54-yard TD run by Campbell. Navy's other slotback, Marco Nelson, had touchdown runs of 22 and 21 yards. Holland threw three TD passes for CSU, setting the school single season record with 23. He hit Johnny Walker on a 22-yarder early in the fourth quarter. Colorado State's Kyle Bell had 122 yards on 22 carries, including a 1-yard TD run on the game's first possession. Navy fullback Adam Ballard had 129 yards on 15 carries.

2005 Fort Worth Bowl

The 2005 edition to the Fort Worth Bowl, the third edition, featured the Kansas Jayhawks, and the Houston Cougars.

2005 Fort Worth Bowl	Line	1	-	2	-	3	-	4	-	Final
Kansas	(-3.5)	7	-	7	-	14	-	14	-	42
Houston	(48.0)	0	-	10	-	3	-	0	-	13

Scoring Summary
Kansas - Murph 85 yard punt return (Webb kick)
Houston - Bell 32 yard Field goal
Kansas - Cornish 13 yard pass from Swanson (Webb kick)
Houston - Kolb 1 yard run (Bell kick)
Kansas - Cornish 30 yard pass from Swanson (Webb kick)
Houston - Lawrence 44 yard Field goal
Kansas - Simmons 32 yard pass from Swanson (Webb kick)
Kansas - Keith 14 yard interception return (Webb kick)
Kansas - Murph 48 yard pass from Swanson (Webb kick)

Associated Press Fort Worth Bowl Game Summary - Jason Swanson started the season hurt. He ended it by leading the Kansas Jayhawks to their first bowl victory and first winning season in 10 years. Swanson threw for 307 yards and four touchdowns, one more than he had in the regular season, and the Jayhawks beat Houston 42-13 Friday night in the Fort Worth Bowl. Houston, with record-setting Quarterback Kevin Kolb, came in as the team touted for its high-powered offense. Instead, the Jayhawks (7-5) had a season-high 538 yards and won for the fourth time in five games — all since Swanson became the starter. Tailback Jon Cornish turned two shovel passes — his only two catches — from Swanson into scores of 13 and 30 yards. He also rushed for 101 yards on 16 carries. Brian Murph, who hadn't returned a kick all season, turned a muffed punt into an 85-yard score in the first quarter that put the Jayhawks ahead to stay. He also caught a 48-yard TD pass. After leading Conference USA with 457 total yards per game during the regular season, Houston (6-6) was held to a season-worst 244. That was 126 yards below their previous low. Kansas had been in only one other bowl since a victory over UCLA in the 1995 Aloha Bowl capped a 10-2 season. The Jayhawks lost 56-26 to North Carolina State in the 2003 Tangerine Bowl that ended Mark Mangino's second year as coach. Swanson started his fifth straight game, going 19-of-29 and earning MVP honors. The senior hurt his leg during the preseason but took over after Adam Barmann and Brian Luke struggled. Houston has lost six straight bowls since winning the 1980 Garden State Bowl. The Cougars' previous postseason appearance was a 54-48 triple-overtime loss to Hawaii in the 2003 Hawaii Bowl that ended coach Art Briles' first season at 7-6. The Cougars slipped to 3-8 last year. Kolb, a junior, started his 36th straight game and already is the career total offense leader at the school where David Klingler and Andre Ware also threw passes. Kolb was 20-of-44 for 214 yards with three interceptions, all turned into scores by Kansas. Kolb had a 1-yard sneak for Houston's only touchdown, and Ben Bell (32 yards) and T.J. Lawrence (44 yards) kicked field goals. Charlton Keith got between Kolb and his intended receiver on a quick-out pass in the fourth quarter. He jumped up and grabbed the pass, then sprinted 14 yards and dived into the end zone. Theo Baines had two interceptions for the Jayhawks. The first set up Cornish's 30-yard TD in the third quarter, and the second led to Murph's TD catch with 9 minutes left for the final touchdown. Five minutes into the game, Murph muffed a punt. The ball rolled several yards away from him before he picked it up, circled around several defenders and ran all the way to the left sideline. He then cut back across the field and slipped past a tackler into the open for the longest Kansas punt return since 1971. Swanson had completions of 31 and 19 yards on the first two plays, but the Jayhawks didn't get another first down on the opening drive. The Cougars then went three-and-out before Justin Laird's 57-yard punt that Murph muffed. Cornish's first TD came in the second quarter. Mark Simmons added a 32-yard score in the third when he caught Swanson's pass near the 20, then was free when he twisted inside, and the defender slipped.

2005 Hawai'i Bowl

The 2005 Sheraton Hawai'i Bowl matched the UCF Knights against the Nevada Wolf Pack. The fourth edition of the Hawai'i Bowl was held in Honolulu, Hawaii, and featured the WAC champions versus the Conference USA runners-up.

2005 Hawaii	Line	1	-	2	-	3	-	4	-	OT	-	Final
Nevada	(-3.0)	7	-	21	-	0	-	14	-	7	-	49
Central Florida	(64.0)	17	-	3	-	10	-	12	-	6	-	48

Scoring Summary
Central Florida – Marshall 51 yard pass from Moffettt (Prater kick)
Central Florida – Smith 78 yard run (Prater kick)
Nevada – Hubbard 4 yard run (Jaekle kick)
Central Florida – Prater 47 yard Field goal
Nevada – Mitchell 1 yard run (Jaekle kick)
Nevada – Mitchell 1 yard run (Jaekle kick)
Nevada – Hubbard 24 yard run (Jaekle kick)
Central Florida – Prater 38 yard Field goal
Central Florida – Marshall 29 yard pass from Moffett (Moffett pass failed)
Central Florida – Smith 3 yard run (Moffett pass failed)
Nevada – Hubbard 5 yard run (Jaekle kick)
Nevada – Branzell 7 yard pass from Rowe (Jaekle kick)
Central Florida – Prater 46 yard Field goal
Central Florida – Marshall 16 yard pass from Moffett (Prater kick)
Nevada – Rowe 4 yard run (Jaekle kick)
Central Florida – Smith 19 yard run (kick failed)

Hawaii Bowl Game Summary - UCF was one of the nation's best stories of the season. They had gone 0-11 the previous season and were during a 17-game losing streak the previous season. They accomplished one of the biggest turnarounds in NCAA history. After starting the season 0-2, they won eight of their next nine games to make it to the Conference USA championship game. At 8-3, and 7-1 in Conference USA, they lost to Tulsa in the championship game to fall to 8-4. UCF started the scoring with Quarterback Steven Moffett throwing a 51-yard touchdown pass to wide receiver Brandon Marshall to make it 7-0 UCF. Four minutes later, running back Kevin Smith took a hand-off and rushed 78 yards for a touchdown giving UCF a 14-0 lead. Robert Hubbard got Nevada on the board with a 4-yard touchdown run cutting the lead to 14-7. UCF's Matt Prater drilled a 47-yard field goal to move the lead back up to 17-7 at the end of the 1st quarter. In the second quarter, running back B.J. Mitchell scored twice on two 1-yard touchdown runs for Nevada to reclaim the lead 21-17. Later, running back Robert Hubbard scored from 24 yards out to extend the lead to 28-17 Nevada. Matt Prater's 38-yard field goal before the half cut the lead to 28-20. Early in the third quarter, Steven Moffett fired a 29-yard touchdown pass to Brandon Marshall. The ensuing two-point conversion failed, and Nevada still led 28-26. With two minutes to go in the third quarter, Kevin Smith scored on a 3-yard touchdown run to give UCF a 32-28 lead. UCF tried for two points again but failed. In the fourth quarter, Robert Hubbard scored on a 5-yard touchdown run to give Nevada a 35-32 lead. With 3:18 to go in the game, Quarterback Jeff Rowe threw a 7-yard touchdown pass to wide receiver Travis Branzell to extend the lead to 42-32. On UCF's next possession, they failed to score a touchdown, and were forced to attempt a long field goal. Kicker Matt Prater nailed a 46-yard field goal to cut the lead to 42-35 with 1:35 left. The ensuing onside kick was recovered by UCF, and they took advantage of it. With 55 seconds left, Steven Moffett threw a 16-yard touchdown pass to Brandon Marshall, to tie the game at 42. This was their third connection of the game. In overtime, Jeff Rowe scored on a 4-yard touchdown run to make the lead 49-42 Nevada. Kevin Smith answered with a 19-yard touchdown run, but Matt Prater missed the extra point, and Nevada escaped with a 49-48 win.

2005 Motor City Bowl

The 2005 Motor City Bowl was held on December 27, 2005 at Ford Field in Detroit, Michigan. The University of Memphis Tigers football team beat the University of Akron Zips football team 38–31. This game is most noteworthy for being the first bowl game the University of Akron Zips football team has played in, and for being the final college game for All-American and All-Pro running back DeAngelo Williams.

2005 Motor City Bowl	Line	1	-	2	-	3	-	4	-	Final
Memphis	(-4.5)	0	-	13	-	7	-	18	-	38
Akron	(50.0)	3	-	0	-	7	-	21	-	31

Scoring Summary
Akron - Swigger 38 yard Field goal
Memphis - Gostkowski 32 yard Field goal
Memphis - D. Williams 1 yard run (Gostkowski kick)
Memphis - Gostkowski 25 yard Field goal
Memphis - D. Williams 2 yard run (Gostkowski kick)
Akron - Arthur 46 yard pass from Getsy (Swigger kick)
Memphis - Gostkowski 50 yard Field goal
Akron - Briggs 72 yard pass from Getsy (Swigger kick)
Memphis - D. Williams 2 yard run (Gostkowski kick)
Memphis - E. Williams 6 yard run (Gostkowski kick)
Akron - Hixon 14 yard pass from Getsy (Swigger kick)
Akron - Arthur 19 yard pass from Getsy (Swigger kick)

Associated Press Motor City Bowl Game Recap - DeAngelo Williams lived up to the hype. Williams set an NCAA record with his 34th 100-yard rushing game and scored three touchdowns, leading Memphis to a 38-31 victory over Akron in the Motor City Bowl on Monday. Williams ran for 233 yards on 30 carries and finished his career with 6,021 yards rushing -- trailing only Ron Dayne, Ricky Williams and Tony Dorsett in Division I-A history -- and an NCAA-record 7,568 all-purpose yards. "I'm really not a statistical guy, but when you mention those guys, it's huge," Williams said. The Tigers (7-5) took a 21-point lead with 3:09 left but needed to recover an onside kick with 55 seconds left to seal the win after Luke Getsy threw his fourth touchdown pass to cut the lead to seven points. Akron (7-6) made a good showing in its first Division I-A bowl game after scoring 21 fourth-quarter points to beat Northern Illinois in the Mid-American Conference championship game. Getsy was 34-for-59 for a Motor City Bowl-record 455 yards and tied Chad Pennington's mark for passing touchdowns in the bowl's nine-year history. Jabari Arthur broke Randy Moss's bowl record with 180 yards receiving, scoring twice on eight receptions. The Tigers led by 10 at halftime after scoring on three straight drives, then pulled away in the second half with three TDs and a field goal in four drives before nearly collapsing in the final minutes. It was a wild finish -- with 46 points scored in the final 15:46 -- after Akron led 3-0 midway through the first quarter. The teams combined for 1,018 yards of offense. Williams, who shared the 100-yard rushing record with Heisman Trophy winners Archie Griffin of Ohio State and Dorsett of Pittsburgh, broke the mark in the third quarter when he ran up the middle and bounced to the outside on an 18-yard carry. Griffin set the mark in 42 games, and Dorsett matched it in 43 games -- one fewer than Williams. It wasn't shocking to see Williams run through and around the Zips with his NFL-caliber speed after Northern Illinois' Garrett Wolfe ran for 270 yards against Akron in the MAC championship game. After Getsy threw a 72-yard TD pass to Brett Biggs early in the fourth quarter to cut Akron's deficit to 23-17, Williams showed his speed and power. He burst through a small hole in the middle of the line and sprinted for a 67-yard gain to set up his 2-yard, linemen-dragging TD for his third score, tying the bowl record. Williams, who finished seventh in voting for the Heisman, was taken out of the game midway through the fourth quarter while Memphis was driving for its 38-17 lead. He finished 4 yards rushing short of the Motor City Bowl record set by Northwestern's Jason Wright against Bowling Green in 2003. "He's got too much at stake to go back in there for 10 yards," West explained. A crowd of 50,616 attended the game in Ford Field, where the Super Bowl will be played in less than six weeks.

2005 Champs Sports Bowl

The 2005 Champs Sports Bowl was the 16th edition of the bowl game and was played on December 27, 2005, featuring the Clemson Tigers and the Colorado Buffaloes. Three weeks prior to the game, Colorado head coach Gary Barnett resigned and so the Buffalos were coached by defensive coordinator Mike Hankwitz against Clemson. James Davis, the Clemson Running back was the Most Valuable Player of the game.

Teams - The Colorado Buffaloes won the Big 12 North. They were soundly defeated in the Big 12 Championship game by eventual BCS Champion Texas 70–3. Texas would go on to win the BCS Championship in the 2006 Rose Bowl. The Buffaloes were 7–2 at one point, losing only to #12 Miami and #2 Texas. Barnett had survived a recruiting scandal and a suspension following derogatory remarks about a female kicker, Katie Hnida, who claimed she was raped by a teammate in 2000. But the losses to Miami, Iowa State, Nebraska and the second Texas drubbing ultimately led to his forced resignation.

2005 Champ's Sports Bowl	Line	1	-	2	-	3	-	4	-	Final
Clemson	(-10.0)	3	-	3	-	7	-	6	-	19
Colorado	(46.0)	0	-	3	-	0	-	7	-	10

Scoring Summary
Clemson – Dean 26 yard Field goal
Colorado – Crosby 35 yard Field goal
Clemson – Dean 18 yard Field goal
Clemson – Whitehurst 6 yard run (Dean kick)
Colorado – Sypniewski 2 yard pass from White (Crosby kick)
Clemson – Davis 11 yard run (kick failed)

Associated Press Champs Sports Bowl Game Summary - James Davis walked out of the Citrus Bowl with the game ball under one arm and the most valuable player trophy under the other. It was obvious who was the key to Clemson's latest victory. Davis ran for a career-high 150 yards and a touchdown, Charlie Whitehurst scrambled for a score and the No. 23 Tigers beat Colorado 19-10 in the Champs Sports Bowl on Tuesday, handing the Buffaloes their fourth consecutive loss. Davis' 6-yard TD run with 1:38 remaining sealed a fourth straight win for Clemson (8-4) and capped a disappointing season for Colorado (7-6). The freshman's performance also showed that the future is bright for the Tigers despite losing their star Quarterback. The Buffs made it close, though, something they didn't do in their previous two games -- losses to Nebraska and Texas by a combined score of 100-6. Backup Quarterback Brian White replaced starter James Cox midway through the fourth quarter and led Colorado on a 69-yard scoring drive that made it 13-10 with 5:45 to play. His 2-yard TD pass to Quinn Sypniewski ended a streak of 14 quarters without a touchdown and gave the Buffs a chance. White rolled right on third down, then threw left to Sypniewski, who was wide open in the end zone. But Davis and Whitehurst answered, moving the Tigers 61 yards in 4:07 to put the game away. It wasn't too surprising considering the duo made big plays all game. Davis ran 28 times and eclipsed the 100-yard mark for the fourth time this season -- a school record for a freshman. Whitehurst, a senior expected to be a first-day selection in next year's NFL draft, was equally efficient and effective. He was 19-of-27 for 196 yards and threw an interception. He showed no signs of shoulder problems after having arthroscopic surgery early this month to relieve pain that had bothered him since September. He also played most of the game without leading receiver Chansi Stuckey, who sat out the second half with a concussion. His absence opened the door for freshman Aaron Kelly, who caught a team-high four passes for 36 yards, including a 23-yarder on the game-sealing scoring drive. It was one of several clutch throws by Whitehurst. His TD run was even bigger, coming on third and goal. He slipped out of Akarika Dawn's grasp at the 5 and strolled in for the score, which made it 13-3. Dawn dropped his head to the ground and pounded the grass with his right fist in frustration. It was that kind of night for Colorado. It also was that kind of season. The Buffaloes were 7-2 at one point, losing only to Miami and Texas, and there was talk about a contract extension for embattled coach Gary Barnett. But consecutive losses to Iowa State, Nebraska and Texas ended that thought as well as Barnett's tenure in Boulder. Barnett had survived a sordid recruiting scandal and a suspension following derogatory remarks about a female kicker who claimed she was raped by a teammate in 2000. But the losses -- most notably the 70-3 drubbing against the Longhorns in the Big 12 title game -- ultimately led to his forced resignation nearly three weeks ago. The school has hired Boise State coach Dan Hawkins to replace Barnett, but defensive coordinator Mike Hankwitz coached the team against Clemson. There was little Hankwitz could do to help the offense. Cox made his second career start, replacing Joel Klatt after the senior starter sustained a severe concussion in the conference title game. Klatt, who hospitalized overnight after the injury, didn't even dress for the game. Cox, who made his first start in 2004 against Iowa State, showed his inexperience. He misfired often, overthrowing and underthrowing receivers and making poor decisions with the ball. He finished 4-of-12 for 26 yards and was sacked three times. He got little help from the running game, which finished with 17 yards on 29 carries.

2005 Insight Bowl

The 2005 edition of the Insight Bowl was the 17th edition of the bowl game. It featured the Arizona State Sun Devils and the Rutgers Scarlet Knights. Arizona State exploded offensively in the game scoring 45 points, and an Insight Bowl record 679 yards of total offense. Rutgers took an early 7–0 lead after Ryan Hart lobbed a 1-yard touchdown pass to Clark Harris. Arizona State responded with a 43-yard touchdown pass from Rudy Carpenter to Matt Miller, tying the game at 7. Rutgers answered with a 31-yard strike from Ryan Hart to Brian Leonard, making it 14–7 Rutgers. Jeremy Ito's 25-yard field goal made it 17–7 and capped the first quarter of scoring. In the second quarter, Jesse Ainsworth kicked a 20-yard field goal to pull the Sun Devils to within 17–10. With 2:30 left in the half, Brian Leonard scored on a 3-yard touchdown run, bumping the Knights' lead to 24–10. Arizona State responded with a 1-yard touchdown pass from Carpenter to tight end Zach Miller making it 24–17 at halftime. In the third quarter, Rudy Burgess scored from 1 yard out for ASU to tie it at 24. Jeremy Ito's 27-yard field goal flipped the lead back over to Rutgers 27-24. Arizona State took its first lead of the game on a 22-yard pass from Carpenter to Terry Richardson, making it 31–27 ASU. Jeremy Ito's 52-yard field goal cut the lead to 31-30 for Rutgers. In the fourth quarter, Rutgers took the lead on a 48-yard Jeremy Ito field goal, giving Rutgers a 33-31 lead. Arizona State came back with a 42-yard touchdown pass from Rudy Carpenter to Matt Miller, and a two-point conversion to make it 39-33 ASU. With 4:26 remaining in the game, Rudy Burgess scored from 4 yards out, but the 2-point conversion attempt failed, making it 45-33 ASU. With 2 minutes left, Ryan Hart threw a 29-yard touchdown pass to Tres Moses making it 45–40 ASU. ASU then ran out the clock to claim the 2005 Insight Bowl. This would be last Insight Bowl played at Chase Field, as Arizona State's Sun Devil Stadium would become the future host of the game.

2005 Insight Bowl	Line	1	-	2	-	3	-	4	-	Final
Arizona State	(-10.5)	7	-	10	-	14	-	14	-	45
Rutgers	(63.0)	17	-	7	-	6	-	10	-	40

Scoring Summary
Rutgers – Harris 1 yard pass from Hart (Ito kick)
Arizona State – Miller 43 yard pass from Carpenter (Ainsworth kick)
Rutgers – Leonard 31 yard pass from Hart (Ito kick)
Rutgers – Ito 25 yard Field goal
Arizona State – Ainsworth 20 yard Field goal
Rutgers – Leonard 3 yard run (Ito kick)
Arizona State – Miller 1 yard pass from Carpenter (Ainsworth kick)
Arizona State – Burgess 1 yard run (Ainsworth kick)
Rutgers – Ito 23 yard Field goal
Arizona State – Richardson 22 yard pass from Carpenter (Ainsworth kick)
Rutgers – Ito 52 yard Field goal
Rutgers – Ito 48 yard Field goal
Arizona State – Miller 42 yard pass from Carpenter (Miller pass from Carpenter)
Arizona State – Burgess 4 yard run (Run failed)
Rutgers – Moses 29 yard pass from Hart (Ito kick)

2005 MPC Computers Bowl

The 2005 MPC Computers Bowl was the ninth edition of the bowl game. It featured the Boise State Broncos and the Boston College Eagles. Though playing at home on its blue "Smurf Turf", where it held a 31-game winning streak, WAC co-champion Boise State was unable to get its usually potent offense on track early, falling behind ACC rep Boston College by 24 at halftime before losing, 27-21.

2005 MPC Computers Bowl	Line	1	-	2	-	3	-	4	-	Final
Boise State	(53.5)	0	-	0	-	7	-	14	-	21
#19 Boston College	(-1.5)	7	-	17	-	3	-	0	-	27

Scoring Summary
Boston College - Gonzales 24 yard pass from Ryan (Ohliger kick)
Boston College - Ohliger 30 yard Field goal
Boston College - Gonzales 13 yard pass from Ryan (Ohliger kick)
Boston College - Blackmon 35 yard pass from Ryan (Ohliger kick)
Boston College - Ohliger 27 yard Field goal
Boise State - James 53 yard pass from Jabransky (Montgomery kick)
Boise State - Zabransky 2 yard run (Montgomery kick)
Boise State - Jones 92 yard punt return (Montgomery kick)

Associated Press MPC Computers Bowl Game Summary - Boston College got offended watching a simple pregame banquet turn into a rally for its opponent. The No. 19 Eagles got even by spoiling Dan Hawkins' last game at Boise State and ending the nation's longest home winning streak. Matthew Ryan threw three first-half touchdown passes and Ryan Glasper intercepted Jared Zabransky's pass in the end zone with 37 seconds left as Boston College held on for a 27-21 win in the MPC Computers Bowl on Wednesday. Several Boston College players said MPC Computers CEO Mike Atkins made fun of defensive end Mathias Kiwanuka's name during the Monday night banquet. Turned out the Eagles needed the strong start. Down 27-0 late in the third quarter, the Broncos tried to rally for their departing coach in the closing moments. Boise State started its final possession at the BC 47 with 1:56 left, and Zabransky completed a 32-yard, fourth-down pass to Vinny Perretta to the 14. A pass-interference penalty moved the ball to the 5, but Zabransky was sacked by Nick Larkin, and then Glasper came up with his interception. The Eagles (9-3) extended the nation's longest bowl winning streak to six and snapped Boise State's 31-game home winning streak. BC's last bowl loss was to Colorado in the 1999 Insight Bowl, and Boise State's last home loss was in 2001 -- a 41-20 loss to Washington State in Hawkins' first home game after taking over for Dirk Koetter. The game was Hawkins' last with the Broncos (9-4), who failed to win 10 games for the first time since 2001. He's headed to Colorado after signing a five-year contract worth $900,000 per year on Dec. 16 -- with the stipulation that he be allowed to coach Boise State in the bowl game. The Broncos were lethargic and lifeless, and bullied by the Eagles in the first half. Ryan took full advantage. The sophomore was rarely pressured and picked apart Boise State's secondary. He threw for 178 yards in the first half and finished with 256 on the famed blue turf that had a slight coat of white after a brief hail and sleet storm in the third quarter. By the time Will Blackmon outmaneuvered three Boise State defensive backs for a 35-yard TD reception with 1:16 left in the first half, Boise State fans were already headed to the tent vendors outside the stadium. It almost became 31-0. On the last play of the half, Ryan completed a 52-yard pass to Blackmon. He caught it at the 6 but was tackled by Colt Brooks at the 1. Blackmon finished with five catches for 144 yards and Ryan Ohliger kicked field goals of 26 and 30 yards for BC. Ryan's first two TD passes went to Tony Gonzalez. The first came on BC's opening drive, when on fourth-down, Ryan sidestepped defensive tackle Nick Schlekeway and found Gonzalez streaking across the back of the end zone for a 35-yard play. Gonzalez's second TD came late in the second quarter after the Eagles came up with a critical turnover. Down 10-0, Boise State put together its most productive drive, marching inside the Eagles 40. Zabransky threw to Jeff Carpenter, who ran to the BC 32, but was hit by linebacker Jolonn Dunbar and fumbled. Ray Henderson scooped up the ball on one bounce and raced 55 yards to the Boise State 13. Ryan connected with Gonzalez on the next play. Boise State was scoreless until late in the third. Zabransky threw a 53-yard TD pass to Drisan James with 1:24 left and then scored on a 2-yard TD run early in the fourth, the Broncos' second score in 2:09. The Broncos got to 27-21 with 3:51 left after Quinton Jones returned a punt 92 yards for a TD. Jones broke two tackles inside his own 10, broke two more and traversed the field for the longest punt return in the bowl's history. Boise State lost for the first time in its hometown bowl. The Broncos beat Iowa State (2002), Texas El-Paso (2000) and Louisville (1999) in the game. Wearing a blue pullover with orange piping and the Boise State logo planted firmly on his chest, Hawkins crisscrossed the field before kickoff, making sure to give every player a pat, handshake and for some, a brief hug.

2005 Alamo Bowl

The 2005 Alamo Bowl was held on December 28, 2005 at the Alamodome in San Antonio, Texas. It was the 13th Alamo Bowl. The Nebraska Cornhuskers, second-place finishers in the Big 12 Conference's North Division, defeated the Michigan Wolverines, third-placed finishers in the Big Ten Conference. This matchup was notable in that it featured the two schools that shared the 1997 national championship. At the time, Michigan and Nebraska were two of only five schools in NCAA Division I history with 800 or more victories.

2005 Alamo Bowl	Line	1	-	2	-	3	-	4	-	Final
#20 Michigan	(-10.5)	7	-	7	-	7	-	7	-	28
Nebraska	(47.0)	7	-	7	-	3	-	15	-	32

Scoring Summary
Nebraska - Nunn 52 yard pass from Taylor (Condon kick)
Michigan - Ecker 13 yard pass from Henne (Rivas kick)
Michigan - Massey 16 yard pass from Henne (Rivas kick)
Nebraska - Swift 14 yard pass from Taylor (Condon kick)
Nebraska - Condon 20 yard field goal
Michigan - Manningham 21 yard pass from Henne (Rivas kick)
Michigan - Henne 7 yard run (Rivas kick)
Nebraska - Ross 31 yard run (Peterson pass from Taylor)
Nebraska - Nunn 13 yard pass from Taylor (Condon kick)

Bentley Historical Library 2005 ALAMO BOWL GAME SUMMARY - Michigan was unable to cap its season with an Alamo Bowl victory, losing 32-28 against Nebraska at the Alamodome. The Wolverines tried to gain the winning points, but their final two possessions ended with an incomplete pass at the goal line and a last-ditch effort on a series of laterals that ended at the Cornhuskers' 13-yard line. Sophomore Quarterback Chad Henne completed 21-of-43 passes for 270 yards and three touchdowns and scored a rushing touchdown on a seven-yard keeper. Senior wide receiver Jason Avant led the receiving effort with eight catches for 71 yards and cracked the 1,000-yard receiving barrier for the season for the first time in his career (1,007). Senior wide receiver/kick returner Steve Breaston gained more than 200 all-purpose yards for the second straight bowl game. The game's Sportsmanship Award recipient, Breaston had 224 all-purpose yards on 13 touches. He set an Alamo Bowl record with 146 kickoff return yards on four attempts and added seven punt returns for 72 yards. He also collected an eight-yard reception. Junior cornerback Leon Hall was named the Alamo Bowl Defensive MVP after gaining two interceptions and four tackles. Senior free safety Willis Barringer registered a career-best nine stops, with sophomore defensive tackle Alan Branch and senior inside linebacker David Harris adding eight tackles apiece. Branch set a U-M bowl record with five tackles for loss. After trading series in the first quarter, Nebraska grabbed a 7-0 lead as wideout Terrance Nunn took a quick slant pass from Quarterback Zac Taylor and went 52 yards for the score. The Cornhuskers' scoring drive covered 73 yards in four plays. Michigan responded on the ensuing possession as Henne completed a 13-yard pass across the field to senior tight end Tyler Ecker for a touchdown. Breaston returned the kickoff an Alamo Bowl record 69 yards to provide the Wolverines with possession at Nebraska's 30-yard line. Henne kept the drive alive with a 14-yard keeper on third-and-12, and Hart added a five-yard carry prior to the second-down scoring play. The Wolverines had an opportunity to take a lead, but junior kicker Garrett Rivas pushed his 25-yard field goal attempt off the left upright. Hall gave U-M possession inside Nebraska territory following an interception at the 39-yard line. Hall collected his second pick on Nebraska's next possession, intercepting Taylor on the first play of the series. The Wolverines converted this time as Henne completed a 16-yard pass across the middle to sophomore tight end Mike Massey for the touchdown, giving U-M a 14-7 lead at 11:43 of the second quarter. Hart gained 12 yards on the first two plays prior to the scoring pass. Nebraska tied the score, 14-14, at 2:37

of the second quarter as Taylor hit wide receiver Nate Swift on a crossing route for the 14-yard touchdown. After halftime, the Cornhuskers scored an apparent touchdown at 8:58 of the third quarter as Taylor completed a three-yard scoring pass that Nunn caught along the ground on a third-and-goal play. The play was reviewed, and the pass was ruled incomplete. Nebraska settled for a 20-yard field goal by Jordan Congdon at 8:54 to regain the lead, 17-14. Michigan answered the field goal and took the lead, 21-17, as Henne threw his Alamo Bowl record tying third TD of the game. Henne floated a 21-yard touchdown pass to freshman wide receiver Mario Manningham in the back right corner of the end zone. The Wolverines had another scoring chance late in the third quarter, but Henne's pass into the back of the end zone was intercepted by cornerback Zachary Bowman. The play was originally ruled incomplete but was overturned by the replay booth. Henne used his feet to increase the Wolverines lead to 28-17 with 11:40 remaining in the contest. Henne was unable to find an open receiver and took off up the middle for a seven-yard keeper and his first rushing touchdown of the season. Michigan started the drive at its 47-yard line after a 15-yard kick catch interference penalty was assessed against Nebraska. Henne completed a key 26-yard pass to Avant on third-and-four that gave U-M possession at 21-yard line and later converted a third-and-eight play from the 19-yard line on a 12-yard run. Nebraska closed the gap to 28-25 as Ross scored on a 31-yard run around the left side of the formation and Taylor completed the two-point conversion pass to Todd Peterson. Michigan gave Nebraska possession at its 48-yard line as Avant was stripped of the ball following a 17-yard completion on the first play following Nebraska's score. The Wolverine defense stiffened and did not allow a first down. U-M turned the ball over for the second straight series and Nebraska gained possession at the Michigan's 17-yard line with 5:56 left in regulation. On a third-down pass play Henne had the ball knocked out of his hand by free safety Bruce Tiedtke, and defensive tackle Ola Dagunduro recovered for Nebraska and returned it 13 yards. The Cornhuskers grabbed the lead for good, 32-28 at 4:29, on a 13-yard TD pass from Taylor to Nunn across the middle. Michigan was unable to gain the go-ahead points on its final two possessions.

2005 Emerald Bowl

The 2005 Emerald Bowl was played on December 29, 2005, at AT&T Park in San Francisco, California. It featured the Georgia Tech Yellow Jackets, and the Utah Utes.

2005 Emerald Bowl	Line	1	-	2	-	3	-	4	-	Final
Georgia Tech	(-8.5)	0	-	10	-	0	-	0	-	10
Utah	(46.0)	13	-	7	-	3	-	15	-	38

Scoring Summary
Utah - LaTendresse 14 yard pass from Ratliff (kick failed)
Utah - LaTendresse 23 yard pass from Ratliff (Beardall kick)
Utah - LaTendresse 25 yard pass from Ratliff (Beardall kick)
Georgia Tech - Copper 31 yard pass from Ball (Bell kick)
Georgia Tech - Bell 29 yard Field goal
Utah - Beardall 23 yard Field goal
Utah - LaTendresse 16 yard pass from Ratliff (Latendresse pass from Ratliff)
Utah - Gardner 41 yard run (Beardall kick)

Associated Press Emerald Bowl Game Summary - Although a whole new bunch of players and coaches are wearing Utah red this season, these Utes still can put on a phenomenal postseason show. In what should stand as the most stunning performance of this bowl season, the Utes (7-5) earned their fifth consecutive bowl victory by drubbing No. 24 Georgia Tech 38-10 in the 2004 Emerald Bowl. The Utah victory featured an offensive performance more than worthy of former coach Urban Meyer's 12-0 team that ran through the Bowl Championship Series in 2004. Travis LaTendresse caught 16 passes for 214 yards and four touchdowns, and Brett Ratliff passed for 381 yards as the Utes rolled up 550 total yards. Quinton Ganther ran for 120 yards and added a 41-yard TD romp in the fourth quarter that gave the Utes their final score. First-year head coach Kyle Whittingham, Meyer's defensive coordinator last season, won his bowl debut in style. The only trouble was, the Utes were so dominant in the second half that they made the favored Yellow Jackets (7-5) look like just another Pittsburgh, last season's Fiesta Bowl opponent. Ratliff, who went 30-of-41, and LaTendresse, the game's offensive MVP, both set Utah bowl records with a superb afternoon of pitch-and-catch against the Yellow Jackets' bewildered secondary. Each of LaTendresse's four TD catches of 14, 23, 25 and 16 yards came on simple post patterns down the middle. Reggie Ball passed for 258 yards for Georgia Tech, which seemed disappointed to be so far from Atlanta for the postseason and it showed. The Yellow Jackets' vaunted defense, ranked among the nation's leaders entering the game, was shredded and stomped by a backup Quarterback and his speedy receivers for its season-high in yards allowed. Cornerback Eric Weddle, the Mountain West Conference's top defensive player and the Emerald Bowl's defensive MVP, did a bit of everything for the Utes - running the ball, engineering a fake field goal as a holder, even throwing a terrible interception. But Weddle was most valuable in his day job, limiting star Georgia Tech receiver Calvin Johnson to two catches for 19 yards. Despite the injury absences of Quarterback Brian Johnson and top receiver John Madsen, the Utah offense was nearly flawless. Ratliff, the backup who led the Utes' overtime win over archrival BYU, made another case for a lively Quarterback competition with Johnson and Oklahoma transfer Tommy Grady in spring ball. Brian Hernandez, a junior who began his college career at Georgia Tech in 2002, added eight catches for 75 yards for Utah. The game essentially was decided early in the fourth quarter, and hundreds of fans from the pro-Utah crowd rushed the field afterward, lifting Ratliff and LaTendresse on their shoulders. Utah opened the game with a drive befitting the nation's 12th-best offense, moving 76 yards in six plays capped by LaTendresse's 14-yard scoring grab. A similar drive later in the quarter ended with his TD catch between Georgia Tech defenders, and the Utes went up 20-0 on LaTendresse's third catch down the middle early in the second quarter. Ball threw two interceptions in the first half but one play after Shaun Harper's pick, the Utes got greedy with a 20-point lead. Weddle, who occasionally runs the ball on direct snaps for Utah's offense, threw a terrible long pass into triple coverage, and Dennis Davis intercepted. Georgia Tech immediately drove for its first touchdown, with Ball hitting tight end George Cooper for a 31-yard score. The Utah offense struggled through the rest of the half, and the Yellow Jackets got within 20-10 with a 65-yard pass to Damarius Bilbo and a field goal shortly before halftime. Georgia Tech never scored again. Utah's offense, meanwhile, was far from finished. Utah faked a field goal inside the Georgia Tech 15 early in the second half, with Weddle running for a first down as the holder - but Ratliff threw an end-zone interception on the next play. The Utes still put it out of reach with a 73-yard scoring drive early in the fourth quarter, with LaTendresse catching his fourth TD pass over the middle and running headfirst into a picture of Willie Mays on the left-field wall at SBC Park, home of the San Francisco Giants. Utah made it 31-10 with a 2-point conversion, with Ratliff throwing to LaTendresse, of course. The Utes final score came on a 41-yard run to the goal line by Ganther. There was plenty of motivation for the Utes to do so after a challenging season. A three-game skid in the middle of the season doomed Utah's hopes of a third consecutive Mountain West Conference title.

2005 Holiday Bowl

The 2005 Holiday Bowl was held at Qualcomm Stadium in San Diego on December 29, 2005, with the Big 12 Conference's Oklahoma Sooners defeating the Pacific-10 Conference's Oregon Ducks, 17–14.

2005 Holiday Bowl	Line	1	-	2	-	3	-	4	-	Final
#6 Oregon	(-3.0)	7	-	0	-	0	-	7	-	14
#25 Oklahoma	(55.0)	3	-	0	-	14	-	0	-	17

Scoring Summary
Oklahoma – Hartley 34 yard Field goal
Oregon – Williams 6 yard run (Martinez kick)
Oklahoma – Runnels 16 yard pass from Bomar (Hartley kick)
Oklahoma – Jones 8 yard run (Hartley kick)
Oregon – Day 3 yard pass from Leaf (Martinez kick)

Associated Press Holiday Bowl Game Summary - Leave it to a Leaf. Brady Leaf has steered clear of older brother Ryan's legacy of boorish behavior, but he couldn't evade another of his sibling's other traits -- throwing interceptions. Oklahoma linebacker Clint Ingram made a leaping interception of Leaf's pass at the 10-yard line with 33 seconds left in the Holiday Bowl to preserve the Sooners' 17-14 upset of the No. 6 Oregon Ducks on Thursday night. Ingram missed the call for a blitz on second-and-9, so he was in position to get in front of Demetrius Williams for the pickoff. Leaf had thrown a 3-yard touchdown pass to tight end Tim Day with 3:30 left to pull the Ducks to 17-14. Oregon's defense held, and Leaf began another drive at his 22 with 3:04 to play. He threw a 38-yard pass to Terrence Whitehead, who zigzagged to the Oklahoma 34. On third-and-14 from the 39, Leaf rolled right, was flushed back to the left and dodged a tackler before side-arming a pass to Jeremiah Johnson for a 19-yard gain. The interception came two plays later. Leaf was booed when he came in for Oregon's third possession of the game, and again when a scoreboard graphic noted that he was Ryan Leaf's younger brother. Ryan Leaf, the bad-boy Quarterback who played for the Chargers for three seasons, was perhaps the biggest bust in NFL history. Brady Leaf had helped rally the Ducks (10-2) in three of their final four regular-season games. The Sooners (8-4) have won six of seven. They were coming off consecutive losses in BCS championship games. It appeared the Ducks and Sooners would play the lowest-scoring Holiday Bowl ever. It turned out to be the second lowest. The Holiday Bowl has a reputation of wild finishes and high scores, with an average of 57 points being scored in the first 27 editions. In the last five Holiday Bowls, the teams combined for an average of 67 points. Oregon led 7-3 after the lowest scoring first half in Holiday Bowl history, but its offense was a no-show for most of the second half. Leaf finally got it going on a 13-play, 78-yard drive that was extended when Oklahoma's Eric Bassey was called for pass interference on a fake field goal. Leaf, the holder for placements, took the snap and threw to Day, who collided with Bassey at the three. One play later, Leaf hit Day for the 3-yard TD. Oklahoma's Adrian Peterson heated up in the second half, finishing with 84 yards on 23 carries. Rhett Bomar threw a 17-yard touchdown pass to fullback J.D. Runnells for a 10-7 Oklahoma lead with 9:20 to play in the third quarter. Late in the third, Peterson's backup, Kejuan Jones, scored on an 8-yard run to make it 17-7. Peterson softened the Ducks with three bruising carries on the drive for 36 yards, including a 20-yard gain when he leveled safety J.D. Nelson. Peterson apparently needed stitches in his forehead in the third quarter after he hit it on the back of a teammate's helmet while celebrating a big play. He was treated on the bench, and when he stood up, had a big bandage on his forehead. Peterson fumbled on the Oregon 1 early in the fourth quarter trying to stretch for the end zone. Oregon at least had the spirit of the Holiday Bowl on its first possession, running two trick plays and then going for it on fourth down before failing to convert. Matt Dragich gained 20 yards on a fake punt before wide receiver Garren Strong threw a pass down the left sideline to Quarterback Dennis Dixon, who dropped it. After taking over on downs, Oklahoma settled for Garrett Hartley's 34-yard field goal. Oregon came back and made it 7-3 on Demetrius Williams' 5-yard touchdown run on an end-around. Bomar was 17-of-30 for 229 yards, with one interception. Leaf was 14-of-24 for 136 yards. Oregon starter Dennis Dixon was 11-of-19 for 107 yards.

2005 Independence Bowl

The 2005 Independence Bowl, the 30th in the history of the bowl game, saw the Missouri Tigers of the Big 12 overcome a 21-0 deficit late in the first quarter to defeat the SEC's South Carolina Gamecocks, 38-31 in the 30th edition of the bowl game.

2005 Independence Bowl	Line	1	-	2	-	3	-	4	-	Final
Missouri	(51.5)	0	-	14	-	7	-	17	-	38
South Carolina	(-4.0)	21	-	7	-	0	-	3	-	31

Scoring Summary
South Carolina – Rice 23 yard pass from Mitchell (Brown kick)
South Carolina – Davis 5 yard run (Brown kick)
South Carolina – Askins 20 yard pass from Mitchell (Brown kick)
Missouri – King 99 yard interception return (Crossett kick)
South Carolina – Davis 2 yard run (Brown kick)
Missouri – Smith 5 yard pass from Coffman (Crossett kick)
Missouri – Smith 32 yard run (Crossettt kick)
Missouri – Smith 4 yard run (Crossett kick)
Missouri – Crossett 50 yard Field goal
South Carolina – Brown 30 yard Field goal
Missouri – Smith 1 yard run (Crossett kick)

Associated Press Independence Bowl Game Summary - As Brad Smith goes, so goes Missouri. South Carolina knew that and the game plan of keeping Smith in check worked great -- for a half, anyway. Then, the Missouri Quarterback broke loose, as he has done so often in his career, rushing for three touchdowns -- including a 1-yarder in the final minutes -- and passing for another to rally the Tigers for a 38-31 victory over the Gamecocks in the Independence Bowl on Friday. Smith, who rushed for 1,151 yards and passed for 2,022 this season, accounted for 431 yards of Missouri's 504 yards as the Tigers staged their biggest comeback victory of the year. Missouri (7-5) trailed 21-0 after the first quarter as Steve Spurrier's Gamecocks dominated the first half. South Carolina (7-5) outgained Missouri 312 yards to 174 in the first half and held the football almost 11 minutes longer (20:02-9:58). The Tigers didn't convert a third-down until the final 58 seconds of the half. Smith completed 21 of 37 passes for 282 yards, with one touchdown and an interception. He passed for 200 or more yards for the 18th time. He also ran for 150 yards and three touchdowns on 21 carries. The Gamecocks needed less than 3 minutes to go 80 yards for their first score. Blake Mitchell's 23-yard pass to Sidney Rice put Carolina up 7-0. Rice finished with 12 receptions for 191 yards. Tony Temple fumbled on Missouri's first play and South Carolina's Ricardo Hurley scooped up the ball. Four plays later Mike Davis, who ran for 125 yards on 18 carries, scored on a 5-yard run for a 14-0 lead. The Gamecocks' third scoring drive covered 69 yards in 1:59. This time Mitchell, who completed 20 of 38 passes for 266 yards, hit Carson Askins with a 20-yard scoring pass to make it 21-0. Mitchell passed for two touchdowns and was intercepted three times. Marcus King gave Missouri its first points, grabbing Mitchell's pass at the goal line and returning it 99 yards to make it 21-7 in the second quarter. After Davis' 2-yard TD run gave the Gamecocks a 28-7 lead, Missouri staged its first long drive of the game. The Tigers went 77 yards and Smith hit Chase Coffman with a 5-yard touchdown pass to make it 28-14 at halftime. Coffman finished with eight catches for 99 yards. On their first drive of the third quarter, Missouri faked a field goal at the Carolina 14. Martin Rucker ran to the 1-yard line, but the Tigers couldn't push it in and

Adam Crossett's 22-yard field goal attempt sailed wide right. Smith pulled Missouri to 28-21 with a 31-yard run with 2:41 left in the third quarter. Another apparent Missouri touchdown was nullified by a 15-yard tripping penalty. Smith finally got the score on a 4-yard run that tied the score at 28 early in the fourth quarter. Crossett kicked a 50-yard field goal to put the Tigers up 31-28, but Josh Brown countered with a 30 yarder that tied it at 31-all. Then, with 2:13 remaining, Smith sealed the Missouri win with a 1-yard TD run.

2005 Music City Bowl

The 2005 Gaylord Hotels Music City Bowl (presented by Bridgestone) was played between the Virginia Cavaliers and the Minnesota Golden Gophers.

2005 Music City Bowl	Line	1	-	2	-	3	-	4	-	Final
Virginia	(59.0)	7	-	3	-	14	-	10	-	34
Minnesota	(-4.5)	14	-	7	-	3	-	7	-	31

Scoring Summary
Minnesota - Valentine 7 yard pass from Cupito (Monroe kick)
Minnesota - Wheelwright 44 yard pass from Cupito (Monroe kick)
Virginia - Williams 6 yard pass from Hagans (Hughes kick)
Minnesota - Ellerson 57 yard pass from Cupito (Monroe kick)
Virginia - Hughes 32 yard Field goal
Virginia - Lundy 7 yard run (Hughes kick)
Minnesota - Monroe 39 yard Field goal
Virginia - Mines 2 yard pass from Hagans (Hughes kick)
Minnesota - Ellerson 23 yard pass from Cupito (Monroe kick)
Virginia - Lundy 2 yard run (Hughes kick)
Virginia - Hughes 39 yard Field goal

Associated Press Music City Bowl Game Summary - Virginia had a distracting December with four coaches departing for new jobs. Marques Hagans and his fellow Cavaliers got their focus back in the Music City Bowl. Connor Hughes kicked a 39-yard field goal with 1:08 left, and Hagans threw for a career-high 358 yards in helping Virginia overcome a 14-point deficit to beat Minnesota 34-31 Friday. Defensive coordinator Al Golden left to coach Temple, taking special teams and linebackers coach Mark D'Onofrio with him as his coordinator, leaving head Coach Al Groh to lead the defense. Offensive coordinator Ron Prince took over Kansas State and associate head coach Danny Rocco went to Liberty. The Gophers (7-5) might have been distracted themselves in what could be Coach Glen Mason's final game at Minnesota. He has a year left, but school officials want to decide by Saturday night when they must either terminate his assistants' contracts or see them roll over to 2006. Minnesota had every opportunity to blow the Cavaliers out and win this bowl for the third time in four years, but the nation's fifth-best offense bogged down after taking a 31-24 lead early in the fourth quarter. The Gophers had one last chance to pull out their fourth straight bowl victory, but Marcus Hamilton intercepted Bryan Cupito's ill-advised pass into double coverage in the end zone with 36 seconds remaining to seal the game for Virginia. It was the Cavaliers' first bowl win since the 2003 Continental Tire Bowl over Pittsburgh. Virginia (7-5) already had forced the Gophers to punt twice, and Hagans overcame an interception in the fourth quarter to rally the Cavaliers with 10 straight points to end the game. The Cavs outgained Minnesota 468-461 in total offense with its best performance of the season. Hagans moved the Cavaliers on drives of 77 and 75 yards in the fourth, with the first capped by Wali Lundy's second TD run of the game -- a 2-yarder that tied the score at 31 with 8:48 left. But the senior Quarterback, who turned 23 on Thursday, was at his best on the Cavs' final drive. Nearly tackled in the end zone for a safety on the opening play from the Cavaliers 3, he escaped back to the line of scrimmage. Then he connected with Deyon Williams on a 19-yarder for a little room, and he later scrambled around before finding Emmanuel Byers for 19 yards on third-and-6 to the Minnesota 25. Four plays later, Hughes kicked his second field goal to clinch the victory. Minnesota led 21-7 and had a chance to pad its lead before turning the ball over on downs when Cupito overthrew Logan Payne on fourth-and-6 at the end of the first half. Hagans used the final 50 seconds to set up Hughes' 32-yarder as time expired to pull within 21-10. That was the first of four straight scoring possessions for the Cavaliers, helping them tie the game at 31. Cupito threw a career-high four TD passes for the Gophers, who jumped out to a 14-0 lead. But the nation's second-best rushing game that had been averaging 279.91 yards per game was held to 198 yards, including only 74 in the second half. Gopher's running back Laurence Maroney finished with 26 carries for 109 yards, giving him a school-record 1,464 for the season. The junior immediately announced he would enter the NFL Draft.

2005 Sun Bowl

The 2005 Sun Bowl, known as the Vitalis Sun Bowl was played on December 30, 2005 in El Paso, Texas. It was the 72nd Sun Bowl. It featured the UCLA Bruins, and the Northwestern Wildcats. UCLA overcame a 22-0 deficit to Northwestern in the first quarter to win 50-38. This is the biggest comeback in UCLA football history. UCLA running backs Chris Markey and Kahlil Bell shared the most valuable player award, the first such shared award in Sun Bowl history. Defensive tackle Kevin Mims of Northwestern won the Jimmy Rogers, Jr. Most Valuable Lineman award. The game would unexpectedly be Randy Walker's last as Northwestern head coach. Walker died of an apparent heart attack the following June.

2005 Sun Bowl	Line	1	-	2	-	3	-	4	-	Final
Northwestern	(74.5)	22	-	0	-	3	-	13	-	38
#17 UCLA	(-3.0)	7	-	22	-	7	-	14	-	50

Scoring Summary
Northwestern - Howells 33 yard field goal.
Northwestern - Mims 30 yard interception return. (kick blocked.)
Northwestern - Philmore 19 yard run. (kick failed)
Northwestern - Roach 35 yard interception return (Howells).
UCLA – Bell 5 yard run (Rotstein kick)
UCLA - Moya 58 yard pass from Olson (Rotstein kick)
UCLA - Bell 6 yard run (Lewis pass from Olson)
UCLA - Everett 8 yard pass from Olson (Rotstein kick)
UCLA - Pitre 5 yard pass from Olson (Rotstein kick)
Northwestern - Villarreal 31 yard field goal.
Northwestern - Philmore 8 yard pass from Basanez (pass failed)
UCLA - Breazell 42 yard kickoff return (Malette kick)
Northwestern - Herbert 5 yard pass from Basanez (Villarreal kick)
UCLA - Breazell 45 yard kickoff return (Rotstein kick)

Associated Press Sun Bowl Game Summary - Brandon Breazell put the perfect wild finish on a wacky Sun Bowl. Twice, in fact. Breazell returned two onside kicks for a pair of highlight-reel touchdowns and Drew Olson recovered from an awful first quarter by throwing three TD passes, leading No. 17 UCLA to a 50-38 win over Northwestern on Friday. This wasn't the first time Breazell had a hand in a thrilling victory. He caught a 21-yard touchdown pass in overtime after the Bruins (10-2) scored 21 points in the final seven minutes of regulation for a 30-27 win at Stanford on Oct. 29. The Wildcats (7-5) pulled within 36-31 with 2:29 remaining when Brett Basanez threw a 9-yard touchdown pass to Mark Philmore, but Breazell -- a receiver lined up to make sure the Bruins kept the ball -- returned the ensuing onside kick 43 yards. After Basanez added a 5-yard TD pass to Shaun Herbert with 23 seconds remaining, Breazell struck again by taking the next onside kick for a 41-yard score, punctuating the highest-scoring Sun Bowl ever. Nobody involved with this year's Sun Bowl had seen it happen twice in one game, let alone within such a short span. It was a fitting ending to a crazy afternoon, where the teams combined to set 11 Sun Bowl records. It figured to be a wild day, as both teams came in ranked among the national leaders in offense but among the nation's worst defenses. Sure enough, the Wildcats set a record with 584 total yards and the teams combined for another record with 1,037 yards. But the kickoff returns? It seemed like too much, even in such a wacky setting. The Bruins also overcame three first-quarter interceptions by Olson, who threw three all season while setting a school record with 31 TD passes. They erased a 22-0 early deficit and survived an injury to star tailback Maurice Drew. With Drew limited to punt returns after a first-half shoulder injury, Chris Markey finished with 150 yards rushing and Kahlil Bell added 136 yards -- career highs for both. Olson had an ugly start, going 2-of-8 for 15 yards with three interceptions. He remembered hearing "almost laughter" after his third, which Nick Roach returned 34 yards to put the Wildcats ahead 22-0. Olson finished 10-of-24 for 143 yards. But Olson regrouped, guiding the Bruins to 29 unanswered points. He threw a 58-yard TD strike to Ryan Moya and Bell scored on runs of 5 and 6 yards. Then Olson added an 8-yard TD pass to Marcus Everett late in the first half as the Bruins took a 29-22 lead. With Drew sidelined much of the first half, Markey filled the void as UCLA established a ground attack. He opened one drive with runs of 24 and 51 yards, setting up Bell's 6-yard TD, and had 120 yards rushing by halftime. Basanez was 38-of-70 for 416 yards passing with two TDs and two interceptions for Northwestern, while freshman Tyrell Sutton, who averaged 126 yards rushing per game this season, had 84 yards.

Sun Bowl Legends - CBS Announcer Verne Lundquist who had been the Sun Bowl broadcaster starting in 1988, and former UCLA Bruins coach Terry Donahue were named Legends of the Sun Bowl.

2005 Chick-Fil-A Peach Bowl

The 2005 edition of the Chick-fil-A Peach Bowl featured two top 10 ranked teams. The ninth ranked Miami Hurricanes battled the tenth ranked LSU Tigers in this contest, the last to be played as the Peach Bowl until 2014.

2005 Chick-Fil-A Peach Bowl	Line	1	-	2	-	3	-	4	-	Final
#9 Miami	(-7.0)	3	-	0	-	0	-	0	-	3
#10 LSU	(41.0)	3	-	17	-	14	-	6	-	40

Scoring Summary
Miami – Peattie 21 yard field goal
LSU – Jackson 37 yard Field goal
LSU – Davis 51 yard pass from Flynn (Stevenson kick)
LSU – Jackson 47 yard Field goal
LSU – Addai 4 yard pass from Flynn (Stevenson kick)
LSU – Addai 6 yard run (Stevenson kick)
LSU – Hester 1 yard run (Stevenson kick)
LSU – Stevenson 35 yard Field goal
LSU – Jackson 50 yard field goal

Associated Press Chick-fil-A Peach Bowl Game Summary - Miami waited until after the Chick-fil-A Peach Bowl to put up a fight. Miami and LSU players exchanged punches in the tunnel as they left the field Friday night after the Tigers' 40-3 victory, the Hurricanes' most-lopsided bowl loss. Matt Flynn threw two touchdown passes in his first start for No, 10 LSU (11-2) and the Tigers attempted two late fake kicks against the No. 9 Hurricanes (9-3). Georgia State Patrol officers intervened in the brawl, with one officer holding a Taser while trying to prevent more players from entering the tunnel. Minutes later, Miami's Andrew Bain, appearing to be dazed, was escorted by officers out of the tunnel, but no players were detained by police, Miami Coach Larry Coker said at the time. Khalil Jones was taken to a hospital for observation, Coker said Saturday morning. While players surged to the tunnel, LSU coach Les Miles was surrounded by reporters on the field. LSU tailback Joseph Addai, who ran for 130 yards and a touchdown and added a touchdown catch, insisted the Tigers "try to play with class." LSU's Jacob Hester, who ran for 70 yards and a touchdown, said trash-talking began as normal banter and involved Tigers receiver Dwayne Bowe, a Miami native. After a few minutes, LSU players were back on the field celebrating the win. Miami players weren't available for comment after the game. Led by Flynn, LSU scored on eight straight possessions starting with a field goal late in the first quarter. Flynn completed 13 of 22 passes for 196 yards with no interceptions and was selected the offensive MVP. Flynn also rushed for 39 yards and was named the offensive MVP. Led by Flynn, LSU (11-2) rebounded from its worst game of the year, a 34-14 loss to Georgia in the Dec. 3 Southeastern Conference championship game, returning to the Georgia Dome and delivering one of its strongest performance of the season. LSU scored on eight straight possessions in a streak that started with a field goal late in the first quarter. Even with a lopsided lead, LSU attempted to add to the rout, faking a field goal while leading 34-3 late in the third quarter and then failing on a fake punt with a 40-3 lead late in the game. Miles said he called for the fake field goal but his players called for the fake punt. Coker wasn't affected by the trickery. LSU piled up 468 yards, the most allowed by Miami this season. The Hurricanes (9-3) entered leading the nation in pass defense and ranked third in total defense. The Tigers were just as impressive on defense, holding Miami to 153 yards and six first downs, none in the second half. Kyle Wright completed only 10 of 21 passes for 100 yards. LSU's dominant performance negated Miami's plan to utilize cornerback Devin Hester as a multiple threat on offense. On Miami's first possession, Hester lined up at tailback and receiver and took a direct snap at Quarterback. Hester had a 24-yard run on the possession to set up a field goal. But overall, the junior and the Hurricanes were contained. LSU had its largest margin of victory in a bowl game, easily surpassing its 45-26 win over Michigan in the 1995 Independence Bowl. Miami's previous most lopsided loss in a bowl game was a 29-0 loss to Arizona in the Fiesta Bowl on Jan. 1, 1994. Addai scored on a 4-yard pass from Flynn in the second quarter and a 6-yard run in the third. With the game tied at 3-3, a key fourth-down stop by LSU's defense early in the second quarter gave the Tigers momentum. On fourth-and-1 from the LSU 35, Wright faked a pitch to his left and then ran right, where he was hit by LSU's Melvin Oliver short of the first down. The Tigers seized the opportunity as Flynn connected with Craig Davis for a 49-yard touchdown pass over Miami cornerback Randy Phillips. After Jackson's 47-yard field goal pushed LSU's lead to 13-3, the Tigers added another touchdown late in the half on Flynn's pass to Addai. Addai went over 100 yards rushing on his second carry of the second half. He rambled 25 yards to the 6, setting up his scoring run on a pitch to the left one play later. With Addai suffering from cramps, Hester filled in on the Tigers' second touchdown drive of the quarter. Hester's dive over the top from the 1 with 5:27 left in the period pushed the lead to 34-

3. The Tigers faked a 46-yard field goal late in the quarter, with Jackson running 12 yards to the Miami 17. Colt David's 35-yard field goal early in the fourth quarter pushed the lead to 37-3. Jackson added a 50-yard field goal with 8:20 left to play.

2005 Meineke Car Care Bowl

The 2005 Meineke Car Care Bowl featured the South Florida and the NC State Wolfpack. The game was the fourth edition to this bowl game, as well as the only shutout in the game's history. The game was played on Saturday, December 31, 2005. It remained the only shutout South Florida ever suffered, until November 12, 2009 when South Florida lost to Rutgers 31–0 for its first shutout in South Florida's regular season. South Florida was in its first bowl in program history.

2005 Meineke Car Care Bowl	Line	1	-	2	-	3	-	4	-	Final
South Florida	(42.0)	0	-	0	-	0	-	0	-	0
NC State	(-4.0)	0	-	14	-	0	-	0	-	14

Scoring Summary
NC State - Clark 9 yard pass from Stone (Deraney kick)
NC State - Brown 1 yard run (Deraney kick)

Associated Press Meineke Car Care Bowl Game Summary - Using stout defense and just enough offense to get the job done, North Carolina State capped its late-season rally with a 14-0 win over South Florida in the Meineke Car Care Bowl on Saturday. Brian Clark caught a 9-yard touchdown pass and Andre Brown scored on a 1-yard run to lead the Wolfpack, who rallied from a 2-4 start to the season to close the year with three consecutive wins. In all, N.C. State (7-5) won five of its final six games. It was a disappointing end for upstart South Florida, which was playing in its first bowl in school history. The Bulls (6-6) launched their program nine years ago, moved up to Division I-A in 2001 and capped their first season in the Big East with a bowl bid. But their 100th game ended in the first shutout in school history as the Bulls managed 295 yards total offense and failed to get Andre Hall -- the Big East's leading rusher -- into the end zone. Hall accounted for most of the offense, finishing with 118 yards rushing and two catches for 49 yards. Credit the Wolfpack defense, particularly linebacker Stephen Tulloch, for stifling South Florida. Tulloch finished with 14 tackles -- five for a loss -- three sacks and a recovery of his own forced fumble to earn the MVP award. Neither team played particularly well on offense nor special teams, with a combined three missed field goals, a South Florida blocked punt, four fumbles and an interception in the end zone to end one of the Bulls' rare scoring threats. So, N.C. State got all it needed with its two touchdowns, both in the second quarter. Toney Baker set up the first score with runs of 22 and 14 yards, allowing Marcus Stone to find Clark in the end zone. The Wolfpack ran the same play twice, with Clark making the first catch out of bounds before grabbing it the second time for the score. Baker used a ton of short runs to set up the second score, then gave way to Brown for the touchdown. Baker finished with 93 yards rushing on 22 carries, while Brown had 51 yards on 12 carries. South Florida spent the entire game just trying to get into the end zone, and had a great chance when Hall broke free for a 41-yard gain to put the Bulls in decent scoring range at the N.C. State 17. But three bizarre play calls -- a run by seldom-used Ricky Ponton, followed by two bad passes -- ended the threat when Garland Heath intercepted Pat Julmiste in the end zone. It was a trend South Florida followed the entire game, trying to add variation to an offense that only has one weapon in Hall. Anytime they tried to stray from involving Hall it backfired, especially during a brief Quarterback change in the third quarter. With Julmiste struggling against the Wolfpack's defense, South Florida sent in freshman Carlton Hill to change the pace. Only Hill fumbled the ball away to N.C. State on two consecutive plays. He lost the first one as he was sacked by Stephen Tulloch. But South Florida got a break when the Wolfpack fumbled it back to them on the next possession -- only to see Hill give it away again on the very next play. In the end, only two things worked for the Bulls: Putting the ball in Hall's hands, and a fake punt late in the fourth quarter that went for a 31-yard gain when holder Brandon Baker connected with S.J. Green. But that never led to a score as South Florida gained only one yard on four tries, leaving Hall angrily ripping off his chin straps as Julmiste was stopped on a futile fourth down run.

2005 Houston Bowl

The **2005 EV1.net Houston Bowl** was the sixth and final edition of the bowl game and was played at Reliant Stadium in Houston, Texas. The game pitted the Iowa State Cyclones from the Big 12 Conference and the TCU Horned Frogs from the Mountain West Conference (MWC). The game resulted in a 27–24 TCU victory.

2005 Houston Bowl	Line	1	-	2	-	3	-	4	-	Final
#14 TCU	(-3.0)	14	-	10	-	0	-	3	-	27
Iowa State	(49.0)	0	-	17	-	7	-	0	-	24

Scoring Summary
TCU - Merrill 20 yard run (Manfredini kick)
TCU - Brown 7 yard run (Manfredini kick)
Iowa State - Blythe 48 yard pass from Meyer (Culbertson kick)
Iowa State - Team safety
Iowa State - Davis 6 yard pass from Meyer (Culbertson kick)
TCU - DePriest 84 yard pass from Ballard (Manfredini kick)
TCU - Manfredini 29 yard Field goal
Iowa State - Blythe 22 yard pass from Meyer (Culbertson kick)
TCU - Locco 44 yard Field goal

Associated Press Houston Bowl Game Summary - After rarely playing since missing three field goals in TCU's only loss of the season, Peter LoCoco was shocked when called on late in the Houston Bowl. But LoCoco got over the surprise and kicked a 44-yard field goal with 5:25 remaining Saturday night to give No. 14 TCU a 27-24 win over Iowa State. The win extended TCU's winning streak to 10 games, the third-longest in the nation behind No. 1 USC (34) and No. 2 Texas (19). LoCoco's field goal was TCU's only score in the second half after the Horned Frogs built a 24-17 halftime lead. The Mountain West champion Horned Frogs were out to prove themselves after being snubbed by the BCS. TCU has the best record among teams from non-BCS conferences. The win gave TCU (11-1, 8-0) 11 victories for the fourth time in school history and the first time since 2003. It was a sloppy game with four fumbles, three interceptions and 20 penalties. Quarterback Jeff Ballard improved to 8-0 as a starter by throwing for 275 yards and a touchdown, despite being sacked six times. TCU had a chance to go ahead early in the fourth quarter but running back Robert Merrill fumbled at the 1-yard line after a 21-yard run, and Iowa State recovered. Bret Meyer threw a 22-yard touchdown pass to Todd Blythe to move Iowa State (7-5, 4-4 Big 12) into a 24-all tie in the third quarter. Blythe lost his helmet following the diving catch. The score was Blythe's school-record ninth touchdown reception of the season. Meyer was 20-of-33 for 254 yards and three touchdowns. Iowa State was doomed by two fumbles, two interceptions and an inability to generate a running game. The Cyclones had just 34 yards rushing. TCU didn't seem rusty, even after a 49-day layoff since its last game. The Horned Frogs jumped out to an early lead when Merrill was untouched on a 20-yard scoring run that capped an 80-yard drive on the team's first series. Merrill finished with 11 carries and 109 yards. The Horned Frogs extended their lead to 14-0 when Aaron Brown scored on a seven-yard run that followed an Iowa State fumble. Iowa State had only 21 yards in the first quarter but took advantage of TCU mistakes to score 17 unanswered points to take the lead in the second quarter. On the last play of the first quarter, Iowa State's LaMarcus Hicks got in front of TCU's Cory Rodgers to make his fifth interception of the season. Two plays later, Blythe outran TCU's Drew Coleman and grabbed a 48-yard touchdown pass from Meyer. It was the first touchdown allowed by the Horned Frogs in 10 quarters. On the ensuing series, TCU punter Brian Cortney chased a high snap out of the back of the end zone for an Iowa State safety. Meyer shook off two would-be tacklers before scampering for a career-long 39 yards to the 6. On third down, he found Jon Davis in the corner of the end zone with a 6-yard touchdown pass, and then hit a wide-open Ben Barkema for the 2-point conversion for a 17-14 lead. A fumble by Meyer set up a bowl-record, 84-yard touchdown reception by Michael DePriest that put TCU back on top. Chris Manfredini kicked a 30-yard field goal just before halftime to leave the Horned Frogs ahead 24-17. It was the second time TCU has faced a Big 12 team this season. The Horned Frogs beat then-No. 7 Oklahoma in their season opener.

2005 Liberty Bowl

The 2005 AutoZone Liberty Bowl was between the Fresno State Bulldogs and the Tulsa Golden Hurricane on December 31, 2005, at Liberty Bowl Memorial Stadium in Memphis, Tennessee. In a closely contested game which went back and forth Tulsa defeated Fresno State 31-24. It was the forty-seventh time the Liberty Bowl had been played.

2005 Liberty Bowl	Line	1	-	2	-	3	-	4	-	Final
Fresno State	(-7.0)	7	-	7	-	3	-	7	-	24
Tulsa	(61.5)	0	-	17	-	0	-	14	-	31

Scoring Summary
Fresno State – Mathis 6 yd run (Zimmerman kick)
Tulsa – Parrish 22 yd run (DeVault kick)
Tulsa – Adams 63 yd run (DeVault kick)
Fresno State – Sumlin 25 yd run (Zimmerman kick)
Tulsa – DeVault 41 yd Field goal
Fresno State – Zimmerman 27 yd Field goal
Fresno State – Fernandez 21 yd pass from Pinegar (Zimmerman kick)
Tulsa – Davis 54 yd pass from Smith (DeVault kick)
Tulsa – Smith 4 yd run (DeVault kick)

Game summary - Early in the first quarter Fresno State put together a long drive, going 54 yards in 15 plays. All but two of these plays were rushes, and none of the plays went for more than 8 yards. On the last play of the drive Fresno State faced 4th and 2 on Tulsa's 10-yard line but failed to convert, coming up empty-handed after eight minutes and 27 seconds. Tulsa was unable to capitalize on the stop and punted the ball away. Starting now from their own 46, Fresno State again drove 54 yards, this time with six plays in just under three minutes. Wendell Mathis ran the ball four times, finally scoring a touchdown on a 6-yard run putting Fresno State up 7-0. Tulsa came right back after Fresno State's score, moving the ball 74 yards in 3:20. The centerpiece of the drive was 22-yard touchdown run by Uril Parrish, tying the score at 7 early in the second quarter. Tulsa scored again at 8:15 on a 64-yard run by Tarrion Adams, which tied his season high against Memphis and put Tulsa up 14-7. Fresno State responded with another of its long drives, a 14-play 79-yarder capped by a 22-yard touchdown run by Bryson Sumlin, which tied the game at 14 with 1:13 left in the half. Tulsa, starting from its own 19, quickly moved the ball to Fresno State's 23-yard line, setting up a 41-yard field goal by Brad DeVault to end the half. Fresno State started the third quarter with a 36-yard kickoff return by Adam Jennings followed by a 24-yard run by Mathis placing them at Tulsa's 35-yard line. Quarterback Paul Pinegar completed a 20-yard pass to Jaron Fairman, putting them on Tulsa's 15. After this strong start, however, Fresno State could not convert and settled for a 27-yard field goal by Kyle Zimmerman, rather than risk the possibility of turning it over on downs as they had in the opening drive of the first quarter. The field goal tied the game at 17. The remainder of the third quarter was marked by missed opportunities and miscues. Fresno State kicker Zimmerman missed a 26-yard field goal. Tulsa QB Smith completed a 25-yard pass to Davis deep inside Fresno State territory, but Davis fumbled the ball. Fresno State took over, but QB Pinegar fumbled and recovered the ball on a 9-yard sack. The quarter ended at a 17-17 tie. To begin the fourth quarter Fresno State continued the drive which had begun on the Tulsa turnover and scored less than a minute in on a 21-yard touchdown pass from Pinegar to Joe Fernandez, putting Fresno State up 24-17. After two inconclusive drives Tulsa scored on a 54-yard touchdown pass from Smith to Davis, tying the game at 24. Tulsa scored again late in the quarter on a 4-yard run by Smith, putting them up 31-24, while Fresno State's efforts were frustrated by two interceptions thrown by Pinegar, the second coming on Tulsa's 32-yard line with two minutes left in the game. Taking possession, Tulsa was able to run out the clock, winning 31-24. Tulsa Quarterback Paul Smith was named the bowl MVP. His 4-yard touchdown run proved the difference in the game and gave Tulsa its first bowl victory since 1991 Freedom Bowl, 14 years ago. The loss ended a three-year bowl winning streak for Fresno State, and frustrated Fresno State Quarterback Paul Pinegar's attempt to be the first QB to go 4-0 in bowl games. Several National Football League teams interviewed Fresno State coach Pat Hill during the off-season, but he elected to remain with Fresno State and received a contract extension through the end of 2010. Tulsa head coach Steve Kragthorpe remained at Tulsa for one more season before departing to coach the University of Louisville. Immediately after the win defensive coordinator Todd Graham departed to become head coach at Rice. Just one year later Graham would return to Tulsa as head coach following Kragthorpe's departure. The 2005 Liberty Bowl is the only edition to feature the Conference USA champion and a Western Athletic Conference team. Beginning with the 2006 Liberty Bowl, the Conference USA champion faced a team from the Southeastern Conference (SEC).

Chapter 2 – 2006-2010

2006 Gator Bowl

The 2006 Gator Bowl was between the Louisville Cardinals and the Virginia Tech Hokies at Alltel Stadium in Jacksonville, Florida, on January 2, 2006. Louisville represented the Big East Conference (Big East), and Virginia Tech represented the Atlantic Coast Conference (ACC) in the competition.

Virginia Tech was selected as a participant in the 2006 Gator Bowl following a 10–2 regular season that included wins over 15th-ranked Georgia Tech and traditional rivals Virginia and West Virginia. A loss to Florida State in the inaugural ACC Championship Game gave Tech a position in the Gator Bowl instead of the more prestigious Bowl Championship Series-run Orange Bowl game. Facing the 12th-ranked Hokies were the 15th-ranked Louisville Cardinals, who finished 9–2 during the regular season of their first year in the Big East Conference. Louisville won its last five games before the Gator Bowl and participated in the Liberty Bowl at the end of the previous season. Pre-game media coverage of the game focused on Virginia Tech's fall from being a contender for the national championship, Louisville's loss of star Quarterback Brian Brohm to injury, the fact that both teams were playing under new conference affiliations, and the rise of Virginia Tech Quarterback Marcus Vick, younger brother of NFL star Michael Vick. The 2006 Gator Bowl began on January 2, 2006, at 12:30 p.m. EST in Jacksonville. Tailback Cedric Humes was named the most valuable player of the game for Virginia Tech, and Quarterback Hunter Cantwell was named the Cardinals' most valuable player. Tech punter Nic Schmitt set Gator Bowl records for punt yardage and average punt distance, kicking the ball six times for 300 yards, an average of 50 yards per kick. Virginia Tech's win was marred by excessive penalties and unsportsmanlike conduct that resulted in the ejection of one player. Following the game, Virginia Tech Quarterback Marcus Vick was released from the team as a result of several incidents of misconduct, including a stomp on Louisville defender Elvis Dumervil's leg during the game.

2006 Gator Bowl	Line	1	-	2	-	3	-	4	-	Final
#12 Virginia Tech	(-8.0)	3	-	7	-	3	-	22	-	35
#15 Louisville	(55.5)	14	-	3	-	0	-	7	-	24

Scoring Summary
Louisville – Urrutia 11 yard pass from Cantwell (Carmody kick)
Virginia Tech – Pace 36 yard Field goal
Louisville – Tinch 39 yard pass from Cantwell (Carmody kick)
Virginia Tech – Harper 33 yard pass from Vick (Pace kick)
Louisville – Carmody 35 yard Field goal
Virginia Tech – Pace 28 yard Field goal
Louisville – Barnidge 29 yard pass from Cantwell (Carmody kick)
Virginia Tech – Humes 24 yard run (Morgan pass)
Virginia Tech – King 5 yard pass from Vick (Pace kick)
Virginia Tech – Anderson 39 yard interception return (Pace kick)

Virginia Tech Media Guide Gator Bowl Game Summary - The Virginia Tech Hokies twice rallied from 11-point deficits, and scored 22 unanswered points in the fourth quarter to knock off Louisville 35-24 in the Gator Bowl played at Alltel Stadium on Monday afternoon in Jacksonville, Fla. The win snapped a two-game losing streak in bowl games for the Hokies and enabled Tech to finish the 2005 season with an 11-2 overall record. Tech recorded 11 wins for just the third time in the program's history. The Hokies trailed 14-3 in the first half, and 17-10 at halftime, primarily because of 75 yards in penalties, all of the 15-yard variety. And in the second half, they found themselves down 24-13 after Louisville Quarterback Hunter Cantwell hit Gary Barnidge on a 29-yard touchdown pass with less than 14 minutes left in the game. After that score, the Hokies got things going. Tech answered by marching 78 yards in just two plays. Tech got a big play from Quarterback Marcus Vick, who hit receiver David Clowney for a 54-yard gain to the Louisville 24. On the next play, Cedric Humes rumbled in from 24 yards out, and the Hokies connected on the two-point conversion when Vick hit Josh Morgan. That made the score 24-21 with just over 13 minutes to go. Tech's Chris Ellis then gave Tech's offense a golden opportunity when he drilled Cantwell on the ensuing possession and forced the Louisville signal-caller to fumble. James Anderson recovered for the Hokies, giving Tech the ball at its own 47. The Hokies capitalized when Vick found tight end Jeff King in the back of the end zone on a 5-yard touchdown pass that gave the Hokies a 28-24 lead with 6:09 left in the game. Tech then put the game away a minute later. Anderson, a redshirt senior from Chesapeake, Va., who enjoyed a huge game, intercepted a Cantwell pass and returned it for a touchdown that made the score 35-24. Louisville had two opportunities to cut into the lead but lost the ball on downs on one occasion and Brandon Flowers intercepted a pass on the Cardinals' final possession of the game. Humes, a redshirt senior from Virginia Beach, Va., took home the game's MVP honors for Tech after rushing for 113 yards and the one touchdown in his final collegiate game. His effort enabled the Hokies to rush for 187 yards, pacing a balanced Tech attack. Vick completed 11-of-21 for 203 yards and two scores. Tech's defense slammed the door on the Cardinals in the second half, allowing just seven first downs and 119 yards. Cantwell threw three touchdowns, but also threw three interceptions.

2006 Outback Bowl

The 2006 Outback Bowl featured the Iowa Hawkeyes, and the Florida Gators. Florida came into the game under first year head coach Urban Meyer with an 8-3 record. Iowa came into the game with a 7-4 record. The Gators represented the Southeastern Conference, while the Hawkeyes represented the Big Ten Conference.

2006 Outback Bowl	Line	1	-	2	-	3	-	4	-	Final
#25 Iowa	(48.0)	0	-	7	-	0	-	17	-	24
#16 Florida	(-1.0)	7	-	17	-	7	-	0	-	31

Scoring Summary
Florida – McCollum 6 yard blocked punt return (Hetland kick)
Florida – Hetland 21 yard Field goal
Florida – Brown 60 yard interception return (Hetland kick)
Iowa – Solomon 20 yard pass from Tate (Schlicher kick)
Florida – Baker 24 yard pass from Leak (Hetland kick)
Florida – Baker 38 yard pass from Leak (Hetland kick)
Iowa – Hinkel 4 yard pass from Tate (Schlicher kick)
Iowa – Hinkel 14 yard pass from Tate (Schlicher kick)
Iowa – Schlicher 45 yard Field goal

Associated Press Outback Bowl Game Summary - When Urban Meyer talks about Florida football, he singles out Vernell Brown. Brown, who broke his leg two months ago, came back Monday and scored on an interception to help Florida beat No. 25 Iowa 31-24 in the Outback Bowl. Chris Leak threw for 277 yards, while Dallas Baker scored on passes of 24 and 38 yards and finished with 10 catches for 147 yards for the 16th-ranked Gators (9-3). With the victory, Meyer matched Ray Graves (1960) and Steve Spurrier (1990) for most victories for a coach in his first season at Florida. Brown, who broke his left leg against Vanderbilt on Nov. 5 and missed the last two games of the season, picked off an overthrown pass and returned it 60 yards. Tremaine McCollum ran 6 yards with a blocked punt for another TD to help the Gators build a 24-7 halftime lead. Meyer also singled out the senior cornerback in making the point that he wants players who are committed to staying in Gainesville, not those who come to Florida to spiff up their NFL resumes. Drew Tate and the Iowa offense had success moving the ball, but the blocked punt on the fifth play of the game, Brown's interception and two costly penalties during an 80-yard touchdown drive Florida put together just before the half left the Hawkeyes (7-5) in a hole too deep to escape. Tate completed 32-of-55 passes for 346 yards and three touchdowns. He rallied his team from a 31-7 deficit in the fourth quarter with TD throws of 4 and 14 yards to Ed Hinkel and then moved Iowa into position for a 45-yard field goal to pull the Hawkeyes within a touchdown with 1:24 remaining. The Gators, making their third Outback appearance in the past four years, had not ended a season with a victory since beating Maryland in the Orange Bowl in 2002. They lost to Michigan in Tampa in the 2003 Outback and to Iowa two years ago -- a game for which some Florida players felt the team was ill prepared. Iowa salvaged its season by rebounding from losses to Michigan and Northwestern to beat Wisconsin and Minnesota to receive its school-record fourth straight trip to a January bowl -- a huge boon for recruiting. Still, five losses have to be a disappointment after going 10-2 and sharing the Big Ten championship with Ohio State in 2004. Florida's season hit a low point with a 30-22 loss at South Carolina. Meyer held a team meeting during the plane ride home, and the Gators responded two weeks later with a dominating 34-7 rout of Florida State that underscored the coach's belief that the program is headed in the right direction. Brown was a freshman wide receiver three years ago when he threw an interception on a trick play that sealed Florida's eight-point Outback loss to Michigan under former Gators coach Ron Zook. He's flattered that Meyer considers him the face of the program. Meyer replaced Zook after last season, moving to the Southeastern Conference after highly successful stints at Bowling Green and Utah. His arrival, however, also brought questions about whether his offense would work in a major league such as the SEC. Leak looked lost in the scheme at times early in the season. But with Monday's win, as well as victories over Tennessee, Georgia and Florida State in the same year for only the fourth time in school history, Meyer's first season was a success.

2006 Capital One Bowl

The 2006 Capital One Bowl was between the Wisconsin Badgers and the Auburn Tigers on January 2, 2006, at the Citrus Bowl in Orlando, Florida. Despite the odds against them, Wisconsin defeated the higher ranked Tigers, 24-10.

2006 Capital One Bowl	Line	1	-	2	-	3	-	4	-	Final
#21 Wisconsin	(53.5)	10	-	7	-	0	-	7	-	24
#7 Auburn	(-10.5)	0	-	0	-	3	-	7	-	10

Scoring Summary
Wisconsin – Williams 30 yard pass from Stocco (Melhaff kick)
Wisconsin – Melhaff 19 yard Field goal
Wisconsin – Daniels 13 yard pass from Stocco (Melhaff kick)
Auburn – Vaughn 19 yard Field goal
Auburn – Taylor 9 yard pass from Cox (Vaughn kick)
Wisconsin – Calhoun 33 yard run (Melhaff kick)

Associated Press Capital One bowl Game Summary - With a masterful offensive performance and a surprisingly stingy defense, the Wisconsin Badgers gave Coach Barry Alvarez a proper send-off. Brian Calhoun rushed for 213 yards, John Stocco passed for 301 and Brandon Williams had 173 yards receiving, lifting the No. 21 Badgers to a 24-10 victory over No. 7 Auburn in the Capital One Bowl on Monday. It was the perfect tribute to a coach who restored pride to a down-and-out program. The 10½-point underdog Badgers (10-3) were in control throughout against the Tigers (9-3), who flopped after ending the regular season with wins over Georgia and Alabama. Alvarez never let his coaching finale be about himself, but the Badgers' near-flawless performance offered a fine opportunity for a little reflection. It was a fitting farewell for Alvarez, who led Wisconsin to eight bowl wins in 16 seasons and will now focus on his duties as athletic director. The Badgers were 1-5 all-time in the postseason before his arrival and sent him off with his fourth 10-win season. Wisconsin amassed 311 yards and a 17-0 lead in the first half, leaving little doubt that Alvarez would get to celebrate another big win. The architect of numerous firsts for Wisconsin, Alvarez became the first Badgers coach to win his finale since Milt Bruhn in 1966. Defensive coordinator Bret Bielema takes over as coach. Alvarez declined to rate the victory. Calhoun, a junior pondering a leap to the NFL, rushed 30 times and scored on a 33-yard run in the fourth quarter. Then he got the highest praise from a coach who has coached star tailbacks like Heisman Trophy winner Ron Dayne. Williams also had four carries for 35 yards as the Badgers dismantled a defense that came in allowing only 294 yards per game. The Tigers tried to edge back into the game in the second half, but the Southeastern Conference's top offense never got going. John Vaughn capped Auburn's first drive of the second half with a 19-yard field goal. Then Taylor Mehlaff missed his second long field goal, a 41-yarder. Auburn then put together a 15-play drive that included two fourth-down conversions. Brandon Cox hit Ben Obomanu for a 13-yard gain on fourth-and-10 from the 19. The Tigers were pushed back 3 yards on their next three plays, but Cox hit a leaping Courtney Taylor in the end zone on fourth down two plays into the final quarter. It was Taylor's first touchdown catch of the season, making it 17-10. The Badgers quickly got the momentum back as Calhoun sprinted for a touchdown. He also had a 60-yarder, a 27-yarder and a 17-yarder to set up Wisconsin's first three scores. Calhoun became just the second player in Division I history to have 1,500 yards rushing and 500 yards receiving in the same season. Pacific's Ryan Benjamin did it in 1991. Calhoun said after the game he hasn't made up his mind on whether he will skip his senior season to enter the NFL draft. He turned in the second-best rushing effort in Capital One history, behind Fred Taylor's 234 in 1998 for Florida. The Tigers were held scoreless in the first half for the first time this season and finished with only 236 yards. Wisconsin gained 548. The Badgers didn't resemble a defense that came in giving up 432.5 yards per game, a nice transition for their next coach, too. Under constant pressure, Cox was 15-of-33 for 137 yards with an interception on the second play of the game. Kenny Irons, the SEC's leading rusher, managed only 88 yards on 22 carries and fumbled on the Tigers' second series. Auburn had won three consecutive bowl games and finished in a tie for the best four-year run in the program's history with 39 wins.

2006 Cotton Bowl Classic

The 2006 AT&T Cotton Bowl Classic was held on January 2, 2006, in Dallas, Texas at the Cotton Bowl. The game featured the Alabama Crimson Tide of the SEC, and the Texas Tech Red Raiders of the Big 12 Conference. During the 2005 season, Alabama — led by Quarterback Brodie Croyle — earned a 9-2 regular season record (all nine wins were later vacated by the NCAA due to violations). Following a 9-0 start, the Crimson Tide's two losses came to SEC West rivals LSU and Auburn. Texas Tech — led by Quarterback Cody Hodges — also suffered two defeats during their season, including a 52–17 defeat to eventual national champion Texas and a 24–17 loss at Oklahoma State. In 2009, the NCAA vacated Alabama's Cotton Bowl win due to infractions committed during the season.

2006 Cotton Bowl Classic	Line	1	-	2	-	3	-	4	-	Final
#18 Texas Tech	(-3.0)	3	-	0	-	0	-	7	-	10
#13 Alabama	(47.5)	7	-	0	-	3	-	3	-	13

Scoring Summary
Alabama – Brown 76 yard pass from Croyle (Christensen kick)
Texas Tech – Trlica 34 yard Field Goal
Alabama – Christensen 31 yard Field Goal
Texas Tech – Hicks 12 yard pass from Hodges (Trlica kick)
Alabama – Christensen 45 yard Field Goal

Cotton Bowl Classic Game Summary - The 70th AT&T Cotton Bowl Classic had it all: warm weather, bright sunshine, a sellout crowd and a Classic finish to remember. Alabama's Jamie Christensen kicked a career-best 45-yard field goal on the final play as time ran out, lifting the Crimson Tide to a 13-10 victory over the Texas Tech Red Raiders. A sellout crowd of 74,222, plus a national FOX TV audience, watched in 70-degree temperatures as the two teams worked their way toward only the second Cotton Bowl decided on the last play. Christensen also made a 31-yarder in the third quarter, giving Alabama a 10-3, advantage. But in the second quarter, he had missed from 39 yards and later had a 38-yarder blocked. His opportunity to kick the game-winner, after Texas Tech tied it, 10-10, with 2:56 left, appeared unlikely considering Alabama's regular-season offensive output in 2005. Alabama, starting at its 14, covered 58 yards in 10 plays. Croyle made it happen, first with a 17-yard pass on third down to Matt Miller, giving the Tide a first down at its 35. He then delivered with an 11-yarder to Brandon Brooks and followed with a 23-yarder to Keith Brown, putting Alabama at the Tech 31 with 49 seconds left. Croyle, completed 19 of 31 passes for 275 yards and one touchdown. Christensen's kick appeared to barely clear the crossbar, squeezing just inside the left upright. Croyle received the Sanford Trophy, which recognizes the game's outstanding offensive player and commemorates Cotton Bowl founder J. Curtis Sanford. Alabama linebacker DeMeco Ryans, who had seven tackles, five solo, and 1½ sacks, received the McKnight Trophy, which recognizes the game's outstanding defensive player and commemorates Felix McKnight, a celebrated Dallas newspaperman and long-time chairman of the Cotton Bowl team selection committee. Alabama grabbed a quick lead on Croyle's 76-yard pass to Brown with 11:37 left in the first quarter. The Tide continued to dominate until the closing three minutes when Tech took advantage of a short field and got the tying score on a 12-yard pass from Cody Hodges to Jarrett Hicks. Alabama's offense controlled the ball for nearly 39 minutes, keeping Texas Tech, No.1 nationally in passing offense and No.2 in total offense, off the field. In the end, Tech could only watch as Christensen ended the Red Raiders' attempt to go to overtime and any dream of Tech taking home the Field Scovell Trophy

2006 Fiesta Bowl

The 2006 Tostitos Fiesta Bowl, played on January 2, 2006, was the 35th edition of the Fiesta Bowl, featuring Notre Dame and Ohio State. Ohio State won the game 34–20.

Selection of teams - The Fiesta Bowl this season was supposed to choose either the Big 12 Conference champion or the Pacific-10 Conference champion as part of the BCS tie-ins for this season. The Rose Bowl served as the BCS National Championship Game this season, and the Pac-10 conference tie-in moved to the Fiesta Bowl as a result. Unlike the 2001 season, the Fiesta Bowl would not be allowed to match the Big 12 and Pac-10 champions, it could choose only one of them. However, neither the Big 12 nor Pac-10 champions would be available to the Fiesta Bowl in the end, as those teams, the Texas Longhorns and the USC Trojans, would finish in the top 2 of the BCS standings and meet in the Rose Bowl. None of the other conference champions that earned an automatic bid were available either, as those teams would go to the Orange and Sugar Bowls. The Fiesta Bowl was left to take the 2 teams that earned BCS at-large bids, Ohio State of the Big Ten Conference and independent Notre Dame, long considered a candidate for membership in the Big Ten.

2006 Fiesta Bowl	Line	1	-	2	-	3	-	4	-	Final
#4 Ohio State	(-4.5)	7	-	14	-	3	-	10	-	34
#5 Notre Dame	(55.5)	7	-	0	-	6	-	7	-	20

Scoring Summary
Notre Dame – Walker 20 yard run (Fitzpatrick kick)
Ohio State – Ginn 56 yard pass from Smith (Huston kick)
Ohio State – Ginn 68 yard run (Huston kick)
Ohio State – Holmes 85 yard pass from Smith (Huston kick)
Notre Dame – Walker 10 yard run (kick failed)
Ohio State – Huston 40 yard Field goal
Ohio State – Huston 26 yard Field goal
Notre Dame – Walker 3 yard run (Fitzpatrick kick)
Ohio State – Pittman 60 yard run (Huston kick)

Associated Press Fiesta Bowl Game Summary - Troy Smith outplayed Brady Quinn and Jim Tressel outfoxed Charlie Weis. Fourth-ranked Ohio State jumped on No. 5 Notre Dame with big play after big play Monday night in a 34-20 Fiesta romp, sending the Irish to their eighth consecutive bowl defeat. So make it four straight bowl wins for the Buckeyes, three of them at the Tostitos Fiesta Bowl. Suspended from last year's Alamo Bowl for taking $500 from a booster, Smith earned a measure of redemption with an offensive MVP performance, hooking up on a pair of long touchdown passes. Santonio Holmes set a Fiesta Bowl record with an 85-yard TD catch, then said he was forgoing his senior season to enter the NFL draft. Ted Ginn scored on a 68-yard end around and caught a 56-yard touchdown pass for the Buckeyes (10-2). Darius Walker scored all three touchdowns for Notre Dame (9-3). The Irish fell to 13-14 overall in bowls, a disappointing end for Weis in his first year as their coach. Smith also sat out this year's opener but has improved steadily since then. He completed 19 of 28 passes for a career-high 342 yards and ran for another 66 in 13 attempts. The junior from Cleveland capped his performance with a pair of third-and-long completions on the Buckeyes' final scoring drive. Antonio Pittman, who rushed for 136 yards in 21 carries, broke free on a 60-yard touchdown run to seal the victory with 1:46 to play. Forget the stereotype of plodding, but powerful Ohio State; the Buckeyes won with sheer speed. Ginn caught eight passes for 167 yards. He zigzagged into the end zone on his long run to help the Buckeyes take to a 21-7 halftime en route to their third Fiesta Bowl victory in four years. Holmes caught five passes for 124 yards. Ohio State had a Fiesta Bowl-record 27 first downs. The Buckeyes' 617 yards were third-most in the bowl's 35-year history. The intricate, efficient offense that Weis brought with him from the New England Patriots sputtered early before the Irish mounted a comeback that cut the lead to seven in the fourth quarter. Hawk, Ohio State's Lombardi Award-winning linebacker and the game's defensive MVP, sacked his girlfriend's brother, Quinn, twice. Hawk also ran down Quinn to stop a third-down play early in the fourth quarter. Quinn, a third-team all-American behind Matt Leinart and Vince Young of Texas, completed 29-of-45 for 286 yards but no touchdowns. He was sacked Walker gained 90 yards in 16 attempts. The teams met for only the fifth time in their storied histories, and for the first in a bowl game. The Irish gave up a 617 yards, third-most in Fiesta Bowl history 275 on the ground. A crucial play came when a video replay nullified what would have been an Ohio State turnover in the third quarter. With Notre Dame trailing 21-13 and the Buckeyes driving, Smith threw over the middle to Anthony Gonzalez, who dropped the ball at the Irish 12. Tom Zbikowski picked it up for Notre Dame and ran 88 yards to the end zone. An illegal block would have brought it back to the Buckeyes' 21, but a video review of the play determined Gonzalez juggled the ball and it was ruled an incompletion. Josh Huston kicked a 40-yard field goal and Ohio State led 24-13 with 2:20 to go in the third quarter. Huston's 26-yard field goal with 10:12 to play made it 27-13. Notre Dame mounted its best drive, 80 yards in 13 plays, to cut the lead to 27-20. Walker's 3-yard run was ruled a touchdown after another video review with 5:27 left. Soon, Ohio State's speed took over. Ginn took Smith's pitch on an end around and raced for a touchdown, leaving three Notre Dame Defenders sprawled on the ground with a cutback from the sidelines 10 yards from the end zone. The Irish led 14-7 with 14:16 left in the first half. Later in the quarter, Ohio State took over at its own 2. No matter. Smith scrambled from the 6 to the 15, then connected with Holmes for an 85-yard scoring play. The previous record for longest pass in the Fiesta Bowl was 79 yards from Tennessee's Tee Martin to Peerless Price against Florida State in 1999 and Oregon's Joey Harrington to Samie Parker against Colorado in 2002. It was the final Fiesta Bowl in Sun Devil Stadium. The game moves to the Arizona Cardinals' new stadium in the west Phoenix suburb of Glendale next year.

2006 Sugar Bowl

The 2006 Nokia Sugar Bowl game was played on January 2, 2006, as part of the Bowl Championship Series. This 72nd edition of the Sugar Bowl featured the West Virginia Mountaineers, champions of the Big East, and the Southeastern Conference Champion Georgia Bulldogs. Double-digit underdog West Virginia's upset victory bolstered the Big East's profile in the wake of losing three members to the ACC, and likely preserved the conference's automatic inclusion in the BCS. **The game was played in Atlanta**, as its traditional site, the Louisiana Superdome, was unfit for use in the aftermath of Hurricane Katrina.

2006 Sugar Bowl	Line	1	-	2	-	3	-	4	-	Final
#11 West Virginia	(45.0)	21	-	10	-	0	-	7	-	38
#8 Georgia	(-7.0)	0	-	21	-	7	-	7	-	35

Scoring Summary
West Virginia – Slaton 52 yard run (McAfee kick)
West Virginia – Reynaud 3 yard pass from White (McAfee kick)
West Virginia – Reynaud 13 yard run (McAfee kick)
West Virginia – Slaton 18 yard run (McAfee kick)
Georgia – Lumpkin 34 yard run (Coutu kick)
Georgia – Brown 52 yard run (Coutu kick)
West Virginia – McAfee 27 yard Field goal
Georgia – Pope 4 yard pass from Shockley (Coutu kick)
Georgia – Bryant 34 yard pass from Shockley (Coutu kick)
West Virginia – Slaton 52 yard run (McAfee kick)
Georgia – McClendon 43 yard pass from Shockley (Coutu kick)

Associated Press Sugar Bowl Game Summary - Georgia had the home-field advantage. West Virginia had the chip on its shoulder. Steve Slaton rushed for a record 204 yards and the No. 11 Mountaineers gave a much-needed boost to the beleaguered Big East, upsetting eighth-ranked Georgia 38-35 Monday night in the first Nokia Sugar Bowl played outside of New Orleans. West Virginia (11-1) stunned all those red-clad fans at the Georgia Dome by jumping to a 28-0 lead by the opening minute of the second quarter. The Bulldogs (10-3) rallied, twice closing within a field goal in the second half, but they couldn't finish one of the greatest comebacks in bowl history. Give most of the credit to Slaton, who wasn't even the Mountaineers' best freshman runner in fall camp and didn't crack the starting lineup until the sixth game of the season. Georgia certainly had no answer for the speedy back, who squirted through big holes and left defenders such as All-American safety Greg Blue in the dust on a pair of 52-yard touchdown runs. Slaton scored three touchdowns and eclipsed the previous Sugar Bowl rushing record, a 202-yard performance by Pitt's Tony Dorsett in a national championship-clinching victory over Georgia in 1977. The Mountaineers saved their biggest surprise for the end. Georgia was poised to get the ball back when West Virginia dropped back to punt on fourth-and-6 at the Bulldogs 48. Phil Brady hauled in the long snap but took off running, gaining 10 yards on the fake and a game-clinching first down. The last of Slaton's touchdowns gave the Mountaineers a seemingly comfortable 38-28 lead with 8½ minutes to go. D.J. Shockley brought Georgia back with his third touchdown pass, a 43-yarder to Bryan McClendon with 5:33 left, but never got his hands on the ball again. The teams combined for 1,003 yards, much of it coming in a wild first half that ended with the Mountaineers holding a 31-21 lead. The 72nd Sugar Bowl was shifted to Atlanta after Hurricane Katrina slammed into New Orleans, flooding the Big Easy and leaving the Superdome in no shape to host a Pop Warner game, much less a major bowl. While poignant, the Sugar was the least heralded of the BCS bowls, a distant fourth to the Fiesta matchup between Notre Dame and Ohio State, the Joe Paterno-vs.-Bobby Bowden showdown at the Orange and, of course, the national championship game between No. 1 Southern Cal and No. 2 Texas at the Rose Bowl. But the Fiesta -- a 34-20 romp for Ohio State -- didn't come close on the excitement meter. And both the Orange and Rose will be hard-pressed to produce a game this thrilling. West Virginia also did its part to stymie criticism of the Big East. OK, so the league isn't as strong since Miami and Virginia Tech bolted to the Atlantic Coast Conference, but the Mountaineers proved they're one of the best teams in the country. They certainly came out with something to prove, facing the champion of the powerful Southeastern Conference just 75 miles from its Athens campus. The Mountaineers, who had lost 11 of their last 12 bowl games, jumped on Georgia with two touchdowns apiece by Slaton and Darius Reynaud. Slaton showed his speed on the first of his 52-yard runs, which capped West Virginia's opening possession. His other first-half score came on an 18-yard burst through a tiny hole, the freshman prancing across the goal line in front of Blue. Reynaud caught a 3-yard pass from Pat White, then caught the Bulldogs off guard on a 13-yard reverse that left all but a couple of defenders running the wrong way. But Georgia didn't fold. Kregg Lumpkin got the Bulldogs on the scoreboard with a 34-yard touchdown run, sparking a little life in the mostly Georgia crowd. They were roaring by the time the teams trotted to the locker room, having cut the deficit to a more manageable 10 points. Thomas Brown had a 52-yard touchdown run for the Bulldogs, getting loose after appearing stuffed at the line by the Mountaineers. West Virginia kept the big plays rolling when fullback Owen Schmitt, a transfer from Division III Wisconsin-River Falls, rumbled for 54 yards on a third-and-1 play. But the Georgia defense finally arrived, stuffing Slaton for a 3-yard loss and forcing the Mountaineers to settle for Pat McAfee's 27-yard field goal. Georgia reclaimed the momentum before halftime with an 11-play, 80-yard drive. The Bulldogs converted on fourth-and-1 at their own 42, then Shockley bailed them out on third-and-10 by scrambling away from pressure and delivering a 32-yard pass to Mario Raley. Shockley followed with a 15-yard run, then connected with Leonard Pope on a 4-yard touchdown pass with 58 seconds left in the wild half. With 62 points by halftime, the teams set both Sugar Bowl and BCS records for one half. The biggest difference was turnovers; Shockley and Danny Ware both fumbled the ball away, and the Mountaineers capitalized each time with TDs. Late in the third quarter, Shockley tossed a 34-yard touchdown to A.J. Bryant, pulling the Bulldogs to 31-28. They never got any closer. Shockley completed 20-of-33 passes for 277 yards and also rushed for 71 yards on eight carries. But it wasn't enough against West Virginia, which ripped through the Bulldogs for 382 yards rushing. Schmitt had 82 yards on the ground, while White rushed for 77 and completed 11-of-14 yards for another 120 yards.

Aftermath - West Virginia capped off an 11-1 season ranked #5 in the nation, while Georgia fell to 10-3. The win was the first of four bowl victories for West Virginia QB Pat White. ESPN ranked the 2006 Sugar Bowl #6 on its list of the best major bowl games of the BCS era.

2006 Orange Bowl

The 2006 Orange Bowl, a 2005–2006 BCS game, was played on January 3, 2006. This 72nd edition to the Orange Bowl featured the Penn State Nittany Lions and the Florida State Seminoles. This game was known for being the eighth, and ultimately final meeting, between the two coaches, Joe Paterno of Penn State and Bobby Bowden of Florida State. On July 23, 2012, the NCAA vacated Penn State's win in the game as a result of the Jerry Sandusky child sex abuse scandal; according to NCAA policies on vacated wins, the game officially had no winner. However, on January 16, 2015, the NCAA restored the result, along with 111 others, making Penn State once again the winner.

2006 Orange Bowl	Line	1	2	3	4	OT	2OT	3OT	Final
#3 Penn State	(-9.5)	7	7	0	2	0	7	3	26
#22 Florida State	(47.0)	0	13	0	3	0	7	0	23

Scoring Summary
Penn State – Scott 2 yard run (Kelly kick)
Florida State – Reid 87 yard punt return (Cismesia kick)
Florida State – Booker 57 yard pass from Weatherford (kick failed)
Penn State – Kilmer 24 yard pass from Robinson (Kelly kick)
Penn State – Team safety
Florida State – Cismesia 48 yard Field goal
Penn State – Scott 1 yard run (Kelly kick)
Florida State – Dean 1 yard run (Cismesia kick)
Penn State – Kelly 29 yard Field goal

Associated Press Orange Bowl Game Summary - This really was one for the ages. For more than four hours, Joe Paterno and Bobby Bowden paced the Orange Bowl sidelines, searching for offense and enduring one missed kick after another. Finally, in the third overtime, at 1 a.m. Wednesday, Kevin Kelly made a 29-yard field goal, giving Paterno and Penn State a 26-23 victory over Bowden's Florida State Seminoles. And one of the most thrilling anyone's ever seen. Paterno had said he didn't want the game to be about him and the 76-year-old Bowden, who rank 1-2 in career coaching victories. It turned out to be about missed opportunities, improbable twists, epic length -- and nearly unbearable suspense. Kelly missed field goal attempts of 29 and 38 yards that would have won the game. It was second down, and Paterno called for a fake field goal. But Florida State's defensive alignment negated that idea. Kelly kicked the winner instead. Florida State counterpart Gary Cismesia missed an extra point in the first half and field goal tries of 44 and 38 yards in overtime -- a familiar problem for Bowden. Missed or blocked field goals have helped the Miami Hurricanes beat him six times, including in the 2004 Orange Bowl. The No. 3-ranked Nittany Lions finished 11-1, with the only loss coming when they gave up a touchdown to Michigan on the game's final play. Paterno's best season in 11 years represented a big rebound after going 7-16 in 2003-04. No. 22 Florida State fell to 8-5, Bowden's worst season since 1981. Also concluding his 40th season as a head coach, he tried to shrug off the defeat. Moments after the game ended, the two old friends came together, stood shoulder-to-shoulder in a crush of cameras and microphones and exchanged warm words. In a bowl season that started before Christmas and has included plenty of lackluster affairs, this one really was worth staying up for. And it served as a perfect warmup to the biggest game yet: No. 1 USC vs. No. 2 Texas in the Rose Bowl on Wednesday. Florida State mostly contained Big Ten MVP Michael Robinson, who threw a touchdown pass with six seconds left in the first half but was limited to 253 yards passing and 21 rushing. One scrum knocked off his helmet. He hit two clutch completions to give Penn State a chance to win the game in regulation. But Kelly, hampered by a shaky hold, was wide left on a 29-yard field goal attempt with 35 seconds left. Cismesia kicked a 48-yard field goal with 4:08 left in regulation to tie the game at 16-all, but on the first series of overtime he was wide right on a 44-yard attempt. Then it was Kelly's turn. He again pushed a try wide left, this time a 38-yarder with a perfect hold.

Austin Scott's 1-yard run put Penn State ahead. B.J. Dean pulled the Seminoles even with a 1-yard scoring run. After Cismesia's 38-yard attempt hit the right upright, Kelly finally came through. The kick gave Paterno his 354th career win, second in Division I-A only to Bowden's 359. Paterno improved to 7-1 against Bowden. The only loss came the last time they met, when Florida State beat Penn State in the 1990 Blockbuster Bowl -- also at Miami. With his first win in the Orange Bowl since 1974, Paterno improved to 21-10-1 in bowl games. Both offenses spent much of the game going backward, but there were fireworks, too. Ethan Kilmer made a leaping 24-yard scoring reception with six seconds left in the first half to give Penn State a 14-13 halftime lead. The Seminoles scored two touchdowns in 80 seconds -- on an Orange Bowl-record 87-yard punt return by Willie Reid, and on a 57-yard reception by Lorenzo Booker. But they totaled only six first downs before Drew Weatherford drove them 65 yards for the tying field goal late in the fourth quarter. Penn State linebacker Paul Posluszny, the Butkus Award winner, hurt his right knee during the drive and was carted off the field. Tony Hunt, a 1,047-yard rusher for Penn State, departed in the first quarter with a left ankle injury. Scott replaced him and ran for 110 yards and two touchdowns. The teams punted 20 times, all in the first three periods. In the second half, they swapped eight possessions before either made a first down -- on a pass-interference penalty. Defense produced the first score of the half. Weatherford, working from his end zone, was called for intentional grounding -- a safety -- when Penn State's Jim Shaw forced a throw. Leading 16-13, the Nittany Lions had a chance to take control with nine minutes left. But on first-and-goal at the 4, Florida State recovered a botched snap. The Seminoles netted 26 yards rushing and were penalized 129 yards. Despite the lack of punch, they stayed in the game thanks to two big plays. They trailed 7-0 when Reid weaved up the middle on a runback, cut left and dashed to the end zone. The punt return broke the Orange Bowl record of 80 yards by former Florida State athletic director Cecil "Hootie" Ingram for Alabama in 1953.

2006 Rose Bowl (BCS National Championship Game)

The 2006 Rose Bowl Game, played on January 4, 2006 at the Rose Bowl in Pasadena, California, served as BCS National Championship Game. It featured the only two unbeaten teams of the 2005 NCAA Division I-A football season: the defending Rose Bowl champion and reigning Big 12 Conference champion Texas Longhorns played Pacific-10 Conference titleholders and two-time defending AP national champions, the USC Trojans. The game was a back-and-forth contest; Texas's victory was not secured until the game's final 19 seconds. Vince Young, the Texas Quarterback, and Michael Huff, a Texas safety, were named the offensive and defensive Rose Bowl Players of The Game. ESPN named Young's fourth-down, game-winning touchdown run the fifth-greatest play in college-football history. The game is the highest-rated BCS game in TV history with 21.7% of households watching it. It is widely considered one of the greatest games in college-football history. Texas's Rose Bowl win was the 800th victory in school history and the Longhorns ended the season ranked third in Division I history in both wins and winning percentage (.7143). It was only the third time that the two top-ranked teams had faced each other in Rose Bowl history, with the 1963 Rose Bowl and 1969 Rose Bowl games being the others. The 92nd-annual Rose Bowl Game was played, as it is every year, at the Rose Bowl Stadium in Pasadena, California, in the United States. This was the final game ever called by longtime broadcaster Keith Jackson (as well as the final Rose Bowl to telecast under ABC Sports branding); the 2007 Rose Bowl would be an ESPN on ABC presentation. This was the first college football game to feature two Heisman Trophy winners in the same starting lineup. USC's Quarterback Matt Leinart and running back Reggie Bush won the award in 2004 and 2005, respectively, although Bush would later forfeit the award.

Pre-game buildup - USC entered the game on a 34-game winning streak. It was the longest active streak in Division I-A. Texas brought the second-longest active streak, having won 19-straight games and entered as the defending Rose Bowl champion, after defeating Michigan in the 2005 Rose Bowl. The teams' combined 53-game win streak was an NCAA record for teams playing each other. The game was also the first to pit against each other the teams ranked first and second in every iteration of the BCS standings. The 2006 Rose Bowl was, in the eyes of many, the most-anticipated matchup in college-football history. Both teams were considered good enough to win the National Championship had they existed in different years instead of having to play each other. USC had been ranked No. 1 since the preseason and Texas had held the No. 2 spot that entire time.

2006 Rose Bowl	Line	1	-	2	-	3	-	4	-	Final
#2 Texas	(70.5)	0	-	16	-	7	-	18	-	41
#1 USC	(-7.0)	7	-	3	-	14	-	14	-	38

Scoring Summary
USC – White 4 yard run (Danelo kick)
Texas – Pino 46 yard Field goal
Texas – S. Young 12 yard run (Kick failed)
Texas – Taylor 30 yard run (Pino kick)
USC – Danelo 43 yard Field goal
USC – White 3 yard run (Danelo kick)
Texas – V. Young 14 yard run (Pino kick)
USC – White 12 yard run (Danelo kick)
USC – Bush 26 yard run (Danelo kick)
Texas – Pino 34 yard Field goal
USC – Jarrett 22 yard pass from Leinart (Danelo kick)
Texas – V. Young 17 yard run (Pino kick)
Texas – V. Young 8 yard run (Pino kick)

Analysis and aftermath - Vince Young was named the Rose Bowl's MVP for the second time in as many years (the first time being the 2005 Rose Bowl). He is only the fourth player in Rose Bowl history (and the only player from the Big 12 Conference) to accomplish this feat. Though USC converted on 57 percent of third downs (to only 27 percent for the Longhorns), it was unable to gain two yards on Texas's defense when doing so might have ensured a Trojan victory. The Trojans also hurt themselves with two turnovers in Texas territory early in the game. Mack Brown, previously maligned for his inability to win big games, thus ended the fourth-longest winning streak in Division I-A history – and the longest since a 35-game streak by Toledo ended in 1971 – and, behind Young, who accounted for 839 yards of total offense in his two Rose Bowl appearances, won the first national title for Texas since 1970. Young accounted for 467 yards in the championship game, which stands as the best performance ever in a BCS Championship game. By winning, Texas assured itself a first place ranking in the USA Today coaches' poll, and its achievement was confirmed when AP polling sportswriters unanimously voted Texas number one on January 5, 2006; USC finished a unanimous second in each poll. On January 11, 2006, Young was awarded the Manning Award, given annually to the nation's top Quarterback. Unlike any other major college-football award, the Manning is based partly on bowl results. This was longtime ABC Sports announcer Keith Jackson's last game and was also the last college-football game aired on ABC under the ABC Sports name, as ABC's sports division began going by the name of corporate sibling ESPN on ABC in September 2006. The victory, Texas' 800th of all time, gave UT its fourth national championship in football. Since the game, the media, coaches, and other commentators have heaped praise upon the Texas team, Vince Young, and the Rose Bowl performance. For instance, Sports Illustrated called the game "perhaps the most stunning bowl performance ever". Both the Rose Bowl win as well as the Longhorns' overall season have both been cited as standing among the greatest performances in college-football history by publications such as College Football News, the Atlanta Journal-Constitution, Scout.com, and Sports Illustrated. The Longhorns and the Trojans were together awarded the 2006 ESPY Award by ESPN for the "Best Game" in any sport. In December 2006, both Sports Illustrated and Time Magazine picked the game as the Best Sports Moment in 2006. Voters on Yahoo Sports also voted it as the Sports Story of the Year for both college football and overall, edging out 12 other stories in the overall voting and receiving 13,931 votes out of 65,641. In the days that followed the Longhorns' victory, the Trinity River in Dallas mysteriously turned a "burnt orange" color. Authorities said that it may have been caused by someone dumping dye into the river. The game received the highest Nielsen ratings for the Rose Bowl since the 1986 Rose Bowl between UCLA and Iowa. In 2007, ESPN compiled a list of the top 100 plays in college football history; Vince Young's game-winning touchdown in the 2006 Rose Bowl ranked number 5. The 2006 Rose Bowl Game and its unreviewed, controversial officials' rulings have been cited as a key reason the NCAA Football Rules Committee added a coach's challenge the following season (ironically USC opted to go without instant replay for its game that season against Notre Dame and then won on the final play when Reggie Bush illegally shoved Matt Leinart over the goal line).

2006 Poinsettia Bowl

The 2006 Poinsettia Bowl was between the TCU Horned Frogs and the NIU Huskies on December 19, 2006 at Qualcomm Stadium in San Diego, California. TCU defeated NIU 37–7 in this game, which was the second year in the bowl's existence.

2006 Poinsettia Bowl	Line	1	-	2	-	3	-	4	-	Final
Northern Illinois	(46.5)	0	-	0	-	0	-	7	-	7
#25 TCU	(-12.5)	6	-	10	-	14	-	7	-	37

Scoring Summary
TCU - Hobbs 4 yd run (Kick blocked)
TCU - Ballard 10 yd run (Manfredini kick)
TCU - Manfredini 25 yd Field goal
TCU - Ballard 1 yd run (Manfredini kick)
TCU - Ballard 6 yd run (Manfredini kick)
Northern Illinois - Tranchitella 32 yd blocked punt return (Nendick kick)
TCU - Hecht 6 yd pass from Ballard (Manfredini kick)

Associated Press Poinsettia Bowl Game Summary - The most exciting ball carrier on the field, at times, was TCU Quarterback Jeff Ballard. It certainly wasn't Northern Illinois' Garrett Wolfe, who ended his career looking more like a third stringer than the national rushing leader. Penned in by a bunch of tough Horned Frogs, Wolfe was held to 28 yards and No. 25 TCU won a San Diego County Credit Union Poinsettia Bowl mismatch against Northern Illinois 37-7 on Tuesday night. The Horned Frogs stopped Garrett cold, and TCU's offense kept trotting back onto the field. Ballard ran for three touchdowns and threw for another. Ballard looked more like a running back as he scored on runs of 10, 1 and 6 yards. He threw a 6-yard TD pass to tight end Brent Hecht and finished with 258 passing yards. There was a 100-yard rusher -- TCU's Lonta Hobbs, who had 109 yards and one TD on 18 carries. Wolfe, a senior from Chicago, came in leading the nation with an average of 158.3 yards rushing and 178.9 all-purpose yards. The Horned Frogs, though, were fourth nationally in run defense after allowing only 67.6 yards per game. TCU kept alive its string of not allowing a 100-yard rusher, one of only four teams to do so this year. Blake had two of TCU's five sacks. NIU had terrible field position most of the night, and TCU brought its safeties close to the line to stuff the box against Garrett. Wolfe, who carried 20 times, came dangerously close to his career-low of 24 yards set in his first game, the 2004 season opener. The Huskies had only five first downs and 60 yards of total offense, compared to 23 first downs and 456 yards for TCU. Wolfe was thrown for losses on four of his 10 carries in the first half, when accounted he for just 8 yards. TCU (11-2) won 11 games for the third time in four years, all under coach Gary Patterson. NIU finished 7-6. The Huskies had minus-13 yards and went three-and-out six straight times before Dan Nicholson completed a 62-yard pass to Matt Simon on third-and-12 from the Huskies' 11-yard line in the second quarter. All that did was set up a missed 51-yard field goal by Chris Nendick. Patterson said Wolfe had poise, patience and great vision, but added that the Horned Frogs had worked on taking away the cutback. NIU's only score came when John Tranchitella returned a blocked punt 32 yards with 14:14 left. Jarret Carter blocked Brian Cortney's punt and the ball bounced back toward Cortney's hands, but Tranchitella swooped in and grabbed it. NIU blocked two punts and a PAT. Hobbs scored on a 4-yard run on TCU's first drive. Early in the second quarter, Ballard dropped back to pass on third-and-9 from the NIU 10. He scrambled left, cut inside and was hit hard as he dived into the end zone. Chris Manfredini kicked a 25-yard field goal as the clock expired for a 16-0 halftime lead. Ballard scored twice in just less than 3 minutes in the third quarter for a 30-0 lead. He ran a 1-yard keeper, then added a 6-yard run when he rolled left, couldn't find a receiver and tumbled into the end zone. Ballard was 19-of-29 passing. Nicholson was 6-of-18 for 80 yards, with one interception.

2006 Las Vegas Bowl

The 2006 Las Vegas Bowl was between the Oregon Ducks and the Brigham Young University Cougars. The Las Vegas Bowl gets its first choice of bowl-eligible teams from the Mountain West Conference (MWC) and the fourth/fifth choice (alternating every year) of bowl-eligible teams from the Pacific-10 Conference (Pac-10). This bowl game was played on December 22, 2006 at 40,000-seat Sam Boyd Stadium in Whitney, Nevada, USA where this bowl game has been played since 1992. It was broadcast on ESPN and ESPNHD. Since 2001, the game has featured a matchup of teams from the MWC and Pac-10.

2006 Las Vegas Bowl	Line	1	-	2	-	3	-	4	-	Final
#19 BYU	(-3.0)	0	-	7	-	17	-	14	-	38
Oregon	(60.0)	0	-	0	-	0	-	8	-	8

Scoring Summary
BYU – McLaughlin 24 yard Field goal
BYU – Brown 6 yard run (McLaughlin kick)
BYU – Harline 41 yard pass from Beck (McLaughlin kick)
BYU – Brown 4 yard run (McLaughlin kick)
BYU – Beck 14 yard run (McLaughlin kick)
Oregon – Paysinger 48 yard pass from Dixon (Johnson run)
BYU – Tonga 17 yard pass from Beck (McLaughlin kick)

Associated Press Las Vegas Bowl Game Summary - Brigham Young Quarterback John Beck stood on the podium above a throng of blue-clad fans so dense the green field below them was barely visible. After five years of frustration and a decade of postseason futility, BYU finally had something to celebrate. Beck passed for 375 yards and two touchdowns, leading the No. 19 Cougars to a 38-8 victory over Oregon on Thursday night in the Pioneer PureVision Las Vegas Bowl. BYU (11-2) closed the season with 10 straight victories, capping the streak with its first bowl win since the 1996 season. Beck was 28-for-46 with two interceptions and got plenty of help. Curtis Brown ran for 120 yards and two TDs, Jonny Harline, voted game MVP, caught nine passes for 181 yards and Justin Robinson intercepted two passes for BYU, which shut out the Ducks (7-6) through three quarters. Beck, Brown, Harline and Robinson were all playing their final game for the Cougars. BYU hadn't had a winning season since going 12-2 in 2001. Oregon lost it's fourth in a row and was never close after BYU scored 17 points in the second quarter. The Ducks had just 120 yards of offense through three quarters and didn't score until Brian Paysinger caught a 47-yard pass from Dennis Dixon with 10:27 left in the game. The Ducks added a 2-point conversion to cut the lead to 31-8. If Oregon was thinking about a miracle comeback, it didn't last long. BYU recovered the ensuing onside kick and scored 1:13 later on a 17-yard pass from Beck to Manase Tonga. Beck also ran for a 13-yard score that put BYU ahead 31-0 early in the fourth quarter. Cougar's fans who packed Sam Boyd Stadium with a record crowd of 44,615 stormed the field after the final play in celebration of the BYU blowout. The Cougars had lost four straight bowl games since beating Kansas State 19-15 in the Cotton Bowl on Jan. 1, 1997. Oregon tried rotating Quarterbacks again with Brady Leaf making his second career start and the quicker Dixon coming in to give the BYU defense a different look. It didn't work. The Ducks allowed two sacks on their first series and Leaf and Dixon combined to throw for 166 yards. Both threw an interception and Oregon finished with 260 yards and lost its fourth straight bowl. It was the largest crowd in stadium history, breaking the previous high of 42,075 fans for UNLV's game against Wisconsin in 2002, and the fans were nearly all wearing BYU dark blue. During the postgame trophy presentation, they chanted "B-Y-U!" Beck, the second-leading passer in school history, stood on the podium with Brown -- BYU's all-time leading rusher -- and led the fans in the BYU fight song. Bronco Mendenhall, who has turned around BYU in just two seasons since taking over after Gary Crowton's resignation in 2004. Crowton, now Oregon's offensive coordinator, witnessed many of the players he brought to Provo playing like the BYU greats of the past. Beck started slowly and had four passes dropped. He started focusing more on Harline and it paid off with a field goal and two touchdowns in the second quarter. Beck and Harline connected on a 41-yard pass in the second quarter that put BYU ahead 17-0, then Brown scored on a 4-yard run just before halftime and BYU led 24-0. Harline's one-handed grab for 18 yards helped set up the game's first touchdown.

2006 New Orleans Bowl

The 2006 R+L Carriers New Orleans Bowl featured the Troy Trojans and the Rice Owls. Rice was making its first bowl appearance since 1961.

2006 New Orleans Bowl	Line	1	-	2	-	3	-	4	-	Final
Rice	(-5.0)	7	-	3	-	0	-	7	-	17
Troy	(53.5)	21	-	7	-	3	-	10	-	41

Scoring Summary
Troy - Haugabook 2 yard run (Whibbs kick)
Troy - Banks 3 yard pass from Haugabook (Whibbs kick)
Rice - Falco 11 yard pass from Armstrong (Fangmeier kick)
Troy - Terry 56 yard pass from Haugabook (Whibbs kick)
Rice - Fangmeier 43 yard Field goal
Troy - Davis 7 yard pass from Haugabook (Whibbs kick)
Troy - Whibbs 26 yard Field goal
Troy - Whibbs 25 yard Field goal
Rice - Dillard 1 yard pass from Armstrong (Fangmeier kick)
Troy - Rutledge 5 yard pass from Haugabook (Whibbs kick)

Associated Press New Orleans Bowl Game Summary - Omar Haugabook was Troy's postseason star, too. The Sun Belt player of the year threw four touchdown passes and ran for another score to lead Troy to its first bowl victory, 41-17 over Rice on Friday night in the R+L Carriers New Orleans Bowl. It was only the second bowl appearance for the Trojans (8-5), who moved up to Division I-A in 2002. Troy earned the bowl bid with its first Sun Belt title. Haugabook, the unanimous MVP of the game, completed 14 of 28 for 217 yards. He also picked up 92 of Troy's 148 yards. Rice (7-6), coming off its first winning season since 1993, and making its first bowl appearance since 1961, was seeking its first postseason victory since 1954. The Conference USA representative was favored going into the game but could not cope with the Trojans' defense. Rice's Joel Armstrong, pressured all night, was intercepted five times and sacked four times. He completed 35 of 54 passes for 305 yards and a touchdown. Rice receiver Jarett Dillard kept his touchdown streak alive. He caught a 1-yard TD pass in the fourth quarter to stretch the streak to 15 games, dating to last season. His 13-game touchdown streak this season set an NCAA record, breaking the mark of 12 set by

Randy Moss in 1997 and matched by Larry Fitzgerald in 2003. Troy, which averaged 21 points a game this year, was up 21-7 after the first quarter. On the first possession, Mykeal Terry's 40-yard reception put the Trojans on Rice's 1. Three plays later, Haugabook's 2-yard touchdown run put Troy on the scoreboard. Minutes later, Armstrong's first pass attempt of the game was intercepted by Boris Lee, who took it back 22 yards to the Rice 1. Haugabook put the Trojans up 14-0 with a 3-yard scoring pass to Gary Banks. Armstrong's 11-yard TD pass to Mike Falco cut Troy's lead to 14-7. Haugabook stretched the Trojans' first-quarter margin with a 56-yard touchdown pass to Terry. After Rice's 43-yard field goal in the second quarter, Haugabook hit Andrew Davis with a 7-yard touchdown pass to put Troy up 28-10 at halftime. The only score in the third quarter was a 25-yard field goal that boosted Troy's lead to 31-10. Kicker Greg Whibbs made it 34-10 in the fourth quarter with a 28-yarder. Haugabook closed out the scoring with a 5-yard TD pass to Toris Rutledge. It was the first bowl game played in the Superdome since Hurricane Katrina devastated the city. The New Orleans Bowl was played in Lafayette last year.

2006 Armed Forces Bowl

The 2006 edition to the Armed Forces Bowl, the 4th edition (previously known as the "Fort Worth Bowl"), featured the Tulsa Golden Hurricane, and the Utah Utes, both former members of the Western Athletic Conference. In addition to the name change the bowl would be sponsored for the first time by Bell Helicopter Textron, the Fort-Worth based defense contractor.

2006 Armed Forces Bowl	Line	1	-	2	-	3	-	4	-	Final
Tulsa	(49.0)	0	-	7	-	0	-	6	-	13
Utah	(-2.0)	3	-	6	-	10	-	6	-	25

Scoring Summary
Utah - Sakoda 45 yard Field goal
Tulsa - Smith 1 yard run (Tracy kick)
Utah - Sakoda 39 yard Field goal
Utah - Sakoda 41 yard Field goal
Utah - Casteel 14 yard lateral run (Sakoda kick)
Utah - Sakoda 34 yard Field goal
Tulsa - Smith 1 yard run (Kick failed)
Utah - Weddle 4 yard run (Kick failed)

Associated Press Armed Forces Bowl Game Summary - Fittingly, the ball was in Utah defensive standout Eric Weddle's hands when the Bell Helicopter Armed Forces Bowl ended. Weddle had an interception on the final play Saturday night, only a minute after scoring on a 4-yard run, to cap the Utes' 25-13 victory over Tulsa. Utah has won six straight bowl games, matching the longest active streak. It was Weddle's final start at Utah, where in a 48-game career he was a two-time Mountain West Conference defensive player of the year who also got plenty of snaps at Quarterback and running back while also holding and returning kicks. The Utes (8-5) have won all their bowl games since 1999, including two years ago when they were the first non-BCS team to play in the Bowl Championship Series and beat Pittsburgh 35-7 in the Fiesta Bowl to cap an undefeated season. Weddle was the holder on all four field goals by Louis Sakoda -- who was selected the game's MVP. Weddle also ran 10 times for 56 yards, including two runs to set up the other Utah touchdown, recovered a fumble and had six tackles. Brett Ratliff was 23-of-34 passing for 240 yards and was credited with a 10-yard touchdown pass in the third quarter, though it was a designed catch-and-pitch similar to a score the Utes had in their Fiesta Bowl romp. Brian Hernandez caught the ball near the line of scrimmage and pitched to Brent Casteel, who ran around the left end and leaped into the end zone. Boston College also has won six straight bowls. The Eagles have a chance to extend their streak next Saturday against Navy in the Meineke Car Care Bowl. Paul Smith scored on a pair of 1-yard keepers for Tulsa (8-5), which finished a once-promising season with its fourth loss in five games. Sakoda kicked a 41-yard field goal on the final play of the first half to give Utah a 9-7 lead. The Utes put the game out of reach by scoring on their first two possessions after halftime, the second when they started at their own 1 after a punt. Utah's latest bowl victory came on the TCU campus, where it played for the first time since a September 2005 game when the Utes' school-record 18-game winning streak ended in a 23-20 overtime loss against the Horned Frogs. On the opening drive after halftime, Weddle took direct snaps on consecutive plays for runs of 7 and 10 yards. That set the Utes up at the 10 for the catch-and-pitch TD that made it 16-7. He carried six straight times on the final offensive series. Weddle also threw a touchdown pass this season and scored three times on defense -- two interception returns and one fumble recovery. After Utah started at its own 1, Ratliffe threw a 7-yard pass to Derrek Richards and ran for 12 yards on the next play. The Utes gained 92 yards on the drive, making up for two 5-yard penalties, before they had to settle for Sakoda's 34-yard field goal. Sakoda kicked a career-long 45-yard field goal on Utah's opening possession of the game. He added a 39-yarder midway through the second quarter. The game provided a first-time matchup of head coaches who were childhood friends. The fathers of Whittingham and Kragthorpe were on Lavell Edwards' staff together at BYU from 1973-79. Smith's 1-yard keeper put Tulsa ahead 7-3 early in the second quarter, only after the play was reviewed to confirm the ball didn't pop out of his hands until after he stretched it across the goal line. That ended an 80-yard drive that almost never got started for the Golden Hurricane after punt returner Idris Moss fumbled. Two Utah players missed chances to recover before freshman linebacker Mike Bryan emerged from the bottom of the pile with the ball. Tulsa finished with only 254 total yards -- 146 below its season average that was second-best in Conference USA.

2006 New Mexico Bowl

The 2006 New Mexico Bowl was held on December 23, 2006 at University Stadium on the University of New Mexico campus in Albuquerque. The game, telecast on ESPN, featured the San Jose State Spartans from the WAC and the hometown New Mexico Lobos from the Mountain West Conference. The game was the inaugural New Mexico Bowl and the first bowl game held in the state. San Jose State controlled the action all game long, jumping out to a 20–3 lead before New Mexico tacked on 9 points in the final few minutes. With the loss, New Mexico's postseason drought was extended to 45 years.

2006 New Mexico Bowl	Line	1	-	2	-	3	-	4	-	Final
New Mexico	(-3.5)	0	-	3	-	0	-	9	-	12
San Jose State	(48.5)	0	-	13	-	7	-	0	-	20

Scoring Summary
San Jose State – Broussard 76 yard pass from Tafralis (Strubeck kick)
San Jose State – Jones 36 yard pass from Tafralis (kick missed)
New Mexico – Byrd 40 yard field goal
San Jose State – Jones 24 yard pass from Tafralis (Strubeck kick),
New Mexico - Team Safety
New Mexico – Smith 15 yard pass from Nelson (Byrd kick)

Associated Press New Mexico Bowl Game Summary - San Jose State linebacker Matt Castelo saw New Mexico halfback Rodney Ferguson hit the hole near the goal line and prepared for a collision. Ferguson never made it to the end zone. Castelo hit Ferguson and his helmet knocked the ball out and right into fellow linebacker Damaja Jones' hands. In a season where San Jose State's defense carried the Spartans to their first bowl game in 16 years, Castelo and Jones teamed up for what may have been the biggest stop of the year. Adam Tafralis threw three touchdown passes and San Jose State beat New Mexico 20-12 on Saturday in the inaugural New Mexico Bowl, extending the Lobos' postseason drought to 45 years. One big pass play by Tafralis and that costly fumble by Ferguson -- both in the first half -- set the tone for the Spartans' first bowl win outside of California. Jones returned Ferguson's fumble 57 yards to the New Mexico 37. Although the Spartans didn't score on that drive, they had the momentum for good. New Mexico (6-7) hasn't won a bowl game since it beat Western Michigan in the 1961 Aviation Bowl and is 0-5 since 1997. For the Spartans (9-4), the win provided a final highlight in a season in which they won more games than they had in the three previous seasons. No doubt the game turned on Ferguson's fumble. Tafralis, who was 11-of-18 for 209 yards, threw scoring passes of 36 and 24 yards to James Jones and 76 yards to John Broussard. The pass to Broussard on the first play of the second quarter -- in which New Mexico's defense totally blew the coverage -- got the Spartans' offense rolling. New Mexico's only touchdown came with 15 seconds left in the game on a 15-yard pass from Chris Nelson to Marcus Smith. The rest of the Lobos' scoring consisted of a 40-yard field goal by Kenny Byrd with 1:11 left in the second quarter and a safety when San Jose State punter Waylon Prather stepped out of the end zone with 1:08 left. Byrd's field goal was his 25th straight from 40 yards or closer and the first made field goal by New Mexico in 10 bowl appearances. San Jose State struck first after the teams combined for seven punts in the first quarter. Tafralis found Broussard 20 yards behind the nearest Lobo. Broussard caught the pass at the 35 and easily scored. New Mexico came right back with a drive that started with DeAndre Wright's kickoff return to the San Jose State 40. Eight plays later the Lobos had a first-and-goal at the 1. The Spartans' defense toughened and on third-and-goal from the 2, Ferguson fumbled. The Spartans made it 13-0 on Tafralis' 36-yard pass to James Jones with 3:59 left in the first half. James Jones caught the ball near the sideline at the New Mexico 16 and slipped out of the grasp of Wright. Matt Strubeck missed the extra point. The Lobos' offense had 377 total yards but was stagnant most of the day. Neither freshman Quarterback Donovan Porterie, who started, nor Nelson, who played in the second half, could sustain drives. What plays did work often were erased by holding penalties and three second-half fumbles, including one by wide receiver Travis Brown at the San Jose State 1 with just over 3 minutes left. Ferguson, who led the Mountain West Conference in rushing this season, had 102 yards on 22 carries. James Jones and Broussard each had 106 yards receiving, Jones with six catches and Broussard with four.

2006 PapaJohns.com Bowl

The 2006 PapaJohns.com Bowl was the first PapaJohns.com bowl game. It was played between the East Carolina Pirates and the South Florida Bulls at Legion Field in Birmingham, Alabama. East Carolina University represented Conference USA and the University of South Florida represented the Big East Conference. The game resulted in a 24–7 South Florida victory. In the inaugural game, South Florida's Benjamin Williams scored the game's first points just over ninety seconds into the game as one of his two touchdowns on the day and earned the game's MVP honors. Notably, South Florida had previously been a member of C-USA. Moreover, East Carolina's then head coach Skip Holtz, would later become USF head coach Jim Leavitt's successor following the 2009 season.

2006 PapaJohns.com Bowl	Line	1	-	2	-	3	-	4	-	Final
East Carolina	(43.0)	7	-	0	-	0	-	7	-	7
South Florida	(-5.0)	14	-	10	-	0	-	0	-	24

Scoring Summary
South Florida - Benjamin 16 yard run (Alvarado kick)
South Florida - Benjamin 1 yard run (Alvarado kick)
East Carolina - Good 48 yard pass from Pinckney (Hartman kick)
South Florida - Jackson 37 yard pass from Grothe (Alvarado kick)
South Florida - Alvarado 38 yard Field goal

Associated Press Papa John's Bowl Game Summary - South Florida started fast, made clutch defensive stops and cashed in on a series of fourth-down gambles. Bowl neophytes? The Bulls hardly looked the part Saturday in a 24-7 victory over East Carolina in the inaugural PapaJohns.com Bowl, the first bowl win for the decade-old program. South Florida's only previous bowl appearance was a shutout loss last year in the Meineke Car Care Bowl. But a team that had ended the regular season with an upset win over West Virginia might have topped that one for the Bulls' biggest victory. The Bulls played the scoreless second half without Quarterback Matt Grothe. The Big East freshman of the year was kicked in the right shin in the second quarter and returned only for the next and final series of the half, but the defense kept turning back East Carolina (7-6). Plus, the Bulls went 5-for-5 on fourth-down conversions on drives that resulted in 17 points. Struggling to make a comeback, the Pirates drove inside the South Florida 30 five times in the second half only to fall short. Sacks, a missed field goal, a fumble and a failed fourth-and-goal pass doomed the threats on trips into the so-called red zone. He said the Bulls had "the fastest defense we've played all year." South Florida racked up six sacks, including two after East Carolina set up first down from the 4-yard line on that late drive led by backup Quarterback Rob Kass. Fittingly, the game ended with the Pirates at the Bulls 12, coming up short once again. In the first bowl game at Legion Field since the 1990 Hall of Fame, East Carolina outgained South Florida 317-286 in total yards. The Bulls jumped ahead with two touchdowns in the first 7 minutes. They kept three scoring drives alive with fourth-down conversions and got an early gift East Carolina's James Pinkney couldn't handle a low shotgun snap on the game's second play and South Florida recovered at the 16. Benjamin Williams scored on a draw on the next play. He scored again on a 1-yard plunge on fourth-and-goal and finished with 67 yards on 17 carries. Both Quarterbacks came up with big touchdown passes after that. First, Pinkney hit Bobby Good for a 48-yard touchdown on third-and-26. Then, Grothe found Amarri Jackson for a 37-yarder on third-and-10. Grothe returned for one series after being helped off the field but didn't play after that. Grothe and backup Pat Julmiste were both efficient if not spectacular. Grothe was 6-for-10 for 81 yards. Julmiste was 6-of-8 for 49 yards and accomplished Leavitt's main second-half goal of avoiding turnovers. Pinkney finished his college career with an ineffective performance and walked off the field late with a heavily iced left elbow. He completed just eight passes in 25 attempts for 125 yards and took a pounding from the defenders. Kass was 10-of-19 for 138 yards. Holtz said he didn't have any information about Pinkney's injury. Good finished with five catches for 116 yards. They needed to start the game better, too. South Florida defensive coordinator Wally Burnham missed the game following the death of his mother, Cora Burnham, of congestive heart failure earlier in the day. That served as motivation for the players.

2006 Hawai'i Bowl

The 2006 Sheraton Hawai'i Bowl was the 5th Hawai'i Bowl ever played. It was played on December 24, 2006, at Aloha Stadium in Honolulu. The game matched the Hawai'i Warriors against the Arizona State Sun Devils and was televised on ESPN. This game received extra attention because Hawai'i Quarterback Colt Brennan was poised to set the NCAA single season record for touchdown passes in a season. Entering the game, Brennan had 53 touchdown passes, one short of University of Houston Quarterback David Klingler's mark of 54 set in 1990. Brennan finished the game having completed 33-of-42 passes for 559 yards and five touchdowns, setting the new single-season record at 58. He shared MVP honors with wide receiver Jason Rivers, who tied a school mark with 14 receptions and set a record with 308 receiving yards, the most in a college bowl game since the NCAA began keeping official records in 1937.

2006 Hawaii Bowl	Line	1	-	2	-	3	-	4	-	Final
Hawaii	(-7.5)	0	-	3	-	21	-	17	-	41
Arizona State	(72.5)	3	-	7	-	0	-	14	-	24

Scoring Summary
Arizona State - Ainsworth 44 yard FG
Hawaii - Kelly 42 yard FG
Arizona State - Smith 37 yard pass from Carpenter (Ainsworth kick)
Hawaii - Rivers 38 yard pass from Brennan (Kelly kick)
Hawaii - Grice-Mullen 7 yard pass from Brennan (Kelly kick)
Hawaii - Grice-Mullen 36 yard pass from Brennan (Kelly kick)
Hawaii - Kelly 43 yard FG
Arizona State - Torain 12-yard run (Ainsworth kick)
Arizona State - Jones 4 yard pass from Carpenter (Ainsworth kick)
Hawaii - Bess 21 yard pass from Brennan (Kelly kick)
Hawaii - Rivers 79 yard pass from Brennan (Kelly kick)

Associated Press Hawaii Bowl Game Summary - Containing Colt Brennan for a half is impressive -- an entire game is almost impossible. Brennan broke the NCAA single season record for touchdown passes, throwing five in the second half to lead Hawaii to a 41-24 victory over Arizona State on Sunday night in the Hawaii Bowl. Brennan, who finished the season with 58 TD passes. Brennan, 33-of-42 for 559 yards, threw a 7-yard scoring pass to Ryan Grice-Mullen on the Warriors' second series of the second half to break the previous mark of 54 set by Houston's David Klingler in 1990, also against the Sun Devils. Jason Rivers also tied a school mark with 14 receptions and set the Hawaii record with 308 yards, the most in a bowl game since 1937. NCAA records don't go back any further. Grice-Mullen grabbed the record TD pass with one hand, made a move and leaped across the goal line for the touchdown that gave Hawaii a 17-10 lead. After throwing the pass, Brennan hugged Coach June Jones and waved No. 1 as teammates lifted the junior into the air and the crowd of 40,623 cheered wildly. Brennan tied the record on the previous series, throwing a 38-yard pass to a wide open Rivers for his 54th TD strike. Brennan and Rivers, selected the co-MVPs for Hawaii, also teamed on the final touchdown pass, a 79-yarder late in the fourth quarter. Hawaii (11-3) matched the school mark for most wins in a season, set in 1992 when the team went 11-2. The Sun Devils (7-6) concluded their disappointing season, unable to send coach Dirk Koetter out with a win. He coached his final game after being fired last month. Dennis Erickson has been hired to take over the team. Koetter went 40-34 in six seasons at ASU, including 2-19 against ranked teams and 21-28 in the Pac-10. He also led the Sun Devils to four bowl games. Brennan finished the season with 5,549 yards to become just the third Quarterback in college history with 5,000 yards and 50 TDs in a season, joining Klingler and Texas Tech's B.J. Symons (2003). Brennan and Grice-Mullen also connected on a 41-yard pass play down the middle for Brennan's 56th TD pass of the season with 2:14 left in the third quarter. Brennan then threw a 21-yard scoring pass to a crossing Davone Bess, giving Hawaii a 34-24 lead with 5:16 left in the fourth quarter. Dan Kelly kicked a 43-yard field goal to put the Warriors up 27-10 early in the fourth, but the Sun Devils trimmed the lead to 10 on Ryan Torain's 12-yard TD run. The score was set up by a 64-yard run by Torain, who finished with 160 yards on 18 carries and was honored as the game MVP for Arizona State. Nate Ilaoa fumbled on the ensuing drive, giving Arizona State the ball on the Hawaii 27. The Sun Devils scored two plays later Rudy Carpenter's 4-yard TD pass to Mike Jones to draw within a field goal with 10:25 left to go. But Arizona State couldn't contain Hawaii's potent offense. The Sun Devils appeared to be in control of the game, holding the nation's No. 1 offense to just three points in the first half using time-consuming drives and an attacking defense. Brennan was intercepted by Josh Barrett and the Quarterback was sacked three times in the half. Arizona State stunned the crowd on Carpenter's 37-yard lob pass to freshman Brandon Smith to take a 10-3 lead. Arizona State drove deep into Hawaii territory on its opening series but came up empty when Torain fumbled at the Hawaii 11 while fighting for extra yards. He lost the ball again on Arizona State's next series, but the Sun Devils recovered, and Jesse Ainsworth's 44-yard field goal put Arizona State up 3-0.

2006 Motor City Bowl
The 2006 Motor City Bowl was played on December 26, 2006 at Ford Field in Detroit, Michigan.

2006 Motor City Bowl	Line	1	-	2	-	3	-	4	-	Final
Middle Tennessee	(51.5)	0	-	7	-	0	-	7	-	14
Central Michigan	(-9.0)	14	-	7	-	7	-	3	-	31

Scoring Summary
Central Michigan - Sneed 1 yard run (Albreski kick)
Central Michigan - Sneed 29 yard pass from LeFevour (Albreski kick)
Middle Tennessee - Gross 3 yard run (Smith kick)
Central Michigan - LeFevour 9 yard run (Albreski kick)
Central Michigan - Kress 56 yard interception return (Albreski kick)
Middle Tennessee - McNair 6 yard run (Smith kick)
Central Michigan - Albreski 43 yard Field goal

Associated Press Motor City Bowl Game Recap - Jeff Quinn made not having the interim tag hang over his head much longer. Ontario Sneed scored a pair of first-quarter touchdowns to lead Central Michigan to a 31-14 victory over Middle Tennessee State in the Motor City Bowl. Central Michigan (10-4) was guided by Quinn, who was named interim coach three weeks ago after Brian Kelly left to take the job at Cincinnati. Quinn helped the Chippewas to their first bowl victory. They had lost the 1990 California Raisin and the 1994 Las Vegas Bowl. Sneed also had a huge hand in the victory, scoring on runs of one and 29 yards in the first quarter to help the Chippewas to a 14-0 lead. Doug Kress returned an interception 56 yards for a score midway through the third quarter, extending the advantage to 28-7. With a large contingent of gold and burgundy filling the stands at Ford Field, the game drew a crowd of 54,113, a record for the Motor City Bowl. Eugene Gross and DeMarco McNair had touchdown runs for Middle Tennessee (7-6), which was playing its first bowl game in school history.

2006 Emerald Bowl
The 2006 Emerald Bowl was played on December 27, 2006, at AT&T Park in San Francisco, California. It featured the UCLA Bruins, and the Florida State Seminoles.

2006 Emerald Bowl	Line	1	-	2	-	3	-	4	-	Final
Florida State	(39.0)	7	-	6	-	10	-	21	-	44
UCLA	(-3.5)	10	-	10	-	7	-	0	-	27

Scoring Summary
Florida State - Booker 25 yard run (Cismesia kick)
UCLA - Breazell 78 yard pass from Cowan (Medlock kick)
UCLA - Medlock 46 yard Field goal
Florida State - Cismesia 39 yard Field goal
UCLA - Taylor 7 yard pass from Cowan (Medlock kick)
UCLA - Medlock 19 yard Field goal
Florida State - Cismesia 21 yard Field goal
Florida State - Cismesia 36 yard Field goal
Florida State - Timmons 25 yard blocked punt return (Cismesia kick)
UCLA - Moline 8 yard run (Medlock kick)
Florida State - Carr 30 yard pass from Weatherford (Cismesia kick)
Florida State - Booker 3 yard run (Cismesia kick)
Florida State - Carter 86 yard interception return (Cismesia kick)

Associated Press Emerald Bowl Game Summary - Although Bobby Bowden has led Florida State to much bigger victories in far grander bowls, a winning season is always sweet - even when it ends with Bowden raising the Emerald Bowl trophy in a chilly baseball park 2,600 miles from Tallahassee. Lorenzo Booker ran for 91 yards, caught five passes for 117 more and scored two touchdowns, leading the Seminoles to a 44-27 victory over UCLA on Wednesday night to put a happy ending on Bowden's 30th straight winning season. Sure, this was no fairy-tale finish for a program that once dominated the sport and won two national titles. Wracked by injuries and beset by coaching turmoil that led to Jeff Bowden's in-season resignation as offensive coordinator, the Seminoles (7-6) finished with their worst record since going 7-4-1 in 1986. But the 77-year-old Bowden still hasn't coached a losing club since going 5-6 in his first season at Florida State - and with 21 points in the fourth quarter against the collapsing Bruins (7-6), the Seminoles are headed into 2007 with more momentum than they've had all season. A 3-5 record in ACC play, including four losses in six games to close the regular season, forced Florida State to finish an ignominious year with the longest road trip in school history. The Seminoles have played in 25 straight bowl games, but the last 15 were played in January, with considerably bigger stakes and payouts. Don't tell that to Booker, a California native who got a chance to impress 130 friends and family members in the stands. This minor bowl was a major win. Drew Weatherford, who overcame a shaky start to pass for 325 yards, 126 in the fourth quarter. Florida State's fourth quarter was dynamite. Greg Carr caught a go-ahead, 30-yard touchdown pass on fourth-and-9, and Booker capped his final college game with a key third-down catch and a 3-yard TD run with 6:17 left. Tony Carter's 86-yard interception return for another score 37 seconds later was the finishing touch in Bowden's 20th bowl victory. Patrick Cowan passed for 240 yards and Chris Markey ran for 144 for the inconsistent Bruins, who came in with a three-game winning streak, highlighted by a 13-9 victory over archrival USC 3 1/2 weeks ago. Yet the Seminoles rolled over the Bruins on offense, defense and special teams in the second half. Lawrence Timmons returned a blocked punt 25 yards for a score in the third quarter, and Carter's return was just one of several big stops. Most in the sellout crowd of 40,331 fans cheered UCLA, but Florida State had a surprisingly solid rooting section for a game on the opposite coast. Florida State took a 23-20 lead in the third quarter when Dekoda Watson blocked a punt and Timmons returned it for a score, but UCLA went back ahead on Chane Moline's 8-yard TD run moments later. When a Florida State drive stalled early in the fourth quarter with the Seminoles trailing by four, Bowden and his son proved they had nothing to lose by boldly going for it on fourth and long. Carr easily made his TD catch a step from the end zone when his defender fell down. Brandon Breazell caught a 78-yard TD pass and Junior Taylor had a scoring catch in the first half for the Bruins, who finished a mediocre regular season playing some of their best football in Dorrell's four seasons. The Bruins led 20-13 at halftime, and a game expected to be dominated by defense featured 501 total yards in the first half alone.

2006 Independence Bowl

The 2006 PetroSun Independence Bowl took place on December 28, 2006 at Independence Stadium in Shreveport, Louisiana. The competing teams were the Alabama Crimson Tide, representing the Southeastern Conference, and the Oklahoma State Cowboys, from the Big 12 Conference. Oklahoma State won the game, 34–31. This was the only 2006–07 bowl game in which both teams finished 6-6 on the regular season, and the first meeting between the programs on the gridiron. With the dismissal of Alabama head coach Mike Shula occurring in November, Joe Kines would serve as the Tide's head coach for this contest, with Nick Saban being hired as coach the following January.

2006 Independence Bowl	Line	1	-	2	-	3	-	4	-	Final
Oklahoma State	(-2.0)	7	-	17	-	0	-	10	-	34
Alabama	(50.0)	7	-	7	-	3	-	14	-	31

Scoring Summary
Oklahoma State – Savage 1 yard run (Ricks kick)
Alabama – Caddell 18 yard pass from Parker-Wilson (Christensen kick)
Oklahoma State – Toston 4 yard run (Ricks kick)
Oklahoma State – Ricks 29 yard Field goal
Alabama – Castille 1 yard run (Christensen kick)
Oklahoma State – Tosten 7 yard run (Ricks kick)
Alabama – Christensen 24 yard Field goal
Oklahoma State – Bowman 11 yard pass from Reid (Ricks kick)
Alabama – Arenas 86 yard punt return (Christensen kick)
Alabama – Smith 2 yard run (Christensen kick)
Oklahoma State – Ricks 27 yard Field goal

Associated Press Independence Bowl Game summary - Jason Ricks had attempted only 10 field goals this season for Oklahoma State, and he had missed a couple of PATs that cost the Cowboys a victory. None of that matter at the PetroSun Independence Bowl on Thursday, when the sophomore kicker teamed with Dantrell Savage to help snatch victory back from Alabama. Ricks kicked a 27-yard field goal with 8.9 seconds remaining after to give Oklahoma State a 34-31 victory over Alabama. Savage ran for 112 yards and a touchdown and made the key play on the winning drive. He took a screen pass from Bobby Reid for 26 yards on third-and-9 to the Alabama 15 to put Ricks in prime position. Alabama tried to ice Ricks with three timeouts. But the sophomore sent the kick through the uprights, and he snatched off his helmet and ran to the sideline with it extended over his head. The kick saved the Cowboys (7-6) from a fourth-quarter collapse and gave them both a winning record and their first bowl victory since 2002. Oklahoma State blew a 14-point lead, setting up the Crimson Tide for the tying touchdown with a fumbled kickoff return. Alabama (6-7) was playing in its NCAA-record 54th bowl game and looking for its 31st bowl victory -- another NCAA record -- but for much of the night the Crimson Tide's vaunted postseason history seemed a distant memory. Bama played flat until late in the fourth quarter. With the Tide trailing 31-17, Javier Arenas returned a punt 86 yards to pull Alabama to within a touchdown with 10:50 left in the game. Then Grant Jones fumbled the ensuing kickoff and Chris Rogers -- who forced the fumble -- recovered, giving Alabama a first down on the Oklahoma State 21. Six plays later, left tackle Andra Smith caught a lateral from John Parker Wilson and ran 2 yards to tie the game at 31. It was a bitter end to a bitter year for the Tide. Playing for the first time since Mike Shula was fired, Bama was unable to dodge its first losing record since 2003, Shula's first season. Alabama is without a coach for next season after being turned down by West Virginia's Rich Rodriguez. Defensive coordinator Joe Kines has handled the head coaching duties in the interim. Oklahoma State -- ranked 16th nationally in total offense -- outgained Alabama 419-276. The Cowboys rushed for 207 yards compared to 108 yards for the Tide. Jeremy Nethon had 11 tackles including seven solo for Oklahoma State and was selected the game's MVP. Reid completed 15 of 29 attempts for 212 yards with a touchdown and an interception, and Keith Toston added 58 yards and two TDs. John Parker Wilson completed 18 of 33 for 168 yards and a touchdown for Alabama. He was intercepted twice. The Cowboys scooped up an Alabama fumble on the Tide's 38-yard line to set up the opening score. Savage ran the final yard to cap a 38-yard drive and make it 7-0 Oklahoma State. Alabama tied it on an 18-yard touchdown pass from Wilson to Matt Caddell with 3:32 remaining in the first quarter. Oklahoma State went ahead 14-7 on Toston's 4-yard run. The Cowboys stretched their lead to 17-7 on a 28-yard field goal by Ricks. Alabama cut the margin to 17-14 on a 1-yard run by fullback Tim Castille. But Alabama was unable to stop the Cowboys final drive of the half. Oklahoma State took it 64 yards, capped by a 7-yard run by Toston for a 24-14 lead at the half. In the third quarter, Jamie Christensen kicked a 24 yard field goal to pull Alabama three points closer. Then Reid hit Adarius Bowman for a 10-yard score to give Oklahoma State a 14 point lead, 31-17.

2006 Texas Bowl

The 2006 Texas Bowl was played on December 26, 2006 at Reliant Stadium in Houston, Texas. The game featured the Rutgers Scarlet Knights and the Kansas State Wildcats.

2006 Texas Bowl	Line	1	-	2	-	3	-	4	-	Final
Kansas State	(44.5)	0	-	10	-	0	-	0	-	10
#16 Rutgers	(-7.5)	14	-	3	-	14	-	6	-	37

Scoring Summary
Rutgers - Brown 14 yard pass from Teel (Ito kick)
Rutgers - Brown 49 yard pass from Teel (Ito kick)
Kansas State - Snodgrass 44 yard Field goal
Kansas State - Figurs 76 yard punt return (Snodgrass kick)
Rutgers - Ito 37 yard Field goal
Rutgers - Frierson 26 yard interception return (Snodgrass kick)
Rutgers - Rice 46 yard run (Snodgrass kick)
Rutgers - Ito 23 yard Field goal
Rutgers - Ito 21 yard Field goal

Texas Bowl Game Summary - Rutgers running back Ray Rice ran for 170 yards and a touchdown, Tim Brown caught two TD passes and the 16th-ranked Scarlet Knights won a bowl game for the first time in program history, beating Kansas State 37-10 in the Texas Bowl. Linebacker Quintero Frierson returned an interception 27 yards for a touchdown on the first play from scrimmage of the second half and Rutgers (11-2) cruised from there, earning an 11th victory for the second time in 137 mostly forgettable seasons. The Scarlet Knights' seventh-ranked defense manhandled Kansas State's offense, holding the Wildcats to 162 total yards and six first downs. Freshman Quarterback Josh Freeman was 10-for-21 for 129 yards with two interceptions. Kansas State (7-6) mustered only 85 yards after Frierson's return of Freeman's first interception put Rutgers up 24-10 just 33 seconds out of halftime. The Wildcats' only touchdown came on Yamon Figurs' 76-yard punt return with 9:37 left in the second quarter. Rice had a 24-yard run on Rutgers' next possession and Teel found Brown deep down the sideline for a 14-0 lead. Brown, a freshman from Miami, had only four catches and one TD reception coming into the game. Rutgers outscored its opponents 103-28 in the first quarter this season. On the first play of the second quarter, Freeman found Jordy Nelson on a crossing route for a 33-yard gain to set up Jeff Snodgrass' 44-yard field goal. Four minutes later, Figurs took Joe Radigan's punt up the middle, sidestepped Radigan and scored Kansas State's seventh special-teams touchdown of the season. Rice, the nation's fourth-leading rusher, had 74 yards rushing at halftime to move into third place on the school's career list. The Wildcats' offense had only one more yard at halftime (77) than Figurs gained on his punt return. Freeman was on the run when Frierson leaped to pick off his wobbly pass. Freeman's 14th interception of the season was his fifth in the Wildcats' last three games. Rice burst through the line and ran untouched through the defense for 46 yards and his 20th touchdown of the season to make it 31-10 with 11:41 left in the third quarter, and that was more than enough for Rutgers. The Wildcats' offense did nothing after that, failing to get a first down for the rest of the third quarter. Freshman Leon Patton, Kansas State's leading rusher, fumbled at the Wildcats' 22 near the end of the quarter, setting up the second of Jeremy Ito's three field goals. Teel finished 16 for 28 for 268 yards without an interception. Brown had four catches for 101 yards and Clark Harris made seven catches for 120. Kansas

State was playing in a bowl for the 12th time in 14 seasons, but for the first time since the Fiesta Bowl following the 2003 season. The Wildcats dropped to 6-6 in those dozen. It was Kansas State's only bowl game with Ron Prince as head coach.

2006 Holiday Bowl

The 2006 Pacific Life Holiday Bowl was played December 28, 2006 in San Diego, California. It featured the Texas A&M Aggies representing the Big 12 against the California Golden Bears from the Pac-10. In the Golden Bears' second trip to the Holiday Bowl in three years, they routed the Aggies, 45-10. Each conference received $2.2 million for the teams playing.

2006 Holiday Bowl	Line	1	-	2	-	3	-	4	-	Final
#21 Texas A&M	(52.5)	7	-	3	-	0	-	0	-	10
#20 California	(-4.0)	7	-	7	-	14	-	17	-	45

Scoring Summary
Texas A&M – Schroeder 19 yard pass from McGee (Szymanski kick)
California – Longshore 1 yard run (Schneider kick)
California – Lynch 2 yard run (Schneider kick)
Texas A&M – Szymanski 32 yard Field goal
California – Lynch 1 yard run (Schneider kick)
California – Hawkins 4 yard pass from Longshore (Schneider kick)
California – Schneider 21 yard Field goal
California – Forsett 8 yard run (Schneider kick)
California – Schutte 3 yard run (Schneider kick)

Associated Press Holiday Bowl Game Summary - Marshawn Lynch ran for 111 yards and two touchdowns, and No. 20 California's defense played impressively in a 45-10 win over No. 21 Texas A&M on Thursday night in the Pacific Life Holiday Bowl. Nate Longshore threw for a touchdown and ran for another, and Lynch's backup, Justin Forsett, ran for 124 yards and one score. Cal (10-3) put an emphatic final touch to its second 10-win season in three years. The Golden Bears had lost to Arizona and Southern California in disheartening fashion before beating rival Stanford and then the Aggies (9-4). In 2004, Cal was in position to end its long Rose Bowl drought but was leapfrogged in the final Bowl Championship Series standings by Texas. Although the fourth-ranked Golden Bears claimed not to be bothered by the snub, they couldn't even hang with No. 23 Texas Tech in the Holiday Bowl and were humiliated 45-31. This trip to San Diego turned out a lot better. Lynch, the Pac-10 offensive player of the year, scored on a 2-yard run in the second quarter to give Cal a 14-7 lead. While Longshore lined up at wide receiver, Lynch was in the shotgun formation, took the snap and bulled into the end zone. Lynch scored on a 1-yard run in the third, leaping over the line and fumbling as he came down in the end zone. The Aggies recovered and referee John O'Neill signaled first down for Texas A&M, then said the play was being reviewed. Replay official Jim Augustyn ruled that Lynch had possession when he broke the plane of the end zone, making it 21-10 Cal. While the Golden Bears moved up and down the field, their defense came up big, too. Jorvorskie Lane, Texas A&M's 274-pound tailback, wasn't much of a factor after tying a 79-year-old school record with 19 rushing touchdowns this year. He was held to 36 yards and no touchdowns on seven carries. Longshore scored on a 1-yard keeper to tie the game at 7 in the first quarter, eight plays after Texas A&M's Stephen McGee threw a 19-yard TD pass to Chad Schroeder. Longshore also threw a 4-yard touchdown pass to Lavelle Hawkins late in the third quarter. He finished 19-of-24 for 235 yards. Texas A&M gambled a few times too many. After Bryce Reed gained 7 yards on a fake punt in the first quarter, the drive bogged down and the Aggies went for it on fourth-and-8 from the Cal 32. McGee was sacked by Nu'u Tafisi. Lynch scored his first TD five plays later. His second touchdown was set up when Texas A&M's Justin Brantly shanked a punt out of bounds for no gain at the Aggies' 41. Lynch scored four plays later. The Aggies failed to convert on another fourth-down play in the fourth quarter. Cal's Eddie Young intercepted Aggies backup Quarterback Ty Branyon with 2:25 left, setting up a 3-yard score by freshman tailback Bryan Schutte.

2006 Music City Bowl

The 2006 Gaylord Hotels Music City Bowl (presented by Bridgestone) featured a contest between the Clemson Tigers and the Kentucky Wildcats. Clemson entered the game with a record of 8-4 after having been ranked in the AP poll for most weeks of the season, as high as #10; Kentucky was 7-5 and unranked. Clemson was favored by 10 points.

2006 Music City Bowl	Line	1	-	2	-	3	-	4	-	Final
Clemson	(-10.0)	0	-	6	-	0	-	14	-	20
Kentucky	(57.5)	7	-	7	-	7	-	7	-	28

Scoring Summary
Kentucky - Johnson 1 yd run (Seiber kick)
Clemson - Barry 32 yd pass from Proctor (kick failed)
Kentucky - Ford 70 yd pass from Woodson (Seiber kick)
Kentucky - Lyons 24 yd pass from Woodson (Seiber kick)
Kentucky - Tamme 13 yd pass from Woodson (Seiber kick)
Clemson - Grisham 18 yd pass from Proctor (Pass failed)
Clemson - Kelly 17 yd pass from Proctor (Palmer pass from Proctor)

Associated Press Music City Bowl Game Summary - Andre Woodson conjured up memories of Tim Couch and made Kentucky a bowl winner for the first time in 22 years. Woodson threw for three touchdowns and 299 yards as the Wildcats surprised Clemson 28-20 in the Gaylord Hotels Music City Bowl on Friday. The junior completed 20 of 28 passes to finish his breakout season with 31 touchdowns -- more than five times his total from last year. He joins Couch, the former No. 1 NFL draft pick, as the only Wildcats to top the 30-touchdown mark in a season. Behind Woodson, the game's Most Valuable Player, the Wildcats (8-5) racked up their highest point total in bowl history. They won their sixth bowl game overall and first since beating Wisconsin in the 1984 Hall of Fame Bowl. Kentucky made its first bowl appearance since 1999 in front of a huge contingency of Wildcats fans, many of whom made the 200-mile trip from Lexington, home of Commonwealth Stadium. Clemson (8-5) took the loss in its 18th bowl game since 1985. The Tigers hadn't ended their season in defeat in three years. Despite beating Wake Forest and Georgia Tech, the teams that played for the Atlantic Coast Conference title, Clemson went into a tailspin down the stretch, losing four of five. While Kentucky's offensive fireworks weren't unexpected, a defense that came into the game ranked second-to-last nationally made the difference. Wildcats held a 4-2 turnover advantage and limited Clemson to just six points until the final seven minutes when Kentucky used a prevent defense. A large early deficit forced the Tigers, one of the country's best rushing teams, into passing situations. Running backs James Davis and C.J. Spiller combined for just 77 yards, and Spiller fell short of the 86 he needed to make the tandem the first in school history with 1,000 rushing yards each. After four straight second-quarter drives ended with turnovers -- two for each team -- Brooks sought a spark with a little razzle-dazzle. Rather than punt from deep in Kentucky territory, punter Tim Masthay threw for the first down. Woodson then lofted a deep pass over the Clemson secondary and found DeMoreo Ford streaking for a 70-yard touchdown -- the longest allowed all season by the nation's 12th-ranked defense. The Wildcats made it 21-6 early in the second half after a Clemson fumble, when Woodson found Dicky Lyons Jr. on a sideline pattern for the 24-yard score. They put the game out of reach with a 13-yard touchdown pass to Jacob Tamme. Clemson cut the deficit to eight points with 44 seconds left when Will Proctor threw a 12-yard touchdown pass to Aaron Kelly and added a 2-point conversion. But Kentucky recovered the onside kick and ran out the clock. The Wildcats drove into Clemson territory on their first drive before Gaines Adams stormed through the line to strip the ball from Woodson. It was one of two sacks on the afternoon for the All-American, giving him 28 in his career to tie Michael Dean Perry for first on the Tigers' all-time list. Phillip Merling picked up the loose ball and seemed to give the Tigers prime field position, but a replay showed Woodson's knee was down before the ball came out. Kentucky took advantage of the second chance and freshman linebacker Micah Johnson, the state's top high school football player last year, scored his first touchdown, plunging in from a yard out. Proctor threw for three touchdowns and 272 yards, but Jad Dean missed two first-quarter field-goal attempts and an extra point after Durrell Barry's 32-yard TD reception made it 7-6 Kentucky.

2006 Liberty Bowl

The 2006 Liberty Bowl was a played on December 29, 2006 at Liberty Bowl Memorial Stadium in Memphis, Tennessee. The game pitted the South Carolina Gamecocks against the Houston Cougars. South Carolina won the game by a score of 44–36.

2006 Liberty Bowl	Line	1	-	2	-	3	-	4	-	Final
South Carolina	(-5.5)	7	-	20	-	3	-	14	-	44
Houston	(56.0)	7	-	21	-	0	-	8	-	36

Scoring Summary
Houston – Marshall 32 yard pass from Kolb (Bell kick)
South Carolina – Boyd 2 yard run (Succop kick)
South Carolina – Pavlovic 1 yard pass from Mitchell (kick failed)
Houston – Hafner 4 yard pass from Kolb (Bell kick)
South Carolina – Rice 19 yard pass from Mitchell (Succop kick)
Houston – Battle 42 yard run (Bell kick)
South Carolina – Boyd 9 yard run (Succop kick)
Houston – Marshall 77 yard pass from Kolb (Bell kick)
South Carolina – Succop 45 yard Field goal

South Carolina – McKinley 43 yard pass from Mitchell (Succop kick)
South Carolina – McKinley 43 yard pass from Mitchell (Succop kick)
Houston – Battle 3 yard run (Bell kick)

Associated Press Liberty Bowl Game Summary - Steve Spurrier's offense was humming along in the first half, but the South Carolina defense was doing nothing to stop Houston. In the final 30 minutes, Spurrier's Gamecocks got a little D to go with their O. Defensive end Jordin Lindsey came up with two turnovers for a defense that made the stops that mattered most, and South Carolina beat Houston 44-36 in the Liberty Bowl on Friday for its first bowl victory under Spurrier. Lindsey, who intercepted a pass and recovered a fumble that set up 13 points, said they knew they had to turn up the pressure or endure Spurrier's wrath. Blake Mitchell tied a bowl record by throwing four touchdown passes, Cory Boyd ran for two more TDs as the Gamecocks (8-5) finished Spurrier's second season with their best record since going 9-3 in 2001. Kevin Kolb, making his 50th start at Quarterback for Houston (10-4) and leading the nation's sixth-best offense, finished 26-of-39 for 386 yards and three touchdowns. Houston, which went 0-11 in 2001, came in with a six-game winning streak and looking to cap its Conference USA championship season. Houston led 28-27 at the half - a Liberty Bowl record for points in a half - but South Carolina held the Cougars to 63 yards in the third quarter when the Gamecocks took control. They sacked Kolb three times, forced two turnovers and stopped the Cougars twice on fourth down in the fourth quarter. The Cougars and Gamecocks combined for 588 yards in the first half, much of it just before halftime. The second quarter took 61 minutes, and a game that was tied at 7 went haywire. In the final three minutes of the half, four TDs were scored in a span 12 plays - the last a 77-yard TD catch by Houston's Vincent Marshall with 11 seconds left. The Cougars didn't score in the second half until Jackie Battle ran in from 3 yards out with 5:42 left. The 2-point conversion cut South Carolina's lead to 44-36. Houston outgained South Carolina 527-512, but the Cougars managed only 200 in the second half. It was the first time in Liberty Bowl history both teams topped 500 yards. Cougar's receiver Vincent Marshall, who set a bowl record with 201 yards receiving, said South Carolina's zone defense took away the middle of the field. With a pair of coaches known for their offensive ingenuity, this had a little of everything: four TDs in a span of 12 plays, a flea flicker for an interception, a punt on fourth-and-goal, a halfback pass and an option by Houston when backed up against its own goal line. Each Quarterback passed for more than 300 yards - a first in the 48-year history of this bowl game. Ryan Succop kicked a 45-yard field goal into winds gusting up to 20 mph on the Gamecocks' opening drive of the second half to put South Carolina ahead to stay at 30-28. Mitchell padded the lead with a pair of 43-yard TD passes to Kenny McKinley, the last with 7:39 to go for a 44-28 lead. Mitchell, the game's Most Valuable Player, was 19-of-29 for 323 yards. Houston ruined its best scoring chance on the drive after Succop's field goal. In the shotgun on third-and-goal at the 8, a bad snap went wide right of Kolb, who tried to chase down the ball and kicked it out of bounds for a penalty. That forced Houston to punt from midfield after having first-and-goal. Briles credited the South Carolina fans with making it tough to hear, forcing the Cougars to go to a silent count. South Carolina linebacker Jasper Brinkley stopped Anthony Alridge short on fourth-and-4 with 9:31 left at midfield, forcing the Cougars to turn it over on downs to kill another drive.

2006 Champs Sports Bowl

The 2006 Champs Sports Bowl was played on December 29, 2006. This 17th edition to the bowl game featured the Maryland Terrapins and the Purdue Boilermakers.

2006 Champs Sports Bowl	Line	1	-	2	-	3	-	4	-	Final
Purdue	(-1.0)	0	-	7	-	0	-	0	-	7
Maryland	(53.5)	7	-	14	-	3	-	0	-	24

Scoring Summary
Maryland – Haynos 4 yard pass from Hollenbach (Ennis kick)
Maryland – Jackson 1 yard run (Ennis kick)
Maryland – Hayward-Bey 46 yard pass from Hollenbach (Ennis kick)
Purdue – Orton 12 yard pass from Painter (Summers kick)
Maryland – Ennis 22 yard Field goal

Associated Press Champs Sports Bowl Game Summary - Maryland methodically and meticulously put away Purdue -- and looked nothing like the team that ended the regular season with two lopsided losses. Sam Hollenbach passed for 223 yards and two touchdowns, Lance Ball rushed for 98 yards, and the Terrapins won the Champs Sports Bowl 24-7 on Friday night. Maryland blew a chance to play for the Atlantic Coast Conference title by losing to Boston College and Wake Forest by a combined 76-40 in November. The Terrapins (9-4) were able to keep Purdue's offense, the NCAA's 10th best at 425 yards per game, in check by blanketing its speedy wideouts, batting down several passes -- and keeping the ball away from the Boilermakers. Keon Lattimore added 86 yards rushing on 20 carries for the Terps, who held the ball for 39:48. It hardly mattered that Dan Ennis' 22-yard field goal with 6:22 left in the third quarter was the only scoring in the second half. Maryland milked the clock with 429 total yards and 20 first downs and Purdue did little when it had a shot. Boilermaker Quarterback Curtis Painter completed 23-of-36 passes for 264 yards, one touchdown and one interception. Maryland's offense was virtually mistake free, but Purdue (8-6) had several costly miscues. The biggest was Dorien Bryant's fumble after a 31-yard reception that would've been Purdue's biggest play of the game on its opening drive of the second half. Purdue never got its ground game on track after falling behind early and finished with 21 yards rushing. Tiller, frustrated with the officiating and 14-0 score, got a 15-yard unsportsmanlike conduct penalty in the second quarter. Shortly afterward, Heyward-Bey showcased his 4.38 speed on a 46-yard touchdown pass. Hollenbach appeared to overthrow him on the sideline route, but the freshman wideout got underneath it for the 21-0 score. Purdue missed its first chance to score by ending a 55-yard first quarter drive with a missed field goal. Ball ran five times for 49 yards on the next series to set up a TD. Out of the shotgun with five wideouts, Hollenbach dumped it to Joey Haynos for a 4-yard score to give Maryland a 7-0 lead. Starting from their own 40, the Terps made it 14-0 after Hollenbach orchestrated another flawless drive. He hit Heyward-Bey over the middle for a 19-yard gain, and Danny Oquendo for 11 yards to the Purdue 4. Cory Jackson ran in from a yard out for the touchdown. The Boilermakers got their only touchdown just before halftime. Painter led them 71 yards in 1:25, hitting Greg Orton for a 12-yard touchdown. Orton and Dorien Bryant's receptions accounted for all Purdue's offense in the drive.

2006 Sun Bowl

The 2006 Brut Sun Bowl featured the Oregon State Beavers of the Pac-10 and the Missouri Tigers of the Big 12 Conference.

2006 Sun Bowl	Line	1	-	2	-	3	-	4	-	Final
#24 Oregon State	(-3.5)	14	-	0	-	7	-	28	-	39
Missouri	(52.5)	7	-	10	-	14	-	7	-	38

Scoring Summary
Missouri – Temple 7 yard run (Wolfert kick)
Oregon State – Stroughter 13 yard pass from Moore (Serna kick)
Oregon State – Moore 1 yard run (Serna kick)
Missouri – Wolfert 30 yard Field goal
Missouri – Alexander 74 yard pass from Daniel (Wolfert kick)
Oregon State – Newton 11 yard pass from Moore (Serna kick)
Missouri – Saunders 29 yard pass from Coffman (Wolfert kick)
Missouri – Temple 66 yard run (Wolfert kick)
Oregon State – Serna 29 yard Field goal
Missouri – Coffman 18 yard pass from Daniel (Wolfert kick)
Oregon State – Bernard 7 yard pass from Moore (Serna kick)
Oregon State – Newton 14 yard pass from Moore (Bernard run)

Associated Press Sun Bowl Game Summary - Oregon State coach Mike Riley was set to take his chances in overtime at the Brut Sun Bowl. Then Missouri called timeout to have Joe Newton's 14-yard touchdown catch with 22.1 seconds to go reviewed, believing he may have bobbled the ball. During that break, Riley decided to go for the win. Yvenson Bernard barely pushed into the end zone on the gutsy 2-point conversion run, giving the 24th-ranked Beavers a 39-38 victory over the Tigers on Friday. The Beavers (10-4) trailed by 14 points with 12:08 to go before rallying for their eighth victory in nine games. Bernard's 7-yard reception had cut the gap to seven with 6:02 to go, and Riley said the senior running back lobbied the hardest to go for two at the end. Tony Temple had 194 yards, four short of the Sun Bowl record, on 20 carries with two touchdowns and Chase Daniel threw two touchdown passes for Missouri (8-5). The Tigers lost four of their last five after a 6-0 start, dropping the finale despite 561 yards of total offense. Temple missed setting a Sun Bowl record for rushing, 197 yards by Charles Alexander of LSU in 1977, after losing 4 yards on his final carry. It was no surprise to Daniel that Oregon State decided to go for broke. He was on the phone with Quarterbacks coach Dave Yost talking strategy for what Missouri might do if the Beavers scored. Daniel, who averaged 20 yards per completion, going 16-for-29 for 330 yards. Matt Moore threw four touchdown passes and ran for a fifth for Oregon State, which helped produce the second-highest scoring game in the Sun Bowl's 73-year history. He was 5-for-7 for 55 yards on the winning drive, set up after Sammie Stroughter's 38-yard punt return to the Oregon State 46. Missouri had seven plays of 29 yards or longer, including Danario Alexander's 74-yard touchdown catch and Temple's 65-yard run. Missouri responded after Newton's first touchdown catch on Oregon State's opening drive of the second half cut the Tigers' lead to 21-17. Tommie Saunders' 29-yard TD catch from tight end Chase Coffman off a lateral gave the lead back to Missouri and Temple's 65-yard untouched touchdown run seemingly put the Tigers in control at 31-21 with 5:58 in the third. The victory was the latest in a series of nail-biters for

Oregon State, which beat Hawaii and Oregon by a combined five points in the last two regular-season games. The Beavers' biggest triumph after a 2-3 start that had fans calling for Riley to be fired was a 33-31 stunner over then-No. 3 Southern California on Oct. 28. Missouri was on the other end of a big bowl comeback last year, rallying behind Quarterback Brad Smith from a 21-point deficit to beat South Carolina 38-31 in the Independence Bowl. Moore was 31-for-54 for 356 yards and set a school record of 182 passes without an interception before getting picked off by Brandon Massey in the third quarter. Oregon State retained possession on the play after Massey was stripped. Oregon State prevailed despite a porous defense that allowed 98 points the last three games. Among Missouri's other big plays were a 40-yard catch by Coffman that led to Temple's 7-yard scoring run on the opening drive. A 47-yard run by Temple was followed by an 18-yard touchdown pass from Daniel to Coffman on the next play for a 38-24 lead with 12:08 left in the game. Newton also caught an 11-yard touchdown pass in the third quarter and had six receptions for 74 yards.

2006 Insight Bowl

The 2006 Insight Bowl was held on December 29 at Sun Devil Stadium on the campus of Arizona State University in Tempe, Arizona, pitted the Texas Tech Red Raiders against the Minnesota Golden Gophers. This game is tied for the biggest comeback in NCAA Division I FBS bowl history. The Red Raiders, after falling behind 38-7 with 7:47 remaining in the third quarter, rallied to score 31 unanswered points to send the game to overtime. The Gophers scored a field goal in overtime, but the Red Raiders responded with a touchdown to win.

Aftermath - Two days after his team's loss in the Insight Bowl, Minnesota head coach Glen Mason was fired. Minnesota athletic director Joel Maturi did not publicly detail the reasons for the firing, but strongly hinted that the Gophers' collapse was the proverbial last straw, saying "If we had not lost the way we lost, we probably wouldn't be here today." This was the latest in a series of Minnesota second-half collapses under Mason, which also included one of the previous three biggest bowl collapses in Division I-A history.

2006 Insight Bowl	Line	1	-	2	-	3	-	4	-	OT	-	Final
Texas Tech	(-7.5)	0	-	7	-	7	-	24	-	6	-	44
Minnesota	(64.5)	14	-	21	-	3	-	0	-	3	-	41

Scoring Summary
Minnesota – Simmons 2 yd pass from Cupito (Monroe kick)
Minnesota – Pinnix 2 yd run (Monroe kick)
Minnesota – Valentine 1 yd run (Monroe kick)
Minnesota – Wheelwright 14 yd pass from Cupito (Monroe kick)
Texas Tech – Woods 1 yd run (Trlica kick)
Minnesota – Payne 3 yd pass from Cupito (Monroe kick)
Minnesota – Monroe 20 yd Field goal
Texas Tech – Filani 43 yd pass from Harrell (Trlica kick)
Texas Tech – Johnson 6 yd pass from Harrell (Trlica kick)
Texas Tech – Harrell 1 yd run (Trlica kick)
Texas Tech – Woods 1 yd run (Trlica kick)
Texas Tech – Trlica 52 yd Field goal
Minnesota – Monroe 32 yd Field goal
Texas Tech – Woods 3 yd run

Associated Press Insight Bowl Game Summary - After spotting Minnesota a 31-point lead, Texas Tech rallied for a stunning 44-41 overtime victory in the Insight Bowl Friday night. Joel Monroe kicked a 32-yard field goal to put Minnesota up 41-38 in overtime, but Shannon Woods scored on a 3-yard run to win it for the Red Raiders. Tech (8-6) appeared finished after Minnesota (6-7) took a 38-7 lead with 7:47 to go in the third quarter. But the Red Raiders mounted a furious comeback, scoring 31 unanswered points in less than 20 minutes. Alex Trlica's 52-yard field goal as regulation expired sent the game into overtime. Tech's comeback began with 4:58 to go in the third quarter, when Graham Harrell hit Joel Filani for a 43-yard score to cut the lead to 38-14. That touchdown started an avalanche that helped beat Minnesota. Trailing 38-35 with no timeouts, the Red Raiders took over at their own 11 with 1:06 remaining. Eight plays later, Trlica tied it. Harrell threw for 445 yards and two touchdowns. Woods rushed for 109 yards and three touchdowns and Filani caught nine passes for 144 yards. For Minnesota, Amir Pinnix ran for 179 yards, Bryan Cupito threw for 263 yards and three touchdowns and Jack Simmons caught seven passes for 134 yards. Minnesota set a school bowl scoring record, and Cupito, a senior, tied Asad Abdul-Khaliq's career record of 55 touchdown passes. The Golden Gophers jumped ahead 7-0 after Texas Tech Coach Mike Leach went for it on fourth-and-1 at his own 45. Harrell was stopped on a sneak, and six plays later Cupito found tight end Jack Simmons for a 2-yard touchdown with 9:27 to go in the first quarter. Four minutes later, Minnesota made it 14-0 after linebacker Mike Sherels intercepted Harrell at Tech's 37. Pinnix capped a six-play drive with a 2-yard run. Another Harrell turnover killed a Tech scoring drive. He fumbled on a sack by Willie VanDeSteeg, and Steve Davis recovered at the Golden Gophers' 13. Minnesota marched 87 yards -- its longest scoring drive of the year -- to take a 21-0 lead on Justin Valentine's 1-yard plunge on the first play of the second quarter. Tech had a chance to slice the deficit when cornerback Antonio Huffman picked off Cupito's pass at the Minnesota 20. But Pinnix jarred the ball loose, and it bounded into the end zone, where the Gophers recovered for a touchback. After Tech's Shannon Woods scored from 1 yard out to make it 28-7, the Gophers answered with an 81-yard drive that ended in a 3-yard touchdown pass from Cupito to Logan Payne in the final minute of the first half. Minnesota looked as if it ended any Tech hopes for a comeback by opening the third quarter with a 16-play, 78-yard drive that consumed 7:13. Joel Monroe's 20-yard field goal gave the Gophers a 38-7 lead.

2006 Meineke Car Care Bowl

The 2006 Meineke Car Care Bowl featured the Navy Midshipmen, and the Boston College Eagles. The game was played on Saturday, December 30, 2006.

2006 Meineke Car Care Bowl	Line	1	-	2	-	3	-	4	-	Final
Navy	(47.0)	7	-	14	-	3	-	0	-	24
#23 Boston College	(-7.0)	6	-	10	-	0	-	9	-	25

Scoring Summary

Boston College - Ryan 2 yard run (kick failed)

Navy - Barnes 31 yard pass from Kaheaku-Enhada (Harmon kick)

Navy - Singleton 5 yard run (Harmon kick)

Boston College - Toal 1 yard run (Aponavicius kick)

Navy - Tomlinson 25 yard pass from Kaheaku-Enhada (Harmon kick)

Boston College - Aponavicius 26 yard Field goal

Navy - Harmon 22 yard Field goal

Boston College - Purvis 25 yard pass from Ryan (Aponavicius kick)

Boston College - Aponavicius 37 yard Field goal

Associated Press Meineke Car Care Bowl Game Summary - It's fitting that Boston College's bizarre month would end with an improbable finish that made a hero out of a walk-on kicker. Steve Aponavicius kicked a career-best 37-yard field goal on the final play and the 23rd-ranked Eagles beat the Midshipmen 25-24 in the Meineke Car Care Bowl to extend the nation's current longest bowl-winning streak to seven. ""The situation" was former coach Tom O'Brien's stunning decision three weeks ago to leave BC for Atlantic Coast Conference rival North Carolina State. Green Bay offensive coordinator Jeff Jagodzinski was hired to replace him but won't join the team until the Packers' season is over. Spaziani, the defensive coordinator and a former Navy assistant, has filled the gap and is expected to stay on as an assistant under Jagodzinski. But several assistants are also expected to join O'Brien's staff. For much of the game, it looked like the distractions would be too much to overcome for BC. Navy, the nation's top rushing team, had 322 yards on the ground and seemingly had the game won. BC (10-3) was out of timeouts and Navy only had to run out the final two minutes. But Reggie Campbell fumbled a pitch from Quarterback Kaipo-Noa Kaheaku-Enhada and BC's Jolonn Dunbar recovered at the Navy 40 with 1:43 left. Matt Ryan completed a 16-yard pass to tight end Ryan Purvis and Aponavicius, who played soccer -- not football -- in high school and replaced the suspended Ryan Ohliger in midseason, calmly kicked the game-winner, setting off a wild celebration. Ryan completed 20-of-29 passes for 242 yards with a touchdown pass and a TD run and overcame two interceptions and three sacks. Shun White rushed for 116 yards and Kaheaku-Enhada threw two touchdown passes for Navy (9-4), which had a four-game winning streak snapped. White's 53-yard run set up Kaheaku-Enhada's 24-yard touchdown pass to Jason Tomlinson, who made a juggling catch in triple coverage, giving Navy a 21-13 lead midway through the second quarter. BC got within 24-22 on Ryan's 25-yard touchdown pass to Purvis with 7:36 left in the game. Forced to go for a 2-point conversion because of Aponavicius' missed extra point in the first quarter, Tony Gonzalez dropped Ryan's pass in the back of the end zone. But Campbell's fumble gave the Eagles -- and Aponavicius -- another chance. Aponavicius, who had never played organized football before going 2-for-2 on field goals against Virginia Tech on Oct. 12, was mobbed by his teammates after the kick, which gave BC its first 10-win season since 1984, when Doug Flutie won the Heisman Trophy. Aponavicius, finished the season 8-for-11 on field goals. Andre Callender rushed for 66 yards for the Eagles, taking over for L.V. Whitworth, who left with an apparent ankle injury late in the first quarter. Until late in the game, Navy's confusing triple-option offense caused the Eagles, who had the nation's 13th best run defense, fits. Kaheaku-Enhada threw touchdown passes to Tyree Barnes and Tomlinson, sandwiched between Zerbin Singleton's 5-yard touchdown run in the first half and Navy appeared poised to beat a ranked team for the first time this season.

2006 Alamo Bowl

The 2006 Alamo Bowl was played in the 65,000-seat Alamodome in San Antonio, Texas on December 30. The game was televised on ESPN and ESPN-HD. It was the most watched bowl game in ESPN history. Alamo Bowl officials announced that both schools sold their entire allotment of tickets, resulting in the fastest sellout in Alamo Bowl history. The attendance for the game was 65,875, which established a new record for the most people to gather in San Antonio to view a sporting event. Texas won the game 26–24.

2006 Alamo Bowl	Line	1	-	2	-	3	-	4	-	Final
#18 Texas	(-9.0)	3	-	7	-	10	-	6	-	26
Iowa	(53.5)	14	-	0	-	7	-	3	-	24

Scoring Summary
Iowa – Young 1 yard run (Schlicher kick)
Iowa – Brodell 63 yard pass from Tate (Schlicher kick)
Texas – Bailey 27 yard Field goal
Texas – Sweed 20 yard pass from McCoy (Bailey kick)
Texas – Bailey 43 yard Field goal
Texas – Charles 72 yard pass from McCoy (Bailey kick)
Iowa – Brodell 23 yard pass from Tate (Schlicher kick)
Texas – Young 2 yard run (Pass failed)
Iowa – Schlicher 38 yard Field goal

Associated Press Alamo Bowl Game summary - Colt McCoy was supposed be a placeholder for Texas at Quarterback this season. Now, he's a record holder. The redshirt freshman who replaced Vince Young turned in another gritty performance with two touchdown passes to rally the No. 18 Longhorns to a 26-24 victory Saturday over Iowa in the Alamo Bowl. McCoy had been cleared to play just a week earlier after suffering a severely pinched nerve in his neck in each of Texas' last two games -- both losses. He also ran 8 yards on fourth down to set up a 2-yard touchdown run by Selvin Young early in the fourth quarter that proved to be the game winner. Vince Young left Texas a year early after leading the Longhorns to the national title last season, and McCoy became the starter before he had ever played a down in college. McCoy finished 26-for-40 for 308 yards. His 29 touchdown passes this season tied the NCAA freshman record set by Nevada's David Neill in 1998. Texas (10-3), the 2005 national champion, won at least 10 games for the sixth straight season and avoided its first three-game losing streak since 1999. Drew Tate passed for 274 yards and two touchdowns, both to Andy Brodell, for the Hawkeyes (6-7), who lost six of their last seven games. The Longhorns were heavy favorites in front of an Alamo Bowl record crowd of 65,875 that was mostly a sea of burnt orange. Texas fans had an easy 70-mile drive from Austin. But Iowa stunned them by taking a 14-0 lead in the first quarter and retaking the lead at 21-20 with 1:08 left in the third when Brodell scored his second touchdown on a 23-yard reception. Brodell had six catches for 159 yards. McCoy, who looked shaky early, had given Texas its first lead -- 20-14 -- with a 72-yard sideline strike to tailback Jamaal Charles in the third. After Young's touchdown with just under 11 minutes left, Iowa pulled within 26-24 when Kyle Schlicher kicked a 38-yard field goal. The Hawkeyes then forced a punt and had the ball near midfield. The Hawkeyes then got tripped up by their own trickery. Texas safety Marcus Griffin tackled Dominique Douglas for a 9-yard loss on a wide-receiver pass on first down. Iowa punted three plays later. Texas won its third straight bowl game and became the first team to win the Alamo Bowl after trailing at halftime. Longhorns fans so disappointed by not making a third consecutive Bowl Championship Series game, will remember this one for McCoy's game effort. Knocked down several times by Iowa's blitz-heavy pass rush, McCoy wasn't sharp at the start. He underthrew several receivers and looked tentative to run and risk another injury. The Longhorns didn't have another scholarship Quarterback available if he got hurt. Longhorns fans were just starting to crank up their "Texas Fight!" chant when the Hawkeyes scored on their first two possessions. Albert Young set up the first with a 26-yard run then scored on the next play on the opening drive. The Hawkeyes needed one play to strike again. Brodell took a short pass, faked out Texas cornerback Aaron Ross, the Thorpe Award winner, and outraced the Longhorns down the sideline for a 63-yard score. McCoy floated a perfect pass to Limas Sweed for a 20-yard score just before halftime to make it 14-10.

2006 Chick-Fil-A Peach Bowl

The 2006 Chick-fil-A Bowl was played between the Georgia Bulldogs and the Virginia Tech Hokies at the Georgia Dome in Atlanta, Georgia. The University of Georgia represented the Southeastern Conference (SEC) and Virginia Tech represented the Atlantic Coast Conference (ACC) in the competition. The game resulted in a 31–24 Georgia victory, even though spread bettors favored Virginia Tech to win by three points. In exchange for the right to pick the first ACC team after the Bowl Championship Series selections, bowl representatives paid US$3.25 million to the ACC, while the SEC, whose fifth team was selected, received $2.4 million. The combined $5.65 million payout was the seventh largest among all college football bowl games, and the fourth-largest non-BCS bowl game payout.

2006 Chick-Fil-A Peach Bowl	Line	1	-	2	-	3	-	4	-	Final
Georgia	(37.5)	3	-	0	-	10	-	18	-	31
#14 Virginia Tech	(-2.5)	0	-	21	-	0	-	3	-	24

Scoring Summary
Georgia – Coutu 39 yard Field goal
Virginia Tech – Ore 1 yard run (Pace kick)
Virginia Tech – Ore 1 yard run (Pace kick)
Virginia Tech – Wheeler 53 yard pass from Royal (Pace kick)
Georgia – Coutu 51 yard Field goal
Georgia – Milner 6 yard pass from Stafford (Coutu kick)
Georgia – Lumpkin 3 yard run (Coutu kick)
Georgia – Colutu 28 yard Field goal
Georgia – Southerland 1 yard run (Coutu kick)
Virginia Tech – Pace 28 yard Field goal

Georgia Media Guide Chick-Fil-A Peach Bowl Game Summary - Georgia stormed back from an 18-point deficit to defeat 14thranked Virginia Tech 31-24 in the Chick-fil-A Bowl in the Georgia Dome in front of a bowl-record crowd of 75,406 and a national ESPN television audience. It marked Georgia's third straight win over a ranked opponent as it closed out the year 9-4. Bulldog linebacker Tony Taylor (two interceptions) and Quarterback Matthew Stafford (129 yards, 1 TD) were named the Defensive and Offensive MVPs. In the fourth quarter, the Bulldogs got scoring runs from tailback Kregg Lumpkin and fullback Brannan Southerland along with one of kicker Brandon Coutu's three field goals (including a Georgia bowl record 51-yarder) to complete the comeback. Georgia fell behind 21-3 by the second quarter, but then held the Hokies to just a fourth quarter field goal. Stafford finished 9-for-21 for 129 yards and a TD after going just 3-for-9 in the first half. Tight end Martrez Milner had three catches for 49 yards and a touchdown, and he caught a critical two-point conversion pass that tied the game at 21-all. Taylor's two picks tied Georgia's bowl record held by Scott Woerner and Ronnie Harris. The Bulldogs had three interceptions and one fumble recovery on the night. In fact, 18 of Georgia's points came off of turnovers. Georgia led 3-0 after the first quarter, but then the Hokies built a 21-3 halftime edge. The final touchdown was a 53-yard lateral pass from Eddie Royal to tight end Sam Wheeler. The Bulldogs' first touchdown was sparked by a successful onside kick by Brian Mimbs who also recovered it. Taylor's interception at the start of the fourth quarter set up the game-tying touchdown. On the Hokies' next possession, Charles Johnson sacked Sean Glennon and caused him to fumble, which Quentin Moses recovered. It led to the go-ahead field goal by Coutu. Then three plays later, Taylor tipped a Glennon pass that was picked off by Paul Oliver who returned it to the 1. Southerland stormed into the end zone for a 31-21 lead.

Chick-Fil-A Game Notes - The 18-point comeback was the largest for Georgia under Coach Mark Richt up to that point. In recognition of their performances during the game, Georgia linebacker Tony Taylor and Quarterback Matthew Stafford were named the defensive and offensive MVPs of the game, respectively. Taylor's two interceptions tied the Georgia bowl record for interceptions, first set by Scott Woerner and Ronnie Harris. The four Virginia Tech turnovers resulted in 18 Georgia points. Georgia's sole turnover resulted in seven points for Virginia Tech.

2006 MPC Computers Bowl

The 2006 MPC Computers Bowl was held on December 31, 2006 at Bronco Stadium in Boise, Idaho. The game featured tie-ins between the Atlantic Coast Conference (ACC), which was represented by the Miami Hurricanes, and the Western Athletic Conference (WAC), represented by the Nevada Wolf Pack. The game was sponsored by the MPC Corporation, which was formerly known as Micron.

2006 MPC Computers Bowl	Line	1	-	2	-	3	-	4	-	Final
Miami	(-3.5)	7	-	7	-	7	-	0	-	21
Nevada	(42.0)	2	-	9	-	3	-	6	-	20

Scoring Summary
Miami - Freeman 1 yard run (Peattie kick)
Nevada - Team safety (Intentional grounding in end zone)
Nevada - Mitchell 27 yard pass from Rowe (pass failed)
Miami - Moore 52 yard pass from Freeman (Peattie kick)
Nevada - Jaekle 33 yard Field goal
Nevada - Jaekle 31 yard Field goal
Miami - Shield 78 yard pass from Freeman (Peattie kick)
Nevada - Jaekle 44 yard Field goal
Nevada - Jaekle 40 yard Field goal

Associated Press MPC Computers Bowl Game Summary - Here's some good news for Randy Shannon. The Miami Hurricanes apparently have plenty of talent coming back for their new coach next season. Kirby Freeman threw for 272 yards and two long touchdowns plus ran for another score, Chavez Grant made a game saving interception with 18 seconds left, and the Hurricanes sent fired coach Larry Coker out with a dramatic 21-20 win over Nevada in the MPC Computers Bowl on Sunday night. Coker was fired Nov. 24 but agreed to stay for the bowl game -- largely, he said, because the players wanted him there. He finished his six years with a 60-15 record and one national title, and by the time the team charter lands Monday morning in South Florida, Shannon will have officially been promoted from defensive coordinator to head coach, with 19 returning starters to work with. And on a cold night, Grant made a great play at the end to secure that Miami would finish with a winning record for the ninth straight year. Nevada had a first down at the Miami 36 in the final minute, but Grant's diving pick sealed the win and got Coker the perfect sendoff that his players wanted. Jeff Rowe threw a 27-yard touchdown pass to Marko Mitchell, and Brett Jaekle kicked four field goals for Nevada (8-5), including 44- and 40-yarders in the fourth quarter to get Nevada within a point. But the Wolf Pack got no closer, thanks largely to Grant's heroics at the end. Freeman threw a 78-yard touchdown pass to Sam Shields with 5:59 left in the third quarter to break what was a 14-14 tie and put the Hurricanes (7-6) ahead for good. Freeman also had a 52-yard scoring pass to Ryan Moore late in the first half. Rowe was 20-of-31 for 192 yards for Nevada, and Robert Hubbard had 60 yards on 20 carries. Shields caught four passes for 101 yards for Miami, while Moore made only two catches, but finished with 96 yards for the Hurricanes, who held a slim 300-297 edge in total offense. Down by seven entering the final quarter against the fifth-ranked defense in the country, Nevada nearly pulled off a comeback -- and may have been denied a great scoring opportunity by a call that didn't go its way. Facing a third-and-10 from the Miami 28, Rowe dropped back to throw to Anthony Pudewell inside the Miami 10. Pudewell was hit by Kenny Phillips as he tried to catch the ball, which bounced in the air. Replays appeared to show that Pudewell trapped the ball between his knees before it hit the turf, but officials ruled it incomplete, and the Wolf Pack eventually settled for a field goal. But at the end, there could be no debate about Grant's game-sealing catch. Rowe was trying to throw toward the right sideline, but Grant broke perfectly for the quick pass, lunged and cradled it as he sprawled to the blue turf -- as the Miami sideline broke into wild celebration. A season that had the Hurricanes endure the shooting death of defensive lineman Bryan Pata, fallout from the on-field brawl against Florida International and then Coker's firing got an ending worth smiling about. So, while battling temperatures in the upper 20s and wind that made it feel 10 degrees colder -- Freeman shouted "I'm freezing" on the sideline at one point -- the Hurricanes found a way to send Coker out a winner.

2007 Outback Bowl

The 2007 Outback Bowl Game was sponsored by Outback Steakhouse. The Outback Bowl has been played annually since 1986 (until 1994 it was known as the Hall of Fame Bowl). The 2007 game was played on January 1, 2007, at Raymond James Stadium in Tampa, Florida. The game pitted the #18 Tennessee Volunteers against the unranked Penn State Nittany Lions and was televised on ESPN.

2007 Outback Bowl	Line	1	-	2	-	3	-	4	-	Final
#17 Tennessee	(-4.0)	3	-	7	-	0	-	0	-	10
Penn State	(41.0)	0	-	10	-	0	-	10	-	20

Scoring Summary
Tennessee - Wilhoit 44 yard field goal
Penn State - Kelly 34 yard field goal
Penn State - Quarless 2 yard touchdown pass from Morelli (Kelly kick)
Tennessee - Coker 42 yard touchdown run (Wilhoit kick)
Penn State - Davis 88 yard fumble return for touchdown (Kelly kick)
Penn State - Kelly 22 yard field goal

Associated Press Outback bowl Game Summary - Joe Paterno insisted all along that he needed his players and assistant coaches more than they needed him in the Outback Bowl. Maybe the longtime Penn State coach was right. With Paterno watching from the press box while recovering from a broken leg, Tony

Hunt ran for 158 yards and Tony Davis returned a fumble 88 yards for a touchdown Monday, leading the Nittany Lions to a 20-10 victory over No. 17 Tennessee. Anthony Morelli threw a 2-yard TD pass to Andrew Quarless and Kevin Kelly kicked two field goals for Penn State, helping Paterno -- the all-time leader in bowl wins -- get his 22nd postseason victory. Penn State (9-4) forced three turnovers in holding Tennessee (9-4) to a season-low point total, and the Nittany Lions improved to 16-6 in New Year's Day bowls under their 80-year-old coach. Paterno broke his shinbone and tore two ligaments in his left knee in a sideline collision during a loss at Wisconsin on Nov. 4. He watched Penn State's next game from home -- the first he'd missed since 1977 -- and returned to Beaver Stadium to watch the season finale against Michigan State from the press box. As late as Sunday, Paterno remained optimistic about being on the sideline for his record 33rd bowl appearance, although he stressed, he would only do so if he felt up to it physically and didn't think it would be a distraction to his players. He wore his signature rolled-up khakis and blue-and-white Penn State jacket and spent a few minutes on the field during pregame warmups. He shook hands with Tennessee coach Phillip Fulmer and other well-wishers before returning to the locker room. Sloppy weather -- the game was played through intermittent rain -- contributed to Paterno's decision to join some of his assistants in a booth high above the field. The sometimes cantankerous coach was shown on television pounding his fist on a table when Kelly's 45-yard field goal attempt sailed wide left in the first quarter. The kicker later missed attempts of 54 and 50 yards with the score tied 10-10. Penn State viewed Monday's game as a final opportunity to assess how far it has come since a lopsided loss to Notre Dame early in the season. The Nittany Lions were more competitive in subsequent losses to Ohio State, Michigan and Wisconsin, and Paterno felt an opponent as highly regarded as Tennessee would be an excellent gauge of where his team is heading. Morelli's TD pass to Quarless finished an eight-play, 92-yard drive -- Penn State's longest of the season -- and gave the Nittany Lions a short-lived 10-3 lead. LaMarcus Coker countered for Tennessee a little more than 2 minutes later, using a nifty straight-arm to fend off linebacker Sean Lee before sprinting through a hole on the left side and outrunning the pursuit to finish a 42-yard touchdown run. It remained 10-10 until Davis picked up a fumble by Tennessee's Arian Fosterand raced untouched up the left sideline to put Penn State ahead for good with 10 minutes remaining. Kelly added his second field goal with 3:29 left. Morelli completed 14 of 25 passes for 197 yards and no interceptions, and Hunt compiled his eighth 100-yard game rushing this season on 31 carries. Erik Ainge was 25-of-37 for 267 yards, but also threw his first interception since Oct. 21 for Tennessee. The Volunteers were threatening to break the 10-10 tie after his 53-yard completion to Chris Brown. However, Lee hit Foster on the next play to force the fumble that Davis returned for his TD.

2007 Gator Bowl

The 2007 Gator Bowl was between the West Virginia Mountaineers and the Georgia Tech Yellow Jackets on January 1, 2007, at Jacksonville Municipal Stadium in Jacksonville, Florida. Down by 18 in the third quarter, West Virginia scored 21 unanswered points to win 38-35. The game matched West Virginia from the Big East Conference against Georgia Tech from the Atlantic Coast Conference. West Virginia entered the game ranked #13 in the AP Poll; it was West Virginia's third appearance in the Gator Bowl in the last four years and sixth overall. Georgia Tech accepted a bid to the Gator Bowl after losing the ACC championship to Wake Forest. It was Georgia Tech's first appearance in the Gator Bowl since 2000 and seventh overall.

2007 Gator Bowl	Line	1	-	2	-	3	-	4	-	Final
#25 Georgia Tech	(47.0)	14	-	14	-	7	-	0	-	35
#13 West Virginia	(-10.5)	7	-	10	-	21	-	0	-	38

Scoring Summary
West Virginia – Schmitt 1 yard run (McAfee kick)
Georgia Tech – C. Johnson 31 yard pass from Bennett (Bell kick)
Georgia Tech – Choice 3 yard run (Bell kick)
Georgia Tech – C. Johnson 48 yard pass from Bennett (Bell kick)
West Virginia – McAfee 24 yard Field goal
Georgia Tech – J. Johnson 27 yard pass from Bennett (Bell kick)
West Virginia – Schmitt 11 yard run (McAfee kick)
Georgia Tech – Choice 5 yard run (Bell kick)
West Virginia – Gonzales 58 yard pass from White (McAfee kick)
West Virginia – Myles 14 yard pass from White (McAfee kick)
West Virginia – White 15 yard run (McAfee kick)

Associated Press Gator Bowl Game Summary - Sometimes even triple coverage isn't enough to stop Calvin Johnson. Johnson leapt between two West Virginia defenders and in front of a third for a 32-yard reception in the third quarter of the Gator Bowl on Monday, one of his nine catches for 186 yards and two touchdowns in Georgia Tech's 38-35 loss. The All-American junior made the Mountaineers' secondary look helpless all day in what may have been his collegiate finale. Johnson is considering forgoing his senior year for the NFL, and the 6-foot-5 wideout looked ready to make the transition. Quarterback Tyler Bennett, thankful for having Johnson to throw to in his second career start. Johnson's yardage total on Monday put him fifth in the Gator Bowl record book -- and in pretty good company. He finished behind Andre Rison, Javon Walker and Fred Biletnikoff and in front of Marvin Harrison. Johnson won the Biletnikoff Award this year as the nation's top receiver and was named the Atlantic Coast Conference player of the year. Before Monday's game, he had 1,016 yards receiving and 13 touchdowns, fourth-best in the country.

2007 Capital One Bowl

The 2007 Capital One Bowl was held on January 1, 2007 at the Citrus Bowl in Orlando, Florida. The game featured the Badgers of The University of Wisconsin, who finished tied for second in the Big Ten Conference, and the Razorbacks of The University of Arkansas, who finished first in the Southeastern Conference's West Division.

2007 Capital One Bowl	Line	1	-	2	-	3	-	4	-	Final
#12 Arkansas	(-2.0)	7	-	0	-	0	-	7	-	14
#6 Wisconsin	(45.0)	10	-	7	-	0	-	0	-	17

Scoring Summary
Wisconsin – Melhaff 52 yard Field goal
Arkansas – Jones 76 yard run (Davis kick)
Wisconsin – Hubbard 22 yard pass from Stocco (Melhaff kick)
Wisconsin – Beckum 14 yard pass from Stocco (Melhaff kick)
Arkansas – Jones 12 yard run (Davis kick)

Associated Press Capital One Bowl Game Summary - John Stocco hoped a win over Arkansas in the Capital One Bowl would help silence those who have questioned the quality of Wisconsin's schedule. He won't have to hear much more of it after helping No. 6 Wisconsin to a 17-14 victory over the No. 12 Razorbacks on Monday. Stocco threw for two touchdowns in the first half, and the Badgers (12-1) held on through a tense second half. Wisconsin won 12 games in a season for the first time, a nice claim for a team overshadowed by Big Ten rivals Ohio State and Michigan. But this was the Badgers' first win over a ranked team. Their only loss was to Michigan, and Ohio State wasn't on their schedule. Arkansas (10-4) had several chances to seize momentum, and each time, Wisconsin held the Razorbacks off. For example, when the Badgers' Ken DeBauche had a punt blocked in the second quarter, he managed to pick up the loose ball, scramble around and complete a pass. The completion didn't count -- Wisconsin had an ineligible man downfield. But because DeBauche picked up the ball and threw instead of merely falling on it, Arkansas had to take the penalty. DeBauche got to kick again, and the Razorbacks ended up losing about 50 yards of field position. Wisconsin frustrated the Razorbacks from the very start. Arkansas' Darren McFadden broke free for a 45-yard gain on his first carry, but defensive back Jack Ikegwuonu managed to run him down at the 9. The Razorbacks came away with no points when Jeremy Davis missed a 30-yard field goal. McFadden, the Heisman Trophy runner-up, hurt his ankle in the Southeastern Conference championship game Dec. 2, and it appeared to be bothering him still. The Razorbacks finished with three straight losses after winning 10 in a row. They were trying for their first 11-win season since 1977. Arkansas committed 12 penalties for 123 yards. The Badgers were held to minus-5 yards rushing for the game, but Stocco threw touchdown passes of 22 yards to Paul Hubbard and 13 yards to Travis Beckum. Wisconsin led 17-7 at halftime. In the third quarter, 35 of the first 41 snaps were in Wisconsin territory, but Arkansas didn't score until Felix Jones' 12-yard run in the fourth. Wisconsin won nine straight to finish the season and can now boast of a second straight Capital One Bowl win over the Southeastern Conference. The Badgers beat Auburn 24-10 last year, although that didn't necessarily silence the doubters. Taylor Mehlhaff opened the scoring for the Badgers with a 52-yard field goal, a career long and a Capital One Bowl record. Jones answered quickly for Arkansas with a 76-yard touchdown run. Jones finished with a career-high 150 yards on 14 carries, outplaying McFadden and Wisconsin's P.J. Hill. Stocco, the game's most valuable player, went 14-of-34 for 206 yards with two interceptions. He also was sacked six times, part of the reason Wisconsin's rushing stats were so bad. But the Badgers passed the ball better than Arkansas. The Razorbacks stuck with their plan to start Casey Dick at Quarterback and bring in freshman Mitch Mustain for the third series. That was Mustain's only appearance of the first half, although he returned for a bit in the second. Dick went 9-of-21 for 98 yards with an interception. Mustain was 5-of-10 for 41 yards with an interception. McFadden left in the third quarter with a sprained right shoulder, although he returned a short while later. He rushed for 89 yards to finish the season with 1,647, the fifth-highest total in SEC history.

2007 Cotton Bowl Classic

The 2007 AT&T Cotton Bowl Classic was played on January 1, 2007, at the Cotton Bowl in Dallas, Texas, USA. The Cotton Bowl Classic featured the Nebraska Cornhuskers versus the Auburn Tigers.

2007 Cotton Bowl Classic	Line	1	-	2	-	3	-	4	-	Final
#22 Nebraska	(46.0)	7	-	7	-	0	-	0	-	14
#10 Auburn	(-2.0)	7	-	7	-	3	-	0	-	17

Scoring Summary
Nebraska – Swift 13 yard pass from Taylor (Congdon kick)
Auburn – Stewart 9 yard pass from Cox (Vaughn kick)
Auburn – Stewart 1 yard run (Vaughn kick)
Nebraska – Jackson 20 yard run (Congdon kick)
Auburn – Vaughn 42 yard Field goal

Cotton Bowl Classic Game Summary - Nearly two decades had passed since Auburn ran its way into the AT&T Cotton Bowl behind the power running of Bo Jackson. This time around, the Tigers relied less on their offense and more on a bruising defense that continually shut down their opponents. The same was said after the 71st AT&T Cotton Bowl Classic. Nebraska brought in a pro-style offense that could roll up large chunks of yards quickly, but Auburn's defense held to form and kept the Cornhuskers in check. Auburn capitalized on two early Husker turnovers, and its defense made a critical fourth-down stop in the closing minutes to help the Tigers secure a 17-14 victory on New Year's Day. Under bright, sunshiny skies, a crowd of 66,777 watched as Auburn's John Vaughn provided the margin of victory with a 42-yard field goal with 6:20 left in the third quarter – marking the second straight year for the Field Scovell Trophy winner to be determined by a three-pointer. Auburn, representing the SEC, finished 11-2 and was 33-5-0 – the school's best three-year record in terms of victories. The Tigers victory marked the fourth straight SEC victory in the AT&T Cotton Bowl. Nebraska, representing the Big 12 Conference as North Division Champions, finished 9-5. Auburn's Courtney Taylor, who caught six passes for 70 yards, received the Sanford Trophy, which honors the game's outstanding offensive player and commemorates Cotton Bowl Classic founder J. Curtis Sanford. Taylor finished his career as Auburn's record holder for 153 career pass receptions. Auburn linebacker Will Herring, who was credited with seven solo tackles, received the McKnight Trophy, which recognizes the classic's outstanding defensive player and commemorates Felix McKnight, a celebrated newspaperman and long-time chairman of the Cotton Bowl Team Selection Committee. Then Nebraska's Stewart Bradley covered Cox's fumble at the Auburn 42 with 5:24 remaining, the Cornhuskers seemed in position to overtake the Tigers. But the Auburn defense stiffened at its 27, stopping a shovel pass for a two-yard loss on third down and forcing an incompletion on fourth down. Nebraska's 15-play, 80-yard scoring drive on the Classic's opening possession was a timely blend of Marlon Lucky's running and Zac Taylor's third-down passing. Taylor's 13-yard throw to Nate Swift helped Nebraska to a 7-0 lead with 7:37 remaining in the first quarter. Momentum swung suddenly in Auburn's direction late in the first quarter on Tiger linebacker Karibe Dede's 52-yard pass interception and return to the Nebraska nine. On second down, Brandon Cox threw a nine-yard touchdown pass to Carl Stewart, enabling the Tigers to even the score with 56 seconds remaining in the period. On the fourth play of the second quarter, Nebraska's fake punt trickery from its 29 backfired, with Auburn's Tristan Davis covering the ensuing fumble at Nebraska's 14. Cox's 12-yard pass to Taylor gave Auburn a first down at the Nebraska one. Stewart scored from there on second down, putting Auburn in front, 14-7. Nebraska evened the score on its next possession, moving 72 yards in seven plays. Brandon Jackson got the touchdown, sprinting 20 yards on a misdirection play over left tackle with nine minutes remaining in the half. The score stayed that way until Vaughn's kick. On fourth down from the Auburn 30 with just under four minutes to play, Nebraska chose not to attempt a possible game-tying field goal. Callahan explained later that the distance was beyond the comfort range set by the coaches before kickoff. Auburn's defense ended up pitching a shutout in the second half, and despite Nebraska's big-play potential, the Tigers clamped down and walked away with a 17-14 victory and the Field Scovell Trophy.

2007 Rose Bowl

The 2007 Rose Bowl Game presented by Citi was played on January 1, 2007 at the Rose Bowl in Pasadena, California. It was the 93rd Rose Bowl Game. In the game, the University of Southern California Trojans, champions of the Pacific-10 Conference, defeated the University of Michigan Wolverines, second-place finishers in the Big Ten Conference, 32–18. USC wide receiver Dwayne Jarrett and USC outside linebacker Brian Cushing were named the Rose Bowl Players of the Game. Historically, the Rose Bowl has pitted the champions the Big Ten and Pac-10. What made the 2007 Rose Bowl a not-so-traditional matchup is that Michigan entered as the runner-up of the Big Ten. The Big Ten champions, Ohio State, were ranked #1 and instead participated in the 2007 BCS National Championship Game. Michigan won their first 11 games in 2006 but lost their last regular season game to the undefeated Buckeyes in Columbus, 42–39.

2007 Rose Bowl	Line	1	-	2	-	3	-	4	-	Final
#8 USC	(Pk)	3	-	0	-	16	-	13	-	32
#3 Michigan	(47.0)	0	-	3	-	0	-	15	-	18

Scoring Summary
USC – Danelo 26 yard Field goal
Michigan – Rivas 43 yard Field goal
USC – McCoy 2 yard pass from Booty (Danelo kick)
USC – Jarrett 22 yard pass from Booty (Danelo kick)
USC – Danelo 26 yard Field goal
Michigan – Arrington 22 yard pass From Henne (2 pt. run good)
USC – Jarrett 62 yard pass from booty (Danelo kick)
USC – Smith 7 yard pass from Booty (Danelo kick)
Michigan – Breaston 41 yard pass from Henne (Rivas kick)

Associated Press Rose Bowl Game recap - Even before his uniform had come off, Dwayne Jarrett's teammates were lobbying him to wear it one more year. After the day he had in the Rose Bowl, it was easy to see why. Jarrett, the sensational Southern California junior, caught 11 passes for 205 yards and two touchdowns to help the eighth-ranked Trojans finish their season with a statement Monday in a 32-18 romp over Michigan. It was an all-encompassing blowout over a solid, third-ranked Michigan squad that positioned USC (11-2) as maybe The Team to watch next season. And that's even if Jarrett takes the bucks and heads to the NFL. Booty was no slouch, either. He threw for 391 yards and four scores to land himself on the early short list of next season's Heisman favorites. Jarrett would be there if he decides to return. Meanwhile, linebacker Brian Cushing had 2 1/2 sacks and defensive end Lawrence Jackson came up with two turnovers on a day when the Trojans must have been thinking about next season, to say nothing of the opportunity it squandered in the one that just ended. This convincing victory came a month after a 13-9 loss to UCLA in this stadium wrecked their chances for another shot at the national title. With most of USC's star underclassmen coming back, Jarrett said he'll sit down with his family to discuss his future. If this was his last college game, it was quite a finale. His 62-yard touchdown behind All-American cornerback Leon Hall put USC ahead 25-11 early in the fourth and showed just how good the 6-foot-5 pass catcher can be. For icing, Jarrett outjumped a pair of Michigan defenders for a 29-yard gain midway through the fourth quarter. A few plays later, Booty threw his fourth touchdown pass -- this one to senior Steve Smith, who finished with seven catches for 108 yards. Joining Hall on the losing end were Chad Henne, Mike Hart and big group of Michigan juniors who also should be a force next season. They came in wondering if maybe they hadn't gotten a raw deal by being left out of the national title game after a back-and-forth 42-39 loss to Ohio State in the wake of Bo Schembechler's death. But these Wolverines didn't look as good as the ones who lost that heartbreaker in November. And they hardly looked like champions. Henne didn't get the Wolverines past the USC 20 until they had fallen behind 19-3. When Michigan finally did reach the end zone to cut its deficit to 19-11, the Trojans came right back with Jarrett's long touchdown. Carr's team lost its fourth straight bowl game and ended the season on a two-game losing streak for the third consecutive year. Granted, there was nothing riding on this game between arguably the two best teams that weren't playing for the BCS championship. Then again, getting stomped like that can make for a tough offseason. The first half was something only Schembechler could have loved -- a 3-3 stalemate that wasn't nearly as interesting as watching the colors change on the San Gabriel Mountains. USC took control early in the third quarter when, after three straight handoffs to Hart, the Wolverines tried a screen pass that Henne threw into a crowd, only to see it land in the hands of Jackson. Thus began a string with Booty throwing on nine straight plays, including four consecutive completions that led to the game's first touchdown and a 10-3 lead. After a three-and-out, Booty moved the Trojans 70 yards, capping it with a 22-yard pass to Jarrett, who easily made the catch over Morgan Trent and celebrated by pretending he was shooting hoops. Cushing got another sack and Jackson recovered the ensuing fumble on the next drive, which led to a field goal and 19-3 lead. From there, the teams went back and forth, giving Jarrett the chance to pad some stats and impress the NFL scouts, who were certainly watching him fashion a successful finish to a frustrating and injury-plagued year. It was a splendid ending to what has been a difficult month and year for the Trojans, who were denied a spot in their third straight BCS title game because of the loss to UCLA. Still, the Trojans and the Wolverines spent the week talking about how happy they were to be in the Rose Bowl, even though the game was relegated to little more than exhibition status. That's because the only game that matters will feature Ohio State and Florida next week in Glendale, Ariz. All USC could do was come out and play its best, and it did. That was more than Michigan could say. Henne finished with good numbers -- 26-for-41 for 309 yards -- but most of them came after the game was out of hand. He also got sacked six times. Hart finished with 47 yards, the first time he's been held under 90 all year. Steve Breaston had seven catches for 115 yards and a late 41-yard score from Henne. None, however, did much when it really mattered.

2007 Fiesta Bowl

The 2007 Tostitos Fiesta Bowl was played annually since 1971, originally at Sun Devil Stadium on the campus of Arizona State University in Tempe, Arizona through 2006, the game was played on January 1, 2007, at the game's new home field, the University of Phoenix Stadium in Glendale, Arizona, and pitted the Big 12 champion No. 8 Oklahoma Sooners against the WAC champion No. 9 Boise State Broncos. The contest was televised on Fox. The game featured a series of "fantastic finishes" – Oklahoma scoring 25 unanswered points to take its first lead with just over one minute remaining in the game, the teams scoring 22 points in the final 1:26 of regulation and 15 points in overtime, culminating with Boise State completing three do-or-die trick plays (the first of which was called with 18 seconds remaining in the fourth quarter) to win the game.

Associated Press Fiesta Bowl Game summary - Boise State proved it belonged in the BCS and started another lively college football debate. The ninth-ranked Broncos completed a perfect season with an exhilarating 43-42 overtime victory over No. 7 Oklahoma in the Tostitos Fiesta Bowl Monday night, leaving Boise State and top-ranked Ohio State as the only teams with perfect records. The Buckeyes will play No. 2 Florida for the BCS national championship on the same field Jan. 8, but the Broncos (13-0) believe they belong in that game. And why not? Boise State showed plenty of heart and resilience in edging the Sooners (11-3) in one of the more amazing games in recent memory. Quarterback Jared Zabransky selected the offensive MVP after completing 19 of 29 passes for 262 yards and three touchdowns. If the Fiesta Bowl was any indication, it would certainly be fun to watch. In one of the most dramatic finishes in BCS history, the Sooners and the Broncos combined for 22 points in the final 86 seconds of regulation. Boise State blew an 18-point lead midway through the third quarter, then twice rallied from seven-point deficits. The Broncos appeared to be finished when Oklahoma cornerback Marcus Walker intercepted Zabransky's pass and returned it 33 yards for a touchdown to put the Sooners ahead 35-28 with 1:02 remaining. The magic came on a stunning 50-yard "hook-and-ladder" touchdown play on fourth-and-18 in the final seconds of regulation. Zabransky hit Drisan James at Oklahoma's 35, and James pitched the ball to Jerard Rabb, who raced into the end zone with 7 seconds to play. Zabransky said the Broncos practice that play almost every day in practice but that it rarely works against the Boise State defense, which usually knows when it's coming. Oklahoma coach Bob Stoops said the Sooners were looking for a trick play. But he said the Broncos ran this one to perfection. That play merely set the stage for more Broncos magic. Oklahoma's Adrian Peterson opened the overtime with a 25-yard touchdown run. It may have been the final college play for Peterson, who ran for 77 yards and two touchdowns in his first game since breaking his left collarbone Oct. 14. The Broncos answered with Vinny Perretta's fourth-down touchdown pass to Derek Schouman. With Boise State down by a point, Petersen decided to go for the victory. On the decisive play, Zabransky looked at three wide receivers to his right, then, with his best Statue of Liberty impression, handed the ball behind his back to tailback Ian Johnson, who raced untouched into the end zone. Moments after Johnson ended the game, he asked his girlfriend, Broncos cheerleader Chrissy Popadics, to marry him. Johnson carried 23 times for 101 yards and a touchdown, and Drisan James caught three passes for 96 yards and two touchdowns. Oklahoma's Paul Thompson threw a career-high three interceptions. He completed 19 of 32 passes for 233 yards and two touchdowns. The wild finish came after Boise State dominated the first 40 minutes, making it clear that the Western Athletic Conference champion deserved a BCS berth. Oklahoma didn't go quietly. The Sooners spotted the Broncos an 18-point lead midway through the third quarter, then rallied to take a 35-28 lead on Walker's interception. That came one play after the Sooners tied it at 28. They Sooners cut it to 28-26 on a 5-yard pass from Paul Thompson to Quentin Chaney with 1:26 to play. After penalties on their first two 2-point conversion tries, the Sooners converted when Thompson hit Juaquin Iglesias. Thompson completed five passes for 59 yards on the tying drive and ran for 8 yards. The Broncos stunned the Sooners with two quick touchdowns to take a 14-0 lead midway through the first quarter. The first came on a 49-yard touchdown pass from Zabransky to James, a Phoenix product. Zabransky froze the defense with a play-fake to Johnson, then fired to James, who was all alone 10 yards behind cornerback Marcus Walker. On the next series, defensive end Mike T. Williams sacked Sooners Quarterback Paul Thompson, who fumbled. Williams recovered at Oklahoma's 9. Two plays later, Johnson scored from 2 yards out to give the Broncos a 14-0 lead with 7:28 left in the first quarter. The Sooners cut the lead to 14-10 before Zabransky and James connected again shortly before the half. But the best was yet to come.

2007 Fiesta Bowl	Line	1	-	2	-	3	-	4	-	OT	-	Final
#9 Boise State	(50.0)	14	-	7	-	7	-	7	-	8	-	43
#7 Oklahoma	(-7.5)	7	-	3	-	7	-	18	-	7	-	42

Scoring Summary
Boise State—James 49 yard pass from Zabransky. (Montgomery kick)
Boise State—Johnson 2 yard run (Montgomery kick)
Oklahoma - Johnson 7 yard pass from Thompson (Hartley kick)
Oklahoma - Hartley 31 yard field goal
Boise State - James 32 yard pass from Zabransky (Montgomery kick)
Boise State - Tadman 27 yard interception return (Montgomery kick)
Oklahoma- Peterson 8 yard run (Hartley kick)
Oklahoma– Hartley 28 yard field goal
Oklahoma– Chaney 5 yd pass from Thompson (Iglesias pass from Thompson)
Oklahoma- Walker 34 yard interception return (Hartley Kick)
Boise State- James lateral to Rabb - 35 yard run (Montgomery Kick)
Oklahoma– Peterson 25 yard run (Hartley Kick)
Boise State– Schouma 6 yd pass from Perretta (Johnson run)

Overtime - Under college football rules, both teams in overtime are given one possession from their opponent's twenty-five yard line. A coin toss gives one team the choice, offense or defense first, or which end of the field. The winner of the toss generally chooses to be on defense first, to know how many points must be scored to win or tie on their offensive possession. The loser of the toss is left to choose the end of the field—usually the one with the largest proportion of their own team's fans so as to increase the crowd noise while their opponents are on offense. The team that is leading after both possessions is declared the winner and in the event of a tie, there is another overtime session with the order of the offensive and defensive possessions reversed. The end of the field is also changed with each overtime session. Boise State won the coin toss and opted to play defense first. Oklahoma scored on their first play with a 25-yard run by Peterson, which would ultimately be his last collegiate touchdown. The extra point was good, making the score 42–35 Oklahoma. On Boise State's drive, the Broncos came down to 4th and 2 on the Sooners' 5 yard line and decided to run their second trick play, a wide receiver rollout option from a variant of the Wildcat offense. Zabransky ran in motion to his left while backup wide receiver Vinny Perretta, lined up as a running back, took the snap, rolled to his right, then threw a touchdown pass to tight end Derek Schouman, who had lined up as a wide receiver, to bring Boise State within one point at 42–41. Instead of kicking the extra-point to tie the game and send it into a second overtime, Broncos coach Chris Petersen risked defeat to go for the two-point conversion to win. He ran their third trick play of the night. It was a variation of the Statue of Liberty play known to the team simply as "Statue Left," which was drawn up by backup Quarterback Taylor Tharp. Boise State lined up three receivers on the right side. After the snap, Zabransky faked a quick pass to his right with his right hand, then quickly handed off the football backhanded with his left hand to running back Ian Johnson, who ran untouched into the end zone for the conversion and the win.

Postgame - During a postgame interview with FOX Sports on-field analyst Chris Myers, Johnson got down on one knee and proposed to his girlfriend, Boise State head cheerleader Chrissy Popadics, on live TV. Myers, however, spoiled the proposal by mentioning it before Johnson went to a knee. She accepted. Ian did not have a ring with him because he originally planned on proposing to Christy at Lagoon on their way home from the Fiesta Bowl, but he could not give up the opportunity to propose on National TV after scoring the game-winning two-point conversion. The couple married on July 28, 2007. According to Ian Johnson, he received about 30 threatening letters which he handed over to the FBI, from people who objected to his nationally televised interracial marriage proposal at the end of the game. Johnson, who is half-black, and Popadics, who is white, hired security for their wedding due to the threats.

Final game facts - Boise State finished their season with a perfect 13–0 record, spurring controversy as to whether teams from non-BCS conferences should have an opportunity to play for a national title.

2007 Orange Bowl

The 2007 FedEx Orange Bowl game was a Bowl Championship Series (BCS) bowl game played on January 2, 2007, at Dolphin Stadium in Miami Gardens, Florida. The game matched the No. 15 Wake Forest Demon Deacons versus the No. 6 Louisville Cardinals and was televised on Fox. Each of the teams selected an honorary captain. Wake Forest chose golf great Arnold Palmer, a Wake alumnus, and Louisville chose boxing legend Muhammad Ali, a Louisville native. Dwyane Wade of the hometown Miami Heat presented the coin for the coin toss.

2007 Orange Bowl	Line	1	-	2	-	3	-	4	-	Final
#15 Wake Forest	(52.0)	0	-	3	-	7	-	3	-	13
#5 Louisville	(-10.0)	0	-	10	-	0	-	14	-	24

Scoring Summary
Wake Forest – Swank 44 yard Field goal
Louisville – Carmody 41 yard Field goal
Louisville – Allen 21 yard pass from Carter (Carmody kick)
Wake Forest – Morton 30 yard pass from Skinner (Swank kick)
Wake Forest – Swank 36 yard Field goal
Louisville – Allen 1 yard run (Carmody kick)
Louisville – Bolen 18 yard run (Carmody kick)

Associated Press Orange Bowl Game Summary - Never mind the turnovers and the sloppy first three quarters. Soon after the No. 5 Louisville Cardinals won the Orange Bowl, they had their sights on bigger things. The Cardinals overcame a rash of mistakes Tuesday night to earn their first major-bowl victory in 15 years, beating Wake Forest 24-13. Brohm threw for 311 yards and Anthony Allen scored two touchdowns, one on a trick play, to help Louisville finish 12-1 and clinch its highest end-of-season ranking ever. Harry Douglas made 10 catches for 165 yards. The Cardinals blew an 18-point lead in their lone loss at Rutgers, which likely cost them a chance to play for the national title. The Cardinals averaged 39 points and ranked second in the nation in total offense this season but fell behind 13-10 in the final period before their high-powered offense got into gear. Touchdown drives of 81 and 71 yards on consecutive possessions sealed their first win in a major bowl since the 1991 Fiesta Bowl. The No. 15 Demon Deacons slipped to 11-3, still their best season. Through three quarters, the Demon Deacons appeared on the verge of an upset, as squandered opportunities plagued the Cardinals. Louisville lost two fumbles in Wake Forest territory, Mario Urrutia dropped a potential 62-yard touchdown pass, and Art Carmody -- the Lou Groza Award winner -- was wide right on a 32-yard field goal attempt, only his fourth miss this season. Alphonso Smith nearly blocked Carmody's errant kick and also harried Louisville's punter into a 14-yard boot that set up a 44-yard field goal by Sam Swank of Wake Forest. Like Louisville, the Demon Deacons failed to convert several scoring chances. They committed three turnovers in Cardinal territory, and after moving 36 yards in the final minute of the first half, Swank missed a 47-yard field goal. But Swank made a 36-yarder to cap a 61-yard drive and put the Demon Deacons ahead 13-10 early in the fourth quarter. The Cardinals responded with an eight-play drive capped by Allen's 1-yard plunge for a 17-13 lead with 12:31 to go. They quickly forced a punt and mounted a 10-play drive that ended with Brock Bolen's 18-yard scoring run. Brohm directed the drives, finished 24-for-34 and was chosen the game's most valuable player. He said he's leaning toward returning for his senior season next fall. His yardage total was the third highest in Orange Bowl history, behind only Michigan's Tom Brady and Southern Cal's Matt Leinart. Wake Forest's Riley Skinner went 21-for-33 for 271 yards with one touchdown and one interception. The Demon Deacons trailed 10-3 at halftime but scored on their first possession of the third period when Nate Morton slipped behind the Louisville secondary to catch a 30-yard TD pass from Skinner. The Cardinals sputtered early but pulled out a trick play to score their first touchdown. Brohm threw a lateral to Carter, who stopped and threw across the field deep to Allen for the score. The 21-yard pass was the first this season by Carter, a Quarterback at Georgia Tech before he transferred. Trick plays backfired early on for the Demon Deacons, who twice tried reverses in the first quarter. The first lost 17 yards and the second lost 10. The bowl game was only the seventh for Wake Forest in 105 seasons.

2007 Sugar Bowl

The 2007 Allstate Sugar Bowl was held on January 3, 2007, in the Louisiana Superdome in New Orleans, it was the 73rd Sugar Bowl. The game matched the Notre Dame Fighting Irish football team against the LSU Tigers football team and was televised on Fox. This game received extra attention because it was the return of the Sugar Bowl to New Orleans. In 2006, the game was played at the Georgia Dome in Atlanta, Georgia due to the damage caused by Hurricane Katrina to the Superdome (that game also featured a virtual "home" team, the Georgia Bulldogs). LSU won the 2007 contest 41–14, tying the Notre Dame-LSU series at 5–5 (with LSU taking a 2–0 lead in bowl game meetings). With the loss, Notre Dame lost a record-setting nine bowl games in a row, including losing their three BCS bowl games by wide point margins.

2007 Sugar Bowl	Line	1	-	2	-	3	-	4	-	Final
#11 Notre Dame	(55.5)	7	-	7	-	0	-	0	-	14
#4 LSU	(-9.0)	14	-	7	-	13	-	7	-	41

Scoring Summary
LSU - Williams 3 yard run (David kick)
LSU – Bowe 1 yard Pass from Russell (David kick)
Notre Dame - Grimes 24 yard Pass from Quinn (Gioia kick)
Notre Dame - Samardzija 10 yard pass from Quinn (Gioia kick)
LSU - Russell 5 yard run. (David kick)
LSU - David 26 yard field goal
LSU - David 37- yard field goal
LSU - LaFell 58 yard pass from Russell (David kick)
LSU - Williams 20 yard run (Gaudet kick)

USA Today/Associated Press Sugar Bowl Game Summary - Maybe Brady Quinn will get a final say in April, hear his name called before that of any other Quarterback in the NFL draft But LSU's JaMarcus Russell gave the far more eloquent, effective performance Wednesday. The junior Quarterback outplayed his decorated Notre Dame counterpart — the second runner-up in last month's Heisman Trophy balloting — in the Allstate Sugar Bowl, throwing for two touchdowns and running for another as the No. 4-ranked Tigers rolled to a 41-14 victory against the Irish. LSU outscored The Fighting Irish 27-0 over the last two quarters and 75 seconds. Russell and the rest of LSU's offense piled up 577 yards, exploiting a Notre Dame defense that surrendered 617 in a Fiesta Bowl loss to Ohio State a year earlier and remained suspect this season. Russell, a unanimous selection as the game's most valuable player, broke a 14-14 tie near the end of the first half, scoring on a 5-yard Quarterback draw. He completed 11 of his first 15 second-half passes, setting up two LSU field goals and providing the night's exclamation point with 18 seconds left in the third quarter. Dodging defensive pressure, he launched a 58-yard scoring strike to freshman receiver Brandon LaFell. LSU (11-2) went on to score the game's final 27 points. The 6-6, 260-pound Russell — also a potential high first-round pick if he forgoes his final season of eligibility to enter the draft — finished 21-for-34 for 332 yards in what might have been his final college game. True freshman Keiland Williams added 107 yards and two TDs rushing. Quinn, a senior who holds 36 Notre Dame Records, also threw for two touchdowns but was intercepted twice in an unsteady-on-the-field audition for the NFL scouts. He completed 15 of 35 passes for 148 yards, sometimes overthrowing, sometimes crossing signals with intended receivers, struggling to find a rhythm. Notre Dame's offense totaled 30 yards in the second half as the Irish lost for a record ninth consecutive time in a bowl. Notre Dame (10-3) bounced back from an early 14-0 deficit and tied the game with 2½ minutes left in the first half. But Russell's took matters in his own hands — and legs — to put the Tigers ahead to stay before the teams went to the locker room. It was a sweet return to the Sugar Bowl for LSU, which claimed the BCS title in the game three years earlier. The stakes in this game weren't quite so high ... or were they? LSU won 75 miles down the road from its Baton Rouge campus, in a city still recovering from Hurricane Katrina, in a building — the Louisiana Superdome — that symbolized the suffering from the storm. A crowd of 77,781 cheered both the bowl's return after a one-year hiatus in Atlanta and the in-state team as a movingly appropriate invitee.

2007 International Bowl

The 2007 International Bowl, held on January 6, 2007 at Rogers Centre in Toronto, Canada. The game pitted the University of Cincinnati against Western Michigan University. It was historically notable for several reasons: It was the first edition of the International Bowl. It was the first significant football game held in Canada under American football rules since 2001, which was the last season in which Simon Fraser University's football team participated in the U.S.-based National Association of Intercollegiate Athletics under American rules. Starting in 2002, Simon Fraser moved its football program to Canadian Interuniversity Sport and began playing under Canadian rules. It was the first major college (American) football game played outside the United States since 1996, when Notre Dame and Navy played their annual regular-season game at Croke Park in Dublin, Ireland. It was the first postseason bowl game (in American football) to be played outside the U.S. since the final Bacardi Bowl was played in Havana, Cuba in 1937. It also made Coach Brian Kelly the first coach ever to beat the same team twice in a season with different teams. The game drew a crowd of 26,717. Besides the historic significance of the game itself, the UC–WMU matchup was of particular interest because newly hired Cincinnati head coach Brian Kelly coached Central Michigan University during the 2006 regular season. Kelly and Central Michigan, the main rival of WMU, defeated Western Michigan 31–7 just eight weeks earlier. In addition, both schools had been charter members of the Mid-American Conference (WMU is still in the conference today, but UC left after the 1952–53 academic year).

2007 International Bowl	Line	1	-	2	-	3	-	4	-	Final
Western Michigan	(42.0)	0	-	17	-	0	-	7	-	24
Cincinnati	(-7.0)	14	-	10	-	0	-	3	-	27

Scoring Summary
Cincinnati - Bowie 26 yard interception return (Lovell kick)
Cincinnati - Goodman 21 yard pass from Davila (Lovell kick)
Cincinnati - Goodman 21 yard pass from Davila (Lovell kick)
Cincinnati - Lovell 37 yard Field goal
Western Michigan - Simmons 76 yard pass from Biggers (Meyer kick)
Western Michigan - Martin 30 yard pass from Cubit (Meyer kick)
Western Michigan - Meyer 30 yard Field goal
Western Michigan - West 7 yard run (Meyer kick)
Cincinnati - Lovell 33 yard Field goal

Associated Press International Bowl Game Summary - Kevin Lovell's 33-yard, fourth-quarter field goal lifted Cincinnati to a 27-24 victory over Western Michigan on Saturday in the International Bowl -- the first college bowl played in Canada and first outside the United States since 1937. Lovell's kick with 8:49 left came after a 7-yard touchdown run by Western Michigan's Brandon West tied it. The Bearcats led 24-0 early in the second quarter, and barely held on. The Broncos had a chance to force overtime with 1:21 remaining, but Nate Meyer's 51-yard field-goal attempt was wide. Brian Kelly enjoyed a winning debut as Bearcats coach. Kelly began the season at Central Michigan before going to Cincinnati on Dec. 4 to replace Mark Dantonio, who went to Michigan State. Kelly led Central Michigan past the Broncos 31-7 on Nov. 10, making him the first NCAA coach to earn beat a school in the same season with two teams. Dominick Goodman, the game MVP with seven catches for 109 yards, had two touchdowns for Cincinnati with John Bowie scoring the other. Lovell added two field goals. Jamarko Simmons and Herb Martin scored touchdowns for the Broncos. Meyer added a field goal. Cincinnati (8-5, 4-3 Big East) made its fifth bowl appearance in seven years and first since beating Marshall 32-14 in the 2004 Fort Worth Bowl. Western Michigan (8-5, 6-2 Mid-American Conference) made its first bowl appearance since 1988 and third in school history. While the Broncos have yet to win one, they've made improvements under Coach Bill Cubit, who took over a program that lost 10 games in 2004. The game was played before a Rogers Centre crowd of 26,717. Bowie opened the scoring, returning an interception 25 yards for the touchdown at 3:28 of the first quarter. Davila's 21-yard touchdown pass to Goodman at 8:33 put Cincinnati up 14-0. The two combined on a second 21-yard touchdown just 30 seconds into the second quarter. Western Michigan used trickery to get on the board. E.J. Biggers, a sophomore cornerback, hit a streaking Simmons on a 76-yard option pass off a double reverse at 5:15. That lifted the Broncos, who forced Cincinnati to punt, then put together a 75-yard march that Ryan Cubit ended with a 30-yard touchdown pass to Martin at 9:25. An interception by Western Michigan's Matt Luderman set up Meyer's 30-yard field goal at 14:52 to pull the Broncos within 24-17 at halftime.

2007 GMAC Bowl

The 2007 GMAC Bowl was played in January 2007, and featured the Southern Miss Golden Eagles, and the Ohio Bobcats.

2007 GMAC Bowl	Line	1	-	2	-	3	-	4	-	Final
Ohio	(42.0)	0	-	0	-	0	-	7	-	7
Southern Miss	(-6.0)	0	-	21	-	7	-	0	-	28

Scoring Summary
Southern Miss - Harrison 44 yard run (McCaleb kick)
Southern Miss - Fletcher 2 yard run (McCaleb kick)
Southern Miss - Denley 12 yard interception return (McCaleb kick)
Southern Miss - Fletcher 9 yard run (McCaleb kick)
Ohio - Christy 13 yard pass from Everson (Lasher kick)

Associated Press GMAC Bowl Game Summary - With big plays, a marathon drive and a smothering defense, Southern Miss gave Ohio a tough lesson on postseason play. The Golden Eagles also gave a pretty good tutorial on how to make a halftime lead hold up in a 28-7 victory over the Bobcats on Sunday night in the GMAC Bowl. After a scoreless first quarter, Southern Miss (9-5) scored 21 second-quarter points then surged out of halftime with a season-long 17-play touchdown drive that effectively ended any comeback threat. Frank Solich's Bobcats (9-5) were making their first bowl appearance since 1968, but that euphoria wore off quickly as the game turned into a mismatch. They are 0-3 in bowl games and failed to match their school record of 10 wins. It was a rough ending to a feel-good story that saw Solich, a former Nebraska coach, revive a struggling program that won only four games in his debut season. By contrast, Southern Miss is accustomed to postseason play, making its fifth consecutive bowl appearance and ninth in 10 years. The Golden Eagles used a series of big plays in the final 8:33 of the first half for the three-touchdown lead. First, backup tailback Tory Harrison scampered for a 43-yard touchdown run, only his second of the season. Jeremy Young then set up Damion Fletcher's second first of two touchdowns -- a 2-yard TD plunge

-- with a 30-yard pass to Josh Barnes on third-and-10. The defense added points, too. James Denley returned an interception of Ohio backup Quarterback Brad Bower 18 yards for a score with 1:13 left before the half. It was the Golden Eagles' seventh non-offensive TD of the season, the most under Bower. After the teams combined for just 82 offensive yards in the first quarter, Southern Miss racked up 150 in the second. The Golden Eagles then monopolized the ball, opening the second half with that ball-hogging, 80-yard drive that worked 9:55 off the clock and severely damaged any hopes for a comeback by Ohio's plodding offense. It was the team's longest drive of the season in both plays and time consumed. Solich and his offense watched helpless from the sidelines for "it seemed like a day and a half," he said. Fletcher ended it by reversing field behind the line and outrunning the defenders for a 9-yard TD. The darting, 175-pound freshman managed just 58 yards on 20 carries, but it was enough for him to earn game Most Valuable Player honors. Young was the offensive MVP after passing for 160 yards. Punter Britt Barefoot claimed special team's honors. Ohio tailback Kalvin McRae capped a difficult week with a 10-carry, 37-yard performance. The two-time All-Mid-American Conference performer only arrived in Mobile Friday evening after his 7-month-old nephew's death. Both offenses struggled. Southern Miss managed just 284 yards compared to 224 for Ohio. Once the Golden Eagles stopped McRae, Austen Everson and Bower were unable to bring their team back. Everson was 14-for-34 for 175 yards, including a 13-yard touchdown pass to John Christy with 9:34 left in the fourth quarter. Bower completed just one of his three attempts for 2 yards. It was the first loss by a MAC team in six GMAC Bowl appearances.

2007 BCS Championship Game

The 2007 Tostitos BCS National Championship Game was played at the University of Phoenix Stadium in Glendale, Arizona, on January 8, 2007. It was the first time that the BCS had staged its own stand-alone national title game (previously the member bowls each took turns serving as the title game). The No. 1 Ohio State Buckeyes lost to the BCS No. 2 Florida Gators, 41–14. The Buckeyes secured a spot by finishing the 2006 regular season undefeated and ranked No. 1 in the BCS. It was the first time the Buckeyes and Gators had ever met on the football field. The 12–1 Florida Gators earned a spot after defeating Arkansas in the Southeastern Conference Championship Game in early December and jumping from No. 4 to No. 2 in the final BCS Rankings, passing No. 3 Michigan and previous No. 2 USC. The game was the first BCS National Championship Game to be televised on the FOX network.

Pre-game buildup - The Ohio State Buckeyes were the No. 1 ranked team for the entire 2006 NCAA Division I FBS football season, anchored by Heisman Trophy winning Quarterback Troy Smith. The Buckeyes were 12–0 with several wins over ranked opponents: the defending national champions, then No. 2 Texas Longhorns, then No. 24 Penn State Nittany Lions, then No. 13 Iowa Hawkeyes, and their then undefeated Big Ten Conference rival, then No. 2 Michigan. The win over Michigan to finish the regular season essentially guaranteed the Buckeyes a spot in the National Championship game. Who they would play remained a highly debated question. Despite the loss to Ohio State, Michigan remained No. 2 in the polls, followed by No. 3 Southern California (USC), No. 4 Florida, and No. 5 Notre Dame. The next week, with both No. 1 Ohio State and No. 2 Michigan's regular season complete, No. 3 USC defeated then No. 5 Notre Dame. Fourth-ranked Florida defeated unranked in-state rival Florida State. With the victory over Notre Dame, USC passed Michigan in the polls, taking over the BCS No. 2 spot. Michigan fell to No. 3 with Florida remaining No. 4 and Notre Dame falling to No. 10. The last week of the regular season was dynamic for the national championship race. Third-ranked Michigan remained idle. Fourth-ranked Florida faced No. 9 Arkansas in the SEC Championship, while No. 2 USC faced unranked, in-city rival UCLA. Both Florida and Michigan cheered as USC fell to UCLA 13–9. Florida defeated Arkansas 38-28 to claim the 2006 SEC Championship Title. USC's loss knocked them out of contention, leaving No. 3 Michigan and No. 4 Florida as the most likely teams to earn the No. 2 ranking and face Ohio State for the BCS National Championship. The final BCS poll passed Florida over Michigan to take the No. 2 spot while Michigan remained unchanged at No. 3, with .0101 points separating the two teams. This small difference was a result of the human polls (the Coaches Poll and Harris Interactive Poll) ranking Florida above Michigan while the computer polls had the two teams tied for second.

2007 BCS Championship	Line	1	-	2	-	3	-	4	-	Final
#2 Florida	(46.0)	14	-	20	-	0	-	7	-	41
#1 Ohio State	(-7.5)	7	-	7	-	0	-	0	-	14

Scoring Summary
Ohio State – Ginn 93 yard kickoff return (Pettrey kick)
Florida – Baker 14 yard pass from Leak (Hetland kick)
Florida – Harvin 4 yard run (Hetland kick)
Florida – Wynn 2 yard run (Hetland kick)
Ohio State – Pittman 18 yard run (Pettrey kick)
Florida – Hetland 43 yard Field goal
Florida – Hetland 40 yard Field goal
Florida –Caldwell 1 yard pass from Tebow (Hetland kick)
Florida – Tebow 1 yard run (Hetland kick)

Associated Press BCS Championship Game Summary - Everybody got it wrong except the Gators. Turns out Florida was too good to be on the same field as Ohio State, and that Heisman Trophy winner Troy Smith and the Buckeyes were the ones who weren't worthy. Coach Urban Meyer's once-beaten Gators dominated the undefeated Buckeyes and streaked to college football's national championship, 41-14 on Monday night. Florida got all but one of the 65 first-place votes in the final Associated Press poll. Ohio State dropped from No. 1 and finished second. Chris Leak and Tim Tebow showed off Meyer's twin Quarterback system to perfection as the Gators became the first Division I school to hold national titles in football and basketball at the same time. Now, only one question remains: What about 13-0 Boise State, the last undefeated team left standing after stunning Oklahoma on the very same field in the Fiesta Bowl on New Year's Day? The No. 5 Broncos got the other first-place vote in the AP poll. Florida's amazingly easy victory left the Gators with a 13-1 record and the Buckeyes at 12-1. That, and with Wisconsin and Louisville also having lost just once, will almost surely renew calls for a playoff system. Ohio State started out like the one-touchdown favorite it was, but only for an instant. Ted Ginn Jr. returned the opening kickoff 93 yards for a touchdown, but then it quickly fell apart for the Buckeyes. Ginn hurt his foot in the touchdown celebration and hobbled off after Ohio State's first offensive play. By the time he returned for the second half on crutches, Florida led 34-14. Leak, maligned for never winning the big one, completed 25 of 36 passes for 213 yards and a touchdown. The Rambo-like Tebow threw for one TD and powered into the end zone for another. Smith, meanwhile, joined a long list of Heisman Trophy Quarterbacks -- Jason White, Eric Crouch and Gino Torretta, among them -- to fall apart in bowl games. He was just 4-of-14 for 35 yards with one interception, sacked him five times and held him to minus-29 yards on 10 runs. Defensive ends Derrick Harvey and Moss made it a miserable night for Smith. Linebacker Earl Everett got into the act, too, running down Smith on one play despite missing his helmet. It was the second national title for Florida, adding to the one Heisman winner Danny Wuerffel brought home in 1996 under Coach Steve Spurrier with a 52-20 romp over Florida State in the Sugar Bowl. This time, the man in charge was the 42-year-old Meyer, once a .200 hitter in the low minors in Atlanta's baseball farm system. Since then, he's made a rocket rise in the coaching ranks, topped off by a title in his second year at Florida. The trophy will make a perfect bookend for the one the basketball Gators won by beating UCLA for the national championship in Indianapolis last spring. Tressel's team, meanwhile, looked as if it belonged at the Holiday Bowl, because it took this night off. Given 51 days to prepare, the Buckeyes were confused from the get-go once Florida got the ball. In the first football matchup between these schools -- they've both played the sport for 100-plus years -- the Gators emphatically stopped Ohio State's 19-game winning streak. The Buckeyes beat a pair of No. 2 teams, defending champion Texas and Michigan, earlier in the season, but they were no match for Florida's speed, strategy and style. Ohio State hoped to win its fifth national title, having taken it behind Maurice Clarett in 2002. But these Buckeyes looked completely flummoxed by Florida's frenetic offense at the outset. Trying to match up with the Gators' shifting formations, they often jumped around at the line and still were out of position. Leak gladly took advantage of the confusion, picking wide-open receivers at will and hitting his first nine passes. Criticized most of his career for a lack of fire, the guy with the soft, green eyes seemed real comfortable. By the end, the numbers were numbing. Florida outgained the Buckeyes 370 yards to 82, led in first downs 21-8 and time of possession 40:48 to 19:12. Meyer's gadgets made it easy pickings for the Gators. They came out in a five-wide set after Ginn's kickoff return, and Leak hit Baker with a tying, 14-yard touchdown pass. The next time they touched the ball, the Gators let Leak, Tebow and scatback Percy Harvin all take direct snaps from center. Harvin later tucked it under his right arm -- the one with a lion tattoo -- and powered for a 4-yard TD. A flanker reverse by Andre Caldwell helped Florida move to a third-and-goal at the 2 as the first quarter ended. When the second period began, Meyer immediately reached into his bag of tricks. Florida put three running backs directly behind Leak -- a power-I-plus -- and gave the ball to the last one. DeShawn Wynn scored on the first play of the quarter, plunging into the end zone right in front of the Gators' band, for a stunning 21-7 lead. Ohio State returned to its roots and ran the ball. Antonio Pittman's 18-yard burst made it 21-14 with 13:32 left before halftime. Undaunted, the Gators came back with something totally out of character, even for them --

field goals. Chris Hetland was only 4-for-13 on kicks this season, and his longest was 33 yards. But Meyer said he would trust him in this game, and Hetland made good, from 42 and 40 yards on the next two possessions. Hetland's second kick came after Tressel showed a little early desperation, gambling on fourth-and-1 at his own 29 and saw Chris Wells stuffed. The Buckeyes got the ball on their 20 with less than two minutes left before halftime and were determined to see a score before the break. They did -- by Florida. Moss sacked Smith and forced him to fumble, and the Gators took over at 5. Tebow ran twice up the middle, then faked a Quarterback draw, rolled to the left and tossed a 1-yard TD pass to Caldwell. At 34-14, fans on both sides were stunned as the teams ran to the locker rooms.

2007 Poinsettia Bowl

The 2007 Poinsettia Bowl was played between the Navy Midshipmen and the Utah Utes played on December 20, 2007 at Qualcomm Stadium in San Diego, California. Utah defeated Navy 35–32 in a game that came down to the final seconds. The third edition of the Poinsettia Bowl was the first of 32 games in the 2007–2008 bowl season.

2007 Poinsettia Bowl	Line	1	-	2	-	3	-	4	-	Final
Utah	(-8.5)	0	-	7	-	14	-	14	-	35
Navy	(65.0)	0	-	10	-	7	-	15	-	32

Scoring Summary
Utah - Mack 6 yard run (Sakoda kick)
Navy - Kaheaku-Enhada 1 yard run (Bullen kick)
Navy - Bullen 39 yard Field goal
Navy - Kettani 43 yard run (Bullen kick)
Utah - Brooks 23 yard run (Sakoda kick)
Utah - Richards 40 yard pass from Johnson (Sakoda kick)
Utah - Johnson 19 yard run (Sakoda kick)
Navy - White 10 yard pass from Kaheaku-Enhada (Bullen kick)
Utah - Mack 1 yard run (Sakoda kick)
Navy - Singleton 58 yard pass from Kaheaku-Enhada (Bullen kick)

Associated Press Poinsettia Bowl Game Summary - Invite the Utah Utes to a bowl game and the odds are pretty good they're going to win. Brian Johnson threw for one touchdown and ran for another, and Utah opened the bowl season with a wild 35-32 victory over the Navy Midshipmen in the Poinsettia Bowl on Thursday night. It was Utah's seventh straight bowl victory dating to 1999. Boston College has won seven straight bowl games going into its matchup against Michigan State in the Champs Sports Bowl next Friday. Running back Darrell Mack, who grew up in the San Diego area, scored the first and last touchdowns for Utah (9-4), which won for the eighth time in nine games. The loss spoiled the head coaching debut of Navy's Ken Niumatalolo, who was promoted from assistant head coach and offensive line coach after Paul Johnson left for Georgia Tech. Navy (8-5) had its four-game winning streak snapped. The Poinsettia Bowl is run by the same group that puts on the Holiday Bowl, so it was fitting that the teams combined for 50 points in the second half. The game came down to a crazy final minute. Navy pulled to 35-32 on Kaipo-Noa Kaheaku-Enhada's 58-yard touchdown pass to Zerbin Singleton with 57 seconds left. Singleton recovered the onside kick at the 42, but Kaheaku-Enhada was intercepted by safety Joe Dale on the second play of the drive to seal the victory. Dale had a team-high 12 tackles. There was a questionable call late in the game. With his Utes leading 28-25, Jerome Brooks caught a 3-yard pass from Johnson and lost the ball as he was diving for the corner of the end zone. The ball hit the pylon and went out of bounds. Officials could have ruled it a touchback for Navy, but after a review, the call on the field stood. On the next play, Mack was stuffed for no gain on fourth-and-goal from the 1. Navy ended up getting stopped on fourth-and-2 from its 9. Afterward, the officials released a statement saying a mistake was made, and the play should have been ruled a touchback, with Navy getting the ball at its 20. Johnson took a hit in the third quarter that seemed to wake him up. He completed 11 straight passes spanning the second and third quarters. He expertly ran Utah's spread-option offense in leading Utes back from a 17-7 deficit by going 9-for-9 for 130 yards in the third quarter. After Brooks scored on a 23-yard end-around pitch to pull the Utes within three, they went ahead on Johnson's 40-yard pass to Derrek Richards with 1:12 left in the third quarter. Johnson scored on a 19-yard scramble early in the fourth quarter to give Utah a 28-17 lead. Navy, which seemed to be wearing down against the larger Utes, got a 10-yard touchdown pass from Kaheaku-Enhada to Shun White, and a conversion run by Kaheaku-Enhada to pull to 28-25 with 8:48 left. Mack's 1-yard TD run with 1:27 left seemed to give Utah a safe lead before Kaheaku-Enhada's big pass play. Johnson was 20-of-25 passing for 226 yards, with one interception. He ran 11 times for 69 yards. After three turnovers in the first 7:20, the teams settled down. Mack scored on a 5-yard run midway through the first quarter for a 7-0 Utah lead. Navy then got its triple-option offense moving to score 17 straight points.

Kaheaku-Enhada scored on a 1-yard run, Joey Bullen kicked a 39-yard field goal and Eric Kettani broke a 46-yard scoring run. Kettani carried 12 times for 125 yards.

2007 New Orleans Bowl

The 2007 R+L Carriers New Orleans Bowl was played on December 21, 2007 at the Louisiana Superdome in New Orleans. The Florida Atlantic Owls, winners of the Sun Belt Conference title for the first time in school history, faced the Memphis Tigers of Conference USA. Both teams had a regular season record of 7-5. The Owls have only played college football since 2001 and the 2007 New Orleans Bowl was their first bowl appearance in history. The seven years between the creation of the FAU college football team and its first bowl appearance in the New Orleans Bowl marked the quickest a team had ever appeared in a bowl game after its establishment. Florida Atlantic led the NCAA in turnover margin. FAU head coach Howard Schnellenberger led the Miami Hurricanes to a National Championship in 1983. At the time of the 2007 New Orleans Bowl, Schnellenberger was the third-oldest head coach in Division I football. The game was Memphis's third bowl game in four years. The Tigers' season was marked by the murder of defensive end Taylor Bradford on September 30, but the team carried on to a winning record and its first bowl appearance since 2005.

2007 New Orleans Bowl	Line	1	-	2	-	3	-	4	-	Final
Florida Atlantic	(-3.0)	17	-	13	-	7	-	7	-	44
Memphis	(67.0)	7	-	13	-	7	-	0	-	27

Scoring Summary
Florida Atlantic - Pierre 4 yard pass from Smith (Leroy kick)
Memphis - Russell 8 yard pass from Hankins (Reagan kick)
Florida Atlantic - Leroy 22 yard field goal
Florida Atlantic - Hedgecomb 29 yard pass from Smith (Leroy Kick)
Memphis - Reagan 38 yard field goal
Florida Atlantic - Bonner 16 yard pass from Smith (Leroy kick)
Memphis - Mack 35 yard field goal
Florida Atlantic - Rose 4 yard pass from Smith (Leroy kick)
Memphis - Williams 19 yard pass from Hankins (Mack kick)
Memphis – Singleton 6 yard pass from Hankins (Mack kick)
Florida Atlantic – Harmon 16 yard pass from Smith (Leroy kick)
Florida Atlantic – Edgecomb 4 yard run (Leroy kick)

New Orleans Bowl Game Notes - The 44-27 victory was the first Florida Atlantic bowl win in school history and Howard Schnellenberger's fifth bowl win as a head coach, bringing him to a perfect 5-0 record in bowl games. FAU became the youngest program in NCAA history to win a bowl game. During the game, Memphis Quarterback Martin Hankins passed the 3,000-yard mark for the season despite missing two games earlier in the year. During the game, he moved into first place all-time at Memphis in season passing yardage, completions, and touchdowns. Heading into the game, Memphis was ranked last in Division I in third-down defense but ran an average of 78 plays on offense per game, enough for 7th in the NCAA.

2007 PapaJohns.com Bowl

The 2007 PapaJohns.com Bowl was played between the Cincinnati Bearcats and the Southern Miss Golden Eagles at Legion Field in Birmingham, Alabama. The University of Cincinnati represented the Big East Conference and the University of Southern Mississippi represented Conference USA (which Cincinnati was once a member of). The game resulted in a 31–21 Cincinnati victory, which did not cover their 11-point spread. The payout for both teams was $300,000, the lowest payout among all college football bowl games. This was the final game for head coach Jeff Bower, ending his 17-season tenure at Southern Miss. Bower was forced to resign after their disappointing season. After Bower's resignation, the selection of Southern Miss was notable as Bower's first game as head coach of the Golden Eagles was also at Legion Field, in the All-American Bowl in 1990. Cincinnati Quarterback Ben Mauk passed for four touchdowns and 334 yards. Southern Miss Quarterback Jeremy Young went 18-for-32 for 122 yards with two touchdowns and three interceptions. After being down 31-14 in the fourth, quarter Jeremy Young cut the lead by scoring a 5-yard touchdown pass to Chris Johnson, but Southern Miss' rally fell short after they couldn't recover an onside kick or convert a fourth-and-1 play on its next possession. Only 35,258 people attended the game, less than half of Legion Field's capacity. Cincinnati distributed 8,352 tickets, a school record for bowl attendance, while Southern Mississippi distributed around 5,000 tickets. Cincinnati's win brought their record to 10-3, their first 10-win season since 1951. With the loss Southern Miss' record ended at 7-5.

2007 PapaJohns.com Bowl	Line	1	-	2	-	3	-	4	-	Final
Southern Miss	(55.5)	7	-	0	-	7	-	7	-	21
#20 Cincinnati	(-11.0)	0	-	14	-	17	-	0	-	31

Scoring Summary
Southern Miss - Nelson 10 yard pass from Young (Estes Kick)
Cincinnati - Goodman 14 yard pass from Mauk (Rogers Kick)
Cincinnati - Goodman 5 yard pass from Mauk (Rogers Kick)
Cincinnati - Jackson 29 yard pass from Mauk (Rogers Kick)
Southern Miss - Young 1 yard run (Estes Kick)
Cincinnati - Giddens 10 yard pass from Mauk (Rogers Kick)
Cincinnati - Rogers 22 yard Field Goal
Southern Miss - Johnson 5 yard pass from Young (Estes Kick)

Associated Press PapaJohns.com Bowl Game Summary - Ben Mauk shrugged off mistakes and Southern Miss defenders alike, and helped Cincinnati (No. 22 ESPN/USA Today, No. 20 AP) make one more entry into an impressive season. Outgoing Golden Eagles coach Jeff Bower, meanwhile, couldn't put another win on his ledger. The hard-to-tackle Mauk passed for 334 yards and four touchdowns, and DeAngelo Smith intercepted three passes Saturday, leading the Bearcats to a 31-21 victory over Southern Miss in the Papajohns.com Bowl. The victory gave Cincinnati (10-3) its second 10-win season and first since 1951, while virtually assuring a spot in the final rankings for the first time. Mauk, the game's most valuable player, completed 30 of 52 passes and overcame three interceptions to become only the third Bearcats player to have a 3,000-yard passing season. It was a nice finish for the former Wake Forest starter, but a difficult one for Southern Miss (7-6) and Bower. It was the final game for Bower after 17 seasons at his alma mater, a stay that ranks behind only that of Joe Paterno, Bobby Bowden and Frank Beamer among current coaches. Bower was forced to resign after a disappointing regular season, leading to the hiring of Oklahoma State offensive coordinator Larry Fedora. Bower walked off the field, his arm draped around daughter Stephanie and admitted he got "a little emotional" in the locker room afterward. Kelly had praise for Bower when they met on the field. Bower's team couldn't convert several chances to at least make the ending interesting. Mostly, though, they couldn't stop Kelly's spread offense. Mauk, who also rushed for 41 yards and frequently broke loose from defenders to make plays, threw three touchdown passes during an 8-minute span extending into the second half. For Mauk, who intends to apply for another season of eligibility because of an injury-shortened junior year at Wake Forest, his scrambling helped in more than the obvious ways. Bower's third-quarter gamble didn't pay off. Cincinnati stopped punter Britt Barefoot on a fake punt on fourth-and-1 from his own 29. Mauk hit Earnest Jackson for a 29-yard TD strike on the next play for a 21-7 lead. Jeremy Young answered with a 1-yard scoring run for Southern Miss before Mauk struck again with a 10-yarder to Antwuan Giddens and set up a 22-yard field goal by Jake Rogers in the final seconds of the third quarter to put the Bearcats up 31-14. Young cut into the lead again with a 5-yard touchdown pass to Chris Johnson. But Southern Miss couldn't recover an onside kick or convert a fourth-and-1 play on its next possession. Smith's third pick ended any hope of a comeback in the final minutes after Brandon Summerall's interception in the end zone gave Southern Miss a slim chance. Damion Fletcher provided most of the offense for Southern Miss. He ran 29 times for 155 yards against a defense that came in allowing just 106 yards on the ground. He also caught seven passes for 50 yards. Young was 18-for-32 for 122 yards and two touchdowns and ran for 55 yards. He was sacked four times and threw the three interceptions. Goodman caught seven passes for 95 yards and a pair of scores for Cincinnati. Connor Barwin (86 yards) and Antwuan Giddens (64) also had seven catches apiece. Leading receiver Marcus Barnett left the game in the first half with a leg injury and didn't return.

2007 Las Vegas Bowl

The 2007 Pioneer Las Vegas Bowl was played between the UCLA Bruins and the BYU Cougars. The Las Vegas Bowl gets its first choice of bowl-eligible teams from the Mountain West Conference (MWC) and the fourth/fifth choice (alternating every year) of bowl-eligible teams from the Pacific-10 Conference (Pac-10). This bowl game was played on December 22, 2007 at 40,000-seat Sam Boyd Stadium in Whitney, Nevada, USA where this bowl game has been played since 1992. It was broadcast on ESPN and ESPNHD. Since 2001, the game has featured a matchup of teams from the MWC and Pac-10.

2007 Las Vegas Bowl	Line	1	-	2	-	3	-	4	-	Final
UCLA	(46.5)	3	-	10	-	0	-	3	-	16
BYU	(-6.0)	3	-	14	-	0	-	0	-	17

Scoring Summary
UCLA - Forbath 22 yard Field goal
BYU - Payne 29 yard Field goal
BYU – Collie 14 yard pass from Hall (Payne kick)
UCLA – Forbath 52 yard Field goal
BYU – Reed 13 yard pass from Hall (Payne kick)
UCLA – Breazell 4 yard pass from Bethel-Thompson (Forbath kick)
UCLA – Forbath 50 yard Field goal

Associated Press Las Vegas Bowl Game Summary - After Brigham Young's defense allowed UCLA to drive 87 yards in the final two minutes, Eathyn Manumaleuna saved the Cougars with his fingertip. Manumaleuna got his right hand on Kai Forbath's field goal attempt as time expired, giving the No. 17 Cougars (No. 19 AP) a 17-16 win over the Bruins in the Pioneer Las Vegas Bowl on Saturday night. Manumaleuna, a 280-pound lineman led the surge that kept UCLA from completing an amazing comeback. The Bruins held BYU to a season-low 265 yards of offense and rallied behind their fourth-string Quarterback and field goals by Forbath. Forbath had made kicks of 22, 52 and 50 yards to keep the Bruins close, but his 28-yarder at the end wasn't quite high enough to clear the defensive line. BYU (11-2) won its 10th straight, getting another magic play at the end. The Cougars converted a fourth-and-18 on their winning drive against rival Utah on Nov. 24. This time it was the defense that came up with the improbable save. UCLA was playing for interim coach DeWayne Walker, the defensive coordinator who took over after Karl Dorrell was fired at the end of the regular season. If it was Walker's only game as UCLA's coach, it was a memorable one. The Bruins' top two Quarterbacks were on the sideline with injuries, but Walker's defense swarmed the Cougars all game and kept the BYU offense in check more than anyone else had this season. UCLA forced BYU to punt with about two minutes left and started the final drive on its own 2-yard line. Walk-on Quarterback McLeod Bethel-Thompson and running back Chris Markey led the Bruins with 87 yards, getting a 36-yard completion from Bethel-Thompson to Logan Paulsen on a third-and-8 play with 30 seconds left. Paulsen caught the ball around the 45-yard line, then rumbled to the 13. The Bruins ran one play, then called timeout with the ball at the 11 and only three seconds left. Forbath, who was 3-for-3, kicked it low enough for Manumaleuna to get a piece of it and keep the ball from getting through the uprights, although there was some confusion on who got the block. In the end, Manumaleuna got the credit, which didn't matter a bit to the Cougars. BYU improved to 2-7 against UCLA, beating the Bruins for the first time since 1983. The Cougars also avenged a 27-17 loss to UCLA in the second week of the season, one of just two losses this year for BYU. The Bruins were just inches away from salvaging the season with a winning record. Hall completed 21 of 35 for 231 yards. Hall was also sacked three times and fumbled on one of them, setting up Forbath's 22-yard field goal that put the Bruins up 3-0 in the first quarter. Markey ran for 117 yards for UCLA, the first runner to break the 100-yard mark against BYU this season. UCLA needed the running game to stay in it with its top two Quarterbacks on the sideline with knee injuries. Osaar Rasshan started and failed to complete his lone pass. Bethel-Thompson replaced him in the second quarter and was solid enough to keep the Bruins close, especially with the way the defense was playing. UCLA got a huge break at the end of the first half when the Cougars decided to run a play instead of running out the clock inside their own 10. Hall handed off to Harvey Unga and Brian Price stripped the ball, which the Bruins recovered at the 4. UCLA scored on a pass from Bethel-Thompson to Brandon Breazell as the second quarter ended and the Bruins were only down 17-13 at halftime instead of 17-6. It was karma for a UCLA blunder that led to an easy score for BYU. Terrence Austin dropped a punt and BYU recovered at the UCLA 14, where Hall lofted a pass on first down to the back corner of the end zone and Austin Collie caught it running at full speed. Collie went tumbling into the padding outside the sideline but came up with the ball and gave BYU a 10-3 lead with 10:32 left in the second quarter. BYU scored again with 1:03 left on a 13-yard pass from Hall to Michael Reed. The Cougars won the Las Vegas Bowl for the second straight year. The last time BYU ended consecutive seasons with bowl wins was 1983 and 1984, when BYU won its only national title.

2007 New Mexico Bowl

The 2007 New Mexico Bowl was held on December 22, 2007 at University Stadium on the University of New Mexico campus in Albuquerque. The game, telecast on ESPN, featured the Nevada Wolf Pack from the WAC and the hometown New Mexico Lobos from the Mountain West Conference. The Lobos topped the Wolf Pack 23-0 to earn their first bowl win since the 1961 Aviation Bowl, a 45-year drought that was the fifth-longest in the nation. Another streak ended in the game, with the shutout of Nevada being the Wolf Pack's first since 1980. New Mexico Quarterback Donovan Porterie made up for a poor 2006 New Mexico Bowl performance with two touchdown tosses and kicker John Sullivan tacked on three long field goals in the win.

2007 New Mexico Bowl	Line	1	-	2	-	3	-	4	-	Final
Nevada	(58.0)	0	-	0	-	0	-	0	-	0
New Mexico	(-2.5)	14	-	6	-	0	-	3	-	23

Scoring Summary
New Mexico – M. Smith 66 yard pass from Porterie (Sullivan kick)
New Mexico – T. Brown 39 yard pass from Porterie (Sullivan kick)
New Mexico – Sullivan 53 yard field goal
New Mexico – Sullivan 45 yard field goal
New Mexico – Sullivan 37 yard field goal

Associated Press New Mexico Bowl Game Summary - For coach Rocky Long, it was just the next game, another brick to continue building his program. For delighted New Mexico fans, it marked the end of a 46-year skid. Paul Baker ran for 167 yards in his first start, and Donovan Porterie threw for a career-high 354 yards and two touchdowns to help New Mexico beat Nevada 23-0 in the New Mexico Bowl on Saturday. The Lobos (9-4) ended a 46-year span without a postseason victory and gave Long, the team's 10th-year coach, his first bowl win in five tries. Long was both defiant and jovial in the interview room, scolding reporters for focusing on the bowl losses -- including Long's 0-4 mark before Saturday. John Sullivan made field goals from 53, 39 and 37 yards, but give credit to New Mexico's defense, which delivered just the second shutout loss for Nevada under Hall of Fame coach Chris Ault. The Wolf Pack (6-7) hadn't gone scoreless since losing 10-0 to Weber State on Sept. 27, 1980, a span of 329 games -- the longest current streak in college football and the second longest in history. It's the first time Nevada was shut out since moving to Division I-A in 1992. It was New Mexico's first bowl victory since beating Western Michigan 28-12 in the 1961 Aviation Bowl at Dayton, Ohio. The Lobos also notched a nine-win season for just the fourth time in school history. New Mexico's defenders pestered redshirt freshman Quarterback Colin Kaepernick all afternoon and made Nevada's "Pistol" offense look more like a popgun. The Wolf Pack averaged 36.2 points and 488.9 yards during the season. Nevada had logged 23 scoring plays that covered at least 25 yards -- second only to Oklahoma's 25 big-play TDs. This time, Nevada had 210 total yards, with only 73 yards rushing. On a chilly day, with the temperature at kickoff 34 degrees, Kaepernick finished 13-of-31 for 137 yards. He had 10 carries for 40 yards rushing. Madsen was selected the defensive player of the game after recording two sacks, two tackles for lost yardage and four total tackles. But he agreed the award could have gone to any New Mexico defender. Long was surely soaked to the bone after his players doused him with icy water at the 2-minute mark, sending up a spirited cheer from the fans who remained from the crowd of 30,223. After the final gun, a handful of New Mexico players jumped into the stands in the north end zone and students swarmed the field to remove the goal post. Baker, meanwhile, made the most of his chance. He moved into the starting lineup this week when Rodney Ferguson, New Mexico's leading rusher over the past two seasons, was ruled academically ineligible. As for Nevada, it was ugly on nearly every front. The Wolf Pack blocked two field goals, Sullivan missed another 43-yard try and the Lobos failed to score after having first-and-goal at the 4 late in the third quarter. But Nevada just couldn't take advantage. Despite the cool weather, Porterie had no trouble warming up. He threw a short slant pass on the third play from scrimmage to Marcus Smith, who raced to the end zone for a 66-yard scoring play. Later in the period, Brown got behind the Nevada defense and Porterie found him on a 39-yard TD pass.

2007 Hawai'i Bowl

The 2007 Sheraton Hawai'i Bowl was played between the Boise State University Broncos from the Western Athletic Conference (WAC) and the East Carolina University Pirates from Conference USA (C-USA) at the Aloha Stadium in Honolulu, Hawai'i on December 23, 2007. Many experts believed East Carolina to be big underdogs to Boise State, which had defeated the Oklahoma Sooners in the 2007 Fiesta Bowl. The 2007 Hawai'i Bowl paid $750,000 to each team's conference in exchange for their participation. The game, which was the sixth edition of the bowl, was expected to be an offensive shootout. Boise State averaged 42.4 points during the 2007 season, while East Carolina averaged 31. That expectation turned out to be justified as East Carolina took a 31–14 lead in the first half. The Broncos fought back in the second half, however, tying the score at 38 late in the fourth quarter after East Carolina's Chris Johnson fumbled the ball, allowing Bronco defender Marty Tadman to recover the ball and return it 47 yards for a touchdown. The game remained tied until the final moments as East Carolina's Ben Hartman made a 34–yard game-winning field goal as time expired. The attendance of 30,467 was the largest crowd to attend a Hawai'i Bowl game that did not feature the host school. Boise State's loss dropped them to a final 2007 record of 10–3, while East Carolina's final-game win earned them a record of 8–5.

2007 Hawaii Bowl	Line	1	-	2	-	3	-	4	-	Final
East Carolina	(58.0)	10	-	21	-	7	-	3	-	41
#24 Boise State	(-10.5)	7	-	7	-	10	-	14	-	38

Scoring Summary
East Carolina – Hartman 36 yard Field goal
Boise State – Smith 89 yard kickoff return (Brotzman kick)
East Carolina – Johnson 68 yard run (Hartman kick)
East Carolina – Lindsay 3 yard run (Hartman kick)
East Carolina – Johnson 18 yard pass from Pinkney (Hartman kick)
Boise State – Putnam 3 yard pass from Tharp (Brotzman kick)
East Carolina – Lindsay 3 yard run (Hartman kick)
East Carolina – Simmons 3 yard run (Hartman kick)
Boise State – Avery 25 yard pass from Tharp (Brotzman kick)
Boise State – Brotzman 31 yard Field goal
Boise State – Harper 1 yard run (Brotzman kick)
Boise State – Tadman 47 yard fumble recovery (Brotzman kick)
East Carolina – Hartman 34 yard Field goal

Associated Press Hawaii Bowl Game Summary - All Chris Johnson could think about after his record-setting night was how let his team down. Johnson set an NCAA bowl record with 408 all-purpose yards, and Ben Hartman kicked a 34-yard field goal as time expired to give East Carolina a 41-38 victory over No. 24 Boise State in the Sheraton Hawaii Bowl on Sunday night. Johnson ran for 223 yards, caught three passes for 32 yards and returned six kickoffs for 153 yards. But he committed a costly fumble late that almost sent it to overtime. It was his first fumble of the season. Hartman's kick gave the Pirates (8-5) their first postseason victory since the 2000 Galleryfurniture.com Bowl. With East Carolina trying to run out the clock near midfield, Marty Tadman scooped up Johnson's fumble and returned it 47 yards for a touchdown to tie it at 38 with 1:25 left. The Pirates took possession at their 39 with 1:16 left and drove to the 17 to set up Hartman's kick. The Pirates stormed the field in celebration and chased after Hartman, who dashed toward the locker room. Hartman said he took off because he was scared about get squashed underneath a pile of teammates. The Broncos (10-3), making their sixth straight bowl appearance, almost repeated their last-minute magic from a year ago when they stunned Oklahoma in overtime in the Fiesta Bowl to finish 13-0. But this time, it was the Broncos who fell a little short without any trick plays and an ailing Ian Johnson. Johnson, who was nursing a sprained left ankle, carried the ball just once for 1 yard in the first quarter and finished with 11 yards on four carries. It was Chris Johnson who stole the show. He was selected the Most Valuable Player for the Pirates. Jeremy Avery, who rushed for 68 yards and caught four passes for 43 yards was Boise State's MVP. Taylor Tharp was 30-of-44 for 266 yards and two touchdowns with two interceptions for Boise State. Patrick Pinkney threw for 117 yards and rushed for 53 more for East Carolina. The Pirates appeared to have the game in hand when they took a 38-14 lead early in the third quarter on Brandon Simmons' 3-yard TD run. The Broncos, however, hung in and reeled off 24 straight points. D.J. Harper's 1-yard TD plunge cut East Carolina's lead to 38-31 with 7:09 left. Most of the crowd was headed out of the stadium after Titus Young fumbled the ball, setting up the Pirates at their 39 with 1:45 left. But East Carolina's star couldn't hang on to the ball as he struggled to add a few more yards to his record, which was previously held by Alabama's Sherman Williams 359 yards set against Ohio State in the 1995 Citrus Bowl. Johnson had 181 rushing yards in the first half alone, including a 68-yard TD run that put East Carolina ahead 10-7. He also caught a screen pass from Pinkney and went 18 yards for a score to make it 24-7. Third-year Pirates coach Skip Holtz said he was proud of his players, especially Johnson. Dominique Lindsay had a pair of 3-yard TD runs in the first half for East Carolina. His second touchdown gave the Pirates a 31-14 halftime lead. The usually explosive Broncos looked rusty and unprepared in the first half. They went three-and-out on their first four possessions, followed by an interception, touchdown and fumble. Boise State, a 10 1/2-point favorite, managed just 3 yards of offense in the first quarter while East Carolina racked up 181 behind Johnson's 106 rushing yards. The Broncos' lone highlight in the first quarter was Austin Smith's 89-yard kickoff return for a TD. In the second quarter, Ryan Putnam caught a 3-yard pass from Tharp to cut East Carolina's lead to 10. Boise State was without its top receiver, Jeremy Childs, who didn't make the trip for violating team rules. East Carolina running back Chris Johnson finished the game with 223 rushing yards, 32 receiving yards, and 153 return yards for a total of 408 all-purpose yards. That mark broke the NCAA bowl record for all-purpose yards previously set by Alabama's Sherman Williams against Ohio State in the 1995 Citrus Bowl. Based on his record-setting performance, Johnson was named the game's Most Valuable Player. On the opposite side of the ball, Boise State tailback Jeremy Avery had a solid, if unspectacular, outing. He produced 69 rushing yards, 43 receiving yards, 41 kick–return yards, and caught a 25–yard touchdown pass. Both Johnson and Avery received the Most Valuable Player award for their respective teams.

2007 Motor City Bowl

The 2007 Motor City Bowl was held on December 26, 2007 at Ford Field in Detroit, Michigan. The Central Michigan Chippewas, who won their second straight Mid-American Conference championship on the same field on December 1, returned to take on the Purdue Boilermakers, who bowl officials invited from the Big Ten Conference. The bowl was a rematch of a game played on September 15 in West Lafayette, Indiana. The Boilermakers won that game, 45–22. CMU had defeated Middle Tennessee in the 2006 game. Purdue dominated the first half of the game, scoring 3 touchdowns in the first quarter to Central's 2 field goals, and by halftime they had assured a 21-point lead over the Chippewas. Central came back in the third quarter, scoring 4 touchdowns to tie the game. The final score was 51–48, with Purdue kicker Chris Summers kicking a game-winning field goal as time expired. Purdue Quarterback Curtis Painter threw for 543 pass yards, setting a Motor City Bowl record and placing him fourth on the list of all-time bowl game performances. His total broke the Purdue school record. The attendance of 60,624 broke the Motor City Bowl record, which had been set in 2006 by Central Michigan and Middle Tennessee (54,113).

2007 Motor City Bowl	Line	1	-	2	-	3	-	4	-	Final
Purdue	(-8.0)	21	-	13	-	7	-	10	-	51
Central Michigan	(71.5)	6	-	7	-	28	-	7	-	48

Scoring Summary
Central Michigan - Aguila 27 yard Field goal
Purdue - Sheets 1 yard run (Summers kick)
Purdue - Orton 29 yard pass from Painter (Summers kick)
Central Michigan - Aguila 47 yard Field goal
Purdue - Keller 62 yard pass from Painter (Summers kick)
Purdue - Summers 30 yard Field goal
Purdue - Summers 21 yard Field goal
Central Michigan - Anderson 49 yard pass from LeFevour (Aguila kick)
Purdue - Sheets 1 yard run (Summers kick)
Central Michigan - Brown 76 yard pass from LeFevour (Aguila kick)
Purdue - Standeford 19 yard pass from Painter (Summers kick)
Central Michigan - Anderson 10 yard pass from LeFevour (Aguila kick)
Central Michigan - LeFevour 9 yard run (Aguila kick)
Central Michigan - LeFevour 4 yard run (Aguila kick)
Purdue - Taylor 13 yard run (Summers kick)
Central Michigan - Anderson 19 yard pass from LeFevour (Aguila kick)
Purdue - Summers 40 yard Field goal

Associated Press Motor City Bowl Game Summary - The Motor City Bowl is low in the postseason pecking order. The Purdue-Central Michigan thriller, however, might be tough to top. Chris Summers kicked a 40-yard field goal as time expired, lifting the Boilermakers to a 51-48 victory over the Chippewas on Wednesday night. The 99 points tied the second-highest total in a bowl game that ended in regulation, trailing only the 2003 Insight Bowl, where California beat Virginia Tech 52-49. Curtis Painter threw for a school-record 546 yards and three touchdowns, helping the Boilermakers build three 21-point leads and set up the winning kick. "It's a fun game to play if you're on this end," he said. Painter was 35-of-54, and both of his interceptions went off receiver Dorien Bryant's hands. Purdue receivers Greg Orton, Jake Standeford and Dustin Keller had at least 112 yards receiving apiece. Central Michigan's Dan LeFevour threw for 292 yards and four scores and ran for 114 yards and two TDs, feeding off the energy from the crowd of 60,624 that created more noise than most Detroit Lions games in the same venue. LeFevour, completed 17 of 34 passes and ran 33 times. Early on, Purdue (9-5) didn't seem inspired perhaps because playing in Detroit isn't exactly what a Big Ten team has in mind when it dreams of playing in the postseason. The Mid-American Conference champion Chippewas (8-6) got the Boilermakers' attention, though, with an interception on the third play of the game and by taking a 3-0 lead. Purdue then seemed to get fired up and appeared to be rolling toward a rout, leading 27-6 midway through the second quarter, 34-13 at halftime and 41-20 early in the third. The Chippewas proved they belonged on the same field. Their comeback started with LeFevour's scoring pass to Bryan Anderson at 10:19 of the third and the Quarterback tied the game with two runs late in the quarter. Purdue answered with Jaycen Taylor's TD run midway through the fourth quarter and seemed to seal the win with a sack when Central Michigan had the ball with 2:15 and no timeouts. But LeFevour wasn't done. He escaped a sack on the next play and got out of bounds. Then, he connected three first downs before lobbing a pass to Anderson from 19 yards to make it 48-all with 1:09 left to play. The sophomore finished the season with 27 passing touchdowns and 19 rushing, falling just short of joining Heisman Trophy winner Tim Tebow of Florida as the only players to have 20 of each in the same season. Painter, who broke the Purdue yardage mark shared by Drew Brees and Kyle Orton, was 4-of-5 for 42 yards on the winning drive.

2007 Holiday Bowl

The 2007 Pacific Life Holiday Bowl was played December 27, 2007 in San Diego. It featured the Texas Longhorns against the Arizona State Sun Devils. Texas won 52–34 and set Holiday Bowl records for the earliest score and for most points scored in the first quarter. Texas also set a school record for most points scored in a bowl game. A bizarre play involving Chris Jessee, a member of the Longhorn football operations staff and the stepson of the Texas head coach, has been cited as one of the strangest plays of the season.

2007 Holiday Bowl	Line	1	-	2	-	3	-	4	-	Final
#12 Arizona State	(62.0)	0	-	10	-	10	-	14	-	34
#17 Texas	(-2.5)	21	-	7	-	7	-	17	-	52

Scoring Summary
Texas – Lokey 2 yard pass from McCoy (Bailey kick)
Texas – Chiles 4 yard run (Bailey kick)
Texas – Charles 15 yard run (Bailey kick)
Arizona State – McGaha 7 yard pass from Carpenter (Weber kick)
Texas – McCoy 7 yard run (Bailey kick)
Arizona State – Weber 32 yard Field goal
Arizona State – Weber 46 yard Field goal
Texas – Finley fumble recovery in end zone (Bailey kick)
Arizona State – Jones 22 yard pass from Carpenter (Weber kick)
Texas – Bailey 21 yard Field goal
Texas – McGee 28 yard run (Bailey kick)
Arizona State – Jones 10 yard pass from Sullivan (Weber kick)
Arizona State – Woods 3 yard run (Weber kick)
Texas – Charles 32 yard run (Bailey kick)

Associated Press Holiday Bowl Game Summary - As wacky plays go, this one certainly earned a spot in Pacific Life Holiday Bowl lore. What made it downright bizarre is that the central character wasn't a player. Texas fans will remember Colt McCoy leading the No. 19 Longhorns (No. 17 AP) to a 52-34 win Thursday night over the Arizona State Sun Devils (No. 11 BCS, No. 12 AP) in the first meeting between the schools and their successful coaches. No one will forget Chris Jessie, the stepson of Texas coach Mack Brown, inadvertently becoming part of the game. With the Longhorns leading 21-0 and the Sun Devils driving early in the second quarter, ASU's Rudy Carpenter dropped back to pass and was hit by linebacker Roddrick Muckelroy. The ball squirted backward, toward the Longhorns' sideline. Jessie, a member of his stepfather's football operations staff, stepped about a yard onto the field and was motioning toward a player when he reached down and appeared to touch the ball with his left thumb. Texas defensive tackle Roy Miller slapped the ball away from the sideline and defensive end Aaron Lewis recovered and returned it to about the ASU 44. After a 12-minute review, officials reversed the play. They ruled that Jessie touched the ball, which is illegal interference, an unsportsmanlike foul. The ball reverted to the Sun Devils and Texas was penalized half the distance to the goal, giving ASU fourth-and-3 at the 7. Carpenter threw a touchdown pass to Chris McGaha. The gaffe didn't end up costing the Longhorns (10-3), other than some embarrassment. The 86 points were the fourth-most in the Holiday Bowl's 30-year history, which is full of crazy plays and wild finishes. Texas set team records for points in a bowl game and with its fourth straight postseason win. McCoy led the way for the Longhorns, throwing for a touchdown, running for another and fumbling into the end zone at the end of a 30-yard run, with tight end Jermichael Finley recovering for a score. McCoy fumbled four times. The Longhorns recovered three and ASU got the other one. Jamaal Charles carried 27 times for 161 yards and two touchdowns for the Longhorns. Brown and Erickson have been friends for years but had never coached against each other. Erickson won two national championships at Miami and Brown coached Texas to the national title two years ago. ASU (10-3) committed five turnovers, with Carpenter throwing two interceptions before leaving the game in the fourth quarter. Carpenter had a horrible night, going 18-of-32 for 187 yards. He was sacked four times. Texas cornerback Brandon Foster had a monster game, with two interceptions, a fumble recovery and a tipped pass that was picked off by teammate Marcus Griffin. McCoy was 21-of-31 passing for 174 yards and carried 16 times for 84 yards. The Longhorns raced to a 21-0 first-quarter lead, including the fastest score in Holiday Bowl history. McCoy threw a 2-yard TD pass to Derek Lokey just 1:21 in. John Chiles scored on a 4-yard run, and Charles had a 15-yard scoring run. After ASU's score following the bizarre play, McCoy added a 9-yard TD run. It looked like he was going to score again in the third quarter when he went zigzagging through ASU's defense. But he fumbled as he was tackled at the 3 and the ball rolled into the end zone. Finley was the third player into the pile and ended up with the ball and the TD. Vondrell McGee scored on a 28-yard run for Texas in the fourth quarter, and Charles added a 32-yard score.

2007 Texas Bowl

The 2007 Texas Bowl was played on December 28, 2007 at Reliant Stadium in Houston, Texas. The matchup had different conference representatives from the inaugural 2006 game (itself the revival of the old Houston Bowl). This time, the teams were the TCU Horned Frogs of the Mountain West Conference and the Hometown University of Houston from Conference USA. The original plan was C-USA versus Big 12, but the Big 12 did not have enough teams eligible for bowl games to fill the remaining slots after Oklahoma won the conference title and Kansas was selected at-large to the Orange Bowl. TCU and Houston had been conference rivals for many years: between 1976 and 1995, they were in the Southwest Conference, and from 2001 to 2004, TCU joined Houston in C-USA. This was their first meeting in a bowl game. The Cougars were led by interim head coach Chris Thurmond after Art Briles left the program at the conclusion of the regular season to take a similar job at Baylor. Radio Shack, the electronics store chain based in Fort Worth, Texas, was the presenting sponsor of the NFL Network telecast. The Horned Frogs won the game 20-13, giving the Cougars their eighth straight bowl loss - at the time the second longest streak in the NCAA (and tied for second-longest streak in NCAA history).

2007 Texas Bowl	Line	1	-	2	-	3	-	4	-	Final
TCU	(-6.0)	0	-	7	-	3	-	10	-	20
Houston	(57.5)	7	-	3	-	0	-	3	-	13

Scoring Summary
Houston - Kohn 67 yard pass from Keenum (Lawrence Kick)
TCU - Dalton 3 yard run (Manfredini Kick)
Houston - Lawrence 39 yard Field Goal
TCU - Manfredini 29 yard Field Goal
TCU - Watts 7 yard run (Manfredini Kick)
TCU - Manfredini 35 yard Field Goal
Houston - Lawrence 32 yard Field Goal

Associated Press Texas Bowl Game Summary - Justin Watts had scored exactly one touchdown in his career at TCU before the Texas Bowl. TD No. 2 for Watts helped the Horned Frogs end the season with a bowl victory for the third straight season, something they haven't done in almost 70 years. The backup running back scored the go-ahead touchdown early in the fourth quarter to help TCU to a 20-13 win over Houston on Friday night in the Texas Bowl. The junior wove through the defense and danced into the end zone for an 8-yard touchdown run that made it 17-10 and gave TCU (8-5) its first lead of the game against its old Southwest Conference rival. He and Ryan Christian split carries against Houston (8-5) after starter Joseph Turner injured his knee in the first quarter and didn't return. Quarterback Andy Dalton also ran for a touchdown for TCU. It was 1936-39 when the Horned Frogs last had a run of bowl victories as long as this one. They started their current bowl winning streak with a win over Iowa State in this bowl in 2005 when it was known as the Houston Bowl. Dalton was 21-of-30 for 249 yards with one interception. Watts and Christian combined for 88 yards rushing on 12 carries. A 15-yard leaping reception by Jimmy Young on third down kept the drive that ended in Watts' touchdown going. Young out jumped Carson Blackmon to grab the ball and managed to keep his left leg in bounds as he landed. It was initially ruled an incomplete pass, but the call was overturned after a review by officials. The Cougars had a chance to tie it with less than 30 seconds to play but Case Keenum's pass sailed just beyond the fingertips of Jeron Harvey in the end zone. He had two more shots at the end zone, but the ball fell short on the first one and Chase Ortiz hit him as he threw the second one to end the game. Keenum was hurried and harassed by TCU most of the night and was sacked five times. He was 23-of-38 for 335 yards. Donnie Avery had 10 receptions for 120 yards. Playing without Coach Art Briles, who left in late November to coach at Baylor, the Cougars extended their bowl losing streak to eight games. Their last bowl win came in the 1980 Garden State Bowl. Interim coach Chris Thurmond led a Houston team that often looked confused and shaky against TCU. The Horned Frogs got to the Houston 2 later in the fourth quarter but had to settle for a 35-yard field goal after a holding penalty followed by a 6-yard loss by Christian on third down. Houston made it 20-13 with a 32-yard field goal by T.J. Lawrence with 1:57 remaining. Houston had a first down from the TCU 14, but Keenum was sacked by Ortiz for a 5-yard loss on third down to bring out Lawrence. The Cougars tried an onside kick after the field goal, but TCU's Brian Bonner recovered the ball. Houston attempted a 48-yard field goal midway through the fourth quarter, but it sailed wide right. TCU's Chris Manfredini hit a 29-yard field goal with 6:30 remaining in the third quarter to tie the game at 10-all. The Horned Frogs shut down Houston's star running back Anthony Alridge. He entered the game with 1,568 yards rushing for the season and managed just 28 yards on 15 carries Friday. A 39-yard field goal by T.J. Lawrence 10 seconds before halftime put Houston ahead 10-7. TCU's Dalton capped an 11-play, 75-yard drive with a 3-yard touchdown run early in the second quarter that tied the game at 7-all. Dalton, who grew up in the Houston suburb of Katy, was the game's most valuable player. Dalton broke TCU's single-season record for completions with 208 when he found Shae Reagan for a 9-yard reception later in the second quarter. The previous mark of 207 was set by Max Knake in 1993. Andre Kohn's 67-yard catch and run near the end of the first quarter put Houston ahead 7-0. Keenum had to scramble away from Ortiz to get the ball off, giving Kohn time to get down the field and ahead of the defense.

2007 Champs Sports Bowl

The 2007 Champs Sports Bowl was the 18th edition of the bowl game. It was played on December 28, 2007 at the Citrus Bowl stadium in Orlando, Florida. The game pitted the Boston College Eagles of the Atlantic Coast Conference against the Michigan State Spartans of the Big Ten Conference. Boston College was in contention for a Bowl Championship Series game bid, but lost the ACC Championship Game to Virginia Tech. Meanwhile, head coach Mark Dantonio led MSU to a bowl game in his first season there.

2007 Champs Sports Bowl	Line	1	-	2	-	3	-	4	-	Final
#14 Boston College	(-5.0)	7	-	7	-	3	-	7	-	24
Michigan State	(58.0)	7	-	3	-	3	-	8	-	21

Scoring Summary
Michigan State – Davis 18 yard pass from Hoyer (Swenson kick)
Boston College – Loyte 1 yard pass from Ryan (Aponavicius)
Boston College – Gunnell 29 yard pass from Ryan (Aponavicius kick)
Michigan State – Swenson 39 yard Field goal
Michigan State – Swenson 23 yard Field goal
Boston College – Aponavicius 28 yard Field goal
Boston College – Gunnell 68 yard pass from Ryan (Aponavicius kick)
Michigan State – Curry 14 yard pass from Hoyer (Davis pass from Hoyer)

Associated Press Champs Sports Bowl Game Summary - Matt Ryan's final game at Boston College made coach Jeff Jagodzinski's first season one of the best in school history. Ryan threw three touchdown passes, two to Rich Gunnell, and the Eagles extended the nation's longest bowl winning streak to eight with a 24-21 victory over Michigan State in the Champs Sports Bowl on Friday. Boston College (11-3) won 11 games for the first time since 1940. It was a great start for Coach Jag, but after an 8-0 start the season had potential to be even better. The Eagles were ranked No. 2 in the country after rallying to beat Virginia Tech in late October. But they ended the regular season losing three of five, including a rematch with the Hokies in the Atlantic Coast Conference title game in Jacksonville, and ended up in the Champs Sports Bowl. With 17 fifth-year seniors playing their final game, motivation came easy. Not surprising, two seniors led the way. Ryan completed 22-of-47 passes for 249 yards. All-America safety Jamie Silva had two interceptions, including one in the end zone, and was the game's most valuable player. The Eagles sealed the win with their fourth interception of the game. Paul Anderson picked off Brian Hoyer's pass and returned it to the Michigan State 29 with 2:29 remaining. Hoyer finished with five turnovers -- four interceptions and a fumble -- for the Spartans (7-6). Michigan State, in its first bowl in four years, played without four academically ineligible players, including defensive end Jonal Saint-Dic, one of the best pass rushers in the Big Ten. Also, ineligible were offensive lineman Abre Leggins, punt returner Terry Love and receiver-cornerback T.J. Williams. Coach Mark Dantonio also suspended senior linebacker SirDarean Adams for violating an unspecified team rule. The Spartans, whose six losses were by a combined 31 points, refused to make excuses. Not Dantonio. Not Hoyer. It was also a tough day for freshman defensive back Chris Rucker, who was playing for the first time since having three medical procedures in the last two months to correct a detached retina and gave up both of Gunnell's long TD catches (29 and 68 yards). Despite Hoyer's struggles, he made it close down the stretch -- thanks mostly to Ryan's fumble. Leading 24-13 in the fourth, Ryan fumbled as he was sacked by Greg Jones. Oren Wilson recovered at the Boston College 37. Hoyer, whose first four turnovers helped stake BC to an 11-point lead, connected with Devin Thomas for a 23-yard gain. Then he rolled right, released the ball just before he stepped out of bounds and found Deon Curry open in the back of the end zone. Hoyer hooked up with Kellen Davis for the two-point conversion that made it 24-21 with 6:04 remaining. The Spartans got the ball back twice in the closing minutes but couldn't pick up a first down. A few minutes later, BC's seniors celebrated their 39th win in the last four years.

2007 Emerald Bowl

The 2007 Emerald Bowl was played on December 27, 2007, at AT&T Park in San Francisco, California, with the Atlantic Coast Conference represented by the Maryland Terrapins against the Oregon State Beavers, representing the Pacific-10 Conference. The Terrapins scored all of their 14 points in the first quarter, while the Beavers scored successive touchdowns in the first, second and third quarters to win the game 21–14. Running back Yvenson Bernard and linebacker Derrick Doggett were the game MVPs.

2007 Emerald Bowl	Line	1	-	2	-	3	-	4	-	Final
Maryland	(47.5)	14	-	0	-	0	-	0	-	14
Oregon State	(-4.5)	7	-	7	-	7	-	0	-	21

Scoring Summary
Maryland - Williams 9 yard pass from Turner (Egekeze Kick)
Oregon State - Rogers 14 yard pass from Canfield (Serna Kick)
Maryland - Heyward-Bey 63 yard pass from Turner (Egekeze Kick)
Oregon State - Bernard 2 yard run (Serna Kick)
Oregon State - Fumble recovered by Rodgers in End Zone (Serna Kick)

Associated Press Emerald Bowl Game Summary - Yvenson Bernard figured the only defense that could have stopped him in the Emerald Bowl was wearing the same uniform as he was. Bernard rushed for 177 yards and a touchdown in his final college game, and Oregon State stopped Maryland's running game cold to emerge from a rainy baseball stadium with a 21-14 victory Friday night. After carrying the ball 38 times and jumping four spots to sixth place on the Pac-10's career rushing yardage list, Bernard felt he had carved out a perfect ending to the Florida native's four-year stint in rural Oregon -- with plenty of help from his stalwart defense, of course. Bernard teamed up with freshman James Rodgers, who rushed for a career-best 115 yards, caught an early TD pass and recovered Bernard's fumble for the second half's only score. With one defensive stand after another, the Beavers (9-4) extended the Pac-10's longest bowl winning streak to four and snapped Ralph Friedgen's three-game postseason winning streak at Maryland. Chris Turner passed for 205 yards and hit Isaiah Williams and Darrius Heyward-Bey with first-quarter TD passes, but the Terrapins (6-7) stalled in the second half of their fifth loss in seven games. The Beavers' vaunted rushing defense -- ranked second in the nation -- was just as good as Maryland feared, holding the Terrapins to 2 yards on the ground in the first three quarters. Maryland ended up with 19 yards on the ground. Oregon State finished with seven victories in its last eight games by surviving the unique challenges of the Emerald Bowl, where both teams stand on the same sideline at the San Francisco Giants' waterfront ballpark. The unorthodox setup got even tougher when officials turned off the malfunctioning play clock in the third quarter. A light rain pelted the largely orange-clad crowd of 32,517 in the second half, with even Terrapins mascot Testudo donning a rain poncho over his shell. Sean Canfield returned from a three-game injury absence to pass for 68 yards in relief of Lyle Moevao, who sprained his left ankle early in the second quarter. Canfield mostly did what Oregon State does best: Hand off to Bernard and Rodgers. Though the Beavers dominated much of the play, they only went ahead when Bernard's fumble at the goal line was recovered by Rodgers, who stretched out for a TD with 10 seconds left in the third quarter. Bernard leapfrogged Arizona's Trung Canidate, UCLA's Gaston Green and USC stars Anthony Davis and Ricky Bell on the conference's career rushing chart with his workhorse performance. With three final quarters of dismal offensive play, Maryland finished with a losing record for the third time in the last four seasons under Friedgen, who hadn't lost a bowl game since the Orange Bowl defeat six years ago after winning the Terps' last ACC title. Maryland opened the game with an impressive 11-play, 80-yard scoring drive capped by Williams' 9-yard TD catch. Turner went 6-of-7 on the drive, with Williams dropping his only incompletion. After Canfield threw a TD pass to Rodgers, Turner hit Heyward-Bey in stride for a 63-yard TD pass down the sideline later in the first quarter, the second-longest scoring play in Maryland bowl history. But Turner also threw two interceptions in the second quarter, and Bernard tied it at 14 with a 2-yard TD run 16 seconds before halftime.

2007 Meineke Car Care Bowl

The 2007 Meineke Car Care Bowl took place on Saturday, December 29, 2007 at Bank of America Stadium in Charlotte, North Carolina. Wake Forest won the game, 24-10. The Connecticut Huskies, making just their second bowl appearance in four seasons since joining the Big East entered the game as co-Big East champions after securing a 9-3 overall record. They faced the Wake Forest Demon Deacons, representing the Atlantic Coast Conference, a school located just 80 miles from Charlotte in Winston-Salem, North Carolina.

2007 Meineke Car Care Bowl	Line	1	-	2	-	3	-	4	-	Final
Wake Forest	(-2.5)	0	-	0	-	14	-	10	-	24
Connecticut	(47.5)	7	-	3	-	0	-	0	-	10

Scoring Summary
Connecticut - Taylor 68 yard punt return (Ciaravino kick)
Connecticut - Ciaravino 29 yard Field goal
Wake Forest - Adams 38 yard run (Swank kick)
Wake Forest - Tereshinski 20 yard pass from Skinner (Swank kick)
Wake Forest - Swank 43 yard Field goal
Wake Forest - Andrews 9 yard run (Swank kick)

Associated Press Meineke Car Care Bowl Game Summary - Put to rest those derogatory nicknames for Wake Forest. There's nothing weak about the Demon Deacons under Coach Jim Grobe. Behind do-it-all receiver Kenneth Moore and a swarming defense full of big plays, Wake Forest rallied to beat fellow upstart Connecticut 24-10 in the Meineke Car Care Bowl on Saturday. Wake Forest WR Kenneth Moore made 11 catches for 112 yards against Connecticut in the Meineke Car Care Bowl. His 98 receptions on the season broke the ACC single season record previously held by NC State's Torry Holt. Often called "Weak Forest" for a long history of ineptitude, Wake Forest (9-4) secured the second-most wins in school history, behind only last year's improbable 11-3 mark that included an Atlantic Coast Conference title and an Orange Bowl berth. While this year wasn't as stellar, Wake Forest finished with nine wins in its last 11 games -- including a bowl win after last year's loss to Louisville in the school's first Bowl Championship Series appearance. The Demon Deacons had to come from behind to do it, reeling off the final 24 points after falling behind 10-0 at halftime against the Huskies, who were playing in only their second bowl game. It was a disappointing end to the Huskies' best season since they completed the move from what used to be called Division I-AA six years ago. UConn was limited to nine first downs and failed to score an offensive touchdown. Edsall bemoaned his team's lack of depth, and UConn had a hard time keeping up with Moore. A senior playing in his hometown in his final game, Moore caught 11 passes for 112 yards and was voted MVP. Riley Skinner completed 29 of 38 passes for 268 yards, one touchdown and two interceptions, and ACC rookie of the year Josh Adams rushed for 81 yards and a score. Micah Andrews finished off UConn with a 9-yard touchdown run with 29 seconds left for Wake Forest, which was playing in bowls in consecutive seasons for the first time and displayed an opportunistic defense. Linebacker Stanley Arnoux highlighted a series of big plays for Wake Forest with an interception and two fourth-down stops. The UConn Quarterback, disrupted all day, completed just 13-of-26 for 98 yards and was sacked twice. Donald Brown rushed for 78 yards for the Huskies (9-4), who's poor second half ended their hopes of being ranked at the end of the season for the first time. While Wake Forest came into the game with a nation-best 10 non-offensive touchdowns, UConn struck first in an unconventional way late in the first quarter. Five-foot-6 Larry Taylor returned a punt 68 yards for a touchdown down the right sideline, getting a crushing block by D.J. Hernandez to break free for the final 20 yards. The Demon Deacons' offense was shut out in a half for the first time all season, with part of the blame pinned on offensive coordinator Steed Lobotzke hectic schedule. Lobotzke was away from the team much of the week while his wife gave birth. Lobotzke returned Saturday morning, and the offense returned in the second half, as Adams' 38-yard run up the middle on the first drive of the second half got Wake Forest on the board. Skinner put the Demon Deacons ahead late in the third quarter by floating a pass to the left corner of the end zone for tight end John Tereshinski for a 20-yard TD. Arnoux's first fourth-down stop, bringing down Brown for no gain, set up Sam Swank's 34-yard field goal that made it 17-10 early in the fourth. Arnoux then broke up Lorenzen's fourth-down pass from the Wake 39. The Huskies, picked to finish seventh in the eight-team Big East, ended the conference's seven-game bowl win streak dating to 2005. Moore was much of the reason. He passed former North Carolina State star Torry Holt's ACC single season record of 88 catches early in the game. He ended up with 98 and was honored on the field after the game as his family -- including his grandmother -- cheered on.

2007 Liberty Bowl

The 2007 AutoZone Liberty Bowl was played on December 29, 2007 at the Liberty Bowl Memorial Stadium in Memphis, Tennessee. The opposing teams were the University of Central Florida (UCF) Knights, winners of the Conference USA Championship for the first time in school history, and the Mississippi State University (MSU) Bulldogs, in their first bowl game under head coach Sylvester Croom. Mississippi State Free Safety Derek Pegues intercepted two passes as part of an outstanding overall defensive effort by the Bulldogs on his way to earning MVP honors. The Bulldogs emerged victorious by a score of 10-3.

2007 Liberty Bowl	Line	1	-	2	-	3	-	4	-	Final
Central Florida	(-3.0)	0	-	3	-	0	-	0	-	3
Mississippi State	(55.0)	0	-	3	-	0	-	7	-	10

Scoring Summary
Central Florida – Torres 45 yard Field goal
Mississippi State – Carlson 22 yard Field goal
Mississippi State – Dixon 1 yard run (Carlson kick)

Associated Press Liberty Bowl Game Summary - Mississippi State's win in the Liberty Bowl was the kind of game coach Sylvester Croom's mentor would have loved. Playing at the site of the Paul "Bear" Bryant's final game 25 years ago, the Bulldogs used power running and a dominant defense to beat Central Florida 10-3 on Saturday and earn a milestone win for the once dormant program. Mississippi State faced three of the top four rushers in the country this season, holding each of them well under their season average. Croom, the Southeastern Conference coach of the year who played and coached under Bryant at Alabama for 11 seasons. Anthony Dixon powered in from the 1 for the winning touchdown with 1:54 to go and most valuable player Derek Pegues picked off two passes in a game featuring anemic offenses and 17 punts. The Bulldogs (8-5) kept the Knights (10-4) out of the end zone and Kevin Smith from breaking the single season rushing record. The junior finished with 119 yards, leaving him 61 shy of Barry Sanders' mark of 2,628 yards set for Oklahoma State in 1988. It was the lowest scoring Liberty Bowl since Penn State beat Tulane 9-6 in 1979, but the pro-Mississippi State record crowd of 63,816 was rewarded for its patience as Dixon and the Bulldogs offense came alive late in the fourth quarter. Croom, in his fourth season with Mississippi State, and the Bulldogs have played this way all year, resurrecting a program that hadn't won more than three games in six seasons. As the Bulldogs did in big wins over Auburn, Kentucky and Alabama this season, they concentrated on the running game -- both on offense and defense. Smith found the going difficult in the second half and finished with an average of 3.4 yards per carry after rushing for 188.3 yards per game during the regular season. Dixon finished with 86 yards and became the seventh Bulldogs runner to go over 1,000 yards (1,066). But like the rest of the Bulldogs, he was ineffective much of the game. The teams were tied 3-3 at halftime, mostly due to conservative play-calling and poor play from the Quarterbacks. Passes were rarely aimed more than 5 yards downfield, and when they were thrown deep, they were dropped or picked off. Neither team converted a third down in the first half (0 for 16) as Mississippi State was held to 84 total yards and Central Florida to 79. UCF Quarterback Kyle Israel had 12 yards passing and two interceptions by halftime and Mississippi State's Wes Carroll had 15 yards and an interception. UCF also didn't get much help from kicker Michael Torres, who gave the Knights a 3-0 lead in the second quarter with a 45-yard field goal but missed from 32 and 37 in the second half. Mississippi State finished with 199 total yards and Blake McAdams tied the Liberty Bowl record with 11 punts. But the Bulldogs came up with just enough big plays after Keith Fitzhugh picked off Israel's pass at the Mississippi State 41 with 5:47 left. Carroll, pulled the series before, returned and responded with two rushes for 17 yards and two completions for 15 yards. All went for first downs and spurred a 10-play, 59-yard drive that consumed 3:53 and finally led to a touchdown. Pegues, fittingly, made the final key defensive play, knocking down a fourth-down pass on UCF's final drive. The Bulldogs held the Knights to 219 yards and forced four turnovers. The junior safety gave Mississippi State two excellent opportunities with interceptions in the first 30 minutes, returning the ball to Central Florida's 6 and 38. The safety's first pick set up a 22-yard field goal by Adam Carlson in the second quarter. As for Croom, the season began with talk about the SEC's first black head football coach needing a winning season to save his job. It ended with the Bulldogs' first bowl victory since the 2000 Independence Bowl and no more questions about job security.

2007 Alamo Bowl

The 2007 Valero Alamo Bowl was played on December 29, 2007 in the 65,000-seat Alamodome in San Antonio, Texas, and nationally televised by ESPN. It was the 15th Alamo Bowl and the first Alamo Bowl sponsored by the Valero Energy Corporation. The game featured the Penn State Nittany Lions and the Texas A&M Aggies, who were both unranked in the national polls. The two teams had met once in the Alamo Bowl in 1999, when Penn State shutout Texas A&M 24–0. The Aggies were coached by interim head coach Gary Darnell, who had taken over after Dennis Franchione resigned, and the Nittany Lions were coached by Hall of Famer Joe Paterno, who marked the 2007 Alamo Bowl as the 500th game of his head coaching career.

Leading into the game - This was the Aggies' 30th bowl appearance, and their third in the Alamo Bowl. This was the Nittany Lions' 40th bowl appearance, and their second in the Alamo Bowl. The 2007 Nittany Lions, who finished 8–4 in their regular season, are led by 42nd-year head coach Joe Paterno, a 2007 College Football Hall of Fame inductee. With a 22–10–1 bowl game record, Paterno is the all-time winningest leader in bowl victories and appearances. The 2007 Alamo Bowl marked Paterno's 34th bowl game appearance and 500th game as Penn State head coach.

2007 Alamo Bowl	Line	1	-	2	-	3	-	4	-	Final
Penn State	(-5.5)	0	-	17	-	7	-	0	-	24
Texas A&M	(51.5)	14	-	0	-	3	-	0	-	17

Scoring Summary
Texas A&M – Goodson 1 yard run (Bean kick)
Texas A&M – Goodson 16 yard run (Szymanski kick)
Penn State – Butler 30 yard pass from Morelli (Kelly kick)
Penn State – Clark 11 yard run (Kelly kick)
Penn State – Kelly 25 yard Field goal
Texas A&M – Szymanski 38 yard Field goal
Penn State – Royster 38 yard run (Kelly kick)

Associated Press Alamo Bowl Game Summary - With Penn State down two touchdowns early, victory for Joe Paterno in his 500th game looked bleak. JoePa said his confidence never wavered, and the Nittany Lions ended the Alamo Bowl like most of Paterno's 499 other games: with a Penn State win. Evan Royster broke a tie with a 38-yard touchdown run, Deon Butler caught a debatable 30-yard TD pass and Penn State erased an early two-touchdown deficit to beat Texas A&M 24-17 on Saturday night at the Valero Alamo Bowl. Penn State's Joe Paterno coached his 500th game Saturday night in a 24-17 win over Texas A&M in the Valero Alamo Bowl. He joined Amos Alonzo Stagg (548) as the only people to reach the 500-game milestone as a major college coach and earned his 23rd career bowl victory. Paterno, college football's leader in bowl appearances (34), led the Nittany Lions (9-4) in a thriller that brought him his record 23rd postseason win. The 81-year-old coach now has 372 career victories, one behind Florida State's Bobby Bowden for the most in major college football. Penn State's Rodney Kinlaw ran for 143 yards on 21 carries and Royster finished with 65 on nine carries. Nervously pacing the sideline in his standard khakis and black sneakers, Paterno couldn't breathe easy until the clock ticked down to zero in a roller coaster of a game. With the Nittany Lions up 24-17, Texas A&M's Stephen McGee led a 15-play drive to the Penn State 2 before losing 4 yards on fourth-and-goal after slipping on an option play with about eight minutes left. McGee said the defense appeared to have snuffed out the play anyway. Another Texas A&M (7-6) drive ended with a punt with 2 minutes left, and Penn State ran out the clock. The Nittany Lions secured their third straight bowl victory and spoiled Gary Darnell's one-game stint as interim head coach for Texas A&M. Darnell took over Nov. 23, when Dennis Franchione resigned, and A&M has hired Mike Sherman, currently offensive coordinator for the Houston Texans, to take over next season. McGee finished 19-of-31 passing for 164 yards and an interception and ran for 34 yards on 10 carries. Down two scores and in need of a change of momentum early in the second quarter, Penn State went for it on fourth-and-4 from the A&M 30. Anthony Morelli threw a wobbly pass to Butler, who had position inside on cornerback Arkeith Brown. The ball sailed just long of Butler, who fell forward in the end zone and appeared to catch the ball just before it hit the ground. It was a close call on whether Butler totally secured the ball as he landed. A replay review confirmed the touchdown that cut A&M's lead to 14-7. Maurice Evans then forced a Goodson fumble on the next drive that was recovered by Penn State's A.J. Wallace. Goodson had 65 yards on 14 carries. Clark, a seldom-used backup, then scrambled to the end zone from 11 yards out on the next play and the game was tied. Penn State had scored 17 straight points to take the lead before Matt Szymanski kicked a 38-yard field goal for A&M to tie it at 17 with 3:57 in the third quarter. The 18-play, 78-yard drive took 8:45, the longest drive by plays and time of possession this season for A&M's often beleaguered offense. The Nittany Lions took the lead for good on the next drive. Morelli connected with Derrick Williams for a 21-yard reception to the Aggie 41 on a third-and-6 before Royster burst up the middle for the decisive score for plays later. It looked rough early for Penn State after falling behind 14-0 on two touchdown runs in a 12-second span in the first quarter by A&M's Mike Goodson. A sea of maroon-clad fans that made up most of the record crowd of 66,166 at the Alamodome roared its approval in hopes of ending a distraction-filled season a high note. It wasn't to be, and the Nittany Lions rallied for their ninth win in their last 11 bowl games. It Penn State's largest comeback win since rallying from 16 points down at Northwestern on Sept. 29, 2005. It was the kind of win that makes Paterno want to keep coaching. Penn State's defense clamped down after Goodson's early runs, and the offense gained traction behind the running of backup Quarterback Darryl Clark and Kinlaw and a couple clutch throws from Morelli.

2007 Independence Bowl

The 2007 PetroSun Independence Bowl took place on December 30, 2007 at Independence Stadium in Shreveport, Louisiana. The competing teams were the Alabama Crimson Tide, representing the Southeastern Conference, and the Colorado Buffaloes, from the Big 12 Conference. Alabama won the game, 30–24. This was the only 2007–08 bowl game in which both teams finished 6–6 on the regular season. It was also the first bowl game for both respective head coaches (Nick Saban and Dan Hawkins) at their current programs.

2007 Independence Bowl	Line	1	-	2	-	3	-	4	-	Final
Alabama	(-3.5)	20	-	7	-	0	-	3	-	30
Colorado	(51.5)	0	-	14	-	3	-	7	-	24

Scoring Summary
Alabama – Tiffin 41 yard Field goal
Alabama – Tiffin 24 yard Field goal
Alabama – Brown 15 yard pass from Parker-Wilson (Tiffin kick)
Alabama – Caddell 34 yard pass from Parker-Wilson (Tiffin kick)
Alabama – Stover 31 yard pass from Parker-Wilson (Tiffin kick)
Colorado – Tyson 4 yard pass from Hawkins (Eberhart kick)
Colorado – Sprague 25 yard pass from Hawkins (Eberhart kick)
Colorado – Eberhart 39 yard Field goal
Alabama – Tiffin 26 yard Field goal
Colorado – Tyson 14 yard pass from Hawkins (Eberhart kick)

Associated Press Independence Bowl Game Summary - Alabama found enough offense Sunday night to win the PetroSun Independence Bowl but stumbled so much that even its star Quarterback acknowledges the Crimson Tide aren't rolling just yet. John Parker Wilson, named the game's most valuable offensive player after the Tide's 30-24 victory over Colorado. Alabama (7-6) stopped a four-game losing streak and avoided consecutive losing seasons for the first time in 50 years. Colorado (6-7) finished below .500 for the second straight year but was vastly improved from a 2-10 mark in 2006. Wilson completed 13 of his first 15 passes for 185 yards and three touchdowns and Alabama raced to a four-touchdown lead. Colorado couldn't complete a comeback, when its attempt at a multi-lateral play as time expired collapsed shy of midfield. The Crimson Tide had averaged 35 points in its first nine games, but only 12 points per game in the last three. Alabama entered Sunday's game having lost four in a row, including an embarrassing outing at home against Louisiana-Monroe. With the Tide up 27-0, Wilson was in firm control until being chased into an intentional grounding penalty with 5 minutes left in the first half. He threw an interception on his next attempt, leading to a Colorado score, and didn't complete another throw in the half. Buffaloes Quarterback Cody Hawkins, meanwhile, recovered from an interception on their first offensive play and finished the half 9-of-10 for 87 yards and two scores. Hawkins' 25-yard pass to Dusty Sprague with 4 seconds left in the half cut Alabama's lead to 27-14. It came less than 2 minutes after Hawkins hit Tyson DeVree with a 4-yard scoring pass. Kevin Eberhart's 39-yard field goal in the third period cut it to 27-17. Alabama amassed 170 yards in the first quarter and had 285 by halftime but added only 103 yards in the second half. Wilson had scoring passes of 15 yards to Keith Brown, 34 yards to Matt Caddell and 31 yards to Nikita Stover. With Leigh Tiffin's two field goals, Alabama led 27-0 early in the second quarter. The Buffaloes, who scored 65 points against Nebraska in their previous game, had a first down on their second play from scrimmage but didn't pick up another until 10 1/2 minutes before halftime. Once Colorado rattled Wilson, though, the fortunes turned. Hawkins was 8-of-8 on the last two drives of the half, while Wilson was 6-of-17 after his hot start and finished the game 19-of-32 for 256 yards. In the second half, having learned they couldn't beat Alabama's linebackers to the corner, Colorado running backs spread out the Tide defense and cut back against the grain to pick up 5 or 6 yards at a time. Alabama's new attention to the run opened routes for Buffaloes receivers. Scotty McKnight, Josh Smith and DeVree caught passes of 11, 22 and 13 yards for key first downs as Colorado drove for a failed 48-yard field goal try on its first drive after halftime. The big plays helped limit the Tide to six plays in the third quarter. Hawkins rallied the Buffaloes to 30-24 with a 14-yard pass to DeVree with 3:51 left, following Tiffin's 26-yard field goal. In the second half, Hawkins had 224 yards passing and finished the game 24-of-40 for 322 yards and three touchdowns. In the third quarter alone, Colorado had nine plays that gained 10 yards or more. Colorado, which had only six turnovers in its six victories this year, gave up the ball twice on interceptions and once on a failed fake punt. Tiffin's first-quarter field goals gave him 105 points for the season, the most for an Alabama kicker. Tiffin added three extra points and the fourth-quarter field goal, giving him 111 points for the season.

2007 Humanitarian Bowl

The 2007 Roady's Humanitarian Bowl was played on December 31, 2007 at Bronco Stadium on the campus of Boise State University in Boise, Idaho. Once again, the invited teams were from the Atlantic Coast Conference (Georgia Tech) and Western Athletic Conference (Fresno State). The Yellow Jackets were in a transition period between previous head coach Chan Gailey, fired in late November, and new head coach Paul Johnson, hired on December 7. Jon Tenuta, the team's defensive coordinator, coached the "Ramblin' Wreck" in this game.

2007 Humanitarian Bowl	Line	1	-	2	-	3	-	4	-	Final
Georgia Tech	(-5.5)	7	-	0	-	14	-	7	-	28
Fresno State	(54.5)	3	-	17	-	14	-	6	-	40

Scoring Summary
Georgia Tech - Thomas 35 yard pass from Bennett (Bell kick)
Fresno State - Stitser 21 yard Field goal
Fresno State - Marlon 6 yard run (Stitser kick)
Fresno State - Lubinsky 3 yard pass from Brandstater (Stitser kick)
Fresno State - Stitser 39 yard Field goal
Fresno State - Smith 43 yard run (Stitser kick)
Georgia Tech - Dwyer 36 yard run (Bell kick)
Fresno State - Brandstater 24 yard run (Stitser kick)
Georgia Tech - Dwyer 2 yard run (Bell kick)
Georgia Tech - Donley 20 yard pass from Booker (Bell kick)
Fresno State - Smith 32 yard run (Stitser kick)

Associated Press Humanitarian Bowl Game Summary - A year ago, Pat Hill was sitting at home during bowl season wondering if his Fresno State program could be revitalized. The fallout of a 4-8 season meant re-establishing the Bulldogs' identity. The task was placed before seniors like Tyler Clutts and Clifton Smith to make sure winning was again the norm in California's Central Valley. The Bulldogs responded and capped their rebound season by adding Georgia Tech -- again -- to their list of conquests from BCS conferences. Smith rushed for 152 yards and two touchdowns, Tom Brandstater threw for a score and ran for another, and the Bulldogs beat Georgia Tech 40-28 in the Roady's Humanitarian Bowl on Monday. Fresno State finished the season 9-4, winning eight of its final 10 and thinking big about 2008, when a talented team will return with aspirations of following Western Athletic Conference brethren Boise State and Hawaii into a BCS bowl game. It's Fresno State's second bowl win over Georgia Tech, after beating the Yellow Jackets 30-21 in the 2002 Silicon Valley Football Classic, and it made the Bulldogs 3-0 against the ACC in bowls. Fresno State has won four of its last five bowl games, all four wins coming against teams from the six conferences with automatic bids to the Bowl Championship Series. While Fresno State can use its surprising offensive eruption as a building block for next year, Georgia Tech will be starting from scratch. Interim coach Jon Tenuta, who took over when Chan Gailey was fired after six seasons, was added to the list of winless stopgap coaches this postseason, joining DeWayne Walker (UCLA), Gary Darnell (Texas A&M) and Chris Thurmond (Houston). While new coach Paul Johnson watched from the press box as a fan, the Yellow Jackets defense, orchestrated by Tenuta, was exposed after being one of the better units in the ACC. Fresno State scored 27 consecutive points after Tech jumped ahead 7-0, and rolled up 571 yards of total offense, the most allowed by the Yellow Jackets this season. Georgia Tech, which led the country in sacks with 47, never got to Brandstater. Brandstater was Tech's biggest problem early on, before Smith took over with 135 yards rushing in the second half and both of his TDs. Brandstater even added a 24-yard TD run in the third quarter, behind an escort from tight end Bear Pascoe. But it was his first half that was most impressive, when Brandstater directed scoring drives of 82, 90 and 91 yards, and the Bulldogs scored 17 points in the second quarter, including 10 in the final 2 minutes. Brandstater, who finished 23 of 30 passing, threw a 3-yard TD pass to Drew Lubinsky with 1:54 left in the half, the first catch of the junior's college career. Georgia Tech drove to the Fresno 47, but on fourth down with 23 seconds left, Quarterback Taylor Bennett was sacked. Brandstater then completed three straight passes and Clint Stitser kicked a 39-yard field goal, his second of the half, to give the Bulldogs a 20-7 lead. Smith then started the second half with a 43-yard TD run to give Fresno State a 27-7 lead. Tenuta's team did show some fight after falling behind. Using young, skill-position backups trying to make an impression on Johnson, the Yellow Jackets got within 34-28 early in the fourth quarter. Backup running back Jonathan Dwyer, taking over for a mostly ineffective Tashard Choice in the third quarter because of an injury, rushed for 62 yards and had touchdown runs of 36 and 2 yards. Backup Quarterback Calvin Booker, in for injured starter Taylor Bennett, threw a towering jump ball that D.J. Donley wrestled from Fresno State defensive backs Moses Harris and Damion Owens, pulling the Yellow Jackets within six with 13:06 left. Brandstater tried to answer, leading the Bulldogs inside the Tech 10. But wide receiver Marlon Moore, who scored on a 6-yard run in the first half, fumbled on a hit by safety Joe Gaston. After Darryl Richard recovered, the Bulldogs' defense held, and Smith capped his career-best day with a 32-yard sprint with 1:50 remaining.

2007 Armed Forces Bowl

The 2007 Bell Helicopter Armed Forces Bowl was played between the California Golden Bears and the Air Force Falcons played on December 31, 2007 at Amon G. Carter Stadium in Fort Worth, Texas, USA.

2007 Armed Forces Bowl	Line	1	-	2	-	3	-	4	-	Final
California	(-4.0)	0	-	14	-	14	-	14	-	42
Air Force	(55.0)	14	-	7	-	6	-	9	-	36

Scoring Summary
Air Force - Carney 1 yard run (Harrison kick)
Air Force - Dekker 7 yard pass from Carney (Harrison kick)
Air Force - Ollis 8 yard run (Harrison kick)
California - Jackson 40 yard pass from Riley (Kay kick)
California - Hawkins 5 yard pass from Riley (Kay kick)
Air Force - Harrison 29 yard Field goal
California - Jordan 18 yard pass from Riley (Kay kick)
Air Force - Harrison 19 yard Field goal
California - Forsett 1 yard run (Kay kick)
California - Forsett 21 yard run (Kay kick)
Air Force - Harrison 47 yard Field goal
California - Riley 1 yard run (Kay kick)
Air Force - Hall 4 yard run (run failed)

Associated Press Armed Forces Bowl Game Summary - Stuck on the sideline for disciplinary reasons, DeSean Jackson and Robert Jordan could do nothing to help as California quickly fell behind by three touchdowns. And they made an immediate impact. Jackson made an acrobatic 40-yard grab for Cal's first touchdown right after entering the game and Jordan had six catches for 148 yards and a score as the Bears rallied to beat Air Force 42-36 in the Armed Forces Bowl on Monday. Ranked No. 2 in the nation in October before losing six of seven games, the comeback gave California (7-6) its sixth straight winning season. Jackson, Jordan and leading tackler Thomas DeCoud were held out of the starting lineup and didn't play the first quarter because of unspecified violations of team rules that occurred before the team got to Fort Worth for the bowl. While the starting receivers watched helplessly, Air Force (9-4) built a 21-0 lead after scoring twice in a 2-minute span early in the second quarter with help of a botched kickoff. Jackson caught three passes on his first possession, including the TD on which he turned and backpedaled a few steps in the end zone before twisting and diving to make the catch. He finished with five catches for 81 yards. Jordan had an 18-TD in the third quarter, then a 52-yard catch to set up the go-ahead 1-yard run by Justin Forsett with 1:33 left in the third quarter. That made it 28-27 and the Bears led the rest of the way. Forsett, playing his final collegiate game only about half-hour from his home with about 300 family and friends watching, ran for 140 yards and two TDs on 23 carries. He added a 21-yard TD run on Cal's next drive. Forsett's first TD came after Air Force lost four-year starting Quarterback Shaun Carney because of a right knee injury when his leg buckled awkwardly while being tackled near the Cal goal line. Carney was running right on a third-and-goal keeper when he was hit head-on by two defenders and from the side by another defender. The Quarterback immediately grabbed his right knee and didn't put any weight on his leg while being helped off the field. Air Force coach Troy Calhoun said after the game Carney had ligament damage. Carney had 15 carries for 108 yards rushing and a TD, a 1-yard keeper on the Falcons' opening drive of the game. He was 5-of-8 passing for 68 yards and a score. Ryan Harrison kicked a 19-yard field goal on the next play to put the Falcons up 27-21, but Jordan's 52-yard catch came soon after. Cal freshman Kevin Riley, who took over for Nate Longshore in the second quarter, was 16-for-19 passing for 269 yards and three TDs and ran for a score. Longshore had been hampered by a sprained right ankle and Tedford wanted to get Riley some action. Riley came in on the same series as Jackson and Jordan, a four-play TD drive, and played the rest of the game. Air Force was then forced to punt for the first time, and the Bears drove 70 yards in 10 plays, Riley's 5-yard pass to Lavelle Hawkins making it 21-14. Cal last had six straight winning seasons from 1947-52. The latest streak, which includes five consecutive bowl appearances for the first time in school history, has come since Tedford took over a team coming off a 1-10 season. After Carney's 7-yard TD pass to Travis Dekker for a 14-0 lead capped a 65-yard drive, the Falcons kicked off into a stiff wind. The high-arching kick bounced off a Bears player who apparently never saw the ball while he retreated to blocking formation. Aaron Kirchoff recovered at the Bears 40, and five plays later Jim Ollis, who ran for 101 yards on 16 carries, scored on an 8-yard run.

2007 Music City Bowl

The 2007 Gaylord Hotels Music City Bowl ("presented by Bridgestone") was the 2007 edition of the Music City Bowl, and it was played on December 31, 2007. It featured the Kentucky Wildcats and the Florida State Seminoles. Both teams entered the game with a 7–5 overall record and a 4–4 conference record; Florida State had been ranked as high as #19 in the season's AP polls, appearing in the rankings for two weeks that season. Kentucky had been ranked as high as #8 (twice) in the season's AP polls and had been ranked for eight weeks during the season. The Seminoles came into the game without 34 players due to various injuries, violations of team rules, and a large academic cheating scandal. For the Wildcats, this was déjà vu all over again, as they had played in last year's edition of the game, entered it with the same 7–5 overall record, and faced an Atlantic Coast Conference team coached by a Bowden, namely the Clemson team coached by Tommy Bowden, son of longtime FSU head coach Bobby Bowden. The attendance of 68,661 set a record for the Music City Bowl.

2007 Music City Bowl	Line	1	-	2	-	3	-	4	-	Final
Kentucky	(-7.0)	7	-	7	-	14	-	7	-	35
Florida State	(57.0)	7	-	7	-	0	-	14	-	28

Scoring Summary
Kentucky - Tamme 14 yard pass from Woodson (Seiber kick)
Florida State - Weatherford 6 yard run (Cismesia kick)
Kentucky - Johnson 13 yard pass from Woodson (Seiber kick)
Florida State - Carter 24 yard interception return (Cismesia kick)
Kentucky - Little 2 yard pass from Woodson (Seiber kick)
Kentucky - Dixon 4 yard run (Seiber kick)
Florida State - Weatherford 1 yard run (Cismesia kick)
Kentucky - Johnson 35 yard pass from Woodson (Seiber kick)
Florida State - Carr 7 yard pass from Weatherford (Cismesia kick)

Associated Press Music City Bowl Game Summary - Kentucky Quarterback Andre Woodson had just handed Bobby Bowden his first December bowl loss, but that didn't stop the cordial Florida State coach from making proper introductions. Bowden may finally have a blemish on his December postseason record, but Woodson is still perfect. In fact, he improved to 2-0 against members of the Bowden family. The senior Quarterback threw four TDs against a depleted Seminoles defense to win MVP honors for the second straight Music City Bowl. The Wildcats hadn't ended consecutive seasons with bowl wins since 1951-52 under Bear Bryant, but they pulled off the feat in Nashville one year after surprising Clemson, coached by Bowden's son, Tommy. Woodson, who came to probation-saddled Kentucky as a freshman and was among a core group that helped turn the program's fortunes. As for the elder Bowden, who has led the Seminoles to 26 straight bowls and two national titles, his December bowl record dropped to 7-1-1. Bowden is major college football's winningest coach with 373 victories -- one ahead of Penn State's Joe Paterno. Florida State was playing three dozen players short due to injuries and suspensions stemming from an academic cheating scandal, and Bowden acknowledged the lack of depth had an impact. Woodson capitalized on the missing players with 358 yards passing and finished the season with 40 touchdown throws, breaking Tim Couch's school-record 37 set in 1998. It was the 19th consecutive game with at least 200 yards passing and a scoring touchdown for Woodson, a senior who figures to be among the first Quarterbacks taken in the NFL draft. The Wildcats took the lead for good midway through the third quarter on Woodson's 2-yard slant to Rafael Little, who ran for a season-high 152 yards on 28 carries. It was the 13th 100-yard rushing game for the senior running back, tying him for second on Kentucky's career list. Antone Smith had a career-high 156 yards rushing for the Seminoles. Florida State Quarterback Drew Weatherford pulled the Seminoles to 28-21 with 8 minutes left on a 1-yard bootleg run -- his first career game with two rushing TDs. Weatherford completed 22 of 48 passes for 276 yards, a TD and two interceptions. Woodson immediately answered, dumping off a short pass that Steve Johnson took for 38 yards for his second TD reception. Johnson led all receivers with 126 yards. Weatherford would add a TD pass to Greg Carr with just over 2 minutes remaining, and Florida State got the ball back at the 1-minute mark behind by one score. Linebacker Micah Johnson appeared to come up with a clinching interception, but a fumble gave the Seminoles another chance. Weatherford's last-second pass fell incomplete in the end zone. Kentucky improved to 4-1-1 against the Seminoles in their first matchup since 1965. It was the first meeting ever between Bowden and Brooks, friends for nearly three decades. The score was 14-all after a first half in which Bowden and others on the Florida State sideline gave the officials an earful after two close calls. The Seminoles disputed an offensive pass interference call on Carr that negated a touchdown. Gary Cismesia wound up missing a field goal -- he didn't make any in the game and finished the season with 27, tied with Sebastian Janikowski for the Atlantic Coast Conference record. Florida State got the ball right back after Carr's penalty, recovering a second fumble by Little. Kentucky ended that possession with a goal-line stand, but the Seminoles' Tony Carter picked off Woodson's next pass and returned it 24 yards to tie the game. Kentucky appeared to pull ahead at the end of the half on a field goal by Lones Seiber, but Florida State was called for personal foul on the play. Brooks decided to try for the TD rather than keep the points, and Seiber eventually missed from 39 yards. Kentucky scored first, taking advantage of a blocked punt. Woodson soon connected with a wide-open Tamme from 14 yards out. The next time Kentucky had the ball, Little fumbled just short of the goal line. Carter grabbed the loose ball and ran 51 yards, stopped only after colliding with teammate Andre Fluellen. Weatherford, not known for dashing speed, scampered 27 yards on Florida State's first play of the next drive and later ran it in from 6 yards out to make it 7-all.

2007 Sun Bowl

The 2007 Brut Sun Bowl was played on December 31, 2007 at Sun Bowl Stadium on the campus of the University of Texas, El Paso, between the South Florida Bulls and the Oregon Ducks. The Ducks were playing without Quarterback Dennis Dixon, who finished fifth in the Heisman Trophy balloting but who had season-ending ACL surgery in November. Redshirt freshman Justin Roper made his first collegiate start in place of Dixon and threw for four touchdowns to tie a Sun Bowl record and lead the Ducks to a 56-21 victory. The game marked the 40th consecutive telecast by CBS Sports. No other network and bowl game has been paired for a longer period.

2007 Sun Bowl	Line	1	-	2	-	3	-	4	-	Final
#23 South Florida	(-6.5)	0	-	14	-	0	-	7	-	21
Oregon	(52.5)	8	-	10	-	28	-	10	-	56

Scoring Summary
Oregon – Roper 7 yard pass from Strong (Evenson run)
South Florida – Alvarado 29 yard Field goal
Oregon – Evenson 39 yard Field goal
South Florida – Johnson 24 yard pass from Grothe (Hill pass from Grothe)
Oregon – Stewart 71 yard run (Evenson kick)
South Florida – Alvarado 35 yard Field goal
Oregon – Williams 14 yard pass from roper (Evenson kick)
Oregon – Dickson 15 yard pass from Roper (Evenson kick)
Oregon – Thurmond 25 yard interception return (Evenson kick)
Oregon – Stewart 7 yard pass from Roper (Evenson kick)
Oregon – Evenson 30 yard Field goal
South Florida – Love 11 yard pass from Gregory (Alvarado kick)
Oregon – DiVincenzo 17 yard interception return (Evenson kick)

Associated Press Sun Bowl Game Summary - If anyone forgot how good Oregon looked earlier this season, Jonathan Stewart and Justin Roper offered a reminder. Stewart set a Brut Sun Bowl record with a career-high 253 yards rushing, while Roper, a redshirt freshman, threw four touchdown passes in his first start to help Oregon beat South Florida 56-21 on Monday. The Ducks (9-4) scored 28 straight points in the third quarter to snap a four-game postseason losing streak, their first bowl win since beating Colorado 38-16 in the Fiesta Bowl after the 2001 season. Oregon made it look easy against the Bulls (9-4), who boasted one of the nation's better defenses. Credit the legwork by Stewart, as smooth a runner as you'll find, and steady play by Roper, who had three weeks to prepare. Roper completed 17 of 30 attempts for 180 yards with no interceptions. His tied a Sun Bowl record with the four TD passes. The Ducks also won for the first time since losing Quarterback Dennis Dixon to a knee injury in November, snapping a three-game losing streak that killed their national title hopes. How easy was it this time for the Ducks? They won a matchup of teams that'd been ranked No. 2 in the nation earlier this season handily, despite setting a Sun Bowl record with 138 penalty yards. But Oregon's offensive and defensive lines set the tone after halftime, and the Ducks never looked back. Roper started the second-half scoring avalanche with a 14-yard TD strike to Jaison Williams and added a 15-yard scoring pass to Ed Dickson. On the next play from scrimmage, Walter Thurmond stepped in front of a pass by South Florida's Matt Grothe and returned it 25 yards for another TD, giving the Ducks a 39-14 lead midway through the third. But these hard-hitting Quackers weren't finished. Grothe had another interception on the ensuing possession, the first of two for Oregon's Jairus Byrd, setting up Roper's 8-yard TD pass to Stewart. On that drive, Stewart got free on a 16-yard gain, breaking the previous Sun Bowl record of 197 yards rushing set in 1977 by LSU's Charles Alexander in a 24-14 loss to Stanford. Just like that, Oregon's 18-14 halftime lead had swelled to 46-14, and fans of the Ducks began wondering if Stewart, a junior, will return next fall. "One more year!" the Oregon fans chanted as Stewart hoisted the Sun Bowl trophy. For good measure, Ducks kicker Matt Evensen added a 30-yard field goal early in the fourth quarter and defensive end Michael DiVincenzo returned an interception for a touchdown with 3:23 remaining. Roper opened the season fifth on the depth chart and ran the scout team until a series of Quarterback injuries -- none more devastating than the loss of Dixon -- reshaped the Oregon roster. Bellotti gave Roper the start over Cody Kempt, another redshirt freshman. Stewart was just as impressive. He broke a 71-yard TD run late in the second quarter, greeted by an enormous hole off left tackle, and raced untouched to the end zone to give the Ducks an 18-11 lead. Stewart kept the momentum going after the break. His 41-yard run on Oregon's first drive of the second half set up Roper's second TD pass for a 25-14 lead, and he logged the ninth-best rushing effort in a bowl game. There was no sign of the turf toe injury that slowed Stewart earlier this season, when Oregon dropped from the national title chase. South Florida, which reached No. 2 in the country in just its 11th season playing football, missed a chance to win 10 games for the first time. The 49,867 fans were treated to lots of penalty flags. The teams combined to break the Sun Bowl record for total penalty yardage -- 202 penalty yards -- and it wasn't even halftime when the old mark fell.

2007 Chick-Fil-A Peach Bowl

The 2007 Chick-fil-A Bowl, formerly known as the Peach Bowl and the Chick-fil-A Peach Bowl. It pitted the Auburn Tigers against the Clemson Tigers. Auburn University represented the Southeastern Conference (SEC) and Clemson University represented the Atlantic Coast Conference (ACC) in the competition. In exchange for the right to pick the first ACC team after the Bowl Championship Series selections, bowl representatives paid $3.25 million to the ACC, while the SEC, whose fifth team was selected, received $2.4 million. The combined $5.65 million payout is the seventh largest among all college football bowl games, and the fourth-largest non-BCS bowl game payout.

2007 Chick-Fil-A Peach Bowl	Line	1	-	2	-	3	-	4	-	OT	-	Final
#15 Clemson	(-2.5)	0	-	7	-	0	-	10	-	3	-	20
#22 Auburn	(46.0)	3	-	0	-	7	-	7	-	6	-	23

Scoring Summary
Auburn – Byrum 36 yard Field goal
Clemson – Spiller 83 yard run (Bucholz kick)
Auburn – Fannin 22 yard pass from Burns (Byrum kick)
Clemson – Bucholz 22 yard Field goal
Clemson – Davis 1 yard run (Bucholz kick)
Auburn – Tate 1 yard run (Byrum kick)
Clemson – Bucholz 25 yard Field goal
Auburn – Burns 7 yard run

Associated Press Chick-Fil-A Peach Bowl Game Summary - The last play of Auburn's 2007 season should give the Tigers good reason to look forward to the start of 2008. Freshman Quarterback Kodi Burns, receiving an expanded role in Auburn's new spread offense, scored on a 7-yard run in overtime to give the Tigers a 23-20 victory over Clemson in the Chick-fil-A Bowl on Monday night. Burns, who shared snaps with senior starter Brandon Cox, threw a 22-yard touchdown pass to Mario Fannin in the third quarter and led Auburn with 69 yards rushing on 13 carries. Just like that, Auburn may have found its next starting Quarterback. After Mark Buchholz kicked a 25-yard field goal on Clemson's opening possession of overtime, Burns scored on a spinning run on a third-and-3 play. Burns said the winning run may have been his most challenging, right from the snap from center Jason Bosley. Burns remembered advice from new offensive coordinator Tony Franklin, who instituted the new offense in bowl practice after he was hired Dec. 12. Burns said blocks from his line and tailback Brad Lester cleared his path to the end zone. Cox ran for a first down on a fourth-and-1 play from the 16 to keep Auburn's overtime possession alive. Auburn (9-4) gained 423 yards on 90 plays -- a winning performance in the debut of the new scheme. "It was tough," Burns said of picking up the new offense after the regular season. Clemson's defense looked tired in the fourth quarter after keeping pace with the no-huddle attack. The pace was even tiring for Tuberville. While Auburn prospered with its two-Quarterback attack, Clemson (9-4) struggled with junior Quarterback Cullen Harper, who was only 14-for-33 passing for 104 yards. Clemson was held to 12 first downs and 293 yards. Harper had arthroscopic surgery on his passing shoulder after the regular season. He tried to stay loose by throwing behind the Clemson bench between possessions, but Clemson coach Tommy Bowden said he didn't think the surgery was a factor in the poor passing numbers. Auburn (No. 23 BCS, No. 22 AP) denied No. 15 Clemson its first 10-win season since 1990. C.J. Spiller had eight carries for 112 yards for Clemson, including an 83-yard touchdown run. James Davis had 23 carries for 72 yards and a touchdown. Clemson linebacker Cortney Vincent said the loss was "heartbreaking." Spiller's long run was the only offensive highlight of the first half for Clemson. On a second-down play from the Clemson 17 early in the second quarter, Spiller appeared to be stopped at the line by Auburn's Josh Thompson and Quentin Groves. But Spiller bounced out to his left, turned the corner and suddenly had open field down the Clemson sideline. Spiller stayed a step ahead of Auburn cornerback Jonathan Wilhite as he watched on the

Georgia Dome video board. The 83-yard run was the longest in a bowl game in Clemson history, the longest in any Chick-fil-A Bowl game and the longest for Clemson in any game since an 89-yard run by Derrick Witherspoon against Maryland on Oct. 30, 1993. Auburn opened the second half with a 10-play, 78-yard touchdown drive. On third and 7 from the Auburn 22, Burns scrambled to his right before passing to Mario Fannin, who ran past Clemson linebacker Josh Miller for the touchdown and a 10-7 lead. A 20-yard run by Spiller helped set up a 22-yard field goal by Mark Buchholz on the first play of the fourth quarter for a 10-10 tie. The tie held until the only turnover of the game. A pass by Cox was deflected by cornerback Crezdon Butler and intercepted by defensive tackle Rashaad Jackson at the Auburn 32. Clemson took advantage. Harper passed to Aaron Kelly for 27 yards to the 4. Davis scored on a fourth-down plunge from the 1 to give Clemson a 17-10 lead. Auburn answered with a 70-yard touchdown drive. A 15-yard run by Burns to the 1 set up a touchdown run by Ben Tate on the next play for a 17-17 tie.

2007 Insight Bowl

The 2007 Insight Bowl was played on December 31, 2007, at Sun Devil Stadium on the Arizona State University campus in Tempe, Arizona. The opponents were the Indiana Hoosiers of the Big Ten Conference and the Oklahoma State Cowboys of the Big 12 Conference. This was the third straight year of the Big 10 and Big 12 tie-ins for this bowl game. Both teams had tumultuous seasons. The Hoosiers' previous head coach, Terry Hoeppner, died in June 2007 and Bill Lynch took over the program. The season-long mantra was "Play 13," as in playing a 13th game, a bowl, after the 12-game regular season. (This is IU's first bowl since 1993.) Meanwhile, Cowboys head coach Mike Gundy became famous throughout North America for a tirade against a sportswriter for The Daily Oklahoman. The outburst was repeated many times on TV sportscasts and online. The Cowboys were 6–6 on the season and unranked nationally. Generally accepted as a disappointing year for the highly touted pre-season offense led by Zac Robinson who replaced Bobby Reid at the starting Quarterback position early in the year.

2007 Insight Bowl	Line	1	-	2	-	3	-	4	-	Final
Indiana	(69.5)	3	-	7	-	7	-	16	-	33
Oklahoma State	(-5.0)	21	-	14	-	7	-	7	-	49

Scoring Summary
Indiana – Starr 43 yard Field goal
Oklahoma State – Savage 3 yard run (Bailey kick)
Oklahoma State – Bryant 24 yard pass from Robinson (Bailey kick)
Oklahoma State – Robinson 7 yard run (Bailey kick)
Oklahoma State – Bowman 14 yard pass from Robinson (Bailey kick)
Indiana – Thigpen 4 yard pass from Lewis (Starr kick)
Oklahoma State – Robinson 1 yard run (Bailey kick)
Indiana – Lewis 1 yard run (Starr kick)
Oklahoma State – Bryant 11 yard pass from Robinson (Bailey kick)
Indiana – Sears 5 yard run (Starr kick)
Indiana – Starr 37 yard Field goal
Oklahoma State – Crosslin 1 yard run (Bailey kick)
Indiana – Bailey 30 yard pass from Lewis (Starr kick)

Associated Press Insight Bowl Game Summary - Back in September, Oklahoma State coach Mike Gundy made headlines by ranting "I'm a man!" But Zac Robinson is the man for the Cowboys. Robinson threw three touchdown passes and ran for two more scores, leading Oklahoma State to a 49-33 Insight Bowl victory over Indiana on Monday night. A sophomore making his 11th college start, Robinson piloted a near-flawless attack in the first half as the Cowboys scored touchdowns on their first five possessions. Robinson completed 24 of 34 passes for 302 yards and threw an interception. Robinson also ran for 70 yards. Dantrell Savage ran for 100 yards and a touchdown for the Cowboys (7-6, 4-4 Big 12), who matched their season-high point total. Dez Bryant caught nine passes for 117 yards and two touchdowns. The loss capped an emotional year for the Hoosiers (7-6, 3-5 Big Ten), who's coach, Terry Hoeppner, died of complications of a brain tumor in June. Kellen Lewis passed for 204 yards and two touchdowns and ran for 83 yards and another touchdown for the Hoosiers in their first postseason appearance since 1993. In last year's Insight Bowl, Texas Tech staged the biggest bowl comeback in major-college history on the same field, rallying from a 38-7 third-quarter deficit to stun Minnesota 44-41 in overtime. This time, the Cowboys sprinted to a 35-10 halftime lead and were never threatened. The Cowboys spotted Indiana an early field goal, then scored touchdowns on their first five possessions. Oklahoma State's attack didn't miss a beat without offensive coordinator Larry Fedora, who left for Southern Mississippi after the regular season. Gundy, their former offensive coordinator, took over the play-calling. Most of the plays involved Robinson, a quick-footed product of Littleton, Colo. He carved up the Hoosiers with his arm and his legs. In the first half, Robinson completed 15 of 20 passes for 192 yards and two touchdowns and led Oklahoma

State with 64 yards rushing and two touchdowns. The Cowboys won their second straight bowl and improved to 2-0 in bowls in Sun Devil Stadium, having beaten Brigham Young in the 1974 Fiesta Bowl. Indiana got off to a good start, taking the opening kickoff and driving 52 yards to set up Austin Starr's 43-yard field goal. That's when the Cowboys took over. On their first five possessions, they drove 67, 53, 54, 57 and 63 yards, scoring touchdowns every time. The longest drive lasted 3:07. The Hoosiers' offense was limited to Lewis, who accounted for all but 10 of their 196 first-half yards. Lewis also scored on a 1-yard run on Indiana's opening possession of the second half. The touchdown came after the Hoosiers faked a field goal on fourth-and-7 and Lewis hit Starr, who bulled for 9 yards to the 1. Starr, who hit his 20th and 21st field goals, extending his single-season school record. Oklahoma State answered with an 80-yard drive, capped by an 11-yard touchdown pass from Robinson to Dez Bryant to push its lead to 42-17. The Hoosiers made it 42-24 on a 5-yard run by Josiah Sears midway through the fourth quarter. Lewis connected with James Bailey for a 30-yard touchdown strike with a second to go to cap the scoring. It was Lewis' 42nd career touchdown pass, tying former Hoosiers star Antwaan Randle El for the most in school history.

2008 Gator Bowl

The 2008 Gator Bowl was played on January 1, 2008. It featured the Red Raiders of Texas Tech University, who finished 3rd in the Big 12 Conference's South Division, and the Cavaliers of the University of Virginia, who finished 2nd in the Atlantic Coast Conference's Coastal Division. Texas Tech won the game on a last-second field goal, securing a 31–28 victory.

2008 Gator Bowl	Line	1	-	2	-	3	-	4	-	Final
Texas Tech	(-6.0)	7	-	0	-	7	-	17	-	31
#21 Virginia	(59.0)	9	-	12	-	0	-	7	-	28

Scoring Summary
Texas Tech – Lewis 10 yard pass from Harrell (Trlica kick)
Virginia – Stupar 3 yard pass from Sewell (Gould kick)
Virginia – Team Safety (intentional grounding in end zone)
Virginia – Simpson 96 yard run (Gould kick)
Virginia – Team Safety (intentional grounding in end zone)
Virginia – Gould 22 yard Field goal
Texas Tech – Amendola 6 yard pass from Harrell (Trlica kick)
Virginia – Simpson 11 yard pass from Lalich (Gould kick)
Texas Tech – Crabtrree 20 yard pass from Harrell (Trlica kick)
Texas Tech – Crawford 4 yard run (Trlica kick)
Texas Tech – Trlica 41 yard Field goal

Associated Press Gator Bowl Game Summary - Texas Tech didn't score 40 or more points, as it had all season. Through three quarters, the nation's top passing offense couldn't score much at all. But Graham Harrell stayed with it, finishing 44-of-69 for 407 yards and three TDs, and the Red Raiders scored just enough to overcome a 14-point deficit and stun Virginia 31-28 on a late field goal in the Konica Minolta Gator Bowl on Tuesday. Alex Trlica hit from 41 yards, despite swirling wind, with two seconds remaining. It was the third game-winner of the senior kicker's career and came at an appropriate time: Earlier in the game, Trlica became the first kicker in school history to score at least 100 points in a season. Tech overcame several mental errors, including pivotal penalties and a fumble, to come back from a 28-14 fourth-quarter deficit. Its aggressive pass offense couldn't score much for three quarters, but Harrell still managed to rack up Gator Bowl records for yards, completions and attempts. In the final period, the Red Raiders finally found the end zone as they were accustomed to all year. Twice and Trlica's field goal did the rest. Just a few minutes earlier, the Cavaliers seemed to be in control. A Tech drive kept alive by two fourth-down conversions sputtered with eight minutes left, and All-American Michael Crabtree couldn't haul in a prayer in the end zone on fourth-and-1. But a few minutes after that, Harrell found him in the same spot against the same defender, and this time it worked -- despite a pass interference call. Then, Virginia gave Tech a gift. The ball was knocked out of backup Virginia Quarterback Peter Lalich's hands at the 4-yard line, Tech recovered, and Aaron Crawford's run a play later tied it at 28. The Red Raiders overcame a tremendous effort by Virginia tailback Mikell Simpson, who ran for 170 yards on 20 carries -- including a NCAA bowl-record 96-yard TD run by a running back -- and caught another touchdown. Pretty impressive, considering he was playing receiver for the Cavaliers until backfield injuries pressed him into service in October. Virginia's offense wasn't the same after losing Jameel Sewell at the start of the fourth quarter. His statistics weren't outstanding -- 14-of-23 passing for 78 yards and a TD -- but he commanded the offense well. Not known for running, the second-year Quarterback had nine carries for 32 yards, and his mobility was key to Virginia's first score. Sewell kept that drive going with two rushes for first downs, one of them on third-and-8, before a 2-yard TD pass for Virginia's first score. He was tackled near the line of scrimmage at the start of the fourth quarter and came up favoring his left leg. Sewell had to be helped off the field and didn't return until Virginia's last possession, when Tech came back and tied things up. By then it was too late -- the Cavaliers couldn't move the ball or stop Harrell, a different story from early in the game. Virginia forced one of the country's most prolific and efficient passers into two safeties in the first half. They happened similarly -- Harrell was backed into his end zone and desperately tossed the ball toward his linemen, earning two grounding calls that counted for safeties. The second time he shouldn't have been in that position anyway. Tech got the ball at its own 11 and then was set back to the 6 with a delay of game penalty. It was one of numerous mental mistakes the Red Raiders overcame. There was also an unsportsmanlike conduct call that gave Virginia new life in Tech territory and a defensive offsides call that ruined a third-down stop, both in the fourth quarter. An illegal block in the third quarter pushed the Red Raiders back to their own 8, and Grant Walker fumbled with less than a minute left in the third quarter and Tech driving. Crabtree, the nation's leading receiver, had nine catches for 101 yards and a touchdown. He hauled in a 20-yard score to put Tech back in the game despite a pass interference penalty. He also beat double coverage to nab a 29-yarder that put Tech in the red zone with about nine minutes left and trailing by 14.

2008 Outback Bowl

The 2008 Outback Bowl was played on January 1, 2008 at Raymond James Stadium in Tampa, Florida. As is the case every year, the opposing teams are from the Big Ten Conference (Wisconsin) and Southeastern Conference (Tennessee). The Volunteers were runners-up in the SEC, having lost to LSU, 21–14, in the SEC Championship Game in Atlanta, Georgia on December 1. The Badgers were trying for a second straight 10-win season under head coach Bret Bielema. Tennessee won, 21–17. Wisconsin had a chance to win the game in the final minute, but Wisconsin Quarterback Tyler Donovan was intercepted on a desperation pass, sealing a Volunteers win. Game MVP Erik Ainge completed 25 of his 43 passes for 365 yards and two touchdowns. Wisconsin running back P.J. Hill ran the ball 16 times for 132 yards.

2008 Outback Bowl	Line	1	-	2	-	3	-	4	-	Final
#18 Wisconsin	(57.5)	7	-	7	-	3	-	0	-	17
#16 Tennessee	(-2.0)	7	-	14	-	0	-	0	-	21

Scoring Summary
Tennessee— Jones 3 yard run (Lincoln Kick)
Wisconsin— Donovan 6 yard run (Mehlhaff Kick)
Tennessee— Briscoe 29 yard pass from Ainge (Lincoln Kick)
Tennessee— Cottam 31 yard pass from Ainge (Lincoln kick)
Wisconsin— Crooks 4 yard pass from Donovan (Mehlhaff Kick)
Wisconsin— Mehlhaff 27 yard Field goal

Associated Press Outback Bowl Game Summary - Phillip Fulmer stepped up to the podium and graciously accepted the Outback Bowl trophy. No. 16 Tennessee overcame injuries, academic suspensions and the impending departure of two key assistant coaches to beat No. 18 Wisconsin 21-17 Tuesday for the Volunteers' first 10-win season since 2004. Erik Ainge threw for 365 yards and two touchdowns in his final game for the Vols, who also got a stellar performance from a defense that has improved dramatically since early season losses to California and Florida. A month after having an interception returned for the winning score in a 21-14 loss to LSU in the SEC championship game, Ainge completed 25 of 43 passes without a turnover to win MVP honors. Fulmer used the 10-point loss to Penn State here last year to motivate players during the offseason. Ainge conceded that finishing his career on winning note was big, even if the Vols fell short of loftier goals. Antonio Wardlow sealed Tennessee's first 10-win season in three years when he intercepted Tyler Donovan's deep throw intended for Paul Hubbard in the end zone in the final minute. The Vols also thwarted another fourth-quarter drive by stopping Wisconsin on downs at the Tennessee 10. Receiver Gerald Jones took a direct snap from center and scored on a 3-yard run, then Ainge tossed TD passes of 29 yards to Josh Briscoe and 31 yards to Brad Cottam to help Tennessee build a 21-7 lead. Donovan's 4-yard TD throw to Andy Crooks trimmed Wisconsin's deficit to 21-14 at the half. The Badgers then pulled within four points on Taylor Mehlhaff's 27-yard field goal in the closing seconds of the third quarter. The Wisconsin Quarterback shrugged off several big hits, including helmet-to-helmet contact when he dove into the end zone on a 6-yard first-quarter run, to help Wisconsin (9-4) stay close by completing 14 of 24 passes for 155 yards. Bielema was upset about the officiating in general but was particularly incensed that Tennessee wasn't penalized for Eric Berry's hit that left Donovan down on his back in the end zone. P.J. Hill returned to Wisconsin's offense after sitting out two games and missing part of two others, running for 132 yards on 16 carries. His 50-yard run was the big play in the drive that stalled at the Tennessee 10 with six minutes left. Donovan launched Wisconsin's last drive from his own 12 with 1:26 to go. The Badgers marched to the Tennessee 36 before the senior overthrew Hubbard, who was racing up the left side of the field. Tennessee played without six players who were declared academically ineligible, including defensive tackle Demonte Bolden, linebacker Rico McCoy and leading receiver Lucas Taylor, who had 73 receptions for 1,000 yards and five TDs this season. Briscoe took up the slack in the absence of Taylor, finishing with seven catches for 101 yards. Both teams rebounded from tough stretches that ruined any hopes of contending for the national title to finish the regular season with nine victories. Tennessee lost two of its first three games before winning eight of nine to earn a berth in the SEC championship game, where the Vols lost to LSU. Wisconsin started 5-0 before losses at Illinois and Penn State dropped the Badgers out of the Top 25. A lopsided loss at Ohio State eliminated any chance of winding up in the Rose Bowl, but the team regrouped to beat Michigan and Minnesota to head to Tampa for its fourth consecutive appearance in a January bowl. The Badgers beat Auburn and Arkansas in the Capital One Bowl the previous two years and would have joined Michigan as the only Big Ten programs to beat SEC opponents in three straight bowl games.

2008 Capital One Bowl

The 2008 Capital One Bowl was held on January 1, 2008 at the Citrus Bowl in Orlando, Florida. The game featured the University of Michigan Wolverines—who finished the 2007 season tied for second in the Big Ten Conference with an overall record of 8–4 (6–2 in the Big Ten)—and the #12 University of Florida Gators—who finished the 2007 season third in the Southeastern Conference's East Division with an overall record of 9–3 (5–3 in the SEC).

2008 Capital One Bowl	Line	1	-	2	-	3	-	4	-	Final
Michigan	(60.0)	7	-	14	-	7	-	13	-	41
#9 Florida	(-10.5)	7	-	7	-	14	-	7	-	35

Scoring Summary
Michigan – Manningham 21 yard pass from Henne (Lopata kick)
Florida – Harvin 10 yard pass from Tebow (Ijjas kick)
Florida – Caldwell 18 yard pass from Tebow (Ijjas kick)
Michigan – Hart 3 yard run (Lopata kick)
Michigan – Arrington 1 yard pass from Henne (Lopata kick)
Michigan – Hart 1 yard run (Lopata kick)
Florida – Tebow 1 yard run (Ijjas kick)
Florida – Caldwell 14 yard pass from Tebow (Ijjas kick)
Michigan – Lopata 37 yard Field goal
Florida – Harvin 10 yard run (Ijjas kick)
Michigan – Arrington 18 yard pass from Henne (Lopata kick)
Michigan – Lopata 41 yard Field goal

Bentley Historical Library 2008 CAPITAL ONE BOWL GAME SUMMARY - The University of Michigan football team sent its seniors and head coach Lloyd Carr into retirement with an emotional victory over ninth-ranked Florida in the 2008 Capital One Bowl, played New Year's Day from the Citrus Bowl. The Wolverines (9-4) concluded the game with 524 yards of total offense, including 373 through the air to seven different receivers. The game marked Lloyd Carr's 162nd and final game as Michigan head coach. He finishes his 13-year head coaching career with a 122-40 overall record and six bowl victories (6-7). The Wolverines opened the playbook and threw its entire offensive arsenal at the Gators, led by senior Quarterback Chad Henne, the game's Most Valuable Player. He completed 25-of-39 passes for 373 yards and three touchdown passes. His primary receiver was senior Adrian Arrington who had career highs of nine receptions and 153 yards and tied a career mark with two touchdowns. Senior tailback Mike Hart again led the ground game with 32 carries, 129 yards and a pair of touchdowns. Junior wide receiver Mario Manningham accounted for Henne's remaining touchdown pass and had five catches for 78 yards. Defensively, the Wolverines held Quarterback Tim Tebow in check for most of the contest, limiting the Heisman Trophy winner to 17-of-33 passing and 154 yards with three touchdown tosses. Senior safety Jamar Adams led the defense with nine tackles, including one sack, while senior Chris Graham and Brandon Harrison added seven tackles apiece. Michigan took the opening kickoff after losing the toss and marched 93 yards in 12 plays for a 7-0 lead as Henne tossed a 21-yard touchdown pass to Manningham. The 4:01 drive started at the seven-yard line and saw the Wolverines gain six first downs. Henne completed all six passes for 63 yards, spreading balls around to four different receivers. Hart rushed four times for 41 yards, including a 23-yard run on the game's second play Arrington caught three passes for 29 yards. Florida moved to the Wolverines' 32-yard line before the drive was stopped on a pass breakup by freshman Donovan Warren on a third-and-five pass by Tebow. Kicker Joey Ijjas' 49-yard field goal attempt sailed wide right to preserve the touchdown advantage for the Wolverines. After holding Michigan on its second possession, the Gators tied the score at seven apiece as Tebow floated a 10-yard touchdown pass to wide receiver Percy Harvin at 2:37 of the first quarter. The seven-play, 59-yard scoring drive saw Harvin rush twice for 16 yards in addition to his TD catch. Tebow had a 19-yard run on the first play of the drive and completed two-of-three passes for 27 yards. The Gators scored an apparent touchdown on a five-yard pass from Tebow to Cornelius Ingram, but Florida was called for an illegal man down field. UF took a 14-7 lead on the next series on a bubble screen from Tebow to Andre Caldwell that covered 18 yards for the touchdown. The three-play scoring drive covered 29 yards in 54 seconds. Tebow completed an 18-yard pass to Harvin who added a two-yard run prior to a series of penalties on both teams that preceded the scoring play. Hart took the ball across the goal line on a three-yard TD run to tie the score at 14-14 with 9:51 remaining in the second quarter. The Wolverines used the abilities of Manningham on the drive, handing him the ball twice on a pair of four-yard runs and Henne tossed an 11-yard pass and a 24-yard third-down completion to him that provided a first-and-goal situation. The 12-play drive covered 56 yards in 4:57 and was capped by Hart's 40th career rushing touchdown. The Michigan defense held firm after allowing a 66-yard run by Harvin at the outset of the following series. The Gators had a first-and-goal situation but a penalty for an illegal formation nullified a scoring pass. Jamar Adams sacked Tebow on third-and-goal from the nine-yard line to end the touchdown drive. Ijjas' 35-yard field goal attempt was blocked by junior nose tackle Terrance Taylor and defensive end Tim Jamison returned the ball 16 yards. The Wolverines were unable to gain the lead as Hart lost his first fumble in 1,005 touches, fumbling on first-and-goal from the four-yard line. U-M gained the first-and-goal opportunity on a backside screen from Henne to tight end Carson Butler that covered 65 yards. Manningharn started the three-play series with a seven-yard run. After holding the Gators to a three-and-out, the Wolverines moved into Florida territory, but turned the ball over as Henne's pass on a trick play was intercepted at the goal line by safety Major Wright. Hart gained one yard on the first play and moved the Wolverines into Florida territory with a draw play that netted 15 yards on the following play. Michigan gained a 21-14 lead on a one-yard touchdown pass from Henne to Arrington with eight seconds left in the half. Henne tossed a one-yard TD pass on an out pattern to Arrington in the right corner of the end zone to give the Wolverines the halftime advantage. Arrington caught an apparent touchdown on a diving pass at the goal line, but the play was reversed and Michigan gained possession at the half-yard line. The 11-play, 62-yard scoring drive covered 2:3 1, with Henne completing three-of-six passes for 46 yards. Manningharn converted two third downs with a seven-yard catch and a 5-yarder that kept the drive alive. Michigan's pepsi kick to open the second half went un-fielded and special teams captain Anton Campbell recovered the miscue to give U-M possession at the Florida 37-yard line. Hart increased the Wolverines lead to 28-14 on a one yard run behind the left side of the line. The key play on the seven-play, 37-yard scoring drive was a 20-yard slant to Arrington from Henne on a third-and-10 play that gave U-M first-and-goal at the two-yard line. Manningharn gained four yards on a run and Hart had an 11-yard carry on the drive. Florida trimmed the deficit in half, 28-21, on a one-yard touchdown run by Tebow. The Gators' longest drive of the game, a 10-play series that covered 56 yards in 4:55, was all Tebow and Harvin Tebow carried four times for 19 yards and completed two-of-three passes for 14 yards. Harvin caught a 10-yard pass to convert a fourth-and-five play and added a 17-yard run and two-yard scamper. Michigan lost another scoring chance at the goal line as Hart fumbled while stretching the ball out and the ball was recovered for a touchback by Major Wright. The Wolverines moved into Gator territory on a 25-yard pass from Henne to Arrington and gained first-and-goal from the five-yard line on a 19-yard pass from Henne to sophomore wide receiver Greg Mathews. Hart took the carry on the ensuing play and gained four yards to the one-yard line where he stretched for the end zone, but Wright put his helmet on the ball. Florida took over at the 20-yard line and moved 80 yards in eight plays to tie the game at 28 as Tebow tossed a 14-yard touchdown pass to Andre Caldwell. The key play on the drive was a fake punt by the Gators, a 15-yard pass from punter Chas Henry to reserve tight end Aaron Hernandez from the UF 23-yard line. With new life, Harvin had a five-yard run and added a 44-yard run to Michigan's 13-yard line on the first two plays after the fake. Michigan regained the lead, 31-28, on a 37-yard field goal by senior kicker K.C. Lopata with 12:16 remaining in the fourth quarter. The Wolverines moved 50 yards in 10 plays, with Hart gaining 26 yards on four carries and Mathews catching passes of six and 10 yards from Henne. Florida took the lead, 35-31, on a 10-yard reverse by Harvin at 5:49 of the final stanza. The Gators gained possession at the U-M 34-yard line after defensive end Jermaine Cunningham tipped a screen pass from Henne and tackle Mike Pouncey intercepted the ball and gained nine yards. Florida used the short field to its advantage, moving 34 yards in five plays, with Tebow rushing twice for 12 yards and completing two passes for 12 yards prior to Harvin's second touchdown of the game. The Wolverines took over at their own 33-yard line and quickly moved to the Florida 24 with a 37-yard completion to Arrington that bounced off a Gator defender. In just four total plays, the Wolverines regained the lead, 38-35, on an 18-yard completion from Henne to Arrington, with the pair accounting for 55 of the 67 yards in the scoring drive which consumed just 1:37. The Gators were held to four-and-out on their ensuing possession, turning the ball over to Michigan at the Florida 24-yard line with 2:42 remaining. Michigan was also held on downs and on fourth-and-10 from the 24, Lopata connected on a 41-yard field goal to extend U-M's lead to 41-35 with 2:21 on the clock. On Florida's final possession, the Wolverine defense again held the Gators on fourth down with four straight incompletions by Tebow, turning the ball over to Michigan at the Florida 23. The Wolverines ran the clock out against the defending national champions, sending Lloyd Carr and the seniors out with an upset and their first bowl victory since

2008 Cotton Bowl Classic

The 2008 AT&T Cotton Bowl Classic was played on January 1, 2008, at the Cotton Bowl in Dallas, Texas, USA. The Cotton Bowl Classic featured the Arkansas Razorbacks from the SEC and the Missouri Tigers from the Big 12 and was televised on FOX. Senior RB Tony Temple of Mizzou set a single game rushing record for the Cotton Bowl Classic with 281 yards and 4 touchdowns. His 281 rushing yards put him in second place all time for total rushing yards in a bowl game.

2008 Cotton Bowl Classic	Line	1	-	2	-	3	-	4	-	Final
#7 Missouri	(-3.5)	7	-	7	-	14	-	10	-	38
#25 Arkansas	(68.5)	0	-	0	-	7	-	0	-	7

Scoring Summary
Missouri – Temple 22 yard run (Wolfert Kick
Missouri – Temple 4 yard run (Wolfert kick)
Missouri – Temple 4 yard run (Wolfert kick)
Missouri – Moore 26 yard interception return (Wolfert kick)
Arkansas – McFadden 3 yard run (Tejada kick)
Missouri – Wolfert 32 yard Field goal
Missouri – Temple 40 yard run (Wolfert kick)

Cotton Bowl Classic Game Summary - The 72nd AT&T Cotton Bowl Classic was hyped as a battle of two Heisman Trophy finalists... Missouri Quarterback Chase Daniel against Arkansas running back Darren McFadden. In the end, one of the Classic's longest-standing records had fallen, but it wasn't Daniel or McFadden entering the record books. Tiger tailback Tony Temple stole the show with an epic day as he raced through the Arkansas defense to amass the second biggest rushing performance in bowl history while leading Missouri to a 38-7 win over the Razorbacks. When the dust settled, Temple finished with the most single game rushing yards in Cotton Bowl history. Temple rushed for 281 yards on 24 carries and four touchdowns breaking Rice halfback Dickey Maegle's record of 265 yards from the 1954 Classic against Alabama. Temple set the rushing record on his final carry, breaking a tackle and spinning away from another for a 40-yard touchdown run in the fourth quarter. He was so spent after his prolific day that his teammates had to carry him from the end zone to the sideline after his record setting trot. The senior from Kansas City also equaled Texas Quarterback Bobby Layne's record of four touchdowns in a game set in 1946 against Missouri, the last time the Tigers were in the Classic. 73,114 fans came out expecting to see fireworks from Daniel, a Dallas-area product, but he wasn't forced to put up big numbers through the air as he had done all year. Rather, all he to do was hand the ball to Temple and watch him work. Daniel finished the day 12 of 29 for 136 yards. McFadden, the two-time Doak Walker Award winner, rushed for a quiet 108 yards on 21 carries, scoring the lone Arkansas touchdown of the day, late in the third quarter. By that time, however, the outcome was nowhere near in doubt. Missouri, the Big 12 North Division Champion, played in its first New Year's Day game since the 1970 Orange Bowl. The Tigers finished a school record 12-2. Entering the Big 12 Championship against Oklahoma, the Tigers were ranked No. 1 in the country. Arkansas, representing the Southeastern Conference, finished the season 8-5. The Razorbacks had endured many highs and lows entering the Classic. In their final regular-season game, the Hogs upset then-No. 1 LSU. Shortly after the big victory, Arkansas head coach Houston Nutt left to fill the head coaching vacancy at Ole Miss. The Razorbacks turned to their defensive coordinator, Reggie Herring, to lead Arkansas against Missouri. It was the first time in Classic history that a team was led by an interim coach. Despite Herring's defensive prowess, the Hogs couldn't find a way to stop Missouri. Temple's 22-yard touchdown run with 2:29 left in the first quarter gave Missouri a 7-0 lead. He added four-yard touchdown runs in the second and third quarters before his record breaking effort in the fourth. Jeff Wolfert's 32-yard field goal early in the fourth quarter accounted for Missouri's other points. For his efforts, Temple was awarded the Sanford Trophy, given to the Outstanding Offensive Player. The trophy commemorates the Cotton Bowl Classic's founder J. Curtis Sanford. Temple also broke his own Missouri bowl game record of 194 yards that he set in the 2006 Sun Bowl against Oregon. Midway through the third quarter, Missouri safety William Moore intercepted a Casey Dick pass and returned it 26 yards to give the Tigers an insurmountable 28-7 lead. Moore was recognized as the Outstanding Defensive Player, winning the McKnight Trophy, presented in honor of the late Dallas newspaperman and former Team Selection Chairman Felix McKnight. Moore was credited with eight solo tackles and five assists. The 2009 Classic marked the end of an era at Arkansas. The game was Cotton Bowl Hall of Famer Frank Broyles' last as Athletic Director. Broyles coached or administered over nine of Arkansas' 11 Cotton Bowl appearances. He was also Missouri's head coach for one season in 1957. The Razorbacks sported all-red jerseys and pants to honor him. Despite all the great story lines entering the game, Temple took the headlines with his record-breaking performance.

2008 Rose Bowl

The 2008 Rose Bowl Game presented by Citi, the 94th Rose Bowl Game, played on January 1, 2008 at the Rose Bowl Stadium in Pasadena, California. The contest was televised on ABC, the 20th straight year the network aired the Rose Bowl, starting at 4:30pm EST. The game's main sponsor was Citi. The 2008 Rose Bowl featured the 7th-ranked USC Trojans hosting the 13th-ranked Illinois Fighting Illini. As with the previous year's game, the contest was a semi-traditional Rose Bowl in that while it was a Big Ten versus Pac-10 matchup, the Big Ten representative was an at-large team because the conference champion, Ohio State, which lost to Illinois earlier in the season, was selected to play in the BCS National Championship Game. USC was making its third straight appearance in the Rose Bowl, while Illinois had not played in the game since 1984. Though Illinois won the Big Ten Conference title in 2001, the then-rotating BCS title game moved them to the Sugar Bowl.

2008 Rose Bowl	Line	1	-	2	-	3	-	4	-	Final
#13 Illinois	(50.0)	0	-	3	-	7	-	7	-	17
#6 USC	(-13.5)	14	-	7	-	14	-	14	-	49

Scoring Summary
USC - Washington 8 yard pass from Booty (Buehler kick)
USC - Reed 34 yard pass from Green (Buehler kick)
USC - Washington 3 yard run (Buehler kick)
Illinois - Reda 28 yard field goal
Illinois - Mendenhall 79 yard run (Reda kick)
USC - Davis 2 yard pass from Booty (Buehler kick)
USC - McKnight 6 yard run (Buehler kick)
USC - Ausberry 15 yard pass from Booty (Buehler kick)
USC - Dennis 3 yard run (Buehler kick)
Illinois - Benn 56 yard pass from McGee (Reda kick)

Associated Press Rose Bowl Game Summary - This would have been a perfect Rose Bowl for the USC Trojans, except for the one part they couldn't control. They couldn't pick their opponent. The sixth-ranked Trojans (No. 7 BCS, No. 6 AP) routed Illinois 49-17 on Tuesday and showed the rest of the country that, yes, maybe they are the best team in college football right now. Certainly, a better test could have come against Georgia or Virginia Tech, or maybe next week against Ohio State in the national title game. But the Rose Bowl presented by Citi wanted a Pac-10-Big Ten matchup, and the national title game didn't want Southern California. So, it wound up being USC-Illinois in the Granddaddy of 'Em All, and the Trojans made the Illini pay. Freshman tailback Joe McKnight finished with 170 of USC's Rose Bowl-record 633 yards. The 49 points tied a record, too, and the blowout gave the Trojans 11 wins for an unprecedented sixth straight season. They have arguably been the country's best team over that span, and might have been the best this season, too. Lacking the playoff that Coach Pete Carroll favors or the trip to the title game he lobbied for, the Trojans (11-2) will have to take this overwhelming display in Pasadena. The game featured 1,078 total yards of offense. Despite the margin, things were truly competitive for a moment. Illinois' Rashard Mendenhall broke a 79-yard touchdown run early in the third quarter to trim what had been a three-touchdown deficit to 21-10. Minutes later, Mendenhall scooted 55 yards with a screen pass from Juice Williams, and Ron Zook's 13th-ranked Illini (9-4) looked as if they might really complete the impossible dream, from 2-19 over the last two years to Rose Bowl champions. But two plays later, Kaluka Maiava popped the ball out of receiver Jacob Willis' hands and USC's Brian Cushing won a scramble in the end zone, one of four Illinois turnovers. Moments later, came the play of the game, when John David Booty threw a sloppy lateral to McKnight, who didn't catch it, but was able to scoop it up on the bounce and run 65 yards. McKnight was chased down by defensive back Vontae Davis -- yes Zook is recruiting some speed to Champaign -- but four plays later, Booty hit Fred Davis with a 2-yard touchdown pass. That made it 28-10 and the rout was on. Booty threw for 255 yards and three scores to set a Rose Bowl record with seven career TDs. USC linebacker Rey Maualuga had three sacks, an interception and a forced fumble for a defense that allowed only 79 yards in the first half. McKnight, hyped as USC's next Reggie Bush, finished with 125 yards rushing and 45 yards receiving, and his broken play in the third quarter wasn't the only time the Trojans made something crazy and unexpected happen. It started in the first quarter, when Booty lateraled to Garrett Green, who is listed as a receiver-Quarterback, and Green threw crossfield to Desmond Reed for a 34-yard touchdown strike and a 14-0 lead. Reed was so open, he could've walked into the end zone, but instead did a leaping front tuck. Stuck the landing, too, but got six points instead of a perfect 10.0, and was docked a 15-yard unsportsmanlike-conduct penalty. That made no difference, and in the end, Illinois' nice little stretch of competitiveness in the third quarter was only a blip, as well. Mendenhall finished with 214 total yards in what could be the last college game for the junior. Williams had 245 yards passing for the Illini, whose last Rose Bowl trip came 24 years ago and ended in a 45-9 loss to Quarterback Rick Neuheisel and UCLA. The score this time was similar, and not totally unexpected. The Illini were 13 1/2-point underdogs -- biggest of any of this season's 32 bowl games -- and the final score only added fuel to the fire of those who criticized the Rose Bowl for insisting on its traditional conference pairing. Many said the Big Ten was weak this season, and while the title game will be the ultimate test of that, this certainly didn't help the image. Meanwhile, USC was said to be playing the best football of anyone when the regular season ended and didn't do anything to debunk that theory. Carroll, a proponent of a playoff, lobbied for the Trojans to have LSU's spot in next week's national title game, the first to include a team with two losses. But a 24-23 loss to 41-point underdog Stanford in October was USC's undoing. On this day at the sun splashed Rose Bowl, it was hard to imagine the Trojans losing to Stanford. Not that they were perfect. Early in the game, a snap sailed over punter Greg Woidneck's head and he had to scramble to get off a 20-yard punt. Later, Justin Harrison picked off Booty's pass and returned it to the USC 20, but Illinois couldn't score off that. Also in the first half, Harrison pulverized receiver Vidal Hazelton and sent the ball flying out, only to redirect into the waiting hands of McKnight.

2008 Sugar Bowl

The 2008 Allstate Sugar Bowl was part of the Bowl Championship Series (BCS) for the 2007 NCAA Division I FBS football season and was the 74th Sugar Bowl. It was played on January 1, 2008, in the Louisiana Superdome in New Orleans.

Because the SEC champion (LSU) was slated to participate in the BCS National Championship Game, the number-five Georgia Bulldogs were selected to host the number-ten, WAC champion Hawaii Warriors, the last undefeated major college football team going into the bowl season. The Warriors were only the third team not in any of the six BCS conferences (not counting major independent Notre Dame) to play in a BCS game. Boise State qualified for the 2007 Fiesta Bowl, and Utah made the same game two years earlier. Both teams won their respective games. The result was less exciting than the build-up. Georgia turned the lights out on Hawaii in the Sugar Bowl en route to an easy 41-10 win. It was already a one-sided affair at halftime with a 24-3 score and it was 41-3 at one point early in the 4th. The closest Hawaii got was 7-3 after a Dan Kelly field goal.

2008 Sugar Bowl	Line	1	-	2	-	3	-	4	-	Final
#10 Hawaii	(69.0)	3	-	0	-	0	-	7	-	10
#4 Georgia	(-8.0)	14	-	10	-	14	-	3	-	41

Scoring Summary
Georgia - Moreno 17 yard run (Coutu kick)
Hawaii - Kelly 42 yard Field goal
Georgia - Moreno 11 yard run (Coutu kick)
Georgia - Coutu 52 yard Field goal
Georgia - Bailey 11 yard pass from Stafford (Coutu kick)
Georgia - Howard fumble recovery (Coutu kick)
Georgia - Brown 1 yard run (Coutu kick)
Georgia - Coutu 45 yard Field goal
Hawaii - Grice-Mullen 16 yard pass from Graunke (Kelly kick)

Associated Press Sugar Bowl Classic Game Summary - Georgia would love to be back at the Superdome next week, playing for the title it really wanted. Instead, the Bulldogs will have to settle for being Allstate Sugar Bowl champs. Overpowering the country's last unbeaten team, black-clad Georgia took out its frustration at getting passed over for a shot at the BCS championship with a 41-10 rout of Colt Brennan and the Warriors on Tuesday night. In nothing else, the Bulldogs got a head start on next season on the first day of the New Year. Georgia (11-2) established itself as a leading contender in 2008 with a total whippin' of the 10th-ranked Warriors (12-1), who cracked the BCS with an unbeaten run through the Western Athletic Conference, then fell flat in their biggest game ever. There was no repeat of the Boise State Miracle. This night was nothing but a four-hour-plus rendition of "Glory, Glory to Ol' Georgia." Knowshon Moreno ran for a pair of touchdowns in the opening quarter and the Bulldogs' defense made life miserable for Brennan, a Heisman Trophy finalist and catalyst for the nation's highest-scoring team. He was sacked eight times, threw three interceptions and lost two fumbles, one of them recovered for a Georgia touchdown. After getting slammed to the Superdome turf one last time by Geno Atkins, Brennan staggered to the sideline, his night mercifully done. The junior had the worst showing of his career in a game played to the finish, going 22-of-38 for just 169 yards, less than half of his 348-yard average this season. The Bulldogs led 24-3 by halftime and quickly snuffed out any chance Brennan might lead an improbable comeback, as he did in bringing Hawaii back from a 21-point deficit in their regular-season finale against Washington. On Hawaii's first possession after the break, Brennan was sacked by Roderick Battle, then picked off by Asher Allen. The Warriors held, getting an interception of their own on a tipped ball, but that merely set up Brennan for more misery. Marcus Howard, who spent as much time in the Hawaii backfield as the guys wearing white, sped by tackle Keoni Steinhoff like he wasn't even there and crashed into Brennan. The ball rolled loose in the end zone and Howard recovered, giving him as many touchdowns as the vaunted run-and-shoot offense that was averaging 46.2 points a game. As it was, Georgia set a school record with the highest-scoring bowl game of its long, proud history, eclipsing a 40-26 win over TCU in the 1942 Orange Bowl. Still, the game's MVP award went to Howard, who had to wait until his senior year to start. He sure went out with a bang in this final college game: three sacks, two forced fumbles and a tipped ball that was intercepted by teammate Dannell Ellerbe. Allen picked off two Hawaii throws. Freshman Rennie Curran chipped in with two sacks. After Ellerbe's pick, defensive coordinator Willie Martinez leaped into his player's arms along the sideline, giddy at the way his unit shut down a team that had eight 40-point games this season. Georgia lobbied for a spot in the title game after the top two teams in the BCS rankings lost on the final day of the regular season. But the Bulldogs, who didn't even make the SEC championship game, had to settle for their third Sugar Bowl appearance in five years. With their title hopes dashed, Richt urged his players to get a good start on 2008, knowing an impressive win over the Warriors would surely set up the Dawgs for a top-five ranking at the start of next season -- and better positioning for a run at No. 1. Consider it done. Hawaii hoped to follow the lead set by WAC rival Boise State, which capped last year's perfect season with a stunning overtime win against Oklahoma in the Fiesta Bowl. In the locker room before the game, Coach June Jones urged his team to "play with confidence, like you belong." They didn't. Brennan ran up against a swarming Georgia defense that was in no mood to give the little guys another day in the sun. In the first half alone, he was sacked five times and turned it over twice, losing a fumble and throwing an interception. Hawaii finally got to the end zone with 10 1/2 minutes to go and backup Quarterback Tyler Graunke running the offense. He tossed a meaningless 16-yard TD pass to Ryan Grice-Mullen while Brennan watched from the sideline. In all fairness to the Hawaii star, this wasn't really a fair fight. The Bulldogs were so much stronger, so much faster, so much better in so many areas. Even so, it was tough to be serenaded with chants of "Overrated! Overrated!" by the Georgia faithful.

Aftermath - Georgia DE Marcus Howard was named the MVP of the Sugar Bowl Game, the first time in its history that a purely defensive player has received the honor. With the win, Georgia Head Coach Mark Richt became the first head coach in Georgia history to win more than one Sugar Bowl (his previous victory was over Florida State University following the 2002 season). Vince Dooley and Wally Butts won one Sugar Bowl each, with Dooley's only win securing the 1980 National Championship. Dooley lost four other Sugar Bowl games.

2008 Fiesta Bowl

The 2008 Tostitos Fiesta Bowl has been played annually since 1971, first at Sun Devil Stadium on the campus of Arizona State University in Tempe, Arizona through 2006, the game was played on January 2, 2008, at the University of Phoenix Stadium in Glendale, Arizona. The game featured the fourth ranked (BCS), Big 12 champion Oklahoma Sooners hosting the ninth ranked (BCS), Big East champion West Virginia Mountaineers. West Virginia defeated Oklahoma by a score of 48–28. The contest was televised on Fox.

2008 Fiesta Bowl	Line	1	-	2	-	3	-	4	-	Final
#11 West Virginia	(63.0)	6	-	14	-	14	-	14	-	48
#3 Oklahoma	(-7.5)	0	-	6	-	9	-	13	-	28

Scoring Summary
West Virginia – McAfee 38 yard Field goal
West Virginia – McAfee 42 yard Field goal
Oklahoma – Hartley 37 yard Field goal
West Virginia – Schmitt 57 yard run (McAfee kick)
Oklahoma – Hartley 24 yard Field goal
West Virginia – Reynaud 21 yard pass from White (McAfee kick)
Oklahoma – Hartley 42 yard Field goal
Oklahoma – Brown 1 yard run (kick failed)
West Virginia – Devine 17 yard run (McAfee kick)
West Virginia – Reynaud 30 yard run (McAfee kick)
Oklahoma – Chaney 19 yard pass from Bradford (run failed)
West Virginia – Gonzales 79 yard pass from White (McAfee kick)
Oklahoma – Iglesias 15 yard pass from Bradford (Hartley kick)
West Virginia – Devine 65 yard run (McAfee kick)

Associated Press Fiesta Bowl Game Summary - Patrick White guided West Virginia to a stunningly easy romp over Oklahoma in the Fiesta Bowl. Then, the option Quarterback made his biggest pitch of the night. White ran for 150 yards and threw for 176 and two touchdowns in a 48-28 victory. After it was over, he endorsed Mountaineers interim coach Bill Stewart to become the permanent successor to Rich Rodriguez, who bolted for Michigan last month. In nine seasons under Bob Stoops, the Oklahoma defense has traditionally been tough to run on. This year had been no different, as the Sooners ranked seventh nationally by giving up just 91.9 rush YPG. Then West Virginia came calling. The Mountaineers had 349 yards on the ground, the most rushing yards ever gained against a Stoops-led OU team. An emotional Stewart wouldn't lobby for the job. But he relished what he called "a colossal win for our program. The Mountaineers (No. 11 BCS, No. 9 AP) didn't need Rodriguez. They had White, a relentless defense and a rushing attack that raced for 349 yards, most allowed by Oklahoma (No. 3 BCS, No. 4 AP) in a bowl game. Since arriving in the desert last week, the Mountaineers (11-2) said they had bonded behind Stewart, who took over when Rodriguez left for Michigan in mid-December. And they vowed to rebound from a 13-9 loss to Pitt that knocked them out of the Bowl Championship Series title game. The Mountaineers were right on both counts, turning in an emotional effort and overcoming the loss of star tailback Steve Slaton to a first-quarter leg injury. Noel Devine replaced Slaton and ran for 108 yards and two touchdowns -- a 17-yarder and a 65-yarder that clinched the game in the fourth quarter. The Mountaineers became the first of six teams to win under an interim coach this bowl season. They improved to 2-0 in the Bowl Championship Series. Oklahoma endured another disappointment on the same field where the Sooners lost a classic Fiesta Bowl to Boise State one year ago. The Sooners have dropped four straight BCS games. Oklahoma (11-3) endured another disappointment on the same field where the Sooners lost a classic Fiesta Bowl to Boise State one year ago. The Sooners have dropped four straight BCS games. The Sooners had no answer for White, whose 79-yard touchdown pass to Tito Gonzales in the fourth quarter was the longest in Mountaineers bowl history. Meanwhile, West Virginia's fourth-rated defense limited the potent Sooners to well below their scoring average of 43.4 points per game, third in the nation. The Mountaineers harassed Oklahoma Quarterback Sam Bradford, sacking the nation's top-rated passer three times and intercepting him in the end zone. Bradford completed 21 of 33 passes for 242 yards and two touchdowns. The Sooners rallied from an 18-point deficit against Boise State last January, taking a late lead before the Broncos forced overtime, where they won on a trick play. This time, OU trailed 20-6 at halftime. But the Sooners cut it to 20-15 on Chris Brown's 1-yard run midway through the third quarter. Then Stoops made two curious calls. First, he decided to go for two points. But Bradford's pass fell incomplete. Then Stoops ordered an onside kick. The ball didn't go 10 yards, and West Virginia took over on OU's 39. The Mountaineers needed six plays to capitalize, scoring on Devine's 17-yard run. West Virginia made it 34-15 on Darius Reynaud's 30-yard run with 20 seconds to go in the third quarter. The Mountaineers went 75 yards in three plays -- 42 on an electrifying run by White, who weaved through tacklers along the left sideline. After the Sooners scored on a 19-yard pass from Bradford to Quentin Chaney, White found Gonzales down the middle for a 79-yard TD that made it 41-21. The rest of the game was garbage time, with numerous personal fouls. Oklahoma was flagged 13 times for 113 yards, and the Mountaineers eight times for 110. At halftime Oklahoma had as many penalties (six) as first downs. The Mountaineers also had discipline problems. But on this night, nothing could stop them -- not the Sooners or the officials.

2008 Orange Bowl

The 2008 FedEx Orange Bowl was between the Virginia Tech Hokies and the Kansas Jayhawks on January 3, 2008, at Dolphin Stadium in Miami Gardens, Florida. Spread bettors favored Virginia Tech by three points, but in a game dominated by defensive and special teams play, Kansas defeated Virginia Tech 24–21. The game between the fifth-ranked ACC champion Virginia Tech Hokies and the eighth-ranked Kansas Jayhawks from the Big 12 Conference (Big 12) was played at neutral-site Dolphins Stadium. Tech served as the home team in the contest. Virginia Tech automatically qualified for the Orange Bowl by virtue of the ACC's tie-in with the bowl, while Orange Bowl selected Kansas over West Virginia—which had been upset by then 4–7 Pittsburgh—and conference rival Missouri. Two weeks after Kansas's selection, controversy erupted when a deal was revealed to put 4th-ranked Oklahoma against Virginia Tech. The deal was vetoed by BCS commissioners, and the selection of Kansas was upheld. The game marked the first time the Jayhawks had been to the Orange Bowl since the 1969 Orange Bowl and was their first bowl game since the 2005 Fort Worth Bowl, when they defeated Houston 41–13. Virginia Tech last played in the Orange Bowl game in December 1996, losing to Nebraska 21–41. The 2008 Orange Bowl was Virginia Tech's 15th consecutive season with a bowl game, a streak dating to the 1993 Independence Bowl.

2008 Orange Bowl	Line	1	-	2	-	3	-	4	-	Final
#8 Kansas	(53.0)	7	-	10	-	0	-	7	-	24
#5 Virginia Tech	(-3.5)	0	-	7	-	7	-	7	-	21

Scoring Summary
Kansas – Talib 60 yard interception return (Webb kick)
Kansas – Webb 32 yard Field goal
Kansas – Henry 13 yard pass from Reesing (Webb kick)
Virginia Tech – Ore 1 yard run (Dunlevy kick)
Virginia Tech – Harper 84 yard punt return (Dunlevy kick)
Kansas – Reesing 2 yard run (Webb kick)
Virginia Tech – Harper 20 yard pass from Glennon (Dunlevy kick)

Associated Press Orange Bowl Game Summary - The high-scoring Kansas Jayhawks brought their usual assortment of tricks to the Orange Bowl. They split their tackles wide alongside the receivers. They threw wrong-handed shovel passes. They pulled off a fake punt. The biggest surprise: They won with defense. While their offense was stymied most of the night, the Jayhawks came up with three interceptions and beat Virginia Tech 24-21 to cap one of the finest seasons in school history. The takeaways led to 17 Kansas points, including Aqib Talib's 60-yard return for the game's first score. He was chosen the game's most valuable player. Kansas (12-1), perhaps the biggest surprise in college football this season, won in its first Bowl Championship Series game to set a team record for victories. A year ago, the Jayhawks went 6-6. The Hokies (11-3) lost their fourth consecutive BCS game. It was a bittersweet finish for the Hokies, who revived campus spirits this season following the April 16 massacre that left 33 students and professors dead. The Jayhawks played in their first major bowl since the 1969 Orange Bowl, and they made a big splash at the start, racing to a 17-0 lead after 23 minutes. Virginia Tech closed the deficit to 17-14 before Sean Glennon was intercepted by Thornton, whose 30-yard return gave Kansas the ball at the 2 with 11 minutes left. Reesing scored on the next play. Chris Harris also had an interception to set up a field goal, and the Jayhawks totaled five sacks while allowing only two scoring drives. Virginia Tech drove 78 yards to score with 3 minutes left on Glennon's 20-yard pass to Justin Harper. The Jayhawks' Raimond Pendleton fielded the ensuing onside kick, and they ran out the clock. Virginia Tech's biggest gain came on special teams. Harper scored on an 84-yard punt return after taking a lateral on a reverse from Eddie Royal, who fielded the kick. Otherwise, Kansas' special teams played well. Joe Mortensen blocked a 25-yard field-goal attempt to preserve a 17-14 Kansas lead. A fake punt kept one drive going, and Kyle Tucker's booming punts kept the Hokies pinned deep. The game was among the chilliest Orange Bowls ever, with a temperature of 57 degrees at kickoff and winds gusting at up to 25 mph. The Jayhawks were the nation's highest-scoring offense this season at 44 points per game, and they took a wide-open approach beginning on the first series. Once they lined up with both tackles flanked wide alongside the receivers, and on another play Reesing threw a left-handed shovel pass for a 9-yard gain. Kansas split a tackle wide again when Reesing completed a pass to convert a fourth-and-1 situation, which led to a touchdown for a 17-0 lead. Reesing hit Marcus Henry with a 13-yard pass for the score, capping a 59-yard drive. Reesing finished 20-for-37 for 227 yards. With only one scoring drive of more than 17 yards, the Jayhawks left most of the big plays to their defense. The biggest was by Talib, who stepped in front of the intended receiver to intercept freshman Tyrod Taylor and ran along the Virginia Tech sideline untouched for a touchdown. It was the first interception return for a touchdown in the Orange Bowl since 1968. Virginia Tech came into the game with the more heralded defense, but the Jayhawks had four sacks in the first quarter. They threw Taylor for losses of 11 and 8 yards on his first two plays as part of the Hokies Quarterback rotation. On Virginia Tech's next possession, Josh Morgan dropped a potential touchdown pass, and Jud Dunlevy missed a 47-yard field goal attempt. Virginia Tech mounted a 68-yard drive late in the first half, and Branden Ore scored on a 1-yard run to cut the deficit to 17-7. Ore was suspended for the first quarter for being late to a practice but still finished with 116 yards rushing. Against the ball-hawking Jayhawks, that wasn't enough.

2008 International Bowl

The 2008 International Bowl was played on January 5, 2008 at the Rogers Centre in Toronto, Ontario, Canada. The game featured the Scarlet Knights of Rutgers University—who finished 5th in the Big East Conference—and the Cardinals of Ball State University—who finished co-champions of the Mid-American Conference's West Division. The game was the only NCAA Division I Football Bowl Subdivision game from the 2007-2008 season to be played outside the United States. Rutgers won by a score of 52–30.

2008 International Bowl	Line	1	-	2	-	3	-	4	-	Final
Rutgers	(-10.5)	14	-	10	-	14	-	14	-	52
Ball State	(61.0)	3	-	6	-	7	-	14	-	30

Scoring Summary
Rutgers - Brown 36 yard pass from Teel (Ito kick)
Rutgers - Rice 1 yard run (Ito kick)
Ball State - McGarvey 47 yard Field goal
Rutgers - Ito 53 yard Field goal
Ball State - McGarvey 24 yard Field goal
Rutgers - Rice 1 yard run (Ito kick)
Ball State - McGarvey 32 yard Field goal
Rutgers - Rice 90 yard run (Ito kick)
Ball State - Love 10 yard pass from Davis (McGarvey kick)
Rutgers - Rice 1 yard run (Ito kick)
Ball State - Hill 6 yard pass from Davis (McGarvey kick)
Rutgers - Underwood 35 yard pass from Teel (Ito kick)
Rutgers - Britt 47 yard pass from Teel (Ito kick)
Ball State - Hill 1 yard pass from Davis (McGarvey kick)

Associated Press International Bowl Game Summary - Ray Rice ran over Ball State and through the 2,000-yard barrier, giving Rutgers its second postseason win in the school's 138-year history and leaving the Scarlet Knights wondering if he'll scamper off to the NFL. The junior, who kept mum on his plans for the draft, ran for 280 yards and four touchdowns, including a career-long 90-yarder to lift the Scarlet Knights to a 52-30 win over the Ball State Cardinals on Saturday. Rutgers (8-5), which played the first college football game, hadn't won a bowl game before last year. Now the program has won two in a row, following a 37-10 win over Kansas State in the 2006 Texas Bowl, another blowout. Ball State (7-6), meanwhile, is still waiting for its first bowl win in six tries. Rice, whose 25 touchdowns this season are a school record, has yet to announce whether he'll skip his senior season and enter the NFL draft. Players who choose to declare for the draft must do so by Jan. 15. On the Scarlet Knights' first drive of the third quarter, Rice took the ball at his own 10-yard line, broke through the line of scrimmage and raced down the left sideline, fighting off two tacklers before diving into the end zone. Rice ended the third with a 12-yard run, making him the first Big East player to break 2,000 yards. Rice's 2,012 yards this season are behind only Central Florida's Kevin Smith and Tulane's Matt Forte. Rice has gone over 100 yards in a school-record eight straight games. Rutgers fans chanted "One more year!" after Rice's fourth touchdown run on a one-yard dive late in the third. Facing a Ball State defense ranked 99th in the nation against the run, Rice set the tone early, running left for a 21-yard gain on Rutgers' first play from scrimmage. Five plays later, Teel found Tim Brown wide open over the middle for a 36-yard touchdown pass as Rutgers took an early 7-0 lead. Rice made it 14-0 on Rutgers' third possession, carrying the ball four straight times and finishing a six play, 70-yard drive with a 1-yard run. Rice did it all by himself on a second-quarter touchdown drive, rushing five times and catching an eight-yard pass from Teel, before another 1-yard plunge gave Rutgers a 24-6 lead. Teel completed 16 of 25 attempts for 303 yards and three touchdowns, including a 35-yard scoring strike to Tiquan Underwood in the fourth. Teel set a school record with his 20th TD pass of the season, a 47-yarder to Kenny Britt at 4:21 of the fourth. Britt finished with six catches for 125 yards. Dante Love scored Ball State's first touchdown on a 10-yard pass from Quarterback Nate Davis in the third. Tight end Darius Hill caught two TD passes in the fourth. Davis completed 25 of 49 for 291 yards and three touchdowns but was sacked seven times. Love caught 13 passes for 169 yards and Ian McGarvey kicked three field goals for the Cardinals. The International Bowl is the only NCAA Division I football game played outside the United States. Cincinnati beat Western Michigan 27-24 in last year's event.

2008 GMAC Bowl

The 2008 GMAC Bowl was the 9th annual game. It was played on January 6, 2008 at Ladd Peebles Stadium in Mobile, Alabama and featured the Tulsa Golden Hurricane against the Bowling Green Falcons. Tulsa Quarterback Paul Smith set an NCAA Division I record with his 14th consecutive 300-yard passing game. The 63-7 final score makes this game the largest margin of victory in bowl history surpassing the 55-point margin set by Alabama over Syracuse in the 1953 Orange Bowl. The game represented just the second matchup of the two teams in football. In 1989, Tulsa also beat Bowling Green in blowout fashion, 45-10.

2008 GMAC Bowl	Line	1	-	2	-	3	-	4	-	Final
Bowling Green	(76.0)	0	-	0	-	7	-	0	-	7
Tulsa	(-4.5)	21	-	14	-	14	-	14	-	63

Scoring Summary
Tulsa - Adams 1 yard run (Tracy kick)
Tulsa - Johnson 13 yard pass from Smith (Tracy kick)
Tulsa - Whitmore 19 yard run (Tracy kick)
Tulsa - Grooms 4 yard pass from Adams (Tracy kick)
Tulsa - Adams 19 yard pass from Smith (Tracy kick)
Tulsa - Johnson 14 yard pass from Smith (Tracy kick)
Bowling Green - Williams 78 yard kickoff return (Vrvilo kick)
Tulsa - Smith 2 yard run (Tracy kick)
Tulsa - Charles 3 yard pass from Smith (Tracy kick)
Tulsa - Whitmore 6 yard pass from Smith (Tracy kick)

Associated Press GMAC Bowl Game Summary - Giving Paul Smith and the nation's top-rated offense extra chances can lead to disaster -- and a plethora of points. Just ask Bowling Green. Smith had his NCAA-record 14th consecutive 300-yard passing game, and Tulsa converted four fumble recoveries into first-half touchdowns on the way to a 63-7 romp over the Falcons in the GMAC Bowl on Sunday night. With all that help, the Golden Hurricane (10-4) ran up a 35-0 halftime lead and capped coach Todd Graham's first season by reaching 10 wins for the first time since 1991. Tulsa had never managed more than 31 points in 14 previous bowl games. They'll do it without the departing Smith, who passed for 312 yards and five touchdowns, the last with 3:22 left in the blowout. He broke the record of 13 300-yard efforts in a row he shared with BYU's Ty Detmer, whose streak stretched over the 1989 and 1990 seasons. Smith and Tarrion Adams joined Houston's David Klingler and Chuck Weatherspoon as the NCAA's only 5,000-yard passing and 1,000-yard rushing tandem. Tulsa outgained Bowling Green (8-5) 562-229 in total yards. Adams scored touchdowns running, passing and receiving before halftime and ran for 112 yards. Trae Johnson caught two scoring passes in the most lopsided bowl game this season, with only the national championship game remaining. Bowling Green, which had won four consecutive bowl games, lost three fumbles in its own territory in the first quarter and never recovered. Taking matters from awful to worse, Quarterback Tyler Sheehan was helped off the field with a sprained left ankle with 24 seconds left in the first half and didn't return. He came out of the locker room on crutches. Sheehan passed for 141 yards and ran for another 21. For Tulsa, all that was left were the records. Late in the fourth quarter, the Golden Hurricane became the first team in NCAA history to have a 5,000-yard passer, 1,000-yard rusher and three 1,000-yard receivers. Smith came in needing 247 yards along with 45 yards receiving from Charles Clay, who reached the milestone with several catches midway through the fourth quarter and finished with 11 for 69 yards. Graham said he told Brandon after the game that he wasn't trying to run the score up. The Mid-American Conference had won five of six GMAC Bowls before the Falcons' fall. Down 42-0, Bowling Green finally got something to cheer about. Roger Williams scored on a 78-yard kick return early in the third quarter for the Falcons' only points. Bowling Green twice drove inside Tulsa's 10 before the half but had the drives stall on a fumble and a failed fourth-down play. The Tulsa defensive players also took umbrage at pre-game predictions of a shootout. Tulsa's offense did its part, at least. Everything from halfback passes to reverses and fake field goals were working for the Golden Hurricane. Tulsa's first scoring drive was kept alive by a fake field goal on fourth-and-2. Holder Paul Jurado flipped a shovel pass to Chris Chamberlain for a first down. In more trickery, Adams threw for a 4-yard touchdown to Kyle Grooms on a halfback pass a minute into the second to push it to 28-0. Smith added a 19-yarder to Adams before the half. Smith wasn't exactly satisfied. Bowling Green defensive tackle Sean O'Drobinak said Tulsa's offense offered few surprises, not that it mattered. The game, which used to be played in mid-December, was moved two years ago in attempt to piggyback for attention on the BCS national championship the following day.

2008 BCS Championship Game

The 2008 Allstate BCS National Championship Game was played at the Louisiana Superdome in New Orleans, Louisiana, on Monday, January 7, 2008, and featured the #1 and #2 college football teams in the United States as determined by the BCS Poll (a combination of polls and computer formulas) to decide the BCS National Championship for the 2007 NCAA Division I FBS football season. The game featured #1 Big Ten champion Ohio State Buckeyes hosting #2 SEC champion LSU Tigers. It also featured the second matchup between head coaches Jim Tressel and Les Miles in five years. The first occurrence was the 2004 Alamo Bowl, when Tressel's Buckeyes defeated Miles' Oklahoma State Cowboys, 33–7.

Team selection - Prior to the last weekend of the regular season, it looked like the national championship game would be played between Missouri and West Virginia. However, Missouri lost to Oklahoma in the Big 12 Championship Game and West Virginia was shocked by their arch-rival Pitt in the Backyard Brawl. This threw the BCS and college football world into upheaval. By virtue of winning the Big Ten and having only one loss, Ohio State looked to be guaranteed a berth in the BCS championship game. After much speculation, LSU was revealed to be the number two team in the ratings, and therefore the Buckeyes' opponent in the title game.

2008 BCS Championship	Line	1	-	2	-	3	-	4	-	Final
#2 LSU	(-4.0)	3	-	21	-	7	-	7	-	38
#1 Ohio State	(48.5)	10	-	0	-	7	-	7	-	24

Scoring Summary
Ohio State – C. Wells 65 Yard Run (Pretorius Kick)
Ohio State - Pretorius 25 Yard Field goal
LSU - David 32 Yard Field goal
LSU - Maxwell 13 Yard Pass from Flynn (David Kick)
LSU - Lafell 10 Yard Pass from Flynn (David Kick)
LSU - Hester 1 Yard Run (David Kick)
LSU - Doucet 4 Yard Pass from Flynn (David Kick)
Ohio State - Robiskie 5 Yard pass From Boeckman (Pretorius Kick)
LSU - Maxwell 5 Yard Pass from Flynn (David Kick)
Ohio State - Hartline 15 Yard Pass from Boeckman (Pretorius Kick)

Associated Press BCS Championship Game Summary - Les Miles unleashed an ear-piercing whoop, then leaned back and exhaled as if he had been holding his breath all night. The second-ranked Tigers danced, dodged and darted their way into the end zone Monday night for a 38-24 victory, turning the title game into a horrible replay for No. 1 Ohio State. They made it look easy with Matt Flynn throwing four touchdown passes. Now the debate begins: Are they the best? In a season of surprises, this was hardly an upset: Ohio State once again fell apart in college football's biggest game. A year after the Buckeyes were routed by Florida 41-14, they barely did better. But this was unprecedented. Playing at their home-away-from-home in the Big Easy, the Tigers (12-2) became the first two-loss team to compete for the title. Still, LSU was a runaway No. 1 in the final Associated Press poll. The Tigers received 60 of 65 first-place votes from a national media panel. Georgia, Southern California, Missouri and Ohio State rounded out the top five. Georgia had three first-place votes while Southern Cal and No. 7 Kansas each had one. And while Miles got to hoist the $30,000 crystal prize, surely many fans around the country were wondering if someone else was equally worthy. Southern California, Georgia, West Virginia, Kansas and Missouri all put on impressive shows in bowl games and will be among the favorites in 2008. The final Associated Press poll was to be released early Tuesday. Shouts of "SEC! SEC!" bounced around the Superdome as the Tigers won their second BCS crown in five seasons. They are the first school to win a second title since BCS rankings began with the 1998 season. LSU rallied from an early 10-0 deficit, taking a 24-10 halftime lead that held up. Jacob Hester bulled for a short touchdown, Early Doucet wiggled loose for a touchdown and Dorsey led a unit that outplayed the top-ranked defense in the nation. Ohio State (11-2) had little to celebrate after Chris "Beanie" Wells broke loose for a 65-yard TD run on the fourth play of the game. LSU, whose two losses both came in triple overtime, became just the fourth favorite to win in 10 BCS championship games. The Tigers added to the crown they won in 2003 -- their other national championship came in 1958. Miles probably got a little extra satisfaction, too. Though he turned down a chance to return home to Michigan, he did something his alma mater hasn't done recently -- beat the Buckeyes. The loss left Ohio State at 0-9 overall in bowl games against teams from the Southeastern Conference. The SEC delights in whipping Big Ten teams in what's become a rivalry that steams up fans on both sides. Better on offense and defense, the Tigers got two big plays on special teams -- Ricky Jean-Francois blocked a field goal, and LSU took advantage of a roughing-the-kicker penalty. Flynn hit Doucet with a 4-yard toss with 9:04 left for a 31-10 lead and the celebration was on in earnest. The Buckeyes made the score more respectable on Todd Boeckman's 5-yard TD pass on fourth down to Brian Robiskie, only to have Flynn come back and throw his second TD pass to Richard Dickson. Flynn finished 19-for-27 for 174 yards and was picked the game's most outstanding offensive player. As the clock ticked down, Boeckman threw a 15-yard touchdown pass to Brian Hartline. Ohio State was trying to win its second BCS title in six years and add to the one that Tressel captured by upsetting Miami 31-24 in double overtime for the 2002 championship. For sure, the Buckeyes were perhaps the most-maligned No. 1 team in recent memory, with critics attacking them all season. Tressel gave his players a 10-minute DVD filled with insults hurled at them by television and radio announcers, hoping it would motivate his team. Instead, the Tigers ravaged the nation's best defense and showed that maybe all those naysayers were right. Known as a punishing runner, Wells got the game off to a quick start. On the fourth play from scrimmage, the Buckeyes' bruising back started left, made a nifty cut right and burst through the middle. Wells was gone, off on the longest run of his career. And so much for SEC speed -- Wells outran All-America safety Craig Steltz for a 65-yard TD. Wells was welcomed by a familiar face once he got back to the sideline. Miami Dolphins receiver Ted Ginn Jr., wearing scarlet and gray Mardi Gras beads, knew all about early strikes. He provided Ohio State's only highlight in last year's BCS title game, returning the opening kickoff for a touchdown. This time, Ohio State made it 10-0 on its next possession. Boeckman hit a wide-open Brandon Saine for 44 yards, setting up Ryan Pretorius' 25-yard field goal. Only five minutes into the game, Ohio State and its all-brass band was blowing away the Tigers. LSU looked dazed and defensive coordinator Bo Pelini -- who now becomes Nebraska's full-time coach -- had few answers. Fortunately for the Tigers, their offense started clicking. On a team full of flash, it was the reliable ol' Hester who settled down LSU. First, he barreled into All-America linebacker James Laurinaitis for a short gain. Both players are the rugged type and in a nice show of sportsmanship, Laurinaitis -- whose dad, Joe, once starred as "Animal" in the "Legion of Doom" wrestling tag team -- helped up Hester. Hester broke off a 20-yard run on the next play, and LSU eventually got a 32-yard field goal from Colt David that made it 10-3. That score late in the first quarter seemed to jazz everyone in purple and gold. The Tigers zoomed into fast motion, the band's Golden Girls suddenly put more bounce in their step and thousands of fans started screaming even louder. Flynn also seemed to recognize exactly what Ohio State was trying to do. LSU Quarterbacks spend a lot of time with an Xbox, playing a custom-made video game to read defenses. Apparently, what worked on the screen did even better on the field. Two big penalties against Ohio State helped set up Flynn's 13-yard touchdown pass to Dickson, who somehow found himself uncovered. Flynn punctuated the strike by hollering, giving a wild fist pump and putting up both hands to signal TD. Tied at 10, the Buckeyes counted on Wells. He delivered one of the season's best stiff-arms on a 29-yard romp, and Ohio State seemed poised to retake the lead. Instead, Jean-Francois crashed through the middle, swung his big right arm and blocked Pretorius' 38-yard field goal try. As Ohio State trudged off the field and LSU ran on, it was all over. It only took a while to confirm it. LSU turned to another of its five dangerous tailbacks, and NCAA sprint star Trindon Holliday zigzagged closer to the goal line. Flynn's perfect pass to Brandon LaFell in the back left corner of the end zone put the Tigers ahead 17-10. Then, it was time for LSU's defense to make the big play. Cornerback Chevis Jackson intercepted Boeckman's loss toss and streaked 34 yards down the right sideline. The Tigers moved to a first-and-goal at 1. On third down, Hester plunged up the middle and it was 24-10.

2008 EagleBank Bowl

The 2008 EagleBank Bowl was the inaugural edition of the EagleBank bowl game and was played at Robert F. Kennedy Memorial Stadium in Washington, DC. The game, formerly known as the Congressional Bowl, before naming rights were purchased by EagleBank, on Saturday, December 20, 2008. The game, telecast on ESPN, pit the Wake Forest Demon Deacons against the Navy Midshipmen. This was a rematch of a September 27, 2008 game between the two teams that Navy won 24-17 at Wake Forest. The Demon Deacons got a measure of revenge by winning the game, 29-19.

2008 EagleBank Bowl	Line	1	-	2	-	3	-	4	-	Final
Wake Forest	(-3.0)	0	-	7	-	7	-	15	-	29
Navy	(43.5)	10	-	3	-	0	-	6	-	19

Scoring Summary
Navy - Harmon 40 yard Field goal
Navy - King 50 yard fumble return (Harmon kick)
Navy - Harmon 47 yard Field goal
Wake Forest - Adams 4 yard run (Swank kick)
Wake Forest - Adams 5 yard run (Swank kick)
Navy - Kaheaku-Enhada 2 yard run (Pass failed)
Wake Forest - Wooster 8 yard pass from Skinner (Brown pass from Skinner)
Wake Forest - Belton 35 yard run (Swank kick)

Associated Press EagleBank Bowl Game Summary - Riley Skinner found a perfect way to obliterate the miserable memory of his painful performance against Navy earlier this season. Skinner went 11-for-11 and threw the go-ahead touchdown pass to Ben Wooster with 7:52 left, leading Wake Forest to a 29-19 comeback victory over the Midshipmen in the inaugural EagleBank Bowl to open the bowl season Saturday. The previous school record for accuracy was a 12-for-14 effort by Mike McGlamry in 1975. Skinner added a completion on a conversion attempt. He finished with 166 yards passing and was named the game's Most Valuable Player. It was a rematch of a September game played at Wake Forest, when Navy took advantage of five turnovers by Skinner - four interceptions and a fumble - to pull off a 24-17 upset. Skinner took the blame for the loss, and in the days leading up to this game, the junior Quarterback expressed an intense desire to "prove something and get a little revenge." The Midshipmen scored the first 17 points in that game, and this time they used a 50-yard fumble return by Rashawn King to take a 13-0 lead. But Skinner didn't flinch. He directed Wake Forest (8-5) to a touchdown in the final minute of the first half and opened the third quarter with a 73-yard drive that ended with a 5-yard run by Josh Harris for a 14-13 lead. Navy (8-5) went back in front when Kaipo-Noa Kaheaku-Enhada scored on a 2-yard run with

12:30 to go, but Skinner went 4-for-4 for 69 yards in an 80-yard drive that ended with his 8-yard pass to Wooster. Skinner then hit Devon Brown in the back of the end zone for the conversion that made it 22-19. Rich Belton added a 35-yard touchdown run with 54 seconds left. That enabled the winningest senior class in Wake Forest football history to enhance its legacy. The Demon Deacons' 16 seniors finished with a 32-19 record, three bowl appearances and the 2006 Atlantic Coast Conference championship. Kevin Harris rushed for 136 yards in his first start since 2006 and Josh Adams scored two touchdowns for Wake Forest. Senior cornerback Alphonso Smith set an ACC record with his 21st career interception, but his fumble while making a rare appearance on offense resulted in a Navy touchdown. The first bowl game held at 48-year-old RFK Stadium drew a crowd of 28,777, many of them Navy fans who made the short drive from nearby Annapolis, Md. After Wake Forest began the game with a three and out, Shun White ran for 39 yards on Navy's first play to set up a 40-yard field goal by Matt Harmon. It was the 12th time in 13 games the Midshipmen scored on their opening drive. The Demon Deacons then picked up a pair of first downs before Smith took off on a reverse. It was the first carry of the year for the cornerback/punt returner, and it was a disaster: He was stripped of the ball by Wyatt Middleton, and King took the fumble into the end zone for a 10-0 lead. King, a senior, missed the Army-Navy game because of the death of his father. It was the second defensive touchdown by the Midshipmen in a bowl game, the other coming in the 1961 Orange Bowl. Navy's next offensive series was a 16-play drive that ended with Harmon's school-record 19th field goal of the season, a 47-yarder. Late in the half, King returned another fumble for a score. But the play was overturned after a replay determined the runner was down by contact, and the Demon Deacons resumed a 98-yard march that produced a 4-yard touchdown run by Adams - the first points against Navy in nearly 161 minutes. Limited to 7 yards passing before the drive, Skinner went 3-for-3 for 58 yards. All three completions went to D.J. Boldin.

2008 St. Petersburg Bowl

The 2008 MagicJack St. Petersburg Bowl was the inaugural edition of the St. Petersburg bowl game, and was played at Tropicana Field in St. Petersburg, Florida. The game was played on December 20, 2008, and was telecast on espn2, saw the South Florida Bulls (based in nearby Tampa) defeat their former conference rivals Memphis Tigers, 41-14.

2008 St. Petersburg Bowl	Line	1	-	2	-	3	-	4	-	Final
Memphis	(54.5)	7	-	7	-	0	-	0	-	14
South Florida	(-11.5)	14	-	10	-	10	-	7	-	41

Scoring Summary
South Florida - Johnson 26 yard pass from Grothe (Bonani kick)
South Florida - Williams 3 yard run (Bonani kick)
Memphis - Hall 3 yard run (Reagan kick)
South Florida - Bonani 22 yard Field goal
South Florida - Busbee 13 yard pass from Grothe (Bonani kick)
Memphis - Calhoun 2 yard pass from Hall (Reagan kick)
South Florida - Bonani 37 yard Field goal
South Florida - Bogan 24 yard pass from Grothe (Bonani kick)
South Florida - Plancher 2 yard run (Bonani kick)

Associated Press St. Petersburg Bowl Game Summary - Matt Grothe and South Florida didn't have a problem getting motivated for what amounted to an extra home game. After floundering the second half of the season, the magicJack St. Petersburg Bowl gave them a chance to feel good about themselves again. Grothe threw for 236 yards and three touchdowns on the way to a 41-14 rout of Memphis on Saturday. The junior Quarterback moved ahead of West Virginia's Pat White as the Big East's career total offense leader, also rushing for 83 yards on 15 carries to earn the most outstanding player award. Grothe and White, a senior who will finish his season in the Meineke Bowl on Dec. 27, are the only players in league history to amass more than 10,000 yards total offense. White has 10,142 in 49 games, and Grothe finished the night with 10,242 in 39 games. USF (8-5) scored on four of its first five possessions to build a 24-14 halftime lead, forcing Memphis (6-7) to play catch-up and essentially taking 1,000-yard rusher Curtis Steele out of the Tigers' game plan. Arkelon Hall threw for one TD and ran for another, however Steele was held to 48 yards rushing on 12 attempts by a stout run defense determined to redeem itself this postseason after giving up 253 yards to Oregon's Jonathan Stewart during USF's lopsided loss in last year's Sun Bowl. Grothe threw TD passes of 26 yards to Taurus Johnson, 13 to Ben Busbee and 24 to Dontavia Bogan before being replaced by Grant Gregory with USF leading 34-14 late in the third quarter. Hall, meanwhile, was 15-of-31 for 154 yards and no interceptions, with much of that coming on a swing pass that Steele turned into a 50-yard gain early in the second half. He ran 3 yards for a first-quarter touchdown, then threw 2 yards to Duke Calhoun for the Tigers' other TD just before halftime. It was the first meeting between the former Conference USA rivals since USF left that league for the Big East in 2005. The teams split four games between 2001 and 2004, and Memphis relished the challenge of facing an opponent from a BCS conference for the first time in five bowl appearances under Coach Tommy West. The Tigers, who won six of nine games to become bowl eligible after a 0-3 start, viewed Saturday as an opportunity to gauge how much they've progressed toward a goal of having a BCS-caliber program. On this day, they were nowhere close to a South Florida team that began the season with high expectations after being ranked as high as No. 2 by the Associated Press in 2007. The Bulls won their first five before stumbling badly in the Big East and winding up in a bowl game just 32 miles from USF's main campus in Tampa. Tropicana Field in downtown St. Petersburg is close enough that Coach Jim Leavitt and his players bused from the team hotel back to campus for practice all week, truly making it seem like an extra home game rather than a bowl trip. Memphis fell to 0-3 against opponents from BCS conferences this season and is 2-13 since 2001.

2008 Las Vegas Bowl

The 2008 Pioneer Las Vegas Bowl was played between the Arizona Wildcats, the fifth pick from the Pacific-10 Conference and the BYU Cougars, third place overall in the Mountain West Conference. This bowl game was played on December 20, 2008 at 40,000-seat Sam Boyd Stadium in Whitney, Nevada and broadcast on ESPN. Since 2001, the game has featured a matchup of teams from the MWC and Pac-10. The announcers were Mike Patrick and Todd Blackledge with the sideline reporting by Holly Rowe. The Wildcats stunned the 16th ranked Cougars in the coldest Las Vegas Bowl in history, 31-21.

2008 Las Vegas Bowl	Line	1	-	2	-	3	-	4	-	Final
#17 BYU	(62.0)	0	-	7	-	7	-	7	-	21
Arizona	(-3.0)	7	-	3	-	14	-	7	-	31

Scoring Summary
Arizona – Grigsby 1 yard run (Bondzio kick)
Arizona – Bondzio 31 yard Field goal
BYU – Unga 1 yard run (Payne kick)
BYU – George 1 yard pass from Hall (Payne kick)
Arizona – Dean 37 yard pass from Tuitama (Bondzio kick)
Arizona – Gronkowski 24 yard pass from Tuitama (Bondzio kick)
Arizona – Tuitama 6 yard run (Bondzio kick)
BYU – Hall 1 yard run (Payne kick)

Las Vegas Sun Las Vegas Bowl Game Summary - When Arizona senior Quarterback Willie Tuitama walked into the interview room Saturday night after the Wildcats' 31-21 upset of No. 16 BYU, coach Mike Stoops immediately stood up and hugged his star player. That warm embrace was more than a congratulatory acknowledgment of Tuitama earning the 17th Pioneer Las Vegas Bowl's MVP award –- it was a show of gratitude for weathering the pain, doubt and criticism that comes with rebuilding a football program. Tuitama completed 24 of 35 passes for 325 yards and two touchdowns while rushing for one more score to signal Arizona football's resurrection in front of 40,047 fans at Sam Boyd Stadium. The Wildcats hadn't appeared in a bowl game since 1998. Although Tuitama will garner much of the spotlight for Saturday's victory, he was the first person to spread credit to his senior teammates. When this current crop of seniors committed to Arizona, the Wildcats had won just nine games in the previous three seasons. As freshmen, they went 3-8. But the Gatorade shower and the confetti explosions almost never happened for the Wildcats. After jumping out to a 10-0 lead early in the second quarter, Arizona soon found itself on its heels. BYU running back Harvey Unga punched in a 1-yard touchdown run to narrow the gap to 10-7 minutes before halftime. Then crisis struck. On the first play of the second half, Tuitama fumbled while trying to avoid a sack and Coleby Claweson recovered for the Cougars. Six plays later, BYU Quarterback Max Hall hit tight end Andrew George in the back of the end zone to put the Cougars on top 14-10 with 11:21 in the third quarter. That's what the Wildcats did as Tuitama connected with Delashaun Dean for a 37-yard touchdown on the ensuing drive to take a 17-14 lead. Arizona ended up posting 21 unanswered points to take a 31-14 lead into the fourth quarter before BYU's final touchdown. Tuitama completed passes to seven receivers while Nic Grigsby rushed 20 times for 88 yards and one touchdown. The Wildcats shredded the Cougars' defense for 416 total yards. Arizona's defense, however, managed to largely contain one of the best passing offenses in the nation. The Wildcats caused five turnovers and sacked BYU Quarterback Max Hall twice. Although Hall completed 30 of 46 passes for 328 yards, he threw for only one touchdown. Arizona also kept BYU star receiver Austin Collie from finding the end zone even though he caught 11 passes for 119 yards. Junior linebacker Xavier Kelley led the Wildcats with 15 tackles, one sack and one forced fumble. What is perhaps more amazing is that since beating Nebraska 23-20 in the 1998 Holiday Bowl to cap off a 12-1 season, Arizona went 39-65 over the next nine years.

2008 New Mexico Bowl

The 2008 New Mexico Bowl was held on December 20, 2008 at University Stadium on the campus of the University of New Mexico in Albuquerque. The game, telecast on ESPN, featured the Colorado State Rams from the Mountain West Conference and the Fresno State Bulldogs from the WAC. Colorado State scored 20 points in the fourth quarter to defeat Fresno State, 40-35 behind running back Gartrell Johnson's 375 rushing and receiving yards, an NCAA bowl record.

2008 New Mexico Bowl	Line	1	-	2	-	3	-	4	-	Final
Colorado State	(60.5)	10	-	10	-	0	-	20	-	40
Fresno State	(-2.5)	14	-	7	-	7	-	7	-	35

Scoring Summary
Fresno State – Miller 1 yard run (Goessling kick)
Colorado State – Stucker 18 yard run (Smith kick)
Fresno State – Harding 2 yard run (Goessling kick)
Colorado State – Smith 29 yard Field goal
Colorado State – Smith 22 yard Field goal
Fresno State – Miller 69 yard run (Goessling kick)
Colorado State – Sperry 22 yard pass from Ferris (Smith kick)
Fresno State – Harding 2 yard run (Goessling kick)
Colorado State – Johnson 1 yard run (Johnson run failed)
Colorado State – Greer 69 yard pass from Ferris (Smith kick)
Colorado State – Johnson 77 yard run (Johnson run failed)
Fresno State – Skidmore 7 yard pass from Brandstater (Goessling kick)

Associated Press New Mexico Bowl Game Summary - Colorado State's Gartrell Johnson was reluctant to talk about his career-high 285 yards rushing, so teammate Tommie Hill took over for him. Sort of. Johnson added 90 yards receiving for 375 total yards and scored two fourth-quarter touchdowns. All day long, he left defenders reaching for the dreadlocks tumbling out of his helmet. Johnson set a Football Bowl Subdivision record for the most combined yards rushing and receiving in a postseason game. His yards rushing were the second-most ever in a bowl, trailing only a 307-yard effort by P.J. Daniels of Georgia Tech at the 2004 Humanitarian Bowl. It was also the second-best rushing performance in school history. Johnson sealed the victory on a 77-yard touchdown burst with 1:46 remaining, igniting a celebration by fans who made the 7-hour drive from Fort Collins, Colo. He was honored as the most valuable offensive player as Colorado State (7-6) won a bowl for the first time since 2001. If only Johnson would speak for himself. He was more focused on his 57-yard run in the first quarter and a 57-yard reception on a shovel pass from Billy Farris in the second period. The reason? He was ribbed by teammates for getting tackled from behind. The Rams took their first lead at 33-28 when Farris threw a 69-yard TD to Rashaun Greer with seven minutes left. Fresno State cornerback Sharrod Davis took a big chance but whiffed on his attempt to bat the ball. Greer made the catch at the 30 and went untouched into the end zone. The loss capped a rough season for the injury-depleted Bulldogs (7-6), who talked in fall workouts about a possible Bowl Championship Series run. They led 28-20 early in the fourth quarter. The loss also spoiled big rushing efforts by Fresno State's Anthony Harding and Lonyae Miller, who each scored twice. Harding finished with 120 yards rushing, and Miller added 113. Fresno State got within 40-35 with 55 seconds to go when Tom Brandstater threw a 7-yard TD pass to Ryan Skidmore. But Colorado State's Kyle Bell had no trouble fielding the ensuing onside kick. Fans came out of the stands as the final seconds ticked off, capping a strong first season for Fairchild. Johnson, who averaged 99 yards rushing this season, had 97 by the end of the first quarter. He went wild against a young Fresno State defense that had allowed 197 yards rushing per game. Tommie Hill, meanwhile, earned most valuable defensive honors after making a key play as Colorado State scored 21 straight points. His interception set up a 1-yard TD run by Johnson that pulled the Rams within 28-26 with 9:45 to play. The Rams trailed 21-20 after 6-foot-6 Kory Sperry caught a perfectly placed ball from Farris and beat two defenders in the corner of the end zone with two seconds remaining before halftime. The Bulldogs played without six starters -- four on defense -- who were lost for the season. But they were in control most of the way. Miller scored Fresno State's first TD on a 1-yard plunge. Then he bounced outside for a 69-yard TD run to put the Bulldogs up 21-13 late in the second quarter. Fairchild got the Rams in a bowl for the first time since the 2005 Poinsettia Bowl and turned a corner from last year's 3-9 record, which led to the dismissal of Sonny Lubick.

2008 New Orleans Bowl

The 2008 R+L Carriers New Orleans Bowl was the eighth edition of the college football bowl game, played at the Louisiana Superdome in New Orleans, Louisiana. The Southern Miss Golden Eagles defeated the Troy Trojans, 30-27 in a dramatic overtime game. Troy had qualified for the game by winning the Sun Belt Conference title, while Southern Miss had roared back from a 2-6 start to fill the game's slot from

Conference USA. Southern Miss was designated as the away team; however, instead of wearing the visitor white jerseys, the Golden Eagles started the game in yellow home jerseys (Troy wore its maroon home jerseys). Due to NCAA rules, Southern Miss was penalized one time out after the opening kickoff and played the first half with two timeouts to Troy's three.

2008 New Orleans Bowl	Line	1	-	2	-	3	-	4	-	OT	-	Final
Southern Miss	(54.5)	7	-	10	-	0	-	10	-	3	-	30
Troy	(-4.5)	14	-	3	-	10	-	0	-	0	-	27

Scoring Summary
Troy - Calvin 17 yard fumble return (Glusman kick)
Southern Miss - Baptiste 64 yard pass from Davis (Barefoot kick)
Troy - Burton 4 yard pass from Brown (Glusman kick)
Southern Miss - Fletcher 8 yard run (Barefoot kick)
Troy - Glusman 20 yard Field goal
Southern Miss - Barefoot 38 yard Field goal
Troy - Glusman 34 yard Field goal
Troy - Jernigan 6 yard run (Glusman kick)
Southern Miss - Massey 35 yard pass from Davis (Barefoot kick)
Southern Miss - Barefoot 46 yard Field goal
Southern Miss - Barefoot 39 yard Field goal

Associated Press New Orleans Bowl Game Summary - It only seemed fitting that Larry Fedora's first bowl game as Southern Mississippi's head coach would feature a stirring comeback and dramatic overtime finish. The Golden Eagles overcame a 10-point fourth-quarter deficit with the help of a fourth-down touchdown pass, and Michael McGee blocked a field goal in overtime for a 30-27 victory over Troy in the R+L Carriers New Orleans Bowl on Sunday night. The victory was the fifth straight for Southern Miss (7-6), which needed the first four to qualify for a bowl and the last one to extend the school's streak of consecutive winning seasons to 15. Troy held Southern Miss to Britt Barefoot's 39-yard field goal on the first possession of OT, but that wound up being enough for the Golden Eagles to win their third New Orleans Bowl in three appearances. McGee knifed in from the left end, diving as he smothered Sam Glusman's 28-yard kick to clinch the win. The Trojans (8-5), winners of the Sun Belt Conference, led 27-17 after Jerrel Jernigan's 6-yard touchdown run late in the third quarter. Southern Miss began its comeback when Austin Davis rolled out on fourth-and-2 and lofted a 35-yard touchdown to tight end Jonathan Massey with 7:20 left in regulation. Barefoot tied it with his 46-yard field goal with 2:50 to go. A lousy start preceded Southern Miss' fantastic finish. When the game began, the Golden Eagles were penalized the loss of a timeout because they wore all-gold uniforms, defying orders that they wear white jerseys as the designated visiting team. They committed a false start while lining up for their first offensive play. Two plays later, Troy took a 7-0 lead on a defensive touchdown as Jorrick Calvin batted down Davis' lateral, then scooped it up for 17-yard fumble return. Later in the first quarter, Southern Miss lost leading receiver DeAndre Brown, who broke his left leg on an awkward landing in the end zone after his attempt at a leaping catch was batten down in the first quarter. Only one series earlier, Brown had set a single-season school record for receptions with 67 on a 9-yard catch. Without his top target, Davis completed 20 of 34 passes for 276 yards and two touchdowns, including a 64-yard scoring pass to New Orleans native Gerald Baptiste on a flea flicker in the first quarter. Southern Miss Career rushing leader Damion Fletcher carried 14 times for 78 yards and a touchdown on an 8-yard end run. Fletcher also caught three passes for 23 yards, while Baptiste finished with five catches for 88 yards. Troy's Levi Brown was 26-of-43 for 255 yards, including a 4-yard touchdown pass to Kennard Burton and Troy never trailed until overtime. After this game, Troy had to be happy to get out of Louisiana, where one of its most crushing losses came in mid-November. Jernigan had nine catches for 65 yards, breaking a 40-year-old Troy record for single-season receptions. He finished with 77 catches on the year, passing Danny Grant, who caught 72 passes in 1968.

2008 Poinsettia Bowl

The 2008 San Diego County Credit Union Poinsettia Bowl was the fourth edition of the college football bowl game, and was played at Qualcomm Stadium in San Diego, California. The game was played Tuesday, December 23, 2008. The game pitted the Boise State Broncos against the Texas Christian Horned Frogs. In the game, TCU overcame a 13–0 deficit to pull off an impressive 17–16 win over Boise State. With Boise State ranked 9th and TCU ranked 11th, this bowl pairing featured teams both ranked higher than the teams playing in a BCS game during the same season, the 2009 Orange Bowl, a first in BCS history. TCU and Boise State would face off in a bowl game again the following season when both played in a BCS game, the 2010 Fiesta Bowl.

2008 Poinsettia Bowl	Line	1	-	2	-	3	-	4	-	Final
#9 Boise State	(45.5)	10	-	3	-	0	-	3	-	16
#11 TCU	(3.0)	0	-	7	-	3	-	7	-	17

Scoring Summary
Boise State - Brotzman 30 yard Field goal
Boise State - Johnson 20 yard run (Brotzman kick)
Boise State - Brotzman 23 yard Field goal
TCU - Brown 16 yard run (Evans kick)
TCU - Evans 32 yard Field goal
TCU - Turner 17 yard run (Evans kick)
Boise State - Brotzman 33 yard Field goal

Associated Press Poinsettia Bowl Game Summary - After getting a pregame pep talk from LaDainian Tomlinson, the TCU Horned Frogs went out and promptly fell behind Boise State 10-0 midway through the first quarter. No big deal. L.T. had told them to do what Frogs do, and in this case, TCU kept it close before wrecking Boise State's shot at an undefeated season. Joseph Turner scored on a 17-yard run midway through the fourth quarter to give the No. 11 Horned Frogs their first lead of the night, which they preserved for a 17-16 victory over No. 9 Boise State in the San Diego County Credit Union Poinsettia Bowl. Boise State (12-1) was trying to finish 13-0 for the second time in three seasons. It was the second time in five years BSU lost a chance at a perfect season by losing its bowl game. In 2004, it lost to Louisville in the Liberty Bowl to finish 11-1. The Broncos took a 10-0 lead on Ian Johnson's 20-yard touchdown run midway through the first quarter, but their high-scoring offense bogged down against TCU's fast, aggressive defense. TCU (11-2) piled up yards if not points until finally wearing down the Broncos' defense in the fourth quarter. The Horned Frogs moved 80 yards in 10 plays on the winning drive, with Turner finishing it off by shedding a tackle inside the 5-yard line and diving into the end zone for a 17-13 lead. Tomlinson, the former TCU standout who's in his eighth season with the San Diego Chargers, jumped in celebration and pumped his fist near the TCU bench. It was a good night to be a Horned Frog, current and past. After Turner's TD, Boise State got to the TCU 14 before having to settle for Kyle Brotzman's 33-yard field goal to make it 17-16. The Broncos got the ball back with 6 seconds left on their 33, but Jeremy Childs' lateral after a catch flip was grabbed by TCU's Matt Panfil. TCU outgained Boise State 472 yards to 250. BSU had only 28 yards rushing. BSU came in averaging 39 points and 456 yards, one of the benefits of dominating the Western Athletic Conference. Johnson scored on a 20-yard run midway through the first quarter. It was his 58th career rushing TD, breaking former San Diego State star Marshall Faulk's WAC record and giving the Broncos a 10-0 lead. Broncos Quarterback Kellen Moore faked a sweep handoff to Childs, then handed to Johnson, who broke outside and found an open field. The Broncos needed the cushion, because TCU's fast, aggressive defense finally clamped down. Boise State defensive end Bryon Hout intercepted Andy Dalton midway through the second quarter, and his 62-yard return included a nice spin move to get away from one TCU player and a stiff arm against another Horned Frog. Hout was a running back in high school. Hout returned the ball to the TCU 11, but the Broncos had to settle for Brotzman's 24-yard field goal and a 13-0 lead. Brown had 102 yards on 14 carries while Turner had 83 yards on 16 rushes. BSU had to settle for field goals by Brotzman three times after getting inside the 20. Brotzman also missed a 38-yard attempt.

2008 Hawai'i Bowl

The 2008 Sheraton Hawai'i Bowl game was played between the Hawai'i Warriors against the Notre Dame Fighting Irish on December 24, 2008, at Aloha Stadium in Honolulu, Hawaii. This seventh edition of the Hawai'i Bowl originally scheduled a matchup between a team from the WAC and another from the Pac-10, however, the Pac-10 failed to produce enough teams. The game was telecast on ESPN. Notre Dame's victory marked it's first in the postseason since the Irish defeated Texas A&M in the 1994 Cotton Bowl Classic to end the 1993 season and ended a NCAA record nine-game bowl game losing streak. Notre Dame Quarterback Jimmy Clausen broke school bowl game records after passing for 401 yards and five touchdowns, and his 84.6% completion rate was the second-best completion percentage for any player in any bowl game in NCAA history. Wide receiver Golden Tate also set Irish bowl records upon catching for 177 yards and three touchdowns. The game set the record for the Hawai'i Bowl's largest attendance, in both tickets sold and turnstile count, breaking the previous record set at the 2006 edition.

2008 Hawaii Bowl	Line	1	-	2	-	3	-	4	-	Final
Hawaii	(49.0)	0	-	7	-	7	-	7	-	21
Notre Dame	(-2.0)	7	-	21	-	21	-	0	-	49

Scoring Summary
Notre Dame – Hughes 2 yard run (Walker kick)
Notre Dame – Grimes 14 yard pass from Clausen (Walker kick)
Hawaii – Bain 10 yard pass from Alexander (Kelly kick)
Notre Dame – Tate 69 yard pass from Clausen (Walker kick)
Notre Dame – Tate 18 yard pass from Clausen (Walker kick)
Notre Dame – Allen 18 yard pass from Clausen (Walker kick)
Notre Dame – Tate 40 yard pass from Clausen (Walker kick)
Hawaii – Bain 21 yard pass from Alexander (Kelly kick)
Notre Dame – Allen 96 yard kickoff return (Walker kick)
Hawaii – Washington 27 yard pass from Funaki (Kelly kick)

Associated Press Hawaii Bowl Game Summary - Jimmy Clausen ended Notre Dame's long bowl drought -- and Hawaii's bid for a fourth straight Sheraton Hawaii Bowl victory -- with a record-breaking passing night. Clausen set Notre Dame Bowl records with 401 yards passing and five touchdowns to lead the efficient Fighting Irish to their first postseason victory in 15 years, 49-21 over Hawaii on Wednesday night. Golden Tate had six catches for 177 yards and three touchdowns, also Notre Dame Bowl records, including a 69-yarder that sparked a 28-point outburst to help the Irish (7-6) end their NCAA-record bowl losing streak at nine. With Weis calling the plays from the coach's box for the first time because of knee problems that require him to walk with crutches, the Irish were unstoppable. The offense scored at will. The blitzing defense shutdown Hawaii's run-and-shoot. And the special teams weren't too shabby, either. After the Warriors (7-7) scored to end Notre Dame's 28-point run, Armando Allen returned a kickoff 96 yards for a score. Allen also caught an 18-yard TD pass on the Irish's opening drive of the second half. Weis said he had an injection in his knee before the game but still couldn't walk. The last time he coached from the box was in 2001. It was evident Weis, who was all smiles after the game, and his players cherished its long-awaited bowl victory. As Notre Dame was presented the Hawaii Bowl's pineapple-football trophy at midfield, each player came around to put their hands on it. Notre Dame's victory was its first in the postseason since it beat Texas A&M in the Cotton Bowl to end the 1993 season. The Irish also avoided consecutive losing seasons. Clausen was confident and sharp, completing 22 of 26 passes. He racked up 300 yards passing and three TDs by halftime alone, sending the crowd home early. The sophomore broke Brady Quinn's postseason school record of 286 yards passing set against Ohio State in the 2006 Fiesta Bowl. With Notre Dame up 14-7, Clausen broke open the game by connecting with Tate on a 69-yard TD play, the Irish's longest play from scrimmage of the season. Clausen faked a handoff, turned and heaved it to Tate, who had blown past cornerback Calvin Roberts along the left sideline. With the catch, Tate became the fifth Irish receiver to break 1,000 yards receiving in a season. The Irish made it 28-7 with a second left in the first half on an 18-yard hookup between Clausen and Tate on third-and-goal. Hawaii challenged the play, but replays showed Tate got his left foot down before stepping out. Tate followed it up in the third quarter with a 40-yard TD reception that pushed the lead to 42-7 and gave the Warriors flashbacks of the pounding they received from Georgia in the Sugar Bowl to end last season. Clausen and Tate shared the MVP award. Hawaii couldn't get much going. Quarterback Greg Alexander was kept off balance and on the run by the Irish defense, which had eight sacks and forced two turnovers. The Warriors, who didn't call a running play until 6 minutes left in the first half, were held to 32 yards rushing. Alexander was 23-of-39 for 261 yards, throwing 10- and 21-yard TD passes to Aaron Bain. Bain had a career-best eight receptions for 109 yards. Hawaii fans had little to cheer about. One of the biggest roars came when the Notre Dame leprechaun's flagstick snapped in half as he charged out to the field.

2008 Motor City Bowl

The 2008 Motor City Bowl saw the Florida Atlantic Owls defeat the Central Michigan Chippewas 24–21. It was played on December 26, 2008 at Ford Field in Detroit, Michigan and aired on ESPN. The underdog FAU team from the Sun Belt Conference was led by game Most Valuable Player Rusty Smith. CMU had finished in third place in the West Division of the Mid-American Conference. The game was the 12th installment of the Motor City Bowl and was attended by 41,399 people, the fourth lowest all time for the Motor City Bowl.

2008 Motor City Bowl	Line	1	-	2	-	3	-	4	-	Final
Florida Atlantic	(66.5)	7	-	3	-	7	-	7	-	24
Central Michigan	(-7.0)	0	-	10	-	3	-	8	-	21

Scoring Summary
Florida Atlantic - Edgecomb 1 yard run (Gornall kick)
Central Michigan - Poblah 5 yard pass from LeFevour (Aguila kick)
Central Michigan - Aguila 35 yard Field goal
Florida Atlantic - Gornall 36 yard Field goal
Florida Atlantic - Bonner 52 yard pass from Smith (Gornall kick)
Central Michigan - Aguila 33 yard Field goal
Florida Atlantic - Gent 18 yard pass from Smith (Gornall kick)
Central Michigan - Brown 15 yard pass from LeFevour (Aguila kick)

ESPN Motor City Bowl Game Recap - Florida Atlantic has played eight seasons of major college football and already has a winning streak in bowl games. Rusty Smith threw for 307 yards and two second-half touchdowns to help the Owls beat Central Michigan 24-21 on Friday night in the Motor City Bowl. Florida Atlantic began playing in the Football Bowl Subdivision in 2001 but has won both its postseason games. The teams were tied 10-all midway through the third quarter when Smith hit Chris Bonner with a 52-yard scoring pass. Smith found Cortez Gent with an 18-yard strike early in the fourth to give the Owls (7-6) a bit of a cushion. Making their third straight Motor City Bowl appearance, the Chippewas (8-5) cut the lead to 24-21 with 3 minutes to play when Dan LeFevour hit Antonio Brown with a touchdown pass and then Kito Poblah for a 2-point conversion. Gent recovered the ensuing onside kick, however. Most of the 41,399 fans at Ford Field cheered the in-state Chippewas, but they were quiet as Florida Atlantic ran out the clock. It was the smallest turnout in the game's 12-year history, yet Motor City Bowl Chairman Ken Hoffman said the game will return to Ford Field in 2009 despite Detroit's dismal economic forecast. Smith, selected the game's MVP, finished 20-for-35. Gent caught seven passes for 98 yards and Charles Pierre had 80 yards on the ground in a happy return to Michigan for Florida Atlantic, shut out at Michigan State on Sept. 13 during a game-long rainstorm. The Owls began the season 1-5 but won five of their final six to become bowl eligible. LeFevour was 28-for-40 for 253 yards with two touchdowns and a first-quarter interception that led to the Owls' first touchdown. Central Michigan dropped its third straight. Central Michigan trailed 17-13 late in the third quarter when Antonio Brown sprang loose for what would have been a 72-yard touchdown run, but Poblah's facemask penalty negated it. The Chippewas were forced to punt a few plays later. The teams went to halftime tied at 10 after Florida Atlantic's Ross Gornall kicked a 36-yard field goal in the final minute of the second quarter. Dilvory Edgecomb scored on a 1-yard run in the first quarter for the Owls, but LeFevour answered in the second with a short touchdown pass to Poblah. Brown caught 11 passes for 91 yards for Central Michigan, which topped Middle Tennessee in the 2006 Motor City Bowl and lost a 51-48 shootout to Purdue last season.

2008 Champs Sports Bowl

The 2008 Champs Sports Bowl was the 19th edition of the college football bowl game that was played on Saturday, December 27, 2008 at the Citrus Bowl in Orlando, Florida. The game, was broadcast on ESPN, pitted the Wisconsin Badgers against the Florida State Seminoles. At the end, the Florida State Seminoles were the winners, 42-13. It was the only bowl game where a punter was named MVP.

2008 Champs Sports Bowl	Line	1	-	2	-	3	-	4	-	Final
Wisconsin	(51.0)	0	-	3	-	3	-	7	-	13
Florida State	(-6.0)	0	-	14	-	14	-	14	-	42

Scoring Summary
Florida State – Nicholson 75 yard fumble return (Gano kick)
Wisconsin – Welch 31 yard Field goal
Florida State – Carr 15 yard pass from Ponder (Gano kick)
Wisconsin – Welch 41 yard Field goal
Florida State – Smith 6 yard run (Gano kick)
Florida State – Jones 14 yard run (Gano kick)
Florida State – Watson 41 yard fumble return (Gano kick)
Florida State – Piurowski 10 yard pass from Ponder (Gano kick)
Wisconsin – Theus 20 yard pass from Sherer (Welch kick)

Associated Press Champs Sports Bowl Game Summary - Bobby Bowden glimpsed into the past, and it made the 79-year-old coach excited about Florida State's future. Bowden saw a big-play offense and a hard-hitting, opportunistic defense in the Seminoles' 42-13 win over Wisconsin at the Champs Sports Bowl on Saturday. Florida State (9-4) finished with more than eight wins for the first time since 2004. Nine victories were once a given for Bowden's Seminoles, who hit that mark in 17 of 18 seasons before tailing off in recent seasons. Derek Nicholson and Dekoda Watson returned fumbles for touchdowns, Christian Ponder threw two TD passes and the Seminoles got a game MVP performance from punter Graham Gano. Watson, Ponder and Gano are all underclassmen. Nicholson, a senior, had two fumble recoveries, including one he returned 75 yards for a first-quarter score. Gano averaged 48.2 yards on five and had three downed inside the Badgers 5 to earn game MVP. Ponder, was 18-for-31 for 199 yards. P.J. Hill ran for 140 yards on 15 carries for the Badgers (7-6), but Quarterback Dustin Sherer completed only four of nine for 55 yards through the first three quarters. His fumble early in the fourth quarter was returned 51 yards for a score by Watson to put FSU up 35-6. It was an ugly finish to a disappointing season for Wisconsin, which was ranked as high as No. 8 early and was expected to contend in the Big Ten. Hill broke runs of 46 and 43 yards, both setting up Philip Welch field goals. But he fumbled deep in FSU territory late in the third quarter and Nicholson recovered to end the threat. Florida State, playing in its NCAA-leading 27th-straight bowl game, improved Bowden's career record to 21-10-1. Antone Smith scored on a 6-yard run off right tackle to put the Seminoles up 21-6 in the third quarter and make the power running Badgers have to go to the pass to catch up. Gano, the Lou Groza Award winner as the nation's best kicker, placed three first-quarter punts inside the 4, including two at the 1. Wisconsin managed drives of 56 and 51 yards after two of those coffin corner punts but had to settle field goals of 31 and 41 yards by Philip Welch. The Seminoles couldn't turn that field position edge into points, though, and when Sherer hit Garrett Graham on a slant for a gain of 43, the game seemed to turn. But on second-and-9 at the Seminoles 19, Sherer took a one-step drop and tried to hit Hill on a quick screen. The ball, clearly a lateral, was deflected by end Neffey Moffett and picked up by Nicholson, who returned it for a score, high stepping the last 20 yards. FSU led 7-0 with about 12 minutes left in the first half. Nicholson's celebration was flagged for unsportsmanlike conduct and after a short squib kick, Wisconsin took over at the Seminoles' 46. Sherer, though, was sacked by Moffett on third-and-2 at the 38 and the Badgers had to punt. Instead of running out the clock deep in their own end in the first half trailing 7-3, Wisconsin passed. FSU forced a punt, taking over at the Badgers' 47 with 40 seconds left. Ponder hit Louis Givens on a swing pass for 26 yards and then found Greg Carr on a fade route in the right corner for a one-handed 15-yard TD catch with 7 seconds left that put the Seminoles up 14-3 at halftime. Wisconsin appeared to have regained the momentum after Welch's second field goal when they recovered a Bert Reed fumble at the Seminoles' 28. Replays showed Reed's knee was down before he lost the ball, and the call was changed.

2008 Meineke Car Care Bowl

The 2008 Meineke Car Care Bowl was the seventh edition of the college football bowl game and was played at Bank of America Stadium in Charlotte, North Carolina. The game was played on Saturday, December 27, 2008. The game, telecast on ESPN, pitted the North Carolina Tar Heels against the West Virginia Mountaineers, with the Mountaineers winning over the Heels 31-30. The crowd of 73,712 was the largest in the bowl's seven-year history and the largest ever to see a college football game in the state of North Carolina. It was also the fourth-largest crowd of the 2008 bowl season, and the second largest for a non-BCS bowl.

2008 Meiniek Car Care Bowl	Line	1	-	2	-	3	-	4	-	Final
West Virginia	(-2.0)	21	-	0	-	3	-	7	-	31
North Carolina	(46.0)	14	-	9	-	7	-	0	-	30

Scoring Summary
West Virginia - Devine 98 yard run (McAfee kick)
North Carolina - Nicks 73 yard pass from Yates (Barth kick)
West Virginia - Arnett 44 yard pass from White (McAfee kick)
North Carolina - Nicks 66 yard pass from Arnold (Barth kick)
West Virginia - Starks 35 yard pass from White (McAfee kick)
North Carolina - Safety, Devine tackled in end zone
North Carolina - Nicks 25 yard pass from Yates (Barth kick)
West Virginia - McAfee 25 yard Field goal
North Carolina - Yates 5 yard run (Barth kick)
West Virginia - Arnett 99 yard pass from White (McAfee kick)

Associated Press Meineke Car Care Bowl Game Summary - During four record-breaking seasons at West Virginia, Pat White made comeback victories and bowl wins routine. His grand finale, though, was unique. The most prolific running Quarterback in college football history had the best passing game of his career, cementing his status as one of the best players in school history and perhaps showing he can take his game to the NFL, too. White threw for 332 yards in his final college game, including the game-winning 20-yard touchdown pass to Alric Arnett midway through the fourth quarter in West Virginia's 31-30 victory over North Carolina on Saturday in the Meineke Car Care Bowl. The senior was voted MVP of a bowl for the third straight year and finished 4-0 in postseason games, helping West Virginia (9-4) end a disappointing season on a positive note. It took a great performance to beat out Hakeem Nicks, who caught eight passes for 217 yards and three touchdowns for the Tar Heels (8-5). But T.J. Yates' otherwise strong game was marred when he was intercepted by Pat Lazear with under 2 minutes left, ending coach Butch

Davis' hopes of a bowl win to complete his turnaround season at North Carolina. As Davis spoke, Stewart was leading the crowd in cheers in a sweet ending to a tumultuous season for the much-maligned replacement for Rich Rodriguez. Entering the season as prohibitive favorites to win the Big East, the Mountaineers started 1-2. They recovered to win five straight, only to go 2-2 over their final four games to end their BCS bowl hopes. White made sure they went out a winner. North Carolina routinely put eight men on the line of scrimmage to stop the NCAA's all-time leading rushing Quarterback. White was held to 55 yards rushing, finishing with 4,480 in his career. Facing questions about whether he can be an NFL Quarterback, White made a strong case. He completed 26 of 32 passes with three touchdowns, one interception, and a clutch fourth-quarter drive. After West Virginia's J.T. Thomas recovered Shaun Draughn's fumble at the Mountaineers 30, White threw a 41-yard pass over the middle to Jock Sanders, picked up nine yards on a running play and then rifled a pass between two defenders to Arnett for the go-ahead touchdown with 7:14 left. The comeback spoiled a remarkable day by Nicks, a junior who could turn pro. The Mountaineers were missing starting defensive backs Brandon Hogan and Sidney Glover to injuries and illness. The 6-foot-1 Nicks, playing in his hometown, responded by setting three school receiving records and shattering his career-high in yards receiving -- before the game was 20 minutes old. It was part of a dizzying offensive display by both teams that had six touchdowns on the board with 10:37 left in the second quarter. Nicks' circus catch midway through the third quarter appeared to put the Tar Heels in good shape. Yates threw a pass behind Nicks on a crossing pattern. Nicks reached back and clutched the ball with his left hand, moved it behind his back and grabbed it with his right hand on the other side of his body for an 8-yard gain. That set up Yates' 4-yard scramble to give North Carolina a 30-24 lead. Nicks caught three TD passes in the first half, and his first will rival his behind-the-back catch for YouTube hits. Yates' deep heave over the middle was underthrown and nearly intercepted by Ellis Lankster, but the ball went through his hands and Nicks caught it behind him, then started to celebrate about 15 yards shy of the end zone. That allowed Keith Tandy to catch up, but Nicks wrestled away from him for the 73-yard touchdown. White was doing his best to keep up in a game that didn't have an incomplete pass or punt until midway through the second quarter. White completed 14 of his first 15 passes and threw two first-half touchdowns, including a remarkable one-handed grab by Arnett for a 44-yard score. But White was intercepted in the end zone at the end of the first half by Deunta Williams, who had earlier tackled Noel Devine in the end zone for a safety. Williams later recovered a fumble, but it wasn't enough for North Carolina. Just too much White. According to the West Virginia sports information staff, White is believed to be the first Quarterback in college football to start four bowl victories.

2008 Emerald Bowl

The 2008 Emerald Bowl was played on December 27, 2008 at AT&T Park, the home field of the Giants in San Francisco, California. The Miami Hurricanes of the ACC were matched against the California Golden Bears (based in nearby Berkeley, California) of the Pac-10, the first appearance by either team in the seven-year history of the Emerald Bowl.

2008 Emerald Bowl	Line	1	-	2	-	3	-	4	-	Final
Miami	(50.)	0	-	7	-	7	-	3	-	17
California	(-9.0)	14	-	0	-	3	-	7	-	24

Scoring Summary
California - Best 1 yard run (Tavecchio kick)
California - Best 42 yard run (Tavecchio kick)
Miami - Byrd 9 yard pass from Harris (Bosher kick)
Miami - Collier 6 yard pass from Harris (Bosher kick)
California - Tavecchio 23 yard Field goal
Miami - Bosher 22 yard Field goal
California - Miller 2 yard pass from Longshore (Tavecchio kick)

Associated Press Emerald Bowl Game Summary - Zack Follett concocted the final pass-rushing move of his California career and slipped past the Miami linemen who taunted him all night. He chased down Jacory Harris from behind, clubbing the ball from the freshman Quarterback's hand with one big swipe. With just enough of the brains, heart and nerve exemplified by their senior linebacker, the Golden Bears proved there's no place like 12 miles away from home with a 24-17 victory in the Emerald Bowl on Saturday night. After Follett forced that turnover deep in Miami territory with 3:28 left, Anthony Miller scored the go-ahead touchdown on his first career catch 47 seconds later. Although the ending was unlikely, with a freshman tight end cradling a perfect pass from a Quarterback who was mostly terrible otherwise, the result was no shock to Cal (9-4). From Follett to Miller, the Bears were determined to capitalize on the decided home-field advantage provided by a baseball stadium teeming with screaming Cal fans. Follett, the defensive player of the game with nine tackles -- four for losses -- and two sacks. Jahvid Best rushed for a bowl-record 186 yards and two touchdowns, yet the Golden Bears still needed a big defensive play and an unlikely hero to hold off the Hurricanes (7-6). Cal Quarterback Nate Longshore shook off a dismal 10-for-21 performance in his final game with that scoring pass to Miller as the Golden Bears won for the fifth time in a school-record six consecutive bowl appearances under Coach Jeff Tedford. Miami stayed in it with strong pass defense and a solid game from Harris, who went 25-of-41 for 194 yards and two TDs in his second career start while subbing for the suspended Robert Marve. Harris had won 31 straight starts dating back to his high school career in South Florida, but his fumble cost the Hurricanes in their first bowl game under Coach Randy Shannon. Laron Byrd and Thearon Collier caught Harris' scoring passes for Miami, which tied it on Matt Bosher's 22-yard field goal with 9:13 to play. After Cal's Giorgio Tavecchio missed a 34-yard field goal with 4:24 left, Follett knocked the ball away from Harris on third down. Cameron Jordan recovered Harris' fumble and returned it to the Miami 2, where Longshore connected with Miller. He was on the field for just three offensive snaps in the Emerald Bowl, and he could remember only four or five occasions when he was on the field for that play all season long. Tedford chose Longshore, the oft-booed senior, to start his final college game instead of Kevin Riley, the Bears' starter for most of this year and the star of last season's comeback victory in the Armed Forces Bowl. If Riley is injured, the Bears won't acknowledge it -- and Longshore struggled all the way until his final throw. Marve was among five Miami players suspended in the days leading up to the game for violating team rules and starting tight end Dedrick Epps was a last-minute scratch from the lineup with a bruised leg. Graig Cooper rushed for 63 yards and Lee Chambers added 60 for Miami, and tight end Craig Zellner made eight catches for 48 yards in Epps' place. Best finished the season with 1,580 yards rushing, the second-best total in school history. Oregon State freshman Jacquizz Rodgers would need 328 yards in the Sun Bowl against Pittsburgh on Wednesday to overtake Best for the Pac-10 rushing title.

2008 Independence Bowl

The 2008 Independence Bowl marked the thirty-third edition of the college football bowl game, and was played at Independence Stadium in Shreveport, Louisiana.

2008 Independence Bowl	Line	1	-	2	-	3	-	4	-	Final
Northern Illinois	(Pk)	7	-	0	-	3	-	0	-	10
Louisiana Tech	(47.0)	7	-	7	-	3	-	0	-	17

Scoring Summary
Northern Illinois – Skarb 8 yard pass from Harnish (Salerno kick)
Louisiana Tech – Livas 97 yard kickoff return (Oestreicher kick)
Louisiana Tech – Porter 11 yard run (Oestreicher kick)
Louisiana Tech – Oestreicher 30 yard Field goal
Northern Illinois – Salerno 20 yard Field goal

Associated Press Independence Bowl Game Summary - Weldon Brown has been a regular at Independence Stadium for most of his life. He played here twice in Peewee football and two more times in high school, but all of those games -- and every one he played in college -- paled compared to the performance the senior defensive back put in Sunday night in Louisiana Tech's 17-10 win over Northern Illinois in the Independence Bowl. Every time the Bulldogs (8-5) needed a big play as the Huskies (6-7) threatened, Brown was there. He stopped one scoring threat with a shoestring tackle to set up fourth down, then batted down the ensuing pass. He recovered a fumbled punt to set up a field goal attempt and ended one of two late drives with the game on the line with an interception. He finished with 14 tackles and was named defensive most valuable player. No matter, Brown and the Bulldogs come out looking just fine after an unexpected invitation to the bowl, which is 70 miles down Interstate 20 from Ruston. Neither the Southeastern Conference nor the Big 12 could produce participants and Louisiana Tech took full advantage. Along with Brown's big plays on defense, Phillip Livas returned a kickoff 97 yards, Daniel Porter rushed for 78 yards and a touchdown and Louisiana Tech scored its first postseason win since the 1977 Independence Bowl with its seventh come-from-behind win of the season. The Bulldogs hadn't won eight games since 1999. The victory over Northern Illinois marks a quick turnaround under Dooley, former protégé of Nick Saban and son of iconic Georgia coach and athletic director Vince Dooley. As his father did, Dooley won his first bowl. And just like ol' dad, he used special teams, defense and the running game to prevail. Two seasons ago such a scenario would be hard to imagine. The Bulldogs won three games, then five last year. But Louisiana Tech kicked off 2008 with an upset of Mississippi State and earned its first postseason trip since the 2001 Humanitarian Bowl by winning four of their last five regular-season games. Much of the scoring and all the big plays came in the first half. Northern Illinois dominated the first quarter with 125 total yards to 23 for Tech. The Huskies scored on Chandler Harnish's 8-yard pass to fullback Kyle Skarb in the left flat, his fifth straight completion for 53 yards on the drive. But poor special teams helped erase the

Huskies' advantage. First, Livas broke a tackle at midfield and shook Chase Carter at the 30 with a dynamic stop-and-go move on the ensuing kickoff. It was the eighth non-offensive touchdown of the season for the Bulldogs, moving them into a tie for the most in major college football. It also was the second longest kickoff return for a touchdown in the Independence Bowl and the first since Mississippi's Deuce McAllister did it in 1998. Livas celebrated the score by throwing the ball into the end zone -- but wasn't flagged for the infraction. After three quick offensive plays, Northern Illinois tried to avoid Livas on the punt, but Mike Salernos shanked a rugby-style kick for 15 yards. Louisiana Tech took over at the Huskies' 42 and got help with a 15-yard facemask penalty on Larry English and a 24-yard pass to Porter. Porter then carried it in from 11 yards out off left tackle for a 14-7 lead with 1:19 gone in the second quarter. Northern Illinois had a chance to tie the game just before halftime, but Brown hit Harnish as he threw toward the end zone, leading to Deon Young's interception. Brown's recovery of Greg Turner's fumble on a punt return ended another chance for the Huskies, though Mike Krause blocked the Bulldogs' ensuing field goal try. The teams traded field goals on their first possessions of the second half, then played to a stalemate the rest of the way. Louisiana Tech managed only 236 total yards and Porter had his string of 100-yard rushing games snapped at four. Northern Illinois had 339 yards, with Harnish going 20-for-40 for 186 yards.

2008 PapaJohns.com Bowl

The 2008 PapaJohns.com Bowl was the third edition of the bowl game, and was played at Legion Field in Birmingham, Alabama. The game was played on Monday, December 29, 2008. The game, telecast on ESPN, pitted the Rutgers Scarlet Knights against the North Carolina State Wolfpack. The game marked the first ever meeting of the two universities' football programs. NC State led 17-6 at halftime but crumbled in the second half after losing starting Quarterback Russell Wilson to a knee injury. Rutgers won, 29-23. This was also the first edition of the bowl game not to feature any current or former members of Conference USA. The selection of NC State did have a connection to past bowl games in Birmingham as the Wolfpack had competed in the last All-American Bowl, held at Legion Field in 1990.

2008 PapaJohns.com Bowl	Line	1	-	2	-	3	-	4	-	Final
NC State	(56.0)	10	-	7	-	0	-	6	-	23
Rutgers	(-7.0)	6	-	0	-	10	-	13	-	29

Scoring Summary
Rutgers - Cervini 6 yard run (Kick blocked)
NC State - Spencer 44 yard pass from Wilson (Czajkowski kick)
NC State - Czajkowski 32 yard Field goal
NC State - Brown 5 yard run (Czajkowski kick)
Rutgers - San San Te 31 yard Field goal
Rutgers - Underwood 10 yard pass from Teel (San San Te kick)
Rutgers - San San Te 28 yard Field goal
NC State - Hill 16 yard pass from Evans (2 pt. conversion failed)
Rutgers - Britt 42 yard pass from Teel (San San Te kick)
Rutgers - San San Te 24 yard Field goal

Associated Press Papa John's Bowl Game Summary - Fitting that Rutgers would end the 2008 season with a come-from-behind win. After winning only one of their first six games, Mike Teel and the Scarlet Knights erased an 11-point second half deficit to defeat North Carolina State 29-23 in the Papajohns.com Bowl on Monday. Leading the comeback -- as he did all season -- was Teel, who passed for 319 yards and two touchdowns, including a 42-yard scoring toss to Kenny Britt to give the Scarlet Knights (8 -5) the lead for good in the fourth quarter. Teel's pass to Britt with 8:30 to play proved to be the winning touchdown. Britt, a third-team All-American, made a juggling catch as he crossed the goal line and finished with six catches for 119 yards. Teel, a senior, was the game's most valuable player. He ended his career on a seven-game winning streak after being booed at home when he was struggling earlier in the season. Schiano said he didn't have to give his team much of a pep talk at the half. NC State (6-7) held a 17-6 halftime edge, led by Quarterback Russell Wilson who was 11-for-23 for 186 yards and a score. But Wilson left the game with a strained knee late in the first half and did not return. His replacements were mostly ineffective and threw three interceptions to aid the Rutgers comeback. Wilson threw one interception all season. North Carolina State coach Tom O'Brien said doctors recommended that Wilson not play in the second half. The Scarlet Knights scored 10 consecutive points in the third quarter on a 31-yard field goal by San San Te and an 11-yard pass from Teel to Tiquan Underwood. Rutgers took a 19-17 lead with 13:31 to play on a 28-yard field by Te after a 10-play 70-yard drive. The Wolfpack came right back as reserve Quarterback Daniel Evans drove them 64 yards in eight plays and hit Anthony Hill with a 16-yard touchdown pass to give NC State a 23-19 lead. But it was only two plays later when Teel hit Britt for the go-ahead score. Rutgers got off to a fast start as cornerback Jason McCourty recovered a Wolfpack fumble on the first play from scrimmage. On the next play, Teel hit Underwood with a 22-yard pass and the Scarlet Knights drove to the NC State 6, where they lined up for a field goal. The holder on the play, Rob Cervini, picked up the ball after the snap and scampered for the touchdown. The extra point attempt was blocked, and Rutgers held an early 6-0 lead. It was Cervini's first play of his career. But the Wolfpack dominated the rest of the first half behind Wilson passing and running. He had 46 yards rushing on eight carries before spraining his knee. North Carolina State took the lead with 7:56 to play in the first quarter when Wilson completed a 44-yard touchdown pass to Owen Spencer, who broke free over the middle. The Wolfpack stretched the lead to 10-6 on a 33-yard Josh Crajkowski field goal late in the first quarter. NC State finished the first half with a 13-play 80-yard drive that was capped with a 5-yard touchdown run by Andre Brown with 38 seconds to play in the half. NC State turned the ball over four times, including one lost fumble and the three second-half interceptions.

2008 Alamo Bowl

The 2008 Valero Alamo Bowl was played on December 29, 2008 in the 65,000-seat Alamodome in San Antonio, Texas, and televised nationally by ESPN. The 2008 Alamo Bowl was the 16th annual edition of the contest and the second to be sponsored by Valero Energy Corporation. The game pit the Missouri Tigers (9–4) against the Northwestern Wildcats (9–3). The 2008 game was dubbed the Journalism Bowl by some in the media, owing to the nationally recognized journalism programs at each school: the Missouri School of Journalism and the Medill School of Journalism.

2008 Alamo Bowl	Line	1	-	2	-	3	-	4	-	OT	-	Final
#25 Missouri	(-12.0)	0	-	10	-	10	-	3	-	7	-	30
#22 Northwestern	(66.0)	7	-	3	-	13	-	0	-	0	-	23

Scoring Summary
Northwestern – Peterman 35 yard pass from Bacher (Villarreal kick)
Missouri – Wolfert 31 yard Field goal
Northwestern – Villarreal 21 yard Field goal
Missouri – Maclin 75 yard punt return (Wolfert kick)
Northwestern – Ward 46 yard pass from Bacher (Villarreal kick)
Missouri – Alexander 11 yard pass from Daniel (Wolfert kick)
Missouri – Wolfert 43 yard Field goal
Northwestern – Lane 23 yard pass from Bacher (Villarreal kick)
Missouri – Wolfert 37 yard Field goal
Missouri – Maclin 7 yard pass from Daniel (Wolfert kick)

Associated Press Alamo Bowl Game Summary - Chase Daniel's last game at Missouri ended with a fitting flourish. The star Quarterback threw a 7-yard touchdown pass to Jeremy Maclin in overtime and the No. 21 Tigers rallied to beat No. 23 Northwestern 30-23 in the Valero Alamo Bowl on Monday night. It was Daniel's first overtime game since leading Missouri to a 27-24 win over Iowa State as a freshman when he took over mid-game following an injury to Brad Smith. Daniel had played sparingly at the end of a couple of games before that, but never when it counted. After the Tigers scored on the opening possession of overtime, their defense delivered, too. Missouri sacked a backpedaling C.J. Bacher, forcing a fumble that left Northwestern with fourth-and-goal from the 32-yard line. Bacher's desperation heave into the end zone was knocked down, and Daniel rushed off the sideline with his teammates to celebrate. The win gave Missouri (10-4) double-digit victories in consecutive seasons for the first time in school history. The Wildcats (9-4) fell to 1-6 in bowl games, with their only win coming in their first bowl appearance in 1949. Playing his final college game, Daniel overcame three interceptions to lead the Tigers back from a three-point deficit in the fourth quarter. Jeff Wolfert made three field goals, including a 37-yarder with 2:49 remaining that tied it 23-all. But he missed a 44-yard attempt that could have won it for Missouri as time expired. Daniel, who finished fourth in 2007 Heisman Trophy voting, matched a season high with his three interceptions. He was 27-of-44 for 200 yards and two touchdown passes. The speedy Maclin, a first-team All-America as an all-purpose player, also returned a punt 75 yards for a score that tied it at 10 in the second quarter. Bacher threw for 304 yards and equaled an Alamo Bowl record with three touchdown tosses. His 23-yard scoring pass to Ross Lane in the back of the end zone gave Northwestern a 23-20 lead at the end of the third. The score came after Brad Phillips grabbed an interception and returned it to the 24. After the Tigers tied it, Northwestern had a chance to drive for a go-ahead score, but Bacher's pass on third-and-3 with less than two minutes remaining fell incomplete. Wildcats kicker Amado Villarreal missed an extra point in the third quarter that could have made the difference in regulation. A 43-yard field goal by Wolfert made it 20-16 Missouri with just under four minutes remaining in the third. That score was set up by an interception and 22-yard return by Brock Christopher. Danario Alexander gave Missouri a 17-16 lead -- its first of the game -- with about seven minutes remaining in the third quarter on an 11-yard touchdown pass from Daniel. Bacher found Rasheed Ward for a 46-yard touchdown pass on the first drive of the second half. Villarreal's extra point bounced off the right upright to leave the score at 16-10 Northwestern. Maclin, who leads the NCAA in all-purpose yards, tied it 10-all with his 75-yard punt return for a touchdown just before halftime. He bolted through the first wave of defenders before getting a good block and zooming past punter Stefan Demos, who had an angle on him but tripped. It was the first punt return TD this season for Maclin. Things started rough for Daniel when his pass was tipped and intercepted by Brian Peters on Missouri's first drive. Northwestern took advantage of that mistake when Bacher found a wide-open Eric Peterman streaking down the middle of the field for a 35-yard touchdown to put the Wildcats up 7-0 early in the first quarter. Northwestern got a 21-yard field goal by Villarreal to make it 10-3 in the second. Daniel's second interception came on an ill-advised throw under heavy pressure from David Arnold in the second quarter. Defensive end Corey Wootton, 6-foot-7, made a diving grab just before the ball would have hit the turf. Northwestern came away empty, though, when Villarreal's 47-yard field-goal attempt sailed wide left. Wootton, who also had a sack, appeared to injure his right leg with about four minutes remaining and did not return. Fitzgerald said he did not have an update on his condition. Missouri's first points came on a 31-yard field goal by Wolfert early in the second quarter.

2008 Humanitarian Bowl

The 2008 Humanitarian Bowl was played between the Maryland Terrapins and the Nevada Wolf Pack on December 30, 2008. It was the two teams' first meeting. The game was played at Bronco Stadium in Boise, Idaho.

2008 Humanitarian Bowl	Line	1	-	2	-	3	-	4	-	Final
Maryland	(60.0)	13	-	15	-	0	-	14	-	42
Nevada	(-2.0)	14	-	0	-	7	-	14	-	35

Scoring Summary
Maryland - Cannon 59 yd pass from Turner (Kick failed)
Nevada - Wellington 1 yd pass from Kaepernick (Jaekle kick)
Maryland - Smith 99 yd run (Egekeze kick)
Nevada - Taua 17 yd run (Jaekle kick)
Maryland - Green 53 yd run (Egekeze kick)
Maryland - Tyler 14 yd pass from Turner (2 pt. conversion good)
Nevada - Taua 17 yd pass from Kaepernick (Jaekle kick)
Nevada - Mitchell 21 yd pass from Kaepernick (Jaekle kick)
Maryland - Scott 49 yd run (Egekeze kick)
Maryland - Scott 2 yd run (Egekeze kick)
Nevada - Kaepernick 15 yd run (Jaekle kick)

Associated Press Humanitarian Bowl Game Summary - Ralph Friedgen's initial reaction was to put Da'Rel Scott and the six other Maryland players who broke curfew leading up to the Humanitarian Bowl on a bus with a one-way ticket back to College Park, Md. Instead of being run out of town, Scott stuck around and ran over Nevada. Benched for 2½ quarters for his curfew violation, an inspired Scott became an unstoppable running force for the final 20 minutes. He carried 14 times for 174 yards and scored two fourth-quarter touchdowns as Maryland held off the Wolf Pack 42-35 on Tuesday. And run Scott did, blowing through a worn down Nevada defense in the final quarter. He sprinted 49 yards nearly untouched to snap a 28-all tie early in the fourth, then added a 2-yard TD gallop to put the Terps up 14 points with 7:44 left. But until he got his first carry midway through the third quarter, doubt lingered in Scott's mind as to if his transgression would keep him off the field. He was one of seven Terps caught by Friedgen, who declined to specify what the players did, but indicated the players had sneaked out a couple of nights before the game. Scott's first carry came with 5:55 left in the third quarter and Maryland needed all of his 174 yards to hold off Quarterback Colin Kaepernick and Nevada's potent "pistol" offense. Kaepernick, who played the second half with a sprained right ankle, misfired in the first half, but found his throwing rhythm after briefly being benched in the third quarter. Kaepernick finished 24-for-47 for a bowl-record 370 yards and three touchdowns and added a 15-yard scoring run with 2:19 left. But Maryland recovered the onside kick and walked away with its fourth bowl victory since 2002. Scott was one of four starters to become statues on the Maryland sideline as Friedgen handed down his punishment. Scott initially started stretching and running after the first quarter ended believing he'd get a shot in the second. The warmup was for naught as he and starting wide receiver Danny Oquendo continued to watch until the second half began. Once Scott got the ball in his hands, he couldn't be stopped. His first run was for 14 yards and he went for 11 on the next play. His 49-yard touchdown dash with 12:21 left put Maryland up 35-28 and vaulted Scott over 1,000 yards for the season -- the seventh back in Maryland history to top 1,000 yards. On Maryland's next drive, Scott accounted for all 66 yards with runs of 11, 23 and 30 yards, and finally his 2-yard score with 7:44 left that proved to be the winning points. Kaepernick, the WAC offensive player of the year, was injured while being sacked late in the first half and moved the rest of the game with a noticeable limp. But he was able to capitalize on a pair of mistakes by Maryland Quarterback Chris Turner to help the Wolf Pack pull even. Nevada's Jonathon Amaya intercepted Turner's pass near midfield midway through the third quarter and returned it to the Maryland 22. Three plays later, Kaepernick hit Vai Taua behind the Maryland secondary for a 17-yard TD score to get the Wolf Pack to 28-21. Late in the third, Turner was hit as he attempted to throw a screen at the Nevada 20. The throw went backward, and Nate Agaiava recovered for the Wolf Pack. Kaepernick needed only five plays and less than two minutes to draw even, hitting Marko Mitchell on a 21-yard TD. The tie lasted only a couple of minutes. Turner hit Torrey Smith for 26 yards on third down, and two plays later Scott ran for his seventh touchdown of the season to give the Terps the lead for good. The wild nature and offensive firepower of this bowl game would have made hometown Boise State proud. While Scott and Oquendo watched from the sideline in the first half, their backups and Turner did more than keep up with a Nevada offense that was averaging 510.6 yards and 37.8 points per game. Turner hit third-string Adrian Cannon for a 59-yard TD on Maryland's opening drive, and found Oquendo's backup, Ronnie Tyler, for a 14-yard score late in the first half to give Maryland a 28-14 lead at the break. Smith added a 99-yard kickoff return and Scott's backup, Morgan Green, added a 53-yard scoring run in the first half.

2008 Texas Bowl

The 2008 Texas Bowl was the third edition of the bowl game, and was played at Reliant Stadium in Houston, Texas. The game was played on Tuesday, December 30, 2008. The game, telecast on NFL Network, featured the hometown Rice Owls against the Western Michigan Broncos. The Owls won the game 38-14, which was their first post-season victory since the 1954 Cotton Bowl Classic.

2008 Texas Bowl	Line	1	-	2	-	3	-	4	-	Final
Western Michigan	(73.5)	0	-	0	-	0	-	14	-	14
Rice	(-2.5)	10	-	14	-	7	-	7	-	38

Scoring Summary
Rice - Clement 26 yard run (Fangmeier kick)
Rice - Fangmeier 30 yard Field goal
Rice - Dixon 6 yard pass from Clement (Fangmeier kick)
Rice - Casey 45 yard pass from Clement (Fangmeier kick)
Rice - Clement 13 yard pass from Dillard (Fangmeier kick)
Rice - Dillard 18 yard pass from Clement (Fangmeier kick)
Western Michigan - Ellsworth 2 yard pass from Hiller (Potter kick)
Western Michigan - Julien 13 yard pass from Hiller (Potter kick)

Texas Bowl Game Summary - Rice's Chase Clement had a hand in all five touchdowns in leading the Owls to a 38-14 victory over Western Michigan in the third annual Texas Bowl at Reliant Stadium. Clement, Conference USA's most valuable player, added the Texas Bowl's outstanding player award by throwing for three TD passes, running for one and even catching a scoring pass from Rice all-America receiver Jarett Dillard. Rice (10-3) won its seventh consecutive game. The senior from Alamo Heights, Tex., High, set Texas Bowl records with 30 completions (in 44 attempts) and those three TD passes. He also rushed for 72 yards on 12 attempts, including the 26-yard run that got the Rice rout started in the first quarter. Clark Fangmeier's 30-yard field goal made it 10-0 Owls after one period, then Clement passes to Toren Dixon for six yards, and to James Casey for 45 yards made it 24-0 at the half. That point total set a Texas Bowl record for the first 30 minutes of play. The reversal of the most productive Quarterback-receiver duo accounted for the Owls' next TD. Clement and Dillard went into the game with an NCAA-record 50 touchdown passes for their careers, but Dillard was the passer and Clement the receiver on their 13-yard scoring play in the third quarter. Then, in the fourth quarter, Clement made it 51 TD passes to Dillard with an 18-yard play to put the score at 38-0. A two-yard run by Kirk Elsworth and a 13-yard pass from Tim Hiller to Schneider Julien gave Western Michigan (9-4) its only points late in the game. The game was watched by 58, 880, the fourth-largest crowd to ever see a bowl game in Houston.

2008 Holiday Bowl

The 2008 Pacific Life Holiday Bowl was played on December 30, 2008 at Qualcomm Stadium in San Diego, California between the Oklahoma State Cowboys and the Oregon Ducks, and nationally televised by ESPN. The Ducks won the contest, 42-31.

2008 Holiday Bowl	Line	1	-	2	-	3	-	4	-	Final
#13 Oklahoma State	(-2.5)	17	-	0	-	7	-	7	-	31
#15 Oregon	(76.0)	7	-	0	-	21	-	14	-	42

Scoring Summary
Oklahoma State – Bailey 45 yard Field goal
Oklahoma State – Bryant 33 yard pass from Robinson (Bailey kick)
Oregon – Johnson 76 yard run (Flint kick)
Oklahoma State – Hunter 3 yard run (Bailey kick)
Oregon – Masoli 1 yard run (Flint kick)
Oregon – Masoli 41 yard run (Flint kick)
Oklahoma State – Hunter 4 yard run (Bailey kick)
Oregon – Masoli 17 yard run (Flint kick)
Oklahoma State – Robinson 1 yard run (Bailey kick)
Oregon – Williams 20 yard pass from Masoli (Flint kick)
Oregon – Blount 29 yard run (Flint kick)

Associated Press Holiday Bowl Game Summary - Jeremiah Masoli and Oregon were a perfect fit for the high-scoring Holiday Bowl. Masoli ran through and over Oklahoma State's defense for three touchdowns and threw for another to lead the No. 17 Ducks to a 42-31 win over the No. 13 Cowboys in a wild, record-setting Holiday Bowl on Tuesday night. Masoli, a junior college transfer, quickly moved up from No. 3 on the depth chart this season due to injuries. He was recruited because Coach Mike Bellotti thought he'd be a great passer, then proved to be quite the runner. Masoli scored on option keepers of 1, 41 and 17 yards in the third quarter, then threw a 20-yard scoring pass to Jaison Williams in the fourth quarter. Masoli ran over OSU free safety Quinton Moore on his 41-yard jaunt. There were big runs, big passes and big hits in a game showcasing two of the nation's most prolific offenses, both of which feature the spread option led by running QBs. Oregon gained 565 yards and OSU had 469. Oregon finished 10-3, the fourth time it's had double-digit wins in Bellotti's 14 seasons as coach. Oklahoma State finished 9-4 under Mike Gundy, the winning Quarterback for Oklahoma State in the 1988 Holiday Bowl. The Holiday Bowl has a history of wild finishes, and this one had five lead changes in the second half.
Oregon's LeGarrette Blount put an exclamation point on the victory with a 29-yard touchdown run during which he hurdled Moore and stiff-armed cornerback Perrish Cox with 3 minutes to play. With the Ducks trailing 17-7, Walter Thurmond returned the second-half kickoff 91 yards to the 3. Masoli scored his first TD two plays later. Masoli gained 106 yards on 16 carries. He completed 18 of 32 passes for 258 yards.
Oregon's Jeremiah Johnson ran 12 times for 119 yards, including a 76-yard TD that eclipsed one of Barry Sanders' Holiday Bowl records. Blount's 74 yards on seven carries gave him 1,002 yards for the season. He and Johnson became the second duo in school history to each have 1,000 or more yards. Johnson finished with 1,201 yards. Oregon and Oklahoma State each erased records from that Holiday Bowl 20 years ago, when Sanders, the Heisman Trophy winner, ran for 222 yards and five TDs in a 62-14 romp over Wyoming. Johnson's 76-yard touchdown run in the first quarter eclipsed Sanders' 67-yard TD in 1988 as the longest run from scrimmage in the Holiday Bowl. Johnson took an inside handoff and seemed bottled up, but worked his way to the left sideline, where he picked up three blocks on his way to the end zone. Oklahoma State wide receiver Dez Bryant set Holiday Bowl records with 13 catches for 167 yards, among them a 33-yard TD that gave the Cowboys a 10-0 lead in the first quarter. The 13 catches were a career high for Bryant, who twice was forced out of the game with a knee injury. The old Holiday Bowl records were 11 catches by BYU's David Mills in 1984 and Texas' Roy Williams in 2001, and 163 yards by Oklahoma State's Hart Lee Dykes in 1988. Bryant said the outcome "probably would have been different" if he hadn't been injured. Oklahoma State Quarterback Zac Robinson took a few big hits yet threw for 329 yards, completing 27 of 50 passes, and ran 16 times for 54 yards and a score. Oregon trailed 17-7 at halftime but came back on Masoli's first two scoring runs to go ahead 21-17 by midway through the third quarter. Oklahoma State's Kendall Hunter answered with his second TD of the game, from 4 yards, before Masoli scored again. The Cowboys took their last lead, 31-28, when Robinson scored on a 1-yard run early in the fourth quarter. Masoli's TD pass to Williams gave the Ducks the lead for good, 35-31. The Ducks dedicated the win to Todd Doxey, a redshirt freshman from San Diego who drowned last summer in Oregon's McKenzie River.

2008 Music City Bowl

The 2008 Gaylord Hotels Music City Bowl was the eleventh edition of the bowl game played at LP Field in Nashville, Tennessee. The game was played on Wednesday, December 31, 2008. The game, telecast on ESPN, pitted the Vanderbilt Commodores against the Boston College Eagles. The Commodores, playing near their Nashville campus, won 16–14, earned their first bowl win in exactly 53 years, and completed their first winning season since 1982.

2008 Music City Bowl	Line	1	-	2	-	3	-	4	-	Final
Boston College	(-4.0)	0	-	7	-	0	-	7	-	14
Vanderbilt	(40.5)	6	-	0	-	7	-	3	-	16

Scoring Summary
Vanderbilt - Hahnfeldt 42 yard Field goal
Vanderbilt - Hahnfeldt 26 yard Field goal
Boston College - Harris 4 yard pass from Davis (Aponavicius kick)
Vanderbilt - Richardson recovered fumble in end zone (Hahnfeldt kick)
Boston College - Larmond 55 yard pass from Davis (Aponavicius kick)
Vanderbilt - Hahnfeldt 45 yard Field goal

Associated Press Music City Bowl Game Summary - Vanderbilt used to be called the worst team in the Southeastern Conference. Cellar dwellers. The private school that just didn't belong in a power football league. No more. Vanderbilt won a bowl game for the first time in exactly 53 years, with Bryant Hahnfeldt kicking a 45-yard field goal with 3:26 left Wednesday for a 16-14 win over Boston College in the Music City Bowl. Vandy hadn't even played in a bowl since 1982 -- the SEC's longest drought. The victory gave the Commodores (7-6) their first winning season since that season. This is just the fourth time in the past 50 years that Vanderbilt has won seven games in a season. So maybe it was only appropriate that Hahnfeldt, a Nashville native who grew up only a few miles away from LP Field where this game was played, provided the winning margin. Hahnfeldt, tied his career-high with three field goals. Boston College (9-5) had won eight straight bowl games, the nation's longest active streak. Playing in a bowl for the 10th straight season, the Eagles also missed a chance at finishing with at least 10 wins for a third straight season. BC lost despite giving up only 200 yards and allowing Vandy to convert only one of its 15 third downs. The Eagles got the ball twice after Hahnfeldt's third field goal. They had to punt the first time, then Myron Lewis picked off Dominique Davis with 1:36 left after having been beaten for the TD that put Boston College up 14-13. Vanderbilt had some of its stars of seasons past cheering from the sideline in Denver Broncos Quarterback Jay Cutler and Chicago Bears teammates Chris Williams and Earl Bennett. PGA Tour golfer Brandt Snedeker also was on hand hoping for his alma mater's first bowl win since beating Auburn 25-13 on Dec. 31, 1955, at the Gator Bowl. They didn't see much offense against a Boston College defense that came in ranked sixth in the nation in yards allowed and tops in the country in turnovers. Vandy scored its lone touchdown when freshman Sean Richardson fell on a punt that bounced off the left knee of BC's Paul Anderson with 10:35 left in the third. Officials huddled, then ruled it a touchdown and a replay review upheld the decision. Vanderbilt played musical chairs at Quarterback, giving redshirt freshman Larry Smith his first career start in the program's biggest game in decades. Chris Nickson also played, and Mackenzi Adams even got in for one play -- on which he was roughed by Eagles linebacker Mark Herzlich, the Atlantic Coast Conference's defensive player of the year, to help set up Hahnfeldt's winning kick. Herzlich said he was just trying to make a play. But Eagles end Jim Ramella also was flagged for a face mask on that game-winning drive for Vanderbilt. The two penalties provided 30 of the 48 yards in that drive. The difference came from Vandy punter Brett Upson. The bowl MVP averaged 42.6 yards on nine punts with a long of 58. A Vanderbilt defense that ranked second in the SEC for interceptions had two more picks for the game's only turnovers. Davis, in only his third career start, put the Eagles up 14-13 with a 55-yard TD pass to Colin Larmond Jr. with 6:38 remaining. The Commodores opened by scoring field goals of 42 and 26 yards from Hahnfeldt for a 6-0 lead. But the Eagles led 7-6 at halftime thanks to Davis' 4-yard TD pass to Montel Harris with 1:27 left in the second quarter. The Eagles lost center Matt Tennant to an injured left elbow early in the second and punt returner Rich Gunnel to an injury. Vanderbilt got its best player hurt a play later. All-SEC cornerback D.J. Moore helped break up Davis' pass to Ifeanyi Momah, and safety Ryan Hamilton intercepted the ball at the Vandy 15. But Momah rolled over Moore's left ankle, and he limped to the sideline. Moore got his ankle taped and played in the second half but couldn't finish. The junior said after the game he would leave early for the NFL draft.

2008 Armed Forces Bowl

The 2008 Bell Helicopter Armed Forces Bowl was the sixth edition of the annual bowl game and featured the Houston Cougars against the Air Force Falcons on December 31, 2008 at Amon G. Carter Stadium on the campus of Texas Christian University in Fort Worth, Texas and telecast on ESPN nationally. The Falcons made their second straight Armed Forces Bowl appearance, having lost the previous year to California, while the Cougars made their fourth straight bowl appearance, having most recently lost to TCU. The Cougars defeated the Falcons 34-28, for their first bowl win since the 1980 Garden State Bowl ending an eight-bowl game losing streak.

2008 Armed Forces Bowl	Line	1	-	2	-	3	-	4	-	Final
Houston	(-4.0)	17	-	0	-	7	-	10	-	34
Air Force	(64.5)	7	-	10	-	3	-	8	-	28

Scoring Summary
Houston - Beall 1 yard run (Mannisto kick)
Air Force - Tew 2 yard run (Harrison kick)
Houston - Keenum 1 yard run (Mannisto kick)
Houston - Mannisto 22 yard Field goal
Air Force - Jefferson 5 yard run (Harrison kick)
Air Force - Harrison 44 yard Field goal
Houston - Keenum 4 yard run (Mannisto kick)
Air Force - Harrison 37 yard Field goal
Houston - Kohn 13 yard pass from Keenum (Mannisto kick)
Air Force - Tew 2 yard run (Harrison kick)
Houston - Mannisto 37 yard Field goal

Associated Press Armed Forces Bowl Game Summary - Kevin Sumlin inherited the nearly three-decade postseason winless drought when he became Houston's coach after last season. Senior linebacker Phillip Hunt had to experience the postseason futility with the Cougars. Such as giving Houston its first bowl victory since 1980, beating Air Force 34-28 in the Armed Forces Bowl on Wednesday to end an eight-game postseason losing streak. Sophomore Quarterback Case Keenum ran for two touchdowns, threw for another and became only the second Houston Quarterback to pass for more than 5,000 yards in a season. Bryce Beall, a freshman, ran for 135 yards and a score. A month after being denied a trip to the C-USA title game with a loss to crosstown rival Rice in the regular season finale, Houston (8-5) avoided a record it didn't want to share with Notre Dame. The Irish won the Hawaii Bowl last week to end their NCAA-record bowl losing streak at nine. In a rematch of a hurricane-disrupted game 3 1/2 months ago that Air Force won, Houston never trailed after the Falcons (8-5) fumbled the opening kickoff and Beall scored on a 1-yard run only 93 seconds into the game. But the Cougars had to overcome two fourth-quarter turnovers, including a fumble at the goal line by Beall. Beall appeared to break into the end zone, but the ball popped loose. Officials initially marked him down at the 1, but after a lengthy review ruled that he fumbled in the end zone and Air Force recovered. But the Falcons failed to get a first down, punting after Hunt's school-record 34th career sack, his second of the game. Air Force ended the season with three consecutive losses, including the regular season finale last month on the same field when the Falcons lost 44-10 to TCU. On the third play after the punt, Keenum hit Andre Kohn for a 13-yard TD for a 31-20 lead with 11 minutes left after Beall's 24-yard burst up the middle. But Keenum, whose 4-yard keeper to start the second half put Houston ahead to stay, later had a pass that deflected off a receiver and was intercepted by Aaron Kirchoff. Fullback Jared Tew finished that drive with five straight carries for 27 yards, the last a 2-yard score that got the Falcons within 31-28 after a 2-point conversion. Tew, getting his first career start because of an injury to starter Todd Newell, finished with 27 carries for 149 yards -- only 30 yards fewer than he had in nine regular season games. But Jordan Mannisto kicked a 37-yard field goal before Air Force's final drive. With Hurricane Ike approaching the Texas coast, the first meeting between Houston and Air Force on Sept. 13 was moved from Houston north to the SMU campus. Kickoff was switched from mid-afternoon to mid-morning and played in windy and rainy conditions in a near-empty stadium. The rematch was under sunny skies before an announced crowd of 40,127. Air Force didn't complete a pass in the first game but held on to win 31-28 after building an early 24-point lead against an understandably distracted Houston team. This time, Spencer Armstrong fumbled the opening kickoff return, though the Falcons quickly tied the game on Tew's 2-yard run. But Houston scored on all three first-quarter possessions, going ahead 17-7 after Keenum's 1-yard run and a 22-yard field goal after Hunt recovered a fumble. Air Force tied the game at 17 on Ryan Harrison's 44-yard field goal with 2:28 left in the first half, and Tyron Carrier fumbled the ensuing kickoff. Harrison then had a 55-yard kick that went through the uprights, but Houston had called timeout and his second try was wide left. The Cougars got to the 13 after an 11-yard run by Beall, still with 8 seconds and a timeout. Carrier caught a screen pass and was running at an angle toward the sideline when he suddenly cut up to try to avoid a defender. The freshman was short of the end zone and time expired.

2008 Sun Bowl

The 2008 Brut Sun Bowl was played on December 31, 2008 at Sun Bowl stadium on the campus of the University of Texas at El Paso in El Paso, Texas. The 75th annual contest pitted the Pittsburgh Panthers and the Oregon State Beavers. Pittsburgh previously appeared in the Sun Bowl in 1975 and 1989. Oregon State previously appeared in the Sun Bowl only once, in 2006. Entering the contest, the teams had a combined 3-0 record in Sun Bowls. Oregon State won 3–0, the lowest scoring bowl game since a 0–0 tie between Air Force and TCU in the 1959 Cotton Bowl and the lowest-scoring Sun Bowl since a 0–0 tie between Arizona State and The Catholic University of America on January 1, 1940. It was the first shutout loss for the Panthers since 1996. This game, however, was special because the only points were scored on a field goal kicked off a botched hold. This game marked the 41st consecutive telecast by CBS Sports. No other network and bowl game has been paired for a longer period.

2008 Sun Bowl	Line	1	-	2	-	3	-	4	-	Final
#24 Oregon State	(-2.5)	0	-	3	-	0	-	0	-	3
#18 Pittsburgh	(52.0)	0	-	0	-	0	-	0	-	0

Scoring Summary
Oregon State – Kahut 44 yard Field goal

Associated Press Sun Bowl Game Summary - Three points, 20 punts and 10 sacks. Go ahead and say it was unsightly, but Oregon State coach Mike Riley saw nothing short of a masterpiece. In the lowest-scoring major bowl game in a half-century, the Beavers shut down No. 20 Pittsburgh 3-0 Wednesday in the Sun Bowl on Justin Kahut's 44-yard field goal. The defensive struggle went on all day. Pitt kicker Connor Lee tried a 58-yard field goal in the closing minutes but the ball, helped by a steady wind, dropped just short of the crossbar. Not since Air Force and TCU played to 0-0 standoff in the Cotton Bowl on Jan. 1, 1959, had a bowl produced so few points. It was also the lowest-scoring Sun Bowl since a scoreless tie in 1940 between Catholic and Arizona State. The Beavers (9-4) improved to 5-0 in bowls since Riley began his second stint as their coach in 2003. Kahut provided the only points with his kick shortly before halftime. Riley liked the way his team rebounded from a 65-38 loss to rival Oregon that denied Oregon State a Rose Bowl berth. Riley stood at the interview table and added: "That is well said." Pitt (9-4), making its first bowl appearance since the 2004 season and the first under Wannstedt, led the Big East in scoring this season, averaging 29.3 points per game. The Panthers managed just 178 total yards. There was no sign of offense in El Paso, not with McCoy held to 85 yards rushing after averaging 116.9 yards per game this season. Quarterback Bill Stull was 7-for-24 for 52 yards with one interception. The Beavers also won without their spectacular brothers, tailback Jacquizz Rodgers and receiver James Rodgers, both out with shoulder injuries. Reserve tailback Jeremy Francis had 76 yards rushing and Moevao was 21-for-42 for 193 yards passing with two interceptions. The Beavers finished with 273 total yards. The Panthers finally got a spark early in the fourth quarter when T.J. Porter returned a punt 36 yards to Oregon State's 42. But three plays later, the big return was wasted because Butler, who had four sacks, stripped Stull and recovered the fumble. Oregon State led 3-0 after Kahut connected on his field goal with 2:18 remaining before halftime. He later missed a 37-yard attempt midway through the third period. The Beavers came up empty on the best touchdown opportunity by either team. Officials ruled tight end John Reese was out of bounds on an apparent 9-yard TD reception 10 seconds before the break.

2008 Insight Bowl

The 2008 Insight Bowl was played at Sun Devil Stadium in Tempe, Arizona. The game, in its 20th year of existence, was played on Wednesday, December 31, 2008. The game, which was telecast on NFL Network, featured the Minnesota Golden Gophers from the Big Ten Conference against the Kansas Jayhawks of the Big 12 Conference, with the Jayhawks winning, 42-21.

2008 Insight Bowl	Line	1	-	2	-	3	-	4	-	Final
Minnesota	(59.0)	14	-	0	-	0	-	7	-	21
Kansas	(-9.5)	14	-	14	-	7	-	7	-	42

Scoring Summary
Kansas – Briscoe 60 yard pass from Reesing (Branstetter kick)
Minnesota – Hoese 1 yard run (Monroe kick)
Minnesota – Hoese 2 yard run (Monroe kick)
Kansas – Meier 4 yard pass from Reesing (Branstetter kick)
Kansas – Briscoe 6 yard pass from Reesing (Branstetter kick)
Kansas – Wilson 4 yard pass from Reesing (Branstetter kick)
Kansas – Briscoe 32 yard pass from Reesing (Branstetter kick)
Minnesota – Decker 6 yard pass from Weber (Monroe kick)
Kansas – Sharp 2 yard run (Branstetter kick)

Associated Press Insight Bowl Game Summary - As night fell in the desert, the haunting Rock Chalk Chant filled Sun Devil Stadium. It was the perfect way for Kansas to celebrate a decisive 42-21 victory over Minnesota in the Insight Bowl on Wednesday. Indeed, the Jayhawks (8-5) have won three straight bowl games, a first for a school renowned for its hoops prowess. The Insight Bowl also marked Kansas' first back-to-back bowl appearances. Kansas sliced up the Golden Gophers (7-6) with a precision passing attack directed by Quarterback Todd Reesing, who threw for four scores. Reesing's favorite target was Dezmon Briscoe, who caught a game-record 14 passes for 201 yards and three touchdowns on his way to game MVP honors. Kerry Meier also had 10 catches for 113 yards, and he caught one touchdown pass and threw another one. Reesing said KU's plan was simple. Reesing completed 27 of 35 passes, hitting on a school-record 14 straight passes in the first half. He threw for 313 yards and was intercepted once. Reesing, a junior from Austin, Texas, has one year left to add to his legacy as the most prolific passer in KU history. He improved to 20-6 as a starter. Eric Decker caught eight passes for 149 yards and a touchdown for the Golden Gophers (7-6), who finished the season on a five-game losing streak and have lost their last three bowl games. But the Gophers can take consolation in earning a bowl invitation one year after a 1-11 season. They started this season 7-1 and cracked The Associated Press Top 25 before a last-second Homecoming loss to Northwestern sent them into a tailspin. Minnesota came to Tempe hoping to erase memories of its last Insight trip, two years ago. The Gophers led Texas Tech 38-7 midway through the third quarter, only to watch the Red Raiders rally for a 44-41 overtime victory -- the biggest comeback in major-college bowl history. This time, Minnesota found itself down by a touchdown after 11 seconds on a sparkling 73-degree afternoon. On the game's first snap, Reesing rolled away from pressure and found Briscoe down the left sideline for a 60-yard scoring play. The Golden Gophers responded quickly to the early deficit. On their first offensive snap, receiver David Pittman hit Decker for a 75-yard pass to the KU 12, and three plays later Jon Hoese bulled over from a yard out to tie it at 7. It was the first collegiate carry for Hoese, a sophomore. Nine minutes later, he scored again, on a 2-yard run, to give Minnesota a 14-7 lead. Mangino said the Gophers surprised KU with some formations they hadn't used during the season. But KU adjusted quickly and throttled Minnesota for most of the last three quarters, even stuffing them on fourth-and-goal at the 1 in the third quarter. KU tied it at 14 on a 4-yard pass from Reesing to Meier late in the first quarter. Reesing added two more touchdown passes -- a 6-yarder to Briscoe and a 4-yarder to Johnathan Wilson -- to give Kansas a commanding 28-14 halftime lead. Minnesota cut it to 35-21 on a 6-yard pass from Adam Weber to Decker early in the fourth quarter, but the Gophers' offense stalled after that. Weber was 19-of-34 for 176 yards and a touchdown. Minnesota's loss dropped the Big Ten to 0-3 in bowls, while the Big 12 improved to 2-1, with both victories coming against Big Ten schools.

2008 Chick-Fil-A Peach Bowl

The 2008 Chick-fil-A Bowl was the 41st annual edition of the Chick-fil-A Bowl, formerly known as the Peach Bowl and the Chick-fil-A Peach Bowl. It pitted the Georgia Tech Yellow Jackets against the Louisiana State Tigers in Atlanta, Georgia. Georgia Tech represented the Atlantic Coast Conference (ACC) and their competitor was from the Southeastern Conference (SEC).

2008 Chick-Fil-A Peach Bowl	Line	1	-	2	-	3	-	4	-	Final
LSU	(52.5)	7	-	28	-	3	-	0	-	38
#14 Georgia Tech	(-4.5)	3	-	0	-	0	-	0	-	3

Scoring Summary
LSU – Scott 2 yard run (David kick)
Georgia Tech –Blair 24 yard Field goal
LSU – Scott 4 yard run (David kick)
LSU – Scott 1 yard run (David kick)
LSU – Dickson 25 yard pass from Jefferson (David kick)
LSU – Williams 17 yard run (David kick)
LSU – Davis 53 yard Field goal

Associated Press Chick-Fil-A Peach Bowl Game Summary - One year after winning a national championship, unranked LSU found renewed reason to hope for a return to glory. Charles Scott ran for three touchdowns; freshman Quarterback Jordan Jefferson completed his first nine passes and LSU made big plays on special teams in a surprisingly easy 38-3 victory win over Georgia Tech in the Chick-fil-A Bowl on Wednesday night. LSU outscored the No. 14 Yellow Jackets 28-0 in the second quarter and led 35-3 at halftime. Scott, who had 65 yards rushing, had two touchdowns in the decisive quarter. LSU (8-5) lost three of its last four regular-season games but regrouped for the dominant bowl victory. Jefferson was 16-of-25 for 142 yards and a touchdown. He added nine carries for 33 yards. The biggest special teams plays all fell in LSU's favor. LSU recovered an onside kick and a Georgia Tech fumbled punt return and made a fourth-down stop on the Yellow Jackets' surprising fake punt from Tech's 22. LSU turned the fumbled punt and stop on the fake punt into quick touchdowns while outscoring Georgia Tech 28-0 in the second quarter. As if to affirm its mastery of special teams, LSU pulled off a successful fake punt in the fourth quarter, with punter Brady Dalfrey running for 21 yards for the first down. LSU led 38-3 when Miles called for the fake, and Georgia Tech fans booed the decision. Georgia Tech (9-4) was denied its first 10-win season since 1998. The Yellow Jackets lost three turnovers, including a fumble by Quarterback Josh Nesbitt on a fourth-down run from the LSU 10 with 2:37 remaining. Scott scored on runs of 1, 2 and 4 yards. Backup tailback Keiland Williams added an 18-yard touchdown run with 1:27 left in the first half. The Tigers' defense, a weakness most of the season, was rarely fooled by Georgia Tech's spread option attack. Nesbitt completed a pass to top running back Jonathan Dwyer for 40 yards on the Yellow Jackets' first play, but that was the only first down of the opening drive. The Yellow Jackets held the ball for 13 plays on their next drive, but LSU cornerback Patrick Peterson deflected a third-down pass for Demaryius Thomas from the Tigers' 7. Georgia Tech had to settle for Scott Blair's 24-yard field goal after holding the ball for more than 7 minutes. After Scott's second touchdown run gave LSU a 14-3 lead early in the second quarter, the Tigers recovered Josh Jasper's onside kick. Stefoin Francois recovered the ball at the LSU 45. LSU had to punt four plays later, but Andrew Smith fumbled the punt at the Georgia Tech 19. Ron Brooks recovered for the Tigers, setting up Scott's third touchdown run for a 21-3 lead. Georgia Tech attempted a fake punt on a fourth-and-8 play from its 22, but defensive end Derrick Morgan gained only 2 yards. Only two plays later, Jefferson completed the touchdown pass to Dickson. The three touchdowns gave Scott 18 for the season, one behind LaBrandon Toefield's school-record 19 in 2001. Colt David's 53-yard field goal late in the third quarter was the longest in the bowl's history. Nesbitt completed a 47-yard pass to Marcus Wright, leaving the Georgia Tech at the LSU 16 as the third quarter ended. The Yellow Jackets couldn't take advantage of the big play, as Nesbitt was sacked by Lazarius Levingston on fourth down from the 13. Nesbitt was 8-for-24 passing for 150 yards with an interception. The Tigers improved to 5-0 in the Chick-fil-A Bowl, including a similarly lopsided 40-3 win over Miami in the 2005 game.

2009 Gator Bowl

The 2009 Gator Bowl was played on January 1, 2009. It featured the Nebraska Cornhuskers, who finished tied for first in the Big 12 Conference's North Division with Missouri, and the Clemson Tigers, who finished fifth in the Atlantic Coast Conference's Atlantic Division. This game was the first meeting between the Clemson Tigers and the Nebraska Cornhuskers since the 1982 Orange Bowl where Clemson defeated Nebraska for their first and only national title.

2009 Gator Bowl	Line	1	-	2	-	3	-	4	-	Final
Nebraska	(55.5)	0	-	3	-	20	-	3	-	26
Clemson	(-2.5)	0	-	14	-	7	-	0	-	21

Scoring Summary
Clemson – McDaniel 28 yard fumble return (Bucholz kick)
Nebraska – Henery 48 yard field goal
Clemson – Kelly 25 yard pass from Harper (Bucholz kick)
Nebraska – Swift 17 yard pass from Ganz (Henery kick)
Clemson – Ford 41 yard pass from Harper (Bucholz kick)
Nebraska – Peterson 19 yard pass from Ganz (Henery kick)
Nebraska – Henery 28 yard Field goal
Nebraska – Henery 28 yard Field goal
Nebraska – Henery 22 yard Field goal

Associated Press Gator Bowl Game Summary - Nebraska Quarterback Joe Ganz was sprawled out on the ground, trainers huddled around him, teammates, coaches and fans wondering whether he would be able to continue playing. Ganz eventually made his way to the sideline, cleared his head, got back in the game and ended up hoisting the Gator Bowl's most valuable player trophy. His comeback provided an appropriate ending for Nebraska's season. After all, the Cornhuskers enjoyed one of college football's best turnarounds. Ganz shook off a horrible first half and a slight concussion, threw for two touchdowns and led Nebraska to a 26-21 victory against Clemson in the Gator Bowl, giving the storied program plenty of optimism following coach Bo Pelini's first season. Nebraska (9-4) ended the season with a four-game winning streak, including a victory against rival Colorado, won six of its final seven games and had success in a January bowl game for the first time in nine years. The senior had a fumble late in the first half that was returned 28 yards for a touchdown and threw an interception in the final minute that was returned 63 yards and led to another score. The Tigers (7-6) took a 14-3 lead into the locker room, but Ganz brought Nebraska back with a 20-point third quarter. He also bounced back from that bone-crushing hit. Although Nebraska didn't score a touchdown after his return, Ganz's value was clear when backup Patrick Witt fumbled on his first play. Clemson picked up the loose ball and returned it for a touchdown and a 27-23 lead, but officials overturned the call after review. Ganz was back the next series. Ganz threw a 17-yard touchdown pass to Nate Swift to open the second half, then hooked up with Todd Peterson for a 19-yard score. Both came on third-and-long situations. Ganz completed 10 of 15 passes for 133 yards in the second half and finished 19-of-36 for 236 yards. Alex Henery kicked four field goals, including three in the second half. Quentin Castille, filling in for injured starter Roy Helu Jr. (knee infection), ran for 125 yards. And Nebraska's defense held Clemson to 91 yards in the second half. Swinney was hoping his team would maintain its late-season momentum. The Tigers won four of their last five games after a 3-3 start that prompted longtime coach Tommy Bowden to resign. Clemson kept this one close by forcing field goals. After Henery's fourth, the Tigers had a final chance to go ahead. They advanced to the Nebraska 10 with

1:54 remaining, but Eric Hagg batted down a pass on first down and sacked Cullen Harper for a 16-yard loss on the next play. Harper nearly hooked up with C.J. Spiller on third down, but Matt O'Hanlon knocked the ball out of Spiller's hands in the end zone. Harper misfired on the final play, and the Huskers ran out the clock from there. The Tigers scored all three of their touchdowns off turnovers. But also had too many of their own. Harper threw two interceptions and was sacked five times, and Spiller and James Davis ran for just 43 yards combined.

2009 Outback Bowl

The 2009 Outback Bowl was played on January 1, 2009 at Raymond James Stadium in Tampa, Florida. The game was telecast on ESPN. The game pitted the South Carolina Gamecocks against the Iowa Hawkeyes. Iowa jumped out to a huge lead, leading South Carolina 21-0 at halftime and 31-0 at the end of the third quarter. Shonn Greene, the MVP, had 30 rushes for 132 yards and three rushing touchdowns.

2009 Outback Bowl	Line	1	-	2	-	3	-	4	-	Final
Iowa	(-4.0)	14	-	7	-	10	-	0	-	31
South Carolina	(43.0)	0	-	0	-	0	-	10	-	10

Scoring Summary
Iowa – Stross 6 yard pass from Stanzi (Murray kick)
Iowa – Greene 1 yard run (Murray kick)
Iowa – Greene 1 yard run (Murray kick)
Iowa – Murray 18 yard Field goal
Iowa – Greene 11 yard run (Murray kick)
South Carolina – Cook 10 yard pass from Smelley (Succop kick)
South Carolina – Succop 48 yard Field goal

Associated Press Outback Bowl Game Summary - From carrying couches to an All-American carrying a football. Now, Big Ten MVP Shonn Greene figures he's ready for the next level. The Iowa running back turned Thursday's Outback Bowl into a farewell party, leading the Hawkeyes past South Carolina 31-10 and then announcing he intends to skip his senior season to enter the NFL draft. Greene ran for 121 yards and three touchdowns. He rushed for more than 100 yards in all 13 of Iowa's games, scored in all but one, and won the Doak Walker Award as the nation's best running back. Greene, of Sicklerville, N.J., finished with school single-season records of 1,850 yards and 20 TDs. Iowa (9-4) won for the sixth time in seven games since losing three straight to fall to 3-3. South Carolina (7-6) lost three straight down the stretch while being outscored 118-30. Greene scored on a pair of 1-yard runs to help Iowa build a 21-0 halftime lead, then added an 11-yarder to make it 31-0 late in the third quarter. South Carolina scored on Chris Smelley's 10-yard TD pass to Jared Cook and Ryan Succop's 48-yard field goal in the fourth quarter. After struggling offensively in lopsided losses to Florida and Clemson, Gamecocks Coach Steve Spurrier decided to start Quarterback Stephen Garcia, a highly regarded redshirt freshman from Tampa who was the centerpiece of his recruiting class in 2007. But Garcia, who nearly undermined his career by being arrested twice within his first month on campus, turned the ball over four times in the first half and was replaced by Smelley after going 9-for-18 for 79 yards and three interceptions. The 20-year-old's homecoming and third career start turned sour in a hurry. His first pass was intercepted and returned 29 yards to set up an Iowa touchdown, then the dual-threat Quarterback fumbled on his first run to give the Gamecocks turnovers on two of their first four offensive plays. The next two South Carolina possessions ended with interceptions. After Bradley Fletcher picked off Garcia in the end zone, Iowa drove 80 yards to take a 21-0 lead on Greene's second touchdown. Ricky Stanzi was intercepted twice before halftime, but neither mistake really hurt the Hawkeyes. Iowa was trying to turn's Garcia's third interception into a quick TD when South Carolina's Chris Culliver made a leaping pick in the end zone. Smelley, who started nine games for South Carolina this season, replaced Garcia at the start of the second half. Moe Brown fumbled on the Quarterback's first completion to set up an Iowa field goal, but the Gamecocks finally had some success moving the ball the rest of the game. Stanzi was 13-of-19 for 147 yards, including a 6-yard TD throw to Trey Stross on the first drive of the game. Smelley finished 16-of-31 for 179 yards and no interceptions. Spurrier fell to 7-8 in bowl games, 1-2 at South Carolina. None of the previous teams making postseason appearances under him scored fewer points.

2009 Capital One Bowl

The 2009 Capital One Bowl was held on January 1, 2009 at the Citrus Bowl in Orlando, Florida. The Georgia Bulldogs of the Southeastern Conference defeated the Michigan State Spartans of the Big Ten Conference by a score of 24–12. The game was televised to a national audience on ABC. The game was supposed to be a "showdown" between MSU RB Javon Ringer and Georgia RB Knowshon Moreno, but both players combined for only 43 carries and 109 yards, with Ringer scoring on a rushing touchdown and Moreno on a receiving.

2009 Capital One Bowl	Line	1	-	2	-	3	-	4	-	Final
#16 Georgia	(-8.0)	3	-	0	-	14	-	7	-	24
#19 Michigan State	(54.5)	3	-	3	-	0	-	6	-	12

Scoring Summary
Georgia – Walsh 32 yard Field goal
Michigan State – Swenson 20 yard Field goal
Michigan State – Swenson 32 yard Field goal
Georgia – Moore 35 yard pass from Stafford (Walsh kick)
Georgia – White 21 yard pass from Stafford (Walsh kick)
Michigan State – Ringer 1 yard run (Pass failed)
Georgia – Moreno 21 yard pass from Stafford (Walsh kick)

Associated Press Capital One Bowl Game Summary - Matthew Stafford gave the type of performance in the Capital One Bowl that'd make a fitting finale to his excellent Georgia career. Whether this was his last game with the Bulldogs, the junior Quarterback hasn't decided. Stafford threw three touchdown passes in the final 18 minutes against No. 18 Michigan State, hitting Knowshon Moreno for the clinching score in the 15th-ranked Bulldogs' 24-12 victory Thursday. Ranked No. 1 by The Associated Press to start the season, the Bulldogs (10-3) gave coach Mark Richt his sixth bowl win in eight tries and put a happy ending on a season that didn't live up to expectations. The first half was ugly for Stafford, projected to be an early first-round NFL draft pick, and Georgia. He was just 6-for-14 and an interception in the first half and Michigan State (9-4) led 6-3. In the second half, he looked more like the Quarterback NFL teams covet. He completed 14 of his final 17 throws, including three TD passes. Figuring out Stafford proved to be a tough task for the Spartans in the second half. Stafford started the comeback by directing a 10-play, 96-yard drive midway through the third quarter. He went 6-for-6 for 92 yards and capped it with 35-yard touchdown toss to Michael Moore. Michigan State coach Mark Dantonio said Georgia made a very effective adjustment in the second half. Stafford was picked as the game's MVP, completing his performance by showing a nice touch in threading a 21-yard TD pass to Moreno late in the fourth quarter. Stafford set a single-season school record with 25 touchdown passes. Georgia's defense helped keep the Bulldogs in the game in the first half. The Bulldogs had four sacks and held an opponent to the fewest points since Sept. 30. The Bulldogs were able to make Michigan State Quarterback Brian Hoyer hurry his throws. Hoyer completed 16 of 31 passes for 159 yards with an interception and gave way to backup Kirk Cousins on a couple of first-half series. He threw 21 yards to Mark Dell on fourth-and-22 late in the fourth quarter and followed that with an interception in the final 40 seconds. The expected showdown between star running backs Javon Ringer and Moreno never materialized. Moreno ran for 62 yards on 23 carries; the All-American Ringer had 47 yards and a TD on 20 carries. Moreno, a third-year sophomore, is also facing a decision on whether to turn professional. Stafford and Aron White hooked up on a 21-yard TD toss with 9 seconds left in the third quarter to put Georgia up 17-6. Ringer scored on a 1-yard run midway through the fourth quarter -- his school-record 22nd -- to make it 17-12, but Hoyer's pass for a 2-point conversion was long. Balmy, 67-degree temperatures were near perfect but a 24-mph cross wind at the Citrus Bowl was a major factor, as both teams depended first on their ground games and star tailbacks with little to show for it. The Spartans got a pair of first-quarter turnovers in Georgia territory but could only turn them into a field goal to tie it at 3. Michigan State took a 6-3 lead with just over two minutes left in the first half on Brett Swenson's 32-yard field goal.

2009 Rose Bowl

The 2009 Rose Bowl, the 95th edition of the annual game, was played on Thursday, January 1, 2009 at the same-named stadium in Pasadena, California. Because of sponsorship by Citi, the first game in the 2009 edition of the Bowl Championship Series was officially titled the "Rose Bowl Game presented by citi". The contest was televised on ABC with a radio broadcast on ESPN Radio. Ticket prices for all seats in the Rose Bowl were listed at $145. The Rose Bowl Game was a contractual sell-out, with 64,500 tickets allocated to the participating teams and conferences. The remaining tickets went to the Tournament of Roses members, sponsors, City of Pasadena residents, and the general public. Scoring 24 unanswered points in the second quarter, the Pacific-10 Conference Champion University of Southern California Trojans defeated the Big Ten Conference co-champion, the Pennsylvania State University Nittany Lions, 38-24, for their third consecutive Rose Bowl victory (in their fourth consecutive appearance, having lost the 2006 BCS title game to the Texas Longhorns). The victory gave the Trojans their 24th Rose Bowl championship, the most by any team in the country. Quarterback Mark Sanchez scored five touchdowns, one rushing and four passing.

2009 Rose Bowl	Line	1	-	2	-	3	-	4	-	Final
#6 Penn State	(45.0)	7	-	0	-	0	-	17	-	24
#5 USC	(-9.5)	7	-	24	-	0	-	7	-	38

Scoring Summary
USC — Williams 27 yard pass from Sanchez (Buehler kick)
Penn State — Clark 9 yard run (Kelly kick)
USC — Sanchez 6 yard run (Buehler kick)
USC — Buehler 30 yard field goal
USC — Johnson 19 yard pass from Sanchez (Buehler kick)
USC — Gable 20 yard pass from Sanchez (Buehler kick)
Penn State — Williams 2 yard pass from Clark (Kelly kick)
USC — Johnson 45 yard pass from Sanchez (Buehler kick)
Penn State — Kelly 25 yard field goal
Penn State — Norwood 9 yard pass from Clark (Kelly kick)

Associated Press Rose Bowl Game Summary - Overwhelming from the start, Southern California put on a championship performance. Too bad for the Trojans, they weren't playing for the national title. Mark Sanchez passed for 413 yards and four touchdowns, USC dominated on defense and the fifth-ranked Trojans beat up No. 8 Penn State 38-24 Thursday in the Rose Bowl Game Presented by Citi. Penn State coach Joe Paterno watched from the press box, where he's been for most of the season because of hip problems. He couldn't have liked what he saw -- at one point in the first half, the TV camera caught him shaking his head as USC (12-1) rolled to a 31-7 lead. But even before the game, the 82-year-old coach said several times he thought USC was at least as good as any team in the country, perhaps better. What was thought to be a weak Pac-10 hurt the Trojans' chances to reach the national championship game in Miami. USC scored four touchdowns and a field goal on five consecutive first-half possessions for a 24-point halftime lead against a team that allowed only 12.4 points per game during the regular season. With the No. 1 defense in the nation, there was no way the Trojans would blow that kind of lead. The Nittany Lions (11-2) scored 17 points in the fourth quarter to make the final score respectable yet fell far short of their 40.2-point average. Paterno, who has won 383 games, including 23 bowls -- both records -- thought the Trojans were every bit as good as advertised. USC won 10 straight after losing to Oregon State, outscoring the opposition 380-80. The Trojans' 31 first-half points were the most they've scored in any of their record 33 Rose Bowl games. They spent most of the second half working the clock while their defense held Penn State in check until the fourth quarter. USC finished with 27 first downs and 474 yards of total offense. The Nittany Lions committed three turnovers and nine penalties for 72 yards. Sanchez, who completed 28-of-35 passes without being intercepted and finished the season with 3,207 passing yards and 34 touchdown throws, might have played his final game for USC. The strong-armed junior has said he will consider making himself available for the NFL draft. The deadline is Jan. 15. Sanchez became the third player to pass for more than 400 yards in the Rose Bowl. Afterward, many in the crowd of 93,293 chanted: "One more year, one more year" to Sanchez. Williams caught a career-high 10 passes for 162 yards and a touchdown and Ronald Johnson caught two TD passes. Daryll Clark completed 21-of-36 passes for 273 yards and two touchdowns with two interceptions. Evan Royster, who averaged 6.5 yards per carry in gaining 1,202 yards during the regular season, came out with an injured left knee in the first quarter after picking up 34 yards on six carries. Carroll's Trojans have won seven straight conference championships and played in seven consecutive BCS bowls -- both records. They're 6-1 in big games -- 5-0 against Big Ten teams such as Penn State -- and 82-9 since 2002, Carroll's second year on the job. They've also won 11 or more games in seven straight seasons -- another record. The Trojans have played in a record-tying four straight Rose Bowls, winning three straight since losing to Texas 41-38 with the national title on the line. They became the first team ever to win three consecutive Rose Bowls. Kaluka Maiava was the top defensive player, becoming the third straight USC linebacker to win that award. It became clear in the first quarter that Penn State's usually dominant defense was vulnerable. Sanchez threw a 27-yard scoring pass to Williams, capping an 86-yard drive. The Nittany Lions, who were 9 1/2-point underdogs, tied it on a 9-yard run by Clark, capping an 80-yard, nine-play drive. Maybe the Big Ten would finally hang in there against USC. Nope. Sanchez scored on a 6-yard Quarterback draw, completing an 80-yard drive that put USC on top for good. David Buehler's 30-yard field goal made it 17-7, and Sanchez threw scoring passes of 19 yards to Johnson and 20 yards to C.J. Gable in a 48-second span late in the second period for USC's 24-point halftime lead. Clark threw a 2-yard touchdown pass to Derrick Williams early in the fourth quarter, capping an 80-yard drive and trimming USC's lead to 31-14. The Trojans wasted no time in answering, going 82 yards on three plays, the last one a 45-yard scoring pass from Sanchez to a wide-open Johnson with 12:02 left. If there was going to be any drama on a typically clear and mild afternoon before a crowd of 93,293 in Pasadena that ended it.

2009 Orange Bowl

The 2009 FedEx Orange Bowl was the 75th edition of the annual Orange Bowl. It pitted the 2008 Atlantic Coast Conference (ACC) champion Virginia Tech Hokies against the Big East Conference champion Cincinnati Bearcats on January 1, 2009, at Dolphin Stadium in Miami Gardens, Florida. Virginia Tech defeated Cincinnati, 20–7.

2009 Orange Bowl	Line	1	-	2	-	3	-	4	-	Final
#12 Cincinnati	(-2.5)	7	-	0	-	0	-	0	-	7
#21 Virginia Tech	(42.0)	0	-	10	-	3	-	7	-	20

Scoring Summary
Cincinnati – Gilyard 15 yard pass from Pike (Rogers kick)
Virginia Tech – Taylor 17 yard run (Keys kick)
Virginia Tech – Keys 43 yard Field goal
Virginia Tech – Keys 35 yard Field goal
Virginia Tech – Evans 6 yard run (Keys kick)

Associated Press Orange Bowl Game Summary - For Virginia Tech, there was no mystery. The Hokies came into the Orange Bowl convinced that if the defense delivered, everything else would fall into place. Oh, how right they were. Darren Evans had 28 carries for 153 yards and a touchdown, Virginia Tech's defense came up with four interceptions and the 21st-ranked Hokies beat the 12th-ranked Bearcats 20-7 on Thursday night to join Southern California and Texas as the only schools to win 10 games in each of the past five seasons. They were the underdogs again Thursday, plus were driven by the chance to avenge last year's Orange Bowl loss to Kansas. For the first 2 minutes, they seemed very much in trouble. But the rest of the way was all Virginia Tech (10-4) -- and Coach Frank Beamer couldn't remember too many sweeter wins than this. Pike -- who wasn't even on Cincinnati's depth chart at the start of the season before blossoming into an all-Big East Quarterback -- threw for 239 yards and a touchdown, but had his night marred mightily by the four picks and getting stopped on a fourth-and-goal in the fourth quarter. Mardy Gilyard had 255 all-purpose yards and a touchdown catch for Cincinnati (11-3), which had its six-game winning streak snapped. Not for Virginia Tech, there wasn't. And not for the Atlantic Coast Conference, either. The Hokies became the first ACC team to win a BCS game since Florida State -- ironically, perhaps -- beat Virginia Tech, then a Big East member, for the national championship to close the 1999 season. The ACC was 0-for-8 in BCS play since. And the oft-maligned league was just 5-12 over the past two seasons in all postseason games before the Hokies broke through. Evans, the game's MVP, got the clinching score early in the fourth, after Pike threw his third interception -- albeit on a highlight-quality play by Virginia Tech defensive end Orion Martin. Deep in his own territory, Pike rolled right and threw back to the left, hoping the misdirection would pay off. Martin never bit, made a diving interception at the Cincinnati 10, and Evans rumbled in from 6 yards out for a 20-7 lead with 11:29 left. Pike got the Bearcats to the Virginia Tech 1 on the next drive, tried to run in on fourth-and-goal, and was stuffed by Barquell Rivers with 7:25 left to end Cincinnati's last realistic comeback chance. His fourth interception came 5 minutes later, capping a night to forget by the Quarterback who wasn't even on the Bearcats' three-deep when spring ball began. The Hokies' best defense was their ball-control offense. Virginia Tech held the ball for nearly 40 minutes. Virginia Tech entered the stadium to the familiar sounds of Metallica's "Enter Sandman" -- the song that usually blares when the Hokies enter Lane Stadium in Blacksburg. Nonetheless, it was Cincinnati at home early in its BCS debut. The Bearcats took the opening kickoff, sent their spread offense onto the field and made the Hokies look very confused. Pike found Gilyard for a 38-yard pickup on the third play from scrimmage, and they hooked up for a spectacular 15-yard touchdown three plays later to open the scoring. Facing a third-and-9 from the right hash, Pike waited ... waited ... waited ... before lofting a fade to the far left of the end zone. Gilyard took off on a sprint, made a diving catch as he sailed out of bounds and managed to just barely drag his right toe on the turf painted in Virginia Tech's colors for a 7-0 Cincinnati lead. It looked easy. Ah, but the nation's seventh-ranked defense would eventually get its bearings. The Hokies held Cincinnati to 137 yards, rendered the Bearcats' running game nonexistent (eight carries, 11 yards) over the remainder of the half, and battled their way to a 10-7 lead by intermission. Virginia Tech Quarterback Tyrod Taylor tied the game with a zig-zigzag rushing effort from 17 yards early in the second quarter. Out of the shotgun on third-and-9, he started straight ahead, darted right, cut back left and then made a sharper move to run just past the pylon -- the Quarterback's seventh rushing score of the season. Cincinnati had a great chance to reclaim the lead later in the second, until Pike made the sort of error he avoided all season, throwing into what essentially was triple coverage while trying to force the ball to Dominick Goodman in the back of the end zone. The miscues just kept coming from there. There were large patches of empty seats in Dolphin Stadium, which wasn't altogether unexpected. Some tickets were available through online resale outlets in recent days -- even Thursday morning -- for $1. Plenty more were offered for well below face value, and the building looked a bit emptier after the Doobie Brothers finished their halftime set. Event officials said 15,781 sold tickets were unused. And by the end, it seemed like only the heartiest Hokies fans remained to regale the back-to-back ACC champs one final time.

2009 Liberty Bowl

The 2009 AutoZone Liberty Bowl is the fiftieth annual college football bowl game, and was played at Liberty Bowl Memorial Stadium in Memphis, Tennessee on January 2, 2009.

2009 Liberty Bowl	Line	1	-	2	-	3	-	4	-	Final
Kentucky	(41.5)	0	-	3	-	13	-	9	-	25
East Carolina	(-3.0)	3	-	13	-	3	-	0	-	19

Scoring Summary
East Carolina – Hartman 22 yard Field goal
East Carolina – Simmons 28 yard run (Hartman kick)
Kentucky – Seiber 21 yard Field goal
East Carolina – Freeney 80 yard pass from Pinkney (Kick blocked)
Kentucky – Jones 99 yard kickoff return (Seiber kick)
Kentucky – Lanxster 19 yard pass from Hartline (Seiber kick)
East Carolina – Hartman 43 yard Field goal
Kentucky – Seiber 34 yard Field goal
Kentucky – Jenkins 56 yard fumble return (Kick blocked)

Associated Press Liberty Bowl Game Summary - Ventrell Jenkins barreled his 285-pound frame 56 yards with the ball in his arm, but it would take some improvisation to reach the end zone and help Kentucky achieve history. Who can blame them? This wasn't your garden-variety, go-ahead fumble return by a lineman. No, this one gave Kentucky a 25-19 win over East Carolina in the Liberty Bowl on Friday and gave the Wildcats a third straight postseason victory -- a distinction not even Bear Bryant's teams were able to achieve decades earlier. Jenkins was an unpredictable MVP after two straight Music City Bowl wins in which Kentucky's former record-setting Quarterback Andre Woodson led the way. Kentucky (7-6) never led in this one until the fourth quarter, when fellow lineman Myron Pryor, who had his own 72-yard fumble return TD earlier this year, forced a fumble with about 3 minutes left. In the scramble for the loose ball, Jenkins came up with it and rumbled down the right sideline untouched. Lones Seiber's extra point attempt was blocked -- the third blocked extra point of the game and second off Seiber's foot. That gave East Carolina (9-5) plenty of time to drive for the win, but the ensuing kickoff was downed at the 1. The Pirates wound up punting four plays later, and Kentucky picked up a first down before running out the clock. Coming off its first Conference USA championship, East Carolina jumped to a 16-3 halftime lead before failing in its attempt to win a third game this season against a team from a BCS conference. Moments before Jenkins' heroics, it appeared Kentucky might get the go-ahead score with another fumble return -- albeit not nearly as long -- by linebacker Micah Johnson. However, instant replay determined East Carolina Quarterback Patrick Pinkney was sacked on the play by Memphis native Jeremy Jarmon, so the Pirates retained possession. Even before that, the Wildcats' defense missed another chance at a game-breaking play in the fourth quarter when Sam Maxwell's interception deep in East Carolina territory was negated by a holding penalty on teammate Winston Guy. Although Kentucky's defensive stars were outplayed in the first half, they saved their best for when it counted. Bryant, who took his Alabama teams to four Liberty Bowls -- including the inaugural game 50 years ago and the final game of his career in 1982 -- was the only other Wildcats coach to lead the program to three straight bowl games. Unlike Brooks, Bryant only won two of them. Kentucky saved virtually all its magic for the second half, in every aspect of the game, and it started when David Jones took the opening kickoff for a Liberty Bowl-record 99-yard TD. Minutes later, Quarterback Mike Hartline, starting for injured freshman Randall Cobb, gave Kentucky its lone offensive TD when he hit Kyrus Lanxster on a crossing pattern for a 19-yard touchdown that tied the game 16-all midway through the third quarter. Hartline completed 19 of 31 passes for 204 yards and one interception. Brooks said he had been sick with the flu and praised his performance. Pinkney finished 18-of-36 for 297 yards for East Carolina, most of it going to Davon Drew and Darryl Freeney. Drew caught five passes for 120 yards, and Freeney had five catches for 112 yards and a touchdown. Trevard Lindley, elected the Wildcats' team MVP, hyperextended his elbow while deflecting a pass in the end zone.

2009 Cotton Bowl Classic

The 2009 AT&T Cotton Bowl Classic was the 73rd edition of the annual college football bowl game. The game featured the Ole Miss Rebels of the Southeastern Conference and the Texas Tech Red Raiders of the Big 12 Conference. The game was played on January 2, 2009, at Cotton Bowl stadium in Dallas, Texas, and was televised in the United States on FOX. This was the final Cotton Bowl Classic to be played at the stadium in the home of the State Fair of Texas, Fair Park. Since 2010, the game has been played at Cowboys Stadium in nearby Arlington.

2009 Cotton Bowl Classic	Line	1	-	2	-	3	-	4	-	Final
#20 Mississippi	(68.0)	7	-	17	-	14	-	9	-	47
#8 Texas Tech	(-4.5)	14	-	7	-	0	-	13	-	34

Scoring Summary
Texas Tech — Britton 45 yard pass from Harrell (Williams kick)
Texas Tech — McBath 45 yard interception return (Williams kick)
Mississippi — Harris 8 yard pass from Snead (Shene kick)
Mississippi — Wallace 41 yard pass from Snead (Shene kick)
Texas Tech — Crabtree 2 yard pass from Harrell (Williams kick)
Mississippi — Harris 21 yard pass from Snead (Shene kick)
Mississippi — Shene 27 yard Field goal
Mississippi — Green 65 yard interception return (Shene kick)
Mississippi — Bolden 17 yard run (Shene kick)
Texas Tech — Britton 12 yard pass from Harrell (Williams kick)
Mississippi — Trahan safety
Mississippi — McCluster 4 yard run (Shene kick)
Texas Tech — Morris 17 pass from Harrell (Kick failed)

Cotton Bowl Classic Game Summary - Ole Miss and Texas Tech ensured the 73rd and final AT&T Cotton Bowl Classic played at historic Fair Park would be one for the record books. Ole Miss prevailed, 47-34, to win its sixth-straight game and finish the season 9-4. Even though the two schools amassed 81 points, first-year Rebels Coach Houston Nutt was quick to praise his defense, which held the Red Raiders scoreless in a third quarter for the first time that season. Ole Miss H-Back Dexter McCluster received the Sanford Trophy given to the outstanding offensive player. McCluster, who rushed for 97 yards and one touchdown on 14 carries and caught six passes for 83 yards. Ole Miss' Marshay Green received the McKnight Trophy given to the outstanding defensive player. The trophy honors the late Dallas newspaperman and former Team Selection Committee Chairman, Felix McKnight. Green had three tackles and returned an intercepted pass 65 yards for an early third-quarter touchdown. Despite controlling the ball for all but three minutes, 20 seconds, the Rebels trailed 14-7, after the first quarter. Ole Miss used relentless defense, hard running and timely passing by Jevan Snead to widen its lead to 38-21 after three quarters. With Tech's quick-strike offense, a comeback still seemed possible after the Raiders recovered a fumble at their two early in the fourth quarter. But the ferocious Rebel defense trapped Tech Quarterback Graham Harrell for a safety on the very next play.

2009 Sugar Bowl

The 2009 Allstate Sugar Bowl was the 75th annual edition of the annual college football, was played on Friday, January 2, 2009 at the Louisiana Superdome in New Orleans, Louisiana. The Sugar Bowl usually takes the champion of the SEC and pits them against an At-Large BCS team. However, with the 2008 SEC Champion, Florida Gators being selected to play for the national championship game, the Sugar Bowl selected two At-Large BCS teams. The bowl kept their traditional ties with the Southeastern Conference for the second consecutive year though, in selecting the Alabama Crimson Tide with an at-large selection. Utah Quarterback Brian Johnson was named Most Outstanding Player of the game. With this win, Utah completed the 2008 season as the only undefeated, 13–0 Division I FBS team in the nation, along with becoming the first team from a non-BCS conference to win two BCS bowls. It was also Utah's first win over a Southeastern Conference school. Andre Smith (Alabama starting left Tackle and 2008 Outland Trophy winner) was suspended for the game because he declined to cooperate with an investigation by the school's compliance staff on the issue with his uncle's illegal contact with a sport's agent. A few days later, he declared himself for the NFL Draft and was the 6th overall pick.

2009 Sugar Bowl	Line	1	-	2	-	3	-	4	-	Final
#7 Utah	(45.5)	21	-	0	-	7	-	3	-	31
#4 Alabama	(-9.5)	0	-	10	-	7	-	0	-	17

Scoring Summary
Utah – Casteel 7 yard pass from Johnson (Sakoda kick)
Utah – Asiata 2 yard run (Sakoda kick)
Utah – Godfrey 18 yard pass from Johnson (Sakoda kick)
Alabama – Tiffin 52 yard field goal
Alabama – Arenas 73 yard punt return (Tiffin kick)
Alabama – Coffee 4 yard pass from Wilson (Tiffin kick)
Utah – Reed 28 yard pass from Johnson (Sakoda kick)
Utah – Sakoda 28 yard field goal

Alabama Media Guide Sugar Bowl Game Summary - Fourth-ranked Alabama battled back from an early 21-0 deficit, cutting its deficit against No. 6 Utah to 21-17 in the second half, but the Crimson Tide was unable to overcome the deficit, falling to the Utes, 31-17, in the 75th Allstate Sugar Bowl in New Orleans. Alabama finished the season with a 12-2 record while Utah finished the season as college football's only undefeated team at 13-0. Utah scored 21 first-quarter points, capitalizing on a John Parker Wilson interception and getting a pair of touchdown passes from Brian Johnson to take a 21-0 lead into the second quarter. Alabama responded with 17 unanswered points, starting the comeback with a 52-yard field goal by Leigh Tiffin and getting a 73-yard punt return for a touchdown by Javier Arenas that cut the largest deficit the Crimson Tide had faced all season to 21-10 at halftime. A fumble on Utah's first possession of the third quarter gave Alabama the ball in the Utes' territory, and a 4-yard touchdown pass from Wilson to Glen Coffee cut the lead to 21-17 with 11:14 to go in the third. Utah, however, closed the game on a 10-0 run. Wilson completed 18 of 30 passes for 177 yards, with one touchdown and two interceptions. Julio Jones was Wilson's leading receiver, finishing with seven catches for 77 yards. Coffee (36 yards) and Mark Ingram (26) combined for 62 yards on the ground. Coffee moved into second place on the Alabama single season rushing list with 1,386 yards. The game was Alabama's first Sugar Bowl appearance since its 34-13 national championship win over Miami to close the 1992 season, and its first Bowl Championship Series appearance since playing in the Orange Bowl in the 1999 season. The game extended Alabama's NCAA-best bowl appearances mark to 56. Utah Quarterback Brian Johnson threw for 336 yards and three touchdowns on his way to being selected the game's most outstanding player, a fitting finish to the career of Utah's winningest Quarterback (26-7). Utah became the first team from a non-BCS conference to win two BCS bowls. The Utes beat Pittsburgh in the 2005 Fiesta Bowl. Johnson was 27-of-41 and was not intercepted as the Utes took charge from the start by bolting to a stunning, 21-0 first-quarter lead. Utah's defense was impressive, intercepting Wilson twice and sacking him eight times, with the seventh sack forcing a fumble that ended the Crimson Tide's last threat with just more than five minutes remaining. The Utes' front seven was significantly outweighed by Alabama's offensive line, playing without left tackle Andre Smith, the Outland Trophy winner who missed the game due to a suspension. Utah did not give ground to the Tide's normally powerful running game that averaged 196.5 yards per game. The Utes' variety of stunts and blitzes appeared to upset Wilson's rhythm. He overthrew a couple of open receivers downfield and finished 18-of-30 for 177 yards and a touchdown. Johnson adeptly spread the ball around, completing passes to seven receivers while the Utes almost completely ignored the running game. Johnson connected with receiver Freddie Brown 12 times for 125 yards. Johnson's touchdowns went for 7 yards to Brent Casteel, 18 yards to Bradon Godfrey and 28 yards to David Reed. Matt Asiata ran for a 2-yard score, set up by Reed's leaping catch at the 2. An Alabama comeback appeared to be building early in the second half, when Dont'a Hightower stripped Johnson, and Bobby Greenwood recovered at the Utah 30. Wilson drove the Tide for a score, hitting Coffee for an easy 4-yard touchdown pass on a rollout to close the gap to 21-17. At the point, it appeared to be only a matter of time before the Tide would overtake the underdog Utes. But Johnson opened Utah's next drive with a 33-yard pass over the middle to Brown. That started a 71-yard scoring drive that ended with Reed's touchdown. The Tide drove right back into Utah territory, but Ingram was stopped for no gain on third-and-2 from the Utah 32. But Tiffin missed a long field goal attempt, hooking a 49-yarder just left of the upright.

2009 International Bowl

The 2009 International Bowl was played between the Connecticut Huskies (UConn) and the Buffalo Bulls at the Rogers Centre in Toronto, Ontario, Canada, on January 3, 2009. Connecticut represented the Big East Conference (Big East) in the game; Buffalo entered as the Mid-American Conference (MAC) champion. Connecticut was selected as a participant in the 2009 International Bowl following a 7–5 regular season where they won their first five games, only to lose five of their last seven contests. Facing the Huskies were the Buffalo Bulls with a regular season record of 8–5, highlighted by an upset win over then-No. 12 and undefeated Ball State in the 2008 MAC Championship Game. Pre-game media coverage focused on the legacy of the 1958 Buffalo Bulls, the first team from the university to be invited to a bowl game. When told that the two African American members of the team would not be allowed to play because of segregation, the team elected to refuse the bowl bid. Buffalo would not play in a bowl until this game, 50 years later.

2009 International Bowl	Line	1	-	2	-	3	-	4	-	Final
Buffalo	(52.0)	3	-	17	-	0	-	0	-	20
Connecticut	(-5.5)	7	-	10	-	7	-	14	-	38

Scoring Summary
Buffalo - Principe 38 yard Field goal
Connecticut - Brown 45 yard run (Teggart kick)
Connecticut - Teggart 32 yard Field goal
Buffalo - Long fumble recovered in end zone (Principe kick)
Buffalo - Principe 29 yard Field goal
Buffalo - Starks 4 yard run (Principe kick)
Connecticut - Lorenzen 13 yard run (Teggart kick)
Connecticut - Brouse 4 yard pass from Lorenzen (Teggart kick)
Connecticut - Lorenzen 11 yard run (Teggart kick)
Connecticut - Deleston 100 yard interception return (Teggart kick)

Associated Press International Bowl Game Summary - Connecticut's Donald Brown showed he has nothing left to prove at the college level. Brown ran for a career-best 261 yards in his final college game, helping the fumble-prone Huskies overcome a mistake-filled first half and defeat Buffalo 38-20 in the International Bowl on Saturday. After becoming the 14th player in major college history to run for 2,000 yards in a season, the junior running back broke the bad news to UConn fans. He then apologized for saying three weeks ago that he planned to return to Connecticut for his senior season. The nation's leading rusher said he made the commitment to return to stop speculation and negate a potential distraction for his team heading into the game at Toronto. He proved that in the first half against the Bulls, when he had 208 yards rushing -- 6 short of matching a career best -- and kept the Huskies in a game. UConn turned the ball over five times in the first 30 minutes. Brown scored on a 45-yard run and then added a career-best 75-yarder to set up Quarterback Tyler Lorenzen's touchdown run. Lorenzen then put the Huskies ahead for good 10 minutes into the third quarter by completing his first pass, a 4-yarder to tight end Steve Brouse for a 24-20 lead. In overcoming a 20-10 deficit, the Huskies (8-5) won their second of three bowl appearances since joining the Big East in 2004. The Mid-American champion Bulls (8-6) had their breakout season under coach Turner Gill end with a loss in their bowl debut. Buffalo scored all its points off turnovers. Gill wasn't too disappointed for a team that registered its first winning season since 1996 and orchestrated one of the most monumental turnarounds in college football. The Bulls were 10-69 in seven seasons prior to Gill's arrival three years ago. The Huskies defense -- ranked 10th in the nation in yards allowed -- played to its stout reputation, containing a Bulls offense that had produced a school-record 404 points. UConn limited Buffalo to 237 yards offense and 10 first downs -- and only five through three quarters. Linebacker Dahna Deleston dealt the final blow, intercepting Drew Willy's pass intended for Naaman Roosevelt at the goal line and returning it 100 yards for a touchdown. Deleston was so exhausted after matching the school's longest interception return, he collapsed in the end zone. Brown, by comparison, was still fresh after being held out for the most of the final quarter with the game in hand. He finished with 29 carries. Edsall's only disappointment in losing Brown to the NFL was a belief the running back didn't get enough recognition for his achievements this season. Edsall said the next step is for Brown to fill out an application to submit to the NFL, a process required by all juniors requesting to enter the draft. Brown ends this season with 2,083 yards rushing -- the 11th best total in college football's top division -- and he set a school record with 18 TDs. The game didn't start well for UConn, a team that looked very much like the one that committed five turnovers in a regular season-ending 34-10 loss to Pittsburgh. Buffalo's Ray Anthony Long recovered Jasper Howard's muffed punt in the end zone. Starks' score came after another Huskies' miscue. Robbie Frey had a kickoff go off his hand and into the end zone. Rather than downing the ball for what would've been a touchback, Frey ran the ball out and had it jarred loose by Justin Winters and recovered by Buffalo's John Syty at the UConn 4. When UConn stopped helping the Bulls, Buffalo couldn't get it done on its own.

2009 Fiesta Bowl

The 2009 Tostitos Fiesta Bowl game was played between the Ohio State Buckeyes and the Texas Longhorns on Monday, January 5, 2009, at University of Phoenix Stadium in Glendale, Arizona. Texas participated in the Fiesta Bowl because the Big 12 champion University of Oklahoma Sooners were participating in the 2009 BCS National Championship Game; however the bowl kept its ties to the Big 12 by selecting the Longhorns, who did not play in the championship game as they beat Oklahoma in the Red River Rivalry, 45-35, then lost to Texas Tech and Texas Tech in turn lost to Oklahoma and dictated that a tiebreaker would decide that the highest BCS ranked team for the Big 12 South the week of November 28, 2008 would be in the title game. The Buckeyes were chosen as an at-large school as co-champions of the Big Ten Conference, having lost the right to play in the Rose Bowl due to a 13-6 loss to Penn State on October 25. This 38th edition of the Fiesta Bowl was televised in the United States on FOX. It was the third meeting in the history of the two schools. The Longhorns are coached by head football coach Mack Brown and led on the field by Quarterback Colt McCoy. The Buckeyes (variously "Ohio State" or "OSU" or the "Bucks") are coached by Jim Tressel and led on the field by Terrelle Pryor. The victory by Texas gave Ohio State their third straight bowl loss, their longest such streak since the early John Cooper era (when they lost 4 bowls in a row from 1989–92). This follows a four game bowl winning streak which tied for longest in OSU history.

2009 Fiesta Bowl	Line	1	-	2	-	3	-	4	-	Final
#10 Ohio State	(52.0)	3	-	3	-	0	-	15	-	21
#3 Texas	(-8.0)	0	-	3	-	14	-	7	-	24

Scoring Summary
Ohio State – Pettrey 51 yard Field goal
Texas – Lawrence 27 yard Field goal
Ohio State – Pretorius 30 yard Field goal
Texas – McCoy 14 yard run (Lawrence kick)
Texas – Cosby 7 yard pass from McCoy (Lawrence kick)
Ohio State – Pettrey 44 yard Field goal
Ohio State – Pryor 5 yard pass from Boeckman (Pass failed)
Ohio State – Herron 15 yard run (Pass failed)
Texas – Cosby 26 yard pass from McCoy (Lawrence kick)

USA Today Fiesta Bowl Game Summary - Texas made its final statement in a long-shot pursuit of the national championship Monday night by overcoming Ohio State 24-21 in the Tostitos Fiesta Bowl. The Longhorns, ranked third in the BCS ratings and both major polls, used a second-half comeback to outlast the Buckeyes (10-3). Quarterback Colt McCoy ran for one touchdown and threw for another in the third quarter and then hit Quan Cosby with a 26-yard scoring pass for the winning score with 16 seconds left. Texas trailed 6-3 at the half after being held to minus-9 yards rushing and giving up 140 to the Buckeyes, 96 to junior tailback Chris "Beanie" Wells, who missed most of the fourth quarter after a blow to the head. McCoy was sacked on a 4th-and-7 situation to squelch one drive and was intercepted at the goal-line by Anderson Russell in the final five seconds after the Longhorns had driven to OSU's 15-yard line. McCoy completed 20 of 27 passes over the first two quarters for an average of only 9.9 yards. But he drove Texas 80 yards for the go-ahead touchdown on the opening drive of the third quarter, covering the final 14 on a Quarterback draw. The Longhorns converted two fourth down plays in the drive, including Rashad Bobino's run on a fake punt on a 4th-and-2. He found Cosby with a 7-yard touchdown pass before the quarter ended for a 17-6 lead. Ohio State scored the next 15 points and took a 21-17 lead on Dan Herron's 15-yard run with 2:05 remaining. The Longhorns then covered 78 yards in 11 plays. Cosby broke free of Anderson Russell's tackle at the 15-yard line over the middle had nothing between him and the end zone. It was the third consecutive BCS bowl loss for Ohio State, the last two which came in the national championship game. Senior linebacker James Laurinaitis said the Buckeyes had their chance Monday but couldn't seal the deal. McCoy finished by hitting 41 of 59 passes for 414 yards and was named the offensive MVP. Cosby had 14 receptions (one shy of the Fiesta Bowl record) for 171 yards, becoming the eighth Longhorn receiver to cross the 100-yard mark in a bowl game. The Buckeyes suffered when Wells went out, but received a lift all game from Todd Boeckman, a senior who lost his starting spot to Pryor after two games despite being a first-team all-Big Ten pick in 2007. In spot duty, Boeckman completed 5 of 11 passes for 110 yards and a touchdown — to Pryor, who lined up at wide receiver. Pryor, the USA TODAY high school player of the year last year, threw for 66 yards and ran for 78, showing versatility that Ohio State will welcome next season. Texas is now 8-3 in bowl games under Brown and its 25 overall bowl victories ranks its fourth. The Longhorns are 1-1 in the Fiesta Bowl. Ohio State, which was playing the Fiesta for the fourth time since 2003, is 4-2 in this competition and 18-22 overall, 4-4 under Tressel.

2009 GMAC Bowl

The 2009 GMAC Bowl was the tenth anniversary edition of this college football bowl game. The contest was played on January 6, 2009 at Ladd Peebles Stadium in Mobile, Alabama and featured the Tulsa Golden Hurricane playing the Ball State Cardinals. For the second consecutive year, the Golden Hurricane won the contest. The game, which was played in a second half driving rainstorm, was won easily by Tulsa 45-13.

2009 GMAC Bowl	Line	1	-	2	-	3	-	4	-	Final
Ball State	(-1.5)	7	-	6	-	0	-	0	-	13
Tulsa	(76.0)	10	-	14	-	7	-	14	-	45

Scoring Summary
Tulsa - Johnson 30 yard pass from David Johnson (Tracy kick)
Ball State - Davis 17 yard run (McGarvey kick)
Tulsa - Tracy 31 yard Field goal
Tulsa - Adams 1 yard run (Tracy kick)
Ball State - McGarvey 40 yard Field goal
Tulsa - Adams 56 yard run (Tracy kick)

Ball State - McGarvey 22 yard Field goal
Tulsa - Shelley 15 yard pass from Johnson (Tracy kick)
Tulsa - Adams 11 yard run (Tracy kick)
Tulsa - Frank 12 yard pass from Johnson (Tracy kick)

Associated Press GMAC Bowl Game Summary - Tulsa raced through the rain to another GMAC Bowl win and a couple more records, too. Tarrion Adams rushed for 207 yards and three touchdowns, David Johnson passed for three scores and Damaris Johnson did a little bit of everything in the Golden Hurricane's 45-13 GMAC Bowl victory over No. 22 Ball State on a soggy Tuesday night. Tulsa (11-3) just kept racking up numbers and wins for a school record in victories. The Golden Hurricane had 439 yards rushing and 632 overall -- hardly slowed down a bit by rain that first formed puddles and then covered nearly the entire field during a second-half deluge. On both sides of the ball. Ball State (12-2) didn't have a first down or completion in the second half, managing a feeble 22 yards after halftime. The nation's No. 1 offense after the other bowls -- No. 2 in the regular season -- was unstoppable. Adams passed Micheal Gunter to become Tulsa's career rushing leader and broke Gunter's single-season mark, too. David Johnson passed for 193 yards, most of that to freshman Damaris Johnson. Tulsa kicker Jarod Tracy became the school's career scoring leader. Adams needed just 19 carries, though one was a season-long 56-yard touchdown scamper. Tulsa's 63-7 win over Bowling Green in last year's GMAC was the most lopsided bowl game in NCAA history. This was another runaway thanks to the no-huddle offense and a capitalistic defense. Ball State fell to 0-5 in bowl games after recording a school-record 12 wins. Damaris Johnson supplied many of the big plays for Tulsa's no-huddle offense and had 274 all-purpose yards. He had 135 yards receiving, 76 yards rushing -- including a tackle-breaking 62-yarder in the fourth quarter -- and returned three kicks for 63 yards. Four Tulsa players ran for at least 58 yards. The Cardinals had been giving up just 142 yards a game on the ground and 348 total. It was a rough debut for Ball State coach Stan Parrish, a 62-year-old promoted from offensive coordinator on Dec. 18 after Brady Hoke left to take over the San Diego State program. The Cardinals lost their final two games after setting a school mark with 12 wins in a perfect regular season. They earned the first national ranking in program history this season. Most of the second half was played in a driving rain, making a comeback attempt by Quarterback Nate Davis and Ball State even more difficult. It might have been the final college game for Davis, who has indicated he was considering skipping his senior season to enter the NFL draft. He was 9-of-29 passing for 145 yards and lost two fumbles and an interception in the first half. Davis was not made available for interviews after the game. He was 0-for-10 in the second half. Parrish said he injured his right, throwing hand in the third quarter and was getting it X-rayed after the game. With help from the Cardinals, Tulsa built a 24-13 halftime lead, with all three touchdowns on plays of at least 30 yards. Ball State hadn't been down going into the locker room this season. Tulsa marched 87 yards on the opening drive of the second half, capping it with David Johnson's 15-yard touchdown pass to Slick Shelley. Ball State couldn't come close to answering, going three-and-out on all three possessions of the third quarter. Leading rusher MiQuale Lewis, who gained over 1,700 yards this season, was limited to 35 on 16 carries. Davis lost fumbles on Ball State's first two drives, with the first setting up David Johnson's 30-yard touchdown pass to Damaris Johnson across the middle. Davis redeemed himself with a 17-yard touchdown run to tie it up late in the first quarter. Then Ball State's Kyle Young blocked a punt at Tulsa's 22-yard line. Three incompletions later, Ball State had to settle for Ian McGarvey's 39-yard field goal and a 17-10 deficit. Adams added his 56-yarder before Davis nearly got the Cardinals back within a score, thanks to a bulldozing, spinning run down to the Tulsa 7 in the final minute. Tulsa stood again, forcing a field goal and Ball State didn't challenge again. Neither the defense nor the rain was able to stop Tulsa's offense.

2009 BCS Championship Game

The 2009 FedEx BCS National Championship Game was played at Dolphin Stadium in Miami Gardens, Florida, on January 8, 2009. It was the national championship game and featured the second-ranked Florida Gators against the top-ranked Oklahoma Sooners. The two participants were determined by the BCS Rankings to decide the BCS National Championship. Television coverage in the United States was provided by Fox, and radio coverage by ESPN Radio. The game was the last BCS Championship to air on Fox; starting with the 2010 game, ABC or ESPN televised the championship.

University of Oklahoma - The Sooners, coached by Bob Stoops, lost one game during their regular season to Texas in the annual Red River Rivalry contest, 45–35 on October 11. During the regular season, Quarterback Sam Bradford, winner of the 2008 Heisman Trophy, led the Sooners on offense to become the highest-scoring team in NCAA history (702 points) and the first team to score 60 or more points in five consecutive games.

University of Florida - Meanwhile, the Gators, coached by Urban Meyer, were looking to win their second BCS championship in three years. They were led by 2007 Heisman winner Tim Tebow. The only blemish on their schedule was a loss to Mississippi (Ole Miss) at home, 31–30 on September 27. By prevailing, Meyer became the first coach to win two BCS championship games, and one of only five coaches in NCAA history to win two titles in his first four years at a college.

2009 BCS Championship	Line	1	-	2	-	3	-	4	-	Final
#1 Florida	(-3.5)	0	-	7	-	7	-	10	-	24
#2 Oklahoma	(71.0)	0	-	7	-	0	-	7	-	14

Scoring Summary
Florida — Murphy 20 yard pass from Tebow (Phillips kick)
Oklahoma — Gresham 6 yard pass from Bradford (Stevens kick)
Florida — Harvin 2 yard rush (Phillips kick)
Oklahoma — Gresham 11 yard pass from Bradford (Stevens kick)
Florida — Phillips 27 yard field goal
Florida — Nelson 4 yard pass from Tebow (Phillips kick)

New York Times BCS Championship Game Recap - After all the penalties, interceptions and missed opportunities in the aesthetically unappealing Bowl Championship Series title game between Oklahoma and Florida on Thursday night, things started to look familiar. There was Florida Quarterback Tim Tebow taking a shotgun snap, lowering his shoulder and simply plowing his way into college football lore. There was Tebow leaping in the air with just over three minutes remaining and delivering a trademark jump pass to David Nelson that clinched the game. And there was Tebow taunting Oklahoma's Nic Harris with a Gator chomp, the most recognizable player in college football adding more indelible moments to his career. Tebow led the Gators to a 24-14 victory against the Sooners on Thursday night, and his familiar image resulted in a familiar spectacle: Florida fans, celebrating their third national title and second in the past three seasons, unleashed the haunting singsong that has become so familiar to college sports fans: "It's great, to be, a Florida Gator." The chants rang through the pro-Gator crowd at Dolphin Stadium as if it were a Saturday afternoon at The Swamp. Florida received 48 first place votes out of 65 in the Associated Press poll released early Friday morning; undefeated Utah finished second (16 first-place votes), followed by U.S.C. (one first-place vote), Texas and Oklahoma. There will be an off-season filled with talk of a burgeoning dynasty in Gainesville. While Meyer affirmed his spot atop the collegiate coaching profession, Oklahoma Coach Bob Stoops's inability to win B.C.S. games is becoming notable. The Sooners have lost the last five B.C.S. games they have played in, and have dropped the last three B.C.S. title games they have appeared in. Among the gaffes that will hound the Sooners in the off-season were two second-quarter trips inside the Gators' 10-yard line that resulted in no points. The Sooners' explosive offense, which had scored more than 60 points in five consecutive games, looked dismal outside of two two-minute spurts, one in the first half and one in the second. Sam Bradford, the Heisman Trophy winner, threw two interceptions, the most critical coming in the fourth quarter when Ahmad Black ripped the ball out of the hands of Oklahoma's Juaquin Iglesias, essentially sealing the game. Tebow's numbers were not imposing either; his two interceptions equaled the amount he had thrown all season. But he took over on Florida's two second-half touchdown drives, much as he did during the Southeastern Conference title game against Alabama. Tebow finished 18 of 30 passing for two touchdowns with two interceptions, but he began tilting the game in Florida's favor with the run. He told Dan Mullen, the Florida offensive coordinator, at halftime that he wanted more carries, and he delivered when he called his own number time and time again on a touchdown drive in the third quarter. Tebow ran the ball seven times for 52 yards on that third-quarter drive, bringing Florida to the doorstep before lining up at H-back and setting up a Percy Harvin touchdown rush on a direct snap. Harvin, who had been questionable with a high-ankle sprain entering the game, also set up what proved to be the clinching field goal with a 52-yard run from the backfield in the fourth quarter. Oklahoma went into halftime tied at 7-7 after having the ball inside the 10-yard line twice in the second quarter and failing to score any points thanks to a pair of baffling sequences. The first gaffe came when tailback Chris Brown failed to punch in the ball on fourth-and-1, as he got corralled behind the line of scrimmage by Florida's Torrey Davis. Oklahoma had first-and-goal from the 9-yard line and ran all four times to Brown, never giving Bradford a chance to pick apart the Gator defense. The second Oklahoma blunder came when Bradford threw an interception at the goal line with three seconds left. Florida's Major Wright came away with the interception, but not before Joe Haden, Ahmad Black and Ryan Stamper, all deflected it. Stoops called Oklahoma's final timeout with the clock already stopped on a first down before the interception. That meant that even if Manuel Johnson had caught the ball, he was short of the goal line and time would have expired. All those Sooner missteps set the stage for Tebow, who with that final jump pass secured another moment that reverberated in college football history.

2009 St. Petersburg Bowl

The 2009 St. Petersburg Bowl presented by Beef 'O' Brady's, formerly known as the St. Petersburg Bowl, was the second edition of the Bowl game and was played at Tropicana Field in St. Petersburg, Florida. The game was played on Saturday, December 19, 2009, was telecast on ESPN and featured the UCF of Conference USA and Rutgers of the Big East. Rutgers defeated UCF 45–24 in a game where Mohamed Sanu, the game's MVP, caught 4 passes for 97 yards and a touchdown in addition to rushing 14 times for 47 yards and two touchdowns. The game marked the Scarlet Knights' fifth consecutive bowl appearance, and their fourth consecutive victory, after not playing in a bowl game from 1979 to 2005. Rutgers was one of nine BCS teams to win a bowl game in each of the last three seasons. This was UCF's third bowl game, the last one was in the 2007 Liberty Bowl. With the loss, Central Florida dropped to 0–3 in the postseason. The bowl game marked the first ever meeting between Rutgers and UCF, both teams being called "Knights".

2009 St. Petersburg Bowl	Line	1	-	2	-	3	-	4	-	Final
Central Florida	(44.5)	7	-	10	-	0	-	7	-	24
Rutgers	(-2.5)	14	-	14	-	10	-	7	-	45

Scoring Summary
Rutgers - Sanu 5 yard run (Te kick)
Central Florida - Aiken 7 yard pass from Hodges (Cattoi kick)
Rutgers - Brown 65 yard pass from Savage (Te kick)
Central Florida - Cattoi 25 yard Field goal
Rutgers - Sanu 1 yard run (Te kick)
Central Florida - Aiken 34 yard pass from Hodges (Cattoi kick)
Rutgers - Anderson 19 yard interception return (Te kick)
Rutgers - Sanu 11 yard pass from Savage (Te kick)
Rutgers - Te 43 yard Field goal
Central Florida - Davis 2 yard run (Cattoi kick)
Rutgers - Munoz 35 yard kickoff return (Te kick)

Associated Press St. Petersburg Bowl Game Summary - Mohamed Sanu was Mr. Everything for Rutgers, and the Scarlet Knights' string of postseason success continues. The multi-threat receiver ran for two touchdowns out of the wildcat formation and also scored on an 11-yard reception from Tom Savage, another true freshman who threw for a career-best 294 yards in Saturday night's 45-24 victory over Central Florida in the St. Petersburg Bowl presented by Beef 'O' Brady's. Rutgers (9-4) claimed a school-record fourth consecutive bowl win to finish with at least nine victories for just the sixth time in 140 years. UCF (8-5) fell to 0-3 in bowl games under Coach George O'Leary. Billy Anderson scored on a 19-yard interception return for Rutgers, which shut down 1,000-yard rusher Brynn Harvey, limiting the running back to 32 yards on 13 carries to end his streak of three consecutive games with at least 129. The first Rutgers player since 1993 to run for a TD, throw for a TD and catch a pass for a TD in the same season, Sanu rushed for 41 yards on 13 carries and had four receptions for 97 yards. He also set up UCF's first touchdown, fumbling a punt that was recovered inside the Rutgers 10. Three plays later, Brett Hodges threw a 7-yard touchdown pass to Kamar Aiken for a brief 7-7 tie. Tim Brown, whose status had been uncertain because of an ankle injury, put the Scarlet Knights ahead for good when he caught a pass over the middle and turned it into a 65-yard TD play. UCF won five of six after a 3-3 start to earn its third bowl bid in six years under O'Leary -- a 106-mile ride from Orlando that's the shortest trip any Football Bowl Subdivision team will make for a postseason game this year. Sanu scored on runs of 5 and 1 yards in the first half. His first reception, a 61-yard gain to the UCF 12 on a pass that was slightly underthrown, set up his 11-yard TD catch that made it 35-17 early in the third quarter. Savage completed 14 of 27 passes and was intercepted once. Hodges was 13 of 28 for 175 yards and two interceptions for UCF before being hurting his shoulder and being replaced by Rob Calabrese late in the fourth quarter. Central Florida had 5 yards net rushing before Calabrese scrambled for 30 for the big gainer in a 10-play, 75-yard march that Jonathan Davis finished with a 2-yard TD run. Hoping for a chance to pull closer than 38-24, UCF tried an onside kick that Rutgers' Damaso Munoz returned 35 yards for the Scarlet Knights' final touchdown with 2:18 remaining. The linebacker did a somersault into the end zone, drawing a penalty but also putting an exclamation point on the victory and setting off a celebration among Rutgers fans in the announced crowd of 29,673. With the game being played so close to Orlando, more than half the tickets were sold by UCF.

2009 New Mexico Bowl

The 2009 New Mexico Bowl was held on December 19, 2009 at University Stadium on the campus of the University of New Mexico in Albuquerque, New Mexico. The game, telecast on ESPN, featured the Wyoming Cowboys from the Mountain West Conference and the Fresno State Bulldogs from the WAC. This was the first trip to the New Mexico Bowl for Wyoming. It was also their first trip to a post-season bowl game since the 2004 season when the Cowboys defeated the UCLA Bruins 24–21 in the Pioneer PureVison Las Vegas Bowl. This marked Fresno State's second straight trip to the New Mexico Bowl; they were defeated 40–35 by Colorado State in the 2008 contest. Before the 2009 New Mexico Bowl, Wyoming and Fresno State had played each other a total of six times, playing in consecutive years from 1992–1997 as rivals in the Western Athletic Conference; the teams have split their matchups with each squad winning three games. The last meeting in 1997 was won by Fresno State, 24–7.

2009 New Mexico Bowl	Line	1	2	3	4	OT	2OT	Final
Fresno State	(-10.5)	0	14	7	7	0	0	28
Wyoming	(55.0)	7	7	3	11	0	7	35

Scoring Summary
Wyoming – Alexander 68 yard run (Watts kick)
Fresno State – Matthews 4 yard run (Goessling kick)
Wyoming – Bolling 21 yard pass from Carta-Samuels (Smith kick)
Fresno State – Hamler 10 yard pass from Colburn (Goessling kick)
Fresno State – Hamler 43 yard pass from West (Goessling kick)
Wyoming – Watts 40 yard field goal
Fresno State – Matthews 5 yard run (Goessling kick)
Wyoming – Leonard 11 yard pass from Carta-Samuels (Carta-Samuels pass to Bolling)
Wyoming – Watts 37 yard field goal
Wyoming – Leonard 13 yard pass from Carta-Samuels (Watts kick)

Associated Press New Mexico Bowl Game Summary - Wyoming trailed by 11 points in the fourth quarter. Its offense was led by a freshman Quarterback, its defense was facing the nation's leading rusher. Time to worry? Not these comeback Cowboys. Freshman Austyn Carta-Samuels threw three touchdown passes, the last a 13-yarder to David Leonard in the second overtime Saturday, and Wyoming rallied past Fresno State 35-28 in the New Mexico Bowl. The first of 34 bowls was a high-scoring matchup that was decided at the end by defense. Wyoming (7-6) stopped the nation's leading rusher, Fresno State's Ryan Mathews, on three rushing attempts from the 1 in the first overtime. The Bulldogs (8-5) tried a Quarterback sneak on third down, and Mathews came up short again on fourth down. The Cowboys, who won four times this season after rallying in the fourth quarter, scored on the first possession in double overtime, then held Fresno State on downs. Wyoming fans spilled out of the stands to celebrate as the school band played "Cowboy Joe." This was Wyoming's first bowl appearance since 2005, and it capped a winning season for Christensen after the Cowboys were picked to finish last in the Mountain West. Mathews, who led the nation in rushing average at 151.3 yards per game, finished with 144 yards on 31 attempts with two touchdowns. But he had a big fumble midway through the fourth quarter, setting up Carta-Samuels to lead a 19-play drive that tied it. Wyoming lineman Mitch Unrein, picked the defensive MVP, stripped the ball. Officials initially ruled Mathews was down but reversed the call after a replay. Wyoming's Ian Watts kicked a 37-yard field goal with 20 seconds left in regulation. After the Cowboys stopped Mathews in the first overtime, Watts was wide left a 40-yard field try that would have won it. Christensen said there was no disappointment on the sideline. Carta-Samuels, the Mountain West's freshman of the year, was chosen the game's offensive MVP after he completed 17 of 31 attempts for 201 yards passing with one interception. He led the Cowboys back after Mathews' 5-yard TD run put the Bulldogs up 28-17 with 13:59 remaining. Carta-Samuels found Leonard on an 11-yard TD pass, then connected with Greg Bolling for a 2-point conversion that got Wyoming to 28-25 with 10:15 to go. Fresno State, trying to build on the lead, was driving when Mathews fumbled at Wyoming's 26. The Cowboys took over with 8:08 left and converted three times on fourth downs -- including a daring fake punt -- on the march that ended with Watts' 37-yard field goal.

2009 New Orleans Bowl

The 2009 R+L Carriers New Orleans Bowl was the ninth edition of the bowl. The game was played at the Louisiana Superdome in New Orleans, Louisiana on Sunday, December 20, 2009. The game was televised on ESPN. The Middle Tennessee Blue Raiders, the Sun Belt Conference runners-up (Troy, the conference champions, took a berth in the GMAC Bowl instead), defeated the Southern Miss Golden Eagles, a team from Conference USA by a score of 42-32.

2009 New Orleans Bowl	Line	1	-	2	-	3	-	4	-	Final
Southern Miss	(-3.5)	14	-	3	-	3	-	12	-	32
Middle Tennessee	(58.5)	0	-	14	-	14	-	14	-	42

Scoring Summary
Southern Miss - Harrison 2 yard run (Run failed)
Southern Miss - Brown 24 yard pass from Young (Brown pass from Young)
Middle Tennessee - Andrews 11 yard pass from Dasher (Gendreau kick)
Middle Tennessee - Blissard 9 yard pass from Dasher (Gendreau kick)
Southern Miss - Hrapmann 20 yard Field goal
Middle Tennessee - Dasher 35 yard run (Gendreau kick)
Southern Miss - Hrapmann 38 yard Field goal
Middle Tennessee - McClover 23 yard pass from Burnette (Gendreau kick)
Southern Miss - Brown 7 yard pass from Young (Pass failed)
Middle Tennessee - Cunningham 2 yard run (Gendreau kick)
Middle Tennessee - Dasher 1 yard run (Gendreau kick)
Southern Miss - Parham 33 yard pass from Young (Pass failed)

Associated Press New Orleans Bowl Game Summary - Dwight Dasher got the best of Southern Mississippi -- and topped Vince Young, too. Dasher ran for 201 yards -- the most by a Quarterback in a bowl game -- and two touchdowns and threw two scoring passes to lead Middle Tennessee to a 42-32 victory over Southern Miss in the R&L Carriers New Orleans Bowl on Sunday night. Dasher completed 15 of 25 passes for 162 yards and ran 26 times. He finished the season with 1,175 yards rushing. He broke the Quarterback bowl rushing record of 200 yards set by Texas' Young in the 2006 Rose Bowl against Southern California. Middle Tennessee (10-3), playing in the second bowl game in school history, concluded its best season since joining the Football Bowl Subdivision in 1999 with a seven-game winning streak and its first bowl victory. Southern Miss (7-6) was playing in its eighth straight bowl game and 12th in the last 13 seasons. The Golden Eagles had won their three previous New Orleans Bowls, including an overtime win against Troy last season. Southern Miss Quarterback Martevious Young completed 18 of 34 passes for 271 yards and three touchdowns. He also threw two interceptions. Southern Miss running back Damion Fletcher ran for 78 yards. He finished the season with 1,015 to become the ninth player in major college football to reach 1,000 in all four seasons. He did it despite a hamstring injury that caused him to sit out one game this season. With 5,302 yards rushing overall, Fletcher passed Herschel Walker (5,259) and LaDainian Tomlinson (5,263) for eighth on the NCAA's career list. Southern Miss started strong, scoring on their first possession as Tory Harrison rushed for a 2-yard touchdown. On their second possession, the Golden Eagles stretched the lead to 14-0 on a 24-yard reception by DeAndre Brown. The Blue Raiders pulled even in the second quarter on an 11-yard reception by Garrett Anders, and -- after Alex Suber intercepted Young's pass on the Southern Miss 12 -- a 9-yard TD catch by Shane Blissard. Southern Miss held a 17-14 edge at halftime thanks to Daniel Hrapmann's 20-yard field goal as time expired. Dasher opened the third quarter with a 35-yard touchdown run. When Dasher left briefly with an ankle injury, Brent Burnette capped 76-yard scoring drive with a 23-yard TD pass to Chris McClover. Hrapmann hit a 38-yard field goal to cut the Blue Raiders lead to eight at 28-20 at the end of three quarters. Southern Miss had a chance to tie it early in the fourth making it 28-26 on DeAndre's 7 yard TD reception, but the 2-point conversion failed. Benjamin Cunningham and Dasher ran for touchdowns to put it out of reach for Middle Tennessee. USM added a final score with 27 seconds left the draw within 10.

2009 Las Vegas Bowl

The 2009 Maaco Bowl Las Vegas was played on Tuesday, December 22, 2009 at 40,000-seat Sam Boyd Stadium in Whitney, Nevada and was broadcast on ESPN. BYU played in the Las Vegas Bowl for the fifth straight year. BYU had gone 2–2 against Pac-10 opponents in the last four Las Vegas Bowls. This was the ninth meeting between the two teams, although the first time they met in this bowl game. Prior to the 2009 Las Vegas Bowl, Oregon State had a 5–3 lead in the series, winning the last meeting 10–7 in 1986. This was the first postseason meeting between the two teams. Bronco Mendenhall, head coach for Brigham Young, is an Oregon State alumnus and it was revealed during the broadcast that he chose Oregon State specifically because Brigham Young did not recruit him, and Oregon State had a game with BYU scheduled for the 1986 season. The 2009 game was the first meeting of two ranked teams in the bowl game's history.

2009 Las Vegas Bowl	Line	1	-	2	-	3	-	4	-	Final
#15 Oregon State	(-2.5)	7	-	0	-	0	-	13	-	20
#16 BYU	(59.0)	14	-	9	-	7	-	14	-	44

Scoring Summary
Oregon State - Canfield 1 yard run (Kahut kick)
BYU - Unga 1 yard run (Payne kick)
BYU - Bauman 34 yard fumble return (Payne kick)
BYU - Payne 28 yard Field goal
BYU - Ashworth 25 yard pass from Hall (Kick blocked)
BYU - Pitta 17 yard pass from Hall (Payne kick)

BYU - Tonga 15 yard pass from Hall (Payne kick)
Oregon State - Rodgers 1 yard run (Kick failed)
BYU - Tonga 18 yard run (Payne kick)
Oregon State - Adeniji 31 yard pass from Katz (Kahut kick)

Associated Press Las Vegas Bowl Game Summary - Max Hall became a regular at the Las Vegas Bowl, and his final performance was his best. The senior Quarterback threw for 192 yards and three touchdowns in the only bowl game he knows, leading BYU (No. 14 BCS, No. 15 AP) past Oregon State (No. 18 BCS, No. 16 AP) 44-20 on Tuesday night. Hall gave the Cougars their third win in five straight bowl appearances in Sin City and ended the Beavers' run of five consecutive bowl wins. Oregon State appeared troubled by cold winds and the lingering sting of missing the Rose Bowl after a close loss to rival Oregon in its season finale. Hall threw a 25-yard touchdown pass to Luke Ashworth, a 17-yard scoring strike to Dennis Pitta and a 15-yard TD pass to Manase Tonga. Hall had 139 yards passing in the first half. Hall won for the second time in the Las Vegas Bowl in three starts, throwing more touchdowns Tuesday night than in his previous appearances. Tonga added an 18-yard rushing touchdown, and Harvey Unga finished with 76 yards rushing and a TD for BYU (11-2). Oregon State (8-5) scored on 1-yard runs by Quarterback Sean Canfield and Jacquizz Rodgers, and a 31-yard pass to Damola Adeniji after the game was out of reach. Adeniji led all receivers with seven receptions for 102 yards. Canfield completed only four passes in the first half as the Beavers struggled to sustain drives. He finished 20 of 41 for 173 yards and an interception. The normally dependable Rodgers fumbled for the first time in his college career in the first quarter, on his 621st touch, and Matt Bauman returned it 34 yards for the go-ahead score. Officials used replay to see whether Canfield's checkdown toss to Rodgers was a lateral or a forward pass and upheld the touchdown. Oregon State finished with three turnovers, including a fumble by Rodgers' brother, James. The Beavers converted once on fourth down in five tries and were 5 for 16 on third-down conversions. Winds gusted up to 50 mph at Sam Boyd Stadium and temperatures fell to 30 degrees. The gusts were so strong that one of Oregon State's punts traveled untouched only 6 yards. Oregon State struck first on Canfield's touchdown. The score was set up by consecutive big plays from the Rodgers brothers -- an 18-yard rush by Jacquizz on the first play of the drive and a 17-yard run by James. BYU responded with a touchdown on its next possession, marching 84 yards on 14 plays in just under six minutes and scoring on Unga's 1-yard run. Oregon State then looked as if it would bounce back from Jacquizz Rodgers' fumble when it seemingly recovered a muffed punt near the goal line. But a holding call forced Oregon State to punt again, and BYU drove 69 yards and kicked a 28-yard field goal.

2009 Poinsettia Bowl

The 2009 San Diego County Credit Union Poinsettia Bowl was the fifth edition of the bowl game and was played at Qualcomm Stadium in San Diego, California. The game was played on Wednesday, December 23, 2009 on ESPN. The Utah Utes defeated the California Golden Bears by a score of 37–27 to win their ninth straight bowl game. The Bears lost their first bowl game since 2004, snapping a winning streak of four post-season victories. The Utes from the Mountain West Conference had won eight straight bowl appearances, including the last season's Sugar Bowl against Alabama. The Utes also faced their former offensive coordinator, Andy Ludwig, who had helped guide them the previous year to a 13–0 record and #2 ranking. Cal played its third bowl game in San Diego in six years, having made two previous trips to the Holiday Bowl in 2004 and 2006. The Bears had not lost a bowl game since 2004. It was the seventh straight year that Cal head coach Jeff Tedford had guided Cal to a bowl appearance, the longest streak in school history.

2009 Poinsettia Bowl	Line	1	-	2	-	3	-	4	-	Final
Utah	(52.0)	7	-	17	-	3	-	10	-	37
California	(-3.0)	14	-	0	-	7	-	6	-	26

Scoring Summary
California - Vereen 36 yard run (D'Amato kick)
California - Young 31yard interception return (D'Amato kick)
Utah - Moeai 6 yard pass from Wynn (Phillips kick)
Utah - Phillips 28 yard Field goal
Utah - Moeai 15 yard pass from Wynn (Phillips kick)
Utah - Brooks 21 yard pass from Wynn (Phillips kick)
Utah - Phillips 29 yard Field goal
California - Vereen 1 yard run (D'Amato kick)
Utah - Phillips 25 yard Field goal
Utah - Sylvester 27 yard interception return (Phillips kick)
California - Ross 24 yard pass from Riley (pass failed)

Associated Press Poinsettia Bowl Game Summary - The Utah Utes flat out know how to win bowl games, whether they're busting the BCS or playing in a lower-tier game before Christmas. True freshman Jordan Wynn threw for a career-high 338 yards and three touchdowns to rally No. 23 Utah from an early two-touchdown deficit to a 37-27 victory over California in the San Diego County Credit Union Poinsettia Bowl on Wednesday night. The Utes scored 27 straight points to win their ninth straight bowl game, the longest current streak in the country and tied for the second-longest ever. Florida State won 11 straight from 1985-96 and Southern California won nine in a row from 1923-45. The Utes' bowl victory streak began with a win over Fresno State in the 1999 Las Vegas Bowl. A member of the Mountain West Conference, the Utes were the original BCS busters, beating Pittsburgh 35-7 in the Fiesta Bowl after the 2004 season. They also beat Alabama 31-17 in the Sugar Bowl last season. Cal is the fifth team from a BCS conference to lose to Utah during the streak. Wynn improved to 3-0 at Qualcomm Stadium, including two section championships while the starter at suburban Oceanside High. Wynn completed 26 of 36 passes and improved to 3-2 as the Utes' starter. Utah's defense came up big, too. The Utes sacked Cal's Kevin Riley five times and intercepted him twice, with linebacker Stevenson Sylvester returning a tipped pass 27 yards for a touchdown late in the game. Riley also lost a fumble. Shane Vereen, who scored twice, was the seventh Cal back to gain more than 100 yards in a bowl, finishing with 122 yards on 20 carries. Utah (10-3) looked overmatched after Cal (8-5) scored twice in 11 seconds midway through the first quarter. Vereen scored on a 36-yard run and Eddie Young intercepted Wynn on the first play of Utah's next drive and returned it 31 yards for a score. After that it was all Utah. Young said the Golden Bears hoped to rattle the young QB. Utah's defense shut down Cal and Utah scored on its last four possessions of the first half. Wynn threw a 6-yard touchdown pass to tight end Kendrick Moeai late in the first quarter and Joe Phillips' 28-yard field goal early in the second quarter pulled Utah to 14-10. Wynn's 15-yard scoring pass to Moeai gave Utah the lead and his 21-yarder to Jereme Brooks made it 24-14 at halftime. Riley fumbled early in the third quarter when he was sacked by Lamar Chapman, with Mike Wright recovering at the 14. That set up Phillips' 29-yard field goal for a 27-14 lead. Cal finally scored again on a 1-yard run by Vereen with 39 seconds left in the third quarter to pull the Golden Bears to 27-21 before Phillips kicked a 25-yard field goal. Riley was 20 of 36 for 214 yards and one touchdown. Cal had only six first downs in the first half. Utah's David Reed set school records for catches (81) and receiving yards (1,188) in a season. Both records came on a 39-yard catch in the fourth quarter.

2009 Hawai'i Bowl

The 2009 Hawaii Bowl was the eighth edition of the bowl game, played at Aloha Stadium in Honolulu, Hawaii. The game was played on Thursday, December 24, 2009, with the SMU Mustangs of Conference USA beating the Nevada Wolf Pack of the Western Athletic Conference 45–10. The 2009 Hawai'i Bowl was SMU's first bowl bid since playing in Hawaii in the 1984 Aloha Bowl, as well as their first since the program was relaunched in 1989 after being shut down for two years due to massive NCAA rules violations. Head coach June Jones made his first appearance as a coach in Aloha Stadium since leaving Hawai'i in 2008 to take over the SMU football program. SMU freshman starter Kyle Padron, who was himself a backup until an injury earlier in the season to then starter Bo Levi Mitchell, was named the game's MVP after throwing for 460 yards and two touchdowns.

2009 Hawaii Bowl	Line	1	-	2	-	3	-	4	-	Final
SMU	(72.0)	17	-	14	-	7	-	7	-	45
Nevada	(-12.5)	0	-	0	-	3	-	7	-	10

Scoring Summary
SMU - McNeal 9 yard run (Syzmanski kick)
SMU - McNeal 2 yard run (Syzmanski kick)
SMU - Syzmanski 22 yard Field goal
SMU - Sanders 17 yard pass from Padron (Syzmanski kick)
SMU - Beasley 2 yard pass from Padron (Syzmanski kick)
SMU - Line 3 yard run (Syzmanski kick)
Nevada - Drake 21 yard Field goal
SMU - McNeal 17 yard run (Syzmanski kick)
Nevada - Wimberly 10 yard pass from Kaepernick (Drake kick)

Associated Press Hawaii Bowl Game Summary - SMU is back from the dead. Freshman Kyle Padron threw for an SMU-record 460 yards, leading the Mustangs to a 45-10 victory over Nevada in the Hawaii Bowl on Thursday night -- SMU's first postseason appearance in 25 years. It was a triumphant return to the postseason and paradise for the Mustangs and second-year coach June Jones, who left Hawaii after nine seasons and has revived a dreadful SMU program hit hard by the NCAA death penalty. Jones is 16-1 at Aloha Stadium since 2006 and 4-1 in Hawaii Bowls. SMU fans chanted "Thank you, June!" in the fourth quarter, but it was his young Quarterback who shone and earned the MVP award. Padron broke Mike Romo's school record of 450 yards passing against North Texas in 1989. It was chaos in the SMU locker room where players were dancing, chanting and screaming. Players couldn't even hear Jones' speech. The Mustangs were motivated by the fact that 91 percent of America picked them to lose online. The 18-year-old Padron, who was 32 of 41 and completed two touchdown passes, was confident and composed on the biggest stage of his young career. He earned the starting job after Bo Levi Mitchell was injured in the seventh game of the season and was largely unknown coming out of Southlake Carroll in Texas, which produced Quarterbacks Chase Daniel and Greg McElroy. Despite the tiny crowd at the game, people are paying attention to Padron -- and SMU. After going 1-11 the previous two years, the Mustangs (8-5) have their most victories since their last postseason game -- also in Hawaii when SMU beat Notre Dame 27-20 in the 1984 Aloha Bowl to finish 10-2. The 12-point underdogs dominated from the opening bell, jumping out to a 17-0 lead in the first quarter and building a 38-0 advantage by the third. Padron had 303 yards passing in the first half alone, breaking SMU's bowl record of 281 yards by Chuck Hixson in the 1968 Astro-Bluebonnet Bowl. Padron's 17- and 2-yard touchdown passes in second quarter gave SMU a 31-0 lead at the half and had the Wolf Pack searching for answers. The 17-yarder was to Emmanuel Sanders, who had seven catches for 124 yards. Sanders finished his career as SMU's career leader in receptions, touchdown catches and yards. Shawnbrey McNeal added 63 yards rushing and three touchdowns, including two in the first quarter. He also had seven catches for 53 yards. The loss was the fourth straight in the postseason for the Wolf Pack (8-5), whose No. 1 rushing offense in the nation was grounded. But it was the Nevada defense that looked as if it was left behind feeding Wheel-of-Fortune machines in Reno. While SMU racked up 534 yards of offense, Nevada had held to just 314, including 137 yards rushing. The Wolf Pack averaged 362.3 yards rushing during the regular season and is the first team in NCAA history to have three 1,000-yard rushers. But Nevada was without two of them in running backs Vai Taua and Luke Lippincott. Taua was ruled academically ineligible, and Lippincott was sidelined with a toe injury. The Mustangs wasted no time getting on the scoreboard and attacking Nevada's anemic pass defense, ranked second worst in the nation. On the second play of the game, Padron found a wide-open Cole Beasley near midfield. Beasley was dragged down from behind at the Nevada 9 for a gain of 71 yards. It was the longest pass in SMU bowl history, breaking Doak Walker's 53-yard pass to Paul Page in the 1948 Cotton Bowl. McNeal scored on the next play. The Mustangs got the ball back on the next series by stopping the Wolf Pack on fourth-and-2. Padron then connected with Sanders for a 58-yard gain, setting up McNeal's 1-yard TD that put SMU up 14-0 less than 6 1/2 minutes into the game. After completing a 53-yard pass to Aldrick Robinson in the third that set up a 3-yard TD run by Zach line, Padron looked at Jones and just shook his head in disbelief. Robinson finished with nine catches for 176 yards. Meanwhile, Nevada Quarterback Colin Kaepernick couldn't get anything going on the ground or through the air. Kaepernick, who rushed for 1,160 yards in the regular season, had just 23 yards rushing on 13 carries. Kaepernick, who was 15 of 29 for 177 yards. He threw a 10-yard TD pass with a minute left in the game.

2009 Meineke Car Care Bowl

The 2009 Meineke Car Care Bowl was the eighth edition of the bowl game and was played at Bank of America Stadium in Charlotte, North Carolina. The game was played on Saturday, December 26, 2009 and was telecasted on ESPN and ESPN360. The Pittsburgh Panthers defeated the North Carolina Tar Heels 19–17 with a 33-yard field goal and .52 seconds remaining in the game.

2009 Meineke Car Care Bowl	Line	1	-	2	-	3	-	4	-	Final
Pittsburgh	(-2.5)	0	-	13	-	3	-	3	-	19
North Carolina	(44.5)	7	-	3	-	7	-	0	-	17

Scoring Summary
North Carolina - Little 15 yard pass from Yates (Barth kick)
Pittsburgh - Hutchins 31 yard Field goal
Pittsburgh - Lewis 11 yard run (Hutchins kick)
North Carolina - Barth 37 yard Field goal
Pittsburgh - Hutchins 31 yard Field goal
Pittsburgh - Hutchins 42 yard Field goal
North Carolina - Little 14 yard pass from Yates (Barth kick)
Pittsburgh - Hutchins 33 yard Field goal

Associated Press Meineke Car Care Bowl Game Summary - Pittsburgh hasn't won this many games since Dan Marino was the Quarterback. The only player in school history to rush for more yards in a season than freshman sensation Dion Lewis is somebody named Tony Dorsett. Thanks to a late-game rally in front of a hostile crowd, the Panthers made a strong case they've returned to prominence. Lewis rushed for 159 yards and a touchdown to move up in the record book and Dan Hutchins kicked a 33-yard field goal with 52 seconds left, giving 17th-ranked Pitt a 19-17 victory over North Carolina on Saturday in the Meineke Car Care Bowl. Winning 10 games for the first time since the Marino era in 1981, Pitt (10-3) overcame a disappointing loss to Cincinnati three weeks ago that cost it a spot in a BCS bowl. The last win in 2009 required a remarkable 17-play drive that lasted nearly 9 minutes, included a key fourth-down conversion, a costly penalty against North Carolina and 13 runs by the dynamic Lewis. Eclipsing Dorsett's freshman rushing record of 1,686 yards in the first quarter, Lewis also moved past Craig Heyward into second on the school's single-season list with 1,799 yards. Dorsett rushed for 2,150 yards in 1976 when he won the Heisman Trophy and Pitt won its last national title. T.J. Yates threw two touchdown passes to Greg Little, but his incomplete pass on fourth-and-10 from his own 49 with 6 seconds left sent the Tar Heels (8-5) to their second straight loss. Yates was 19 of 32 for 183 yards and an interception while Little caught seven passes for 87 yards and Ryan Houston rushed for 83 yards. But North Carolina's defense, which came in sixth in the nation overall and ninth against the run, struggled to contain the shifty Lewis and continued a trend of struggling to close out games over the past two seasons under coach Butch Davis. It took Wannstedt's big gamble to lift Pitt after North Carolina took a 17-16 lead late in the third quarter on Yates' 14-yard TD pass to Little. Facing a fourth-and-1 from his own 30 with 6:36 left, senior Bill Stull got 3 yards on a Quarterback keeper. Lewis was later stuffed on third down, leaving Wannstedt with another decision on fourth-and-2 from the North Carolina 30 with 1:30 left. He brought out the field goal unit, but Pitt used a hard count and North Carolina's Cam Thomas jumped offsides, giving Pitt a first down. Lewis got 13 yards on the next play, and his 6-yard run into the middle of the field on his 28th carry set up Hutchins' fourth field goal. Lewis broke Dorsett's 36-year-old freshman mark on a 24-yard run late in the first quarter that ended with him fumbling the ball through the end zone for a touchback when E.J. Wilson knocked the ball free. The speedy Lewis made up for it an 11-yard touchdown run that put Pitt ahead 10-7 early in the second quarter. The 5-foot-8 Lewis had eclipsed 100 yards by halftime, his 10th 100-yard game of the season and his eighth straight. Not bad for a lightly recruited player deemed too small by most of the major schools. Davis compared him to Clinton Portis, and Lewis was already fielding 2010 Heisman Trophy questions after the game. North Carolina couldn't overcome its numerous mistakes in falling to 0-3 in the Charlotte bowl. Erik Highsmith's fumble set up a Pitt field goal, and Yates was picked off by Dan Mason near the goal line in the second quarter. Even Yates' 15-yard TD pass to a double-covered Little in the first quarter ended with a 15-yard penalty when Little punted the ball into the stands.

2009 Emerald Bowl

The 2009 Emerald Bowl was the eighth edition of the bowl game and was played at AT&T Park in San Francisco, California. The game was played on Saturday, December 26, 2009. The game was telecast on ESPN.

2009 Emerald Bowl	Line	1	-	2	-	3	-	4	-	Final
Boston College	(45.0)	0	-	13	-	0	-	0	-	13
USC	(-7.5)	7	-	7	-	3	-	7	-	24

Scoring Summary
USC - Havili 53 yard pass from Barkley (Congdon kick)
USC - Havili 5 yard pass from Barkley (Congdon kick)
Boston College - Harris 7 yard run (kick failed)
Boston College - Gunnell 61 yard pass from Shinskie (Aponavicius kick)
USC - Congdon 38 yard Field goal
USC - Barkley 1 yard run (Congdon kick)

Associated Press Emerald Bowl Game Summary - Southern California ended a disappointing season with a bowl win that the Trojans hope will vault them into a more successful 2010. Matt Barkley threw touchdown passes to Stanley Havili on Southern California's first two possessions and added a touchdown run in the fourth quarter to help the Trojans beat Boston College 24-13 in the Emerald Bowl on Saturday night. The victory was far from impressive, but it did put a positive ending on the worst season at USC (9-4) since Pete Carroll's first back in 2001. The Trojans lost three of their final five regular-season games to fall out of the national rankings for the first time since that year. That left USC in an unfamiliar bowl setting after making it to the Bowl Championship Series the past seven years, including four straight Rose Bowl bids. But the Trojans made the most of it, handing Boston College (8-5) its second straight bowl loss after an eight-year bowl winning streak. Damian Williams caught 12 passes for 189 yards in what could be his final game for the Trojans, grabbing long passes to set up Havili's second score and Barkley's 1-yard sneak that gave USC a 24-13 lead with 11:53 remaining. Williams will decide in the next few days whether to skip his senior season to enter the NFL draft. The Eagles stayed close with the Trojans for most of the game before Dave Shinskie threw an interception to Shareece Wright early in the fourth quarter. On the next play, Barkley connected on a 48-yard pass to Williams, who made a leaping grab between three defenders.

Barkley scored on the next play. The Trojans won despite playing without leading rusher Joe McKnight, who was not cleared to play as the school investigates whether he violated rules by using an SUV that doesn't belong to him. McKnight is USC's first 1,000-yard rusher since 2005, with 1,014 yards on 6.2 yards per carry and eight touchdowns. USC struggled on the ground without McKnight but was able to move the ball consistently through the air as Barkley often found receivers on slant patterns. Barkley was 27 of 37 for 350 yards in the second 300-yard game of his freshman season. He also threw two interceptions that allowed Boston College to stay close until the fourth quarter. The Trojans got a fast start by scoring touchdowns on their two possessions with passes from Barkley to Havili to go up 14-0. But USC didn't score again in the half, with Barkley throwing an interception deep in BC territory to end one potential scoring drive. The Eagles got right back into the game with a 7-yard run by Montel Harris. Steve Aponavicius hit the upright on the extra point attempt, ending a streak of 81 straight makes since late in the 2007 season. BC got help from a big mistake by USC to get another score late in the half. Michael Morgan was called for pass interference on a third-and-21 toss to Chris Pantale that went only 2 yards. But the infraction gave the Eagles an automatic first down and Shinskie connected with Rich Gunnell on a 61-yard TD pass on the next play to make it 14-13. Gunnell finished with six catches for 130 yards, breaking Pete Mitchell's school record for yards receiving with 2,659 in his career. The Eagles missed a golden opportunity to score after intercepting Barkley on the first play of the second half to give them the ball at the 9. Harris fumbled a handoff two plays later, costing BC a chance to take its first lead of the game. Harris finished with 102 yards on 23 carries for his fifth straight 100-yard game, but BC struggled to move the ball in the second half. The Eagles had just 19 yards in the third quarter and never mounted a sustained drive in the second half until the game had been decided.

2009 Little Caesars Pizza Bowl

The 2009 Little Caesars Pizza Bowl was played on December 26, 2009 at Ford Field in Detroit, Michigan and aired on ESPN. The game was the 13th installment of the bowl game played in Detroit. A lack of eligible teams from the Big Ten Conference made a spot available in the game for Marshall. **Line judge Sarah Thomas became the first female to officiate a college football bowl game.**

2009 Little Caesars Pizza Bowl	Line	1	-	2	-	3	-	4	-	Final
Marshall	(49.0)	14	-	7	-	0	-	0	-	21
Ohio	(-3.0)	0	-	7	-	10	-	0	-	17

Scoring Summary
Marshall - Ward 12 yard run (Ratanamorn kick)
Marshall - Booker 58 yard punt return (Ratanamorn kick)
Marshall - Ward 2 yard run (Ratanamorn kick)
Ohio - Ballard 75 yard fumble return (Weller kick)
Ohio - McCrae 8 yard pass from Scott (Weller kick)
Ohio - Weller 46 yard Field goal

Little Caesar's Pizza Bowl Game Recap - Marshall sprung to a 21-0 lead, then held on to defeat Ohio 21-17 in the Little Caesars Pizza Bowl at Ford Field in Detroit. The 21-0 lead was built on a pair of Martin Ward rushing touchdowns sandwiched around a 58-yard Andre Booker punt return. The Thundering Herd was driving to potentially make it 28-0 before Darius Marshall fumbled and Shannon Ballard returned it 75 yards for Ohio's first points. Two punt blunders by Marshall helped Ohio cut the lead to 21-17 in the 3rd quarter. A 15-yard punt gave the Bobcats the ball at the Marshall 37-yard line and Terrence McCrae scored on an 8-yard TD reception from Theo Scott five plays later. Marshall's next possession ended in a blocked punt that led to a 46-yard Matt Weller field goal to close the scoring. Ohio leads the series 29-18-6, but Marshall has won the last five meetings. Despite having campuses that are less than 90 miles apart, these teams had not met since Marshall left the MAC after the 2004 season to join CUSA. 2010 will mark a renewal of the rivalry during the regular season. The Herd dominated the MAC during its brief stay, capturing the conference title five times in its 8-year league history. Marshall won four straight conference titles during its first four years of MAC membership, lost the title game in its fifth year, and recaptured the crown in its sixth. The Herd played in each of the Motor City Bowl's first four games and won the last three after dropping the first. It was the 11th consecutive bowl loss for MAC teams and the 3rd straight in this bowl. Ohio fell to 0-4 overall in bowl games while Marshal improved to 6-2. Ohio was making its first appearance in the Detroit bowl but was playing its second consecutive game at Ford Field. The Bobcats may not want to see it again anytime soon after ending the season with two straight losses at the venue, including a 20-10 setback to Central Michigan in the MAC Championship game on December 4. Had Ohio won that game, it would have secured its first MAC title since 1968, and its first 10-win season since that same year. Frank Solich saw his overall bowl record drop to 3-5, including 0-2 with Ohio.

2009 Music City Bowl

The 2009 Gaylord Hotels Music City Bowl was the twelfth edition of the bowl game, and was played at LP Field in Nashville, Tennessee. The game was played on Sunday, December 27, 2009 and was telecast on ESPN. Music City Bowl officials originally wanted to select North Carolina as the ACC representative. This would have set up a contest between two traditional college basketball powers (the Wildcats and Tar Heels are first and second, respectively, in all-time college basketball wins). This plan came undone, however, when the Chick-fil-A, Gator, and Champs Sports Bowls all passed on Clemson, which lost the 2009 ACC Championship Game to Georgia Tech. This forced the Music City Bowl to take Clemson. Under the ACC's bowl selection rules in 2009, the conference title game loser could not fall below the Music City Bowl, which had the fifth pick among bowl-eligible ACC teams. The Tar Heels accepted a bid to the 2009 Meineke Car Care Bowl. Since 2002, the name of the bowl game has been known as The Gaylord Hotels Music City Bowl, being named after its primary sponsor, Gaylord Hotels. The 2010 game marked the first time since then that a new company has taken over as title sponsor of the game, as Franklin American Mortgage will take over. Gaylord Hotels continued to be a major sponsor of the game. This was Kentucky's third appearance in the bowl game in four years. It was Clemson's second appearance in the bowl. The game was a rematch of the 2006 game in which Kentucky won by a score of 28–20. The two teams had met a total of 12 previous times with Kentucky winning 8 of the previous games. Aside from the 2006 Music City Bowl, the schools also met in the 1993 Peach Bowl, a game won by Clemson 14–13.

2009 Music City Bowl	Line	1	-	2	-	3	-	4	-	Final
Kentucky	(52.5)	7	-	3	-	3	-	0	-	13
Clemson	(-7.0)	7	-	7	-	0	-	7	-	21

Scoring Summary
Kentucky - Matthews 17 yard pass from Newton (Seiber kick)
Clemson - Ford 32 yard pass from Parker (Jackson kick)
Kentucky - Seiber 39 yard Field goal
Clemson - Harper 1 yard run (Jackson kick)
Kentucky - Seiber 44 yard Field goal
Clemson - Spiller 8 yard run (Jackson kick)

Associated Press Music City Bowl Game Summary - C.J. Spiller went out a winner in the final game of his record-setting career at Clemson. Kentucky coach Rich Brooks? Well, the 68-year-old coach apparently is ready to call it a career. Spiller scored a touchdown and had 172 all-purpose yards in his final college game, leading Clemson to a 21-13 victory over Kentucky on Sunday night in the Music City Bowl. The Tigers (9-5) hadn't won a bowl since the 2005 Champs Sports Bowl. The Tigers (9-5) hadn't won a bowl since the 2005 Champs Sports Bowl. Kentucky (7-6) was trying to make program history by winning a fourth straight bowl game. The Wildcats certainly had the home-field advantage with blue filling nearly two-thirds of the lower bowl at LP Field. Spiller, the Atlantic Coast Conference player of the year, scored his 51st career touchdown -- a Clemson record -- on an 8-yard run with 10:14 left in the fourth quarter to make it 21-13. Spiller scored three plays after Clemson linebacker Kavell Conner stripped Gene McCaskill after a short catch and Jarvis Jenkins recovered the ball at the Kentucky 19 for the game's only turnover. Kentucky tried to answer. Punter Ryan Tydlacka ran for 9 yards on fourth-and-3, then Brooks used his last timeout with 5:38 left before going for it again on fourth-and-8 at the Clemson 32. The Cats couldn't convert. Freshman Quarterback Morgan Newton scrambled only to be tackled by Ricky Sapp a yard short. Spiller helped the Tigers run out the clock and start the celebration. He finished with 68 yards on 15 carries and 57 yards on three catches to earn game MVP honors. But the Wildcats did a decent job of slowing down one of the country's most dynamic players. He became the first ACC player to rush for at least 1,000 yards and have at least 500 yards receiving in the same history at the end of the third quarter when he took a shovel pass 3 yards. "He got it done," Swinney said of Spiller needing 55 yards receiving to notch that accomplishment. He didn't return a kick longer than 30 yards. Kentucky kicker Lones Seiber perfectly placed one kickoff into the right edge of the end zone near the pylon for a touchback, and Spiller caught another near the same spot for another touchback. Kentucky held onto the ball for more than 34 minutes and ran 22 more plays. Brooks credited Clemson with using the time before the bowl to prepare well to defend Kentucky's version of the wildcat offense because the Tigers still outgained the Wildcats 321-277. The Tigers also held on to the ball for the final 5:27. Winds gusting to 22 mph affected both teams on a cold night. Richard Jackson's 44-yard field goal for Clemson into the wind came up just short with 4:32 left in the third. Kentucky called a timeout with 2 seconds left in the third, and Dawson Zimmerman's punt went just 24 yards before bouncing back for the Wildcats. The Tigers forced Kentucky three-and-out, and Tydlacka had to deal with that wind himself. His punt went only 14 yards. Clemson led 14-10 at halftime as Kyle Parker found Jacoby Ford all alone in the end zone for a 32-yard TD pass to cap a four-play, 90-yard drive Spiller jump started with a 42-yard catch-and-run. Seiber put Kentucky up 10-7 in the second with a 39-yard field goal, then Spiller had a 30-yard kickoff return. Tailback Jamie Harper handled all the work on a five-play drive as he picked up 60 yards and capped it with a 1-yard plunge to put the Tigers ahead 14-10 in the second quarter. The Wildcats' only TD came on their opening drive when Newton found Chris Matthews in the end zone for a 17-yard TD pass and a 7-0 lead.

2009 Independence Bowl

The 2009 AdvoCare V100 Independence Bowl was the thirty-fourth edition of the bowl game, and was played at Independence Stadium in Shreveport, Louisiana. The game was played on Monday, December 28, 2009. The game was Georgia's second appearance in the bowl game. As for Texas A&M, the Aggies made their third appearance in the Independence Bowl and now hold an overall record of 1–2. The game was fifth time that the two schools have faced each other in a game. Texas A&M previously held the series advantage 3–1 (now 3-2). The last time, prior to the bowl that the two teams met was a 42–0 victory by Georgia in 1980. The two teams have played in a bowl game against each other once before, as they met in the 1950 Presidential Cup Bowl.

2009 Independence Bowl	Line	1	-	2	-	3	-	4	-	Final
Texas A&M	(66.5)	0	-	7	-	7	-	6	-	20
Georgia	(-7.0)	0	-	14	-	10	-	20	-	44

Scoring Summary
Texas A&M - McCoy 15 yard pass from Johnson (Bullock kick)
Georgia - Boykin 81 yard kickoff return (Walsh kick)
Georgia - King 2 yard run (Walsh kick)
Texas A&M - Michael 14 yard run (Bullock kick)
Georgia - Walsh 49 yard Field goal
Georgia - White 24 yard pass from Cox (Walsh kick)
Georgia - White 2 yard pass from Cox (Walsh kick)
Georgia - King 1 yard run (Walsh kick)
Georgia - Chapas 5 yard run (Kick blocked)
Texas A&M - Morrow 5 yard pass from Johnson (Pass failed)

Associated Press Independence Bowl Game Summary - Brandon Boykin's teammates were giving him all kinds of kudos after his school record-setting kickoff return for a touchdown sparked Georgia's win over Texas A&M in the Independence Bowl. Boykin wanted none of it, though. To hear him tell it, all he did was run. His third kickoff return for a score of the season -- an 81-yarder late in the second quarter -- hardly qualified as a miracle, but it was just what the Bulldogs needed to fuel a 44-20 victory on Monday. Fifty-six seconds later Georgia blocked a punt, setting up another touchdown, and a game that was supposed to be an offensive showdown turned into yet another contest decided by the unit most folks usually forget about. Boykin set the school record and tied the Southeastern Conference mark with his kick return TD, Georgia blocked two kicks and Joe Cox threw his first touchdown pass after a snap sailed over the Texas A&M punter's head in the third quarter. In all, special teams play led to 24 points for Georgia, which also got a 49-yard field goal from Blair Walsh. Add in an unexpectedly strong defensive effort and the Bulldogs managed to salvage a smile after a disappointing season. Boykin may have deflected the credit, but everyone else called his return the "spark" that kicked the moribund Bulldogs to life. Instead of trailing going into halftime, Georgia was up 14-7. Joe Cox hit offensive MVP Aron White on touchdown passes of 24 and 2 yards in the second half and the Bulldogs (8-5) scored a bowl record 30 points in the final two quarters for their fourth straight postseason victory. It was the fourth straight postseason loss for the Aggies (6-7), who have not won a bowl since 2001. The Bulldogs sealed the win by intercepting Jerrod Johnson twice in the third quarter, an unexpected outcome for a defense that was playing with just one full-time assistant after the firing of defensive coordinator Willie Martinez and two others. All the offense expected from two teams with porous defenses and stars on offense such as Johnson and Georgia receiver A.J. Green never really developed. The teams had more punts than first downs in the first 25 minutes of the game. Texas A&M finally got moving in the waning moments of the second quarter behind Johnson, whose 15-yard TD pass to Jamie McCoy with 2:33 left in the first half had the feel of a momentum builder. But on the ensuing kickoff, Boykin tied the score at 7. Even after the late first-half collapse, the Aggies seemed to have life. Christine Michael scored from 14 yards out on Texas A&M's first drive of the second half to make it 14-14. Their next three drives were disastrous, though. The first ended on the botched snap over the punter's head, which gave Georgia the ball at the Texas A&M 24. Three plays later, Cox hit White with a touch pass down the middle of the field with a rusher in his face to make it 24-14. Johnson threw interceptions on the next two Aggies' possessions. Georgia was unable to score after the first turnover, but Reshad Jones' 59-yard interception return on the second gave the Bulldogs the ball at the Aggies 28. Five plays later, Cox faked the handoff from the 2, rolled right on a naked bootleg and found the wide-open White in the right corner of the end zone for a 31-14 lead. Caleb King, who scored twice, and Shaun Chapas tacked on TD runs in the fourth quarter to pad Georgia's lead and gave the Bulldogs a share of the Independence bowl record with six touchdowns. The Bulldogs improved to 7-2 in bowls under Richt and put a positive finish on a season that didn't go as expected.

2009 Champs Sports Bowl

The 2009 Champs Sports Bowl was played between the Wisconsin Badgers of the Big Ten Conference and the Miami Hurricanes of the Atlantic Coast Conference. Played at the Citrus Bowl in Orlando, Florida, the game was played on Tuesday, December 29, 2009 and was televised by ESPN. Wisconsin won the game 20-14. The 2009 game marked the last time in the foreseeable future that the Big 10 was represented in the bowl game. A four-year contract was signed so that starting in 2010 the Big East will send a team to the bowl instead. Miami made its third appearance in the bowl, they last played in the game in 1998 where they easily defeated North Carolina State 46–23. The Canes won their two previous appearances. Meanwhile, Wisconsin made its second appearance in as many years. They were defeated in the 2008 game by Florida State 42–13. The bowl game marked the fourth time that the two schools have faced each other and the first time in the post-season. Miami previously held a 2–1 series advantage (now 2-2) with the last meeting being a 51–3 thrashing by the Hurricanes in opening game of the 1989 season. Miami would go on to win their 3rd National Championship that year.

2009 Champs Sports Bowl	Line	1	-	2	-	3	-	4	-	Final
#14 Miami	(-3.5)	7	-	0	-	0	-	7	-	14
#24 Wisconsin	(57.0)	7	-	10	-	0	-	3	-	20

Scoring Summary
Miami - Cooper 16 yard run (Bosher kick)
Wisconsin - Clay 3 yard run (Welch kick)
Wisconsin - Clay 3 yard run (Welch kick)
Wisconsin - Welch 37 yard Field goal
Wisconsin - Welch 28 yard Field goal
Miami - Collier 14 yard pass from Harris (Bosher kick)

Associated Press Champs Sports Bowl Game Summary - All that Miami speed was no match for the big, bad Badgers. John Clay had 121 yards rushing and two touchdowns, powering Wisconsin (No. 25 BCS, No. 24 AP) past Miami (No. 15 BCS, No. 14 AP) 20-14 in the Champs Sports Bowl on Tuesday night. Clay ran through, over and around the Hurricanes to help the Badgers (10-3) earn their first victory over a ranked opponent this season and claim a big win for the Big Ten. Scott Tolzien threw for 260 yards, and Montee Ball added 61 yards rushing for a Wisconsin team touted as too big and too slow for the dynamic Hurricanes. None of that seemed to matter when the Badgers were powering the ball down the field. Miami's Jacory Harris struggled before throwing a touchdown pass to Thearon Collier with 1:22 remaining. The Hurricanes recovered the onside kick, but Harris threw incomplete on fourth down to end any hope of a comeback. Harris, who threw for 188 yards, was slowed by an injured right thumb, a brace around his left leg and a Badgers team that smothered him with five sacks. Wisconsin's running game helped it hold the ball for nearly 40 minutes, leaving little time for Miami to work. Miami also lost Graig Cooper to a right knee injury in the second quarter, a big reason why the Hurricanes (9-4) will have to wait at least another year to end their drought of 10-win seasons. The Badgers made sure of that. Even if they didn't show it at the start. Sam Shields took a reverse from Cooper on the opening kickoff, zipped up the middle, then cut down the left sideline for a touchdown. But an illegal block in the back on the play returned the ball to the Wisconsin 16-yard line. Shields was credited with an 84-yard return, a Hurricanes bowl record. Cooper had a 16-yard touchdown run on the next play that gave Miami the lead 23 seconds into the game. That was about the only thing that went wrong for the Badgers. Their big and bulky lines bullied the fleet Hurricanes, whose all white jerseys -- almost all complete with long sleeves on the brisk 50-degree night -- parted to a sea of Wisconsin red on both sides of the ball. Clay had all sorts of seams to run through, and he bulldozed his way to the rest of his yards. The Big Ten offensive player of the year ripped through a hole for a 52-yard run and followed that with his second 3-yard TD run of the game to put Wisconsin ahead 14-7 in the second quarter. Phillip Welch added a 37-yard field goal with 12 seconds left in the half and a 29-yarder with 4:01 remaining in the game that made it 20-7. But they blew a chance to send Miami home early. Garrett Graham caught a 20-yard pass at the Hurricanes 5, fumbled after a hard hit by Brandon Harris and the ball was recovered by Miami's Randy Phillips in the end zone. The Hurricanes never could take advantage. Harris later fumbled after being sacked by O'Brien Schofield with 7:49 remaining. The ball was recovered by J.J. Watt. The Hurricanes tried to rally late, but Harris' errant pass to Collier on fourth down ended Miami's hopes of its first 10-win season since 2003. Only adding to

Miami's offseason problems was Cooper's nasty fall. He took a kickoff 27 yards before he lost his footing and tumbled to the ground on the patchy Florida Citrus Bowl field. He clutched his right knee and was examined by trainers for about 5 minutes. Cooper was barely able to stand as he was helped off the field by teammates Javarris James and Damien Berry.

2009 EagleBank Bowl

The 2009 EagleBank Bowl was held on December 29, 2009. It marked the second edition of the EagleBank Bowl, played at RFK Stadium in Washington, D.C. The game, in which UCLA of the Pacific-10 Conference defeated Temple of the Mid-American Conference 30–21. The game was telecast on ESPN and was organized by the DC Bowl Committee, Inc., the Washington Convention and Sports Authority and its title sponsor.

2009 EagleBank Bowl	Line	1	-	2	-	3	-	4	-	Final
UCLA	(-5.0)	7	-	3	-	7	-	13	-	30
Temple	(45.5)	7	-	14	-	0	-	0	-	21

Scoring Summary
Temple - Maneri 26 yard pass from Charlton (McManus kick)
UCLA - Rosario 46 yard pass from Prince (Forbath kick)
Temple - Pierce 11 yard run (McManus kick)
Temple - Brown 2 yard run (McManus kick)
UCLA - Forbath 40 yard Field goal
UCLA - Austin 32 yard pass from Prince (Forbath kick)
UCLA - Forbath 42 yard Field goal
UCLA - Ayers 2 yard interception return (Rosario pass from Prince)
UCLA - Team safety

Associated Press Eagle Bank Bowl Game Summary - Sure, Temple was playing its first bowl game in 30 years, but what about those Bruins from UCLA? They were playing in the school's first cold-weather, East Coast bowl on a field so icy it caused the coaches to change the game plan at halftime. Wearing those soft blue and gold hues that don't look right in subfreezing weather, UCLA rallied from a two-touchdown, first-half deficit Tuesday to spoil the new bowl kids' day, beating Temple 30-21 in the EagleBank Bowl. Akeem Ayers returned an interception 2 yards for a go-ahead touchdown in the fourth quarter and UCLA's defense allowed Temple to complete only one pass in the second half. The Bruins (7-6), completing their second season under coach Rick Neuheisel, finished with a winning record for the first time since 2006. UCLA's mini slump of losing seasons paled next to the decades of futility endured by the Owls (9-4), whose only previous bowl appearances in school history were the inaugural Sugar Bowl in 1935 and the Garden State Bowl in 1979. But Temple coach Al Golden has engineered a four-year turnaround after inheriting a program that went 0-11 in 2005, exciting a fan base led by No. 1 alum, comedian Bill Cosby. The temperature was 32 at kickoff with the wind chill at 19. Still, both teams said they were less affected by the cold and more by a field Neuheisel described as "an ice rink." One of UCLA's halftime adjustments was to run plays that required little or no change of direction. "The icy field affected everything we did," said fullback Chane Moline, who benefited with a straight-ahead running style that produced 69 yards on 15 carries. The biggest difference was a UCLA defense that limited Vaughn Charlton to 1-for-7 passing for 6 yards with two interceptions in the second half. Charlton's strong practices gave him the starting nod over Chester Stewart, who had started Temple's last four regular-season games, and the choice seemed like the right one when Charlton went 12 for 16 for 153 yards in the first half. Temple also played much of the game without Bernard Pierce, who left after re-injuring his shoulder. Pierce ran for 1,308 yards and 15 touchdowns in the regular season, but he had only 12 carries for 53 yards and a touchdown on Tuesday -- all in the first half. The ice played a factor in the interception that gave UCLA the lead when the Bruins were trailing 21-20. Ayers slipped at the beginning of the play, but he recovered and found himself in the perfect spot to step in front of Charlton's screen pass and stroll into the end zone with 6:01 remaining. It was Ayers who also had one of the most amazing interceptions of the college football season in October, when he leaped to snag a pass in the back of the end zone in a loss to Oregon. The Bruins got a 2-point conversion, then added two more when Temple snapped the ball over its punter's head and out of the own end zone for a safety with 4:29 to play. Kevin Prince completed 16 of 31 passes for 221 yards with two touchdowns and one interception for the Bruins. He had a 46-yard TD throw to Nelson Rosario, who made a juggling catch down the left sideline in the first quarter, a play set up by Terrence Austin's 47-yard punt return. In the second half, Austin caught a fourth-and-1 pass in the flat and took it 32 yards up the right sideline for a score. Temple tried to answer, but Matt Brown was stopped on fourth-and-1 at the UCLA 9, and Bruins sophomore Rahim Moore's 10th interception of the season ended another Owls drive. Moore leads major college football in interceptions. The game drew 23,072 to RFK Stadium, a decline of more than 5,000 from last year's inaugural game. Organizers had to dig deep for participants because the original matchup -- Army vs. an Atlantic Coast Conference team -- didn't pan out because Army finished with a losing record and the ACC lacked enough bowl-eligible schools. But UCLA and Temple weren't complaining -- not even in the cold.

2009 Humanitarian Bowl

The 2009 Humanitarian Bowl was the thirteenth edition of the Humanitarian Bowl, and was played at Bronco Stadium in Boise, Idaho, on the campus of Boise State University. The game was played on Wednesday, December 30, 2009. As of this game, the Humanitarian Bowl was the longest continuously running cold weather bowl. The 2009 game was Idaho's first bowl game in more than a decade, when they defeated Southern Mississippi in the 1998 Humanitarian Bowl. Bowling Green, in its debut at the Humanitarian Bowl, filled a spot usually reserved for the Mountain West Conference: however, the MWC champion TCU was selected to play in the Fiesta Bowl and the conference did not have enough bowl-eligible teams to fill out its usual bowl commitments. Bowling Green played in the GMAC Bowl the previous season, where it lost 63–7 to Tulsa. The game also marked the first time the two schools had met in competition. Both teams entered the game with 7-5 records in the regular season: Idaho began the 2009 season at 6–1 but lost four of its last five. Meanwhile, Bowling Green was 1–4 early in the season, but won six of its last seven games.

2009 Humanitarian Bowl	Line	1	-	2	-	3	-	4	-	Final
Bowling Green	(-1.5)	14	-	0	-	7	-	21	-	42
Idaho	(68.0)	7	-	7	-	14	-	15	-	43

Scoring Summary
Bowling Green - Barnes 35 yard pass from Sheehan (Norsic kick)
Idaho - Bjorvik 3 yard pass from Enderle (Farquhar kick)
Bowling Green - Geter 59 yard run (Norsic kick)
Idaho - Greenwood 7 yard pass from Enderle (Farquhar kick)
Idaho - Woolridge 8 yard run (Farquhar kick)
Idaho - Woolridge 13 yard run (Farquhar kick)
Bowling Green - Scheidler 14 yard pass from Sheehan (Norsic kick)
Bowling Green - Barnes 5 yard pass from Sheehan (Norsic kick)
Idaho - Davis 30 yard pass from Enderle (Farquhar kick)
Bowling Green - Geter 2 yard run (Farquhar kick)
Bowling Green - Barnes 51 yard pass from Sheehan (Farquhar kick)
Idaho - Komar 16 yard pass from Enderle (Davis pass from Enderle)

Associated Press Humanitarian Bowl Game Summary - As his offense trotted back on the field, that fleeting voice of consciousness popped into Robb Akey's head. Was this the right move for Idaho? Why not play for overtime, instead of risking everything on a 2-point conversion with 4 seconds left? No one is going to question the Vandals coach now. Not after the gold and black celebration on the famed blue turf of Idaho's rival, capping a finish that'll be hard to match by any other bowl game this postseason. Max Komar cradled a sliding 16-yard touchdown catch with 4 seconds left and Nathan Enderle found Preston Davis alone in the back of the end zone for the 2-point conversion, lifting the Vandals to a dramatic 43-42 victory over Bowling Green in Wednesday night's Roady's Humanitarian Bowl. The score capped a wild final four minutes where Bowling Green scored twice to take then lead, then watched Idaho go 66 yards in 28 seconds to pull off the win -- and by the same score rival Boise State beat Oklahoma in the Fiesta Bowl three years ago. The Falcons took a 42-35 lead with 32 seconds left on a 51-yard pass from Tyler Sheehan to Freddie Barnes, who slipped behind the Idaho secondary for his 17th catch of the game and No. 155 in his record-setting season. But Idaho answered with a 50-yard heave from Enderle to Davis that got the ball to the Bowling Green 16. After an incompletion with 8 seconds left, Enderle found Komar -- the Vandals' leading receiver who dropped several passes -- sliding across the goal line to snag the low throw. It was Komar's only catch of the game. Akey decided before the Vandals even took possession that if they scored, he'd go for two. Just to make sure, he called timeout after the touchdown to confirm with his offensive coaches the play called would work. That's when the slightest bit of doubt arrived too. He didn't need to worry. With most of the 26,729 in attendance roaring their approval, Enderle had plenty of time to connect with Davis near the back line, setting off a wild, premature celebration. One overly joyous fan ran on the field to the Idaho bench, only to get shoved down by one of the Vandal players. Idaho (8-5) was penalized but Trey Farquhar's kickoff bounced inside the Bowling Green 5 and the fans finally got to celebrate for real when Jahmal Brown was tackled at the 22. Some thought they never would after the Vandals cycled through three coaches in three years and Akey spent much of his first two seasons shoveling out players not interested in his intense, folksy style. The Vandals had three wins in two years but turned it around in 2009 starting out 6-1 and closing the year with the second bowl victory in school history. Those hopes of capping the season with a win seemed finished when Barnes struck again in his banner senior season. Needing just five receptions to set an NCAA Bowl Subdivision record, Barnes finished with 17 grabs for 219 yards and three touchdowns, the final one putting Bowling Green in prime position for its fifth victory in its last six postseason trips. But Komar gave the Vandals decent field position with a solid kickoff return and Enderle's long throw landed in the arms of Davis, who finished with four catches for 119 yards and a 30-yard TD reception in the fourth quarter. Komar then made his sliding grab and Akey confidently went for 2. Meanwhile, the Falcons were left to figure out how this one slipped away. They trailed 28-14 midway through the third quarter, only to stage a furious rally with 28 of the next 35 points and two touchdowns in the final four minutes. Willie Geter's 2-yard plunge with 3:51 left tied it at 35. Idaho drove to the Falcons 40 but had to punt and Bowling Green took over with 1:49 left. Facing third-and-11 at their own 49, Barnes got lost in Idaho's zone coverage and ran free down the sideline for the score. De'Maundray Woolridge carried Idaho with 22 carries for 126 yards and two third-quarter touchdowns. Enderle was 15 of 28 for 240 and four touchdowns after starting the game 1 of 6. Sheehan was 33 of 47 for 387 yards and four TDs for Bowling Green (7-6). But it was the 14th consecutive bowl loss for the Mid-American Conference.

2009 Holiday Bowl

The 2009 Holiday Bowl was the thirty-second edition of the bowl game and was played at Qualcomm Stadium in San Diego, California. The game was played on Wednesday, December 30, 2009. The game was telecast on ESPN. The Nebraska Cornhuskers defeated the Arizona Wildcats 33–0 for the first shutout in the history of the bowl. This was a rematch of the two teams, who faced each other in the 1998 Holiday Bowl, where Arizona defeated Nebraska 23–20.

2009 Holiday Bowl	Line	1	-	2	-	3	-	4	-	Final
#22 Arizona	(40.5)	0	-	0	-	0	-	0	-	0
#20 Nebraska	(-1.5)	10	-	13	-	10	-	0	-	33

Scoring Summary
Nebraska - Lee 4 yard run (Henery kick)
Nebraska - Henery 47 yard Field goal
Nebraska - Burkhead 5 yard run (Henery kick)
Nebraska - Henery 50 yard Field goal
Nebraska - Henery 41 yard Field goal
Nebraska - Henery 22 yard Field goal
Nebraska - Paul 74 yard pass from Lee (Henery kick)

Associated Press Holiday Bowl Game Summary - After developing a reputation for high-scoring games and crazy finishes, the Holiday Bowl finally got the first shutout in its 32-year history. It wasn't close, either. Zac Lee threw a 74-yard touchdown pass to Niles Paul in the third quarter to highlight a 33-0 rout by Nebraska against Arizona on a rainy Wednesday night. The coaches expected a defensive game, and the Huskers delivered, earning their first shutout in 46 bowl appearances. Defensive tackle Ndamukong Suh, the AP College Football Player of the Year and a Heisman finalist, had only three tackles, including one for a loss, in his final college game. But he helped the Huskers harass Arizona Quarterback Nick Foles all night. Suh even went out for a pass early in the third quarter on second-and-4 from the Arizona 5, but Lee didn't throw his way. Suh had been on the bench for most of Arizona's final drive but came back in for a goal-line stand, along with some other starters. The Wildcats had the ball fourth-and-3 at the Nebraska 8-yard line with 1:41 to go before safety P.J. Smith batted down Foles' pass to preserve the shutout. Then again, the Wildcats were never in this one. Nebraska free safety Matt O'Hanlon intercepted Foles on the third play from scrimmage and returned it 37 yards to the Arizona 5. Lee scored on a 4-yard run two plays later. It was the fastest score in Holiday Bowl history, coming just 75 seconds in. Arizona set Holiday Bowl records for futility, with six first downs, 109 yards of offense, 51 offensive plays and nine punts. The Wildcats didn't get into Nebraska territory until the first drive of the third quarter. The previous Holiday Bowl record for fewest first downs was 12 by Nebraska in a 23-20 loss to Arizona in 1998. The previous record for fewest yards was 185 by BYU in a 65-14 loss to Texas A&M in 1990, and the previous record for the most punts was eight, by five teams. Nebraska got its first 10-win season since 2003. Arizona finished 8-5. This loss mirrored Arizona's first bowl appearance, a 38-0 loss to Centre (Ky.) in the rain in the 1921 East-West Christmas Classic in San Diego. Pelini earned bragging rights in Youngstown, Ohio, where he and Stoops grew up and played at Cardinal Mooney High. Nebraska's Alex Henery set a Holiday Bowl record with four field goals, from 47, 50, 41 and 22 yards. The Huskers even ran a handful of plays out of the wildcat formation, including a 5-yard run by Rex Burkhead early in the second quarter for a 17-0 lead. With Nebraska leading 26-0 late in the third quarter, Paul hauled in Lee's long pass at the Arizona 40 and cruised into the end zone. He spiked the ball and flexed his muscles in a pose to the crowd, drawing a 15-yard unsportsmanlike conduct penalty. Paul had four catches for 123 yards.

2009 Armed Forces Bowl

The 2009 Armed Forces Bowl was the seventh edition of the bowl game and was played at Amon G. Carter Stadium in Fort Worth, Texas. The game was played on Thursday, December 31, 2009. The game was telecast on ESPN and earned a 1.6 rating.

2009 Armed Forces Bowl	Line	1	-	2	-	3	-	4	-	Final
Houston	(-4.5)	0	-	6	-	14	-	0	-	20
Air Force	(64.0)	14	-	10	-	10	-	13	-	47

Scoring Summary
Air Force - Clark 36 yard run (Soderberg kick)
Air Force - Tew 6 yard run (Soderberg kick)
Houston - Hogan 33 yard Field goal
Air Force - Clark 22 yard run (Soderberg kick)
Houston - Hogan 33 yard Field goal
Air Force - Soderberg 27 yard Field goal
Houston - Carrier 79 yard kickoff return (Hogan kick)
Air Force - Warzeka 100 yard kickoff return (Soderberg kick)
Houston - Edwards 10 yard pass from Keenum (Hogan kick)
Air Force - Soderberg 27 yard Field goal
Air Force - Jefferson 1 yard run (Soderberg kick)
Air Force - Tew 71 yard run (Kick failed)

Associated Press Armed Forces Bowl Game Summary - With Asher Clark and Jared Tew grinding out yards and Air Force controlling the ball for more than 41 minutes, there were few chances for Case Keenum and Houston's potent offense. Then when Keenum got on the field in the Armed Forces Bowl, he was often under pressure or getting picked off -- or both. Air Force's top-ranked pass defense had six interceptions and Clark and Tew each ran for more than 100 yards and two touchdowns to lead the Falcons to a 47-20 victory on Thursday. After the Falcons (8-5) went ahead on Clark's 36-yard TD to cap the opening drive of the game, Keenum's first pass attempt deflected off his falling receiver and was grabbed by Anthony Wright, who had three interceptions. That set up Tew's 6-yard TD run for a 14-0 lead. When it was over, Keenum had thrown a career-high six picks and was 24 of 41 for a season-low 222 yards for the Cougars (10-4). Before throwing three interceptions with five TDs and a school-record 56 completions in a loss to East Carolina in the Conference USA championship game last month, Keenum had only six picks the first 12 games this season. The junior Quarterback who played his 40th career game had previously said he plans to be back next season, when the Cougars return nine offensive starters, including three 1,000-yard receivers. Keenum finished this season with a nation-leading 5,671 yards with 44 touchdowns and 15 interceptions. Air Force ran for 402 yards and Tim Jefferson was effective through the air, hitting 10 of 14 passes for 161 yards. He had a 71-yard TD run with 3:32 left in the game after Keenum's fifth interception. Clark ran 17 times for 129 yards for the Falcons, who had lost in the Armed Forces Bowl the past two seasons, including 34-28 to Houston a year ago. Air Force had lost three straight postseason games. Houston's bowl win last year capped Sumlin's debut season and snapped an eight-game postseason losing streak that had spanned 28 years. This time, the Cougars missed out on their first 11-win season since 1979. After Houston was held without a touchdown before halftime, Tyron Carrier returned the opening kickoff of the second half 79 yards for his fourth TD this season. He took the ball near the left sideline, then ran to the middle of the field before shooting through a gap and running untouched to get the Cougars within 24-13. Air Force immediately responded with its first kickoff return for a touchdown since 1985. Jonathan Warzeka fielded the ball and stepped back into the end zone before running 100 yards. Five Houston players got their hands on him but couldn't get him down. According to STATS, it was only the sixth major college game since 1996 with kickoff return touchdowns on consecutive plays. None of them had been in a bowl game. After the kickoff returns, Keenum threw a 10-yard TD to Patrick Edwards to make it 31-20. That gave Keenum a TD pass in 30 consecutive games, but this was the first time in that streak that he had more picks than scores. Houston managed only 331 total yards after coming in with a nation-best 581 yards per game and averaging 44 points. When Jefferson slipped down trying to run on third-and-goal from the 2 with 17 seconds and no timeouts left just before halftime, he quickly got the offense off the field and the kicking team got out in time for Erik Soderberg's 27-yard field goal.

2009 Texas Bowl

The 2009 Texas Bowl was the fourth edition of the bowl game, and was played at Reliant Stadium in Houston, Texas. The game was played on Thursday, December 31, 2009. The game was telecast on ESPN for the first time in bowl history after being televised by the NFL Network for the first three games. This was the first time that either team appeared in the Texas Bowl. It was the seventh year in a row that Navy appeared in a bowl game, and a team record fifth year in a row that Missouri made a post-season appearance. Missouri came off two straight bowl wins while Navy had lost three bowl games in a row. The game marked the third time that the two teams had played each other and the second time they had met in a bowl game. Prior to the 2009 Texas Bowl, Missouri held a 2–0 advantage with a 35–14 victory in 1948 and a 21–14 win in 1961 in the Orange Bowl.

2009 Texas Bowl	Line	1	-	2	-	3	-	4	-	Final
Navy	(53.0)	7	-	7	-	7	-	14	-	35
Missouri	(-6.5)	7	-	3	-	0	-	3	-	13

Scoring Summary
Missouri - Gabbert 58 yard pass from Alexander (Ressel kick)
Navy - Dobbs 1 yard run (Buckley kick)
Navy - Dobbs 13 yard run (Buckley kick)
Missouri - Ressel 31 yard Field goal
Navy - Doyle 3 yard pass from Dobbs (Buckley kick)
Missouri - Ressel 31 yard Field goal
Navy - Curry 11 yard run (Buckley kick)
Navy - Dobbs 1 yard run (Buckley kick)

Associated Press Texas Bowl Game Summary - Ricky Dobbs listened to the chatter from Missouri's defense and knew Navy had the Tigers beat. Dobbs ran for 166 yards and three touchdowns, and the Midshipmen manhandled Missouri with their triple-option offense in a 35-13 victory in the Texas Bowl on Thursday. Dobbs also threw a touchdown pass to Bobby Doyle and Marcus Curry ran for a score as the Midshipmen (10-4) rushed for 385 yards against Missouri's 12th-ranked run defense. Navy won time of possession by nearly 22 minutes and ran 81 offensive plays to only 57 for the Tigers. The old-fashioned, run-first (and second and third) offense put the Midshipmen on equal footing with bigger, faster opponents all season. They nearly upset Ohio State in the season opener and beat Notre Dame on Nov. 7. Dobbs sensed that Navy was going to take down another heavyweight when he heard the frustrated Tigers complaining about the Midshipmen's low blocks. The Midshipmen matched a school record for victories in a season, securing only the third 10-win campaign in its history. They wore the same uniforms they donned for their 17-3 win over Army on Dec. 12 -- gold on the shoulders and lined with red on the beltline and arms to honor the Marine Corps. Navy coach Ken Niumatalolo conceded Missouri's size and speed advantage leading up to this one. The undersized defense still managed to hold the Tigers to only 65 rushing yards. Blaine Gabbert threw a 58-yard touchdown pass to Danario Alexander on Missouri's second play from scrimmage, but the Tigers mustered only 298 yards the rest of the game -- largely because the Navy offense kept the ball for almost 41 minutes. Missouri (8-5) lost for the second time in its last five bowl appearances. Gabbert also threw two interceptions and was sacked four times, even though Navy had up to eight players dropped into pass coverage on some plays. Alexander, who led the nation in receiving yards coming into the game, took a short pass from Gabbert and outran the Navy defense just 24 seconds into the game. It was Alexander's 14th TD catch of the season and eighth covering more than 50 yards. Navy didn't panic, stuck to its game plan and the Tigers never came up with an answer. Dobbs broke a 24-yard run on Navy's second possession, diving into the end zone with 2:58 left in the first quarter. It was Dobbs' 25th touchdown run of the year, adding to his NCAA single season record for a Quarterback. Tiger's defensive end Aldon Smith sacked Dobbs on the first play of the second quarter, setting a Missouri record with his 12th sack of the season. Dobbs wasn't sacked again, and the Midshipmen drove to the Missouri 22 late in the half. Dobbs ran up the middle, but Missouri safety Jasper Simmons forced a fumble just before Dobbs crossed the goal line and the Tigers recovered in the end zone. It only slowed down the Middies temporarily. Missouri's Derrick Washington fumbled on the next play, Navy recovered and Dobbs, unfazed by his miscue, scored on a 12-yard run with 45 seconds left before halftime. Grant Ressel's 31-yard field goal on the last play before the break to make it 14-10. But Navy had already set the tone for the game, rushing for 216 yards in the first half. Dobbs' 3-yard touchdown pass to Doyle finished the first drive of the third quarter and put Navy up 21-10. Ressel kicked another 31-yarder to make it 21-13, then Navy pulled away Dobbs joined Craig Candeto (2003) and Chris McCoy (1997) as the only Midshipmen to run and pass for over 1,000 yards in a season.

2009 Sun Bowl

The 2009 Brut Sun Bowl game was the 76th edition of the Sun Bowl. It was the two teams' fifth meeting. The game featured two conference tie-ins: the University of Oklahoma represented the Big 12 Conference and Stanford University represented the Pacific-10 Conference. The game was played at the Sun Bowl Stadium on the University of Texas at El Paso campus in El Paso, Texas. The game featured Stanford's 13th-ranked offense including Toby Gerhart, a Heisman finalist who led the NCAA Division I FBS subdivision with 1,736 rushing yards and 26 touchdowns, against the seventh-ranked Oklahoma defense.

This was the first time the two teams played each other in a bowl game. They had faced each other 4 previous times in the regular season with Oklahoma holding a 3–1 advantage. The last contest played by the schools was a 19–7 victory in Norman, Oklahoma by the Sooners in 1984.

2009 Sun Bowl	Line	1	-	2	-	3	-	4	-	Final
Oklahoma	(-9.5)	10	-	7	-	14	-	0	-	31
#19 Stanford	(55.0)	7	-	17	-	0	-	3	-	27

Scoring Summary
Oklahoma - Broyles 30 yard pass from Jones (O'Hara kick)
Stanford - Marecic 1 yard run (Whitaker kick)
Oklahoma - O'Hara 28 yard Field goal
Stanford - Gerhart 19 yard run (Whitaker kick)
Oklahoma - Broyles 13 yard pass from Jones (O'Hara kick)
Stanford - Gerhart 16 yard run (Whitaker kick)
Stanford - Whitaker 35 yard Field goal
Oklahoma - Broyles 6 yard pass from Jones (O'Hara kick)
Oklahoma - Murray 1 yard run (O'Hara kick)
Stanford - Whitaker 21 yard Field goal

Sun Bowl Classic Game Summary - The combination of Landry Jones and Ryan Broyles was almost unstoppable for the Oklahoma Sooners. And while OU's steely defense couldn't quite stop Toby Gerhart, yards were hard to come by for the Heisman Trophy runner-up. Broyles set a Sun Bowl record with three touchdown receptions, Jones passed for 418 yards and Oklahoma slowed Gerhart just enough to beat No. 19 Stanford 31-27 on New Year's Eve. Jones took over as Oklahoma's Quarterback after 2008 Heisman Trophy winner Sam Bradford was injured in an opening loss to BYU. Broyles finished with 156 yards receiving and set Oklahoma's single-game record with 13 receptions in front of a Sun Bowl record crowd of 53,713. Broyles was named the C.M. Hendricks Most Valuable Player and the John H. Folmer Most Valuable Special Teams Player for his efforts. He is the first player in the history of the game to win both awards. Jones found Broyles on TD strikes of 30, 13 and 6 yards, and the Sooners led for good at 31-24 after DeMarco Murray flipped across the goal line late in the third quarter. The victory capped an injury-plagued season that opened with national title hopes, but coach Bob Stoops said he was proud that the Sooners (8-5) never quit. Gerhart, who led the nation with 1,736 yards rushing, ran for 135 on 32 carries and scored two TDs in the first half in what was his final game for Stanford. Oklahoma rallied with 14 straight points in the third quarter, then held on after Patrick O'Hara missed a 32-yard field goal try with 3:19 remaining. Stanford (8-5) got a final opportunity but turned it over on downs, starting a celebration for fans wearing crimson and cream. The Cardinal pulled to 31-27 on a 22-yard field goal by Nate Whitaker, capping a series that began when Broyles mishandled a punt. Oklahoma protested because Stanford's Johnson Bademosi hit Broyles just as the ball arrived, but officials gave possession to the Cardinal.

2009 Insight Bowl

The 2009 Insight Bowl was the 21st edition of the bowl game, played at Sun Devil Stadium in Tempe, Arizona. The game matched the Iowa State Cyclones against the Minnesota Golden Gophers and was played on Thursday, December 31, 2009. The game was telecast on the NFL Network. The game marked the Cyclones' first postseason trip since 2005, and Minnesota's third Insight Bowl appearance in the last four years. Cyclones first-year coach Paul Rhoads turned around a team that finished 2–10 in 2008 and was winless in eight Big 12 games. Given the relatively proximity between them, the two schools have played each other a total of 25 times. Minnesota has dominated the matchup holding the series lead 22–2–1 up until the bowl game. However, only one of the games has been played in Iowa and the two teams have only played each other three times since 1924. The last meeting between the opponents was a 53–29 Gophers victory in 1997. This was the first bowl game played between the two schools.

2009 Insight Bowl	Line	1	-	2	-	3	-	4	-	Final
Minnesota	(-2.0)	3	-	0	-	10	-	0	-	13
Iowa State	(48.5)	0	-	14	-	0	-	0	-	14

Scoring Summary
Minnesota - Ellestad 36 yard Field goal
Iowa State - Arnaud 9 yard run (Mahoney kick)
Iowa State - Williams 38 yard pass from Arnaud (Mahoney kick)
Minnesota - Tow-Arnett 23 yard pass from Weber (Ellestad kick)
Minnesota - Ellestad 21 yard Field goal

Associated Press Insight Bowl Game Summary - Iowa State made its two-win 2008 season seem like a long time ago. With a 14-13 victory against Minnesota in the Insight Bowl on Thursday night, the Cyclones locked up their first winning season since 2005. Then they partied on New Year's Eve with a band of followers in Sun Devil Stadium. Alexander Robinson ran for 137 yards, and Austen Arnaud threw for one touchdown and ran for another as the Cyclones (7-6) won for only the third time in 10 bowl games -- and the second in Arizona. As for the Golden Gophers, they can't wait for next year -- and, they hope, a chance to end a four-bowl losing streak. Minnesota (6-7) made an unwanted bit of history by becoming the first three-time Insight Bowl loser. Minnesota's Adam Weber threw for 261 yards and a score, and Kyle Theret picked off two passes and caught a 40-yard pass on a fake punt, but it wasn't enough to prevent the Big Ten's fourth straight Insight Bowl loss to the Big 12. A crowd of 45,090 turned out on a 63-degree afternoon at Sun Devil Stadium, capacity 56,000, for a game that was more interesting than pretty. The Cyclones won it the hard way. They overcame four turnovers by Arnaud, who threw two interceptions and lost two fumbles. Rhoads, the first Iowa State coach to post a winning record in his debut season since George Veenker in 1931. The Cyclones nearly had a fifth turnover, when Robinson fumbled on a long completion and the Golden Gophers recovered. But the officials gave the ball back to the Cyclones after a lengthy video review. Iowa State also conceded 434 yards and committed eight penalties. But the Cyclones' defense twice came up with turnovers to repel the Gophers deep in Iowa State territory. The first came with the Cyclones leading 7-3 late in the first half. Iowa State's David Sims picked off a pass in the end zone with 1:23 to go. That led to the Cyclones' most impressive possession -- a lightning 89-yard drive in 1 minute. Arnaud hit Jake Williams for a 38-yard score after Theret fell, leaving Williams all alone. That gave the Cyclones a 14-3 halftime lead, and they romped off the field to the cheers of their red-and-yellow-clad faithful. Still down 14-3 midway through the third period, the Gophers stunned the Cyclones with a brilliant trick play. On fourth-and-4 at Minnesota's 37-yard line, punter Blake Haudan hit a wide-open Theret for 40 yards -- the junior defensive back's first career reception. One play later, Weber found tight end Nick Tow-Arnett for a 23-yard touchdown to cut Iowa State's lead to 14-10. It was Minnesota's first offensive touchdown since Nov. 7, a span of 10 quarters. The Gophers took advantage of another Arnaud fumble -- this one at Minnesota's 40 -- to drive 50 yards for a 21-yard field goal by Ellestad, trimming the deficit to 14-13 after three quarters. Minnesota had trailed in all six of its regular-season wins, and four times rallied from a fourth-quarter deficit to win. The Gophers seemed poised for another comeback when they marched to Iowa State's 17 late in the fourth quarter. But backup Quarterback MarQueis Gray, inserted as a running threat, fumbled on a keeper, and Iowa State's Ter'ran Benton recovered. The Cyclones ran out the final 4:04, with Arnaud and Robinson each rushing for first downs. Iowa State beat its border rival for only the third time in 26 meetings -- and for the first time since 1898.

2009 Chick-Fil-A Peach Bowl

The 2009 Chick-fil-A Bowl was played between the Virginia Tech Hokies and the Tennessee Volunteers on December 31, 2009, in the Georgia Dome, Atlanta, Georgia. Virginia Tech defeated Tennessee 37–14. The game, the 42nd edition of the Chick-fil-A Bowl was televised in the United States on ESPN and the broadcast was seen by an estimated 4.87 million viewers. In recognition of his performance during the game, Virginia Tech running back Ryan Williams was named the game's most valuable player. By the end of the game, he had set a school record for most rushing yards in a season and conference records for most rushing touchdowns and most total touchdowns. Following the game, Tennessee head coach Lane Kiffin resigned to become head coach of the University of Southern California Trojans football team. Several players from each team participated in postseason all-star games and a handful were selected to play in the National Football League through the 2010 NFL Draft.

2009 Chick-Fil-A Peach Bowl	Line	1	-	2	-	3	-	4	-	Final
#12 Virginia Tech	(-5.5)	7	-	10	-	7	-	13	-	37
Tennessee	(49.0)	0	-	14	-	0	-	0	-	14

Scoring Summary
Virginia Tech - Williams 1 yard run (Waldron kick)
Virginia Tech - Williams 3 yard run (Waldron kick)
Tennessee - Hardesty 4 yard run (Mathis kick)
Tennessee - Moore 2 yard pass from Crompton (Mathis kick)
Virginia Tech - Waldron 21 yard Field goal
Virginia Tech - Taylor 1 yard run (Waldron kick)
Virginia Tech - Waldron 46 yard Field goal
Virginia Tech - Wilson 3 yard run (Waldron kick)
Virginia Tech - Waldron 22 yard Field goal

Associated Press Chick-Fil-A Peach Bowl Game Summary - Ryan Williams isn't keeping track of his records. Probably, but in just one season Williams has already made a quite an impression. He capped a brilliant debut season with a record-setting game, running for two touchdowns to power Virginia Tech (No. 11 BCS, No. 12 AP) past Tennessee 37-14 in the Chick-fil-A Bowl on Thursday night. The Hokies (10-3) took the lead with a field goal in the final seconds of the first half and outscored Tennessee 20-0 in the second half on their way to a sixth straight 10-win season. The only team with a longer active streak is Texas with nine. Williams, a redshirt freshman, had 117 yards rushing to become Virginia Tech's single season rushing leader with 1,655 yards. Williams also set Atlantic Coast Conference records with 21 rushing touchdowns and 22 total touchdowns this season but said "I really don't care about records." The Hokies outrushed Tennessee (7-6) 229-5. Tennessee's star running back, Montario Hardesty, could not keep up with Williams. The Volunteers' senior had 18 carries for 39 yards and a touchdown. Tennessee Quarterback Jonathan Crompton was taken to a local hospital after the game for precautionary reasons, according to a school spokesman. Crompton suffered an undisclosed injury late in the game. Vols junior safety Eric Berry confirmed after the game he will enter the NFL draft. Tennessee was hurt by two turnovers which led to 10 points for Virginia Tech, and a dropped pass that cost the Vols a touchdown. Rashad Carmichael intercepted a pass by Crompton in the first quarter to set up Williams' first touchdown run. Crompton fumbled when sacked by Nekos Brown late in the fourth quarter. John Graves recovered at the Tennessee 13 to set up Matt Waldron's third field goal, a 22-yarder. Virginia Tech players dumped a cooler of water on Beamer seconds later. Virginia Tech fans in the sellout crowd of 73,777 cheered, and Beamer raised his fists in response. Williams sat out the fourth quarter after a left ankle sprain. Virginia Tech fans cheered when Williams left the trainer's table and ran on the sideline, but Beamer gave the fourth quarter carries to Josh Oglesby and David Wilson. Wilson had a 3-yard touchdown run with 5:14 remaining. Williams passed Kevin Jones' school-record record 1,647 yards rushing in 2003. North Carolina's Don McCauley held the ACC records with 19 rushing touchdowns and 21 total in 1970. Clemson's C.J. Spiller matched the total touchdown mark this season. Georgia Tech's Robert Lavette also rushed for 19 touchdowns in 1982. Williams passed Jones with his seventh carry of an eight-play touchdown drive in the third quarter. He had long runs of 21 and 32 yards in the drive before setting the record on a 6-yard run to the 3. Tyrod Taylor scored from the 1 for a 24-14 lead. He completed 10 of 17 passes for 201 yards with an interception. Crompton completed 15 of 26 passes for 235 yards with a touchdown and an interception. Waldron, who had a 21-yard field goal at the end of the first half, added a 46-yarder -- the longest of his career -- to push the lead to 27-14 early in the fourth quarter. Tennessee's had a chance to get back into it, but wide-open Denarius Moore dropped a deep pass from Crompton on the Vols' next drive. Kiffin said the play "really took the wind out of our sails. Williams had two short touchdown runs to give the Hokies a 14-0 lead in the second quarter. Tennessee then responded. Hardesty ran through 301-pound defensive tackle Cordarrow Thompson's tackle for a 4-yard run to cap an 80-yard drive. Janzen Jackson's interception set up Crompton's 2-yard touchdown pass to Moore with 18 seconds remaining in the first half. Instead of running out the clock, Taylor threw from his 33 to Jarrett Boykin, who was stopped inside the Vols' 5 as the clock apparently expired. Tennessee players left the field but were summoned back as a video review showed Boykin's knee hit the ground with 2 seconds remaining. Waldron's 21-yard field goal gave Virginia Tech a 17-14 halftime lead. The Hokies, who won the Orange Bowl last season, have back-to-back bowl wins for the first time in school history.

2010 Outback Bowl

The 2010 Outback Bowl was the 24th edition of the bowl game, and was played at Raymond James Stadium in Tampa, Florida. The game was played on Friday, January 1, 2010. The game was telecast on ESPN and matched Auburn University against Northwestern University. The game drew 5.69 million viewers (up 30% from the previous year), making it the 7th highest viewing on cable television for the week. The game marked Auburn's third appearance in the Outback Bowl. It was the team's first appearance in the bowl since a 1996 43-14 loss to Penn State. The game marked Northwestern's first appearance in the Outback Bowl. The Wildcats sought their first postseason win since the 1949 Rose Bowl. The two teams had never played each other prior to the Outback Bowl. Darvin Adams, the MVP, had 12 receptions for 142 yards.

2010 Outback Bowl	Line	1	-	2	-	3	-	4	-	OT	-	Final
Northwestern	(55.0)	7	-	0	-	14	-	14	-	0	-	35
Auburn	(-8.0)	14	-	7	-	0	-	14	-	3	-	38

Scoring Summary
Auburn - Burns 1 yard run (Byrum kick)
Auburn - McFadden 100 yard interception return (Byrum kick)
Northwestern - Brewer 39 yard pass from Kafka (Demos kick)
Auburn - Carr 46 yard pass from Todd (Byrum kick)
Northwestern - Brewer 35 yard pass from Kafka (Demos kick)
Northwestern - Dunsmore 66 yard pass from Kafka (Demos kick)
Auburn - Tate 5 yard run (Byrum kick)
Auburn - Tate 12 yard run (Byrum kick)
Northwestern - Kafka 2 yard run (Kick failed)
Northwestern - Steward 18 yard pass from Kafka (Mitchell pass from Brewer)
Auburn - Byrum 21 yard Field goal

Associated Press Outback Bowl Game Summary - Pat Fitzgerald reached into Northwestern's bag of tricks one more time, hoping to pull out the perfect play to give his team a dramatic victory over Auburn in the Outback Bowl. Wes Byrum kicked a 21-yard field goal in overtime, and Auburn (8-5) overcame several mistakes, including a costly pair of penalties, that gave Northwestern chances for their first bowl victory in 61 years. On the game's final play, the Wildcats sent backup kicker Steve Flaherty onto the field seemingly to try to force a second overtime. But with regular kicker Stefan Demos on the sideline after being injured earlier in the overtime, Fitzgerald had no intention of trying to tie the score. Receiver Zeke Markshausen took a handoff between the legs from holder Dan Persa and circled right end to try to win the game. Auburn's Neiko Thorpe stopped him after a 3-yard gain to the 2. The Tigers intercepted Mike Kafka five times -- twice in the end zone -- and Walter McFadden returned one of the picks 100 yards for a touchdown that helped Auburn to an early 14-0 lead. Kafka threw for a career-best 532 yards and four TDs. He rallied Northwestern from a two-touchdown deficit in the closing minutes of the fourth quarter, and the Wildcats wasted a chance to win it at the end of regulation. Auburn finished its first season under Chizik with the second-most wins by a first-year coach in school history. Only Terry Bowden, who went 11-0 in 1993, produced more wins in his initial season on the job. Northwestern fell to 1-7 all-time in postseason games. The lone win came against California in the 1949 Rose Bowl. Ben Tate ran for 108 yards and two TDs for Auburn, which led 35-21 before Northwestern stormed back with a pair of touchdowns and a 2-point conversion to force overtime. Tate's fourth-quarter fumble and a late face mask penalty against the Tigers' Nick Fairley helped the Wildcats' cause. Demos squandered a chance to win it in regulation, hooking a 44-yard field goal attempt wide right with no time remaining. Byrum gave Auburn the lead on the first possession of the extra period, and then things got real interesting. Thinking they had won the game when officials ruled Kafka fumbled when he was sacked for a 10-yard loss, the Tigers rushed off the sideline to celebrate until the call was overturned in the replay booth. Four plays later, Demos lined up for a 37-yard field goal to tie but hit the right upright, setting off another premature celebration. This time, Aairon Savage was penalized for roughing the kicker, giving Northwestern new life -- but also leaving the Wildcats without Demos, who limped off the field. Kafka only threw seven interceptions during the regular season and entered Northwestern's first New Year's Day game in more than a decade with a streak of 116 consecutive passes without one. The fifth-year senior, part of Walker's final recruiting class, completed 47 of 78 passes, both Outback Bowl records. Kafka looked like he might be able to overcome the early mistakes when threw TD passes of 35 yards to Andrew Brewer and 66 yards to Drake Dunsmore within a span of 2:15 to make it 21-21 heading into the fourth quarter. Brewer also caught a 35-yard TD pass, and later took a pitch for Kafka on a gadget play and threw to Brendan Mitchell for a 2-point conversion that tied it 35-35 with 1:15 remaining in regulation. Markshausen had 12 receptions for 84 yards and Sidney Stewart finished with 10 for 97 yards and one TD. Darvin Adams led Auburn with 12 catches for 142 yards, and Quindarius Carr scored on a 46-yard reception from Chris Todd, who was 20 of 31 for 235 yards and no interceptions.

Northwestern - Kafka set the all-time bowl record with 47 completions and 78 attempts. He set Northwestern and Outback Bowl records with 532 passing yards and an Outback Bowl record with 5 interceptions.

2010 Gator Bowl

The 2010 Gator Bowl game was played between the Florida State University Seminoles from the ACC, and the West Virginia University Mountaineers representing the Big East, and was played on Friday, January 1, 2010, at Jacksonville Municipal Stadium in Jacksonville, Florida. It was the sixty fifth edition of the bowl game.

Bobby Bowden's final game - In the final game of Bobby Bowden's storied 44-year career as a head coach. Bowden finished with a 389-129-4 record, and most importantly to him, a 33rd consecutive winning season. West Virginia's school-record four-game bowl winning streak came to an end with the loss. Florida

State won five of its final seven games of the season after a three-game losing streak. In his 33rd and presumably final bowl game, Bobby Bowden won again, bringing his career bowl record to 22-10-1. His .682 bowl winning percentage is the best in NCAA history among coaches to coach in at least 20 bowl games.

2010 Gator Bowl	Line	1	-	2	-	3	-	4	-	Final
#18 West Virginia	(-2.5)	14	-	0	-	0	-	7	-	21
Florida State	(60.0)	3	-	10	-	10	-	10	-	33

Scoring Summary
West Virginia - Brown 31 yard run (Bitancurt kick)
Florida State - Hopkins 26 yard Field goal
West Virginia - Devine 1 yard run (Bitancurt kick)
Florida State - Thomas 12 yard run (Hopkins kick)
Florida State - Hopkins 42 yard Field goal
Florida State - Hopkins 22 yard Field goal
Florida State - Thomas 19 yard run (Hopkins kick)
West Virginia - Clarke 5 yard run (Bitancurt kick)
Florida State - Manuel 2 yard run (Hopkins kick)
Florida State - Hopkins 37 yard Field goal

Associated Press Gator Bowl Game Summary - Bobby Bowden rode only a few bouncy steps on his players' shoulders, then hopped off. Time to say goodbye. As a winner, too. Jermaine Thomas ran for 121 yards and two touchdowns, MVP E.J. Manuel threw for 189 yards and ran for another score and Florida State knocked off West Virginia (No. 16 BCS, No. 18 AP) 33-21 Friday at the Gator Bowl in the final game of Bowden's storied 57-year coaching career. Bowden finished with a 389-129-4 record, and most importantly to him, a 33rd consecutive winning season. Next week, Jimbo Fisher takes over at Florida State, which finished 7-6 for the third time in the last four years. That run of mediocrity was the 80-year-old Bowden's downfall -- he wanted to stay at least one more season but was essentially forced into retirement after Florida State offered him a lesser role for 2010. But on this day, none of that mattered to the Florida State faithful, which serenaded him with "Bob-by! Bob-by!" chants throughout the day, saving their loudest cries for the very end. "Eat your heart out, Florida State," Ann Bowden, the coach's wife, said afterward. "Eat your heart out." With 1:39 left, Bowden trotted down to the Florida State band section, removing his autographed white cap and tossing it into the seats -- and the celebration began. When it was over, Bowden was surrounded by a wall of photographers, trying to make his way over to shake the hand of West Virginia coach Bill Stewart -- who was a 177-pound walk-on for Bowden's first Mountaineers team in 1970. Bowden leaves as major college football's second-winningest coach. Joe Paterno earned his 394th victory Friday in the Capital One Bowl as Penn State beat LSU 19-17, now the official winner of the back-and-forth race to be the game's all-time win leader, something that wasn't lost on Bowden. Paterno could win No. 400 next year. By his own math, Bowden's already beyond that benchmark. This retirement thing is already working. Noel Devine rushed for 168 yards and a touchdown for West Virginia (9-4), which ran out to a 14-3 lead, then sputtered the rest of the way. There was even a "wide right" -- in Bowden's favor, for a change. West Virginia's Tyler Bitancurt pushed a 33-yard field goal try past the right upright midway through the third quarter, a big break for the Seminoles. Bowden's teams lost four epic matchups with archrival Miami over the years, and probably at least two national championships, because of FSU field goals going wide right. Let it be noted that on the last field goal his team tried, FSU made it. This was Bowden's day, and the Seminoles made sure he wouldn't be denied. FSU safety Jamie Robinson, who helped turn the game around with a second-quarter interception. Everything about the matchup was arranged with celebrating Bowden in mind, and that didn't change on game day. Deion Sanders, Warrick Dunn and more than 350 of Bowden's former players were there as guests, and thousands of fans -- many of whom arrived 2 hours before Bowden -- braved 52-degree air and steady rain to line the route the coach and his wife would take into the stadium, followed by the rest of the Seminole roster. There was a pregame video of Bowden highlights. He got a new car, a gift from Toyota and the Gator Bowl. And then came a rare treat even for Bowden, the right to take the flaming FSU spear from Chief Osceola and slam the point into the turf at midfield, one of Florida State's most revered pregame traditions. Bowden was head coach at Samford from 1959-62, led West Virginia from 1970-75 and took over at Florida State the next season. The tributes didn't stop at kickoff, either. A fan donned a No. 12 Thad Busby jersey, changed some letters and -- voila! -- The former Florida State Quarterback's surname went from BUSBY to BOBBY. The Florida State band, instead of spelling out "Noles" at halftime, stood in "Bobby" formation. And on the West Virginia sideline, fans mindful of his stint there as head coach from 1970-75 tacked a "We [heart] U Bobby" banner to the wall. During the game, Bowden's demeanor didn't change much from what's become the norm in his final seasons. He often kept to himself, hands either clasped behind his back or at his sides. He talked to players individually, sometimes offered a quick thought to Fisher, and then would go back to pacing about. A few times, Bowden took a quick look around the stadium, almost as if he was taking a mental picture of it all. Bowden spent much of the afternoon hugging his former players. Some of them now were middle-aged men, their hair tinged with gray. West Virginia took the opening kickoff and scored without much resistance; an easy drive capped by a 32-yard touchdown rush by starting Quarterback Jarrett Brown -- who was injured in the second quarter. The Mountaineers went up 14-3 on their second possession, after Devine broke off a 70-yard run to get inside the Florida State 5, then scored from 1 yard out. After that, all Florida State. The Seminoles led 23-14 entering the fourth, and after West Virginia got within two, Manuel's 2-yard touchdown burst put Florida State up 30-21. It would be the last touchdown anyone would score for Robert Cleckler Bowden, and soon, the man who saved Florida State's program -- it almost folded before he was hired in 1976 -- would start hugging anyone he could get his arms around on the sideline. An hour later, Ann Bowden wrapped her arms around her husband, tousling his gray hair. "Time to go home, baby," she said.

2010 Capital One Bowl

The 2010 Capital One Bowl was the sixty-fourth edition of the bowl game, and was played at the Citrus Bowl in Orlando, Florida. The game was played on January 1 and matched the LSU Tigers against the Penn State Nittany Lions. Although the game marked LSU's third appearance in the Capital One Bowl and Penn State's fifth, it was the first time the two teams faced each other in the bowl's history, and only the second time the two teams met overall (the first being the 1974 Orange Bowl). The two teams represented the highest ranked SEC team and Big 10 team not appearing in a Bowl Championship Series (BCS) bowl game. The game was notable for its poor field conditions. Eight state high school championship games had been played at the stadium in recent weeks, but the turf was replaced immediately after the last games on December 19. The Champs Sports Bowl played ten days later, badly damaged the new turf. The grounds crew worked frantically over the next three days to get the field in shape for the Capital One Bowl, but ultimately failed. As a result, this was the last Capital One Bowl to be played on grass as artificial turf was installed at the Citrus Bowl several months later.

2010 Capital One Bowl	Line	1	-	2	-	3	-	4	-	Final
#11 Penn State	(-2.0)	7	-	6	-	3	-	3	-	19
#13 LSU	(43.5)	0	-	3	-	7	-	7	-	17

Scoring Summary
Penn State - Moye 37 yard pass from Clark (Wagner kick)
LSU - Jasper 25 yard Field goal
Penn State - Wagner 26 yard Field goal
Penn State - Wagner 18 yard Field goal
Penn State - Wagner 20 yard Field goal
LSU - LaFell 24 yard pass from Jefferson (Jasper kick)
LSU - Ridley 1 yard run (Jasper kick)
Penn State - Wagner 21 yard Field goal

Associated Press Capital One Bowl Game Summary - Dampened by rain, slowed by mud and trailing late in the fourth quarter, Daryll Clark was determined to get Penn State some points. The Nittany Lions (No. 13 BCS, No. 11 AP) and their star Quarterback emerged from the muck for a thrilling 19-17 win over LSU (No. 12 BCS, No. 13 AP) in the Capital One Bowl. The late-game drive led by Clark helped set up Collin Wagner's 21-yard field goal with 57 seconds left, and Penn State staved off a last-ditch effort by the Tigers to preserve the victory. Penn State coach Joe Paterno got his record 24th bowl win and handed Les Miles his first loss in five bowls as LSU coach. It was just the second game ever between two popular college football programs. But the drama extended well beyond the high-profile coaches. A driving rainstorm turned the field into a mosh pit in some places. LSU rallied from a 13-point deficit late in the second half to take a 17-16 lead on Stevan Ridley's 1-yard touchdown run with 12:49 left. And LSU had one final chance after Wagner's game-winner. The junior kicker said it was the first time he had ever hit four field goals in a game. The Tigers got to midfield, but right guard Lyle Hitt was whistled for a disputed personal foul penalty that pushed them back to their own 40. Quarterback Jordan Jefferson hit Rueben Randle for a 25-yard gain on the game's last play to the Penn State 35, but Randle fumbled as time expired. LSU was still fuming after the game. This game will be remembered as much for the messy beginning as the dramatic finish. Bad footing and dropped passes were normal in the first half, and Clark fumbled the snap exchange twice -- though both were recovered by Penn State. Nevertheless, Clark had a good time in the mud. Clark, nagged by questions of whether he can win a big game, ended his college career on a high note. Similarly, critics noted Penn State hadn't beaten a ranked team all season despite its gaudy record. JoePa has something to smile about in wrapping up his 44th season on the sideline. Clark finished 18-of-35 for 216 yards and 37-yard touchdown pass to Derek Moye in the first quarter. Clark also nearly came close to throwing a couple interceptions Friday -- if LSU had held on to wet balls. The Nittany Lions emerged at halftime with a 13-3 lead, but LSU gained traction after rain subsided in the second half. LaFell's 24-yard touchdown pass from Jefferson with 13 seconds left in the third quarter drew the Tigers within 16-10 to awaken the slumbering LSU crowd. Jefferson was 13-of-24 for 202 yards with the TD and one interception, while LaFell finished with five catches for 87 yards. Penn State stalled on its next drive, and Trindon Holliday -- the reigning NCAA 100-meter dash champion -- returned a punt 37 yards to the LSU 49 to help set up Ridley's TD run. The teams exchanged stalled drives before Penn State took over for its game-winning drive with 6:54 left. Clark hit a Graham Zug one third-and-4 from the LSU 42 for a key conversion to keep the chains moving. The field took another pounding after poor conditions hampered the Champs Sports Bowl earlier in the week on the same turf. Eight state high school championship games were also played at the stadium in recent weeks. The grounds crew worked frantically all week to get the field in shape for Friday's game. Rain started falling about a couple hours before game time, and the field took a pounding during pregame warmups. Routines by the marching bands didn't help either. Conditions were so bad for both offenses early on that the teams combined for 15 punts -- shattering the bowl record of 10 set Miami, Ohio and Florida in 1973.

2010 Rose Bowl

The 2010 Rose Bowl, the 96th edition of the annual game, was played on Friday, January 1, 2010 at Rose Bowl Stadium in Pasadena, California. It featured the Ohio State Buckeyes against the Oregon Ducks. The Buckeyes won 26–17. Ticket prices for all seats in the Rose Bowl were listed at $145. The Rose Bowl Game was a contractual sell-out, with 64,500 tickets allocated to the participating teams and conferences. The remaining tickets went to the Tournament of Roses members, sponsors, City of Pasadena residents, and the general public. This was the 22nd and final Rose Bowl televised by ABC. Corporate sibling ESPN took over coverage in 2011. This game was a separate BCS game from the National Championship Game, which the Pasadena Tournament of Roses also hosted.

Teams - Ohio State represented the Big Ten Conference in the Rose Bowl as the conference's automatic bid after winning their 5th consecutive Big Ten championship by defeating Iowa 27–24 on November 14, 2009. Oregon represented the Pac-10 as the conference's automatic bid after defeating Oregon State 37–33 in the Civil War on December 3, 2009. The pairing of the two conferences in the Rose Bowl is the oldest college football agreement between two major conferences in the United States. The two teams had met seven times prior to this game, with the last coming on September 19, 1987, in Columbus, Ohio, where Ohio State defeated Oregon 24–14. This was the second time the two teams faced one another in the Rose Bowl. Ohio State defeated Oregon 10–7 in the 1958 Rose Bowl. Prior to the 2010 game, Ohio State was 7–0 all-time against Oregon in football. It was the first time the outright Big Ten champion met the outright Pac-10 champion in the Rose Bowl since the 2004 Rose Bowl between Michigan and Southern California. Ohio State wore its white jerseys on the west sideline while Oregon wore its dark jerseys on the east.

Game notes - Oregon won the coin toss to begin the game and decided to defer to the second half. Ohio State Quarterback Terrelle Pryor was selected the game's offensive Most Valuable Player. His performance included passing for a season-high 266 yards and rushing for 72 yards. Oregon defensive end Kenny Rowe was the game's defensive Most Valuable Player. He recorded 3 sacks, tying a Rose Bowl Record. The game time temperature was 71 degrees, wind at 5 mph ESE, on a sunny afternoon.

2010 Rose Bowl	Line	1	-	2	-	3	-	4	-	Final
#8 Ohio State	(50.5)	10	-	6	-	3	-	7	-	26
#7 Oregon	(-4.0)	0	-	10	-	7	-	0	-	17

Scoring Summary
Ohio State - Saine 13 yard pass from Pryor (Pettrey kick)
Ohio State - Barclay 19 yard Field goal
Oregon - Flint 24 yard Field goal
Oregon - Blount 3 yard run (Flint kick)
Ohio State - Barclay 30 yard Field goal
Ohio State - Pettrey 45 yard Field goal
Oregon - Masoli 1 yard run (Flint kick)
Ohio State - Barclay 38 yard Field goal
Ohio State - Posey 17 yard pass from Pryor (Pettrey kick)

Associated Press Rose Bowl Game Summary - Terrelle Pryor jumped on a golf cart and rode up the Rose Bowl Game presented by Citi tunnel in his grass-stained uniform, heading out to pick up a trophy. A clutch of departing Ohio State fans caught sight of his No. 2 jersey and let loose the sort of wild cheer Pryor always imagined would be the soundtrack to his career. Ohio State's bowl woes were over, thanks to a

Quarterback who finally played up to his enormous potential -- and a sturdy defense that grounded Oregon's high-flying offense. Pryor passed for a career-high 266 yards and two touchdowns, rushed for 72 more and threw a 17-yard scoring pass to DeVier Posey with 7:02 to play, ending the No. 8 Buckeyes' three-game BCS skid with a 26-17 victory over No. 7 Oregon on Friday. From the opening days of bowl preparation, Pryor's teammates sensed a new focus in their sophomore leader, whose much-publicized recruitment had led to two solid seasons, but not the transcendence many expected from the mobile passer. With a Rose Bowl effort that evoked memories of Vince Young's breakout performance in the same stadium four years ago, Pryor shook off his early mistakes and led the Buckeyes (11-2) confidently through a tense fourth quarter. Turns out nothing was wrong with the Buckeyes' sophomore Quarterback that winning the Rose Bowl couldn't cure. Even with two Big Ten titles and two wins over Michigan, Pryor hadn't matched his hype until this steady, sometimes spectacular performance on the biggest stage of his career. His frustrations with the sometimes-staid Ohio State offense evaporated with a surprisingly wide-open game plan against Oregon (10-3), taking advantage of his legs and arm. With Ohio State nursing a two-point lead in the fourth quarter, he took charge during a 13-play, 81-yard drive eating up more than six minutes -- part of the Buckeyes' Rose Bowl-record 41:37 time-of-possession advantage. After arriving in Los Angeles, Pryor disclosed he'd been playing with a partially torn knee ligament, and he came up limping early in the game. But Pryor said the knee didn't bother him, and you sure couldn't tell by the way he played. Pryor converted a third-and-13 play near midfield with about nine minutes to play on a 26-yard catch by tight end Jake Ballard, who leaped high to snatch it. After another third-down conversion, Posey made an impressive TD catch, turning both directions and snagging Pryor's pass away from his body before tumbling over the goal line. Posey had eight catches for 101 yards, and Brandon Saine caught an early TD pass for the Buckeyes, making their first Rose Bowl appearance since 1997. Yet Ohio State's defense did much of the work, limiting the Ducks' no-huddle offense to its worst passing game of the season. Jeremiah Masoli threw for just 81 yards and LaMichael James rushed for 70. A series of big plays and kick returns by Kenjon Barner kept the 96th Rose Bowl close until Pryor sealed it. Oregon made a remarkable comeback from its season-opening loss to Boise State to win its first Pac-10 title since 2001, but the Ducks haven't won the Rose Bowl since the game's third edition in 1917, back when the Granddaddy of Them All was a toddler. Masoli's 1-yard TD run put Oregon up 17-16 early in the third quarter, but the Ducks' powerful offense never scored again. Oregon ran for 179 yards, the second-most allowed by Ohio State this season, but the Ducks were one-dimensional. Oregon, in its first Rose Bowl since 1995, had scored at least 37 points in its previous six games. After Oregon's Morgan Flint missed a 44-yard field goal -- his first miss since Oct. 3 -- Pryor drove the Buckeyes one more time, finishing with emphasis by gaining a first down with a 12-yard run right after Oregon called its final timeout. LeGarrette Blount scored an early touchdown for the Ducks, but the once-suspended tailback also fumbled out of the end zone in the third quarter, ending a potential scoring drive. The cheers Blount received on the way on and off the field highlighted a tumultuous season for the bruising tailback, who was suspended for eight games after punching a Boise State player in frustration after the Ducks' season-opening loss. Ohio State marched 19 plays for a short field goal 1:05 before halftime, and Ross Homan's 20-yard interception return moments later put the Buckeyes in position for Aaron Pettrey's 45-yard field goal at the gun to make it 16-10.

2010 Sugar Bowl

The 2010 Allstate Sugar Bowl was part of the Bowl Championship Series (BCS) and was the 76th Sugar Bowl. The contest was played on Friday, January 1, 2010, in the Louisiana Superdome in New Orleans, Louisiana between the Florida Gators, who lost the 2009 SEC Championship Game and the Cincinnati Bearcats, winners of the Big East Conference. The Bearcats were coached by Offensive Coordinator Jeff Quinn after Head Coach Brian Kelly left Cincinnati to take the head coaching position at Notre Dame on December 10, 2009. This would be Quinn's only game as head coach for Cincinnati, as he had already accepted the head coaching position of the University of Buffalo's football team effective after the Sugar Bowl.

This was Florida's 8th trip to the Sugar Bowl, having gone 2–5 in their previous seven appearances, the last being a 37–20 loss to Miami in 2001. For Cincinnati, this was their first appearance in the Sugar Bowl and their second in a BCS bowl game. In the only previous matchup of these two teams, in 1984, the Gators defeated the Bearcats 48–17. Urban Meyer, the head coach of Florida in the 2010 Sugar Bowl, was a member of that Cincinnati team in 1984. Florida Quarterback Tim Tebow broke two records for the Bowl Championship Series. He threw for a BCS record 482 passing yards and set another BCS record with 533 total yards. Cincinnati Wide Receiver/Returner Mardy Gilyard also broke Sugar Bowl records for return yards in the game. On December 26, 2009, Meyer announced that he would take a leave of absence as head coach after the Sugar Bowl due to health and family reasons.

2010 Sugar Bowl	Line	1	-	2	-	3	-	4	-	Final
#4 Cincinnati	(57.0)	0	-	3	-	7	-	14	-	24
#5 Florida	(-12.0)	9	-	21	-	14	-	7	-	51

Scoring Summary
Florida - Hernandez 7 yard pass from Tebow (Kick blocked)
Florida - Sturgis 40 yard Field goal
Florida - Thompson 7 yard pass from Tebow (Sturgis kick)
Florida - Moody 6 yard run (Sturgis kick)
Cincinnati - Rogers 47 yard Field goal
Florida - Cooper 80 yard pass from Tebow (Sturgis kick)
Florida - Moody 2 yard run (Sturgis kick)
Cincinnati - Waugh 2 yard pass from Pike (Rogers kick)
Florida - Tebow 4 yard run (Sturgis kick)
Cincinnati - Binns 3 yard pass from Pike (Rogers kick)
Florida - Rainey 6 yard run (Sturgis kick)
Cincinnati - Alli 6 yard pass from Pike (Rogers kick)

Recap by Sugar Bowl historian Marty Mulé

"Wow." That was the verbal reaction of football fans in the Superdome - and across the sporting world. But the actual words were uttered by the man of the hour, Tim Tebow, after taking his customary victory jog to salute the Florida fans. "I wanted my final night as a Florida Gator to be very special, and it was," he said in a bit of an understatement. The game itself was over by the half - 30 minutes in which Tebow had already rung up the best statistical outing of his four-year college career. He started the Sugar Bowl by completing the first seven of his passes for 61 yards, culminating with a seven-yard touchdown pass to Aaron Hernandez. Tebow finished the first quarter 10-of-10 for 124 yards. He went 12-of-12 before missing a receiver. Throwing another TD pass and guiding the Gators to two more in the second quarter, Tebow ended the first half 20-of-23 for a season-high 320 yards. When Tebow launched an 80-yard strike to receiver Riley Cooper to make the score 30-3 at intermission, the game was, of course, over for all practical purposes. Cincinnati, who came within a hair of playing for the national championship, had no kryptonite - and no answers. And it wasn't as if Florida was doing anything gaudy offensively against the Bearcat defense. Most of Tebow's passes were short-distance plays, or screens, to receivers who drew single and loose coverage, giving them plenty of room to maneuver after the catch. Even the 80-yard touchdown pass was a short sideline toss that Cooper broke and galloped off to the races. Six Gator receivers had three or more receptions. And the Florida defense was just as dominant. The Bearcats picked up a first down on their second play of the night, then couldn't get another until 6:37 of the second quarter, at which time Florida was on cruise-control with a 23-0 lead. Pike, who threw three touchdown passes to make the score a bit closer than it seemed. All the Florida scoring did help Mardy Gilyard set a Sugar Bowl record. He returned eight kickoffs for 207 yards. By the end of the night, though, nothing eclipsed Tebow's 482 yards passing and 51 yards rushing - the best overall performance not only the Sugar Bowl, but also in the 13-year annals of the BCS. To put his game in perspective, consider that Florida gained a total of 659 yards, and Tebow was responsible for all but 126 yards of that. It was a heckuva way to say goodbye.

2010 PapaJohns.com Bowl

The 2010 PapaJohns.com Bowl was played between the Connecticut Huskies (UConn) of the Big East Conference and the South Carolina Gamecocks of the Southeastern Conference (SEC), on January 2, 2010 at Legion Field in Birmingham, Alabama. Connecticut was selected to play in the 2010 PapaJohns.com Bowl following a tumultuous 7–5 regular season that included five losses by a total of just fifteen points, a double-overtime victory at Notre Dame, and the murder of cornerback Jasper Howard. The Huskies faced South Carolina, who also had 7–5 regular-season, highlighted by wins over then-No. 4 Mississippi and then-No. 15 Clemson. Pregame coverage focused on the tragedy that marked the Huskies' season, as well as on head coaches Randy Edsall of Connecticut and Steve Spurrier of South Carolina. Dixon was named player of the game and finished with 126 rushing yards and one touchdown. Connecticut wide receiver Marcus Easley and South Carolina linebacker Eric Norwood were among four players from the teams to be selected in the subsequent 2010 National Football League (NFL) Draft.

2010 PapaJohns.com Bowl	Line	1	-	2	-	3	-	4	-	Final
Connecticut	(51.0)	10	-	3	-	0	-	7	-	20
South Carolina	(-4.0)	0	-	0	-	0	-	7	-	7

Scoring Summary
Connecticut - Moore 37 yard pass from Frazer (Teggart kick)
Connecticut - Teggart 33 yard Field goal
Connecticut - Teggart 44 yard Field goal
Connecticut - Dixon 10 yard run (Teggart kick)
South Carolina - Maddox 2 yard run (Lanning kick)

Associated Press PapaJohns.com Bowl Game Summary - The Connecticut Huskies made a statement in the Southeastern Conference's backyard, while Steve Spurrier and South Carolina left embarrassed by what the coach described as a "sad, sad effort." Andre Dixon rushed for 126 yards and a touchdown and resilient Connecticut ended a trying season with a 20-7 victory over the Gamecocks in the Papajohns.com Bowl on Saturday. It was a choppy one. The Huskies (8-5) are 3-1 in bowl games since moving up to Division I-A (now FBS) in 2002, but this was their first win over an SEC team -- and it came in the powerhouse league's home base. They won their final three regular-season games and overcame the October stabbing death of cornerback Jasper Howard to reach a bowl. UConn won't get much argument from the Gamecocks (7-6). The nation's 95th-rated pass defense throttled South Carolina and Quarterback Stephen Garcia while the offense relied on Dixon's 33 carries to control the ball. The senior said he and his teammates drew motivation from Howard's memory. He was killed in a fight outside a school-sponsored dance Oct. 18. Dixon was the Most Valuable Player and joined teammate Jordan Todman as 1,000-yard rushers, the first time two UConn backs have surpassed that mark in the same season. Garcia completed just 16 of 38 passes for 129 yards while gaining 56 yards on 15 carries. He lost a fumble, was intercepted once and didn't get much help. An emotional Garcia called the Gamecocks' performance "very disappointing." He said they never got it going, "and it shows on the scoreboard." UConn had a pristine performance, with zero penalties. Linebacker Lawrence Wilson called it "the most complete game we've played all year." The Gamecocks avoided their first shutout in three seasons on Brian Maddox's 2-yard touchdown run with 3:24 left. Their only other possession ending in UConn territory resulted in a botched field goal attempt. It was another difficult postseason chapter for the Gamecocks, who are now 4-11 in bowl games and 1-3 under Spurrier. They have been outscored 51-17 the past two years including a loss to Iowa in last season's Outback Bowl. This one was marred by dropped passes, a missed interception and costly penalties that kept a mostly garnet-and-black clad crowd subdued -- and steadily shrinking by the fourth quarter. Spurrier couldn't blame them for leaving early. Leading receiver Alshon Jeffery was held to three catches for 28 yards, all in the first half. Tailback Kenny Miles had just six carries for 24 yards. Dixon's 10-yard touchdown with 13:12 left effectively put the game away. Jesse Simpson had set the Huskies up at the Gamecocks' 29-yard line by forcing Garcia to fumble, knocking it away from behind at the end of a run. A South Carolina team that pounded Clemson with 58 runs in a win to finish the regular season finished with 26 rushes for 76 yards. UConn jumped ahead 13-0. Kashif Moore snagged the ball one-handed down the right sideline for a 37-yard touchdown catch from Zach Frazer in the first quarter. Dave Teggart then hit field goals of 33 and 44 yards. The first kick was set up when Garcia was stopped on a sneak on fourth-and-1 from South Carolina's 32. South Carolina didn't even manage its initial first down until midway through the second quarter, and that took Garcia converting a third-and-16. South Carolina's sloppy play continued into the second half. Running into the kicker and roughing the passer calls helped UConn keep its first drive alive for more than seven minutes, though it ended with a fumble. Then, cornerback Akeem Auguste dropped an easy interception with nothing between him and the end zone.

2010 Liberty Bowl (January)

The 2010 Liberty Bowl was the fifty-first edition of the bowl game, and was played at Liberty Bowl Memorial Stadium in Memphis, Tennessee. The game was played on Saturday, January 2, 2010. The game was telecast on ESPN and matched the Arkansas Razorbacks against East Carolina University, the Conference USA Champion. The game marked Arkansas' fourth appearance in the bowl. It was their first appearance since 1987 and their first win in the bowl. East Carolina also made its fourth appearance in the game. The Pirates played in the 2009 game, a 25–19 loss to Kentucky. Arkansas entered the game with a 7–5 record. East Carolina entered the game with a 9–4 record. It was the first ever meeting between the two schools.

2010 Liberty Bowl	Line	1	-	2	-	3	-	4	-	OT	-	Final
Arkansas	(-7.5)	0	-	0	-	17	-	0	-	3	-	20
East Carolina	(61.5)	0	-	10	-	7	-	0	-	0	-	17

Scoring Summary
East Carolina - Lindsay 3 yard run (Hartman kick)
East Carolina - Hartman 34 yard Field goal
Arkansas - Tejada 25 yard Field goal
Arkansas - Thomas 37 yard interception return (Tejada kick)
East Carolina - Harris 13 yard pass from Pinkney (Hartman kick)
Arkansas - Wright 41 yard pass from Mallett (Tejada kick)
Arkansas - Tejada 37 yard Field goal

Associated Press Liberty Bowl Game Summary - Alex Tejada kicked the ball through the uprights, turned around and ran toward the opposite end of the field. His Arkansas teammates chased him all the way to the end zone amid a wild scene of celebration and relief. Tejada's 37-yard field goal in overtime gave Arkansas a 20-17 win in the Liberty Bowl on Saturday night after East Carolina's Ben Hartman missed two field goal attempts late in regulation and another in the extra session. Tejada, who missed an overtime kick in a loss to LSU to end the regular season, redeemed himself by helping the Razorbacks overcome the upset-minded Pirates. Tejada missed a crucial kick in a loss to Florida in October, and his miss against LSU prevented the Razorbacks from forcing a second overtime. Tejada missed from 43 yards in the fourth quarter Saturday, but his struggles were nothing compared with Hartman's. The East Carolina senior missed four attempts in all, each at the same end of the field. He was short from 45 yards in the first quarter, then hit the left upright from 39 yards with 1:03 remaining in regulation with the score tied. He missed from 39 yards again on the final play of the fourth quarter, then missed from 35 in overtime. Arkansas (8-5) had won only two of its previous 14 bowls, and the Razorbacks insisted they were unusually focused on this one. It didn't show. Arkansas' vaunted offense had the ball for only 22:05. Mallett was named most valuable player, but he went only 15 of 36 for 202 yards and a touchdown. The Liberty Bowl is right across the Mississippi River from Arkansas, but the Razorbacks were playing in the game for the first time since 1987. Except for a small section of purple in one corner, the crowd was a sea of Arkansas red. Those fans watched their team go 0 of 13 on third down. The low point came toward the end of regulation: After Hartman's miss with just over a minute remaining, the Razorbacks went three-and-out in only 29 seconds, allowing the Pirates (9-5) to set up Hartman again. This potential game-winner went wide right. Hartman's field goal and two extra points in the game were enough to break the school's career scoring record, but that was small consolation. Hartman wasn't made available to reporters afterward. East Carolina lost in the Liberty Bowl for the second straight season. Last time it was a late fumble return by Kentucky that did in the Pirates. Dominique Lindsay rushed for 151 yards on 33 carries for East Carolina. His 3-yard touchdown run opened the scoring in the second quarter, ending a 99-yard drive by the Pirates. It was 10-0 at halftime, the first time the Razorbacks had been shut out in the first half since September against Alabama. Arkansas had been averaging 37 points per game. The Razorbacks tied it in the third quarter with a defensive touchdown when Tramain Thomas intercepted a pass and ran 37 yards to the end zone. East Carolina took the lead again on Patrick Pinkney's 13-yard touchdown pass to Dwayne Harris with 5:52 left in the third. Arkansas answered 36 seconds later when Mallett threw a 41-yard scoring pass to Jarius Wright to make it 17-all. Still, it was a struggle for the Razorbacks, who became only the second major college team this season to win without converting a third down. Colorado State went 0 for 8 while beating Weber State in September, according to STATS LLC. Pinkney, a sixth-year senior, went 17 of 33 for 209 yards with a touchdown and two interceptions. The last time Arkansas played in the Liberty Bowl, the Razorbacks lost to Georgia 20-17 on a last-second field goal by John Kasay. That kick was from 39 yards, the same distance as Hartman's fourth-quarter misses.

2010 Alamo Bowl (January)

The 2010 Alamo Bowl (known via corporate sponsorship as the Valero Alamo Bowl) was played at the Alamodome in San Antonio, Texas on Saturday, January 2, 2010. It was the 17th edition of the Alamo Bowl. The game featured the Michigan State Spartans against the Texas Tech Red Raiders. The 2010 game was the last one to feature a team from the Big Ten Conference. In the fall of 2009, it was announced that the Pacific-10 Conference's second-place team would take part in the Alamo Bowl instead of the Holiday Bowl. This was the third Alamo Bowl appearance and first Alamo Bowl win for the Texas Tech Red Raiders. Their previous appearance was a 19–16 loss to Iowa in the 2001 game. Michigan State played in one previous Alamo Bowl, losing the 2003 game to Nebraska, 17–3. The game also marked the first-ever meeting between the two schools. With approximately 5,553,630 households watching it, the game was the most viewed Alamo Bowl in history. It also drew the highest rating of any bowl ever shown by ESPN. Behind the BCS bowl games and the Capital One Bowl, it was the most viewed bowl shown up to that point in the 2009–10 bowl season.

2010 Alamo Bowl	Line	1	-	2	-	3	- -	4	-	Final
Michigan State	(60.0)	7	-	7	-	14	-	3	-	31
Texas Tech	(-7.5)	7	-	13	-	7	-	14	-	41

Scoring Summary
Texas Tech - Batch 3 yard run (Williams kick)
Michigan State - Baker 46 yard run (Swenson kick)
Texas Tech - Williams 21 yard Field goal
Texas Tech - Leong 2 yard pass from Potts (Williams kick)
Michigan State - Martin 48 yard pass from Cousins (Swenson kick)
Texas Tech - Williams 38 yard Field goal
Michigan State - Nichol 7 yard run (Swenson kick)
Texas Tech - Franks 14 yard pass from Potts (Williams kick)
Michigan State - White 8 yard pass from Martin (Swenson kick)
Michigan State - Swenson 44 yard Field goal
Texas Tech - Lewis 11 yard pass from Sheffield (Williams kick)
Texas Tech - Batch 13 yard run (Williams kick)

Associated Press Alamo Bowl Game summary - No questions about Mike Leach. No questions about Adam James. Those were the ground rules Texas Tech Quarterback Steven Sheffield laid down Saturday night after saving the day in a thrilling Alamo Bowl victory that his fired head coach would've loved. Let him enjoy it somewhere else, the Red Raiders said. This isn't his team anymore. After a week like that, the Red Raiders can finally unwind a little. With everyone still talking about Leach -- and who can blame them? -- the Red Raiders blocked out the distractions and rallied to beat Michigan State 41-31 in front of an anxious, almost angry crowd that clearly wanted their "Head Pirate" back on the sideline. They also wanted James gone. Texas Tech fired Leach on Wednesday amid allegations that he mistreated James, son of ESPN analyst Craig James, after the sophomore wide receiver was diagnosed with a concussion. James declined comment after a night in which fans booed him so loud, it drowned out the marching band at halftime. He was flanked by two security guard as Texas Tech (9-4) celebrated and looked relaxed for the first time since arriving in San Antonio. The Red Raiders heard the boos. They saw the posters -- "Man up, Adam!" among them. But offensive lineman Brandon Carter had a message for fans: James isn't the one to blame. Interim coach Ruffin McNeill said he also was disappointed in James' reception. The tone of the crowd changed after the win. A chorus of "Ruffin! Ruffin!" went out in a thank-you to Leach's defensive coordinator, who navigated the Red Raiders through a week the school is desperate to forget. The controversy surrounding Leach didn't even quiet long enough to let Saturday belong to the game. Hours before kickoff, Texas Tech released an affidavit in which school athletic trainer Steve Pincock says he told James he was "sorry" for having placed the player inside an equipment shed near the practice field. Pincock told Tech officials he didn't agree with that "form of treatment for anyone." Just another layer to a bowl game that cornered the market on turmoil. No bowl teams in the country kicked off with more upheaval than Texas Tech and Michigan State (6-7). Leach's firing did Michigan State the favor of drawing attention from its own black eye: 14 players who didn't make the trip in the wake of a Nov. 22 dormitory brawl. Nine Michigan State players face charges of misdemeanor assault. But the short-handed Spartans held their own. They took a 28-27 lead into the fourth quarter and appeared to get a break when Tech Quarterback Taylor Potts left the game after injuring his non-throwing hand. He left with an Alamo Bowl-record 372 yards and two touchdowns. But this was still a Leach-built team. And in his offense, Quarterbacks thrive. With Tech down 31-27, Sheffield marched the Red Raiders downfield in eight plays, the last an 11-yard touchdown pass to Detron Lewis. Batch tacked on a 25-yard touchdown run to put it away. Texas Tech will savor this win -- especially because the future may not be so rosy. Leach vows he's not done with Texas Tech, and a nasty legal battle likely looms. The Red Raiders also must find a successor to the winningest -- and perhaps most popular -- head coach in Texas Tech history. McNeill wants the job, and this win might help. Players were unanimous in wanting McNeill back, too. It was just a year ago that Leach had the Red Raiders unbeaten and ranked No. 2 in late November. Even Texas Tech's toughest critics were finally acknowledging the Red Raiders as a legitimate contender, and no longer just a gimmicky pest that withered against the nation's elite. A four-loss encore this season was a letdown, to be sure. But Leach still brought Texas Tech to a ninth bowl game under his watch, more than any of his predecessors. A mostly full Alamodome crowd of more than 64,000 showed their appreciation. In Leach vs. Texas Tech, there was no doubt where the fans sided Saturday. Pirate flags fluttered in the parking lot. Posters venerating Leach and dogging James -- "EVERY SUCCESSFUL PIRATE KNOWS BETRAYAL" hanged prominently behind the Texas Tech bench -- were en vogue in just about every aisle. Gray-haired alumni made "Fire (Texas Tech AD Gerald) Myers" stickers a popular accessory, and scores of Texas Tech students arrived in "Team Leach" T-shirts. Even a 10-year-old wore a shirt taking a shot at the James family. If Adam James noticed, he didn't act like it. He wandered the sideline wearing his No. 82 jersey and a black stocking cap, standing mostly off to the side with other inactive players. James might have been on the Red Raiders' sideline for the last time. Acting offensive coordinator Lincoln Riley stopped short this week of saying he wanted James back -- and that was after Riley said far worse things about the 21-year-old in e-mails to university administrators. Riley wrote James was "unusually lazy and entitled" to save Leach's job. He sent it on Dec. 26. A week later Saturday, Texas Tech was ready to go home. And leave everything else in San Antonio.

2010 Cotton Bowl Classic

The 2010 AT&T Cotton Bowl Classic game was played between the Oklahoma State Cowboys, from the Big 12 Conference and the Ole Miss Rebels, from the Southeastern Conference that took place on Saturday, January 2, 2010, at Cowboys Stadium in Arlington, Texas. The 2010 game was the first game in Cowboys Stadium after leaving its namesake venue and was the concluding game of the season for both teams involved. Ole Miss has the distinction of playing in the last ever Cotton Bowl Classic held in the old Cotton Bowl stadium and playing in the first ever Cotton Bowl Classic held in its new home at Cowboys Stadium. This was Ole Miss' second consecutive Cotton Bowl Classic appearance as the Rebels also played in the 2009 Cotton Bowl Classic where they defeated Texas Tech 47–34. This was also the second meeting between Ole Miss and Oklahoma State in a Cotton Bowl Classic game. The two teams met in the 2004 Cotton Bowl Classic, which Ole Miss won 31-28 on the arm of Quarterback Eli Manning. This was Oklahoma State's third appearance in the Cotton Bowl Classic. Their first was a 34–0 win over TCU in 1945. This was Ole Miss' fifth appearance in the Cotton Bowl Classic. Aside from the 2004 and 2009 games, Ole Miss defeated TCU 14–13 in 1956 and lost to Texas 7–12 in 1962. In this 2010 edition of the Cotton Bowl Classic, Ole Miss defeated Oklahoma State by a score of 21-7. With the win, Ole Miss became the first team to win back-to-back Cotton Bowl Classics since Notre Dame did so in 1993 and 1994. Ole Miss' Dexter McCluster was awarded the offensive MVP, making him only the second back-to-back offensive MVP in the Cotton Bowl Classic's 74-year history. The other was SMU's Doak Walker in 1948 and 1949. McCluster's 86-yard run for a touchdown was the longest actual completed run in Cotton Bowl Classic history but is not the longest officially. In the 1954 Cotton Bowl Classic, Rice University's Dicky Moegle began a run from his team's 5-yard line down the sideline near the University of Alabama's bench. As Moegle passed Alabama's bench, Alabama player Tommy Lewis jumped off the bench, wearing no helmet, and tackled Moegle at the 42-yard line. The referee saw what happened and signaled touchdown therefore making it officially a 95-yard run for a touchdown.

2010 Cotton Bowl Classic	Line	1	-	2	-	3	-	4	-	Final
#21 Oklahoma State	(50.5)	0	-	0	-	7	-	0	-	7
Mississippi	(-3.0)	0	-	7	-	0	-	14	-	21

Scoring Summary
Mississippi - McCluster 86 yard run (Shene kick)
Oklahoma State - Youman 1 yard pass from Toston (Bailey kick)
Mississippi - McCluster 2 yard run (Shene kick)
Mississippi - Trahan 34 yard fumble recovery (Shene kick)

Cotton Bowl Classic Game Summary - The first AT&T Cotton Bowl Classic at Cowboys Stadium promised a "new beginning" for the 74-year-old Classic, but it was déjà vu for Ole Miss and Dexter McCluster. The Rebels defeated Oklahoma State, 21-7, to win the AT&T Cotton Bowl for the second straight year — third time since 2004 — and McCluster repeated as the Sanford Trophy winner, which recognizes the outstanding offensive player and commemorates AT&T Cotton Bowl Classic founder J. Curtis Sanford. Playing in the largest domed structure in the world, the event drew 77,928 spectators — second largest in Cotton Bowl Classic history — plus a national FOX TV audience. By unanimous vote in 2010, McCluster became of first player since University of Houston linebacker David Hodge in 1979 and 1980 to win consecutive outstanding player honors and the first offensive player since SMU's Doak Walker in 1948 and 1949 to earn offensive recognition in the AT&T Cotton Bowl Classic. As Nutt pointed out, McCluster is the first player in Southeastern Conference (SEC) history to account for more than 1,000 rushing yards and 500 receiving yards in a single season. McCluster finished this year with 1,167 rushing yards and 565 receiving yards, including his 182 rushing and 45 receiving yards and two touchdowns in his final game. Of a possible record-setting afternoon, which included a career high 32 carries, he said he really wasn't worried. Following a scoreless first quarter, McCluster gave the Rebels a 7-0 lead on an electrifying 86-yard touchdown run with 11:19 remaining in the first half. The run was the second longest in Classic history behind Rice's Dicky Maegle gallop of 95 yards against Alabama in 1954. Following an Oklahoma State turnover with 6:15 to play in the fourth quarter, McCluster scored his second touchdown on a two-yard leap with 4:03 to play, giving Ole Miss a 14-7 advantage. Ole Miss' got its final touchdown with 3:12 to play on a 34-yard fumble return by Patrick Trahan. Andre Sexton's interception of an Ole Miss pass led to Oklahoma State's only touchdown — a 1-yard jump pass from Keith Toston to Wilson Youngman with 7:13 remaining in the third quarter. Sexton received the McKnight Trophy, which recognizes the outstanding defensive player and commemorates long-time Dallas newspaperman and Cotton Bowl Team Selection Chairman

Felix McKnight. Oklahoma State Coach Mike Gundy congratulated Ole Miss, commiserated about his team's turnovers and praised the AT&T Cotton Bowl Classic for its legendary hospitality.

2010 International Bowl

The 2010 International Bowl was the fourth and final edition of the bowl game, and was played at Rogers Centre in Toronto, Ontario, Canada. The game was played on Saturday, January 2, 2010. The game was telecast on espn2, and the South Florida Bulls defeated the Northern Illinois Huskies 27–3.

2010 International Bowl	Line	1	-	2	-	3	-	4	-	Final
South Florida	(-7.0)	3	-	0	-	10	-	14	-	27
Northern Illinois	(49.5)	0	-	3	-	0	-	0	-	3

Scoring Summary
South Florida - Scwartz 39 yard Field goal
Northern Illinois - Salerno 21 yard Field goal
South Florida - Scwartz 19 yard Field goal
South Florida - Love 46 yard pass from Daniels (Scwartz kick)
South Florida - Love 7 yard pass from Daniels (Scwartz kick)
South Florida - Ford 24 yard run (Scwartz kick)

Associated Press International Bowl Game Summary - Mike Ford played the best game of his career in just two quarters. Ford ran for a career-high 207 yards and scored one touchdown, B.J. Daniels threw two scoring passes to A.J. Love, and South Florida beat Northern Illinois 27-3 in Saturday's International Bowl. Ford had just one carry in the first half, an 18-yard gain in the second quarter. He broke out in the third, rushing 12 times for 106 yards, then capped his day with a 24-yard touchdown run in the fourth. Ford set the tone for his big second half by breaking off a 36-yard run, his longest of the day, three plays after the break. Ford had holes to choose from as fatigue slowed Northern Illinois' defense in the second half. It's the third straight year a Big East running back has topped 200 yards in the International Bowl. Ray Rice of Rutgers turned pro after rushing for a game-record 280 yards and four touchdowns in 2007, while Connecticut's Donald Brown ran for 261 yards in last year's game. Carlton Mitchell caught six passes for 94 yards for the Bulls, who won back-to-back bowls for the first time. South Florida beat Memphis 41-14 in last year's St. Petersburg Bowl, part of a streak of five straight bowl appearances. Daniels threw for 217 yards but was sacked five times. South Florida scored 24 unanswered points in the second half after the teams traded field goals in a dreary first half. Making consecutive postseason appearances for the first time, the Huskies lost their third straight bowl and extended the Mid-American Conference's bowl game losing streak to 14 games. Spann carried 20 times for 93 yards, giving him 1,038 for the season. Big East teams have defeated their Mid-American Conference opponents in all four International Bowls, the only bowl game played outside the United States. Cincinnati beat Western Michigan in the inaugural game in 2007, followed by victories for Rutgers over Ball State in 2008 and Connecticut over Buffalo in 2009. The Bulls took the lead for good on the opening drive of the third quarter. Ford's 36-yard run set up Daniels' 31-yard pass to Mitchell, who shook off a tackle and raced down the sideline to the 6. It was a record-setting catch for Mitchell, giving him 680 yards on the season and breaking Hugh Smith's school mark of 661 set in 2002. The Bulls couldn't punch it in but went ahead on Eric Schwartz's 19-yard field goal. Daniels hooked up with Love for the game's first touchdown on the Bulls' next possession, rolling to the outside before firing a 46-yard strike off his back foot and capping an eight-play, 81-yard drive. Cornerback Jerome Murphy picked off Huskies Quarterback Chandler Harnish on the next possession, giving South Florida the ball at its 48. Ford carried five times to get the Bulls to the 7, where, on the first play of the fourth quarter, Daniels connected with Love again, making it 20-3.

2010 Fiesta Bowl

The 2010 Tostitos Fiesta Bowl game was played between the #4 TCU Horned Frogs, champions of the Mountain West Conference, and the #6 Boise State Broncos, champions of the Western Athletic Conference. The game was played Monday, January 4, 2010, at University of Phoenix Stadium in Glendale, Arizona. For the second consecutive year, TCU and BSU faced off in a bowl game of historic significance. In the 2008 Poinsettia Bowl, TCU and Boise State played in the first non-BCS game ever in which both teams were ranked higher than both participants in a BCS bowl game in the same season (specifically the 2009 Orange Bowl), with the Horned Frogs winning 17–16.

2010 Fiesta Bowl	Line	1	-	2	-	3	-	4	-	Final
#6 Boise State	(55.0)	7	-	3	-	0	-	7	-	17
#3 TCU	(-7.5)	0	-	7	-	3	-	0	-	10

Scoring Summary
Boise State - Thompson 51 yard interception return (Brotzman kick)
Boise State - Brotzman 40 yard Field goal
TCU - Clay 30 yard pass from Dalton (Evans kick)
TCU - Evans 29 yard Field goal
Boise State - Martin 2 yard run (Brotzman kick)

Associated Press Fiesta Bowl Game Summary - Boise State pulled "Riddler" out of its bag of tricks. Presto: the Broncos stunned Texas Christian in a Fiesta Bowl duel of unbeaten BCS busters. After a gutsy fake punt at the Broncos' own 33-yard line, Doug Martin scored the decisive touchdown to give No. 6 Boise State a 17-10 victory over third-ranked TCU on Monday night. For the second time in four years, the Broncos (14-0) won the Fiesta Bowl with a YouTube- worthy play. Last time, the victim was Oklahoma. This time it was TCU (12-1), which fizzled in its BCS debut. A 10-10 stalemate came alive with a play straight out of Boise State's goofy playbook. It's called "Riddler," and TCU couldn't solve it. Petersen called it on fourth-and-9 at the Broncos' 33. Punter Kyle Brotzman hit wide-open Kyle Efaw with a 30-yard strike on fourth-and-9. TCU coach Gary Patterson said the Horned Frogs had worked on the fake in practice, but they were caught flat-footed. TCU never recovered. Broncos Quarterback Kellen Moore, who threw for 211 yards, connected on three straight passes to move Boise State to the TCU 2-yard, and then Martin vaulted over a tackler from 2 yards out to put the Broncos up 17-10 with 7:21 to go. The trickery evoked memories of Boise State's BCS debut three years ago, when it pulled out a passel of gadget plays to defeat Oklahoma on the same field. Unlike the thriller against OU, this game offered little drama for the first three quarters. It was the first time two schools from conferences without automatic BCS bids have met in one of college football's biggest bowls. But for long stretches TCU and Boise State played as if they belonged in the Poinsettia Bowl, site of TCU's 17-16 victory over Boise State in December 2008. Boise State entered as the nation's highest-scoring team (44.2 points per game), and the Horned Frogs were fourth (40.7). But their expected offensive duel turned into a tedious series of punts. Neither team could muster an offensive touchdown until the final minute of the first half, when TCU's Andy Dalton hit Curtis Clay for a 30-yard score to make it 10-7 at halftime. TCU's Ross Evans kicked a 29-yard field goal to tie it at 10 heading into the fourth quarter. The game appeared to be dragging toward overtime until Petersen's gutsy call. After taking the lead, the Broncos called on their unheralded defense to lock up the win. TCU took over at its own 1 with 1:06 remaining and marched to the Boise State 30 before cornerback Brandyn Thompson disrupted a pass by Dalton, and Winston Venable picked it off with 18 seconds remaining. Thompson had two interceptions. He returned the first 51 yards for the game's first score, and his second one set up the Broncos' winning drive. Dalton had thrown only five interceptions in 279 pass attempts during the regular season, when he earned first-team All-Mountain West Conference honors. But the Broncos put pressure on Dalton from the start; late in the first quarter, unblocked defender Kyle Wilson blitzed and flattened Dalton, who came out for one play. Dalton finished with 272 yards and a score through the air but was intercepted three times. Western Athletic Conference champion Boise State earned its second BCS victory -- as many as Michigan, Penn State and Alabama have combined. The Broncos are one of only three remaining unbeatens, along with Texas and Alabama, which will play for the national title on Thursday night. Petersen has resisted entering the national title debate, but it's clear he thinks his spunky team can play with anyone.

2010 Orange Bowl

The 2010 FedEx Orange Bowl game featured the Georgia Tech Yellow Jackets and the Iowa Hawkeyes on Tuesday, January 5, 2010, at Land Shark Stadium in Miami Gardens, Florida. Iowa won the game 24–14, securing the Hawkeyes' first major bowl win since the 1959 Rose Bowl. Georgia Tech was selected to participate in the Orange Bowl after an 11–2 season that culminated in a 39–34 victory in the 2009 ACC Championship Game. Iowa was selected as the other half of the matchup after a 10–2 season that ended with a 12–0 win against Minnesota. It was the coldest Orange Bowl in Miami's history with a kick-off temperature of 49 degrees. The game was televised in the United States on FOX and marked the end of the broadcast agreement between the BCS and FOX, as ESPN took over all BCS broadcast rights in 2011. This was Iowa's second Orange Bowl appearance (first appearance in 2003 Orange Bowl), and Georgia Tech's sixth appearance, but first since 1967. It was the first time that the two teams had played against each other.

2010 Orange Bowl	Line	1	-	2	-	3	-	4	-	Final
#10 Iowa	(50.5)	14	-	0	-	3	-	7	-	24
#9 Georgia Tech	(-4.5)	7	-	0	-	0	-	7	-	14

Scoring Summary
Iowa - McNutt 3 yard pass from Stanzi (Murray kick)
Iowa - Sandeman 21 yard pass from Stanzi (Murray kick)
Georgia Tech - Tarrant 40 yard interception return (Blair kick)
Iowa - Murray 33 yard Field goal
Georgia Tech - Allen 1 yard run (Blair kick)
Iowa - Wegher 32 yard run (Murray kick)

Orange Bowl Classic Game Summary - Iowa Earns First BCS Win - In a game that featured one of the most dynamic offenses in the nation against one of the country's stingiest defenses, it was the No. 10 Iowa Hawkeyes solving No. 9 Georgia Tech's triple option attack for a 24-14 victory at the 2010 Orange Bowl. Despite a temperature of 49 degrees at kickoff, the coldest in the 76-year history of the football classic, the Hawkeyes had the Yellow Jackets feeling the heat from the start. Iowa earned its first BCS bowl win, matched the school record for victories and could claim their highest final ranking since finishing No. 3 in 1960. Atlantic Coast Conference champion Georgia Tech (11-3) totaled nine first downs and 155 yards, both season-lows. Defensive end Adrian Clayborn led Iowa's defensive charge with two sacks and nine tackles and was chosen the game's most outstanding player. Iowa earned its first Orange Bowl win. The game marked the sixth appearance for Georgia Tech in the Orange Bowl, but first since 1967. The Hawkeye offense was led by Quarterback Ricky Stanzi, who went 17-for-29 for 231 yards and threw two early touchdowns, and true freshman running back Brandon Wegher, who carried the ball 16 times for 113 yards and one score.

2010 GMAC Bowl

The 2010 GMAC Bowl, the eleventh edition of the bowl game, was played at Ladd-Peebles Stadium in Mobile, Alabama on January 6, 2010. The game was telecast on ESPN and matched the Central Michigan Chippewas, champions of the Mid-American Conference, against the Troy Trojans, champions of the Sun Belt Conference. Central Michigan won in double overtime, 44-41, on a 37-yard field goal by Andrew Aguila, his fifth of the game. The opponent for the MAC team was scheduled to be the ninth selection of a team from the Atlantic Coast Conference. However, the ACC only produced seven bowl-eligible teams in 2009. Therefore, the GMAC Bowl was able to select an at-large team that was bowl eligible and did not have a prior conference tie-in. Many had felt that the invitation would go to Notre Dame, who finished the season at 6-6. After lengthy meetings the Notre Dame administration made the decision that they will not go to a bowl game following the 2009 season. Also, Notre Dame would only have been eligible to fill the slot after all available teams with 7 or more wins had been accommodated. Several sportswriters pointed to the comparatively low payout of the bowl and the potential humiliation if Central Michigan (then the likely opponent) defeated the Irish. Troy ultimately filled the slot after Southern Miss claimed Conference USA's slot in the 2009 New Orleans Bowl. Although that game has a guaranteed berth for the Sun Belt champion, the organizers used their prerogative to invite the conference's second-place team, Middle Tennessee, not wishing to repeat its Troy–Southern Miss matchup from 2008. As a 9-win team, Troy had priority over any 6–6 teams not already tied to specific bowl games.

2010 GMAC Bowl	Line	1	-	2	-	3	-	4	-	OT	-	2OT	-	Final
Central Michigan	(-3.5)	3	-	6	-	10	-	15	-	7	-	3	-	44
Troy	(63.0)	7	-	3	-	14	-	10	-	7	-	0	-	41

Scoring Summary
Troy - Harris 9 yard pass from Brown (Taylor kick)
Central Michigan - Aguila 28 yard Field goal
Central Michigan - Aguila 35 yard Field goal
Troy - Taylor 22 yard Field goal
Central Michigan - Aguila 44 yard Field goal
Troy - Southward 1 yard run (Taylor kick)
Central Michigan - Aguila 42 yard Field goal
Central Michigan - Brown 7 yard run (Aguila kick)
Troy - Harris 6 yard run (Taylor kick)
Troy - Harris 1 yard run (Taylor kick)
Central Michigan - Brown 95 yard kickoff return (Aguila kick)
Central Michigan - Anderson 4 yard pass from LeFevour (Poblah pass from LeFevour)
Troy - Taylor 46 yard Field goal
Central Michigan - LeFevour 13 yard run (Aguila kick)
Troy - Southward 1 yard run (Taylor kick)
Central Michigan - Aguila 37 yard Field goal

Associated Press GMAC Bowl Game Summary - LeFevour finished with flair. Central Michigan's relentless Quarterback moved into second place on the career total yards list, accounted for two late touchdowns and scored one of his biggest wins in his last game by rallying the Chippewas (No. 25 AP) to a

44-41 double-overtime victory against Troy in the GMAC Bowl on Wednesday night. All in a night's work for one of college football's most overlooked Quarterbacks. Antonio Brown started the rally with a 95-yard kickoff return. LeFevour followed with a touchdown pass to put the sluggish Chippewas (12-2) ahead with 1:17 left and scored from 13 yards out in the first overtime to set up Andrew Aguila's 37-yard game-winning field goal after Central Michigan appeared to fade away. LeFevour completed 33 of 55 passes for 395 yards and finished his career with 15,853 total yards, trailing only Hawaii Quarterback Timmy Chang (16,910). He also moved into fifth place in the FBS in career completions and 10th in yards passing before being selected the game's most valuable player. It was the 10th 400-yard game of a decorated career. It also was vintage LeFevour, showing off everything he's learned in four years. He was harassed by Troy much of the game, watched receivers drop several passes and had minus-1 yards rushing through four quarters. Yet when it seemed like the Chippewas were fading, he snapped to attention and put on a nearly flawless drive to rally his team. He completed 8 of 11 passes for 90 yards, hitting Bryan Anderson with a 4-yard touchdown for the lead with 1:17 left. He then completed another pass for the 2-point conversion to make it 34-31. The teams traded touchdowns in the first overtime with LeFevour scoring on a 13-yard misdirection run, then Vince Agnew blocked Michael Taylor's 31-yard field-goal attempt to start the second overtime. Central Michigan played it conservative before Aguila set a GMAC record with his fifth field goal. The Trojans (9-4) led much of the game behind DuJuan Harris' three touchdowns. But after taking a 31-19 lead midway through the fourth quarter, they gave LeFevour and the Chippewas an opening. The game-turning drive was in stark contrast to the rest of the night. The Chippewas and LeFevour were sluggish and plagued by small mistakes that kept Aguila busy. He hit from 28, 35, 44 and 42 yards in regulation, keeping Central Michigan in it until LeFevour rallied the team. He completed 31 of 56 passes for 386 yards and became the 41st Quarterback to pass for 4,000 yards in a single season. The senior opened the scoring with a 9-yard pass to Harris and was sharp on third down as the Trojans converted 13 of 20. Harris rushed for 112 yards and scored rushing touchdowns of 6 and 1 yards. The last score midway through the fourth quarter appeared to put the Trojans out of reach, but Brown had different plans. He took the ensuing kickoff up the right side and raced nearly untouched to the end zone to cut the lead to 31-26. He also scored on a 7-yard touchdown run and finished with 403 all-purpose yards (178 receiving on 13 catches, 203 on kickoff returns and 22 rushing).

2010 BCS Championship Game

The 2010 Citi BCS National Championship Game was the finale of the 2009 NCAA Division I FBS football season and was played between the Texas Longhorns and the Alabama Crimson Tide. It was hosted by the Pasadena Tournament of Roses Association at the Rose Bowl Stadium in Pasadena, California, January 7, 2010. It was the 12th BCS National Championship Game, and the second consecutive year the champion of the Southeastern Conference (SEC) was matched against the champion of the Big 12 Conference. The game was the ninth meeting of Texas and Alabama, though the first since the 1982 Cotton Bowl Classic. Prior to the game, Texas led the all-time series with a 7–0–1 record, with the first meeting in 1902. The match-up was the third game in which the Tournament of Roses hosted the BCS National Championship game in Pasadena, and the fifth time, overall, that it has hosted a No. 1 versus No. 2 match-up. However, this was the first time the Tournament of Roses hosted the game as a separate event from the Rose Bowl Game. They had previously hosted BCS Championship games in the 2006 and 2002 Rose Bowls, and pre-BCS No. 1 versus No. 2 matchups in the 1969 and 1963 Rose Bowls.

2010 BCS Championship	Line	1	-	2	-	3	-	4	-	Final
#2 Texas	(45.0)	6	-	0	-	7	-	8	-	21
#1 Alabama	(-3.5)	0	-	24	-	0	-	13	-	37

Scoring Summary
Texas - Lawrence 18 yard Field goal
Texas - Lawrence 42 yard Field goal
Alabama - Ingram 2 yard run (Tiffin kick)
Alabama - Richardson 49 yard run (Tiffin kick)
Alabama - Tiffin 26 yard Field goal
Alabama - Dareus 28 yard interception return (Tiffin kick)
Texas - Shipley 44 yard pass from Gilbert (Lawrence kick)
Texas - Shipley 28 yard pass from Gilbert (Run good)
Alabama - Ingram 1 yard run (Tiffin kick)
Alabama - Richardson 2 yard run (Kick failed)

Alabama Media Guide BCS Championship Game Summary - The No. 1-ranked Alabama football team held true to its ranking, defeating second-ranked Texas, 37-21, in the 2010 BCS National Championship at the Rose Bowl in Pasadena. The 2009 national championship was the 13th in Alabama history. The Crimson Tide defense ended any hopes of a Longhorn comeback when blitzing linebacker Eryk Anders forced a fumble by Texas Quarterback Garrett Gilbert with only 3:08 remaining in the game. Alabama would force two more turnovers and score two touchdowns to seal the 2009 national championship. After Texas jumped out ahead 6-0 in the first quarter, the Crimson Tide took the lead with running back Mark Ingram punching in a two-yard rush putting Alabama up 7-6 with 14:18 remaining in the second quarter. Trent Richardson joined in on the ground attack when he busted a 49- yard touchdown run at the 7:59 mark of the second quarter to stretch Alabama's lead to 14-7. Placekicker Leigh Tiffin extended the Tide's lead by connecting on a 26- yard field goal. Two plays later, defensive tackle Marcell Dareus intercepted Gilbert's shovel pass and returned it 28 yards for an Alabama touchdown. The 10-point swing gave the Crimson Tide a 24-6 lead heading into halftime. With Texas' offense scoring 11 unanswered points in the second half and pulling within 24-21, Anders forced a fumble at the three-yard line with linebacker Courtney Upshaw recovering for the Tide. The Texas fumble led directly to Ingram's one-yard touchdown run, putting Alabama up 31- 21. Javier Arenas came up with his second interception of the night with 1:55 remaining in the game and Richardson turned the turnover into points once again, scoring a touchdown on a two-yard run. Tiffin missed the extra point attempt, making the final score 37-21. With the win Alabama head coach Nick Saban became the first head coach in major college football history to win a national championship at two different schools, also winning the BCS national championship in 2003 at LSU. Saban also became the second head coach to win two BCS national championships, joining Urban Meyer of Florida. The victory in Pasadena came 84 years after Alabama won its first national championship in the 1926 Rose Bowl game and marked the fifth Alabama team to end a national championship campaign at the Rose Bowl in Pasadena.

2010 New Mexico Bowl

The 2010 New Mexico Bowl was held on December 18, 2010, at University Stadium on the campus of the University of New Mexico in Albuquerque, New Mexico. The organizers introduced a new logo to celebrate the 5th anniversary of the game on September 29, 2010. The game, which was telecast on ESPN, featured the UTEP Miners from Conference USA and the BYU Cougars from the Mountain West Conference. Both are former members of the Western Athletic Conference where the Cougars dominated the series with a 28–7–1 record. BYU, making its 29th bowl appearance, came into the game winning five out of seven games after a 1–4 start. UTEP, in just its 13th bowl, had dropped six of seven after opening the season 5–1. Both teams were making their first New Mexico Bowl appearance. UTEP was the first team from outside the WAC or MWC to play in the game due to the bowl organizers wanting a more regional matchup. BYU won the game in dominating fashion by a score of 52–24. Freshman Quarterback Jake Heaps took home MVP honors with a game-record four touchdown passes, helping his team to a 31–3 second quarter lead. UTEP has lost five straight bowl games, the second-longest streak in the nation.

2010 New Mexico Bowl	Line	1	-	2	-	3	-	4	-	Final
BYU	(-11.5)	17	-	14	-	14	-	7	-	52
Texas-El Paso	(50.5)	3	-	7	-	7	-	7	-	24

Scoring Summary
BYU - Kariya 4 yard run (Payne kick)
BYU - Heaps 9 yard pass from Ashworth (Payne kick)
Texas-El Paso - Warren 52 yard Field goal
BYU - Payne 38 yard Field goal
BYU - Heaps 31 yard pass from Hoffman (Payne kick)
BYU - Heaps 3 yard pass from Hoffman (Payne kick)
Texas-El Paso - Vittatoe 67 yard pass from Adams (Warren kick)
BYU - Luigi 2 yard run (Payne kick)
Texas-El Paso - Vittatoe 37 yard pass from Adams (Warren kick)
BYU - Heaps 29 yard pass from Hoffman (Payne kick)
BYU - Quezada 8 yard run (Payne kick)
Texas-El Paso - Vittatoe 49 yard pass from Adams (Warren kick)

Associated Press New Mexico Bowl Game Summary - Jake Heaps is BYU's bowl-winning Quarterback, and that's no easy feat for a freshman. Heaps threw four touchdown passes, connecting with Cody Hoffman on three scores, and finished with 264 yards passing to help BYU beat overmatched Texas-El Paso 52-24 on Saturday in the New Mexico Bowl. While he was one of the nation's top recruits a year ago, Heaps has come a long way from earlier this season when he was sharing snaps with Riley Nelson, who later was injured, and struggling to throw TD passes for the first time in his life. Heaps showed some toughness, too. He disclosed in the interview room that he has had a broken rib since BYU's last game, a 17-16 loss to Utah on Nov. 27. The victory capped a triumphant turnaround for the Cougars (7-6), whose 1-4 start included a rare loss to instate rival Utah State. At that point, Mendenhall told his team it would be a remarkable feat to reach a bowl game and win it. Mission accomplished after the Cougars won five of their last seven regular-season games to become bowl eligible. In the first game of college football's bowl season, Mendenhall's team showed just how far BYU came by dominating the Miners (6-7). Hoffman had eight catches for 137 yards, while Joshua Quezada ran for 101 yards and J.J. DiLuigi added 98 yards on the ground to help the Cougars in their final contest before they begin play as an independent in football next season. Heaps became the first freshman Quarterback to start any of BYU's 29 bowl games. For most of the day, he looked like a polished veteran and showed why he was one of the nation's top recruits coming out of high school in the Seattle suburbs in 2009. He completed seven of his first nine attempts, with both of those incompletions on drops. The Cougars raced to a 14-0 lead. J.D. Falslev returned the game's first punt 43 yards to set up a 4-yard TD run by Bryan Kariya. Heaps threw a 9-yard strike to Luke Ashworth, a 31-yard pass to Hoffman and made it 31-3 midway through the second quarter on a 3-yard pass to Hoffman. On that play, Heaps also broke Ty Detmer's 22-year-old BYU freshman record for most passing TDs in a season. Heaps, who finished with 15 TD passes on the year, was 25 of 34 with one interception and was selected the game's most valuable offensive player. BYU also got two interceptions and one of the team's four sacks from Andrew Rich, voted the most valuable defensive player. Afterward, Rich said Heaps has worked hard to lead BYU's younger players and the older players noticed. UTEP's season went in the opposite direction compared to BYU, with the Miners losing six of seven after opening 5-1. They still reached a bowl game for the first time since 2005 but dropped to 0-5 since beating Mississippi 14-7 in the 1967 Sun Bowl. Trevor Vittatoe, who postponed surgery on his left ankle so he could play in the postseason, threw three TD passes, all to Kris Adams on plays of 67, 37 and 49 yards. But that was the bulk of the offense for the Miners, whose 233 total yards included minus-12 yards rushing.

2010 Humanitarian Bowl

The 2010 Humanitarian Bowl (officially known as the UDrove Humanitarian Bowl) was the fourteenth edition of the bowl game, and was played at Bronco Stadium in Boise, Idaho, on the campus of Boise State University. The game was played on Saturday, December 18, 2010 and was telecast on ESPN. The game featured the Fresno State Bulldogs from the Western Athletic Conference (WAC) versus the Northern Illinois Huskies from the Mid-American Conference (MAC). Despite having been abandoned by their coach of three years, Northern Illinois defeated Fresno State 40–17.

2010 Humanitarian Bowl	Line	1	-	2	-	3	-	4	-	Final
Northern Illinois	(-1.5)	6	-	17	-	10	-	7	-	40
Fresno State	(58.0)	7	-	3	-	0	-	7	-	17

Scoring Summary
Fresno State - Colburn 11 yard pass from Hamler (Goessling kick)
Northern Illinois - Harnish 7 yard run (Kick failed)
Northern Illinois - Harnish 28 yard run (Cklamovski kick)
Northern Illinois - Cklamovski 45 yard Field goal
Fresno State - Goessling 45 yard Field goal
Northern Illinois - Harnish 22 yard pass from Skarb (Cklamovski kick)
Northern Illinois - Cklamovski 51 yard Field goal
Northern Illinois - Spann 18 yard run (Cklamovski kick)
Northern Illinois - Spann 8 yard run (Cklamovski kick)
Fresno State - Colburn 11 yard pass from Evans (Goessling kick)

Associated Press Humanitarian Bowl Game Summary - After Northern Illinois lost a conference title and its head coach, Tom Matukewicz's first objective was to make the Huskies' bowl trip fun. He constantly cracked jokes. He made the coaches go one-on-one in practice. No matter what happened, Matukewicz was going to take a lighter approach. The reward? That came Saturday night when the Huskies closed out the best season in school history in resounding fashion. Quarterback Chandler Harnish ran for two touchdowns and threw for another, and Northern Illinois made Matukewicz a winner in his only game in charge with a 40-17 victory over Fresno State in the uDrove Humanitarian Bowl. Northern Illinois (11-3) earned a school-record 11th victory and ended an emotional two-week stretch that started with a loss to Miami, Ohio in the Mid-American Conference title game, then was compounded 48 hours later by the departure of head coach Jerry Kill for Minnesota. The players uniformly credited Matukewicz for bringing stability and focus -- and a little fun -- at a time the Huskies needed it most. He started his postgame comments saying he was going to "milk this thing out" since he'll no longer be the guy in charge. He jokingly told Harnish he was getting an extra postgame meal after paying the coach a compliment. Lighthearted worked for these Huskies. Any changes that might be coming when Wisconsin defensive coordinator Dave Doeren is done game planning for the Rose Bowl and becomes the new head coach -- with Matukewicz staying on as linebackers coach -- were secondary. That's why the Huskies chanted "Tuke! Tuke!" on the field and doused him with a water bucket in the final seconds, then celebrated on Boise's blue turf as snow started swirling. Harnish finished 17 of 26 for 300 yards passing and another 72 yards rushing. It helped his receivers made highlight catches -- like Perez Ashford's fingertip grab on the sideline and Willie Clark's mid-route adjustment for 32-yard gain -- and Fresno State's defensive line got no pressure on Harnish. Running back Chad Spann added 95 yards and two touchdowns, giving him 22 rushing TDs on the season and, for now, put him one ahead of Oregon's LaMichael James for most in the country. And the Huskies were beyond good, they dominated. NIU never punted and scored on seven straight possessions after falling behind 7-0. The only times they were stopped were a pair of failed fourth-down attempts and the end of the game. They sacked Fresno State Quarterback Ryan Colburn six times, including three -- all in the first half -- by Jake Coffman. Bulldogs' running back Robbie Rouse, who ran for nearly 300 yards in a game earlier this season, was held to 32 yards. While Matukewicz was happily cracking jokes postgame, Fresno State coach Pat Hill was again looking at a troubling trend. Fresno State (8-5) continued its postseason track of playing up against BCS opponents but struggling against those from non-automatic qualifying conferences. In its last 11 bowl appearances, the Bulldogs are 4-1 against BCS teams and 0-6 against the others. And for how much respect Hill has shown Boise, he might not want to come back here for quite a while. This season, the Bulldogs were outscored 91-17 on the blue turf. In their last three trips here, it's 152-27. Fresno State looked fine early, scoring on its opening drive when Colburn hit Jamal Hamler on an 11-yard TD. Not much went right from there. Colburn threw for 273 yards and added a late TD pass to Rashad Evans. After failing on fourth down at the Fresno State 31 on their opening possession, the Huskies were not stopped. They scored the next seven times they touched the ball, getting touchdown runs of 7 and 28 yards from Harnish, and a 22-yard TD pass to Kyle Skarb in the final minute of the first half to take a 23-10 lead. Michael Cklamovski added a career-best 51-yard field goal on the Huskies first possession of the second half to extend their lead to 26-10. Colburn and the Bulldogs looked poised to make one final push, but he was sacked by Devin Butler and fumbled deep in the Huskies end. After Colburn's fumble, the Huskies went 89 yards, capped by Spann's 28-yard dash for a 33-10 lead. Spann added one more, an 8-yard run, to give the Huskies a 30-point lead. It set a school record for TDs in a season and capped a nearly perfect night for the Huskies. But before he stepped away, Matukewicz had one more message.

2010 New Orleans Bowl

The 2010 R+L Carriers New Orleans Bowl was the tenth edition of the bowl. The game was played at the Louisiana Superdome in New Orleans, Louisiana on Saturday, December 18, 2010. The contest was televised live on ESPN. The game featured the Ohio Bobcats of the Mid-American Conference versus the Troy Trojans from the Sun Belt Conference.

2010 New Orleans Bowl	Line	1	-	2	-	3	-	4	-	Final
Ohio	(57.5)	7	-	0	-	7	-	7	-	21
Troy	(-2.0)	14	-	24	-	10	-	0	-	48

Scoring Summary
Troy - Jernigan 12 yard run (Taylor kick)
Ohio - Goulet 34 yard pass from Jackson (Weller kick)
Troy - Gill 31 yard pass from Robinson (Taylor kick)
Troy - Jernigan 16 yard pass from Robinson (Taylor kick)
Troy - Taylor 50 yard Field goal
Troy - Gill 17 yard pass from Robinson (Taylor kick)
Troy - Gill 26 yard pass from Robinson (Taylor kick)
Troy - Taylor 33 yard Field goal
Ohio - Foster 5 yard pass from Jackson (Weller kick)
Troy - Harris 2 yard run (Taylor kick)
Ohio - Dunlop 18 yard pass from Jackson (Weller kick)

Associated Press New Orleans Bowl Game Summary - Corey Robinson punctuated a formidable freshman season by helping Troy rewrite the R+L Carriers New Orleans Bowl record books. Robinson threw for 387 yards and four touchdowns, and Troy set a New Orleans Bowl scoring record with a 48-21 victory over Ohio on Saturday night. Robinson completed 23 of 29 passes for 285 yards and four TDs in the first half alone, when Troy (8-5) raced to a 38-7 lead and was 32 of 42 overall. While Robinson was chosen the game's MVP, he was quick to credit his experienced receivers, who made Ohio regret trying to cover them man-to-man. Tebiarus Gill had a New Orleans Bowl-record three touchdowns, all on receptions in the first half. Fellow senior Jerrel Jernigan had seven catches for 48 yards, including a 16-yard touchdown. Troy finished with 602 offensive yards -- also a New Orleans Bowl record. The Trojans had a 371-39 advantage in offensive yards through the first two quarters, by which time it was apparent Ohio (8-5) was going to drop to 0-5 in its bowl history. So dominant were the Trojans that they didn't punt until the fourth quarter and even outrushed Ohio, which runs a variation of the option Solich used when he was at Nebraska from 1998-2003. Troy finished with 220 yards on the ground while the Bobcats had 99. Troy's Dujuan Harris ran for 105 yards and a score. The Trojans have won or shared the past five Sun Belt Conference titles and are 2-3 in bowl games since becoming a full member of the Football Bowl Subdivision in 2002. Both wins came at the New Orleans Bowl, where the Trojans have played three times. Before the game, Trojans players expressed hope that a second bowl victory on national television might bring them a little more recognition. At the very least, fans across the country saw that the Trojans have a Quarterback with the potential to rack up a lot of yards by the time his college career is done. Robinson connected four times with Gill for 80 yards and four times with Jason Bruce for 59 yards. Robinson finished his freshman campaign with 3,726 yards and 28 TDs. The Bobcats, who were second in the Mid-American Conference's East Division, came in knowing they'd be in trouble if they didn't play well on defense and control the ball on offense. They struggled on both counts. The Bobcats' Boo Jackson passed for 209 yards and three TDs, but he did not start after missing some recent practices to clear up some academic matters. Solich started Phil Bates, whose first pass was intercepted deep down the sideline by Jimmie Anderson. Troy then marched 78 yards in 10 plays, with Jernigan scoring on a 12-yard run out of the wildcat formation to make it 7-0. Jackson entered the game during Ohio's second offensive season and completed a 34-yard touchdown pass to Steven Goulet to tie it at 7. Troy went back in front when Robinson lofted a 31-yard timing pass down the left sideline to Gill. Jernigan capped Troy's next series with a 16-yard TD catch on which the receiver took a short pass near the 10 and dodged three tacklers. Michael Taylor's New Orleans Bowl-record 50-yard field goal nudged Troy's lead up to 24-7. Gill's 17-yard TD catch made it 31-7, marking the first time a team had scored that many points in a half of any of the 10 New Orleans Bowls. Troy wasn't done, though. The third Robinson-to-Gill TD connection, covering 26 yards, came in the final minute of the second quarter.

2010 Beef 'O' Brady's Bowl

The 2010 Beef 'O' Brady's Bowl St. Petersburg was the third edition of the bowl game formerly known as the St. Petersburg Bowl. It was played at Tropicana Field in St. Petersburg, Florida, on Tuesday, December 21, 2010. The game was telecast on ESPN and featured the Southern Miss Golden Eagles from Conference USA versus the Louisville Cardinals from the Big East Conference. Louisville was a member of Conference USA from 1996 through 2004.

2010 Beef 'O' Brady's Bowl	Line	1	-	2	-	3	-	4	-	Final
Southern Miss	(58.5)	14	-	7	-	0	-	7	-	28
Louisville	(-2.5)	0	-	21	-	0	-	10	-	31

Scoring Summary
Southern Miss - Pierce 32 yard pass from Davis (Hrapmann kick)
Southern Miss - Johnson 62 yard run (Hrapmann kick)
Louisville - Graham 11 yard pass from Burke (Philpott kick)
Southern Miss - Pierce 11 yard pass from Davis (Hrapmann kick)
Louisville - Chichester 10 yard pass from Burke (Philpott kick)
Louisville - Powell 6 yard run (Philpott kick)
Southern Miss - Walters 8 yard pass from Davis (Hrapmann kick)
Louisville - Wright 94 yard kickoff return (Philpott kick)
Louisville - Philpott 36 yard Field goal

Associated Press Beef 'O' Brady's Bowl Game Summary - Charlie Strong is making good on his pledge to turn around the Louisville Cardinals. A lot sooner than some people expected, too. Justin Burke threw for two touchdowns and Jeremy Wright scored on a 95-yard kickoff return Tuesday night to help Louisville beat Southern Mississippi 31-28 in the Beef 'O' Brady's Bowl and finish its first winning record in four years. Strong, the former Florida defensive coordinator who took over the Cardinals last December, inheriting a team that went 4-8 and lost six of seven games in the Big East in 2009. Burke tossed scoring passes to 11 yards to Cameron Graham and 10 yards to Josh Chichester while the Cardinals (7-6) were overcoming an early 14-point deficit, then produced a go-ahead field goal in the fourth quarter. Austin Davis threw 205 yards and two touchdowns to become Southern Mississippi's career TD pass leader, moving ahead of Brett Favre and Lee Roberts in the Golden Eagles record book with 53 in three seasons. The Southern Miss Quarterback also scored on a 17-yard reception from receiver Quentin Pierce. Wright's long kickoff return made it 28-all early in the fourth quarter. Chris Philpott's 36-yard field goal gave the Cardinals their first lead with 6:30 remaining. Davis completed 19 of 32 passes, including TD throws of 32 yards to Pierce and 8 yards to Zeke Walters for the Golden Eagles (8-5). In addition to becoming the Southern Miss career TD pass leader, the junior moved into second place on the school's career passing list with 7,396 yards -- 299 short of the 7,695 Favre threw for from 1987-90. Meanwhile,

Desmond Johnson scored on a 62-yard run and finished with a season-high 107 yards rushing. Bilal Powell rushed for 75 yards for Louisville -- well below his season average of 120.9 -- however the 215-pound senior was instrumental in helping the Cardinals exhaust most of the clock after finally taking the lead. Although they were meeting for the first time in a bowl game, there's a long history between the former conference rivals. The Cardinals and Golden Eagles faced each other every season from 1978 to 1991 and both were members of C-USA 1996 to 2004, the season before Louisville moved to the Big East. Southern Miss scored on its first two possessions, taking a quick 14-0 lead on Pierce's TD reception and Johnson's long run that left Louisville's defense, which ranked 11th nationally during the regular season, looking sluggish and bewildered. The Cardinals didn't flinch, though, methodically climbing back into the game with help from linebacker Antwone Canady's fumble recovery, which set up Powell's 6-yard touchdown run and enabled Louisville to pull even at 21-all late in the first half. Strong took over a team that many picked to finish last in the Big East. He wound up being co-coach of the year after a 3-4 finish in the conference, achieved despite not having starting Quarterback Adam Froman for the team's four games in November. Burke completed 20 of 32 passes for 178 yards in his fifth consecutive start for the Cardinals, who went 3-2 in those games. He scrambled 19 yards on third-and-3 before throwing his TD pass to Graham to trim Louisville's deficit to 14-7 early in the second quarter. Southern Miss answered with a seven-play, 64-yard march that Davis finished with his first his only reception of the season. The 6-foot-2, 200-pound Quarterback from Meridian, Miss., circled to his right out of the backfield after handing off to receiver Kelvin Bolden, who handed to Pierce as he was heading around left end. Davis became the Golden Eagles' career TD pass leader on the first play of the fourth quarter, finding Walters in the right corner of the end zone to snap a 21-21 tie. The lead lasted 15 seconds, as Wright took the kickoff on the left side of field and eventually made his way to the right sideline to finish the longest return in the short history of the Beef 'O' Brady's Bowl.

2010 Maaco Bowl

The 2010 Maaco Bowl Las Vegas was played Wednesday, December 22, 2010 at 40,000-seat Sam Boyd Stadium near Las Vegas and the broadcast was on ESPN. The game featured Utah against Boise State.

2010 Maaco Bowl	Line	1	-	2	-	3	-	4	-	Final
#20 Utah	(59.0)	3	-	0	-	0	-	0	-	3
#10 Boise State	(-16.5)	0	-	16	-	7	-	3	-	26

Scoring Summary
Utah - Phillips 44 yard Field goal
Boise State - Martin 84 yard run (Brotzman kick)
Boise State - Brotzman 29 yard Field goal
Boise State - Shoemaker 25 yard pass from Moore (Run failed)
Boise State - Pettis 18 yard pass from Moore (Brotzman kick)
Boise State - Brotzman 21 yard Field goal

Associated Press Maaco Bowl Game Summary - It wasn't the bowl Boise State wanted to be in, and for the better part of the first half Wednesday night, the Broncos played as if they were thinking about the one that got away. Then Doug Martin raced 84 yards up the middle, and suddenly the MAACO Bowl didn't look so bad after all. Martin shook Boise State out of its brief postseason funk with his long touchdown run midway through the second quarter, and the 10th-ranked Broncos dominated the rest of the way to beat Utah 26-3 in a game that wasn't as close as the final score indicated. The victory was small consolation for Boise State, which missed out on a possible Rose Bowl appearance on two missed field goals last month at Nevada. But the dominating win against a team that was at one time ranked No. 6 in the country was a reminder why the Broncos rode high in the polls before suffering their only loss in two years. It may also be a reminder for next year's poll voters not to write off a team that won every game over the past two years except the one that really mattered. The loss to Nevada not only cost the school millions of dollars in a BCS bowl bid, but some of the grudging respect others had finally given Boise State. Count Utah (No. 19 BCS, No. 20 AP) coach Kyle Whittingham among the believers. Neither of those things happened, of course, forcing Boise State to go begging for a decent bowl bid despite its gaudy record. The Broncos landed in this gambling city, where the bookies quickly established them as 17-point favorites to beat a Utah team that also had its BCS dream dashed late in the season. But Boise State came out flat and seemed disinterested. Kellen Moore fumbled on the third play of the game and the Broncos turned the ball over three times to help Utah to a 3-0 lead. Martin then scampered up the middle and headed down the left sideline on the first play from scrimmage following a Utes punt. Martin's run came after a mistake-prone first quarter in which Boise State kept giving the ball away and making costly errors. Utah wasn't much better, and when the Broncos began finding their stride the game quickly turned one-sided. Moore, who also threw an interception in the first quarter, rebounded with a 25-yard touchdown pass to Tyler Shoemaker in the closing seconds of the first half to give Boise State a 16-3 lead. He added another 18-yard TD pass to Austin Pettis in the third quarter. Meanwhile, Boise State's defense held Utah to just 200 yards, forcing the Utes to punt again and again. The Broncos shut down both the running and passing game and Utah never scored after its opening field goal. Boise State (12-1) was ranked as high as No. 2 in The Associated Press Top 25 poll this year, but early on looked little like the team that was everyone's favorite BCS buster. That changed with Martin's run, with the Broncos taking control on both sides of the ball against a team that was a BCS team itself two years ago and had won nine straight bowl games. Moore, who finished fourth in Heisman voting earlier this month, finished with impressive numbers despite his rocky start. He completed 28 of 38 passes, including 12 to Pettis, who was playing the final game of a college career in which his team won 51 of 53 games. The game was the last for Utah (10-3) before going into the Pac-12 Conference, where the Utes can play for an automatic big bowl bid. Boise State is also switching conferences, heading to the Mountain West where the Broncos still will have to impress both voters and computers to get a Bowl Championship Series bid. Boise State was plenty impressive against Utah, shutting down Quarterback Terrance Cain and the Utes running game. Utah didn't help itself by losing three fumbles and being penalized 10 times for 83 yards in a sloppily played game. Boise State kicker Kyle Brotzman, who's chip-shot misses cost his team a BCS bowl game and his school dearly, became the all-time NCAA leader in points kicking with a 29-yard field goal in the second quarter. Brotzman added another field goal in the fourth quarter but had a mixed night, getting one attempt blocked and dropping a pass while wide open on a fake punt.

2010 Poinsettia Bowl

The 2010 San Diego County Credit Union Poinsettia Bowl was played between the San Diego State Aztecs and the Navy Midshipmen on December 23, 2010 at Qualcomm Stadium in San Diego, California. The sixth edition of the annual Poinsettia Bowl, which the Aztecs won 35–14, and was broadcast on ESPN.

2010 Poinsettia Bowl	Line	1	-	2	-	3	-	4	-	Final
Navy	(60.0)	0	-	14	-	0	-	0	-	14
San Diego State	(-3.5)	14	-	7	-	0	-	14	-	35

Scoring Summary
San Diego State - Hillman 22 yard run (Perez kick)
San Diego State - Brown 53 yard pass from Lindley (Perez kick)
Navy - Jones 30 yard pass from Dobbs (Buckley kick)
San Diego State - Hillman 37 yard run (Perez kick)
Navy - Dobbs 1 yard run (Buckley kick)
San Diego State - Hillman 15 yard pass from Lindley (Perez kick)
San Diego State - Hillman 1 yard run (Perez kick)

Associated Press Poinsettia Bowl Game Summary - Once workers pumped away 1.5 million gallons of rainwater that had flooded Qualcomm Stadium, it was smooth sailing for freshman Ronnie Hillman and San Diego State. Hillman scored four touchdowns and matched his career best with 228 yards rushing on 28 carries to lead the Aztecs to their first bowl victory since 1969, 35-14 over Navy in the San Diego County Credit Union Poinsettia Bowl on Thursday night. The only thing that slowed Hillman in the slightest was a wet sock. One of his cleats came off late in the third quarter and he hopped off the field, trying to keep that foot dry. Six plays later, he pulled in a 15-yard scoring pass from Ryan Lindley after a beautifully executed fake. Lindley faked a handoff to Brandon Sullivan into the line, then hid the ball down by his right hip as Navy stood up the fullback at the line. Lindley hit a wide-open Hillman in the right corner of the end zone for a 28-14 lead on the first play of the fourth quarter. Hillman, the Mountain West Conference Freshman of the Year, scored on a 2-yard run midway through the period to go along with first-half scoring runs of 22 and 37 yards. SDSU (9-4) hadn't won a postseason game since beating Boston University in the 1969 Pasadena Bowl. The Aztecs had been in only three bowl games since, most recently the 1998 Las Vegas Bowl, which they lost to North Carolina. Hillman broke the previous Poinsettia Bowl record of 129 yards rushing by Navy's Adam Ballard in 2005. Hillman also ran for 228 yards in a loss at Missouri on Sept. 18. The Aztecs outrushed Navy 279-235. The game was played on a slick field after all that rainwater was pumped out of Qualcomm Stadium overnight. Players went slipping and sliding all night, but organizers met their promise of kicking off on time after several days of torrential rain flooded the field and a portion of the parking lot. Navy (9-4) was making its third Poinsettia Bowl appearance since the game's inception in 2005. Hillman's 228 yards broke the school bowl record of 164 yards rushing by Marshall Faulk in the 1991 Freedom Bowl. SDSU took a 14-0 lead in the first quarter on Hillman's 22-yard TD run and Lindley's 53-yard TD pass to Vincent Brown. Navy pulled to 14-7 on Ricky Dobbs' 30-yard scoring pass to Greg Jones early in the second quarter. Hillman put the Aztecs up by two touchdowns again as he ran untouched 37 yards up the middle with 3:15 before halftime. Navy closed within one score on Dobbs' 1-yard keeper 7 seconds before halftime. SDSU held Navy on the opening drive of the second half, when Dobbs' pass went off Bo Snelson's fingertips in the end zone on fourth-and-goal from the 3. Lindley completed 18 of 23 passes for 276 yards. Brown had eight catches for 165 yards, also a Poinsettia Bowl record. The old record was 126 yards by David Anderson of Colorado State in 2005.

2010 Hawai'i Bowl

The 2010 Sheraton Hawaii Bowl was the ninth edition of the bowl game. The game was played at Aloha Stadium in Honolulu, Hawaii on Friday, December 24, 2010. The contest was televised live on ESPN. The game featured Tulsa of Conference USA versus Hawai'i of the Western Athletic Conference.

2010 Hawaii Bowl	Line	1	-	2	-	3	-	4	-	Final
#24 Hawaii	(-10.0)	0	-	14	-	14	-	7	-	35
Tulsa	(73.5)	10	-	17	-	21	-	14	-	62

Scoring Summary
Tulsa - Singleton 3 yard run (Fitzpatrick kick)
Tulsa - Fitzpatrick 42 yard Field goal
Hawaii - Austin 1 yard run (Enos kick)
Tulsa - Flanders 54 yard interception return (Fitzpatrick kick)
Tulsa - Arnick 54 yard interception return (Fitzpatrick kick)
Hawaii - Salas 18 yard pass from Moniz (Enos kick)
Tulsa - Fitzpatrick 28 yard Field goal
Hawaii - Salas 5 yard pass from Moniz (Enos kick)
Tulsa - Owens 15 yard pass from Kinne (Fitzpatrick kick)
Hawaii - Green 1 yard run (Enos kick)
Tulsa - Johnson 67 yard run (Fitzpatrick kick)
Tulsa - Roberson 47 yard pass from Kinne (Fitzpatrick kick)
Hawaii - Pollard 33 yard pass from Moniz (Enos kick)
Tulsa - Johnson 3 yard run (Fitzpatrick kick)
Tulsa - Johnson 9 yard pass from Kinne (Fitzpatrick kick)

Associated Press Hawaii Bowl Game Summary - Damaris Johnson ran sideways through defenders and down the sidelines past them. He didn't stop until he had an NCAA record and a big pineapple-shaped trophy. Johnson broke loose for a career-high 326 all-purpose yards to break the NCAA career record and Tulsa took advantage of six first-half turnovers to beat No. 24 Hawaii 62-35 in the Sheraton Hawaii Bowl on Friday night. The Golden Hurricane (10-3) grounded the nation's No. 1 passing offense most of the night and broke it open with a 21-point third quarter for their seventh straight win and third consecutive bowl victory. The short and speedy Johnson earned MVP honors, rushing for 98 yards and a touchdown on five carries and catching four passes for 101 yards and another score. He had two big plays in the decisive third quarter -- a 59-yard reception and a 67-yard TD run that put Tulsa up 41-28. He also had five kickoff returns for 109 yards and an 18-yard punt return. Johnson hauled in Tulsa's final touchdown, a 9-yarder from G.J. Kinne with 1:16 left. Johnson raised his nation-leading all-purpose average from 191.8 to 202.2 yards. Greg Salas also had a record night for Hawaii (10-4). The senior had 13 receptions for career-high 214 yards and two touchdowns and set Hawaii single-season records in receptions and receiving yards. Hawaii, 3-3 in its hometown bowl, had 550 yards of offense to Tulsa's 531. But it was Johnson who ran wild in paradise. The junior has 7,796 all-purpose yards, breaking Western Michigan standout Brandon West's record of 7,764 set in 2006-09. Johnson broke the record on a 12-yard run in the fourth quarter. He entered the game fourth on the career list, 294 yards shy of tying the mark, and quickly passed up Memphis' DeAngelo Williams and Clemson's C.J. Spiller. Kinne was 17 of 31 for 343 yards and three second-half touchdowns. He had just 107 yards passing in the first half. Tulsa entered the game ranked 119th in the nation in pass defense, but used an aggressive pass rush up front and had its linebackers drop back into coverage on the Warriors, who shared the Western Athletic Conference title with Boise State and Nevada. The Golden Hurricane forced a fumble and intercepted five passes in the first half, including two picks by Curnelius Arnick. Hawaii's six first-half turnovers led to 24 Tulsa points and gave the Hurricane a 27-14 halftime lead. On Arnick's second interception, he stepped in front of Bryant Moniz's errant throw and returned it 54 yards along the sideline, leaping for the score to put Tulsa up by 17. Arnick celebrated by flexing his bulging biceps in front of the booing Hawaii fans. Moniz broke the 5,000-yard passing mark for the season, throwing for 411 yards and three touchdowns. But he had a disastrous first half with four interceptions. His 33-yard pass to Royce Pollard cut it to 48-35 with 9:27 left, but the Warriors wouldn't get any closer as the Golden Hurricanes seemed to move the ball at will. Hawaii pulled to 27-21 on a 5-yard TD pass from Moniz to Salas to open the second half. But Tulsa answered with Kinne lobbing a short pass to the speedy Johnson, who cut right, across the field for a 59-yard gain. Kinne found Jameel Owens for a 15-yard score on the next play to push the lead back to 13. Hawaii's offense finally got going late in the first half. Salas caught an 18-yard TD pass from Moniz to cut Tulsa's lead to 10 with 2:20 left in the half. The score was set up by highlight-reel reception with Salas outjumping two defenders and hauling it in for 55 yards. The reception was Salas' 109th of the season, breaking Davone Bess' single-season record of 108 set in 2007. Earlier in the game, Salas broke Ashley Lelie's mark of 1,713 yards receiving set in 2001. However, the sure-handed Salas fumbled a punt return, leading to a Tulsa field goal just before halftime. Salas finished his career at Hawaii with 285 catches for 4,345 yards and 26 touchdowns.

2010 Little Caesars Pizza Bowl

The 2010 Little Caesars Pizza Bowl was played on December 26, 2010 at Ford Field in Detroit, Michigan and aired on ESPN. The bowl game matched up the Florida International Golden Panthers of the Sun Belt Conference against the Toledo Rockets of the Mid-American Conference.

2010 Little Caesars Pizza Bowl	Line	1	-	2	-	3	-	4	-	Final
Florida International	(56.5)	0	-	7	-	14	-	13	-	34
Toledo	(-1.5)	7	-	14	-	3	-	8	-	32

Scoring Summary
Toledo - Thomas 4 yard run (Claus kick)
Toledo - Thomas 87 yard run (Claus kick)
Florida International - Perry 1 yard run (Griffin kick)
Toledo - Noble 10 yard pass from Owens (Claus kick)
Toledo - Claus 29 yard Field goal
Florida International - Hilton 89 yard kickoff return (Griffin kick)
Florida International - Perry 7 yard run (Griffin kick)
Florida International - Hilton 10 yard pass from Carroll (Griffin kick)
Florida International - Griffin 31 yard Field goal
Toledo - Owen 14 yard run (Pass good)
Florida International - Griffin 34 yard Field goal

Little Caesar's Pizza Bowl Game Recap - Jacob Younger caught the pass near midfield, flipped the ball to his team's top player and hoped for the best. T.Y. Hilton took the lateral and dashed toward the sideline, trying to reach the first-down marker and keep Florida International's final drive alive. The officials ruled Hilton reached the marker before stepping out of bounds, giving FIU an improbable conversion on fourth-and-17. Moments later, Jack Griffin's 34-yard field goal as time ran out gave the Golden Panthers a delirious 34-32 victory Sunday night in the Little Caesars Pizza Bowl. And this game set the bar high for the many bowls still to come this season. It featured two wild comebacks by FIU in the second half alone, the second of which came after Toledo took a one-point lead on a touchdown and a 2-point conversion with 1:14 remaining. Add in FIU's frantic hook-and-lateral, and it was quite a debut on the big stage for a program in only its ninth season. FIU made the transition to what is now called the Football Bowl Subdivision in 2005. The team has seldom had a chance to celebrate like this. Three years ago, FIU finally snapped a 23-game losing streak, and the program also had to deal with the fallout from a 2006 brawl against Miami. Earlier this year, the Panthers dealt with tragedy after running back Kendall Berry was stabbed to death on campus. Now, the program once known for a long losing streak has a perfect record in bowls. The Panthers trailed 24-7 in the third quarter before Hilton returned a kickoff 89 yards for a touchdown. FIU (7-6) went on to score 24 straight points, taking a 28-24 lead on Hilton's 10-yard touchdown catch and adding a field goal with 3:18 remaining. Terrance Owens, who had thrown three interceptions in the second half, patiently led Toledo (8-5) back on a 62-yard drive that ended when he kept the ball himself for a 14-yard touchdown run. When the Rockets decided to go for two, Owens found Eric Page on a slant pattern to put them ahead. It appeared Toledo had pulled the game out, to the delight of many of the 32,431 in attendance. Toledo is about an hour from Detroit and had plenty of fans at Ford Field. But after taking a 32-31 lead, the Rockets tried a squib kick to keep the ball away from Hilton. FIU ended up taking over near midfield. Although a sack knocked FIU back, the Panthers had one trick play left. The initial ruling was that Hilton had gotten the first down, and the officials didn't overturn it after a replay review, putting the ball at the Toledo 42. Much of the pregame anticipation surrounded Page and Hilton, two shifty wide receivers who are also dangerous return men. Page set up an early touchdown with a 21-yard punt return and nearly won the game for Toledo with his late 2-point conversion. Hilton scored two touchdowns -- and his biggest play was nowhere near the end zone. The win gave the Sun Belt Conference bragging rights over the Mid-American Conference. The leagues are matched up in three bowls this season, but the Sun Belt has already won the first two. This was also a rubber match of sorts between FIU and Toledo after the teams split games in 2008 and 2009. Perry ran for 132 yards and two touchdowns for the Panthers. Adonis Thomas rushed for a career-high 193 yards and two touchdowns for the Rockets, including an 87-yard touchdown run as Toledo built a 21-7 halftime lead -- long before anyone realized what an enthralling game this would become.

2010 Independence Bowl

The 2010 AdvoCare V100 Independence Bowl was the thirty-fifth edition of the bowl game and was played at Independence Stadium in Shreveport, Louisiana. The game was played on Monday, December 27, 2010. The game was telecast on ESPN2 and featured the Georgia Tech Yellow Jackets from the Atlantic Coast Conference (ACC) versus Air Force from the Mountain West Conference (MWC), the nation's top two rushing teams.

2010 Independence Bowl	Line	1	-	2	-	3	-	4	-	Final
Air Force	(-2.5)	3	-	3	-	0	-	8	-	14
Georgia tech	(55.5)	7	-	0	-	0	-	0	-	7

Scoring Summary
Air Force - Bell 42 yard Field goal
Georgia Tech - Allen 5 yard run (Blair kick)
Air Force - Bell 41 yard Field goal
Air Force - Tew 3 yard run (Run good)

Associated Press Independence Bowl Game Summary - Air Force was struggling to run the ball and failed to convert a few great opportunities in the passing game. Instead of growing frustrated and losing focus, the Falcons kept plugging along. Their persistence paid off. Air Force cashed in when Georgia Tech muffed a punt in the second half of the AdvoCare V100 Independence Bowl, getting a go-ahead touchdown run from Jared Tew in a 14-7 victory Monday. It was a matchup between the two best rushing teams in the country, but the game was largely decided by special teams. Backup kicker Zack Bell converted the first two field-goal attempts of his career before Tew's 3-yard run gave the Falcons (9-4) the lead for good. Air Force's only touchdown came four plays after Daniel McKayhan's second muffed punt of the game -- the third of four Georgia Tech turnovers. Georgia Tech's 327 yards rushing per game this season edged Air Force's 317.9 average for the nation's top spot. Both teams use a heavy dose of option, which often catches opponents off guard because it's a relatively rare offense. But with each defense familiar with the scheme, there were no surprises, and both teams were held under their season rushing average -- Georgia Tech with 279 and Air Force with 170. Air Force's Tim Jefferson completed 11 of 23 passes for 117 yards. Bell's field goals came from 41 and 42 yards. Georgia Tech's Tevin Washington rushed for 131 yards and Anthony Allen added 91 as Georgia Tech outgained Air Force 320-287. But the Yellow Jackets had three costly fumbles. Georgia Tech (6-7) came into the game hobbled by injuries, academic casualties and misbehavior. Joshua Nesbitt, the ACC's career leading rusher for a Quarterback, missed the game because of a broken right arm. Top receiver Stephen Hill and starting safety Mario Edwards were among four players declared ineligible because of various academic issues. The Yellow Jackets announced Sunday that defensive end Anthony Egbuniwe and defensive backs Michael Peterson and Louis Young would miss the first half because of a curfew violation. Even with all those issues, Georgia Tech probably would have won if not for the turnovers. Instead, the Yellow Jackets dropped their sixth consecutive bowl and posted their first losing season in 14 years. Bell's 42-yard field goal gave Air Force the lead in the first quarter, but Georgia Tech responded with a 12-play, 69-yard drive capped by Anthony Allen's 5-yard touchdown run. The clock-chewing possession was all running plays stayed as the Yellow Jackets ran over and around the Falcons' defense. Air Force was much more willing to take shots through the air, throwing 17 passes in the first half, but couldn't take advantage of its opportunities. Jonathan Warzeka dropped what looked to be a sure touchdown pass in the second quarter, and the Falcons couldn't convert on three fourth-down opportunities in the first half -- including one that was well within field-goal range. Bell's 41-yard kick as time expired in the second quarter cut Georgia Tech's lead to 7-6 at halftime. The Yellow Jackets appeared to take control of the game in the second half, but a handful of crucial mistakes proved to be too much for them to overcome. A nearly nine-minute drive opening the third ended when Washington fumbled on the Air Force 5. Then McKayhan's muffed punts -- including the one at the Georgia Tech 14 that led to Air Force's winning touchdown -- gave the Falcons terrific field position. After Tew's scoring run, the Falcons converted the 2-point conversion on a Warzeka run. Georgia Tech had one last chance to tie it, but a last gasp pass toward the end zone was intercepted by Jon Davis.

2010 Champs Sports Bowl

The 2010 Champs Sports Bowl was played on December 28, 2010. The game matched up the NC State Wolfpack from the Atlantic Coast Conference versus the West Virginia Mountaineers from the Big East Conference. The game was played at Florida Citrus Bowl Stadium, Orlando, Fla.

2010 Champs Sports Bowl	Line	1	-	2	-	3	-	4	-	Final
#22 West Virginia	(-2.5)	0	-	7	-	0	-	0	-	7
NC State	(48.5)	7	-	3	-	6	-	7	-	23

Scoring Summary
NC State - Greene 16 yard pass from Wilson (Czajkowski kick)
West Virginia - Bailey 32 yard pass from Smith (Bitancurt kick)
NC State - Czajkowski 45 yard Field goal
NC State - Czajkowski 38 yard Field goal
NC State - Czajkowski 40 yard Field goal
NC State - Williams 7 yard pass from Wilson (Czajkowski kick)

Associated Press Champs Sports Bowl Game Summary - If this was Russell Wilson's football finale, he sure made the most of it. Wilson threw for 275 yards and two touchdowns, leading North Carolina State past No. 22 West Virginia 23-7 in the Champs Sports Bowl on Tuesday night. The Atlantic Coast Conference's leading passer this season now must decide whether to make an early move toward a professional baseball career or come back to lead the Wolfpack again next year. Wilson also had 41 yards rushing, Josh Czajkowski made three field goals and the Wolfpack (9-4) won nine games for the first time since 2002. Geno Smith had 196 yards passing and an injured Noel Devine ran for 50 yards for the Mountaineers (9-4), whose five second-half turnovers ended any hopes of a cheerful send off for some of Bill Stewart's staff. Stewart is being slowly moved out as coach, with Dana Holgorsen, Oklahoma State's offensive coordinator, taking over at the same position next year at West Virginia before moving into Stewart's job in 2012. The game was current offensive coordinator Jeff Mullen's last game. How it will all work remains a mystery. Wilson, who earned the bowl's MVP honor, may very well have played his last football game for the Wolfpack. He spent much of the summer playing second base in the Colorado Rockies' minor league system, and his career in baseball has always seemed more promising. The Wolfpack can only hope he returns. Wilson was 28-for-45 passing, had no interceptions and shredded a West Virginia defense that had been solid. It was the most points that the Mountaineers -- who had never given up more than 21 points -- allowed all season. Wilson's 16-yard touchdown pass to Mustafa Greene put the Wolfpack up 7-0 in the first quarter, and they never had trouble moving the ball after that. Scoring, at least early, was another matter. NC State's offense stalled several times after crossing into Mountaineers' territory. The Wolfpack also faked a potential 43-yard field goal in the second quarter that was a disaster: Holder Corey Tedder threw an over-the-shoulder pass from his knees that skipped off the new field turf, kicker Czajkowski was hit amid the scramble and West Virginia took possession. West Virginia capitalized when Smith threw a 32-yard touchdown pass to Stedman Bailey, who reached over defensive back David Amerson to catch the ball and tie the game. But the Mountaineers ended any chance of a comeback with late turnovers. Smith fumbled a handoff; Devine lost the ball after a hit by Amerson and then Smith was intercepted by Brandon Bishop. As if that wasn't enough, Jock Sanders fumbled a punt on the West Virginia 7-yard line that led to a 3-yard TD catch by Jarvis Williams to seal the victory. Smith also had another fumble in the final minutes. The win put Wilson in elite company with only one other Wolfpack Quarterback: Only the 2002 team that went 11-3, led by Philip Rivers, had won at least nine games. Even if he does opt to leave school early, Wilson said he isn't giving up on either of his dreams.

2010 Insight Bowl

The 2010 Insight Bowl was the 22nd edition of the bowl game, played at Sun Devil Stadium in Tempe, Arizona on Tuesday, December 28, 2010. It featured the Missouri Tigers from the Big 12 Conference versus the Iowa Hawkeyes from the Big Ten Conference.

2010 Insight Bowl	Line	1	-	2	-	3	-	4	-	Final
#14 Missouri	(-2.5)	3	-	7	-	14	-	0	-	24
Iowa	(46.5)	7	-	10	-	3	-	7	-	27

Scoring Summary
Iowa - Coker 1 yard run (Meyer kick)
Missouri - Ressel 23 yard Field goal
Iowa - Coker 62 yard run (Meyer kick)
Iowa - Meyer 34 yard Field goal
Missouri - Josey 10 yard run (Ressel kick)
Iowa - Meyer 21 yard Field goal
Missouri - Gabbert 7 yard run (Ressel kick)
Missouri - Egnew 3 yard pass from Gabbert (Ressel kick)
Iowa - Hyde 72 yard interception return (Meyer kick)

Associated Press Insight Bowl Game Summary - Micah Hyde snatched the ball near the sideline, ran toward the middle of the field, even backward for a few yards before sprinting up the far sideline. Fill-in freshman Marcus Coker took a more direct approach at the Missouri Tigers: he ran right over them. Coker bulled his way through Missouri's defense in place of suspended starter Adam Robinson and Hyde scored the decisive touchdown on a meandering, 72-yard interception return in the fourth quarter, helping Iowa close out a difficult season with a 27-24 win over Missouri on Tuesday night in the Insight Bowl. Undermanned due to injuries and suspensions, Iowa (8-5) turned to Coker, a backup who had 403 yards and a touchdown during the regular season. The bruising freshman had no trouble taking over for Robinson, running over and occasionally around the Tigers to set school records with 219 yards and 33 carries while scoring two touchdowns in front of an Insight Bowl-record 53,453 fans. Behind Coker, Iowa piled up 425 yards against one of the nation's stingiest defenses to overcome two rare turnovers by Ricky Stanzi and win three straight bowls for the first time. Missouri (10-3) had its way with Iowa's once-stout defense most of the night, rolling up 512 yards, including a school bowl record 434 passing by Blaine Gabbert. Gabbert finished 41 for 57 to set two more school records, but inexplicably threw the ball right to Hyde, who dodged several tackles and seemingly every Missouri player for the second-longest interception return in Insight Bowl history. Missouri had one final chance, but a fourth-down reception at Iowa's 33-yard line by T.J. Moe with 2:15 left was overruled on review and Coker helped grind out the clock. Moe finished with an Insight Bowl record 15 receptions for 152 yards for the Tigers in their second straight bowl loss. Once fierce rivals, these teams hadn't met in a century, despite being separated by less than 250 miles. The 12-game rivalry plagued by dirty play, riots and racial discrimination ended following a particularly brutal game in 1910, and a planned four-year series from 2005-08 also fell through, putting an interesting twist on this Midwest battle in the desert. Missouri was looking to cap one of its best seasons, even after having its Big 12 and BCS bowl chances dashed with consecutive losses to Nebraska and Texas Tech. The Tigers won their final three games to get into the Insight Bowl and were in position for their third 11-win season as a program. Iowa had a different kind of momentum going. After opening the season No. 9 in the polls, the Hawkeyes were plagued by injuries and an inability to close out games. They played most of the season without defensive coordinator Norm Parker, who had a foot amputated due to complications from diabetes, had five losses by a combined 18 points and entered the bowl having lost their final three. Turned out to just be the prelude to their problems. Since the regular season ended, the Hawkeyes have lost their career leading receiver, top rusher and two other running backs. Receiver Derrell Johnson-Koulianos was the first to go, booted off the team after being arrested on drug charges in early December. Robinson then was suspended for breaking team rules, and was arrested Monday night for marijuana possession, jeopardizing his career at Iowa. Promising running back Jewel Hampton also decided to transfer, and fullback Brad Rogers was out to undergo cardiological tests. Johnson-Koulianos and Robinson combined for 21 touchdowns during the season, which put more pressure Coker and wideout Marvin McNutt. Neither seemed to be bothered by the added spotlight. McNutt hauled in a 49-yard catch on Iowa's first drive and Coker punctuated it with a 1-yard touchdown run. Coker followed that by blowing through a big hole on the right side early in the second quarter for a 62-yard touchdown run -- Iowa's longest of the season -- that put the Hawkeyes up 14-3. He had 113 yards on 16 carries in the first half. Gabbert was doing what he does best going the other way, picking apart Iowa's defense with short and intermediate throws. He was 23 for 31 for 284 yards in the first half, setting up a 23-yard field goal by Grant Ressel in the first quarter and Henry Josey's 10-yard touchdown run that made it 17-10 in the second. Gabbert had the Tigers moving again late in the half, but the drive ended when Brett Greenwood picked off a deflected pass in the end zone. Coker and Gabbert continued to counterpunch in the second half. Coker ran over Missouri linebacker Jarrell Harrison on a 35-yard run early in the third quarter, setting up Mike Meyer's second field goal, from 21 yards. Gabbert kept winging passes all through Iowa's defense. He set up his 7-yard touchdown run, then followed the first of two interceptions thrown by Stanzi, who had four in 324 attempts in the regular season, by hitting tight end Michael Egnew on a 3-yard TD pass that put the Tigers up 24-20 heading into the fourth quarter. After all those yards, Iowa finally held, getting the game-changing interception by Hyde and holding -- thanks to the review -- on Missouri's final drive to close out a tumultuous season with an impressive win.

2010 Military Bowl

The 2010 Military Bowl presented by Northrop Grumman was the third edition of the bowl game previously called the EagleBank Bowl. It was played as scheduled at RFK Stadium in Washington, D.C. on December 29, 2010, and was telecast on ESPN. The event remains sponsored by EagleBank and is organized by the DC Bowl Committee, Inc. and the Washington Convention and Sports Authority.

2010 Military Bowl	Line	1	-	2	-	3	-	4	-	Final
East Carolina	(68.5)	0	-	3	-	10	-	7	-	20
Maryland	(-7.5)	6	-	10	-	21	-	14	-	51

Scoring Summary
Maryland - Dorsey 45 yard pass from O'Brien (Kick blocked)
Maryland - Baltz 23 yard Field goal
East Carolina - Barbour 37 yard Field goal
Maryland - Adams 1 yard run (Baltz kick)
Maryland - Adams 1 yard run (Baltz kick)
East Carolina - Lewis 20 yard pass from Davis (Barbour kick)
Maryland - Adams 1 yard run (Baltz kick)
East Carolina - Barbour 31 yard Field goal
Maryland - Scott 61 yard run (Baltz kick)
Maryland - Scott 91 yard run (Baltz kick)
Maryland - Adams 4 yard run (Baltz kick)
East Carolina - Jones 14 yard pass from Wornick (Barbour kick)

Associated Press Military Bowl Game Summary - Ralph Friedgen soaked in the chants and fought back a few more tears. He gave a parting gift to his alma mater -- the highest point total Maryland has ever posted in a bowl game -- then followed it with a parting shot at the administration that fired him. Already the Atlantic Coast Conference coach of the year, already the engineer of the second-biggest regular season turnaround in the country, Friedgen ended his 10-year run with the Terrapins on Wednesday with a 51-20 victory over East Carolina in the Military Bowl Presented by Northrop Grumman. Patrolling the Maryland sideline one last time, holding his customary play sheet and wearing a white cap with the word "Terps" in red, Friedgen wound up a 9-4 season and a 75-50 Maryland decade that includes a 5-2 record in bowl games. Fans held up signs and banners proclaiming, "Thanks Ralph" and chanted his name through much of the second half. He got the customary ice-bucket bath from his players with 2 1/2 minutes left in the game. New Maryland athletic director Kevin Anderson announced last week that Friedgen was being dismissed, effective after the bowl game, with the school buying out the final year of the 63-year-old coach's contract for $2 million. Friedgen said preparing for the game was like "a slow death." He found it hard to hold back his emotions and was concerned that his players wouldn't be focused. He needn't have worried. Running back Da'Rel Scott (13 carries, 200 yards) spoke for his teammates when he said they were determined to "make sure coach Friedgen went out with a bang." Much of the game was more ceremony than competition. The Terrapins piled up 478 yards against the nation's worst defense and forced four turnovers. Scott had second-half touchdown runs of 61 and 91 yards on back-to-back Maryland offensive plays, and D.J. Adams had four short touchdown runs. Dominique Davis completed 35 of 57 passes for 268 yards with one touchdown and two interceptions for East Carolina (6-7), which committed 15 penalties and never got its high-octane offense in rhythm. The temperatures were in the mid-40s, a tolerable break from a mostly frozen December but nothing like from the balmier destinations Maryland expected after tying for third in the Atlantic Coast Conference. Bowl after bowl bypassed the Terrapins until they were chosen by the Military Bowl with the No. 8 ACC selection, a disappointment caused mainly by concerns about the waning fan base in College Park. There were even rumblings that Terrapins fans would be vastly outnumbered at RFK Stadium, only a few miles from campus, but red and purple appeared just about even among the 38,062, a record turnout for the three-year-old bowl. The first half included 12 penalties, four turnovers, a blocked extra point and a missed 25-yard field goal. The Terrapins scored on a 45-yard touchdown pass from ACC rookie of the year Danny O'Brien to Kevin Dorsey, a 1-yard run by Adams and a 23-yard field goal by Travis Baltz to take a 16-3 lead at the break. East Carolina finally got on the board with a field goal with 6:08 left in the first half -- the longest the Pirates had gone into a game without scoring this season. Hours before kickoff, Maryland declared four players academically ineligible for the game. Sitting out were defensive lineman Drew Gloster, offensive lineman Pete White and receivers Quintin McCree and Ronnie Tyler. Afterward Maryland receiver Torrey Smith said he will declare himself eligible for the NFL draft. But such news was mere housecleaning. Friedgen was the star of the day.

2010 Texas Bowl

The 2010 Texas Bowl was the fifth edition of the bowl game, and was played at Reliant Stadium in Houston, Texas. The game was played on Wednesday, December 29, 2010. The game was telecast on ESPN for the second time in bowl history after being televised by the NFL Network for the first three games. The bowl matched the sixth selection from the Big 12 Conference, Baylor, versus the sixth selection from the Big Ten Conference, Illinois.

2010 Texas Bowl	Line	1	-	2	-	3	-	4	-	Final
Illinois	(62.5)	6	-	10	-	8	-	14	-	38
Baylor	(-1.0)	0	-	0	-	7	-	7	-	14

Scoring Summary
Illinois - Dimke 38 yard Field goal
Illinois - Dimke 28 yard Field goal
Illinois - Dimke 43 yard Field goal
Illinois - Leshoure 5 yard run (Dimke kick)
Illinois - Leshoure 13 yard run (2 pt. conversion)
Baylor - Finley 3 yard run (Jones kick)
Baylor - Wright 39 yard pass from Griffin (Jones kick)
Illinois - Leshoure 5 yard run (Dimke kick)
Illinois - Scheelhaase 55 yard run (Dimke kick)

Associated Press Texas Bowl Game Summary - Mikel Leshoure isn't sure whether he'll declare for the NFL draft or return to Illinois for his senior season. But if Wednesday night's Texas Bowl ends up being his college send-off it will certainly be remembered as a good one. Leshoure ran for 184 yards and a career-high three touchdowns and set five school records as Illinois earned its first bowl victory since 1999, beating Baylor 38-14. The Illini spoiled the Bears' first bowl appearance in 16 seasons. Both teams finished at 7-6. Leshoure had a 5-yard TD run in the second quarter, a 13-yard score in the third quarter and another 5-yard touchdown run in the fourth period. The performance gave him school records for single-season rushing yards (1,697), single-season scoring (122 points), total touchdowns in a season (20), 100-yard rushing game in a season (9) and consecutive 100-yard rushing games (5). The Illini built a 24-0 lead and Leshoure's last touchdown put the game out of reach. Illinois coach Ron Zook was informed late in the game that Leshoure needed 23 yards to set the rushing record. Baylor's Robert Griffin III threw for 306 yards and a touchdown, but his two fumbles in the first half put the Bears behind. Baylor coach Art Briles couldn't focus on the strides his team made this season in finishing with its first winning record since 1995. Leshoure was chosen the most valuable player and wore a cowboy hat as he hoisted the trophy above his head after the game while the small but vocal group of Illinois fans cheered. He kept the hat on when he spoke to reporters after the game. The Bears cut the lead to 24-14 when Griffin found a diving Kendall Wright on a 39-yard touchdown pass on fourth-and-14 early in the fourth quarter. Illinois finished with 291 yards rushing and 533 yards of total offense to give Zook his first bowl win as a head coach in his fourth try. Scheelhaase, a freshman, got off to a sensational start, completing all of his 13 passes in the first half, and finished 18 of 23 for 242 yards. He scored on a 55-yard touchdown run with 41 seconds to play to make it 38-14. His 13 completions were the most to start a game in school history. Illinois opened the second half with an 87-yard drive capped by a 13-yard touchdown run by Leshoure. Leshoure also scored the 2-point conversion to extend the lead to 24-0. Baylor finally found its offensive touch on its first possession of the second half. Griffin completed five of seven passes on that drive, which ended with a 4-yard touchdown run by Jay Finley to get the Bears within 24-7 with about eight minutes remaining in the third quarter. The Illini held Finley in check for most of the night and Baylor's 1,000-yard rusher finished with 12 carries for 63 yards. Illinois led 9-0 before a 5-yard touchdown run by Leshoure about 10 minutes before halftime stretched the lead to 16-0. That score was set up by a 52-yard reception by Ryan Lankford a play earlier. Baylor was driving with about 3 1/2 minutes left in the first half when a pass by Griffin was intercepted by Terry Hawthorne. But the Bears got a second chance when Corey Liuget was penalized for roughing the passer, giving Baylor the ball back. The Bears still came away empty though when Griffin fumbled a few plays later to give Illinois the ball back on its own 32. Griffin, set Baylor's career passing record with 6,073 yards. Baylor's problems started early with Griffin fumbling on the first possession. Travon Bellamy recovered that fumble and returned it 46 yards. The Illini couldn't get anything going on that drive and settled for a 38-yard field goal to take a 3-0 lead.

2010 Alamo Bowl (December)

The 2010 Valero Alamo Bowl game was the 18th edition of the annual bowl game known previously as the Alamo Bowl. It was played on December 29, 2010 between the Arizona Wildcats and the Oklahoma State Cowboys. ESPN television broadcast the game.

2010 Alamo Bowl	Line	1	-	2	-	3	-	4	-	Final
#16 Oklahoma State	(-5.0)	17	-	6	-	10	-	3	-	36
Arizona	(66.0)	7	-	0	-	3	-	0	-	10

Scoring Summary
Oklahoma State - Smith 6 yard run (Bailey kick)
Oklahoma State - Blackmon 71 yard pass from Weeden (Bailey kick)
Arizona - Criner 5 yard pass from Foles (Zendejas kick)
Oklahoma State - Bailey 40 yard Field goal
Oklahoma State - Martin 62 yard interception return (Kick failed)
Arizona - Zendejas 42 yard Field goal
Oklahoma State - Blackmon 3 yard pass from Weeden (Bailey kick)
Oklahoma State - Bailey 50 yard Field goal
Oklahoma State - Bailey 44 yard Field goal

Associated Press Alamo Bowl Game Summary - Justin Blackmon could've strolled into the end zone. But the Oklahoma State star instead turned left and trotted along the goal line until he almost reached the sideline, finally forced to make the touchdown official. Maybe he was taking it all in. Because the nation's top receiver might not be back. Blackmon caught two touchdowns, including his 71-yard strike that he savored long as possible before scoring, and Oklahoma State (No. 14 BCS, No. 16 AP) finished its first 11-win season with a 36-10 victory over Arizona in the Valero Alamo Bowl on Wednesday night. Blackmon, the Biletnikoff Award winner as the nation's top receiver, later set an NCAA record with his 12th straight game with at least 100 yards receiving and a touchdown. The sophomore caught nine passes for 117 yards in perhaps his last college game. He's a projected high NFL pick who's already won Big 12 offensive player of the year and surpassed former Pitt star Larry Fitzgerald for most receiving yards by a sophomore. Brandon Weeden was 25 of 41 for 240 yards for Oklahoma State (11-2) in the final game plan for Cowboys offensive coordinator Dana Holgorsen, who is leaving to become the coach-in-waiting at West Virginia. Oklahoma State, which led the nation in total offense, won its first bowl game in three tries and scored at least 33 points for the 11th time this season. Arizona (7-6) ended the year with five straight losses. Coach Mike Stoops said he'll enter the offseason taking a hard look at his program, which fell shy of the 8 wins it posted in the previous two seasons. This last, lopsided defeat made Arizona's 7-1 record and No. 13 ranking in November seem like that was much longer ago. Nick Foles completed 32 of 50 passes for 280 yards and a touchdown, but he threw three interceptions, including one returned by Markelle Martin for a 62-yard score. The Wildcats had their chances early. But six possessions inside Oklahoma State territory in the first half resulted in just one touchdown. Oklahoma State now awaits whether this was a farewell victory lap for its biggest stars. Weeden and Blackmon are both projected NFL draft picks if they leave early. Blackmon seems poised to follow former teammate Dez Bryant as a first-rounder and may have little incentive to return after being chosen as the Big 12 offensive player of the year. Both players say Holgorsen's departure won't influence their decision. Holgorsen won't be back, but he helped give his duo another big night. After Arizona couldn't convert a fourth down at the Cowboys' 29-yard line on its opening possession, Weeden found Blackmon practically uncovered down the sideline. Weeden said Blackmon, a little frustrated with the lack of throws his way, told him to throw him the "daggum ball" before tossing the long strike his way. Arizona fans didn't appreciate the showboating. Blackmon scored for a second time on a 3-yard pass in the third quarter, breaking the game open after Alex Zandejas' 42-yard field goal put Arizona back within two scores. Arizona's only other score came in the first quarter when Juron Criner caught a 5-yard touchdown from Foles, who was playing back in the Alamodome where he was a Texas prep star. The Cowboys can take comfort even if forced to replace more than Holgorsen: They lost Bryant and switched to a new Quarterback this season, only to shatter practically every school passing record. They're also toasting the most wins in school history after debuting seven new defensive starters. It's why the Cowboys began the season picked to finish fifth in the Big 12 South. Instead, Oklahoma State came within a wild fourth quarter against Oklahoma of playing for its first Big 12 title. Nebraska handed the Cowboys their only other loss. Arizona was denied a third consecutive eight-win season and absorbed another bowl pummeling after losing 33-0 to Nebraska in the Holiday Bowl last year. The Pac 10 returned to the Alamo Bowl for the first time since 1994 after the game ended a 15-year run with the Big 10. The Pac 10's deal with the Alamo Bowl runs through 2013.

2010 Armed Forces Bowl
The 2010 Armed Forces Bowl was the eighth edition of the bowl game, and the first of two editions to be played at Gerald J. Ford Stadium on the campus of Southern Methodist University (SMU) in University Park, Texas. From the bowl's inception as the Fort Worth Bowl in 2003, it had been held at Amon G. Carter Stadium on the campus of Texas Christian University, but a renovation project that began immediately after the 2010 regular season led to a temporary move to the SMU campus. The event returned to TCU in 2012. The game was played on Thursday, December 30, 2010. The game was telecast on ESPN and matched the SMU Mustangs from Conference USA, playing on their home field, with the Army Black

Knights. Army's appearance in the 2010 edition of the game marked the fourth consecutive year that a service academy played in the bowl. Air Force competed in the contest in the years, 2007, 2008, and 2009.

2010 Armed Forces Bowl	Line	1	-	2	-	3	-	4	-	Final
Army	(52.0)	13	-	3	-	0	-	0	-	16
SMU	(-7.0)	0	-	0	-	7	-	7	-	14

Scoring Summary
Army - McNary 55 yard fumble recovery (Carlton kick)
Army - Brown 13 yard run (Kick failed)
Army - Carlton 44 yard Field goal
SMU - Robinson 8 yard pass from Padron (Szymanski kick)
SMU - Johnson 28 yard pass from Padron (Szymanski kick)

Associated Press Armed Forces Bowl Game Summary - Second-year coach Rich Ellerson already has a season to cherish at Army. Josh McNary and 24 other seniors get to leave on a winning note. McNary scooped up a fumble and returned it 55 yards for a touchdown and Army held on to beat SMU 16-14 in the Armed Forces Bowl on Thursday, giving the Black Knights their first winning season since 1996. When Ellerson was hired, Army (7-6) was coming off three consecutive 3-9 seasons and had won only 30 games since its 1996 Independence Bowl appearance that was the last winning season -- until now. The Black Knights led 16-0 at halftime on SMU's home field, then ran out the game's final 4 minutes after Matt Szymanski was wide left on a 47-yard field goal attempt that would have put the Mustangs (7-7) ahead. After Quarterback Trent Steelman converted a pair of third downs, Ellerson was doused with the contents of a water cooler and the Black Knights celebrated a long-awaited victory. It was only the fifth bowl game for the Black Knights, who hadn't won a postseason game since the 1985 Peach Bowl. SMU, with only four seniors among its 22 starters, still hasn't had consecutive winning seasons since resuming play in 1989 after being the only team ever given the NCAA's so-called death penalty. The Mustangs last season ended a 25-year bowl drought with a win in the Hawaii Bowl that gave them an 8-5 record. That was only the second winning season since the death penalty, and this was the second .500 record in that span. Jones removed his name from consideration for the Maryland job this week, saying he was committed to the Mustangs. They are 15-12 since going 1-11 in Jones' first season after he left Hawaii following an undefeated regular season and BCS appearance. Steelman ran for 6 yards on third-and-5 after SMU called its final timeout. On a third-and-4, he rolled right and had only his second completion, a 22-yarder before a final kneel-down. Jared Hassin ran for 82 yards to lead Army's triple-option offense, which got 199 of its 229 total yards on the ground. SMU's Kyle Padron completed 23 of 34 passes for 302 yards, including touchdowns on consecutive drives in the second half before the Mustangs got their last chance. He had two interceptions and a fumble before halftime. Padron hit Aldrick Robinson for a 45-yard pass on the first play of the game, but two plays later fumbled while being sacked by Zach Watts. The Mustangs kept their next drive alive when Szymanski, also the punter, ran 18 yards to convert fourth-and-6 from their 33. But Szymanski was wide right on a 35-yard field goal attempt at the same open end of the stadium into the breeze. Padron threw the first of consecutive drive-ending interceptions when SMU got the ball back, making it three straight drives inside the Army 30 without any points. After Malcolm Brown took a pitch left 13 yards to put Army up 13-0, the extra point was blocked by 6-foot-8 Margus Hunt, a world-class shot put and discus thrower from Estonia who had never played football before getting to SMU last year. It was his third blocked kick this season and the 10th in his career, already a school record. Alex Carlton, kicking at the same end where Szymanski had both of his misses, made a 44-yard field goal with 2:39 left in the first half. Zach Line ran 17 times for 103 yards for SMU, which finally scored when Padron capped a 92-yard drive with an 8-yarder to Robinson, the eighth consecutive game the senior receiver caught a TD pass. Padron later threw a 28-yard touchdown to Darius Johnson.

2010 Music City Bowl

The 2010 Franklin American Mortgage Music City Bowl was the 13th edition of the bowl game and was played at LP Field in Nashville, Tennessee. The game was played on Thursday, December 30, 2010.

2010 Music City Bowl	Line	1	2	3	4	OT	2OT	Final
North Carolina	(-1.5)	7	10	0	3	7	3	30
Tennessee	(50.5)	7	7	0	6	7	0	27

Scoring Summary
North Carolina - Draughn 58 yard run (Barth kick)
Tennessee - Jones 29 yard pass from Bray (Lincoln kick)
North Carolina - Barth 28 yard Field goal
Tennessee - Rogers 45 yard pass from Bray (Lincoln kick)
North Carolina - Highsmith 39 yard pass from Yates (Barth kick)

Tennessee - Hunter 8 yard pass from Bray (Lincoln kick)
North Carolina - Barth 40 yard Field goal
North Carolina - Yates 1 yard run (Barth kick)
Tennessee - Stocker 20 yard pass from Bray (Lincoln kick)
North Carolina - Barth 23 yard Field goal

Associated Press Music City Bowl Game Summary - For North Carolina, the crazy finish to the Franklin American Mortgage Music City Bowl was just another twist in a trying season that ended on a high note. Tennessee had a much different viewpoint, and an all-too-familiar feeling. Casey Barth kicked a 23-yard field goal in the second overtime to send North Carolina past Tennessee 30-27 in a game that will be remembered much more for the crazy finish of regulation than how it ended Thursday night. The Volunteers thought they had capped coach Derek Dooley's first season in Knoxville with a dramatic victory when the officials told them to return to the sideline and gave the Tar Heels one last chance to tie it in the fourth quarter. Barth kicked a 39-yard field goal after officials reviewed what had been the final play of the game and decided to penalize the Tar Heels for having "more than 11 men" on the field. The Big Ten officiating crew also announced T.J. Yates had spiked the ball with 1 second left. That allowed Barth to run out and kick the field goal that tied it at 20. Barth's winning kick in the second overtime completed a season marred by an NCAA investigation into agent-related benefits and academic misconduct that eventually forced 14 Tar Heels to miss at least one game. Seven missed the entire season. Tennessee was stunned at the sudden switch in the final seconds. Tyler Bray threw a 25-yard TD in the first overtime, but Quan Sturdivant picked him off to end the Vols' last chance in the second OT. It was the second time this season that a flag for too many men on the field played a role in a Tennessee loss. The Vols lost to LSU on Oct. 2 when they got caught having too many defenders, giving the Tigers another chance to pull out a 16-14 win. Dooley said it was "chaos again." His Vols were celebrating. Just like LSU, a case of painful deja vu, officials told them it wasn't over yet. Tennessee had the home-field advantage with LP Field painted orange from top to bottom, and the Vols' fans had been celebrating ever since Bray's 8-yard TD pass to Justin Hunter put them up 20-17 with 5:16 left. But Donte Paige-Moss blocked Daniel Lincoln's extra point, and that provided the edge North Carolina needed to force overtime with Barth's second field goal. Paige-Moss already had a bloody nose and puffy face after his helmet came off sacking Bray and teammate Quinton Coples' helmet smashed into his head. Tennessee had a chance to clinch the victory when the Vols got the ball back with 1:36 left but punted it back to North Carolina with 31 seconds remaining to set up the bizarre finish. Everyone was on the field after the clock appeared to run out when North Carolina got caught -- and flagged -- with too many men on the field. A handful of Tar Heels were running toward the sideline when Yates took the snap and spiked the ball with the holder behind him as if preparing for a field-goal attempt. Davis took the blame for the confusion. He said the offensive players were doing what they'd been told a couple plays before, while the field-goal unit started running out. The Vols celebrated with the Tar Heels dejected. Officials suddenly announced that the end was under review. They announced the replay showed North Carolina had "more than 11" players on the field for a 5-yard penalty. But they said Yates had spiked the ball with 1 second remaining. Dooley noted college football doesn't have the NFL rule that would have run out the clock to punish the offense for the penalty. Davis, who coached the Cleveland Browns for four seasons and won two Super Bowls as an assistant in Dallas, said, "Our game isn't the NFL." Barth ran out and kicked the field goal to force overtime. Angry fans began tossing bottles and other trash onto the field. Tennessee defensive end Gerald Williams chucked his helmet in disgust, bouncing it down the field. Officials threw yet another flag, this one for unsportsmanlike conduct. That set North Carolina up in the first overtime at the Tennessee 12, and Yates scored on a 1-yard keeper to put the Tar Heels up 27-20. Bray answered almost immediately. He found Luke Stocker with a 25-yard TD on the very next play. This time, Lincoln kicked the extra point to tie it. North Carolina chose to go on defense in the second overtime. Sturdivant intercepted Bray on second-and-9 to give the Tar Heels a chance at victory. The Tar Heels intercepted Bray three times and finished with four sacks. North Carolina also held Tennessee to 27 yards rushing on 29 attempts, outgaining the Vols 385-339 in total offense. Shaun Draughn ran for 160 yards and a TD, and Yates threw for 234 yards and a score. Yates scored on a 1-yard keeper for North Carolina in the first overtime, and Draughn helped moved the Tar Heels down to the Vols 6. Davis ran Barth out for the winning field goal to spark a North Carolina celebration while a couple of Vols slumped to the field in disbelief.

2010 Pinstripe Bowl

The 2010 New Era Pinstripe Bowl was the first edition of this bowl game, and was played at Yankee Stadium in Bronx, New York. The game was played on December 30, 2010 and was telecast on ESPN. The game featured the Syracuse Orange of the Big East Conference and the Kansas State Wildcats of the Big 12 Conference. New Era Cap Company was the title sponsor of the game. It ended with Syracuse defeating

Kansas State, 36-34. The game was played four days after one of the worst blizzards in New York City history, affecting travel for the teams and their fans.

2010 Pinstripe Bowl	Line	1	-	2	-	3	-	4	-	Final
Kansas State	(Pk)	7	-	7	-	7	-	13	-	34
Syracuse	(47.5)	7	-	7	-	13	-	9	-	36

Scoring Summary
Kansas State - Thomas 51 yard run (Cherry kick)
Syracuse - Sales 52 yard pass from Nassib (Krautman kick)
Syracuse - Sales 36 yard pass from Nassib (Krautman kick)
Kansas State - Thomas 10 yard run (Cherry kick)
Syracuse - Carter 7 yard run (Krautman kick)
Kansas State - Harper 10 yard pass from Coffman (Cherry kick)
Syracuse - Carter 15 yard run (Kick failed)
Kansas State - Thomas 1 yard run (Cherry kick)
Syracuse - Sales 44 yard pass from Nassib (Pass failed)
Syracuse - Krautman 39 yard Field goal
Kansas State - Hilburn 30 yard pass from Coffman (Pass failed)

The Bronx Salute - The Call - With 1:13 left in the game, Kansas State's Adrian Hilburn scored a 30-yard touchdown to pull KSU within two points of a tie. Following the score, Hilburn made a military hand salute toward the crowd and was penalized for unsportsmanlike conduct. Because of the 15-yard penalty, Kansas State had to attempt a two-point conversion from the 17-yard line. The conversion failed, accounting for the margin in the final score. The call was considered highly controversial, and according to ESPN determined the outcome of the game. Due to the impact from this call, the NCAA chose in the next year's rule changes to not penalize celebrating in general but to penalize only taunting. The call was called "one of the most infamous plays of the college football season in 2010" and was given the name "The Bronx Salute." It later was used as an example of incorrect interpretation of the new celebration rules.

Associated Press Pinstripe Bowl Game Summary - The first Pinstripe Bowl turned into a home run derby, with Syracuse and Kansas State trading big plays and touchdowns in one of the most exciting games of this postseason. A little too much enthusiasm, though, cost the Wildcats. Delone Carter ran for career-high 198 yards and two touchdowns, Marcus Sales caught three long TD passes and Syracuse got some help from a celebration penalty on Kansas State to beat the Wildcats 36-34 on Thursday at Yankee Stadium. Adrian Hilburn slipped a tackle and raced to a 30-yard touchdown catch with 1:13 remaining to pull Kansas State within two. Hilburn saluted the crowd behind the visitor's dugout and was flagged 15 yards for unsportsmanlike conduct, which pushed the 2-point conversion attempt back to the 17-yard line. Coffman overthrew Aubrey Quarles in the end zone, and when Kansas State (7-6) couldn't come up with the onside kick, Syracuse (8-5) only had to take a knee to win a bowl game for the first time since 2001. Daniel Thomas ran for three touchdowns for Kansas State, which was making its first bowl appearance since 2006. In a bowl season filled with blowouts so far, the first bowl game in New York in 48 years turned out to be a hit. The team's traded long gainers right from the start -- Thomas went 51 yards for a score on the second play from scrimmage -- and scored touchdowns on the first five second-half possessions. Both teams pulled off successful flea-flickers, with Syracuse's going for its first touchdown. Kansas State coach Bill Snyder, sensing field goals would not be enough, called for a fake with 4:50 left in the fourth from the 11, but Syracuse stacked up Ryan Doerr on the run. Snyder passed on commenting on the celebration penalty, instead blaming himself for the fake field goal. Carter, a fifth-year senior who has endured a major hip injury and plenty of losses during his time at Syracuse, broke free for a 60-yard run on the next play. It set up Ross Krautman's 40-yard field goal with 3:08 left that made it 36-28. Too much time. Coffman, who played brilliantly in his last college game, led the Wildcats into Syracuse territory and connected with Hilburn near the sideline about 10 yards down field. After winning a footrace to the end zone, he dropped the ball, did a quick salute and turned to celebrate with teammates. Hilburn, caught five passes for 84 yards. Big Ten referee Todd Geerlings said both the head linesman and the back judge threw flags for excessive celebration -- rule 9-1-1d -- because Hilburn was drawing attention to himself. The 2-point attempt turned into a desperation play. Syracuse linebacker Doug Hogue said he was "all smiles" when he noticed those flags. Coffman finished 17 for 23 for 228 yards and two touchdowns. Thomas was held to 90 yards on 22 carries by a defense that was geared to stop him. Ryan Nassib passed for 239 yards and hooked up with Sales on touchdowns of 52, 36 and 44 yards in Syracuse's first bowl appearance since 2006. Second-year coach Doug Marrone, a Bronx native whose grandfather was an usher at the original Yankee Stadium, has quickly turned around a Syracuse program that was flailing when he arrived. It was Big East against the Big 12 in the first bowl game in New York since the Gotham Bowl matched Nebraska and Miami at the original Yankee Stadium in 1962. The final score in that one, by the way, Cornhuskers 36-34. The weather Thursday was pretty much as expected: cold. But temperatures in the 30s were more than tolerable for the crowd of 38,274 -- more than 44,000 tickets were sold, the Yankees said -- especially considering 16 inches of snow got dumped on the city four days earlier. And the snow piled as much as 8 feet high next to the outfield walls and behind the end zone where home plate usually sits just added to the scenery. Those who decided to brave the chill or make the long trip from the Little Apple (Manhattan, Kan.) to the Big Apple were rewarded with doozy of a game. It was tied at 14 at the half, and Syracuse started the second attacking Kansas State's faulty run defense, which ranked 118th in the country after the regular season. Carter's easy 7-yard TD run gave Syracuse a 21-14 lead. Coffman tied it at 21 with a 10-yard TD toss to Chris Harper and Carter came right back with a 15-yard TD run. But Krautman knocked the point after wide and Syracuse led 27-21 heading into the fourth quarter. Thomas gave Kansas State a 28-27 lead on a 1-yard run on fourth-and-goal with 11:03 left in the fourth. Sales, who came in with one touchdown on the season, got his third of the game with 7:52 left, but Syracuse's 2-point attempt failed, and it was 33-28 Orange.

2010 Holiday Bowl

The 2010 Holiday Bowl (also known as Bridgepoint Education Holiday Bowl) was the thirty-third edition of the bowl game and was played at Qualcomm Stadium in San Diego, California. The game was played on Thursday, December 30, 2010 and matched the Nebraska Cornhuskers against the Washington Huskies. The game was telecast on ESPN. The Washington Huskies won 19-7.

2010 Holiday Bowl	Line	1	-	2	-	3	-	4	-	Final
#17 Nebraska	(-14.0)	0	-	7	-	0	-	0	-	7
Washington	(53.0)	10	-	0	-	7	-	2	-	19

Scoring Summary
Washington - Polk 3 yard run (Folk kick)
Washington - Folk 39 yard Field goal
Nebraska - Reed 15 yard pass from Martinez (Henery kick)
Washington - Locker 25 yard run (Folk kick)
Washington - Team safety

Associated Press Holiday Bowl Game Summary - Jake Locker ended his college career with a win that has the Washington Huskies headed back to respectability. Locker bounced back from an injury he said looked worse than it was, scoring on a 25-yard run in the third quarter to help Washington to a 19-7 victory over punchless Nebraska (No. 18 BCS, No. 17 AP) in the Bridgepoint Education Holiday Bowl Thursday night. Tailback Chris Polk ran for 177 yards and a score as the Huskies (7-6) avenged a 56-21 loss to the Huskers (10-4) in Seattle on Sept. 18. The Cornhuskers piled up 533 yards of total offense in that game, including 383 rushing. While Washington was a winner in its first bowl game since 2002, the Huskers came out flat in their second straight Holiday Bowl appearance. They were manhandled on both sides of the line and imploded with 12 penalties for 102 yards. Washington outgained Nebraska 340 yards to 189, including 268 to 91 rushing. Locker, who passed up the NFL draft last spring to return for his senior season, capped the opening drive of the second half with a 25-yard scoring run to give Washington a 17-7 lead. He faked a handoff and then ran right, bouncing off a defender and staying on his feet to score. The Huskies were 0-12 in 2008 before Steve Sarkisian took over as coach. Locker ran 13 times for 83 yards. Polk had 34 carries. Locker was shaken up in the second quarter when he scrambled, slid headfirst and was hit helmet-to-helmet by Nebraska safety Austin Cassidy. Locker was on the ground for a few minutes before walking off on his own power. He was replaced by Keith Price for the rest of the series, which ended when a fourth-down run by Chris Polk was stuffed. Locker returned for the next series after safety Nate Fellner intercepted Taylor Martinez's pass. Martinez limped off the field in the third quarter. He was replaced by Cody Green, who had a nice scramble deep in his own territory. But guard Ricky Henry was called for holding in the end zone for a safety, giving Washington a 19-7 lead. Martinez missed the regular-season finale against Colorado because of injuries to his right ankle and left foot. Nebraska played as bad a first half as possible and trailed just 10-7 at halftime. The Huskers fumbled twice on the game's opening drive, once by Martinez as he was sacked, which was recovered by guard Keith Williams. Four plays later, Rex Burkhead took a direct snap, fumbled as he was hit by Victor Aiyewa, with Washington's Alameda Ta'amu recovering and returning it 14 yards to the Nebraska 21. Polk scored three plays later, running in untouched from the 3. The Huskies made it 10-0 on Erik Folk's 39-yard field goal. The Huskers came back and salvaged a drive on which they were whistled for consecutive delay-of-game penalties. Martinez gained 20 yards on a keeper on third-and-13, and a late hit out of bounds by Nate Fellner gave the Huskers the ball at the 17. Three plays later, Martinez threw a 15-yard touchdown pass to Kyler Reed to pull to 10-7. Folk was wide left on a 48-yard field goal try 2 seconds before halftime.

2010 Meineke Car Care Bowl

The 2010 Meineke Car Care Bowl was the ninth edition of the bowl game and was played at Bank of America Stadium in Charlotte, North Carolina. The game was played on Friday, December 31, 2010 and featured the South Florida Bulls of the Big East Conference against the Clemson Tigers of the ACC. The bowl was telecasted on ESPN and ESPN3. This game was the last game of the series to be called the "Meineke Car Care Bowl", as the bowl organizers terminated their title sponsorship agreement with the parent company of Meineke, effective in 2011.

2010 Meineke Car Care Bowl	Line	1	-	2	-	3	-	4	-	Final
South Florida	(40.5)	7	-	10	-	7	-	7	-	31
Clemson	(-5.5)	3	-	10	-	0	-	13	-	26

Scoring Summary
Clemson - Catanzaro 27 yard Field goal
South Florida - Murray 25 yard pass from Daniels (Bonani kick)
South Florida - Bonani 27 yard Field goal
South Florida - Bogan 15 yard pass from Daniels (Bonani kick)
Clemson - Catanzaro 44 yard Field goal
Clemson - Harper 1 yard run (Catanzaro kick)
South Florida - Plancher 2 yard run (Bonani kick)
South Florida - Daniels 8 yard run (Bonani kick)
Clemson - Ford 6 yard pass from Boyd (Kick failed)
Clemson - Ford 10 yard pass from Boyd (Catanzaro kick)

Associated Press Meineke Car Care Bowl Game Summary - Skip Holtz came to South Florida in a tough spot, replacing a popular coach whose firing left some bad feelings in the locker room. The 3-3 start fueled by a shaky offense didn't help matters. Slowly, Holtz got a grip on the young program and thanks to an impressive comeback from an injury by his Quarterback, the Bulls have reached another milestone. B.J. Daniels threw two touchdowns passes and ran for a third and in South Florida's 31-26 victory over Clemson on Friday in the Meineke Bowl that gave Holtz a strong finish to his first season and left his team full of smiles. Mo Plancher also ran for a score for the Bulls (8-5), who took control after Tigers Quarterback Kyle Parker left at halftime with a cracked rib. South Florida secured its fifth straight eight-win season and earned its first bowl win over a team from a BCS automatic-qualifying league. Holtz's grin was in stark contrast to Clemson coach Dabo Swinney after a bad ending to a rough season that left him not ruling out changes to his coaching staff. The Tigers were 2-0 before an overtime loss to No. 1 Auburn set off an avalanche of bad news and losses. Parker's final game before embarking on a baseball career ended abruptly when he was tackled near the goal line at the end of the second quarter. Backup Tajh Boyd was picked off by JaQuez Jenkins on the first play of the fourth. His 48-yard return set up Daniels' 8-yard TD run to make it 31-13 and gave the Tigers (6-7) their first losing season in 11 years. It was a triumphant return to North Carolina for Holtz, who left East Carolina in January to take over at South Florida after coach Jim Leavitt's surprise ouster after he was accused of mistreating a player left a divided locker room. Holtz had insisted all week he'd split the snaps between Daniels, who had missed the regular-season finale against Connecticut with a thigh injury, and freshman walk-on Bobby Eveld. But a steady Daniels didn't need to share, completing 20 of 27 passes for 189 yards and an interception to win the MVP award. It wasn't the final season Parker had in mind when the first-round pick forfeited $800,000 from the Colorado Rockies to put off baseball for a year. After getting benched in the regular-season finale against South Carolina, he contemplated skipping the bowl game. Turned out, he was done at halftime after completed 11 of 17 passes for 134 yards and an interception. He finished with 12 touchdowns and 11 interceptions. South Florida stormed to a 17-3 second-quarter lead behind Daniels' TD passes to Demetris Murray and Dontavia Bogan. The Bulls added a field goal following Quenton Washington's 45-yard interception return. Parker led two scoring drives to end the first half, but he was hurt on a 1-yard run before Jamie Harper punched it in from yard out to make it 17-13 at halftime. Plancher's 2-yard TD run early in the third quarter gave South Florida a comfortable cushion again and the elusive Daniels was able to keep Clemson's stout defense at bay. Da'Quan Bowers, who came in with a nation-best 15 1/2 sacks, never got to Daniels and failed to set the school's single-season sacks record in what might be his final college game. Bowers is projected to be a high first-round draft pick. Clemson made a last-gasp comeback bid. Boyd threw a 6-yard touchdown pass to Brandon Ford with 1:47 left. The Tigers recovered the onside kick and Boyd found Ford again for a 10-yard TD. But Clemson's second onside kick was touched by the Tigers about a half yard short of the 10 it needed to travel, and USF took over. Clemsons's difficult season ended with small group of its disgruntled fans making the 2 1/2 drive to Charlotte to see them.

2010 Liberty Bowl (December)

The 2010 Liberty Bowl, also known as Autozone Liberty Bowl, was the fifty-second edition of the bowl game, and was played at Liberty Bowl Memorial Stadium in Memphis, Tennessee. The game was played on December 31, 2010. The game was telecast on ESPN and matched up the Georgia Bulldogs of the SEC against the University of Central Florida Knights, the C-USA champions.

2010 Liberty Bowl	Line	1	-	2	-	3	-	4	-	Final
Georgia	(-6.5)	3	-	0	-	3	-	0	-	6
Central Florida	(55.5)	0	-	3	-	0	-	7	-	10

Scoring Summary
Georgia - Walsh 20 yard Field goal
Central Florida - Cattoi 22 yard Field goal
Georgia - Walsh 41 yard Field goal
Central Florida - Murray 10 yard run (Cattoi kick)

Associated Press Liberty Bowl Game Summary - Latavius Murray scored on a 10-yard touchdown run with 9:01 left, and UCF held on to beat Georgia 10-6 Friday in the AutoZone Liberty Bowl and cap the best season in school history with the program's first postseason victory. The Knights (11-3) had never won more than 10 games in a season and had lost their first three bowl games, including their last visit here in 2007. The Conference USA champs made this win even sweeter by knocking off a Southeastern Conference team in the process, just their second win over that league. The Knights had been 1-13 with the lone win over Alabama in 2000. Georgia (6-7) snapped a four-game bowl winning streak with its first loss since the 2006 Sugar Bowl. Worse for the Bulldogs is notching their first losing season since going 5-6 in 1996. Georgia coach Mark Richt didn't accept the runner-up trophy, instead telling an official to get it to him later. The Bulldogs had the ball longer and last, converting two fourth downs before Kemal Ishmael knocked down Aaron Murray's final long throw into the end zone as time expired. And in an ending reminiscent of Thursday night's Music City Bowl finish to regulation, the game seemed to be over before it actually was. Murray's first deep throw into the end zone landed incomplete and the clock appeared to run out. But replay officials reviewed the play and ruled the clock should have stopped with 2 seconds left. Players from both teams went back to their sideline. The Bulldogs had one more shot to pull out the win. Murray rolled to his left and heaved the ball into the end zone, but Ishmael knocked it to the ground with one hand to start the Knights' celebration. They had to move under cover quickly because a storm front that caused tornadoes in Arkansas hit minutes after the game ended, prompting security to order everyone off the field and out of the stands due to lightning. Latavius Murray finished with 104 yards on 18 carries, but it was the Knights' defense that pulled out this victory. UCF came in with C-USA's stingiest defense and 18th best in the nation. The Knights held Georgia to 280 yards total offense, well below the Bulldogs' average of 393.8. Senior captain and two-time C-USA defensive player of the year Bruce Miller had 1 1/2 sacks in the fourth quarter, including one on the final drive. They picked off Murray twice and sacked him a total of three times. So, Georgia has a disappointing end to a season that started with so much promise before junior receiver A.J. Green sat out a four-game NCAA suspension for selling a bowl jersey. Richt tried to use Green as much as possible, even putting him out to return punts after he had fielded only one this season. Green fair caught two and returned the other for 18 yards. The junior, who could be high NFL draft pick if he decides to leave school early, also caught eight passes for 77 yards. The Bulldogs got the ball back three times after Murray's TD. They went three-and-out on the first two, and Georgia got the ball back for the final time with 2:20 left. They also started both halves driving down field easily before bogging down and settling for field goals of 20 and 41 yards by Blair Walsh. These teams went to halftime tied at 3-3 after a first half in which both Georgia and UCF wasted chances at the end zone. Richt kicked the first field goal despite having fourth-and-1 at the UCF 3. He said he would've gone for the TD if he'd known what the final score would be. But he still thinks he made the right decision at the time. UF had its struggles moving the ball. The Knights finished with 241 yards on offense and Georgia picked off freshman Jeff Godfrey twice, including once in the end zone. In fact, four of the first nine possessions ended with interceptions. They moved the ball when it mattered most, and Murray capped the 65-yard drive with the winning TD.

2010 Sun Bowl

The 2010 Hyundai Sun Bowl game was the 77th edition of the bowl game. It was played on December 31, 2010 between the Miami Hurricanes from the ACC and the independent Notre Dame Fighting Irish, in a revival of a long-dormant rivalry. CBS television broadcast the game. Hyundai took over as the title sponsor.

2010 Sun Bowl	Line	1	-	2	-	3	-	4	-	Final
Notre Dame	(47.0)	14	-	13	-	3	-	3	-	33
Miami	(-3.0)	0	-	3	-	0	-	14	-	17

Scoring Summary
Notre Dame - Floyd 3 yard pass from Rees (Ruffer kick)
Notre Dame - Floyd 34 yard pass from Rees (Ruffer kick)
Notre Dame - Wood 34 yard run (Ruffer kick)
Notre Dame - Ruffer 40 yard Field goal
Notre Dame - Ruffer 50 yard Field goal
Miami - Bosher 47 yard Field goal
Notre Dame - Ruffer 19 yard Field goal
Miami - Hankerson 6 yard pass from Morris (Bosher kick)
Miami - Streeter 42 yard pass from Morris (Bosher kick)
Notre Dame - Tausch 34 yard Field goal

Sun Bowl Classic Game Summary - Freshman Tommy Rees passed for 201 yards and two touchdowns to Michael Floyd as Notre Dame beat Miami 33-17 in the Sun Bowl on Friday, making Kelly the first Fighting Irish coach to win a bowl game during his first season. After a 20-year break, it was all Irish in the latest installment of a storied rivalry that became known during the 1980s as Catholics versus Convicts. Notre Dame (8-5) reached the end zone on three of its first four possessions. Rees tossed TD passes of 3 and 34 yards to Floyd and Cierre Wood broke free on a 34-yard scoring run before David Ruffer added field goals from 40, 50 and 19 yards. The Hurricanes trailed 30-3 going into the fourth quarter, completing a season in which their coach was fired with an ugly loss. Rees hardly looked like a freshman, completing 15 of 29 attempts without an interception. He struggled in the season-ending victory over USC but his performance against Miami marked the first time a first year starting Quarterback at Notre Dame won a bowl game. Floyd had a big day, too, with six catches for 109 yards receiving, and he was close to hauling into two more scores. The game sold out in 21 hours, the fastest in the Sun Bowl's 77-year history, and the crowd of 54,021 set a bowl attendance record. Many fans wore Notre Dame Jackets to ward off the 34-degree weather as a round of overnight snow dusted the Franklin Mountains. The warm-weather Hurricanes – many wearing head covers under their helmets – struggled much of the afternoon. Miami scored twice in the fourth quarter when Stephen Morris threw a 6-yard TD pass to Leonard Hankerson and a 42-yard scoring play to Tommy Streeter, but it was too late by then. The Hurricanes also had 10 penalties for 106 yards. The Canes trailed 27-0 late in the first half and the player with the most catches from a Hurricanes Quarterback was Irish safety Harrison Smith, who intercepted three passes. Robert Blanton also had an interception during Miami's turnover binge. Not everything went perfectly for Notre Dame. Ruffer was wide right a 36-yard try late in the third quarter, his first miss on 24 career attempts. Linebacker Manti Te'o sat out most of the second half with a knee injury but could have played if needed. Jacory Harris started at Quarterback for the Canes after Morris sprained an ankle in practice this week. Harris couldn't get anything going, completing just 4 of 7 with three interceptions. Morris took over the second quarter and finished 22-of-33 for 282 yards passing with two TDs.

2010 Chick-Fil-A Peach Bowl

The 2010 Chick-fil-A Bowl is the forty-third edition of the bowl game, and was played at the Georgia Dome in Atlanta, Georgia. It was played Friday, December 31, 2010, and featured the #23 Florida State Seminoles versus the #19 South Carolina Gamecocks.

2010 Chick-Fil-A Peach Bowl	Line	1	-	2	-	3	-	4	-	Final
#19 South Carolina	(-3.0)	0	-	3	-	7	-	7	-	17
#23 Florida State	(54.5)	6	-	7	-	6	-	7	-	26

Scoring Summary
Florida State - Hopkins 29 yard Field goal
Florida State - Hopkins 48 yard Field goal
Florida State - Thompson 27 yard run (Hopkins kick)
South Carolina - Lanner 40 yard Field goal
Florida State - Hopkins 35 yard Field goal
South Carolina - Garcia 3 yard pass from Sanders (Lanning kick)
Florida State - Hopkins 45 yard Field goal
South Carolina - Maddox 7 yard run (Lanning kick)
Florida State - Easterling 7 yard pass from Manuel (Hopkins kick)

Associated Press Chick-Fil-A Peach Bowl Game Summary - E.J. Manuel's days as a backup appear to be over. Manuel threw a fourth-quarter touchdown pass to stop a South Carolina rally and lead Florida State to a 26-17 victory over the turnover-plagued Gamecocks in the Chick-fil-A Bowl on Friday night. Manuel took over after senior Quarterback Christian Ponder left early in the second quarter with a concussion. The sophomore looks ready to assume the starting role next season. Manuel completed 11 of 15 passes for 84 yards and a touchdown and had seven carries for 46 yards. He was 7-for-7 passing on the fourth-quarter touchdown drive. Manuel has a knack for postseason success. He was the MVP of the Seminoles' Gator Bowl win over West Virginia to end the 2009 season. Dustin Hopkins kicked four field goals for the No. 23 Seminoles (10-4), who reached 10 victories for the first time since 2003. Hopkins tied his own school record for a bowl, and the four field goals also matched the Chick-fil-A Bowl record. No. 19 South Carolina (9-5), which was seeking its first 10-win season since 1984, lost star running back Marcus Lattimore when he was hit hard on the Gamecocks' first drive. Coach Steve Spurrier's team also committed five turnovers. Stephen Garcia, who threw 11 interceptions in 13 games leading up to the bowl, was picked off by Michael Harris, Kendall Smith and Xavier Rhodes in the Gamecocks' turnover-filled first half. Including Lattimore's lost fumble on South Carolina's opening drive, the Gamecocks had turnovers on each of their first three possessions and four in the first half. Spurrier said he considered making a change at Quarterback. Garcia recovered to lead two long touchdown drives that trimmed Florida State's lead to 19-17 before Manuel answered with the 7-yard scoring pass to Taiwan Easterling. Florida State cornerback Greg Reid, whose hits caused the fumbles by Lattimore and Jeffery, deflected a fourth-down pass by Garcia with 3:23 remaining to end the Gamecocks' last hope. Garcia completed 19 of 34 passes for 243 yards and also scored on a nifty play in the third. On a third-down play from the Florida State 3, Garcia threw a screen pass to Ace Sanders, who threw back across the field to Garcia alone in the right side of the end zone. The Seminoles answered with Hopkins' fourth field goal, from 45 yards, to push the lead to nine. Hopkins also kicked four field goals in the Seminoles' Gator Bowl win over West Virginia. Garcia responded by leading a 79-yard drive, capped by Brian Maddox's 7-yard TD run. Garcia helped set up the score with a 29-yard pass to Jeffery. Reid's hit on Lattimore knocked the freshman out of the game with an injury announced as a cut to his mouth. Spurrier said after the game that Lattimore also had "a little bit of a concussion" and was taken to a hospital for stitches. Linebacker Kendall Smith picked up the fumble after Reid's hit and returned it 46 yards as Lattimore remained on his back. Trainers hurried off the sideline to surround Lattimore before the play ended. He was helped off the field and had an ice pack on his chin for the Gamecocks' next possession. The lost fumble was the first of Lattimore's career. Ponder started in his return from a right elbow injury but appeared to be less than full strength while completing only 1 of 5 passes for 6 yards. Ponder badly underthrew a fourth-down pass from the South Carolina 2-yard line early in the second quarter and Manuel took over on the Seminoles' next possession. Fisher said Ponder suffered the concussion when he was hit on the play before his fourth-down incompletion. Ponder missed Florida State's Atlantic Coast Conference championship game loss to Virginia Tech with the elbow injury.

www.ingramcontent.com/pod-product-compliance
Lightning Source LLC
Chambersburg PA
CBHW082109230426
43671CB00015B/2653